APPLICANTS FOR WORK RELIEF

LONDON : HUMPHREY MILFORD
OXFORD UNIVERSITY PRESS

APPLICANTS FOR WORK RELIEF

A STUDY OF MASSACHUSETTS FAMILIES UNDER THE FERA AND WPA

BY

ELIZABETH W. GILBOY

SECRETARY, HARVARD UNIVERSITY COMMITTEE ON RESEARCH IN THE SOCIAL SCIENCES

CAMBRIDGE, MASSACHUSETTS
HARVARD UNIVERSITY PRESS
1940

PRINTED AT THE HARVARD UNIVERSITY PRESS
CAMBRIDGE, MASSACHUSETTS, U.S.A.

To

G. G.

PREFACE

THIS STUDY was begun in 1934 under the auspices of a Harvard Committee and the Massachusetts Emergency Relief Administration. At that time a number of projects on various phases of unemployment in this state were started. The data for the original sample of 397 ERA cases in Cambridge were collected with the assistance of ERA workers. The study was later expanded to include over 2100 work relief cases, who had been made eligible for work relief under the ERA and continued on the active list under the WPA, as well as some 400 cases who had been separated from the work relief rolls after 1935. These data were taken from ERA and WPA records made available by the Massachusetts Works Progress Administration. The research and statistical work involved in the larger study, as well as the preparation of the manuscript, has been financed by the Harvard University Committee on Research in the Social Sciences. I am also indebted to the Committee for assistance in publication.

I should like to express my gratitude to Colonel John J. McDonough, formerly Administrator of the Massachusetts Works Progress Administration, now Director of Region One, who made it possible for me to use the official records and to talk with members of the Administrative staff. Every facility was granted me, without restriction, for securing the available information. I am also extremely grateful to the Division of Research of the Works Progress Administration (now the Works Projects Administration) in Washington, D. C. Published and unpublished material was put at my disposal by Mr. Howard B. Myers, Director, and members of his staff. Dr. A. Ross Eckler, then Assistant Director, has been most helpful at every phase of the investigation. He has given freely of his time in discussing the project and in criticizing the final manuscript.

It would not have been possible to complete this study without the information and assistance of the Works Progress Administration. I should like to make it clear, however, that at no time has any attempt been made to influence the course of the investigation or the conclusions to be drawn from the data. I was given a free hand to use and interpret the evidence as I saw fit. And I alone am responsible for the conclusions.

A good deal of information has been secured as a result of interviews with relief officials. They were frank about giving opinions, some of which are included in the final study. For obvious reasons references cannot be given in these instances. But I have felt that such intangible evidence, coming as it does from those actively engaged in administering the relief program, has its place.

There are numerous others who have given great assistance in the course of the investigation. Professors W. L. Crum and Edwin Frickey of Harvard University have been kind enough to read and criticize the manuscript. The work could never have been finished without the aid of four research assistants, Margaret Brainerd Rolph and Helen Sorenson, in the early days of the investigation; Winifred Asnault and Martha Sharpless at the later stages. Althea MacDonald has tackled uncomplainingly the laborious task of typing and retyping the manuscript and checking the footnotes.

I am indebted as well to the editors of the following journals for allowing me to include material previously published in their pages: The Quarterly Journal of Economics, The American Economic Review, and The American Sociological Review. Detailed references will be found in the footnotes.

Although the manuscript was completed in the summer of 1939, an attempt has been made to include the most important developments in relief administration and references to current data occurring since then. The main body of the material, however, relates to the period preceding 1939 and it is recognized that references to more recent material and events are by no means complete.

ELIZABETH W. GILBOY

Cambridge, Massachusetts
January 1940

CONTENTS

STATISTICAL TABLES IN THE TEXT

NOTE: Complete statistical tables, containing more detailed information than will be found in the summary tables of the text, are in Appendix B, designated by Arabic numerals. References to them are given in the text. They are not listed here.

INTRODUCTION

The attempt to deal on a national scale with the problem of unemployment is a very recent development in the United States. The heterogeneous nature of the population, the social and business philosophy of individualism, the political creed of states' rights have precluded the development of social insurance, unemployment compensation, and relief measures such as has occurred abroad. Nearly all the European nations have well-developed systems of social insurance, including accident, sickness, old age, and unemployment. Nearly all of them have experimented with work relief and direct relief. They have as well tried monetary and trade measures to stimulate employment. In other words, they are familiar with the difficulties of widespread unemployment and their social philosophy reached the point long ago where it was recognized that the country as a whole must do something about it.

Americans are just beginning to recognize that philosophy. Many of them even yet refuse to adopt it. Undoubtedly this Administration has accelerated its development, but it would have come with any administration. The impact of unemployment upon the public mind was very great in the past depression, especially since many had deluded themselves into believing that a new era of prosperity had come into being before 1929. One heard vaguely of the large-scale unemployment in other countries but the general attitude of most Americans may be expressed by the phrase "It can't happen here." It did happen here, on an unprecedented scale, and something had to be done. The first measures were taken in traditional fashion. Local governments attempted to deal with their own unemployment. It soon became too much for them. Then the state governments stepped in, and finally the federal government. The story of the development of relief in Massachusetts which is told in the first two chapters will, despite some characteristics peculiar to New England, illustrate the evolution of unemployment and relief from a local to a national concern.

Work relief, as it has been developed in this country, must be seen as one of a number of measures for dealing with unemployment. It has no concern, theoretically, with those among the unemployed who are unable to work for reasons of age, health, and so on; or with those who are a chronic relief problem. It is designed to provide legitimate work for those thrust out of their jobs by economic causes which they can in no way control, during the period of unemployment. Such work is supposed to keep up skill and morale, and provide a minimum living, until the unemployed can again find work in private industry. Work relief in no way attempts to prevent unemployment; it deals with it once it has arisen.

Direct relief is also a means of supporting the unemployed, and there are many who believe it preferable to work relief, not only on the ground of expense, for work relief is admittedly more costly, but on the ground of the failure of work relief to accomplish its avowed purposes, namely the preservation of working efficiency and morale, and the return of those on work relief to private employment. The work relief program of the present Administration, particularly the WPA, has been attacked as much if not more than any other measure. It has been maligned and derided. WPA workers have been sneered at as bums and ne'er-do-wells. Unfortunately very few individuals are supplied with factual information as to the works programs and those benefiting from them. The subject is usually discussed in an atmosphere of emotionalism and politics.

It seems important to present at this time some facts about work relief recipients and the work relief system as it was set up in this country. Work relief is now undergoing reorganization, and if it is to benefit by the experiences of the past few years, all available facts and opinions as to its actual effectiveness should be subjected to impartial examination. Under the new Federal Works Agency it ought to be possible to coordinate work relief and to plan it more effectively and efficiently. Those who believe that the work relief program should be abolished, and direct relief established in its stead, will do well to examine the facts concerning the operation of the work relief program as impartially as possible. If some other relief program succeeds work relief, still the experience of the last few years should not be neglected.

It should be understood at the start that this book is no general study of unemployment or of measures for dealing with unemployment. It is not even a general study of relief. It is restricted to an investigation of work relief, particularly of those on work relief, in one section of the country. Although every effort has been made to ultilize comparable data for other parts of the country and to indicate to what extent the Massachusetts experience has been typical, general conclusions should not be drawn from this investigation. However, it does provide factual data for a case study of those on work relief and it is in many ways more complete than other such investigations.

A word should be said here as to the nature of the data, although more precise information is given in Appendix A. For the most part the data are taken from records made under the FERA and WPA. They are therefore accurate only within a very approximate range. Wherever possible the information so obtained was checked by similar material from other sources. It is thought that the results are roughly correct, but no great statistical accuracy is claimed for them, and the very simplest statistical methods were used. Other information was obtained from studies carried out by the personal interview method. Statistically speaking such data on income and expenditures, and the facts about the life of human beings, are extremely unprecise. Yet, on the whole, the material thus gathered presents an internally consistent picture. In any case, the data, the methods used, and the difficulties encountered are laid before the reader and he can judge as to the reliability of the conclusions drawn. No one, however, can be more completely aware of the inadequacies of the data and the complexities of the problem than the author.

Notwithstanding the deficiencies of studies such as this from a scientific standpoint, they have distinct value. If economists were to restrict themselves to investigations allowing the application of strict scientific method, they would have little left to investigate. But the attempt to analyze a current and controversial problem coldly and impartially and to subject it to whatever statistical procedure is possible may serve to illuminate it markedly. It is not often possible for those in the middle of such a problem to see it as a whole. How can administrators and politicians, responsible for the active carrying out of the work relief program, beset by the necessity for immediate decision, subjected to pressure of many sorts, be expected to survey the program and assess its worth? That is certainly one of the jobs of the professional economist. The present study will supply, it is hoped, an unbiased report of the work relief system in the past few years, and an impartial analysis of the people who were on relief in one section of the country.

PART I

THE PROBLEM OF WORK RELIEF

CHAPTER I

THE ADMINISTRATIVE BACKGROUND IN MASSACHUSETTS

MASSACHUSETTS is one of the states still dominated by the Elizabethan concept of poor relief. In common with the other New England states, settlement laws and the administration of local relief officials play a considerable part in the handling of the relief problem. In the course of time various types of cases, such as those applying for relief as a result of old age, dependent children, insanity or feeble-mindedness, have been put under state jurisdiction. There still remains, however, a large proportion of cases which are handled under local public welfare administrations. Some of these cases, those considered employable, have been put on the federal work relief programs in recent years, but a considerable residue are still taken care of by the towns and cities.

Eligibility for local relief of any kind in Massachusetts results from five years' residence in a town or city, with no previous recourse to relief, as well as family need. If a family has acquired settlement in one town and then moves to another and there becomes dependent upon public aid, the town of settlement is responsible for the cost of the family's relief. Those cases with no settlement in any local community are the responsibility of the state. It is easy to see how a complicated legal and financial situation has arisen as a result of these settlement laws. Many town officials are engaged in the attempt to collect relief costs from other towns and from the state, and are in turn being sued by other towns. Costly legal machinery has been set up to handle such cases. The net result of the transfer of such funds among towns is a small proportion of the total amount of money involved. Time and money are wasted by the complex legal machinery involved. Sometimes the ability of a town to collect depends rather on the cleverness of its legal representatives than on the justice of the case. Many small towns cannot afford and do not attempt to collect from other localities. It is small wonder that the Special Commission on Taxation and Public Expenditures recommended that the present settlement laws be repealed and that the state bear a certain proportion of local relief costs [1] in all cases.

The administration of relief for which the state is responsible was incorporated in the Department of Public Welfare, created by legislative act in 1919. The powers of the department are primarily supervisory, although its participation in local relief has grown immensely since that date, particularly in the field of old age and mothers' aid. As far as general relief is concerned the state still has jurisdiction only over the unsettled cases. The Department has not made the most of its powers despite their limitations. By the promulgation of administrative standards of case work methods, personnel standards, etc. it might have been possible for the state to stimulate a more uniform handling of relief cases in the localities. The state, however, has apparently been afraid to antagonize local officials who are inclined to resent any usurpation of their functions by the state. The result has been a wide variation in local administrative practice. Even the statistics are frequently not comparable. The state has restricted itself to the annual inspection of the unsettled cases. Sometimes there has been a difference in the amounts given by the states and the localities to general relief cases under their respective jurisdictions. In other words, the administration of relief and the relation be-

[1] *Report of the Special Commission on Taxation and Public Expenditures*, Part II, Public Welfare, with Recommendations for an Emergency Relief Tax, January 24, 1938, Mass. House Document No. 1702.

tween the towns and the state have been far from satisfactory on the whole.[2]

With the rapid increase in relief applicants after 1930, it soon became apparent that the situation was beyond the powers of localities, and even of the state, to handle financially. State authorities became alarmed at the extent of unemployment and the unprecedented burden falling upon relief sources. The state attempted to relieve unemployment by emergency appropriations for public works, such as repair of buildings, roads, mosquito control, etc. Eight acts authorizing such appropriations "As a Measure of Relief during the Present Unemployment Emergency" were passed from January 1931 to March 1933.[3] A 2 year program for the "Acceleration of Building Construction, in order to Alleviate the Present Unemployment Emergency" was also enacted by law in April 1930 and was financed by the issue of 4 year notes.[4] In March 1933 an Emergency Finance Board was created to supervise the borrowing by cities and towns from the state for public welfare expenses. Both the municipalities and the state could issue notes for this purpose under certain conditions. An act in July 1933 further defined the conditions under which towns and cities might borrow and provided that funds received by the state under the Emergency Relief Act of 1933 for these towns

[2] *Ibid.* This report gives a summary of the administration of relief in Massachusetts and recommendations for a revised state and local administration. Unfortunately the plan for revising the Department of Public Welfare is linked in the report with a plan for a sales tax to finance it. Consequently, the merits of the Public Welfare revision have been overlooked in the furious arguments which have arisen concerning the sales tax.

[3] *Acts and Resolves of Massachusetts*, 1931, Chapters 1, 14, 112, 465; 1932, Chapters 69, 212, 307; 1933, Chapter 89. These appropriations, secured from the gasoline tax, short term loans, and including $7 million for work relief on highways, were administered by the State Department of Public Works. $30 million was authorized for such relief loans. *FERA Monthly Report*, May 1935, p. 58.

[4] *Ibid.*, 1931, Chapter 268.

should be applied to the payment of these bonds and notes.[5] It is evident that the state tried to provide employment in public works and to extend local funds available for relief by enabling towns and cities to borrow for the emergency with greater ease. Still the problems of relief and unemployment were not solved.

Several commissions were appointed by successive governors to investigate unemployment and to make recommendations as to state procedure. Although these commissions were concerned rather with unemployment than relief as such, their reports are of considerable interest, particularly in connection with work relief. It is perhaps characteristic of the early years of the depression that they did not at first urge the expansion of relief agencies to handle unemployment. Their primary concern was with individuals. Persons and industries were urged to join in ways of expanding employment and providing for emergencies. The commissions were on the whole against extensive federal participation in the mitigation of unemployment, with one or two rare exceptions. The unemployed who were the concern of the successive commissions dealt with below were those whom work relief under the ERA and WPA was designed to assist. In the early days of the depression, at least, those called upon to investigate the situation in the state had no thought of as extensive a program of work relief as was later developed.

The philosophy underlying efforts to cope with the relief problem at this stage of the depression is exemplified by a statement of "principles on which efforts in behalf of the unemployed in Boston should be based" which appeared in the Boston Council of Social Agencies' *Bulletin* in December 1930.[6] Among these principles were the following: "Help through employment is better than help through relief"; "Relief when necessary should be administered through the regularly estab-

[5] *Ibid.*, 1933, Chapters 49, 307.

[6] Pp. 5 and 6.

lished relief agencies . . ."; "Decentralization rather than concentration of remedial activities should be the rule." It is natural that a council of social agencies should recommend the use of existing agencies and it is typical of the state that any centralization should be opposed. These views were very widely held at this stage and it was with slow reluctance that the necessity for the coordination of relief and for state and federal assistance was admitted.

An Emergency Committee on Unemployment was appointed by the governor in October 1930. The Committee was composed of a number of individuals prominent in civic, industrial, and religious life. Similar committees were formed under their guidance in 210 towns and cities in the state with the purpose of investigating and alleviating the unemployment situation. The main objectives of these committees were to stimulate employment by urging public and private agencies and individuals to undertake necessary work in advance of the usual time for such work, to urge that those whose incomes had not been reduced should spend as usual, and to get some numerical estimate of the extent of unemployment in the state. A great deal of newspaper publicity was given to the activities of the Committee which stated in its report that "we believe it can be said that a very large number of people have been employed as a result of the activities of this Committee. . . ."[7] The final report of the Committee estimated that 34,366 persons had been employed for 21 weeks at an average wage of $12.19 per week as a result of the efforts of the Committee in stimulating the creation of jobs.[8] At the same time the state was increasing its appropriations for public works.

The Committee was not able to obtain, however, an accurate

[7] *Preliminary Summary of Work from October 29, 1930, to December 31, 1930, Massachusetts Emergency Committee on Unemployment*, p. 20.

[8] *Final Report of the Massachusetts Emergency Committee on Unemployment from October 29, 1930 to April 15, 1931*, p. 9.

estimate of unemployment and could come no closer than the belief that the unemployed at that time were between 150,000 and 200,000. Towns were urged to set up means for registering the unemployed and to keep accurate records of those registering. Only 167 towns attempted this and they reported 57,396 unemployed. The Committee was aware that the estimates of unemployment received were inaccurate and continued to emphasize the necessity for a precise record of unemployment. When the Committee disbanded in April 1931, and turned over its activities to the Department of Labor and Industries, it recommended a plan for obtaining a census of unemployment in the state through local relief agencies, Chambers of Commerce, and municipal officers. The census of unemployment was finally made with the assistance of the CWA and FERA in 1934.

A special Commission on the Stabilization of Employment was appointed by the Governor in July 1931, in accordance with the Resolves of 1931. This Commission undertook considerable research upon the problems of employment and unemployment in general and upon possible methods of preventing and handling unemployment in Massachusetts.[9] The Commission's final report, in fact, presented a long and careful analysis of the causes of unemployment, and of the situation in Massachusetts. It was pointed out that unemployment as a result of seasonal, cyclical, and secular fluctuations and technical progress had existed in Massachusetts for some time and had been a serious problem since the 'twenties as a result of the declining trend of Massachusetts industry. Unemployment was no new Massachusetts problem but one greatly magnified by the past depression. The Commission's final recommendations embodied the following:

[9] The activities and recommendations of the Commission may be found in its *Preliminary Report*, House Document No. 1100, December 1931; its *Final Report*, House Document No. 1200, December 1932; and its *Supplementary Report*, House Document No. 1301, January 1934.

(1) Reorganization of the state system of public employment offices under the Department of Labor and Industries; (2) an Act to provide for the regulation of private employment offices; (3) an Act to establish a Public Works Planning Board; and (4) an Act to provide for the establishment and administration of unemployment reserves.

These measures will not be described or analyzed in any detail here since their bearing on the relief problem is indirect. The reports of the Commission are of interest for our purpose, however, in revealing the Commission's conviction that unemployment is beyond the individual's control. He is laid off or discharged as a result of forces which act upon the entire economic system and which carry individuals, both employees and employers, before them. The Commission's attitude towards unemployment was quite different from the general New England view that any individual who really wants work can find it. The Commission proposed to attack the problem in three ways: first, by setting the system of employment exchanges on a more efficient basis so that individuals might quickly find out about any jobs which do exist. In the second place, public works were to be outlined sufficiently in advance (the proposed Act contemplated a successive 5 year plan) so that new well-planned projects might be started when unemployment became serious. Upon the third proposal the Commission lavished a great deal of attention. The unemployment reserves were to be compulsory upon employers who must contribute up to a certain maximum for each employee. When employees were laid off, they were to receive a certain proportion of their wages after a 4 weeks' waiting period, for a period of weeks defined in the Act. The details of the proposal cannot concern us at this time, nor the means of financing it, nor the arguments for and against it. It is important to note, however, that the Commission believed that the plan for relieving unemployment should be financed by employers and that the working man should not and could not be expected to save towards the eventuality of being unemployed. To the question of the final incidence of the unemployment payments, the Commission gave very little attention. The Commission was aware that their plan of unemployment reserves could not take care of long-continuing unemployment; that it was a temporary measure at best. They felt, however, that relief sources would be relieved of a considerable burden if their plan went into effect, though they admitted that relief would have to be relied upon after the maximum period of unemployment benefits had been exhausted. An Act setting up a system of unemployment compensation was finally passed in August 1935 and amended in 1936 to bring it under the provisions of the Social Security Act.[10]

In April 1932, as a result of the recommendation of the Special Commission on the Stabilization of Employment, a separate Division of Public Employment Offices was created under the jurisdiction of the Department of Labor and Industries.[11] The Boston offices were moved to larger quarters and the work of the new Division was considerably expanded. In 1933 the state Division became affiliated with the United States Employment Service in accordance with the provisions of the Wagner-Peyser Act which established a national employment service.[12] Six new offices were opened in the state and certain federal

[10] *Acts and Resolves of Massachusetts*, 1935, Chapter 479; 1936, Chapters 12, 249. An Unemployment Compensation Commission under the Department of Labor and Industries was created to administer the Act. It would take us too far afield to examine the details of the Act. It is of considerable interest to note, however, that several important recommendations of the Commission were not followed, largely as a result of the provisions of the Social Security Act. Both employers and employees were to contribute under the provisions of the Act as passed, and the regulations for investing the fund set up from these contributions differed considerably from those recommended by the Commission.

[11] *Report of the Department of Labor and Industries*, November 30, 1932, p. 144.

[12] *Report of the Department of Labor and Industries*, November 30, 1933, p. 97.

funds were allotted to Massachusetts as one of the states accepting the provisions of the Act. From then on the work of the state employment offices as part of the national system continued to expand. They were used as the referral agency for the CWA, PWA, and at first for WPA projects. All workers on federal work relief were supposed to be registered with them.

From 1932 on the federal government began seriously to enter into the business of relief. The Emergency Relief and Construction Act of 1932 authorized the expenditure of funds to increase employment both by direct loans to the states on the part of the Reconstruction Finance Corporation and by a large appropriation for federal public works. The sum of 120 million dollars was set aside for emergency construction of federal highways. The Massachusetts share of this money was nearly 2 million dollars.[13] Massachusetts was one of six states, however, which received no direct advances from the Reconstruction Finance Corporation.[14]

During this period the state governments were forced in general to assist local units financially in connection with unemployment relief. Some states set up their own emergency relief administrations (for instance, New York and New Jersey) and most states appointed some kind of relief board under the governor's control, with a paid administrator. Nothing of this sort was done in Massachusetts except for the creation of the Emergency Finance Board. Although state assistance in enabling the towns to borrow in order to meet their relief expenses was furnished and some attempt was made to expand the state's public works program, no further coordination of relief agencies was attempted. Relief was administered as usual by the De-

[13] *Report of the Department of Labor and Industries*, November 30, 1932, p. 45.

[14] A. C. Millspaugh, *Public Welfare Organization*, The Brookings Institution, Washington, D. C., 1935, ch. XIII.

partment of Public Welfare and the town and city boards of public welfare.[15]

The Federal Emergency Relief Act of 1933 created the FERA, which operated under a Federal Administrator appointed by the President. No direct grants for relief could now be made to the states except with the approval of the Federal Administrator. With this approval the states could be granted money both for direct and work relief. In Massachusetts federal funds were granted almost entirely for work relief.[16] The FERA was a federal grant-in-aid system and ordinarily the states were empowered to spend the money under a state emergency relief administration, with general supervision from Washington. The act of 1933, however, authorized that "control may be assumed in any State where in the judgment of the Federal administrator more effective and efficient cooperation between the State and Federal authorities may thereby be secured. . . ."[17] A presidential Executive Order of November 22, 1933 further defined the control of the Federal Administrator in such cases, authorizing him to appoint directly a state emergency relief administration, the personnel of which were to be responsible to him alone.[18] This was done in Massachusetts on March 7, 1934.

Two acts were passed by the Massachusetts legislature in July 1933 with the purpose of enabling the state and cities and towns to take advantage of funds for public works which were

[15] Millspaugh, *op. cit.*, p. 312. Decentralization was characteristic of all state relief administration before this depression. For a brief history of poor relief laws before the depression and the trend towards centralization appearing in the depression, see *Legislative Trends in Public Relief and Assistance*, WPA Division of Social Research, Series III, No. 2.

[16] *Ibid.*, p. 321.

[17] Public Resolution No. 15, 73d Congress, sec. 3b, as quoted in *Chronology of the Federal Emergency Relief Administration* by Doris Carothers, Works Progress Administration, Research Monograph, VI, 1937.

[18] Executive Order 6442 as summarized in Carothers, *op. cit.*, pp. 32–3.

to be granted under the PWA.[19] An Emergency Public Works Commission was set up to approve state projects. Local projects were to be approved by the Emergency Finance Commission. In addition all projects had to be approved by the governor before being submitted to Washington. No method of handling FERA funds was devised by the legislature, however, except through the Emergency Finance Board, and no state relief administration, other than that already existing, was set up.[20] A state act of July 1, 1933 did provide that loans from the state to towns and cities for public welfare should be paid off in part by money received by the Commonwealth under the FERA Act of 1933 for these cities and towns.[21]

Federal funds for work relief in Massachusetts were under the direct control of the FERA Administrator in Washington. Massachusetts was one of three states in which the state emergency relief administration was appointed and controlled by Washington in 1934.[22] The situation in Massachusetts, therefore, was not typical of the country during the period of FERA control of work relief. In most states the Federal Administrator wielded only indirect powers once the money had been granted. Direct federal control of work relief in the states, however, was universally established under the Works Progress Administration in 1935. Sometimes the state emergency relief organiza-

[19] The PWA was created under Title II of the National Industrial Recovery Act (June, 1933) and Secretary Ickes was appointed Administrator.

[20] *Acts and Resolves of Massachusetts*, 1933, Chapter 344.

[21] *Acts and Resolves of Massachusetts*, 1933, Chapter 307.

[22] Millspaugh, *op. cit.*, p. 321. The other states were Oklahoma and North Dakota. Three additional states were put under federal control in 1935; Ohio, Louisiana, and Georgia. *FERA Monthly Report*, April 1935. "In Massachusetts the control of the emergency work program was assumed by the FERA on March 7, while the administration of direct relief was left to the individual cities and towns . . . a Federal disbursing system, under the supervision of the Disbursing Division of the U. S. Treasury, was established to handle all disbursements of Federal relief funds." *FERA Monthly Report*, March 1934, p. 17.

tion was liquidated when the WPA came into existence, but in many cases the state organization continued to function parallel to the WPA.

The Civil Works Administration was inaugurated by executive order in the fall of 1933 as a temporary program of relief for unemployment and as a stimulus to spending. It was a brief affair which ended in the spring of 1934. About half of the CWA workers were employable cases taken from the relief rolls. The CWA in the states was directly administered by Washington. One of the CWA projects in Massachusetts was the state census of unemployment, made as of January 2, 1934, under the direction of the Division of Statistics of the Department of Labor and Industries. The census was later completed with FERA funds.

The FERA was superseded by the WPA in 1935, which was set up as a centrally administered federal system of work relief from the start. It was definitely a program to take care of unemployment and it was made clear in the President's message that only employable workers out of a job were to be considered eligible. Unemployables were to be left to the care of states and localities. Need ceased to be the sole criterion of eligibility, as in practice it had been under the FERA. Employability became, at least in theory, an equally important standard.

In Massachusetts at the present time relief of all kinds is divided among local, state, and federal jurisdictions. The state and the municipalities have been largely relieved of the burden of employable cases by the WPA. Other types of relief cases have been given federal assistance under the provisions of the Social Security Act. The state report previously cited, however, looks forward to a time when employable cases will again become the concern of Massachusetts.[23] There has been some talk of making the WPA a permanent federal institution, but that

[23] The Commonwealth of Massachusetts, *Report of the Special Commission on Taxation and Public Expenditures*, Part II, pp. 36–39.

has not as yet eventuated. The proposal has met strong opposition in many directions. Certainly in Massachusetts, where local self-government is still tenaciously adhered to, the permanent centralization of work relief administration would probably arouse many enemies. The 1939 relief bill has created a Federal Works Agency under which the WPA and PWA both are controlled. It remains to be seen what differences in control will result from this agency. It is not, however, a permanent federal institution, in the sense of a government department, although such an institution was proposed in the original Byrnes bill on the reorganization of relief. The same relief bill cut drastically work relief appropriations. Consequently, a good many employables, in the WPA sense, have been forced back upon direct relief in recent months, not only in Massachusetts, but all over the country.

CHAPTER II

THE MASSACHUSETTS ERA

IN THIS BOOK I shall deal primarily with those on work relief in Massachusetts under the ERA and WPA in 1935. The sample selected is one representative of Massachusetts work relief conditions at the time. The families which will be described in later chapters were largely supported by work relief. It must be remembered, however, that these families are representative of only a portion of those on relief. Most of the families had at least one employable member and were therefore among the cases most likely to be a temporary rather than a permanent relief problem.[1] The probability of their return to private employment will be examined later on in the book. The theory behind work relief, admittedly a more expensive form of relief than direct aid, is that work relief will preserve the skills and morale of those unemployed who are out of work through no fault of their own, but as a result of the movement of business and economic forces beyond their control. Some of these employable cases may be reabsorbed in private industry. For those who are unemployable there is no such possibility. They are the ones who are the main concern of the state and local relief administrations at the present time and they will probably remain a permanent relief problem.

Some idea of the relative importance of the various kinds of relief cases in Massachusetts may be obtained from the following figures on the case load for 1935 which have been secured from the records of the WPA in Boston.[2]

[1] This was not as true of the ERA as the WPA. Since need was a more important criterion than employability under the ERA, a number of unemployables were put on ERA projects.

[2] Complete monthly figures from May 1934 to July 1939 are to be found in Appendix B.

TABLE A

Total Number of Relief Cases * in Massachusetts, 1935

	Direct Relief [a]	ERA
January	103,547	101,346
February	102,222	108,327
March	98,871	116,084
April	91,807	119,115
May	86,648	117,648
June	81,665	116,275
July	79,311	115,022
August	85,797	110,119
September	80,941	103,693
October	79,789	100,997
November	85,194	86,731
December	93,239	23,335 (109,833 WPA)

* Number of families and single persons combined.

[a] Includes Public Welfare and Soldiers' Relief.

In 1935 a maximum of 119,000 cases (rounded figures) were on ERA in April. During the year the monthly figure varied from 23,000 in December, when the ERA was about to be superseded by the WPA, to the above maximum. From October to December ERA cases were gradually being transferred to the WPA. Consequently, the ERA figures for these three months do not represent accurately the work relief case load. The WPA figure for December has been used in Chart I as more nearly representative of the case load. (See explanation in Table 1, Appendix B.) Ordinarily the number of cases employed by the ERA each month was around 100,000. The number of cases taken care of by direct relief, largely Public Welfare, started at 104,000 in January and declined during the year to a monthly figure which hovered about the level of 80,000. Except for January, the work relief case load was consistently greater than that on direct relief by a proportion varying from 1 to 45 per cent.

Chart I plots the course of the direct relief and work relief

Chart I — Relief Case Load in Massachusetts, May 1934–May 1938

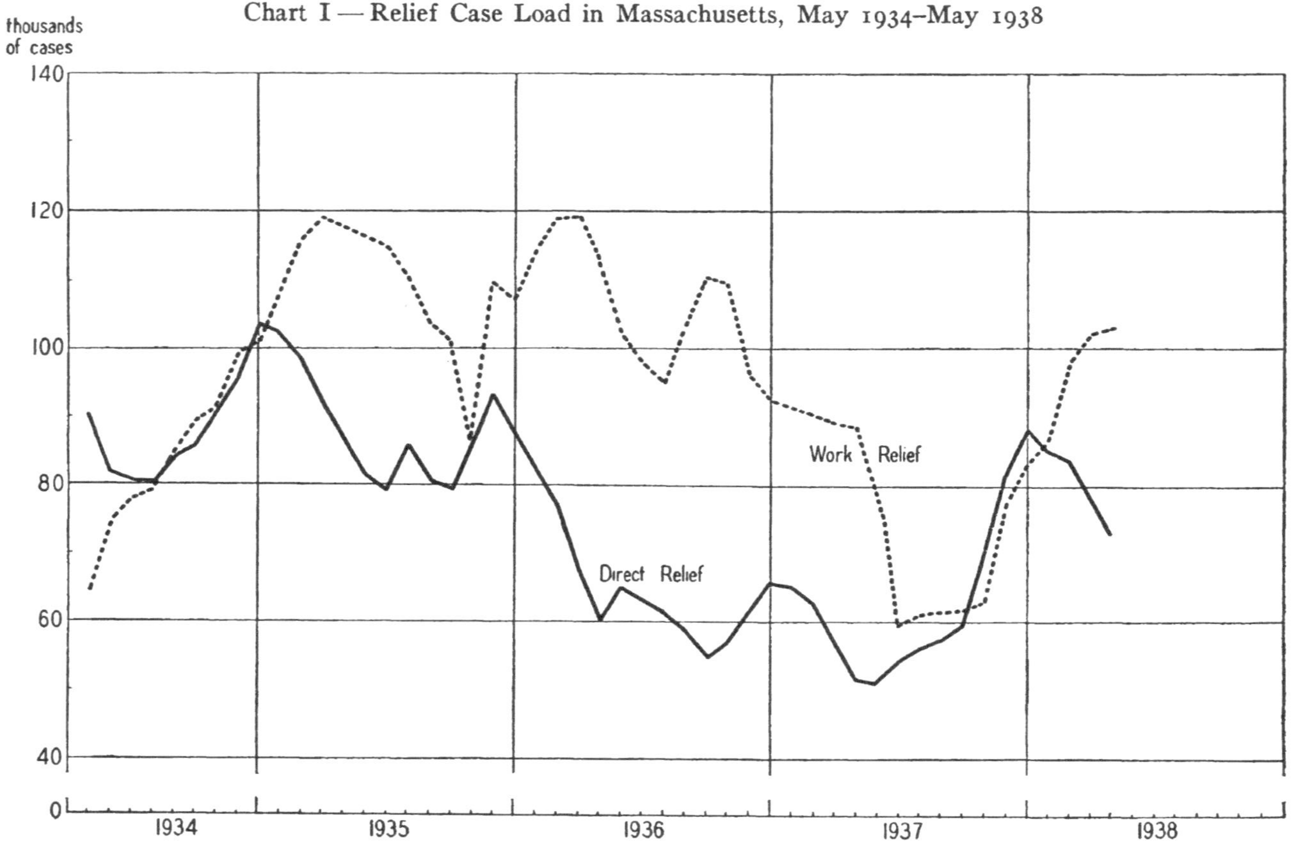

case load in the state by months from May 1934 through May 1938. It is apparent that, except for 1934, the latter part of 1935, and the last few months of 1937, the case load for work relief was much heavier than that for direct relief. In 1934 the ERA was just getting started and was not yet sufficiently well organized to take care of a large number of cases. The winter of 1934–35 was a bad one. All over the country the peak of the relief load came at that time. In Massachusetts both direct and work relief cases increased rapidly to January 1935. Then the direct relief case load fell off, although the work relief figures continued to increase to their high point in April and held that high level until the end of the year. In November and December the transfer from ERA to WPA necessitated a rise in direct relief to handle an interim situation, although by the end of December the transfer of cases had been largely completed. In the last three months of 1937, when the business "recession" began to be felt, both work relief and direct relief cases increased in number. Again, as in 1935, direct relief cases attained their peak in January and then fell off, while work relief cases continued to increase throughout the winter.

In general it may be said that in Massachusetts a greater number of relief cases were cared for by work relief than by direct relief during these four years. The state and localities were therefore relieved of a considerable part of their relief burden by federal participation in relief. This is confirmed by data on the relative expenditure of the localities, the state, and the federal government in connection with relief in Massachusetts.[3] In the first quarter of 1933 local funds provided 100 per cent of emergency relief expenditures. By the middle of the year the federal government had begun to contribute, and for the year as a whole the local contribution was 81.6 per cent, the federal 17.7 per cent, and the state .7 per cent. Federal

[3] *Statistical Summary of Emergency Relief Activities*, January 1933–December 1935, FERA.

funds continued to increase, so that in 1934 the localities' contribution to emergency relief had dropped to 45 per cent, the state's to .2 per cent. In 1935 this trend continued with the federal government supplying nearly 64 per cent of relief funds, the localities 36 per cent, and the state .1 per cent. The extremely small part played by the state in financing emergency relief is brought out by these figures. Vermont is the only other New England state in which the state contributed as little, though in Connecticut and Maine the state contribution was usually small, around 10 per cent. In Rhode Island the state supplied around 25 per cent of emergency relief funds throughout this period, and in New York from 15 to 20 per cent. In New Jersey, on the other hand, the state began as the chief source of relief funds, and the federal government's contribution served to relieve the financial strain on the state rather than on local governments. It is true in some degree, however, of all the New England states, and of New York, that the entrance of the federal government into relief eased the tremendous pressure upon local funds.

Certain differences in the fluctuations of the work relief and direct relief case loads are to be noticed. The trend of direct relief was distinctly downward from the beginning of 1935 to the last three months of 1937. Except for the decrease occasioned by the shift from ERA to WPA at the end of 1935 which is exaggerated by the ERA figures, the trend of work relief cases did not begin to go down until the spring of 1936. Then it went down sharply, except for an unexplained upswing in August, September, and October 1936. It may be coincidence that this upswing, which is clearly out of line with the general movement for that year, took place in the three months preceding the November elections. The WPA contends that this is coincidence and that the similar increase in work relief cases in the late summer of 1936 throughout the country was a result of the expansion of relief in the drought states. Although Massachusetts was not affected by the drought, it is suggested that there is a possibility of a sympathetic movement even in this state.[4]

It is interesting to observe that the two relief series show a clear seasonal fluctuation. As might be expected, the case load rises to a maximum in the winter. The timing, however, is different. Cases on direct relief are usually at their highest in January. From then on they decline. The high point for the work relief case load was consistently in April until 1937.

The sample of work relief cases with which this book is concerned was selected at random from 20 towns and cities in Massachusetts chosen to represent a cross section of industrial and economic conditions in the state.[5] Evidence concerning their representativeness will be presented later on. As far as work relief cases in our sample are concerned, the total case load for these towns and cities follows almost exactly the movement of the case load series for the state through the end of 1935. Monthly figures for the individual towns were not obtainable after that date. For direct relief the correspondence is not as close. The total of direct relief cases in our sample does not exhibit the sharp downward movement which is characteristic of direct relief cases for the state from the beginning of 1935 to 1937. The trend of direct relief in our sample appears to have been practically level for the whole period. Shorter movements, however, are almost exactly the same for our sample as for the state, both in direction and in timing, although the amplitude differs. In the middle of 1935, and again at the beginning of 1937, direct relief cases in our sample fluctuated more violently than in the state as a whole.

There are too many factors involved to be certain whether there exists any tendency for direct relief to take up the slack

[4] See Chapter XI for a more detailed analysis.

[5] A complete description of these towns and cities with their economic background is given in Chapter III.

in relief when work relief is reduced. Obviously the case load of both direct and work relief will depend on business conditions in general and upon the resources of individual families as well as upon local funds available. Most of the unemployed do not apply for relief in the first stages of unemployment but use their available assets first. There is some evidence which indicates that direct relief varied inversely at times with work relief. For the state figures this is notably apparent in the last three months of 1935. The annual peak of direct relief in all other years came in January, but in 1935 direct relief reached its maximum a month earlier and increased to a greater degree than it would have if the transition from ERA to WPA had not cut down work relief at this time. The inverse relation between direct relief and work relief is more apparent in the individual towns which make up our sample. Up to the last few months of 1934, the movements of the two kinds of relief cases are distinctly inverse in New Bedford, Cambridge, Somerville, Framingham, and the Small Towns. In Cambridge and Newton a very large increase in direct relief cases occurred in December 1935. Most of the other towns showed an increase in direct relief at that time, or a very small decline, as in Brookline, Hudson, Maynard, and New Bedford. On some occasions and in some places direct relief and work relief worked to supplement each other.[6]

Eligibility for work relief under the ERA depended upon family need, employability, and settlement. At least one member of the family must be employable, and if there were several, one was selected as the "economic head" of the case. ERA assignment would go to the "economic head." Family need was determined by a minimum standard budget set up in accordance with the size of the family, age of members, and local economic

[6] An inverse movement should be noticeable whenever large numbers of cases are transferred from relief to ERA and WPA or vice versa, according to a WPA official.

conditions. A standard budget is now used by the WPA in part to determine the eligibility of relief applicants although they are paid on the basis of a security wage.

Under the ERA if total family income was less than the standard budget set up for that family, work relief was given to the employable member selected as "economic head" of the family to make up the income deficiency. In other words work relief was frequently a means of supplementing inadequate family income. Family income was determined by totalling income received from all sources by members of the family considered as making up the family case. The income of children, brothers and sisters, or other less immediate family members, was not counted in full, however. Income from property was net. In a normal family group consisting of husband, wife, and children, all of the income of husband and wife was counted, but only two-thirds of the income of any of the children who were working. Property-ownership in itself was no bar to relief eligibility. If the income from property was less than the budget set up for the family, the case was considered eligible. It was therefore possible for a family to receive income from private employment, property, and other sources and still be eligible for ERA work as long as income from non-relief sources continued less than the family's bugetary minimum. It will be apparent when the data for our sample are analyzed that income from many non-relief sources was received by a number of families who also had ERA income. An attempt was made to allocate work relief so that supplementary ERA income would not raise the family income above the budgetary standard for individual families. It will be noted, however, that in most instances the addition of ERA income did not enable family income to meet the minimum of expenditure considered necessary for the family in question.

The ERA standard budget will be examined later on in connection with the expenditure data of our sample. It will be of some interest to describe it at this point, however, and compare it with the Boston Public Welfare budget and that of the WPA. The ERA budget included allowances for food, fuel, and light, rent, clothing, and incidentals. Each person was allowed $1.50 to $2.00 a week for food, depending on age, $.75 for clothing. The family was allowed in addition $5.00 a week for rent, $1.50 for fuel and light, and $1.00 for incidentals. Frequently the full allowance for clothing and incidentals was not made in practice when the budget for a family was computed. The WPA standard budget, a state maximum which varies with localities and which is used to determine eligibility, is very similar. The allowances for food, rent, and clothing are the same as in the ERA budget. Fuel and light were allowed $3.00, however, and incidentals could vary from $1.00 to $2.00 a week. Actually the allowances for clothes and incidentals have not been permitted by the State Administrator except in special cases (up to 1939), on the ground that those in need of food and housing should be taken care of first. The WPA has recently revised its standard budget and it now includes small allowances for clothing and incidentals.

The Boston Public Welfare budget (as of April 6, 1939) indicates a somewhat different basis. In the first place, although size of family is considered, $15.00 a week is the maximum relief allowance given, under any circumstances. There was no such fixed maximum under the ERA. The general relief budget is as shown in Table B.

Similar budgets, varying with local prices and economic circumstances, are set up from time to time in the towns and municipalities of the state. It should be remembered in the case of the work relief standard budgets that the maximum indicated a standard of family living to be attained by ERA assistance. It did not as a rule indicate the sum which would be paid. Departments of Public Welfare, however, were usually in the position of having to pay out their budgetary maximum

TABLE B

BOSTON PUBLIC WELFARE BUDGET

No. in family	Food	Rent	Gas & light	Total
1	no budget	$2.00	$3.00 (living expenses) *	$5.00
2	$3.15	2.50	1.00	6.65
3	4.88	2.75	1.00	8.63
4	6.21	3.00	1.00	10.21
5	7.37	3.25	1.00	11.62
6	8.69	3.50	1.00	13.19
7 & over	10.30	3.75	1.00	15.00

* For single persons a blanket sum for living expenses was allowed. The food and fuel items were not budgeted individually.

in full. In the case of the WPA, the standard budget indicated a minimum which the family income must fail to attain in order to be eligible.

ERA and WPA wages were determined on another basis. Under the ERA, "prevailing" wage rates in the locality were to be paid, with a minimum of 30 cents an hour set by the federal administrator. Family need indicated which families were eligible and to what extent. The amount of work to be given an individual depended roughly on the income deficiency of his family. Elasticity in the amount of ERA income an individual earned was brought about by varying his total hours of work within a definite time period and within the limits set by the Federal Administrator. The wage to be paid fluctuated with state and local standards and with occupational skill. Controversy has arisen concerning the work relief wage rates all over the country. There are those who claim it is too high; others that it is too low. In Massachusetts the rate has been determined in relation to the union wage for the trade involved. In other states somewhat different bases have been used.[7] What-

[7] The wage policy of the FERA was defined as the "prevailing rate for the given type of work in the locality in which the work is performed."

ever standard is used, and whether the rate is the same as or lower than that paid in private employment, some relation between the relief wage and the industrial wage has been noted. In New Jersey, where the relief wage was low, it was claimed that industrial wages were lowered as a result.[8] In Massachusetts it has been argued that relief wages were too high, with the result that it has frequently been difficult for private employers, particularly small ones, to get sufficient help at the wage they wish to pay. Some workers would rather stay on work relief and work shorter hours although their total income might be less than what they could earn in private employment. Trade unions, on the other hand, proclaim that very low relief wages tend to undermine the wage standards they have spent years in establishing. Whatever the justice of these arguments, it seems clear that there is some interaction between relief and industrial wages.[9]

It is a complicated problem. No fair-minded person wishes

The actual rate was to be determined either by (a) a wage rate committee composed of one representative each of organized labor and the local relief organization, and one local business or professional man selected by the other two, or by (b) the local relief administrator. If wage agreements between organized labor and employees existed in any locality, they were to be the prevailing rates. *FERA Monthly Reports*, January 1935, A Survey of Common Labor Rates Paid on the Work Program, p. 4.

[8] See R. A. Lester, *Some Aspects of Unemployment Relief in New Jersey*, unpublished Ph.D. thesis at Princeton.

[9] See Leah H. Feder, *Unemployment Relief in Periods of Depression*, 1936. Also *FERA Monthly Reports*, *op. cit.* The survey of ERA wages paid concluded that they reflected the rates paid by private industry on the whole. There were distinct geographical variations and also differences related to the degree of urbanization. Massachusetts was in the highest wage area, with a prevailing wage of 40 cents an hour or more.

Under the WPA, there have been a number of cases of skilled workers who earn their total security wage in a small number of hours and undercut rates for non-relief workers on free days. See Testimony of Carl Watson, WPA Administrator of Ohio, in the *Hearings before a Special Committee to Investigate Unemployment and Relief*, U. S. Senate, 75th Congress, vol. I, pp. 721–23.

to make work relief so attractive that workers will prefer to stay on relief rather than return to private employment. Until government control of industry goes to far greater lengths than it has at present, return to employment in private industry will be considered the goal for work relief applicants. That this is the assumption of the federal government is indicated by the emphasis laid by Washington officials on the actual return to private employment of relief workers in periods of industrial upturn, the establishment of a federal system of public employment exchanges, and the attempt to organize work relief jobs so as to preserve the skill of the unemployed. The President has stated on several occasions that work relief is a temporary expedient and that everything will be done to hasten the return, at least of the employables, to private work. To what extent this desideratum has been attained or can be attained is another matter. Many work relief projects have been organized so hurriedly and so inefficiently, for a number of reasons which will not be discussed at this point, that best use could not be made of the skills of the workers involved. More progress has been made in the direction of efficiency under the WPA than under the ERA. The fact that the average age of those on work relief is somewhat greater than that of the working population will make it more difficult for those on work relief to get jobs in private industry.[10] And the fact that there is less stigma attached to work relief than to direct relief may induce those on work relief to relax their efforts to get a private industrial job more quickly. These are but a few of the factors involved. The problem will be discussed more adequately when we have examined our sample of those on work relief who received cancellations, and the reasons for cancellation.

On the other hand, relief should be given on the basis of some standard of adequacy or the whole purpose of work relief

[10] The age difference is probably not more than two or three years, according to WPA evidence.

will be defeated. Skill and morale, to say nothing of health and decency, cannot be preserved on a starvation diet or under markedly inadequate living conditions. The minimum budgetary standard set up under the FERA was barely adequate, but there are many who thought it too high. In New England at least, the popular view that no one would be on relief if it were not in some way his fault still exists and has not yet been superseded entirely by the view that many unemployed are unable to secure work in private industry. The FERA took the attitude that reported figures for direct and work relief in New England did not accurately represent the relief problem, but understated it, because of the social stigma attached to being on relief. As one of their reports put it:

> ". . . the peculiar method of relief distribution which is still almost entirely in the hands of the township governments and the overseers of the poor . . . especially with respect to the distribution of direct relief, has tended to retain almost all of the social stigma which customarily attached itself to all those who, in that region of the country, are said to be 'on the town.' "[11]

Work relief was given a somewhat higher social status, being "frequently regarded as equivalent to a 'job' and not relief."[12] The latter view, however, was by no means general at this date, and is not even now.

In the following chapters a representative sample of Massachusetts work relief cases will be examined. Their economic status at the time of their application for relief, their income, their property, their debts will be presented. We shall also analyze their occupations and their age. In some cases their weekly expenditure is known; in others we have only the standard budget set up for them by the ERA. A smaller sample of cases which received cancellations from the ERA or WPA will also be analyzed. In the majority of cases the reason for cancellation was given as well as the general economic data for the

[11] *FERA Monthly Report*, November 1934, p. 7. [12] *Ibid.*

family. The comparison of our data with other investigations (such as those made by the Division of Research of the WPA, formerly the Division of Social Research), by other organizations and individuals in many parts of the country will give some indication as to the representative nature of the conclusions which will be drawn.

It seems clear that our relief sample may safely be taken to represent Massachusetts work relief cases, and possibly those of New England. To what extent Massachusetts is typical of the situation in the whole country it is not possible to say. Detailed information on relief cases and administration is not generally available, except for a few states and cities.[13] There are some difficulties, however, in considering a Massachusetts sample as representative, even of the industrial section of the country. Chief of these is the fact that Massachusetts industries have been subject to a declining trend which began long before the last depression. The emphasis on local administration of relief, if not peculiar to the New England states, is more strongly characteristic of states like Massachusetts. Less centralization of relief activities was undertaken on its own initiative than in many states during the depression.[14] Despite these

[13] D. H. MacNeil, *Seven Years of Unemployment Relief in New Jersey, 1930–36*, a report prepared for the Committee on Social Security of the Social Science Research Council; *The Relief Problem in Hamilton County*, Ohio, 1937; L. V. Armstrong, *We Too Are the People*, Boston, 1938, are among the best studies giving information for other states. Mrs. Armstrong, formerly ERA Administrator of a Michigan county, gives many details on relief cases and administration in Michigan.

[14] The FERA states that New England was one of the regions with "reasonably effective local welfare departments" which existed as a "nucleus of organization." In many states there was not even this and relief administration had to be "built from the ground up." *FERA Monthly Report*, November 1934, pp. 5 and 6. Nevertheless, Massachusetts made almost no moves to centralize these local departments until centralization was forced upon the state by the FERA. This centralization applied only to work relief. Direct relief is still almost completely in the hands of town and city welfare boards.

considerations the occupational distribution of relief workers in Massachusetts shows a remarkable similarity to that in the United States.

Even if our data and conclusions can be taken as typical only of the region to which they directly refer, however, they are important. There has not been previously as complete an analysis of any section of the relief population. It is certainly desirable to know what kind of people are on relief and how long they are likely to stay on relief. The problem of relief is one of the most important confronting us today, and the more facts available concerning it, the better. It is believed that the following analysis will contribute to the collection of facts necessary for competent understanding of the relief situation.

CHAPTER III

A GENERAL PICTURE OF THE WORK RELIEF APPLICANT

GENERALIZATIONS are constantly being made concerning those who are on relief. In many instances they seem to be considered as a race apart by those who have never had to apply for relief. One of the purposes of this investigation is to present information based on facts concerning the people who are on relief. What are their occupations? Do they own property? Are they "bums" or ne'er-do-wells? Do they have any sources of income other than relief? How do they spend their money? These are some of the questions which will be given at least a partial answer for Massachusetts in this book.

The information has been taken, for the most part, from records of the Massachusetts ERA for the calendar year 1935; [1] 2,180 cases from twenty towns and cities in the state serve as the main statistical sample. In selecting the towns from which the cases were to be drawn, the attempt was made to represent all conditions in Massachusetts. Cambridge and Somerville, for instance, typify both urban and industrial conditions; Maynard, Hudson, and Framingham are examples of small industrial towns in rural parts of the state; New Bedford exemplifies the depressed textile areas; Newton and Brookline are residential towns; and a number of small towns such as Hopkinton, Lincoln, Stow, Sudbury, and Sherborn were combined into one

[1] The records used were 25A (the home visit report) and 15A (the ERA application blank). Wherever possible the home visit report was used, as it was the opinion of one of the administrative staff that it was a more accurate record of family circumstances, and inspection of the records indicated that this was indeed the case. The home visit reports were the reports of ERA investigators who interviewed the families in order to check the information given by the family on application for work relief.

group to represent the rural villages of the state. When the cases from all the towns were combined, without any weighting except that resulting inevitably from the selection of the towns and the size of the sample from each town, it was found that the results compared surprisingly well with those obtained by the WPA in their 1935 inventory of work relief cases in Massachusetts. The details of this comparison will be considered later. It may be said here, however, that every test indicates that the two thousand odd cases which are the subject of this survey are representative of those on Massachusetts work relief in 1935, and, to the extent that the state represents other industrial sections of the country, of the industrial United States.[2]

These cases are all families the head of which applied for and received work relief on the ERA some time in 1935. These records were taken from the active file in the WPA district offices during 1937, which means that they had been on and off work relief continuously up to the end of 1937. They may have been shifted from project to project with lapses of time during which they did not work. They may have returned to private employment for a few days or weeks. But eventually they returned to the relief rolls. From such cases which have been more or less continuously active since 1935 may result a permanent work relief problem.[3] An analysis of the economic status of these families is thus of considerable importance.

In this chapter the entire sample will be considered as a whole, irrespective of the individual towns. Other sections of

[2] Part IV deals in some detail with the question of the typicalness of Massachusetts and the sample.

[3] Since our sample is drawn from the continuing relief cases, it has been questioned (by a WPA official) whether it typifies the entire 1935 work relief load. It has been suggested that these cases analyzed represent the "hard core" of unemployment and not those who got off relief between 1935 and 1937 and stayed off. The comparison between this sample and a smaller one of separated cases (in Chapter VIII) will illuminate this question further. Still, the statistical comparisons made with available data indicate a close relation between our sample and the entire 1935 case load.

the book will analyze in some detail the differences among the towns, as well as other aspects, such as income and occupational status. It must be remembered, too, that these relief cases are confined to those who were made eligible for work relief. Although income from other relief sources was sometimes given them to supplement their ERA income, they are not primarily direct relief cases.

The average family on work relief (in our sample) was slightly larger than the average family in Massachusetts: 4.3 as against 4 persons. The difference, however, is not as great as might be supposed. It has been found that relief families are usually larger than the average family in comparable non-relief populations. This does not mean, necessarily, that larger families are less able to withstand hard times. It may well be explained by the preference given large families by relief agencies.[4] The economic heads of the families (the members selected by the ERA as the most employable) were predominantly male, only 442 or one-fifth of the sample being female. Nearly half of the women heads of families were in the smaller families; for example, 51 per cent of the single persons, and 35 per cent of the heads of families of two, were women. The number of female economic heads in the other size of family groups varied from 8 to 18 per cent. The average work relief applicant in this group was, then, a man who was the economic head of a family of 4 or 5 persons.

He was likely to be a semi-skilled or white collar worker, a skilled craftsman, or an unskilled laborer, in the order named.

[4] In New Jersey, the 1934 investigation found that over one-third of the relief families had five or more members and that relief families were on the average larger than other families in the general population. (They give no comparative figures, however.) *Neighbors in Need*, Report No. 1, N. J. ERA, 1935, p. 12. In Chicago, among complete native white families investigated for the Consumer Purchases Study, the relief families averaged 4.3 persons per family in comparison with 3.5 persons for non-relief families. *Family Income in Chicago*, Bull. 642, Bureau of Labor Statistics, 1939, p. 37.

Those four occupational groups comprised 86 per cent of our sample, as may be seen from Table 4 (Appendix B). Domestic workers, farmers and their laborers and inexperienced workers formed a very small proportion of the group. Among white collar workers, the number of office workers and salesmen was about twice as great as professional people and proprietors. The WPA figures for Massachusetts [5] show an extremely close similarity with the occupational distribution of our sample. The only marked differences occur in the white collar and semi-skilled groups. There were 5 per cent more white collar workers

TABLE C

WORK RELIEF AGE DISTRIBUTION IN MASSACHUSETTS, 1935

Years	Massachusetts *		New Bedford	
16–24	13.9%		14.0%	
25–34	23.0		19.1	
35–44	26.8	61.0	29.2	66.8
45 and over	34.2		37.6	

* Sample study based on 5 per cent of the cases studied for the labor inventory of March 1935. The data were made available to me through the kindness of Mr. Howard B. Myers, Director of Research, WPA.

and 2 per cent fewer semi-skilled workers in our sample than in the WPA occupational inventory. These differences may be attributed in part to errors of sampling and in part to the fact that the WPA survey relates only to March 1935 whereas our sample relates to the entire calendar year, and includes only those who were still on the work relief rolls in 1937.

The majority of relief workers were over 35 years of age in Massachusetts. The WPA conducted a sample study of age distribution at the time of their labor inventory. Table C states their results and includes as well the age distribution for New Bedford.[6]

[5] Taken from the labor inventory of 1935.

[6] The age distribution was obtained only for New Bedford for our sample. Limitations of time and the fact that the age data were not easily available from the records made it impracticable to secure the age distribution of the whole sample.

If the Massachusetts figures are taken as typical of those on work relief in 1935, it is apparent that 61 per cent were 35 and over, and that 34 per cent were 45 and over. In our New Bedford sample the proportion of older workers was 6 per cent higher, the group 25 to 34 years of age 4 per cent lower, and the percentages the same for the youngest group of 16 to 24 years. Since New Bedford is a cotton textile town which has not only been hit hard by the depression, but is also subject to the declining secular trend characteristic of Massachusetts textiles, it may be that the older workers were particularly

TABLE D

UNEMPLOYMENT IN MASSACHUSETTS, 1934

Years	Total Unemployed		Temporarily Employed on Government Work		Full Time Employed	
14–24	32.8%		21.6%		17.9%	
25–34	19.2		23.0		26.2	
35–44	17.1	48.0	24.8	55.4	23.6	55.9
45 and over	30.9		30.6		32.3	

affected in that city. Probably if the age distribution of all our towns had been recorded the results would be more in line with those of the WPA. The question of the age of relief workers becomes peculiarly important when the problem of re-employing them in private industry is faced. Discrimination by private industry against workers over 40 years old has been charged frequently.

The results of the Massachusetts Unemployment Census for 1934 are consistent with the above conclusions with respect to age. Table D shows that the majority of the workers employed on government relief projects in 1934 were over 35 years of age. It is interesting to note that unemployment in general was relatively more prevalent among the younger workers, below 24 years of age. Government work relief, however, tended to favor the older workers, particularly those between 25 and 44 years. It is also of some interest that more than half of the full-time employed were over 35 and that a third of these were 45 or over. If there is discrimination against re-employing older workers who have been on relief, it apparently does not extend to older employees who are already at work.

What is the economic status of an unemployed worker at the time he applies for relief? Is he a person who couldn't keep his job and gladly relied on the government to support him? Is he one of the many who had never owned property or saved and therefore could not be expected to support himself and his family during bad times? There are such on the relief rolls, of course, but the following information on property holdings at the time of application for relief is revealing as to the economic class from which many relief applicants come. It must be borne in mind, however, that our sample represents the most employable portion of the relief population. Those accepted for work relief must be able to do some kind of work and are more likely to have a good occupational history. On the other hand, our sample is taken from those who had been on relief more or less constantly since 1935 and had not been able to obtain and hold jobs in private industry during the course of three years.

At the time of their application for work relief in 1935 the families included in our sample owned property as shown in Table E. The information on telephones applies to only two towns, Somerville and Newton, and it is difficult to know whether the lack of information for the other towns means inaccuracy of recording or that no telephones were rented by the families. In all cases there is undoubtedly a good deal of inaccuracy in the records and the probability is that property-ownership was understated rather than exaggerated, since ownership of too much property might render a person ineligible for relief. Approximately one-fifth of the families owned their own homes, of which more than four-fifths were mortgaged. There were

TABLE E

WORK RELIEF PROPERTY-OWNERSHIP

	Number	Per cent
Total number of cases	2221°	100.0
Number having telephones †	29	1.3
Number owning homes	450	20.7
Number mortgaged	379	82.6*
Number owning other Real Estate	10	0.5
Number with Insurance	805	36.2
Number owning automobiles	164	7.4
Number owning Securities	6	0.3
Number with savings (bank accounts)	46	2.1
Number owning other Property	13	0.6

° Some schedules could be used for the property analysis, although not for the more detailed income, expenditure, debt analysis. Therefore, we have more than 2180 cases for this purpose.

* Per cent of homes owned which were mortgaged. All the other per cents are in terms of the total number of cases.

† Not strictly property but included as indicative of economic status.

many other cases recorded on the schedules where houses had been owned but had been taken over by banks or towns for lack of payments. More than one-third of these families had insurance policies, usually industrial policies for small amounts. Many more of them had had policies but had been forced to let them lapse, or, where possible, had turned them in for cash. The only other property ownership which is at all significant is that of automobiles and only 7.4 per cent of the cases had them. Usually the ownership of an automobile was allowed only when it was essential in connection with the work of the family head or when it was so old and decrepit that its turn-in value was nil. The ownership of other property was negligible. A few families had other real estate or property of some kind, or securities or savings, but only a very few. Property-ownership differed considerably with the town or city. A village family, for instance, was much more likely to own its own home than to have insurance. Such differences will be analyzed in considerable detail when the individual towns are dealt with.

It is fairly safe to say that at least one-third of our group, possibly more, came from the class of workmen who owned a home, held a small insurance policy, and may have had some kind of car. Probably more of the group had been in this class but had been forced to use their assets to support themselves and their families in the period intervening between loss of employment and work relief. A number of studies have shown that the unemployed ordinarily subsist on savings, loans, cashed-in insurance policies, and credit before application for relief is made. Our investigation of cancelled work relief cases, described in Chapter VII, gives some information on the source of support of some 400 cases between their loss of employment and certification for the ERA in five of the towns. The chief sources of support were, in order: odd jobs and temporary work, friends and relations, public welfare, savings, other relief agencies, insurance and loans, and credit. About 7 per cent went on ERA at once, a very small proportion of the sample. It is noteworthy that slightly over 40 per cent relied on temporary jobs and the help of relatives and friends. (See Table 5, Appendix B.)

It appears to be characteristic of low-income families that they spend more than they earn and rely on credit for a considerable proportion of their expenditures.[7] Relief families are no exception. Applicants were asked to enumerate their debts when they applied for relief and in some towns the ERA standard budget was set up to include a weekly payment towards their debts when they applied for relief. It is unlikely that the debt figures are precise and it is hard to say whether the amounts were overstated or minimized. There might be a tendency to overemphasize the extent of debt in order to make out

[7] Releases of the results of the Consumer Purchases Study indicate that families with incomes of $1,250 a year or below usually spent more than they earned in 1935–36.

a good case for the necessity of relief. On the other hand, families may have tried to conceal their debts or have forgotten many of them. Undoubtedly the debts reported were of fairly recent origin.

Massachusetts relief applicants, as represented by our sample, were almost universally in debt. At the time of application the average debt per family was about $234. Table F indicates the items for which the average family was in debt.

TABLE F

MEAN DEBT PER FAMILY (2,180 cases)

	Amount	Per cent		Amount	Per cent
Food	$19	8.1	Furniture	$11	4.7
Rent	45	19.2	Medical	25	10.7
Taxes	18	7.7	Unspecified	55	23.5
Personal Loans	41	17.5	Mortgage	7	3.0
Industrial Loans	13	5.6	Total	234	100.0

Nearly a quarter of the indebtedness was unspecified. A fifth of the indebtedness went for rent, slightly more than a fifth for loans, and one-eighth for medical care. The families owed, on the average, small amounts for food, taxes, furniture, and on mortgages. It should be noted that the averages were computed for all cases, whether or not the family was actually in debt for that particular item, counting as zero those cases for which there were no debts. The actual amount of indebtedness for the families which were in debt for any item was higher than the average figure given here by $52.

The size of the average debt for the various items was also very much greater when the average is based on the number having such debts. Table G presents these averages and the per cent of the total sample with such indebtedness. Over four-fifths of these families had some kind of indebtedness. Thirty-five per cent owed an average of $128 for rent, and $155 for unspecified debts. Twenty-eight per cent were in debt for taxes, and for medical care. Food bills were outstanding for twenty-seven per cent. The proportion in debt for loans and mortgages was small, but the average amounts were large.

TABLE G

MEAN DEBT PER CASE WITH DEBTS

Item	Average (based on number having debts)	Per cent of Cases with Debts for Each Item
Total Debts	$285	82
Food	70	27
Rent	128	35
Taxes	63	28
Personal Loans	288	14
Industrial Loans	236	5
Furniture	91	12
Medical	90	28
Unspecified	155	35
Mortgages	258	3

Not only were these families in debt when they applied for relief but they continued to subsist on credit for part of their current expenses. Their average income was consistently below their average expenditure. The interpretation of the expenditure figures which are given in the ERA records is uncertain because it is not always possible to tell whether the expenditures represent what was actually spent by the family at the time of application, or the ERA standard budget for that family in that district. Apparently it depended on the district supervisor as to which was recorded. It seemed fairly clear from the records, however, that in Newton, Somerville, Cambridge, and Framingham, the attempt was made to record actual weekly expenditures. In the other towns the expenditure figure was probably a statement of what the family was entitled to spend according to ERA standards. The average figure for the sample, therefore, is a mixture of standard and actual expenditures. The interesting thing is that however the expenditures may be interpreted, they were consistently higher than weekly income, by, on the average, $4.08.

Table H lists the average income, divided as to sources, and the average expenditure, divided as to items, for the entire sample.

TABLE H

AVERAGE WEEKLY INCOME AND EXPENDITURE

Weekly Income	Amount	Per cent	Weekly Expenditure	Amount	Per cent
Total	$13.50	100%	Total	$17.58	100%
Private Employment	1.41	10.4	House	6.53	37.1
Rents	.43	3.2	Food	8.25	46.9
Lodgers	.19	1.4	Clothing	1.57	8.9
ERA	10.40	77.0	Insurance	.33	1.9
Public Welfare	.41	3.0	Other	.90	5.1
Other Relief	.41	3.0			
Miscellaneous	.25	1.9			

As might be expected, the average income of $13.50 per week was derived for the most part from relief sources. From the ERA came 77 per cent, and 3 per cent each from Public Welfare and other relief sources. Private employment, usually odd jobs or contributions from other working members of the family, amounted to $1.41 a week, or 10 per cent of the family income. There were some, of course, who subsisted entirely on relief, and a few who, although on the active ERA list, were temporarily engaged in private employment. Rents, boarders and lodgers accounted for only 4.5 per cent of weekly income on the average although in a few families this was an important source of income.

On the average, although the group supplemented relief income in many ways, they were still unable to meet the main expenses of living. They spent or were budgeted for $6.50 for rent, light, and fuel per week, $8.25 for food, about $1.60 for clothes, $.33 for insurance, and $.90 for miscellaneous. Expenditure for insurance was quite general and is undoubtedly an account of an actual expenditure, for no allowance for insurance was made in the ERA standard budget. It is more than likely that actual expenditures of these families included many more items such as tobacco, the movies, medical care, etc. A detailed study made of some 400 families in Cambridge in 1935 made it clear that relief families do not cut out expenditures on tobacco, movies, newspapers, etc. even if it is necessary to obtain credit for more necessary budgetary items such as food and rent.[8]

A comparison of our income figures with those derived from certain WPA studies indicates close correspondence. Sample cases in 13 cities, selected as being typical of the relief situation throughout the country, were investigated in 1935 and 1936. The median income of these certified cases from all sources was, in March 1936, $58.30 for the month, or $13.45 per week.[9] This is almost identical with our average weekly income figure. In May 1935 a similar survey had been made of cases in the same cities. Those with relief income only and those with relief income plus income from other sources were treated separately. The median income for supplemented cases was $44.10 per month, or $10.17 per week; the mean income $50.60 per month, or $11.60 per week.[10] These figures are below the average income of the families in our sample.

A few other facts need to be mentioned before the general picture of our relief sample is complete. Out of 2,165 cases

[8] See "The Expenditures of the Unemployed" by Elizabeth W. Gilboy in the *American Sociological Review*, December 1938.

[9] *Survey of Cases Certified for Works Program Employment in 13 Cities*, WPA Division of Social Research, Series IV, No. 2. Estimated weekly income was obtained by multiplying their monthly figure by 12 and dividing by 52.

[10] *The 1935 Relief Population in 13 Cities:* A Cross Section, WPA Division of Social Research, Series I, No. 23. Estimated weekly income was obtained as below.

which reported on the question of citizenship, 98.5 per cent were U. S. citizens and 1.3 per cent had taken out their first papers. Even if the few who did not report were aliens, they would have formed a negligible proportion of the total group.

Of the 2,221 cases for which race was given nearly 97 per cent were white and almost 3 per cent were colored. One person was listed as belonging to a race other than white or Negro and the rest were unknown. In only two cities were more than 6 colored persons registered. Cambridge had 25 Negro families, and New Bedford 28. Thus, our sample consists almost entirely of white persons. For that reason the small number of Negroes were not treated separately. It is interesting to note, however, that the per cent of Negroes in our sample of unemployed was nearly twice that of the working population of the state.[11]

The data on education were limited. Apparently the ERA districts were not uniform in recording this information. There was nothing on the subject in the Somerville records, and very little in those of Cambridge, Newton, and Framingham. On the other hand educational data were fairly complete for cases in the Small Towns, New Bedford, Maynard, and Hudson. In all, 514 cases had records of their education. Approximately 56 per cent of the economic heads of these families had had 4 to 8 years of schooling, and 31 per cent had been to high school. Almost 7 per cent had been to college or had technical education of some kind. About 6 per cent had been limited to 1 to 3 years of school. The majority had gone no further than grammar school.

Presumably the skilled craftsmen would be the principal workers eligible for union membership. There were 466 skilled craftsmen among the heads of families. Only 87 of them, or 19

[11] According to the 1930 census, only 1.3 per cent of the Massachusetts population were other than white. D. Davenport and J. Crosston, *Unemployment and Prospects of Employment in Massachusetts*, p. 12.

per cent, reported that they belonged, or had at one time belonged, to a labor union. Here again, the absence of information does not necessarily mean that those for whom information was lacking were not union members.

It is now possible to describe in average terms the 1935 ERA applicant in Massachusetts as represented by our sample. He is a man over 35 years old and head of a family of 4 or 5 persons. He is a citizen of the United States, white in color, and he has had 4 to 8 years of school. He is probably a semi-skilled or unskilled laborer. It is probable that his capital assets, such as a house, insurance, or savings, have been liquidated by the time he applies for relief. He is already in debt, to the extent of nearly $250, principally for personal and industrial loans, rent, and medical care. He also owes small amounts for food, furniture, and clothes. His weekly income comes largely from relief, work on ERA projects supplemented by Public Welfare and other relief agencies. He gets as well a small weekly sum from the private employment of himself or other members of his family. Income from rents, boarders and lodgers, and other sources serves to eke out his weekly earnings further. Still he spends, or is allowed to spend according to the ERA standard for his family, $4 more than he receives each week, even for the main necessities of life such as shelter, heat and light, food, and clothes.

The above description probably applies roughly to the majority of these relief applicants. But there are other types who must not be forgotten in the general picture. The man may be a skilled craftsman or a white collar worker; a youth just out of school under 25 years of age who has been unable to get a job; a woman with no specialized training who is forced to work to support her family. These all represent important sections of the group. Or he may be one of the fortunate third who have managed to hang on to his insurance, or of the fifth who still own their own homes.

The danger of relying on an average picture, however, must not be forgotten. The diverse nature of our sample will be brought out in succeeding chapters which will examine the data for the individual towns and cities, and other groups within the sample. The reliability of any typical description of a sample of families such as ours must depend, statistically, on how representative the average is. If there is considerable dispersion of the cases, and no pronounced grouping about the statistical average used, the figure becomes nothing but a statistical device with little meaning. We have seen that many different occupations and ages are included in the group of families investigated and their proportionate strength has been indicated. As far as income and expenditure are concerned, the statistical averages may be tested more precisely to determine their representative character. An income frequency distribution has been drawn up to indicate the concentration of cases in the various income classes. The result for the whole sample appears in Table I.

TABLE I

FREQUENCY DISTRIBUTION OF INCOMES

Income Class	Per cent of Total Cases
$ 0– 3.99	12.9
4– 7.99	5.7
8–11.99	5.2
12–15.99	45.5
16–19.99	13.6
20–23.99	6.5
24–27.99	5.5
28–31.99	2.6
32–35.99	.8
36–39.99	1.0
40 and over	.7

It will be noted that the grouping about the income class interval which contains the average income ($12–15.99) is fairly good. Nearly half the cases fall within this class, and an additional 18 per cent are in the classes immediately below and above it. The average income, then, is adequately descriptive of almost two-thirds of our families. There is another concentration of cases, however, in the very lowest income group. Thirteen per cent of the families investigated had incomes between zero and $3.99 for the week in question. When charted these two points of concentration appear distinctly and the distribution looks almost bimodal. In none of the expenditure distributions did this phenomenon appear. The distributions are skewed towards the lower expenditure classifications, but there is no marked grouping of cases, except about the average.

In trying to describe the typical relief applicant of our group of families, therefore, the nature of the income distribution cannot be neglected. While some two-thirds of the families may be represented as deriving an income of $13.50 a week from various sources, principally relief, there are 282 families who had practically no income. The statements about the average relief applicant must be qualified with reference to the differences which occur within the whole group. Nevertheless, an attempt to describe the group in average terms has some advantages if the proper qualifications are made. It is possible to become too concerned with the diversities of the families and to fail to see the characteristics which they have in common.

CHAPTER IV

LOCAL DIFFERENCES IN WORK RELIEF

A NUMBER of significant differences between the towns and cities included in our sample appear with respect to the relief situation. In order to make these local variations clear it is necessary to go briefly into their economic background. Three cities with a population of slightly over 100,000 (in 1934) represent quite diverse conditions. Cambridge is a manufacturing city within the radius of metropolitan Boston. Its chief industries in 1936 were food (bakery products and confectionery), printing and publishing, foundry products and furniture.[1] Although these industries are listed by Dr. Davenport [2] as ones in which there is a prospect of a return to the predepression level and possibly of expansion, Cambridge heads the list of our towns in per cent of unemployment, 26.1.[3] This is probably explained by the fact that many of the minor industries, such as boots and shoes, were subject not only to the depression but to the general declining trend of manufacturing in the state. Also more than half of the employable workers in Cambridge are not employed by the city industries. Many of them work in Boston, which suffered an even greater industrial decline during the depression than Cambridge. There has been

[1] The industrial data for Cambridge and the other cities and towns are taken from the Massachusetts Census of Manufactures for 1936, supplied to me through the kindness of Dr. Roswell Phelps, Director of Statistics, Massachusetts Department of Labor & Industries.

[2] *Unemployment and Prospects for Reemployment in Massachusetts*, Business Research Studies, No. 15. Harvard Graduate School of Business Administration. Much of the information on the present and future status of Massachusetts industries comes from this study.

[3] *Massachusetts Census of Unemployment.* This was not the case in the Biggers census of 1937. Cf. figures on p. 52.

a slight upward trend in wage earners employed since the low point of 1932, but in 1935 the number employed was well below the high point of 1926.

Somerville is another city within the metropolitan Boston area, in many respects similar to Cambridge. It is less of a manufacturing city, employing only about a third as many wage earners in its industries as Cambridge. Its principal industries are food, furniture, structural metal, and printing and publishing. Approximately eight-ninths of its employable workers were employed outside of Somerville in 1934. It stood next to Cambridge in the unemployment ranking, with 25 per cent.

The other large city, New Bedford, is one of the chief cotton textile cities in the state. Since 1927 this industry has declined sharply in Massachusetts, as a result of a geographical shift in the industry. The depression only intensified a problem of unemployment which appears to be permanent. There has been a considerable increase in the number of wage earners employed since 1932, but there were still nearly one-third less in 1935 and 1936 than in 1927. The ratio of unemployed to employable workers in 1934 was 22.5 per cent. The development of silk and rayon mills, of which there were 7 in 1936, may help to absorb some of the unemployed and the development of minor industries may aid in solving the problem. The fact remains, however, that New Bedford is primarily a one-industry city which has been doubly hit by the depression and the long-term declining trend in cotton textiles.

Another group of towns also are indicative of manufacturing conditions in the state. Framingham, Ashland, Hudson, and Maynard are all small towns, set in rural areas, with a few manufacturing establishments supporting them. Framingham and Ashland are adjacent and have been considered together. They had in 1934 a population of some 25,000. The chief industries in Framingham are paper goods, rugs, and worsted goods; in Ashland, electric clocks. Although Massachusetts has been losing its relative share in the paper industry since 1919, the industry itself is subject to a slow upward trend and there seems no reason to suppose that it will not return to its former level. The jewelry industry, under which the making of clocks is classed, is one of the few prosperous industries in the state and was less hard hit by the depression than most of the others. Nevertheless, the per cent of unemployment in Framingham in 1934 was 24; in Ashland, 25.

Maynard is a town of about 7,000 inhabitants supported almost entirely by the woolen industry. Hudson, a town of similar size (8,000 population), depends upon worsted goods and boots and shoes for its work. Although the woolen industry is losing in importance in the country, Massachusetts has managed to keep its share, and the industry showed a surprising recovery from the depression. The leather industry is the chief industry in the state from the standpoint of wage earners employed and value of products. It is a declining industry and there seems little hope that it will reach its pre-depression level. As a whole, however, both Maynard and Hudson had a low percentage of unemployment in 1934, 18.6 and 17.7 respectively.

Brookline and Newton are wealthy residential towns within metropolitan Boston. One would expect them to have survived the depression better than industrial cities and towns. That such is the case is shown by their unemployment ranking. They are below all the other towns in our sample with percentages of 12.7 in Brookline, and 16.4 in Newton. Yet a certain limited amount of industry goes on in both places. In 1936 Newton had 56 establishments, chiefly for radio apparatus and knit goods employing about 3,000 workers. This figure is almost as high as the 1929 level and employment in Newton industries has risen steadily since 1932. However, nearly four-fifths of Newton's employable workers have jobs outside of Newton. The same is true of Brookline to an even greater degree. It had 23 establishments, of which the principal ones were for steel engraving and advertising novelties. These were small, employing only 413 workers in 1936.

The Small Town group is composed of the following: Acton, Concord, Holliston, Hopkinton, Lincoln, Littleton, Sherborn, Stow, Sudbury, Weston, and Wayland. All these are small rural or residential towns, with a total population of about 29,000. Concord is the largest, with some 6,000 inhabitants; Weston and Wayland are around 3,000 in population. The others are all below 3,000 population, and Sherborn, for example, contains only 944 people. Very little manufacturing goes on in these towns, although Concord has a few small furniture and wool shoddy factories, and Acton has a plant for the manufacture of explosives. Despite the fact that Lincoln, Weston, and Wayland may be considered to some extent as Boston suburbs, they are farming communities, and the other small towns are far enough away to be outside the metropolitan influence. It was found by Dr. Davenport that rural communities, defined as towns of a population under 2,500, suffered to a greater extent from unemployment in 1934 than industrial and urban centers. Taking our Small Town group as a whole, that does not seem to be the case. The unemployment per cent was 20 in 1934, between that of New Bedford and Maynard, but less than that of Cambridge, Somerville, and Hudson. Of course, our Small Town group is not strictly comparable with that defined by Dr. Davenport, since it includes as well some towns in the 2,500 to 10,000 class which had the lowest per cent of unemployment of any category. Although the rural section of our sample may not be completely representative of rural localities in Massachusetts, it appears to approximate the rural sections of the state in matters which can be compared statistically, such as occupational distribution.

The occupational distribution of our Small Town group parallels very closely that of the rural section of Massachusetts given in the WPA occupational survey of 1935, although their definition of rural is based on a population below 2,500 and ours is not. The chief differences occur in the white collar, the domestic, and inexperienced classes which are represented in our rural sample in somewhat greater proportion (3 to 4 per cent). In both samples the farm classification is almost identical. The differences may be due to lack of similarity in definition of rural, to errors of sampling, to the difference in the time of survey, or to the influence of Boston upon some of our towns. However that may be, the correspondence between the occupational distribution of the two samples appears sufficient to warrant the use of our Small Town group as representative of relief applicants in rural sections of the state.

On the whole, our sample seems to represent economic conditions in Massachusetts fairly well. Most of the principal industries are included, and rural and residential areas each play their part. Possibly the extent of unemployment is somewhat understated, for nearly all these towns except Cambridge had unemployment ratios below the state average, according to the 1934 census.

The unemployment percentages of the towns, however, are quite different when computed from figures given by the voluntary census of 1937. In this case, New Bedford has the highest proportion of unemployed to employable, with Cambridge considerably lower. In fact all the percentages are reduced in comparison with the 1934 figures except that for New Bedford. The inaccuracy of the Biggers data and the fact that the extent of error varied from place to place and group to group makes comparisons uncertain. Also we have been forced by lack of data to use the 1934 figure for employables in computing the percentages. Consequently the 1937 percentages may be worth little or nothing. Yet it is true that one would expect unemployment to be greater relatively in New Bedford than in Cambridge, for instance, and the 1934 census figures show the reverse.

TABLE J

RELATIVE UNEMPLOYMENT IN MASSACHUSETTS, 1934 AND 1937, BY TOWNS

Town	Per cent of unemployed to employables	
	1934 *	*1937* °
Cambridge	26.1	16.9
Somerville	24.8	15.7
Framingham	24.0	15.2
New Bedford	22.5	32.7
Small Towns	20.0	...
Maynard	18.6	...
Hudson	17.7	...
Newton	16.4	7.3
Brookline	12.7	8.0
The State	25.0	...

* From Massachusetts Census on Unemployment.

° Percentages are calculated from data on totally unemployed and emergency workers given in the Biggers voluntary census of 1937 and the 1934 employable figures from the Massachusetts Census.

The figures on the case load in Massachusetts and for these towns and cities, both for ERA and direct relief, indicate that our sample is typical of the relief situation in the state. The movement of the case load figures for the state and for the total of the towns (see discussion and charts in Chapter I) is very similar, with the exception that in the last half of 1935, direct relief, as compared with work relief, was used in these towns to a greater degree than in the state.

In all of the towns except Brookline, a substantial majority of the work relief applicants were men. However, 47 per cent of the Brookline cases were women. The per cent of women was considerably below the proportion for the whole sample (20 per cent) in the case of Newton, Cambridge, Framingham, and Hudson, and somewhat above for Maynard, Somerville, and New Bedford.

The distribution of families of various sizes among relief applicants was markedly different among the towns. It might be expected that the average size of the family would be larger for the industrial towns. Such is not the case. The average size of family was largest in Newton with 5 members. Cambridge and Framingham arc next with average families of 4.9 and 4.8 respectively. New Bedford, Hudson, and the Small Towns had smaller average families of 4.2, 4.0, and 3.9 respectively. Maynard and Brookline, towns very dissimilar in economic background, had average families of 3.1 persons. There appears to be no relation between the economic status of a town and the average size of the family on work relief. The wealthy residential suburbs of Newton and Brookline are at the top and bottom

TABLE K

PER CENT OF TOTAL CASES IN EACH TOWN ACCORDING TO SIZE OF FAMILY

Town	1	2	3	4	5	6	7	8	9 & over
Somerville	8.7%	20.1%	22.7%	16.7%	13.6%	7.5%	4.7%	3.5%	3.5%
Cambridge	2.3	6.9	20.5	20.8	14.2	13.2	8.3	7.3	6.6
New Bedford	8.1	17.6	21.1	17.8	12.8	5.9	6.7	3.6	6.5
Brookline	26.7	20.8	14.2	15.8	12.5	2.5	4.2	2.5	.8
Newton	.9	6.4	20.4	21.3	17.4	12.8	7.2	7.2	6.4
Framingham	3.5	11.3	17.0	17.4	19.6	12.2	8.3	2.6	8.3
Maynard	23.5	29.4	14.7	11.8	5.9	5.9	2.9	..	5.9
Hudson	10.9	19.5	24.2	12.5	10.9	3.9	5.5	6.3	6.3
Small Towns	7.6	22.9	24.3	14.6	11.8	4.9	6.3	4.2	3.5

of the list. The rural section, represented by the group of small towns, ranks with the manufacturing centers of New Bedford and Hudson. Possibly a difference in the interpretation of eligibility requirements in the individual towns may offer a partial explanation of the variation.

Table K exhibits the distribution of family size in the towns. About one-quarter of the cases in Brookline and Maynard were single persons. In all the other towns except Hudson single persons form less than 10 per cent of the cases, and in Newton there were only .9 per cent in the one-person class. Families of two make up 30 per cent of the cases in Maynard and one-fifth of all families in Brookline, Cambridge, New Bedford,

Hudson, and the Small Towns.[4] About one-half of the families in Brookline and Maynard were either families of two or single persons. In all the other towns 70 per cent or more of the cases were composed of families larger than two persons.

In every town a very large majority of the family heads (over 90 per cent) were citizens. The greatest number of aliens were to be found in Cambridge, New Bedford, and the Small Towns. The number and proportion of colored and races other than white were extremely small. The few colored cases were concentrated in Cambridge where 8 per cent of the cases were Negroes; in New Bedford, 6 per cent, and in Newton, 2 per cent.

The information on the education of the head of the family is incomplete. Four towns only record a sufficient number of cases to be mentioned. About one-quarter of the New Bedford cases (195) reported on education. Of these, the majority had had 4 to 8 years of schooling, and 19 per cent had been to high school. Of the 44 Brookline families for which the facts were given, half had been to high school and half had had 4 to 8 years of school. For Maynard, 23 family heads were listed and of these 12 had been to school for 4 to 8 years, and 7 went to high school. In Hudson, out of 117 cases for which the facts were given, one-half had had 4 to 8 years of school and one-third had been to high school. The 110 cases in the Small Town group reported 42 per cent as having been to high school and 42 per cent to grammar school for 4 to 8 years. In all the towns a few individuals had had only 1 to 3 years of school, and some had been to college or technical school. In the Small Towns and Brookline, in particular, the average of education was high, in so far as the cases reported on are representative.

Except for New Bedford, the only data on age available for the individual towns are to be found in the Massachusetts

[4] The proportion of alien cases was small, about 5 to 6 per cent, in these localities.

Census of Unemployment. Even there the information is given only for New Bedford, Somerville, Brookline, Newton, and Cambridge. Table 7 in Appendix B summarizes the data. A slight majority of the total unemployed in every town was, in 1934, 34 years of age or under, and about one-third were 24 or under. In selecting family heads for work relief age was consistently given preference, although to a lesser extent in Brookline and Newton than in the other cities. Of those temporarily working on relief projects, only one-fifth were of the youngest age group. This is true of all five cities. From the age of 25 on older workers were favored to a greater degree for work relief than their proportion among the total unemployed. This appears to be the case especially for the age group 35 to 44. Brookline and Newton favored the 25 to 34 year old class more than the other towns, and workers over 45 less. Possibly this may be explained by the fact that more older workers, proportionately, were fully employed in Brookline and Newton than in the other towns.

Some information on age is given by the WPA study of a 5 per cent sample of employable cases on relief in Massachusetts in 1935. The distribution was given for urban and rural sections of the state as well as for the whole. The percentage distribution of the ages of urban relief workers is almost identical with that for the whole state. Certain differences may be observed, however, among rural work relief recipients. It appears that more rural relief workers were in the very old and young age groups than is the case with urban relief recipients.

We have seen that our sample is somewhat overweighted with white collar workers. This is undoubtedly a result of the larger proportion of white collar workers in Brookline and Somerville, and to a lesser degree, Newton. (See Appendix B, Table 4.) Nearly 40 per cent of the Brookline family heads were in the white collar group, and 33 per cent of the Somerville cases. Newton was next with 24 per cent. Skilled workers were most prevalent in Newton and Framingham (30 per cent), with Maynard and Somerville next (23 and 22 per cent). Semi-skilled workers predominated in the factory towns of Hudson (56 per cent), New Bedford (36 per cent), and Maynard (31 per cent). Brookline, too, had a large percentage of semi-skilled, a result of the number of dressmakers included in their case records. Cambridge, Newton, and Maynard had the highest proportion of unskilled laborers on work relief. The Small Town group was the only one considerably above the per cent for the whole sample for both the domestic and farm categories. Over one-fifth of the relief applicants in these communities were classified in one or the other of these two groups.

We were able to check the occupational distribution of the whole sample with that of the inventory made by the WPA in 1935. Similar information for cities of a population of 100,000 or more was given separately.[5] For Somerville, Cambridge, and New Bedford we are therefore able to compare our occupational distribution with that of the WPA. For Somerville the WPA distribution includes a relatively large proportion of white collar workers, but not as large as in our distribution. It is apparent that our Somerville sample overweights white collar workers and underrepresents, though not as much, the skilled and laboring occupations, as compared with the WPA inventory. The two Cambridge distributions are very similar and none of the differences is large. The greatest is in the case of skilled craftsmen which compose 3 per cent less of our sample than of the WPA group. In New Bedford our sample is clearly underrepresented with respect to semi-skilled workers in comparison with the WPA distribution. There is a difference of nearly 9 per cent in the proportion of semi-skilled workers in the two samples. Our New Bedford sample, on the other hand, is overweighted with office workers and inexperi-

[5] I am indebted to Mr. Howard Myers, Director of Research, WPA, for sending me copies of these occupational distributions.

enced persons. Despite these discrepancies, the occupational distributions for the three towns are clearly very like the WPA distributions. The differences observed may be a result of real differences in the time of the two studies, or the result of errors of sampling. In any case, they are not sufficiently large to throw out our samples as non-representative.

Property ownership among the unemployed of our sample was concentrated in Newton, the Small Towns, and Somerville. Homes were owned by nearly half the Small Town families, more than one-third of the Newton families, and one-fifth of the Somerville cases. Most of these homes were heavily mortgaged. Automobile ownership was high relatively in the country districts (one-quarter of the Small Town sample had cars), where cars are an essential method of transportation and where many of the automobiles were trucks used for work. One-eighth of the Newton families also owned automobiles at the time of their relief application. One might expect that savings would take the form of durable consumption goods, such as homes or automobiles, more readily in the rural sections of the state and that insurance would be more prevalent in urban and industrial centers. In general this was the case. A high proportion of the Hudson, Framingham, Cambridge, and Maynard relief families had insurance. Cambridge relief applicants had little else, in fact, which was also the case in Brookline. Framingham, Hudson, and Maynard also took on the characteristics of rural communities, with a significant extent of home ownership. In Newton, too, insurance as well as home ownership was extensive, with more than half of the relief applicants holding policies. New Bedford relief families had few assets of any kind. It is apparent that the property-holders among our relief applicants were to be found, for the most part, either in the rural villages, in Newton, or in the white collar city of Somerville.[6]

[6] For greater details on property see Table 8 in Appendix B.

Indebtedness was common among all the relief applicants, particularly so in Newton and Somerville, where skilled and white collar workers with considerable assets predominated. Debts were relatively great among New Bedford families as well but quite small in Hudson. As Table L indicates, the average family debt becomes even higher when computed on the basis of those having debts, and the ranking of the towns by size of debt changes. This is a result of the fact that in some localities, such as the Small Towns, Maynard, Brookline, and

TABLE L

AVERAGE DEBT BY TOWNS

Town	Mean Total Debt (all cases)	Mean Total Debt (those having debt)	Per cent having debt
Newton	$393	$416	95
Somerville	304	355	86
New Bedford	257	290	89
Framingham	202	223	90
Small Towns	166	257	65
Maynard	162	290	56
Brookline	133	286	47
Cambridge	116	142	82
Hudson	88	154	57

Hudson fewer of the families were in debt, but the debts of those who had them were frequently as high as those in the larger cities. Debts were most frequent in Newton, Framingham, New Bedford, Somerville, and Cambridge.

Average weekly income varied from $9.62 per family in the Small Towns to $18.11 in Newton. Framingham and Somerville came next with $15.77 and $14.27. For the other towns average weekly income was around $11 or $12. The sources of income will be dealt with in some detail in the next chapter. Suffice it to say here that income from ERA made up the bulk of income in all towns. Supplementary income from private employment was highest in Newton, Brookline, and Framingham, and of small importance in New Bedford, Maynard, and the Small Towns. Earnings from ERA were largest in Newton, Framingham, Maynard, and Somerville, all towns in which the proportion of skilled craftsmen and white collar workers was high. Framingham was the only town in which income from miscellaneous sources was of any importance.

In discussing the meaning of the average income figure for the whole sample, it was pointed out that the income distribution was such that there were two points of concentration of the cases. A majority of them were grouped about the average, but there was as well a smaller concentration in the lowest class interval. This is even more true for some of the individual towns and cities.[7] In the Small Towns, for example, nearly one-third of the families received incomes below $4 a week. In Hudson and New Bedford the proportion of families within this low income range was 16 and 15 per cent respectively. On the other hand, the concentration of cases at the lower limit of the income distribution was not marked in Newton, Framingham, and Maynard. It should be remembered, therefore, that the representativeness of the average income varies greatly among the towns and means something quite different in Newton and the Small Towns, to name the extremes.

There are only four towns in our sample in which any attempt was made to record the actual weekly expenditures of the families, as far as could be determined from the records themselves and information received from WPA officials. These towns are Somerville, Cambridge, Newton, and Framingham. And even in these cases there were some instances in which the weekly expenditures were obviously based on the ERA standard budget for a family of that size. The expenditure items recorded for the other towns were those of the standard budgets, and deviations occurred only when some item, such as

[7] The income frequency distributions for the towns will be found in Table 20 of Appendix B.

the clothing or miscellaneous allowance, was omitted for certain families. Whether the weekly expenditure averages for each town represent actual expenditures or standard, they are consistently above income, except in the case of Maynard. Newton, Somerville, Hudson, and Framingham had the highest weekly expenditure averages of $20.34, $19.11, $19.05, and $17.79 respectively. Maynard and Brookline were the lowest with an average weekly expenditure per family of $12.58 and $15.13.

It was explained in Chapter II that the standard budget is a device used by relief agencies to determine the minimum upon which a family should be expected to live, and that ERA earnings were adjusted to some extent, with attention to supplementary income, so that the family might attain that minimum income while on relief. This at least was the theory. The standard budget was based on the number of persons per family, to some extent on the age of the family members, and on prices and standards in that locality. The scale used to compute the standard budget by the ERA in the localities included in our sample is as follows:

Food	$2 per week per person
Fuel and light	$1.50 per week per family
Rent	$5 per week per family
Clothing	$.75 per week per person
Incidentals	$1 per week per family

This scale offered the maximum ERA budget. Actually the standard computed for any one family varied below this maximum. Sometimes $1.50 per week was allowed for food for children under 16, and incidentals and clothing were not always allowed. The rent figure is the maximum; if actual rent payments were under this amount they were usually substituted.

As a matter of interest the maximum budget possible under the ERA scale, with allowances for all items included, has been computed for each town. Table M compares these budgets with the average expenditure and income derived from the records.

TABLE M

COMPARISON OF INCOME AND EXPENDITURE WITH ERA BUDGET, BY TOWNS

Town	Average Size of Family	Maximum ERA Standard *	Average Expenditure	Average Income
Somerville	3.9	$18.23	$19.11	$14.27
Cambridge	4.9	20.98	16.79	12.81
New Bedford	4.2	19.05	16.24	11.81
Brookline	3.1	16.03	15.13	11.32
Newton	5.0	21.25	20.34	18.11
Framingham	4.8	20.70	17.79	15.77
Maynard	3.1	16.03	12.58	12.89
Hudson	4.0	18.50	19.05	12.81
Small Towns	3.9	18.23	15.75	9.62

* Based on ERA standard for the computed family size in each town.

One fact is apparent at once. The average income of these relief recipients in every town was well below that of the ERA maximum allowance based on the average size of family in each town. Far from being overpaid, these families did not receive enough, on the average, to meet the requirements of the ERA budget. In this connection, it is well to remember the nature of the income distributions which showed that many families were receiving less than $4 a week.

Let us examine the towns in which the expenditure figures approximate actual outgo. In Somerville the average family spent $1 more per week than the maximum possible allowance under ERA standards. The average Cambridge family spent $4 less than could have been allowed by the ERA budget. Although average family expenditure was high in Newton, it was still a dollar less than the highest possible ERA allowance. In Framingham average weekly expenditure was almost $3 lower than the maximum ERA standard for that town. Only in Somerville were ERA applicants spending enough to meet the minimum standard of consumption set up by the ERA.

In the other towns the expenditure figures represent an average of the actual budgets set up by relief administrators for each family. Variations in expenditures allowed, resulting from individual family circumstances, account for the differences between the actual and theoretically possible budgets. In Brookline and Hudson the difference between the possible and actual budgetary expenditure standard was small, indicating that most Brookline and Hudson relief families were allowed the maximum. On the other hand, the average allowance is considerably lower than the maximum possible ERA budget in the Small Towns, Maynard, and New Bedford. Even so, income did not approximate these actual standards, except in Maynard.

At the present time we shall not examine the individual items of expenditure in each town, nor the specific categories of debts. Later chapters will be devoted to the analysis of incomes, expenditures, and debts, not only with respect to the individual towns, but also with respect to occupations and family size.

From the mass of details concerning relief workers in the individual towns there emerge certain clear-cut distinctions. In the first place unemployment as a whole was less of a problem in Newton and Brookline than in any of the other towns we have examined. There the similarity between the two metropolitan suburbs ends. Work relief seems to have been utilized by quite different economic classes in the two cities. Skilled craftsmen, clerks, salesmen, and other white collar workers, people who had had savings, insurance, and property and who often had managed to hold on to some of these assets, were not unusual recipients of work relief in Newton from 1935 to 1937. They had been, for the most part, substantial citizens, on the basis of the economic evidence, and they had been able to get a good deal of credit. One might say that they represent the upper stratum of our relief cases.

The Brookline relief applicants form a somewhat peculiar group, in the sense that so many of them were women and such a large proportion of single persons were among them. Although less than half of them were in debt, most of them had few assets. Their relief income was low, as the average was markedly affected by the $10 a week wage paid women on sewing projects.

It was anticipated that Cambridge and Somerville would be similar in their relief population since they are both industrial cities closely affiliated with Boston. Marked differences appear, however, in the characteristics of relief applicants in the two places.[8] Cambridge relief workers in our sample appear to belong to the laboring class. Most of them had been semi-skilled or unskilled workers, with very little property. Their debts — and credit — were small. They had insurance, but little else. Somerville relief applicants, on the other hand, seem to have belonged to a different economic group. They were, for the most part, white collar workers and skilled craftsmen who owned their own homes, and were considerably in debt. From an economic point of view they are more like the Newton work relief families than those in Cambridge.

The New Bedford relief applicants were usually semi-skilled workers in the textile mills. Their debts were above the average for the sample but they had practically no assets when they applied for relief. In many respects, the Cambridge relief group resembles them.

Relief applicants in the small factory towns of Framingham, Maynard, and Hudson were better off than those in New Bedford. They were often able to combine factory work with gardening and other rural advantages. They were more apt to

[8] It has been suggested to me that these differences are a result of the keeping of the records. It was obvious that the Somerville records were in far better shape than the Cambridge ones and it is possible that this is a factor in the situation. But the same differences, in occupational distribution at least, occur in the WPA data resulting from the 1935 inventory. See p. 56.

be home-owners, to have insurance or automobiles. Their average income was higher and there were fewer applicants in the lowest income group.

The relief applicants of the Small Towns were of still another variety. In any one town there were relatively few. In the group as a whole the occupations were less concentrated in a few classes, making it more difficult to select a typical example. They might be of the laboring class, usually unskilled or semi-skilled, or farmers. They probably owned their own homes and they may have had a car. Their total weekly income was very low, about $9.60 on the average; and one-third of them had almost no income. They were not badly in debt and fewer of them were in debt than was the case in the industrial cities. Although their income, including work relief, was unusually low (about half that in Newton, for instance) it must be remembered that in a small town or rural community they were more likely to receive personal assistance from friends and neighbors. Also they probably had a garden which supplied them with a good deal of food and they may have had to pay no rent. Many of the homes owned were owned free of debt.

Before examining the data on debts, income, expenditure, and occupations more thoroughly, we can point out tentatively six kinds of relief applicants included in our sample. There was the middle-class white collar worker or skilled craftsman of Newton and Somerville, usually with property, insurance, and large debts. There was the property-less factory worker of New Bedford, also considerably in debt. There was the factory worker or skilled man in the rural factory towns who still had some property and had probably had more, with relatively moderate debts. And there was the rural farmer or laborer, with his own home. There was also the single woman semi-skilled worker of Brookline who had insurance but nothing else. And there were the applicants with family incomes of less than $4 a week, people who must have been in desperate need. Some of them existed in every one of the towns and cities, but they were most frequent in the Small Towns and New Bedford. In addition, there were many other types of work relief applicants, but it may be said that the six varieties mentioned are represented most frequently in our sample.

PART II

A STATISTICAL ANALYSIS OF WORK RELIEF APPLICANTS

CHAPTER V

THEIR SOURCES OF INCOME

THE INCOME of families on work relief was, in many cases, supplemented by income from other sources. In some instances, earnings from odd jobs, or from the employment of other members of the family, rents, payments from boarders and lodgers helped to increase total family income. All these supplements were allowed by the ERA as long as total family income kept within the budgetary standard set up for that particular family. In computing family income certain concessions were made by the ERA in considering earnings of children, or relatives other than the husband and wife. Only two-thirds of the earnings of a daughter or son were counted as family income. In the case of rents, net income alone was considered as being part of family income. Thus it was possible for actual family income to be higher than the figure recorded by the ERA. Our figures, however, are for total family income, without ERA deductions. All the earnings from private employment of any member of the family were included, as well as gross rent. In the latter instance housing costs were added to expenditures. Our income averages, therefore, would differ from similar figures given by the ERA and in an upward direction.

It was not always possible to estimate the monetary equivalent of goods given to these families. Fuel, food orders, clothing etc. were often donated by public and private charitable agencies. Sometimes a record of these transactions was made on the family schedule. In most such instances no clue was given as to the amount of money these goods represented, and they were perforce omitted from our income figures.

It should be pointed out at this juncture that the weekly income averages afford no basis for computing the annual income of these families.[1] The data used were recorded on the application schedules of the family head and the incomes given were received by the applicant shortly after acceptance for and placement on an ERA project. In the cases in which there was no ERA income, or no income of any kind, the applicant, although eligible, had not yet been put on ERA work. Most of these relief recipients were on and off work relief during the course of 1935. They did not as a rule work continuously for a whole year. Since we examined the application schedules for the entire calendar year, our data are a cross section of the eligible work relief applicants for the week after acceptance for work relief. At any given time some of them would be working on projects and others would not; some would have private employment and others none, and so on. For any individual family the picture might be entirely changed, let us say, for the week after that recorded on the schedule. For the group as a whole, however, it is thought that our data present an adequate cross section for the average week after acceptance in 1935.

Table 9 (Appendix B) presents an analysis of our sample, both as a whole and with respect to the individual towns, classified according to sources of income. The classification was set up in such a way that comparisons could be made with a similar study of the WPA. The WPA results are listed in the last column.[2] A majority of the relief workers which make

[1] In Chicago, the mean and median incomes of complete native white relief families in 1935–36 was $461 and $395 respectively. However, the relief figures are probably an understatement, as direct relief was not included, and the relief figures are considered unreliable. Consumer Purchases Study, *Family Income in Chicago*, Bull. 642, Bureau of Labor Statistics, footnote 13, p. 12.

[2] *Survey of Cases Certified for Works Program Employment in 13 Cities*, Series IV, no. 2, Division of Social Research, Washington, 1937. Table 26,

up our sample were supported entirely by income from relief; 65 per cent of them were in receipt of what the WPA calls "non-supplemented" income. A little more than half of the whole sample had no income but what they received from the ERA. Those whose income was supplemented got their weekly income from various combinations of relief and non-relief sources, only a few of which are separately classified. The proportion receiving both relief and non-relief income was small, 17 per cent. Still less (10 per cent of the group) had income from private employment in addition to relief. Private employment was the only source of income for 4 per cent, and other non-relief combinations provided the income for 3 per cent; 241 cases, or 11 per cent of the sample, had no income at all during the cross-section week of our survey.

The WPA survey of March 1936 which covers 13 cities selected as typical of the relief situation throughout the country provides figures for sources of income which are not very different from ours. The percentages of cases receiving income from relief only, ERA only, and relief and non-relief sources together, are almost identical. A greater proportion of cases in the 13 cities derived their sole income from private employment, 11 per cent as against 4 per cent, and considerably less had no income, 2 per cent in comparison with 11 per cent of our sample. These differences may be attributed to the variation in time of the two surveys and to the differences in regions covered. Opportunities for private employment were probably greater in 1936 than in 1935.[3] In general, it may be said that the Massachusetts work relief applicants had the same sources of income and to the same degree as those in the 13 cities.

---

p. 43. The categories are not quite comparable to those in our study, but are combined as well as possible to correspond.

[3] It has also been suggested to me that higher earnings from private employment may reflect the failure of the WPA to cancel cases whose need for relief had disappeared since certification.

Approximately 82 per cent of our sample, and 83 per cent of the cases from the 13 cities examined by the WPA in 1936, were supported in whole or in part by relief. About one-half of the cases had no other source of income than the ERA, and only 17 per cent were able to supplement their relief with other sources of income. These data apply to the whole sample. Let us examine the variations in each town.

In all the towns except Newton, more than half of the cases received income from relief alone. The percentages range from 47 (Newton) to 79 (Maynard). The ERA alone supported a majority of the relief recipients in all localities with the exception of Newton, Brookline, and the Small Towns. Other relief (usually Public Welfare) was important as a source of income in Maynard, Brookline, Newton, New Bedford, and Cambridge. Supplemented income was most important in Newton and Framingham, and in Newton over one-quarter of the cases supplemented private employment earnings with relief. Private employment as the sole source of income was of no great significance, except in Brookline, with 10 per cent of its cases thus supported. In most localities the cases with no income were 10 per cent or under, but in the Small Towns nearly 28 per cent had no earnings at all, and in Hudson, 16 per cent.

It is apparent that in the industrial towns relief provided the only source of income for far more families than was the case in the rural districts and the prosperous suburbs of Newton and Brookline. Supplementation of relief income was most prevalent in Newton, Framingham, and Somerville, with private employment providing the main supplement in Newton, and other sources, such as rents and boarders, in Framingham and Somerville. Relief applicants not on ERA projects at the time of our survey found it easiest to get private employment of some kind in Brookline and Cambridge. Cases with no income at all were relatively more prevalent in the rural districts, where, fortunately, it would be easier for them to secure food and the elements of mere existence than in an industrial center.

The above data are of interest in indicating the extent to which the relief population in our sample was dependent upon relief and non-relief sources for their subsistence. Table 10 (see Appendix B) lists the mean and median income by source. It should be made clear at this point that the averages for the whole group include cases for which income as a whole and from any source was 0. The income classifications by source exclude by definition those cases which had no income at all, and those which had no income from the specific source in question.

Both the arithmetic mean and the median have been derived for each category and each town, partly so that the results may be comparable with those of various WPA studies of income in which the median is ordinarily used. As far as our sample is concerned there is some reason for thinking the mean a better measure of average income than the median.[4] As may be observed in the table, the median income from relief alone, from relief among supplemented cases, and from all sources, is $12 per week. This is true for almost all the towns individually as well as for the whole sample. Considerable variation occurs among the means. Since ERA earnings dominate the entire sample and almost all the towns, it is apparent that the median reflects the current ERA wage of $12 a week almost exclusively. The mean, however, being influenced by extreme variations where the median is not, reflects to some extent variations from the ERA wage. In so far as we wish to analyze the variations in income which occurred in diverse places, the mean becomes a better average for our purposes. We know at the start that the usual ERA wage was $12 a week and that the majority of the cases were receiving it. We wish to know in addition to what extent other sources of income increased this wage, on

[4] The typical nature of any average of data such as these, however, is questionable; see p. 45 for analysis of income frequency distribution. This difficulty has been taken into account wherever possible.

the average, and it is only by letting the relatively few extreme cases affect the average that we can determine this. We shall continue to use the mean, therefore, in our analysis of the data. It is of some interest to observe, however, that Newton was the only town in which the median income from relief alone differed from $12. It was, in the case of Newton, $17.59. Some differentiation was made by the ERA between skills, and white collar workers and skilled craftsmen frequently received a higher wage. Such was probably the case in Newton. The median income from all sources deviates from $12 only for Somerville and Newton. As far as Somerville is concerned, the number of cases receiving supplementary income was sufficient to affect the median.

Average income from relief only, which was the income of 1416 cases, ranged from $11.72 in Brookline to $17.83 in Newton. The factory towns of Hudson and Maynard gave a relief income of little over $13, and the same was true of Cambridge. The Framingham figure was slightly higher, $14.30, and the New Bedford level a little lower, $12.73. The Small Town figure was still less, $12.30. In all cases the usual ERA wage appears to have been supplemented by other relief of some kind. The ordinary rate for unskilled labor was $12, for skilled labor $14–16. Owing to the predominance of single women among the Brookline cases, the average is influenced obviously by the $10 wage usually paid to women on ERA sewing projects. The average size of family for those who were supported by relief alone was almost exactly the same as that for the whole sample, 4.3 persons. In the separate localities families varied from 2.7 persons in Brookline to 4.9 persons in Newton.

The 371 families who managed to add income from other sources to their ERA earnings were able to increase their total income considerably above that of those who relied on relief alone. In all the towns their average weekly income was considerably higher than the income from relief alone and also the ERA budgetary standard.[5] Their average weekly income varied from $18.07 in Brookline to slightly over $25 in Hudson and Framingham. In some towns the average relief income received by this group was more than the average relief income received by those who had no other source of income. This was true in Cambridge, New Bedford, Maynard, and the Small Towns, and, to a slight degree, of the average for the whole group. The supplementary income varied in amount from $5.36 in the Small Towns to $12.33 in Hudson. The higher relief income and the extent of supplementary income may be explained by the larger size of these families. For the whole sample the families in this category had 4.9 members as compared with 4.3 members for those on relief only. It is therefore dubious whether their higher income left them any better off financially. This may have been true in New Bedford and Maynard, the only towns where families with supplemented income were smaller than relief families.

There were 81 families who were supported entirely by the private employment of some member of the family. The average family income from private employment was markedly below average income from relief alone, except for Somerville and Brookline. The actual amounts ranged from $7.71 in New Bedford to $15.15 in Somerville. The average for all the cases is $11.13 as compared with $13.65 for those with income from relief alone. Maynard had no cases receiving income from private employment only and but 4 families who supplemented relief income from other sources. Taking the sample as a whole, the difference between income received from relief and private employment cannot be explained by differences in family size. Families whose income came solely from private

[5] Since we have included total income of all members of the family from all sources, our figures are higher than the ERA figures for total family income, which exclude certain deductible amounts. See p. 69.

employment contained 4.4 members, and those whose income was entirely from relief contained 4.3 members. These are average figures for the whole sample. Yet relief families had an average weekly income greater by some $2.50 than those whose income was privately earned. In 4 cities (Somerville, New Bedford, Brookline, Newton) families supported by private employment were larger than those supported by relief. In two of these cities, Somerville and Brookline, the average earnings of these families with jobs were also higher than average income secured by relief families. But in New Bedford and Newton, the reverse was true. The families supported entirely by private employment earned markedly less than those on relief so that the larger families had less income. In the other localities, relief families were larger and relief income was also larger. We cannot be sure that families supported by private employment alone suffered a distinct financial disadvantage, compared to those receiving relief income alone, except in New Bedford and Newton, but for the entire sample differences in family size do not appear to explain the differences between relief and industrial income.

The positive difference between relief income and that derived from private employment might seem to support those who argue that relief families find it more profitable to stay on relief than to try and get private employment. It is true that in some instances the relief wage is greater than that which a workman could get for equivalent hours in private industry. But our data are capable of other explanations. The influence of family size has been examined, and does not seem an adequate explanation. However, our sample is composed of active relief cases. Any employment secured by the heads of the families was therefore temporary, as long as the recipient was still considered eligible for work relief. Temporary odd jobs of this kind would necessarily pay little and are not comparable to the kind of work for which a person would leave the relief rolls. Also the proportion of cases supported by private employment is small, and the average wage received by these 81 cases may not be typical. However, the marked discrepancy between the relief income and that received from private employment is suggestive, particularly in connection with the question of the permanency of the relief problem. This question will be taken up at some length in a later chapter.

In Chapter I we gave a few comparative income figures from studies made of cases in the 13 cities by the WPA Division of Social Research. Table N summarizes the results in somewhat more detail.

TABLE N

WORK RELIEF INCOME

MAY 1935 *

Source	Mean Monthly	Mean Weekly	Median Monthly	Median Weekly
Non-supplemented				
Relief Income	$28.10	$ 6.50	$24.10	$ 5.56
Supplemented Income —				
Combined	50.60	11.60	44.10	10.17
Relief	27.20	6.27	23.10	5.33
Private Employment	24.20	5.60	17.20	4.00

* Source: *The 1935 Relief Population in 13 Cities:* A Cross Section, WPA Series I, No. 23. See footnote 9, Chapter III, for method of deriving weekly figures.

MARCH 1936 *

Source	Median Monthly	Median Weekly
Total	$58.30	$13.45
WPA only	58.10	13.40
WPA and Private Employment	79.50	18.36
Private Employment only	68.30	15.76
WPA and Relief	64.30	15.22

* Source: *Survey of Cases Certified for WPA Employment in 13 Cities*, WPA, Series IV, No. 2.

Comparing these tables with Table 10 it is apparent that in May 1935 the median and the mean weekly incomes both for straight relief and supplemented cases were considerably below those given for our sample. It is possible that the definition of relief is somewhat different and it is clear that private employment is the only source of supplementary income considered. It is interesting to observe that the relief income received by supplemented cases is somewhat less than that received by those who were dependent on relief alone, although the former had larger families (3.7 as against 2.7 persons for relief families).

The classifications in the study of March 1936 are more clearly defined. The median weekly income from all sources was $13.45, higher than our median and about the same as the mean. The same is true for the income from WPA only when it is compared with our figures for relief only. The median weekly income of $15.76 received in these 13 cities by those who had income from private employment alone is much higher than our median of $10, or our mean of $11.13 for the same classification. This is consistent with the previous conclusion that opportunities for private employment were far better in 1936 than in 1935. Those who had income from WPA and private employment made less than those in our sample who had both relief and non-relief income. However, the difference in definition and in the areas makes comparisons uncertain.[6]

The importance of relief and supplementary sources of in-

[6] These comparisons are used, not because they are accurate, but because they seem to be the only ones available. It is fully realized that a comparison between data referring to employable workers in 13 cities all over the country and a representative sample of Massachusetts relief workers leaves much to be desired. However, Massachusetts is a predominantly urban state and it is thought that the comparisons may be useful in indicating whether the Massachusetts figures are completely out of line with those referring to work relief people in other urban areas.

come for the individual towns in our sample is presented from still another point of view by the table (11, Appendix B) which shows the proportion of average income derived from each source. The relative amount of income contributed by relief in Maynard, New Bedford, and the Small Towns was 80 per cent or more, the highest in the sample, although their average incomes were by no means the largest. Public Welfare was most important in Brookline, nearly 9 per cent of the average income being procured from this source. From this point of view, private employment was of greatest significance in Brookline, Newton, and Hudson, where it formed 18, 15.5, and 15 per cent of average income respectively. The proportion of average income contributed by rents and boarders was usually small. In the case of Somerville, this source of income was the highest, relatively, being 7 per cent of the average. Miscellaneous sources were even less important, except in Framingham, where 8 per cent of average income was made up in this way. Again it is evident that relief, and of relief sources, the ERA, was the chief source of income for relief recipients in these towns. Some differences in the ranking of the towns may be observed when the importance of the various sources of income is measured in this way rather than by number of cases or amount of income. Cambridge, for example, had a greater proportion of cases being supported by employment than was true of Hudson or Newton. Yet average income in these two towns was affected to a greater degree by earnings from private employment than in Cambridge.

Since the amount of relief given was to some extent dependent upon size of family, since large families were favored in the ERA eligible lists, and since private earnings might be expected to be greater the larger the family and the more members available for work, it is not surprising to find that the averages of total weekly income vary directly with the size of the family. (See Table 12, Appendix B.) The average income for a single person was $7.81 per week; for a family of nine or more persons, $20.11 per week. Without exception, average income increased steadily with the number of persons in a family. The same tendency was apparent in that portion of income derived from the ERA, although it was less marked. The average ERA income for a single person was $7.15; for our largest family group $12.43. Families of five, six, and seven persons all had ERA earnings of about $11.50. Public welfare grants show a direct variation with family size, the two largest family groups having far more, on the average, from this agency than any other. The same is noticeable in other relief sources. Income from private employment rose from an average of six cents a week for a single person to $4.42 for a family of nine and over. Income from rents, boarders and lodgers, and miscellaneous sources, on the other hand, obviously had no relation to the number of persons in a family. These sources contributed so small a part of average income, however, that the direct relationship between income and family size is little influenced.

In every town the same direct relation between family size and average income is apparent, although deviations, probably a result of the smallness of the sample in some cases, occur. The variation in the amounts received by the different-sized families in the towns is of some interest. The average income of single persons, for instance, ranged from $4.47 in Cambridge to $9 in Newton. Most of the single persons were to be found in Brookline, Somerville, and New Bedford, with average incomes of $6.59, $8.91, and $8.70 respectively. The families of nine or more persons had average incomes as low as $14.56 in New Bedford and as high as $26.46 in Newton. Families of four, on the other hand, got more in Newton ($18.10) than the largest New Bedford families, and as little as $10.49 in the Small Towns. Every sized family, in fact, except families of two, reached much higher incomes in Newton than in any other town.

Another tendency to be observed is that, although the amount of average income from relief increases directly with the size of family, the proportionate amount contributed by relief decreases as the family size becomes larger. This is true of the individual towns as well as of the entire sample. Other sources of income are of relatively much greater importance for the larger families, particularly earnings from private employment.

According to every statistical measure which we have used, relief income was the principal means of support of our sample of work relief cases. A bare majority of the families had no income other than that from their ERA wage. The amount of average income was also determined largely by relief, which was relatively the most significant source of income. Nearly one-fifth of the families, however, were able to add earnings from private employment, or rents, or other miscellaneous sources to their relief income. They were larger families as a rule than those who relied on relief alone, and, on the average, they received a slightly higher relief income, despite their ability to draw on other sources of income. In all, over 80 per cent of our sample was wholly or partially dependent on relief for subsistence.

What happened to the remaining fifth of the group? How did they support themselves? A few, 81 in all (4 per cent of the sample), had private jobs, the earnings from which were the only family source of income. Their average income was less than that of those on relief although they had families as large on the whole. Still fewer managed to get some income from other sources. But 11 per cent of the sample had no income whatever. Since our data afford a cross-section view of our sample for the year 1935, we must conclude that in any given week after application, selected at random, around 10 per cent of the cases would have had no visible means of support.[7] How could they live? Although they may have been receiving relief in other weeks of the year it is doubtful if they could have saved, particularly as average income was below the ERA budgetary standard. Doubtless they borrowed from friends, went into debt if they could, and when their assets and credit were nil, begged or starved. An illuminating description of such cases is given by Saya Schwartz during the month in Philadelphia when relief funds were held up by legislative difficulties.[8] These people were destitute and many of them were supported by friends and neighbors, landlords, grocery stores, and even total strangers during this period. Others begged and pilfered, and nearly starved, in a quite literal sense.

A few marked differences between the towns are apparent. In a town like Newton, where unemployment was relatively small, families on relief fared better than in any other locality we have studied. Not only was relief income higher, but opportunities for private employment were more numerous, so that for nearly 40 per cent of the families relief income supplemented other earnings. In Brookline the problem was somewhat different. Relief income was low, as a result of the predominance of single women and small families, but opportunities for private employment were as good as in Newton. It is in the manufacturing towns that the extent of the relief problem becomes apparent. Three-quarters of the New Bedford cases, for example, were entirely dependent on relief, and nine per cent more were on relief although they had some other sources of income. Eleven per cent had no income. Relief income in New Bedford was low and it was difficult to get private employment. The same situation held in Maynard,

[7] The possibility of inaccurate records must also be considered. This may account for some of the cases, although the income data seem to have been fairly carefully checked.

[8] Mimeographed report in the files of the WPA Division of Social Research, Washington, D. C., *Off Relief*, Philadelphia County Relief Board, July 31, 1936.

but Hudson and Framingham relief workers were somewhat better off. Their relief income was higher and they found it easier to get private jobs. On the face of it, the position of relief applicants in the Small Towns was even worse. Nearly 70 per cent were wholly or partially supported by relief, and about a quarter of them had no income. The relief income was the lowest of any of the regions. The only mitigating circumstance is that in such small communities it is less difficult for families to receive individual assistance from friends and neighbors, and easier for them to supplement their food supply by gardening.

The two most striking characteristics of income among our relief applicants appear to be, 1, the fact that a considerable number of them were, in any given week in 1935, without income of any sort; 2, that those who were able to add to their relief income from other sources frequently received a relief income as high as, if not higher than, that obtained by those without other resources.[9] I do not wish to overemphasize these points, since they apply to a small portion of our sample, and even if they are applicable in Massachusetts, may not be elsewhere. However, the first point is substantiated in some degree by the fact that in 13 cities a small proportion of the cases were without income in 1936, although opportunities for private jobs were then more prevalent than in 1935. As far as the second point is concerned it may be explained partially, at least, by the ERA standards, which took into account size of family in determining relief income, and allowed certain deductions for earnings of other members of the family. We have seen that the larger families were better able to supplement income, and they would be allowed larger relief and total family income. Whatever the explanation, it is possible that this situation, if it became at all general, would act as a deterrent to a decrease in the relief rolls.

[9] A WPA official comments that this may merely show poor relief administration — failure to put cases on a proper supplemented basis.

CHAPTER VI

THEIR PROPERTY OWNERSHIP AND DEBTS

MONEY INCOME is by no means a complete measure of the total income of the relief families of our sample. Many of them were living on credit for a substantial amount of current living expenses and almost all of them were in debt and had been in debt for some time. At the same time some of them still owned capital assets in the form of real estate, insurance, automobiles, etc. We have discussed in the preceding chapters the average amount of debt for the whole sample, the kinds of debt, and the extent to which property was owned. We have also examined the general differences between the towns in this respect, finding that the Small Towns, Newton, and Somerville led the group in the possession of capital assets and that the average debt per family was highest in Newton and Somerville. In this chapter we shall investigate debts and the ownership of property still further, with attention to factors such as the influence of occupations and size of family.

Up to this point we have dealt mainly with average figures. The total amount of debt incurred by the families in our sample is of some interest, however, and Table O lists the summary figures, both by towns and by occupations. The 2,180 families in our sample were in debt to the extent of half a million dollars at the time of their application for relief. Three-quarters of this amount was owed in Somerville, New Bedford, and Newton, although the cases in these towns form only a little over one-half of our sample. They also were the towns in which the average debt per family was largest. The skilled and semi-skilled occupations were responsible for almost a quarter of a million dollars in debts, and the unskilled ranked next with 11 per cent of the total. When one realizes that the cases included in our sample formed a small proportion of the total case load in the state in 1935, the total amount owed by those on relief becomes a problem of sizeable proportions. It means that those on relief were being supported not only in the regular way, by relief funds taken out of taxes, but by many members of the community who assumed or were forced to assume this additional relief burden.

TABLE O

TOTAL DEBT BY TOWN AND OCCUPATION

Town	Amount	Per cent of Total	Occupation	Amount	Per cent of Total
Somerville	$149,529	29.5	Professional	$ 21,249	4.2
Cambridge	35,242	6.9	Proprietors	40,200	7.9
New Bedford	127,203	25.1	Office workers	53,721	10.5
Brookline	16,011	3.2	Salesmen	38,921	7.7
Newton	92,275	18.2	Skilled	124,190	24.5
Framingham	46,346	9.1	Semi-skilled	119,600	23.6
Maynard	5,518	1.1	Unskilled	57,917	11.4
Hudson	11,234	2.2	Domestic	12,928	2.6
Small Towns	23,860	4.7	Farm	10,275	2.0
			Inexperienced	22,574	4.5
Total	$507,218	100.0	Unknown	5,643	1.1
			Total	$507,218	100.0

The kinds of debt most prevalent were for food, rent, taxes, loans (both personal and industrial), furniture, mortgages, and medical care. Nearly one-quarter of the total debts were not specified. Approximately $100,000, or a fifth of the total, was owed by our group for rent; $88,000 had been loaned to them on a personal basis, mostly by friends and relatives; and they had borrowed about $28,000 from banks, insurance companies, and commercial loan agencies. They owed $55,000 for medical care and $41,000 for food. Back taxes, unpaid interest and principal on mortgages, and overdue payments on furniture made up the rest of the debts.

The proportion of the average debt per family for each item is given in Chapter II. Let us see whether these proportions vary noticeably for the towns. (Table 13, Appendix B.) Obviously the families in each town differed considerably, on the average, as to the items for which they were most in debt. In the first place the unspecified items are largest for New Bedford, Maynard, Hudson, and the Small Towns.[1] There is no way of knowing what these unspecified debts were for, and the comparison between items is somewhat obscured by this lack of information. The highest proportion owed for food was in Framingham (14 per cent), Newton (12 per cent), the Small Towns and Hudson (11 per cent). As a whole the food debts were not large. People have to eat, and as their credit evaporates, they can be forced to pay for food more easily than for other commodities and services. For rent, on the other hand, the debts were much higher. Landlords hesitate a long time before going to the expense and trouble of eviction, especially as public sentiment has been against it. In Cambridge, Somerville, Newton, and Brookline, one-fifth to one-third of the average debt was for rent. In the Small Towns, Maynard, and Hudson, where home ownership was important, unpaid rent formed a negligible per cent of the average debt. Back taxes unpaid, however, were important in the rural villages and towns, where property ownership was more prevalent. In the industrial cities most of these families were liable only to the poll tax, which was usually owing for several years.

The proportion of personal loans was high in Somerville, Brookline, Maynard, and Newton. Industrial loans were negligible except in Newton. Cambridge families owed the highest

[1] The accuracy with which the kinds of debt — and other information — were listed varied markedly with the town. In many cases, it was obvious that the applicant had been asked how much he owed and had replied with an approximate lump sum which was put down on the records without further detail.

per cent for furniture (10 per cent). Doctors' bills and other medical expenses were relatively the most important in Brookline, Framingham, the Small Towns, and Somerville.

It is apparent that the extra-burden of relief, represented by the debts incurred by our relief families, rested largely on the shoulders of friends and relatives, landlords, and doctors. One-half the average debt was divided between these three groups in Somerville, Brookline, and Cambridge. In fact, except in the two towns (Hudson and New Bedford) in which the proportion of unspecified debt was very large, doctors, landlords, and friends are the chief creditors. The Town itself was an important creditor in Framingham, Maynard, and the Small Towns, and grocers suffered particularly in the Small Towns and Framingham.

How were these relief applicants able to secure so much credit? One might expect that their credit would depend to a large extent on their past economic status, their occupations, their ownership of property, etc. An occupational analysis has been made in order to determine to what degree debts and previous occupation are related. The total amount of debts by occupational groups is given in Table O on p. 85. In order to determine whether occupation as such was related to indebtedness, independent of the weight of the occupational group in the sample, a very simple method was used to eliminate the effort of the size of the sample. In Chart II the distribution of indebtedness was derived as follows. For each occupation, the ratio of $\frac{\text{total debt per occupation}}{\text{total debt of whole sample}}$ to $\frac{\text{number of cases in occupational group}}{\text{total number of cases}}$ was taken. The line at 100 on the charts represents, therefore, the extent to which each occupation would have contributed to the total debts of the group if its relative weight in our sample were the determinant. In so far as indebtedness of an occupation deviates from this norm, we can say that the debts of that occupational group were more or less than might be expected on the basis of its relative contribution to the size of the sample. Of course, other factors besides the occupation itself may determine these deviations, but at least the relative size of the occupational group is not one of them.

The distribution of all debts, charted on this basis, indicates that the relative contribution of the professional men, white

Chart II — Relative Indebtedness by Occupation
Active Cases

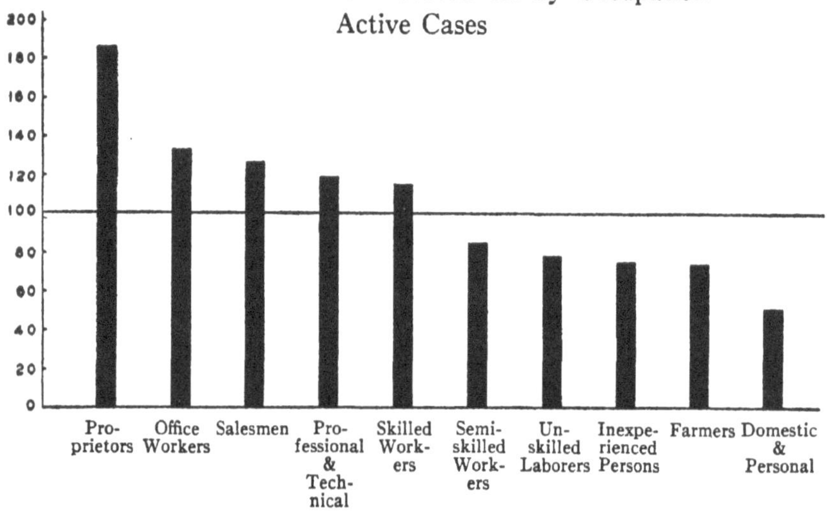

collar workers, and skilled craftsmen to the total debts of our groups was greater than their relative size. Proprietors, managers, and officials headed the list with respect to relative debts. Office workers, salesmen, professional men, and skilled workers came next in the order named. All the other occupational groups were relatively less in debt than their number would warrant. The class of domestic and personal workers were least in debt on this basis.

The results of this analysis tend to confirm the idea that previous occupational and economic status was of importance in determining the amount of credit which individuals and their families could get and the number of debts they incurred. The classification of proprietors, managers, and officials included men who had owned their own businesses, men who had been salaried executives, etc. who had probably made good incomes and had considerable assets.[2] They would ordinarily be looked upon as good credit risks and would probably be allowed to run up debts for a long time before it became apparent that they were no longer good risks. The same applies to the office workers, salesmen, and professional men, and to a less degree to the skilled workers. In the occupational classes which contributed more than their proportionate share to the total indebtedness were those which ordinarily form the solid middle class of any community and whose expenditure had been on a relatively high basis.

Total debts for individual items were analyzed by occupational groups on the same basis. It may be observed that certain occupations tend to contribute more than their share to the total debt for certain items. The same groups of white collar and skilled workers were most in debt for personal loans. Friends of professional men apparently were more willing or more able to make personal loans than those of office workers or salesmen. Proprietors, salesmen, and skilled workers had relatively large debts for unpaid rent. The proportion of medical debts owed by salesmen was well in excess of their relative number and also considerably above the share of any other group. Professional workers, proprietors, office and skilled workers, and inexperienced persons, however, also had proportionately high medical debts.

The occupational distribution changes noticeably for the other types of debts. Unspecified debts were owed to a greater proportionate degree by proprietors, semi-skilled workers, farmers, skilled and office workers, and professional men, in

[2] Small business owners such as peddlers, owners of small stores, etc. were included as well.

order. Unpaid grocery bills were relatively large for skilled and unskilled workers, inexperienced persons and proprietors. The greatest proportion of taxes was owed by office workers, farmers, proprietors, unskilled and skilled laborers. Industrial loans were relatively important only for office workers and proprietors. Professional men and semi-skilled workers were the only classes who owed more than their share for furniture. Mortgage debts were relatively high for the four white collar classes and for farmers. In all cases, the debts of domestic and personal workers were markedly below their normal contribution, and in most cases those of the inexperienced and farm classes.

To most of the specific debts, as to debts as a whole, the white collar classes, led by proprietors, and the skilled craftsmen made the largest proportional contribution. The exceptions are of some interest. All of the white collar groups except proprietors were well below their normal share of debts for food. The same was true with respect to salesmen and professional workers in regard to taxes. Professional men were the only white collar group with proportionately large debts for furniture.

An analysis similar to the foregoing has been made for property ownership. Chart III gives the distribution of home-ownership by occupation as an illustration. The line at 100 indicates what would have been the proportion of property owned by each occupation, if it were the same as their relative share of all the cases in the sample. The results are somewhat unexpected. One would have thought that the higher paid occupational groups, probably those with the most debts, would be the ones to own relatively the most property. Such is frequently not the case. For example, the occupational group with the greatest proportion of homes owned was the inexperienced persons. Proprietors, farmers, professional, and skilled workers are next. Unskilled laborers own almost their normal share and the other groups are below. The distribution of automobile ownership is more nearly in accordance with expectations. Farmers have the largest relative participation in automobile ownership, with the four white collar groups and skilled workers next. The possession of insurance is relatively high for farmers, skilled, office, and unskilled workers in the order named. Domestic and personal workers, usually below

Chart III — Relative Home Ownership by Occupation
Active Cases

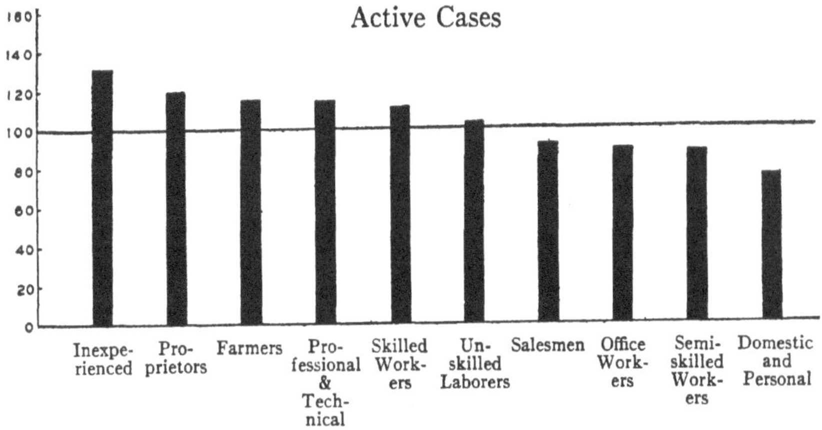

normal with respect to their relative debts, have almost exactly their relative share. With insurance, however, none of the occupational groups are much above or below the normal line. Very few families in our sample had any savings. But of the few who did, more of them were, relatively, professional men, farmers, or proprietors than of any other group. The proportion was high, too, for domestic workers, inexperienced persons, office workers, and salesmen. The three groups of industrial labor contributed far less than their relative share to the possession of savings.[3]

We have seen in Chapter II that the ownership of property was most prevalent in the rural sections and in Newton and

[3] The samples are so small, however, except for insurance and home ownership, that the results cannot be relied upon.

Somerville. Consistent with this conclusion is the fact that farmers were first in proportion of insurance, automobiles owned, second in savings, and third in home ownership, and that proprietors, professional, and skilled workmen were also in the higher ranks. It is somewhat surprising to find, however, that inexperienced persons ranked first in relative home ownership.[4] It is clear, too, although debts were consistently high in proportion among all the white collar occupations, that the relative concentration of property ownership is not as marked among them. Indebtedness and the ownership of property, at the time of application to relief, quite evidently are not related to past occupational status in the same way.

The influence of family size upon the amount of debt incurred is open to conjecture. Although a large family might have to go in debt to a greater extent than a small family, we have seen that the incomes of large families were consistently higher than those of small. Also there is no reason to suppose that credit ratings and the ability to incur debt are related to family size. In fact, one would anticipate that they would be based on general economic standing, income, occupation, etc. Nevertheless the average debt per family increases with family size up to a family of five persons. This group had the largest average debt. For families of six or more there is no apparent relation between amount of indebtedness and the number of persons in the family. In the case of food it may be said that the average amount owed for food was on the whole more for the bigger families. For the other items there is no clear relationship.

As one of the occupational classes about which little is

[4] This may be explained by the probability that inexperienced persons had broken or incomplete families. It is consistent with the Consumer Purchases Study results in Chicago, where it was found that incomplete families had relatively more home owners than the complete families. *Family Income in Chicago*, vol. I, Bull. 642, Bureau of Labor Statistics, p. 81.

known a somewhat more detailed analysis was made of inexperienced persons. There were 132 family heads who were put into this category. As a group they owed $22,574, although this amount was relatively below what they might have been expected to owe according to their relative size. Except for food, industrial loans, and medical debts, they were consistently below the 100 per cent line. In these three types of debt, particularly food, their indebtedness was relatively high. We have seen that they, as a group, owned homes to the greatest proportion of any of the occupational groups. They were also above their normal proportion for relative savings. The number of inexperienced persons was largest in Somerville, New Bedford, and the Small Towns, although all the towns in our sample included some case in this category. The group was predominantly female, since only 28, or 21 per cent, were men. The families headed by inexperienced males were large, 6 persons on the average. Those headed by females were smaller, 4.2 persons, or about the size of the average family for our whole sample. The usual inexperienced person in our group was, then, a woman with a family of 4 or 5 to support, and with no training to assist her in getting a job. She may have owned a house and had some savings. She was also in debt, particularly for food and doctor's bills, and she had probably attempted to get some kind of commercial loan.

The analysis of inexperienced persons was undertaken in the hope that some information might be secured on the extent of "broken families" on the work relief rolls. Other studies have indicated that they are more prevalent on relief than in the general population.[5] The term means that the usual family head is unable to support his family for one reason or another,

[5] In New Jersey, for instance, broken families, headed mostly by females, formed approximately one-third of the relief population in 1934. Such families were particularly frequent among the Negroes. *Neighbors in Need*, p. 14.

and that the burden of family support falls upon one of the children, or the wife. Unfortunately our data are not sufficiently complete to make certain that the inexperienced persons in our sample headed broken families. However, the large proportion of females and the average size of family are indirect evidence that many of the families in this group may well be broken families.[6]

The usual broken family is one in which the man, ordinarily the head of the family, is dead, incapacitated, or missing, so that some other member of the family is forced to assume the burden of family support. As a rule, the wife becomes the chief wage earner and is frequently inexperienced in an occupational sense. Sometimes one of the children becomes the chief wage earner, often a youngster just out of school who has never worked before. It was found in New Jersey that broken families were more prevalent on relief for two reasons.[7] If the chief wage earner had been unable to support his family before they went on relief, they were less able to withstand the difficulties of the depression and more likely to apply for relief. Also the apparently insurmountable difficulties of unemployment often discouraged the man of the family so much that he deserted. There were also deliberate desertions, to enable the rest of the family to get relief.[8] When there was no employable member of the family their problem became entirely one of government support. That is not so with our inexperienced cases, as they would not have been eligible for work relief if some member of the family had not been considered employable by the ERA. Still they represent a difficult problem and more

[6] The results of the Consumer Purchases Study investigation in Chicago indicate that three-fifths of the broken families, most of whom were classified in the independent business group, were headed by females. *Family Income in Chicago*, *op. cit.*, p. 26.

[7] Lester, *op. cit.*

[8] There is no statistical evidence for this statement, but it is made on the basis of the opinion of a WPA official.

of a permanent one than that of many other relief families.

The extent of the debts piled up by relief families both before and after they go on relief is a question of some importance and one that has not been sufficiently emphasized. Various studies of relief families have shown that they have gone heavily into debt before coming on relief, and have emphasized that rent was frequently the chief item owed.[9] In a previous investigation of Cambridge families, which were not typically relief families on the whole, although one-third to one-half of their income came from relief, it was found that these families were constantly in debt, for current expenses, as well as for past consumption.[10] In this study the debts were minimized, as loans from friends and relatives were counted as part of income. Their debts were largely for rent, medical care, and food. It was pointed out that the incidence of relief expenses, through the prevalence of debts, fell to an extraordinary degree upon landlords, doctors, and grocers.

This previous investigation of Cambridge families is not strictly comparable with our present study, even for Cambridge. Although the families were selected at random from the Cambridge ERA list, many of them were not on relief and had private employment. They were rather "underemployed" than unemployed as was the case with the majority of families in the sample now under analysis. Also, the Cambridge families were personally investigated and considerably more and better information was obtained. Data on annual income, expenditure, and debts were secured. We are now forced to rely on the weekly information obtained from ERA records, the validity of which we were not able to check per-

[9] E. Clague, E. W. Bakke, W. J. Couper, *After the Shutdown*, Yale University, 1935; E. Clague, W. Powell, *Ten Thousand Out of Work*, 1933; R. A. Lester, *op. cit.*

[10] Gilboy, "The Unemployed: Income and Expenditure," *American Economic Review*, June 1937.

sonally. Despite these difficulties it is interesting to find that the conclusions concerning debt are very similar for our relief families and for the underemployed in Cambridge. The families in our sample were also in debt, as a whole for half a million dollars. The principal creditors were landlords, friends and relatives, doctors, and grocers. These represent debts already incurred at the time of application for relief. We can also infer that our relief families were currently running a deficit since average weekly income was consistently less than average weekly expenditure, whether actual expenditure or that of the ERA standard budget.

It is possible that the amount of indebtedness in our sample is somewhat exaggerated for typical relief cases. The occupational classes which contributed relatively the most to indebtedness were the white collar workers and skilled craftsmen. And our sample is probably somewhat overweighted with white collar workers, particularly those from Newton and Somerville. Nevertheless indebtedness remains a considerable problem, especially as most of these debts will probably never be repaid. It would be interesting to know what the repercussions of this situation have been. Obviously landlords and doctors and grocers and other creditors must have had reduced incomes. Probably their standard of living was decreased. It may be that many of them, particularly the marginal ones, were themselves forced on relief. If so the problem becomes circular. However, we have at present no data which give information on the situation and can only speculate. That the problem is not entirely restricted to those on relief is shown by the recently released income and expenditure figures from the Consumer Purchases Study. It was characteristic of low income families that they operated on an annual deficit for 1935–36.

Not only were our families in debt but many of them owned property. Regionally, property ownership and debt were both concentrated in Newton and Somerville, with some exceptions.

New Bedford was high in debts but low in property holdings. The reverse was true of the Small Towns. Occupationally debts were relatively high for all four classes of white collar workers and skilled craftsmen and low for domestic servants and inexperienced persons. Property ownership, however, was not relatively high for the same occupations with the greatest proportional debts, as a rule. Farmers, inexperienced persons, and proprietors held relatively large amounts of property. Approximately one-third of our group had capital assets still remaining, in the form of houses, insurance, etc. when they went on relief. One cannot say therefore that the ownership of property was typical of relief cases. One can say, however, that one type of relief applicant, by no means infrequent, was the owner of his own home, or of insurance, or of an automobile when he became an eligible ERA worker. His property may have been more of a liability than an asset and it was not supposed to provide him with income, except a very limited amount, according to ERA rulings. Nevertheless he owned it. The implication is that a number of ERA workers came from an economic status somewhat above the lowest on the economic scale. Whatever their previous economic condition, however, most of them were in debt by the time they became ERA workers.

CHAPTER VII

THE EXPENDITURE OF THEIR INCOME

ONE OF THE FUNDAMENTAL AIMS of work relief is the preservation of the health, both mental and physical, and the skill of those who are employable. It was recognized at an early stage that the wage paid on work relief projects must meet some standard of adequacy. The standard budget set up for each eligible family in each district under the ERA was supposed to establish the minimum amount of money upon which that family could live without physical deterioration. The amount of money received by the family from work relief was adjusted to meet this minimum. The WPA attempted to do more than provide bare physical needs. Its wages were supposedly determined by the principle of a "security wage"[1] so that they were more than enough to meet minimum physical standards and yet not sufficiently high to compete with private business. The material in this chapter will afford some basis for judging whether the work relief aim of providing a minimum level of living for its recipients was fulfilled.

The ERA standard budget for Massachusetts has been described previously. We have also called attention to the fact that on the average the income of the families in our sample was not sufficient to meet the maximum budgetary standard which could have been set up according to ERA rules in the various towns.[2] Although there is no way of knowing how many of these families were able to meet or to surpass a minimum standard of physical efficiency before the depression, the data on property ownership and debts would seem to indi-

[1] See President's comment on establishing the WPA, *FERA Monthly Report*, April 1935.

[2] See p. 61.

cate that a considerable number had previously attained a much higher level of living. It is probable that many of them suffered a severe reduction in living standards, although it is an open question whether the unemployed have borne all or most of the incidence of unemployment in the form of reduced living conditions.[3]

In Massachusetts, work relief wages were paid in cash [4] and no official attempt was made to direct the actual expenditure of families in accordance with ERA rules. How they spent their money was their own concern. Little information exists, however, on the expenditure of relief families, in Massachusetts or elsewhere.[5] I have been able to collect some information for relief families in Cambridge and Professor Zimmerman has turned over to me data on relief families in five Massachusetts towns.[6] In addition I tried to secure expenditure data for the sample which forms the basis of the analysis in this book. As has been explained before, it is uncertain whether

[3] Professor Bakke contends that the burden of unemployment falls for the most part upon the unemployed in the form of a decline of living standards. (See *After the Shutdown*, by E. Clague, W. J. Cowper, and E. W. Bakke, Institute of Human Relations, Yale University, 1934, p. 112.) David Lasser, President of the Workers' Alliance, also believes that the unemployed themselves have carried the burden of unemployment. (See his testimony before the *Special Committee to Investigate Unemployment and Relief*, vol. 2, Hearings, S. Res. 36, Feb. 28–April 8, 1938, pp. 1031–32.) Some further discussion of this point may be found in Gilboy, "Unemployed: Income and Expenditure," *American Economic Review*, June 1937, pp. 320–23.

[4] According to the Emergency Reconstruction Act of 1933 ERA wages could be paid in kind, in cash, or by check. In New Jersey, for instance, work relief wages were frequently paid in kind. *FERA Monthly Report*, May 1933.

[5] The Consumer Purchases Study collected some information on relief income and some scant data on relief expenditures. The latter were too incomplete to be of statistical value.

[6] The results have been summarized in an article by the author in the *American Sociological Review* for December, 1938. Some of the tables and text are reprinted in this chapter by permission of the editor.

the weekly expenditures of the families which were recorded on the ERA records refer to the actual expenditures of the families or to the ERA budget set up by the District office. It is obvious in some cases that the expenditures are those of the standard budget. In four towns, Newton, Somerville, Cambridge, and Framingham, it seemed reasonably certain that an attempt was made to record actual expenditures. The Newton records gave the standard budget and the actual expenditures for each family. The expenditure data from these four towns, with that of Cambridge and the five Massachusetts towns, will serve as the basis for the analysis of the expenditures of those on relief in this chapter.

TABLE P

AVERAGE WEEKLY EXPENDITURE BY TOWNS

Towns	No. in Family	Total Income	Total Expenditure	Food	House	Clothing	Insurance	Other
Newton	5.0	$18.11	$20.34	$9.04	$8.82	$1.16	$.55	$.76
Somerville	3.9	14.27	19.11	8.51	7.76	1.54	.39	.91
Cambridge	4.9	12.81	16.79	8.88	6.25	.66	.45	.56
Framingham ...	4.8	15.77	17.79	8.47	6.71	1.58	.53	.50

Table P presents the expenditure data for the four Massachusetts towns and cities for which the data seemed reasonably adequate. During a typical week in 1935 an average family of 5 on work relief in Newton spent a little over $20. Out of this sum $9 went for food and almost $9 for housing. Of the remainder $1.16 was spent for clothing and the rest was divided between insurance and miscellaneous expenditures. The expenditures in Newton were consistently higher than in the other towns, except for clothing and miscellaneous. On a per capita basis, however, Somerville, where the average family was smaller, spent the most. The average family member in Somerville spent $4.90 as against $4.07 in Newton, $3.70 in Framingham, and $3.42 in Cambridge. In every item except insurance, per capita expenditures were highest in Somerville. With respect to house and clothing, Cambridge spent the least, both on a family and a per capita basis, though for food expenditure Cambridge equalled Newton.

On a percentage basis, the distribution of total expenditure weekly between the various items is very similar for both Newton and Somerville. In both cities 44 per cent went for food, and slightly less for housing. Clothing was next in importance, with 8 per cent for Somerville and nearly 6 per cent for Newton. Insurance and miscellaneous accounted for the remaining 6 or 7 per cent. The percentage spent on food was higher in Cambridge and Framingham, particularly in Cambridge, than the proportion in Newton and Somerville. Over half of the weekly expenditure in Cambridge went for food. The proportions spent on housing and clothing were correspondingly less, although the percentages for insurance and other were very like those in the other three towns. In Framingham, the chief relative reduction was in housing, since clothing was nearly 9 per cent of the budget, the highest proportion for any of the four towns, and the other items were about the same.

TABLE Q

AVERAGE WEEKLY EXPENDITURE BY TOWNS (per cent)

	Food	House	Clothing	Insurance	Other	Total
Newton	44.4	43.4	5.7	2.7	3.8	100.0
Somerville	44.5	40.6	8.1	2.0	4.8	100.0
Cambridge	52.9	37.2	3.9	2.7	3.3	100.0
Framingham	47.6	37.8	8.9	3.0	2.9	100.0

These two tables bring out the fundamental likeness between the Newton and Somerville samples, which has been noted before. The number of property owners among relief applicants was relatively high; the proportion of white collar workers and skilled craftsmen was also large. It is apparent, too, that their distribution of expenditures in the family budget was very similar. Cambridge, on the other hand, seems to stand by itself, with a much greater relative expenditure on food than in any other case.

Several previous studies afford interesting comparisons with the above data. A sample of 397 Cambridge families was taken

TABLE R

AVERAGE EXPENDITURE IN CAMBRIDGE (397 cases) *

Items	Annual	Weekly [a]	Per cent of Total Expenditure
Food	$425	$8.17	44.6
House inc. operation & furnishings	333	6.40	34.9
Clothing	52	1.00	5.5
Transportation inc. auto	27	.52	2.8
Recreation inc. tobacco & reading	32	.64	3.3
Personal care	7	.14	.7
Medical	31	.60	3.2
Education	3	.06	.3
Gifts	7	.14	.7
Other expenditure	38	.73	4.0
Total	$955	$18.34	100.0
Income	$804	$15.46	84.2

Average size of family 4.2 persons.

* The figures in this table are taken from Tables 1 and 5 printed in "The Expenditure of the Unemployed," *American Sociological Review*, December 1938.

[a] The weekly figures have been derived by dividing the annual figures by 52.

from the 1935 ERA list of eligible cases and detailed information upon their income and expenditure was secured by personal investigators.[7] The expenditure data secured are on an

[7] See the following articles for a more detailed account of the results: "The Unemployed: Income and Expenditure," *American Economic Review*, June 1937; "The Expenditure of the Unemployed," *American Sociological Review*, December 1938, by E. W. Gilboy; and "The Economics of Low Income Diets," *Quarterly Journal of Economics*, August 1937, by H. L. Sorenson and E. W. Gilboy.

annual basis and far better than anything which could be derived from the WPA records for our present sample. This Cambridge sample appears to represent a somewhat more fortunate group economically than the majority of those in our present sample. The average family in this study was less dependent on relief and had more chances for private employment. Nevertheless, a comparison of the data from the two studies is informative. Table R lists the expenditure of these Cambridge families.

On a weekly basis the average family in the Cambridge sample spent $18.34 and earned $15.46, considerably more in both instances than was received or spent by the average Cambridge family in our main sample. Yet the weekly food expenditure for our second Cambridge sample was slightly higher in amount than the first, which may be a result of a slightly larger family. In fact the weekly food expenditure for the underemployed group was less on the average than in any one of the four towns. Expenditure on housing was about the same for both Cambridge samples and was less than that recorded for Newton, Somerville, and Framingham. One dollar a week was spent on clothes by the Cambridge underemployed; 66 cents by the work relief applicants. The other three towns all listed clothing expenditure as more than a dollar. As far as food and housing go, in both Cambridge samples expenditure for the average family was roughly the same. Yet the family was smaller in size in the underemployed sample and total expenditure was greater. The active relief cases of our second sample still maintained their food and housing standards at the level, at least, of the underemployed. It is of some interest to recall that in comparing the expenditures of the 397 Cambridge families with those of an employed group in Boston we found that the Cambridge families, half of which were on relief, attempted to maintain their food and housing standards at a level comparable to that of the employed group. Economies were made chiefly in clothing and in luxury expenditures which were cut down but not entirely eliminated.[8]

The chief difference to be found between the expenditures of the underemployed in Cambridge and the unemployed in our four towns lies in the miscellaneous items. The average underemployed family spent about $3.00 a week on recreation, personal care, medicine, etc. Thirty-eight cents of this was for insurance. The active work relief cases in the four towns, however, had on the average anywhere from fifty to ninety cents a week to cover all their miscellaneous expenses except insurance. They could not have had very much recreation or personal or medical care on that amount. Of course, miscellaneous expenses were not itemized on the ERA records, and many of them were probably not recorded. It seems almost impossible to believe that these unemployed families did not on occasion go to the movies, smoke, buy a newspaper, or have a haircut. If their miscellaneous expenses were actually greater than is shown by the records, their weekly deficit must also have been greater. As we have seen, the average weekly income in the four towns was below the average weekly expenditure recorded on the ERA blanks.

It must be remembered, too, that the weekly income and expenditure figures for the underemployed in the separate Cambridge study apply throughout the year. During 1934-35 these families earned and spent on the average the amounts given every week. For the active cases in the four towns there is no such assurance. The income and expenditure figures refer to only one week for each family and our data reveal a cross-section picture of income and expenditure for the average family during one week in the year. There is no way of knowing what was earned or spent in other weeks, or what annual income and expenditure might have been. It is known, however, that these cases were not kept on ERA continuously

[8] See Gilboy, *op. cit.*, *American Sociological Review.*

throughout the year. The presumption is that their annual income, and probably their annual expenditures, would be considerably less than the weekly figure multiplied by 52.[9] From this point of view the work relief cases were much worse off than those families in our group of the underemployed.

A brief survey of income and expenditure was made by Professor Zimmerman in five Massachusetts towns in connection with a study of rural conditions. The income and expenditure information was collected by personal investigators. The figures have not previously been published, although they have been referred to.[10] The towns, Dracut, Gilbertville, Marlboro, Sudbury, and Winchester were selected by Zimmerman to represent varying rural conditions. Dracut, Gilbertville, and Marlboro are rural-industrial towns comparable to Framingham and Maynard in our sample. Winchester is a metropolitan suburb with some industry of its own, somewhat like the Newtons. Sudbury is a farming community which is becoming popular with professional people as a place of residence. It is somewhat in the category of Lincoln or Wayland and is similar to the towns included in the Small Town group in our sample. The families interviewed were all on some kind of relief and receiving relief at the time the survey was conducted. More were on public relief than work relief, consequently they are not quite comparable to the samples previously discussed. Tables S and T list the income and expenditures in these five towns for relief cases. The samples are small and the averages must therefore be interpreted with generous limitations.[11]

[9] A WPA official remarks that miscellaneous employment might rise after the initial ERA acceptance and that the ERA grant might be higher in later weeks. This may be true, but there is still no guarantee of continuous work relief employment.

[10] See articles previously mentioned by the author. There was not sufficient space in these papers to include the tables.

[11] In rechecking the figures it was discovered that some inaccuracy in grouping had taken place in the original computations. Since this occurred

The expenditures in these rural towns are characterized, as was the case with the underemployed Cambridge sample, by a considerably larger surplus for items other than food, housing, and clothing than is true of our active work relief cases.

TABLE S

AVERAGE WEEKLY EXPENDITURE IN THREE MASSACHUSETTS TOWNS (Relief Cases)*

	Gilbertville	Marlboro	Winchester
No. of cases	58	39	83
Average size of family	4.2	4.7	4.9
Total Income	$13.42	$15.76	$18.26
Total Expenditure [a]	16.28	18.80	23.55
Expenditure on			
Food	9.13	7.45	9.17
Household	3.02	5.93	7.23
Clothing	.84	.87	1.34
Health	.65	1.63	1.26
Insurance	1.03	.56	1.11
Investment	.08	.75	1.30
Farm	.10	.01	.08
Education	...	.01	.02
Reading	.12	.18	.20
Auto	.37	.33	.66
Miscellaneous	1.11	1.06	1.18

* The data are given in annual form. Weekly figures were computed by dividing by 52.

[a] Except in the case of Winchester the total expenditure figures do not correspond exactly to the sum of the individual items, because the averages for total expenditure and for each item were calculated separately so that there is a small difference (not over one per cent) in the decimal places.

The Winchester relief families spent nearly $6.00 a week for miscellaneous items, over half of which went for health, insurance, and investment. The same is true for Marlboro,

largely in connection with the non-relief cases, it need not concern us here, except to make it even more important to realize the very approximate nature of the final figures. Dracut and Sudbury figures have been omitted as being too few to be worth anything.

although their total expenditure for miscellaneous was less, $5.00 per week, on the average. Relief families in Gilbertville were more like those of our Cambridge ERA families, with $3.00 to spend each week on other items.

As far as food is concerned, relief families in all the towns except Marlboro spent as much per week as our Boston families, and more than the Framingham families which they might be supposed to resemble. Housing expenditure was consistently low. Except for Winchester, the amount spent was well below that for the cases in our other samples. Clothing expenditure was about the same in all the towns, running about one dollar per week. The total weekly expenditure for the necessities of life, food, housing, and clothes, was about the same for Winchester and Newton, the latter being a little higher. The total for the other towns was below that of Framingham, which they resemble. Gilbertville and Marlboro spent considerably less, although their expenditure for all items was not low.

It will be noted that family size varied considerably in these towns. The average family in Gilbertville was exactly the same in size as that of the separate Cambridge sample, 4.2 persons. Winchester and Marlboro had somewhat larger families, of nearly 5 persons, as was also the case of Newton, Cambridge, and Framingham.

The per cent of total expenditure allocated to the various budgetary items is given in Table T. The percentages indicate a number of interesting things about the rural towns. In Gilbertville the proportion spent for food was extremely high, 55 per cent, comparable to the relative food expenditure in the Cambridge sample of active work relief cases. The chief thing to be noted, however, is the proportion of weekly incomes available for expenditures other than food, household, and clothing. This percentage varied from 21 per cent in the case of Gilbertville to 25 per cent in the case of Winchester. We have seen that for the Cambridge sample of underemployed, 15 per cent was available for other expenditures, and about half of that proportion for the four cities in our ERA sample.

On the basis of diversity of expenditure, then, the relief families in the rural towns were somewhat better off, with the possible exception of Gilbertville, than the families in our separate Cambridge sample; and markedly better off than

TABLE T

AVERAGE WEEKLY EXPENDITURE IN THREE MASSACHUSETTS TOWNS

(Relief Cases)

PER CENT OF TOTAL EXPENDITURE

	Gilbertville	Marlboro	Winchester
No. of cases	58	39	83
Food	55.4	39.6	38.9
Household	18.3	31.5	30.7
Clothing	5.1	4.7	5.7
Health	4.0	8.7	5.4
Insurance	6.3	3.0	4.7
Investment	.5	4.0	5.5
Farm	.6	.1	.3
Education	..	.1	.1
Reading	.7	.9	.9
Auto	2.3	1.8	2.8
Miscellaneous	6.8	5.6	5.0
	100.0	100.0	100.0

those in our present ERA sample. The average work relief family in Newton, Somerville, Cambridge, or Framingham was forced to spend all but 6 or 7 per cent of its total expenditures during that week on food, house, and clothing. It must be remembered, too, that this weekly expenditure was not continuous throughout the year, whereas the weekly figures for the other relief samples are based on annual data.

There are reasons for thinking that the apparent differences in level of living between the 1935 ERA sample of work relief cases and those in the separate Cambridge sample and in the five rural towns have some basis in fact. In the first place there is a difference in time which may affect the results. Data of our present sample refer to a cross section week in 1935. The information for the first Cambridge sample is for the year June 1934 to June 1935. Professor Zimmerman's material refers to the period June 1933 to June 1934. From the point of view of time alone it is not surprising that 1935 relief cases were worse off than those in preceding years. It has been found that most relief applicants will exhaust their own resources before applying for relief, and those who waited until 1935 to apply may have reduced themselves to a greater dependence on relief sources than those who applied earlier.

A more cogent argument, however, lies in the probability that our ERA sample for Massachusetts is more representative of the continuing work relief case, whereas the other data apply perhaps more accurately to the upper fringes of the unemployed group. The Massachusetts cases were selected at random from WPA cases active in 1937 which had been declared eligible in 1935 under the FERA. The majority of their income came from relief. They appear to be typical of the ordinary work relief family in 1935 in occupation, income sources etc. (see Chapter III) but their continuance on the work relief rolls indicates that they are the ones who will be most likely to provide a continuing relief problem. In the other Cambridge sample, however, only half the families were on relief at the time of the survey and relief was not, on the whole, their main source of income. Their occupational distribution was also somewhat different from that of the active work relief population. Less is known about the relief cases in the five rural towns, but it is clear that relief was not their predominant source of income, and that they are more like the families in the underemployed Cambridge group, allowing for geographical differences, than those in our present work relief group. We appear to be dealing with two different but allied strata of the unemployed, those who were (and perhaps are) continuing work relief cases, whose main income came from work relief, supplemented by income from other sources; and those who relied on work relief as a supplement to their income from private employment, boarders, etc. It is more accurate to designate the latter as the underemployed rather than the unemployed, as suggested by Dr. Eckler.[12] It seems clear that the underemployed were able to maintain a somewhat higher and more diverse standard of living than the unemployed.

The data are statistically too inaccurate to lead to satisfactory results in the analysis of income-expenditure relations. However, a rough analysis of this sort was made, with the best results being obtained from the data of the first Cambridge sample of the underemployed.

The weekly expenditure figures for Newton, Somerville, Framingham, and Cambridge were classified according to income groups and charted on a double logarithmic scale. The results are extremely erratic. For some items the income-expenditure points did not fall along a curve at all, and in most cases the curves changed in shape and were often discontinuous at various income levels. It may be said tentatively that inelasticity of income-expenditure relations appeared to be indicated and that there was a fairly consistent negative elasticity for the lower income classes.[13] On the whole, however,

[12] See Gilboy, *op. cit.*, *American Economic Review* and *American Sociological Review*, for more details.

[13] Elasticity is used here to denote the relation between a proportionate change in income and expenditure. If the proportionate change in expenditure is greater than the proportionate change in income, income-expenditure relations are elastic. If the reverse is true, they are inelastic. If the proportionate change is the same, income-expenditure elasticity is 1. Negative elasticity indicates that expenditure and income change inversely.

the dubious nature of the expenditure figures and the smallness of the samples makes it unsafe to draw any conclusions.

It is of some interest to observe the percentage changes in expenditure as income rose. The per cent spent for housing went down with an increase in income fairly consistently for all three towns. The proportion spent for food tended to remain level or increase, indicating a very low standard of living. As Professor Zimmerman has explained, this is not really inconsistent with Engel's laws, one of which is ordinarily interpreted to state that as income increases the proportion spent on food decreases. A minimum level of food consumption must be attained before the law can be expected to operate.[14] Very possibly the relief families in these four towns were below that minimum. The per cent spent on the remaining budgetary items remained fairly stable as income increased, except for "other" which showed a slight tendency to increase. Roughly it looks as if these relief applicants preferred to reduce their relative housing expenditure in favor of more and better food, as their income went up. This was particularly clear in Cambridge and Framingham, but not as marked in Newton or Somerville.

The analysis of income-expenditure relations for the Cambridge underemployed proved fairly successful. The distribution of average expenditure by amounts and per cents according to income classes will be found in Table 14,[15] Appendix B. It will be noted that the per cent spent for food and housing went down as income rose, the per cent for housing to a lesser extent than that for food. Of the other items, the proportion spent increased consistently for clothing, recreation, medical expenditure, automobile, and savings (including insurance). The ex-

[14] See Zimmerman, *Quarterly Journal of Economics*, "Ernst Engel's Law of Expenditures for Food," November 1932.

[15] These data were reproduced and briefly analyzed in "The Expenditure of the Unemployed," *American Sociological Review*, December 1938.

penditure on books decreased, relatively, and the per cent spent on tobacco, travel, other etc. appears to vary erratically.

In all cases the actual amount spent increases with income. When these amounts were charted against average total expenditure for the respective income class intervals on a double logarithmic scale, fairly good curves resulted. It was therefore possible to measure income-expenditure elasticity graphically very approximately. Housing expenditure was elastic up to an income level of $500 and inelastic above that. Food expenditure was slightly inelastic throughout the whole income range, with a coefficient of .9. Auto, recreation, medical care, clothing, tobacco, and personal care were definitely elastic throughout, and in the order named. Other, insurance, travel, and books were elastic for most of the income range. In other words, most of the budgetary items, with the exception of housing and food, had an income-expenditure elasticity greater than unity. As income increased more was spent proportionally on items other than food and clothing. This conclusion was confirmed by a similar analysis of the income and expenditure data in per capita terms. When the influence of size of family is thus eliminated, income-expenditure elasticity is greater than unity for everything except food and housing. Food had an income-expenditure elasticity of .8 and housing of unity. We may conclude tentatively, therefore, that nearly all of the expenditures of this group were highly elastic.

This conclusion does not check with the apparent inelasticity of income-expenditure relations for the work relief group in the four towns. Possibly the difference may be explained by the fact that the two groups are not entirely similar and represent somewhat unlike economic levels. The main explanation, however, lies in the uncertain nature of the data, particularly the expenditure figures for the four towns, and the limited income range there represented.[16]

[16] Also the record of miscellaneous expenditures was extremely poor.

Much more confidence may be placed in the expenditure data for the Cambridge underemployed and in the income-expenditure analysis. One would expect, too, considerable elasticity in expenditure for groups who had not been able to satisfy their wants, even for food and housing, at a very low income level.

The most important item in the budget and the one which comprised the greatest amount and proportion of weekly expenditure was food, both for the unemployed and the underemployed. It is of some interest to determine whether this expenditure enabled these low income groups to obtain an adequate diet. Some information was secured on this point for the Cambridge underemployed, of which 203 families kept a detailed account of expenditures, mainly for food, for one or more weeks.[17] In comparing the food expenditures of these underemployed families with the four standard diets set up by the Bureau of Home Economics, it was found that all the income classes in Cambridge were able to obtain the restricted diet, the lowest standard set up. The cost of these standard diets per adult male unit in Cambridge at the time of the survey was approximately as follows:

Restricted diet	$1.51
Adequate diet at minimum cost	1.98
Adequate diet at moderate cost	2.67
Liberal diet	3.24

The lowest income group spent a little more than that required for the restricted diet, and the next income class exceeded the necessary expenditure for an adequate diet at minimum cost. It is not, however, until the 300-399 income level was reached that 3,000 calories per day per adult male was attained and the expenditure for food approached that of

[17] This information has been published in an article by Helen L. Sorenson and the present author in the *Quarterly Journal of Economics* for August 1937. The material is summarized here.

the adequate diet at moderate cost. In the highest income group more than enough was spent to secure the liberal diet.

An income-expenditure analysis of the items in Table U indicated that the income elasticity of food expenditure in general was slightly below unity, confirming the previous analysis of the data classified in another way. Other food expenditures, fruit and vegetables, and meat and fish had income

TABLE U

FOOD EXPENDITURE IN CAMBRIDGE

INCOME CLASS (dollars per year per AMU)

Food Item	100–199	200–299	300–399	400–499
Meat and Fish	$ .368	$ .556	$ .658	$1.152
Eggs	.097	.163	.197	.266
Milk [1]	.247	.369	.396	.557
Butter	.079	.128	.148	.180
Other Fats	.064	.054	.062	.087
Fruits and vegetables	.181	.266	.353	.658
Potatoes	.062	.087	.088	.118
Bread and Cereals	.355	.443	.374	.551
Sugars	.077	.105	.101	.143
Other [2]	.128	.135	.207	.388
Total	$1.658	$2.316	$2.582	$4.100

[1] Includes fresh and canned milk, cheese, and cream.

[2] Includes expenditures on non-alcoholic beverages, condiments, pastry, meals out and miscellaneous items.

elasticity coefficients above unity and may be classed as definitely elastic items of food expenditure. Eggs and milk were the next most elastic items, with coefficients of .9 and .8 respectively. Fats, sugars, potatoes, and bread and cereals were distinctly inelastic in relation to income, with the latter having an approximate coefficient of .4. As income rises, therefore, expenditure on food rises in almost the same proportion, as does the expenditure on eggs and milk. The expenditure on miscellaneous foods, fruit and vegetables, and meat and fish increases relatively to a greater extent, while that on the other kinds of food increases to a smaller degree. It is noteworthy that absolute expenditures on all the food items increase consistently with income, even on the inelastic items such as bread and cereals.

The diet of these Cambridge families was characterized by a concentration on meat and potatoes, and particularly for the lowest income groups, a deficiency in milk and vegetables. The Cambridge diet was thus quite different from the adequate diet at minimum cost which is centered around milk and cereals. It looks as if these families were trying to maintain the same type of food consumption which they had enjoyed before the depression period, with undoubtedly some reduction in quality, rather than reorganizing their food budget to apply to their new conditions of reduced income. The deficiency in protective foods such as milk and vegetables becomes serious when one realizes that it is in the lower income group that the large families were concentrated. On the whole, however, these underemployed families were able to maintain a diet somewhere between that of the adequate diets at minimum and moderate cost.

We have no such detailed information on the diets of the families comprising our other samples. Other evidence has indicated, however, that the relief families in the five rural towns are of a similar economic class. Gilbertville, at any rate, had a weekly food expenditure somewhat higher than the average for these Cambridge families, with the same size family. In the other four towns, the family was somewhat larger in size, and weekly food expenditures were slightly more in Dracut and Winchester; slightly less in Marlboro and Sudbury. It is probable that these relief families in the rural towns fared at least as well in the matter of diet as the families in the original Cambridge sample. Perhaps they fared better, since the rural nature of the communities made it possible for many of them to have gardens which would supplement their food budget.

Both the average and per capita expenditure on food in the four work relief samples of Newton, Somerville, Cambridge, and Framingham would have enabled these families to support a diet somewhere between the restricted diet and the one at minimum cost, at least in that cross section week. They appear to be comparable to the two lower income groups in the first Cambridge analysis. This means that their food consumption was likely to be lacking in sufficient milk and vegetables and in total calorie content. What happened to their diet in the weeks when the head of family was not assigned to a work relief project it is difficult to say. Certainly it is the opinion of trained social workers on the Massachusetts WPA staff that the allowance of $2 a week per person was not enough for an adequate diet, and we have seen that many families did not average that expenditure per person in the cross section week. It is more than likely that the work relief families in our main sample were distinctly undernourished and to a far greater extent than those in the underemployed groups.

The distribution of surplus commodities to needy families by the Federal Surplus Commodities Corporation may have helped to supplement the food consumption of these families. Since they were mainly dependent on work relief, however, it is unlikely that they shared in the surplus commodities to as great an extent as the welfare cases. Table 15, Appendix B, lists the amount and kind of commodities shipped to Massachusetts for distribution from 1933 to 1938.[18] In 1935, the year to which the major portion of our data refers, the following foods, in order of amount shipped, were sent to Massachusetts: canned beef, white potatoes, dried prunes, canned mutton, canned veal, cabbage, cheese, rice, and evaporated

[18] This information has been supplied to me through the kindness of Dr. Norman Gold of the Federal Surplus Commodities Corporation.

milk. To some degree the distribution of these commodities would tend to improve the adequacy of diet, although there was not as much emphasis on vegetables and dairy products as would be desirable from the standpoint of nutrition. The FSCC, however, finds itself in the position of distributing the surpluses which exist at any particular time. Obviously such surpluses are the result of factors quite unallied to the nutrition problem, such as the general farm production policy of the AAA, the weather etc. It is interesting to observe, however, that in the years following 1935, far more dairy products, fruit and vegetables were sent for distribution than in preceding years. Doubtless, existing surpluses were a large factor in determining the change, but it is also true that the FSCC has become increasingly aware of the nutrition problem, and the necessity for raising the dietary standards of these low income groups in certain directions.

As to the adequacy of other budgetary items we can only comment briefly. In Cambridge and the five rural towns approximately a dollar a week was spent per family on clothing. This is inadequate even in comparison with a farm standard of $150 a year for a family of 5.[19] The work relief families in our main sample had less than a dollar to spend on clothing and must have been even more insufficiently clothed. Sometimes clothing was distributed to such families by welfare and religious agencies and given them by friends. Also the FSCC contributed surplus cotton and wool, sheep skin etc. which was made into clothing for distribution to such families.

We have little information on actual housing conditions, though it is known that they are very inadequate for such low

[19] This was the lowest clothing budget set up for farm families in the Eastern states and assumed that most of the clothing would be made at home. It is based on 1932 prices. U. S. Department of Agriculture Extension Service, Mimeographed report, No. 6358, by Florence Hall.

income families. It was found that many work relief families had banded together to cut housing expenses, that many families had lost their previously mortgaged houses. Obviously there was a severe reduction in housing standards for these families during their dependence on relief. Yet as incomes rose, at least within the limits of the data here analyzed, housing was one of the last expenditures to increase.

Perhaps the most striking difference between the underemployed and the unemployed, as indicated by our figures, lies in the amount available for miscellaneous and luxury expenditures. The underemployed had a few dollars to spend each week on newspapers, cigarettes, personal care, movies, etc. The unemployed had only a few cents a week. Now it may be that they actually spent more on such items and did not report them. If so, they were either in debt to a greater extent than is shown in our figures, or their dietary, housing, and clothing consumption was even more insufficient. It may be hazarded that both are probably the case in some degree.

The expenditure analysis may be briefly summarized by stating that our data, rough and approximate as they are, lead one to conclude that our underemployed and unemployed families certainly belong to the ill-nourished, ill-clad, and ill-housed third of the nation referred to by President Roosevelt and by many others. On all counts the underemployed fared better than the unemployed, but particularly in the matter of diet and miscellaneous expenditures. Those who were dependent almost entirely on relief for their support were not, on the average, able to indulge themselves on their relief wages or amounts given. Even the standard budgets set up by the ERA were inadequate for a minimum standard of living, and family income rarely came up to this standard. As Mrs. Armstrong puts it, on the basis of her experience as ERA Administrator of a Michigan county,—"All rumors to the contrary notwithstanding, none of these relief cases, chiselers or otherwise, were living in sinful luxury on the relief granted them by our office."[20]

[20] Louise V. Armstrong, *We Too Are the People*, Boston 1938, p. 281. Of 1050 cases on the ERA (both direct and work relief) in this county during an average month in 1935, 62 per cent received less than $20 a month, 16 per cent between $20 and $30, 10 per cent between $30 and $40.

For those interested in the human side of the relief problem and the reactions of a competent social worker to the relief system, this is an excellent book.

PART III

THE CHANCES OF RE-EMPLOYMENT

CHAPTER VIII

CANCELLED WORK RELIEF CASES

THE FINAL JUSTIFICATION of work relief must be found on grounds other than its money cost, for it is undoubtedly a more expensive form of relief than straight relief, the cost ratio on a comparable basis being 100 : 73.[1] The arguments in favor of work relief run in terms of the following: (1) although more expensive it contributes to increasing the wealth of the country by the tangible results of its various projects; (2) it enables those who become unemployed in a period of depression to remain employable by using their skill in work for which they are trained and by maintaining their morale; (3) it thereby facilitates their return to private employment. We shall be concerned in this section largely with the third argument and to some extent with the second.

In order to determine what chances of re-employment might be expected to obtain for those on work relief, it was decided to examine a sample of cases, certified during 1935, who had received "cancellations" from work relief thereafter. Therefore 408 cases were selected at random for Framingham, Newton, Somerville, the Small Towns, and New Bedford from the inactive WPA file in 1938.[2] For 279 of these cases the reason for their separation from the work relief rolls was given. Nearly all of the data which have been presented for the continuing work relief sample were also available for those who had been

[1] Ratio estimated by WPA Division of Research.

[2] These cases were cancelled during the period from 1935 to 1938. The Framingham sample is very small, only 20 cases. No individual analysis of Framingham is attempted, but these 20 cases are included in the totals for the whole sample.

discontinued. It was thought that the comparison of the sample of separated cases with our other sample, since both samples are composed of cases certified in 1935, might give some information on two points: (1) whether there was any difference to be observed in the occupational, age, or economic characteristics of those who had left relief and of those who had stayed on, and (2) to what extent the separated cases had returned to private employment. If there are any differences between those who had remained more or less constantly dependent on work relief from 1935–1938 and those who had left it by 1938, our information might indicate where these differences lay. Are the continuing work relief cases, for instance, older, less skilled, from a lower economic class, less well educated, etc? Are they the marginal workers of our society who are continually on the verge of unemployment and representative of a long range social problem rather than a short period depression phenomenon? Are they the relief cases we have always with us who have merely been shifted to work relief from the public welfare rolls?

Certain characteristics of the average person who had been on work relief ought now to be clear after the preceding chapters. We are dealing with a group composed largely of semiskilled and skilled workers, around 40 years of age, the chief wage earners of families of 4 or 5 persons. They are almost entirely dependent on work relief for their existence and they do not earn enough to meet either the work relief budget or their actual weekly expenditures for the main necessities of life. Most of them have been to grammar school, some of them to high school. Almost all are U. S. citizens. Nearly a third of them have managed to hang on to property in the form of mortgaged houses or insurance of some kind. Probably a majority of them owned some substantial form of property before they lost their jobs. All are constantly in debt and most of them have several hundred dollars of accumulated debt

TABLE V

Reasons for Cancellation from WPA

	No. of Cases	Sufficient Income		Return to Private Employment	Transfer to Other Relief Agency	Drunkenness	Inefficiency	Insubordination	Did not Report	Other
		Private Employment	Concealed Assets							
New Bedford	38	31	..	3	1	..	..	..	..	3
Newton	83	13	1	37	1	1	4	2	1	23
Framingham	20	5	2	6	2	..	..	..	..	5
Somerville	105	25	4	40	..	1	..	..	..	35
Small towns	33	6	6	12	3	..	..	..	..	6
Total	279	80	13	98	7	2	4	2	1	72
Per cent	..	28.7	4.7	35.1	2.5	.7	1.4	.7	.4	25.8

behind them. There is no evidence to show that the typical work relief case in our sample was initially in any sense a chronic relief case. Undoubtedly there were these in our group but they were outweighed on the whole by those who are normally hard-working factory workers or skilled artisans, living an average existence, able to save a little, perhaps, or own their own homes, but without sufficient margin to withstand the exigencies of unemployment.

How do they compare with their fellow work relief applicants who left work relief? Before examining the characteristics of the separated cases, it is of some interest to know why they left work relief. We have the cause for 70 per cent of the sample of inactive cases and there is no reason to suppose that they were any different from the cases for which we were unable to secure this information.[3] Table V indicates that about one-third of the cases were separated from the work relief rolls for reasons of sufficient income; that slightly more than one-third had definitely returned to private employment. The remaining third were cancelled for a number of miscellaneous reasons, including transfer to another relief agency (2.5 per cent). There were two cases each of drunkenness and insubordination, and four cases of inefficiency.

It is clear that the majority of these cases left work relief for private employment. It is uncertain, however, whether the private employment cases listed under sufficient income actually returned to private employment. There is reason to suspect that in some instances, at least, the family had concealed sources of income from private employment (mostly of other family members) in order to get on work relief. In other cases,

[3] Cancellation slips were in some cases unavailable because they had not yet been sent to the Army Base, where the inactive files were stored. For the cases where the reason for leaving work relief was really unknown, however, there would be some difference. Such cases would include no administrative separations and probably a good many who had secured private jobs and had never reported again to their work relief project.

some member of the family had secured a job after the head of the family had become eligible for work relief and as a result family income was considered sufficient. Because of the uncertainty of the interpretation of these cases they have been classified separately and not with the cases in which there was definitive evidence of a return to private employment.

There is no doubt, however, as to the fact that fraud was involved in connection with the thirteen families who concealed their assets. Investigation, the data of which were included in the case files, indicated that they should never have been on relief at all.[4] There was, indeed, considerable evidence in these files of careful investigation of the eligibility of the relief cases. Unfortunately, in a number of instances the investigation was slow and a number of months elapsed before enough evidence was gathered to declare a person ineligible. In the meantime, he had been receiving work relief. Lack of sufficient investigators, official red tape, the difficulty of securing evidence as to bank accounts and assets, and lax administration may all be blamed for the existence of this situation.

Approximately two-thirds of the group left work relief to be supported by wages from private employment. Another five per cent had sufficient funds to support themselves. The remaining 28 per cent still had to be supported in some way by the government or private charity. The chances are that most of them fell back on public welfare if they could.

One important difference between this group and our main

[4] Many of the case files contained some very amusing human interest stories, and voluminous correspondence from the persons involved. There were certainly some persons who felt that since the government was supplying relief they ought to get their share, whether they needed it or not. In a few of the cases I examined apparently an anonymous letter had started off the investigation. Some disgruntled neighbor of the work relief family would write to the relief official and state that so and so ought not to be on relief because he had savings, or a new car, or his mother sent him money and so on. Very often these allegations were found to be true.

sample of continuing work relief cases has been established. Nearly three-quarters of the inactive cases became capable of supporting themselves for the time being, at least, and thereby removed themselves from the necessity of government aid. Were they dissimilar in other respects to the cases who continued to be dependent on work relief for their support?

Very little difference is to be found as far as the sex of the heads of families is concerned. The proportion of males was a bit higher among those who left WPA, 82 per cent as against 80 per cent. Such a small difference, however, may well be due to sampling errors. The most marked increase in the percentage of males is to be found in New Bedford and Somerville where it rose from 75 to 86, and 75 to 81 respectively. In both groups males predominated among the family heads, with perhaps some tendency for an even greater male predominance among those who had left work relief in the industrial cities.

The occupational distribution of the heads of the families among the active WPA workers and the cancelled cases is very similar. The proportion of white collar workers and semi-skilled was almost exactly the same. The only differences occur in the per cent of skilled, unskilled, and domestic workers. The group which had been removed from the work relief rolls had a slightly higher proportion in all three groups. For both samples, however, the majority of family heads were semi-skilled, skilled, or white collar workers.

The age of the head of the family was secured for all cases in the separated group. Table W indicates the age distribution for the whole sample and for each town.

In all instances well over half of the heads of families were 35 years of age or over, and the average age of the family head was, for the entire sample, 39 years. The individual towns show some differences. The age distribution in New Bedford and Somerville, for instance, is more biased towards the younger men. For those cities, the average age was 37 years, and only about 30 per cent were 45 and over. The reverse is true of Framingham and Somerville, where the average age is 41 and 42 respectively, and where 40 per cent of the cases were 45 and over. The age distribution in Newton, however, was practically identical with that for the whole sample. The average age of those who left work relief was, then, about 39, and probably about the same as the average age of active

TABLE W

Age Distribution, Cancelled Cases, by Towns

(per cent of total number of cases)

Years	Framingham	New Bedford	Newton	Small Towns	Somerville	Total
16–24	15.0%	25.0%	16.0%	9.4%	22.1%	18.3%
25–34	25.0	22.0	23.0	28.2	21.2	23.5
35–44	20.0	24.0	25.0	20.0	25.9	23.8
	} 60.0	} 53.0	} 60.0	} 62.4	} 56.7	} 58.1
45 and over	40.0	29.0	35.0	42.4	30.8	34.3
Unknown	0	0	1.0	0	0	.1
	100.0	100.0	100.0	100.0	100.0	100.0
Number of cases	20	100	100	85	104	409
Average age	41 years	37 years	39 years	42 years	37 years	39 years

WPA workers in 1935. Certainly the age distribution of WPA workers in Massachusetts in 1935 (see Chapter II, Table C) was almost the same as that of our inactive group; 61 per cent were 35 or over, and 34 per cent 45 or over, showing somewhat greater concentration in the older age groups.

For our first sample of active cases there is available the age distribution for New Bedford only. This distribution differs markedly from that obtained for cancelled cases in the same city. The average age of the family head among the active work relief recipients was 40, as against 37 for those who left work relief. Nearly half of the second sample were under 34 years, whereas only a third of the first sample were in the younger age groups. There is some evidence here to substantiate the hypothesis that those who left work relief were, in New Bedford, somewhat younger than those who remained on the relief rolls.

Property ownership appears to have been slightly more extensive among those who left work relief than among those

TABLE X

PROPERTY OWNERSHIP, CANCELLED AND ACTIVE CASES

Kind of Property	Cancelled Cases Number°	Cancelled Cases Per cent	Active Cases Number°	Active Cases Per cent
Telephone†	14	3.4	29	1.3
Home owned	123	30.1	459	20.7
Mortgaged*	103	83.8*	379	82.6*
Other real estate	10	2.4	10	.5
Insurance	123	30.1	805	36.2
Automobile	81	19.8	164	7.4
Cash securities	3	0.7	6	.3
Savings	22	5.4	46	2.1
Other property	5	1.2	13	.6

° Total number of cases — 409 cancelled, 2221 active.

* Per cent of homes mortgaged based on number of homes owned. All other per cents based on total number of cases.

† Reported in Newton and Somerville only; not property, but indicative of economic status.

who remained on the rolls. Table X lists ownership for both samples. For every item except insurance the per cent owned was higher than that for the active relief cases. Nearly one-third of those who left relief owned their own homes and had insurance. One-fifth owned automobiles, and five per cent had savings. For our first sample of active relief cases 20 per cent owned houses, 36 per cent had insurance, 7 per cent automobiles, and 2 per cent savings. In both groups over four-fifths of the homes were mortgaged. In both samples, too, there is considerable difference in the extent of property ownership among the individual towns and cities. The Small Towns lead in the ownership of homes and automobiles in both groups. In these rural areas 43 per cent of the active WPA workers in our sample owned their homes, and 23 per cent had automobiles, in comparison with a 53 per cent home ownership, and a 41 per cent automobile ownership among those who left work relief. Newton is second in rank in both samples but it is of some interest to note that the per cent of homes and insurance was slightly less for the separated Newton cases than for the active ones. Automobile ownership, however, was more than twice as prevalent among those who had left relief in Newton. The proportion of property owned was greater than among active cases for all items in Somerville and Framingham among the separated cases. Even in New Bedford where few relief families owned property in either sample, there was some increase in the per cent of homes and automobiles owned for those no longer on WPA. Apparently those who left the relief rolls after 1935 had been able to hang on to their property to a larger extent than those who remained dependent upon work relief, if our sample is at all representative.

Table 16 (see Appendix B) gives the detailed information on income, expenditure, and debts for the sample of separated work relief cases. The data have been analyzed in the same way as was done for the larger sample of active work relief families, so that comparisons may easily be made. It should be stated that the expenditure data refer only to the work relief budgets set up by the ERA for each family, and not to actual expenditures, as far as could be told from the records. Even the standard budgets were not recorded for nine cases in the Small Towns.

As a whole the families in this group had, at the time of their application for work relief, an average weekly income of approximately $14.00. Their weekly expenditure, according to the ERA budgets for 399 of them, should have been about $19, or $5 more than they could secure in income. They had accumulated an average debt of $322. Compared with the active work relief families, they had a slightly larger weekly income — about fifty cents more a week — and were in debt to a greater extent, nearly $100.

At this point an examination of the frequency distribution of income will assist in determining the extent to which the

TABLE Y

INCOME FREQUENCY DISTRIBUTION, CANCELLED AND ACTIVE CASES

Income Class	Per cent of Total Cases Cancelled Cases	Active Cases
0– 3.99	17.4	12.9
4– 7.99	6.1	5.7
8–12.99	4.2	5.2
13–15.99	38.5	45.5
16–19.99	13.5	13.6
20–23.99	7.6	6.5
24–27.99	5.4	5.5
28–31.99	1.5	2.6
32–35.99	2.7	.8
36–39.99	1.0	1.0
40–43.99	1.0	.4
44 and over	1.1	.3

average is typical of the whole group. A similar analysis was made of the first sample in Chapter III and brought out the fact that there was a marked concentration of cases in the lowest income class as well as about the average. This was even more true of the income distribution of the cancelled cases, as may be seen by the comparison in Table Y. The income distribution of those who left work relief differed from that of the continuing cases in the following respects: (1) a higher proportion of the families were in the lowest income group, (2) a somewhat larger per cent were in the higher income classes, (3) although a majority of the cases were concentrated in the class interval in which the average was found and the two classes above and below, the majority was smaller. In other words, the average income for the cancelled cases is less typical for the group than that of the first sample. In both groups the attempt to picture the typical case or family must be modified by the realization that a considerable group of families stood at the lower extreme of the income distribution. The larger proportion of cancelled cases in this low income group is determined to a considerable degree by the peculiar income distribution in the Small Towns, where 40 per cent of the cases were in the 0 to 3.99 class interval.[5]

Perhaps the most interesting differences between the two groups are to be found in their sources of income and their debts. Those families who left work relief were, even while still eligible, less dependent on relief sources of income. The average family derived twice as much from private employment as was earned from this source by families who remained on work relief. This matter is worth further examination, as it may bear on the question of the ability of the typical work relief recipient to get a job in private industry. Some importance may also be attached to the analysis of debt, as the amount of credit which a person can obtain has some possible relation to his economic status and personal credit rating. Although the sample of inactive cases has been subjected to the same statistical treatment as the first and larger sample of active relief families, the comparative results will merely be summarized except in these two instances, income and debts.

These data were taken from precisely the same kind of ERA records as in the case of the first sample. They refer, therefore, to a cross section week in 1935 before these families were re-

[5] It has been suggested that some of these cases were in process of transfer and were recorded at the moment of no income. On the other hand, they may simply have been unassigned to work relief projects, though eligible at the time.

moved from work relief. The data in Table 17 (see Appendix B) bring out even more clearly that the families in the sample of separated cases had on the average been much less dependent on relief than the continuing relief cases. A bare majority (49.5 per cent) had income from relief alone, and 41 per cent were supported entirely by the ERA. The comparable proportions for the active cases are 65 per cent and 53 per cent. As one might expect, supplemented relief income and earnings from private employment were also much more prevalent. The proportion of those having earnings from private employment in addition to relief was almost twice as great among separated cases as among the continuing ones. Approximately 8 per cent subsisted on earnings from private employment alone among the separated cases as compared with 4 per cent among the active cases. The only inconsistent element in the analysis results from the fact that a greater proportion of the inactive cases had had no income during the cross section week, 16 per cent as against 11 per cent in the first sample. Quite obviously the figure for the whole group is influenced by Newton and the Small Towns which showed a considerable increase in those with no income for the sample of cancelled cases.[6]

The individual towns evidence, for the most part, the same characteristics concerning sources of income in both samples.[7] New Bedford work relief families relied most exclusively on relief as the sole source of income, and those in Newton the least. It is to be noted, however, that the proportion so dependent in the second New Bedford sample of separated cases

[6] I do not know what the explanation is. Possibly it lies in the fact that the inactive file included those cases separated from WPA because of transference to other relief agencies, and for reasons of inefficiency, etc., as well as those who had gone back to private industry. These cases might be the ones least likely to have any earning power as a result of age or personality defects.

[7] Framingham will be disregarded on account of the smallness of the sample.

dropped very sharply. The proportion of those whose only source of income was private earnings tripled in Newton and quadrupled in New Bedford among the separated cases. Over twice the percentage were able to supplement relief earnings by private employment in Somerville.

This evidence that the families taken off the relief rolls had less difficulty in securing some form of private employment than active relief workers checks with our analysis of cancellations. (See p. 126.) In Newton and Somerville, a high proportion of the cancellations were due to a definite return to jobs in private industry.

Table 18 (Appendix B) lists the mean and median incomes for the various income sources for those who had left work relief, and is comparable to Table 10 (Appendix B). The incomes derived from relief by the cancelled cases differ very little from those received by families in the active relief group. Relief income was generally around $14, as measured by the arithmetic mean, or $12 as measured by the median. In both samples it varied in the individual towns largely as a result of occupational distribution, for different work relief rates were set for unskilled and skilled craftsmen, and white collar workers. The chief difference to be observed is the uniformly higher amount derived, on the average, from non-relief sources by families in the sample of inactive cases. Those who supplemented relief income from other sources received a supplementary income of nearly $12 a week as compared with $9 a week for the continuing cases. Earnings from private employment alone amounted to $13 as compared with $11. And we must remember that a larger proportion of the separated families had received this type of income so that more of the group benefited from the higher earnings. There is no doubt that the separated cases had had a higher earning power even where they were on relief than those who were on relief at the same time, and stayed there.

It has been pointed out that the average debt per family for those who were taken off work relief was higher than for those who stayed on.[8] The total debts of the inactive group amounted to approximately $131,000, those of the active work relief families about half a million. If our second sample had been the same size as the first, and of the same characteristics, its total debt would have been about three-quarters of a million dollars. Table Z presents the information on total debts, divided into the constituent items.

TABLE Z

TOTAL DEBTS, ITEMIZED, CANCELLED AND ACTIVE CASES

Items	Cancelled Cases Total Amount	Cancelled Cases Per cent	Active Cases Total Amount	Active Cases Per cent
Food	$ 7,352	5.5	$40,786	8.0
Rent	18,454	14.0	98,489	19.4
Taxes	11,931	9.0	38,993	7.7
Personal Loans	25,895	19.6	88,372	17.4
Industrial Loans	8,322	6.7	27,633	5.4
Furniture	2,434	1.8	23,535	4.7
Medical care	9,966	7.4	55,002	10.9
Unspecified	3,198	2.7	119,714	23.6
Mortgage	43,737	33.3	14,693	2.9
Total	$131,290	100.0	$507,217	100.0

The distribution of the total debt was not very different for the two samples. The inactive cases were relatively less in debt for food, rent, furniture, and medical care, and relatively more in debt for loans, both personal and industrial, for taxes, and for mortgages. There is some indication here that the continuing relief cases tended to contract debts to a greater extent for the immediate necessities of life whereas the other

[8] The average referred to here is based on all cases. If the average had been based only on those having debts, the figure would have been higher. Such an average was derived for the first sample of inactive cases but not for the separated cases.

group, possibly with a better credit rating, were able to secure more loans, either from friends or on a commercial basis.

The relative distribution of indebtedness by occupations is quite dissimilar for the two groups.[9] Among the families who left the work relief payroll in 1935, salesmen, proprietors, inexperienced persons, domestic and personal workers, in the order named, were all in debt to a greater degree than one would expect in comparison with their relative numbers. Among the continuing relief cases, however, proprietors were proportionately the most in debt, with all the white collar workers, plus the skilled artisans, contributing more than their share as well. Inexperienced persons and domestic and personal workers were relatively less in debt. In both groups one of the white collar occupations ranks first in indebtedness.

Salesmen among the inactive cases were relatively very heavily in debt for personal loans and unspecified items. Proprietors had run up considerable indebtedness for rent, taxes, personal loans, industrial loans, and mortgages in proportion to the size of their group. Inexperienced persons were most in debt proportionately for food, rent, taxes, personal loans, and industrial loans. Domestic and personal workers were relatively quite extensively in debt for medical care. Farmers in both samples owed a proportionately high amount for taxes. Examination of the debt analysis of the first sample in Chapter IV will bring out a number of differences between the relative contribution to various types of debt in the two samples. Skilled and semi-skilled workers, for example, were far more in debt for items like food, among the group in the first sample. It is difficult to tell how significant these differences are. They may be due largely to the difference in size of the sample. It can be said, however, that the inactive relief families were more in debt when they applied for relief and that the burden

[9] See Chapter IV, p. 87 for explanation of method of determining relative indebtedness.

of debt seems to have been borne by somewhat different occupations than in the case of the active work relief families.

The average debt among the individual towns follows almost the same ranking in accordance with size for both samples. Newton and then Somerville have the highest average debt per family. The Small Towns, however, change their rank from fifth to third with an increase of average debt of $100 per family in the second sample as compared with the first sample. This may be explained by the prevalence of debt among the inexperienced and domestic workers, who were more heavily concentrated in rural communities. It is noticeable that the average debt of the separated cases rose markedly in Somerville and the Small Towns, as compared with that of the active relief cases in these cities and towns. The average amount owed was about the same in both samples for Newton and New Bedford, and less for Framingham.

It is now possible to describe briefly the group of discontinued work relief recipients which we have investigated. In the first place, the majority of these families were removed from the relief rolls for two main reasons; either the head of the family had actually returned to private employment, or the family was adjudged to have an income sufficient for its support. In the latter instance, sufficient income was due, for the most part, to income from private employment obtained by one or more members of the family. Surely this group may be considered as employable. They were on relief temporarily but they were able to go back into private employment. We do not know, however, how long they remained in private employment, whether they ever went back on WPA, or whether their new jobs in private industry were of the same type as they had held before. Such information could be secured only through a complete follow-up of individual cases after they had left relief.

Although there is no information as to the return to work

relief of these particular cases, the Massachusetts WPA Administrator (now Director of Region One), Colonel John J. McDonough, has supplied the figures in Table AA concerning separation from and return to the relief rolls because of private employment for the whole state. On the basis of the 1938 and 1939 figures, about one-half as many returned to relief from private employment as had left the relief rolls for private jobs during the same year. The net return to private

TABLE AA

WPA TERMINATIONS FOR AND RETURNS FROM PRIVATE EMPLOYMENT, MASSACHUSETTS

TERMINATION FOR PRIVATE EMPLOYMENT	
June 1 to December 30, 1936	7,819
January 1 to December 30, 1937	14,056
January 1 to December 30, 1938	27,001
January 1 to June 17, 1939	13,867
RETURNING TO WPA FROM PRIVATE EMPLOYMENT *	
Last twenty weeks in 1937	1,268
January 1 to December 30, 1938	12,602
January 1 to June 17, 1939	6,799

* These figures were not kept before the 28th week in 1937 and Colonel McDonough advises that, as a result of the time necessary for the procedure to get going, the early figures are not precise.

employment from WPA in Massachusetts was a little over 14,000 cases in 1938, and about 7,000 cases for the first half of 1939. It is not known how many of the same cases later returned to work relief after having left for private employment, but studies made by the WPA Division of Research, which will be examined in the next chapter, indicate that many of the jobs for which work relief recipients left the rolls were of short duration.

Inactive relief families had the same occupations, were about the same size, and had approximately the same total income on the average as the active relief families, at the time of their application for relief. The main differences between the two groups may be listed as follows:

1. The heads of families among the cancelled cases were somewhat younger, especially in the industrial cities.
2. The separated relief families were less dependent on relief.
3. The separated families derived more income from private employment while they were on relief.
4. The separated families were in debt to a greater extent.
5. More of the separated families owned houses, automobiles, and had savings, even when they applied for relief.

In other words, the younger cases, who had retained more contact with private industry while on relief, who had secured a larger amount of credit, and who had managed to hang on to more of their property were the ones who got jobs in 1935 and thereafter. This result coincides with the opinion of one of the relief officials in the Massachusetts administration, that the most employable of the work relief people had been reabsorbed into private positions by the end of 1935. The residue, of which our sample of continuing work relief cases may be representative, he thought could be divided into three classes: those who were employable but would find difficulty in securing jobs because of their age (45 or over); youths just out of school who had never had jobs and who were in danger of becoming unemployable; and chronic relief cases.[10]

[10] The character of the work relief rolls changed markedly in late 1937 when the business recession caused further unemployment. Many new applicants were forced to apply for work relief and many former work relief recipients returned to the rolls at that time.

CHAPTER IX

IS THERE A PERMANENT RELIEF PROBLEM?

ONE OF THE MOST VITAL ISSUES connected with relief is that of the re-employability of those on relief. What chances have relief workers of becoming employed in private industry, and, further, what are the chances of their staying in such jobs once they get them? In dealing with those on work relief, we are investigating the most employable portion of those on relief. As a report on the Cincinnati relief situation puts it: "Presumably the WPA workers were the cream of the relief clients, and from this standpoint would stand a better chance of securing private employment, being better workers." [1] The study of our sample of work relief cases indicates that even among this preferred group there is a differentiation as to employability. Certain members of the work relief group may be expected to have far greater prospects of re-employment than others. One of the most important factors determining employability appears to be age; another is length of unemployment.

In recent years a good deal of evidence has been compiled on the question of the re-employability of work relief recipients. Much of the data has resulted from studies made by the WPA Division of Research on cases separated or "closed" from relief for various reasons. Some of these studies will be examined later on in this chapter. One study just published deals intensively with a group of cases which left relief for private employment.[2] Its importance lies in the fact that it gives data on what happened to these people after they left

[1] *The Relief Problem in Hamilton County, Ohio*, 1937.

[2] *Former Relief Cases in Private Employment*, by J. C. Bevis and S. L. Payne, WPA Division of Research, 1939.

relief, during a one year period, how long their jobs lasted, and so on. In fact, the Introduction to this report states in such clear terms the factors involved in the relation between work relief and private employment, that part of it is quoted here:

> The return to self-support through private employment is the one solution of the relief problem upon which business, industry, Government, taxpayers, and relief recipients can agree. Yet it is obvious that this solution is no more permanent than the private employment which terminates a relief case. Much of the confusion that has grown up around the fact that the relief rolls do not disappear when business improves is the direct result of failure to realize this simple fact. From the very beginning of the FERA to the present time private employment has been taking people off relief. For some of these workers relief is an incident happily brought to a conclusion, but for others the employment is a matter of only a few weeks or months and then unemployment again forces them back on public assistance rolls.
>
> This constant change in the personnel of the relief population, or turnover, has been apparent from the start. In addition to the new cases added each month, and the old cases closed, *reopened* cases — that is, families returning to relief on WPA rolls after a period of separation — contribute to the changing picture of the relief load. Despite this knowledge there has been a tendency to think of cases that have been "closed for private employment" not only as removed from immediate need of assistance but also from the likelihood of need in the near future. Unfortunately, as this report shows, the fact of private employment often provides no definite assurance that the return to self-support is more than a temporary change in status.
>
> Whether or not private employment actually closes a relief case in more than a temporary or technical sense depends upon a complex of factors among which the fluctuation of industrial activity, the worker's skill or industrial quality, and the wages paid are of prime importance. Until more is known of just what does happen to families which leave the relief rolls because of private employment, it is impossible even to identify all these factors, much less to evaluate them.[3]

[3] J. C. Bevis and S. L. Payne, *op. cit.*, p. vii.

Before analyzing the conclusions of this report on cases who definitely left work relief for private employment, a brief description of the more general WPA "separation" studies will be given, in which the cases were closed for a number of reasons, including purely administrative ones. Although these studies deal with small samples in sections of the country frequently not comparable with Massachusetts, some of the results will be summarized here as they give evidence on the general problem of the re-employability of relief cases. Three specific and three general studies have been selected as illustrative of the analysis of closed cases.

In Baltimore County, all relief cases were "closed for re-examination" in March 1935. The relief authorities felt that private employment opportunities were increasing and that pressure should be exerted to see that relief cases took advantage of them. Within the three months following March, in which the follow-up survey was made, the relief load averaged about one-third of what it had been before. The study deals with the 1022 cases out of the original 1629 who did not return to relief in the three month period after the relief rolls had been closed to them. The main conclusion of the survey is that "a majority of these households were raising themselves successfully above a relief status."[4] Employment increased steadily; average monthly income rose from $20.50 in March, when they were still on relief, to $40.30 in June. There were in June, however, 145 cases with no persons employed, and with an average monthly income of $2.30. It was discovered that in securing private jobs there was some tendency for occupational status to be lowered. Also, although most of the group appear to have adjusted themselves to non-relief conditions, there is no evidence to indicate how perma-

[4] *A Survey of 1022 Relief Cases Closed in March 1935, Baltimore County, Maryland*, by W. O. Brown and Mary L. Trippe, WPA Bulletin, Series II, No. 10, p. ii, January 1936.

nent this adjustment was. There is some reason, indeed, to think that a good deal of the employment was seasonal, since much of it was in agriculture.

An investigation was undertaken in Sioux Falls, South Dakota, of 147 closed from the relief rolls as a result of "widespread rumors that relief clients were refusing employment in the harvest fields." [5] More than half of the cases, however, had already been closed as a result of a return to private employment before the special relief suspension order went through on July 21, 1935. The remainder, selected families with one or more employable members, were taken off relief as a direct result of the order. As in Baltimore County, it was found that private employment and average monthly income increased (from $38.89 to $47.50) within three months after the closing. But 50 of the 110 cases interviewed were forced back on relief in ten weeks' time and only one-sixth of the group considered their employment as likely to be permanent. Harvest work turned out to be a much exaggerated source of jobs, as many of the farmers were too poor to hire extra hands. Less than a third of the families had members who were able to get such jobs, and their income averaged only about $34 over a period of eight weeks. Temporarily, these closed cases were able to support themselves, but how long they could continue seemed dubious, unless employment conditions changed radically.

A study made of rural families closed for administrative reasons from the relief rolls in four South Dakota counties indicates that those dependent entirely on agriculture for their support suffered a sharp diminution of cash income in the months following the closure.[6] Non-agricultural families, on

[5] *Survey of Cases Closed from Relief Rolls in Sioux Falls, South Dakota, in July 1935*, WPA Division of Social Research, Series II, No. 11, Jan. 1936.

[6] *Survey of Rural Relief Cases Closed for Administrative Reasons in South Dakota, November 1935*, WPA Division of Social Research, Series II, No. 12, Jan. 1936.

the other hand, were able to get private employment and their incomes rose from $27.83 to $40. For both groups private income was much larger, rising from $5.48 to $11.89 for the agricultural families, and from $10.80 to $40 for the non-agricultural cases. Again, however, the investigators concluded that a great deal of this private employment was seasonal and temporary. The majority of the agricultural families were working their own farms and had suffered serious loss from dust storms and drought. Though they were not primarily dependent on employment, farming conditions indicated that they would need some kind of assistance for a long time to come. Those who were dependent on private employment must be assured of other than temporary jobs, if they were not to fall back on relief again.

A more general study of separations was made in 1936, when certified WPA workers were reduced by about 750,000 partly for administrative reasons and partly for re-examination of eligible relief workers. Eight areas, in which 4,552 cases were investigated, were selected throughout the country.[7] It was found that one-half of the cases found private jobs in the month after separation and secured their main income from them; that one-quarter went on general relief or received their income from miscellaneous sources; and that one-quarter were transferred to work on other government projects. Those with private employment received $23 more income per month than when they had been on relief, three-fifths of all cases had higher monthly incomes, and a tenth had the same incomes. On the whole those who got private employment did much better than on relief. They made more than the security wage

[7] *Survey of Workers Separated from WPA Employment in Eight Areas During the Second Quarter of 1936*, WPA Division of Social Research, Series IV, No. 3. The areas were: Worcester, Mass.; Allegany and Steuben Counties, N. Y.; Marion County, W. Va.; Kanawha County, W. Va.; Marion County (Indianapolis), Ind.; 8 rural counties, Ind.; Ogden, Utah; San Francisco, Calif.

and most of them got jobs in their own occupation or a higher one. No information is given as to the permanence of their employment, nor the probability of their return to relief.

In general, up to 1937 these investigations indicate that those families who left relief or were separated from the rolls fared better, temporarily at least, than they had on relief. More of them were privately employed and those that were got higher incomes. Still, in each case where closings were made for administrative reasons, a considerable portion of the cases studied did not succeed in finding jobs and had to go on public welfare, return to work relief, or rely on community resources. For this group, work relief offered a better living than they were able to procure for themselves.

A similar, but more detailed, investigation of closed cases in nine areas was made in the spring of 1937, with results far less optimistic.[8] The separations in this case were partly voluntary and partly administrative and amounted to a reduction of 550,000 certified workers all over the country. A sample of 1,370 cases was interviewed in October and November 1937. These workers were far less successful in supporting themselves after they had left work relief than had been the case with the 1936 group. To some extent this may have been the result of the greater proportion of administrative cancellations in 1937, and the dismissal of aliens. The decline in industrial jobs as a result of the 1937 recession was undoubtedly another reason. Fewer of the 1937 workers found jobs, one-half of the group as compared with two-thirds of the 1936 cases. In three-fifths of the cases their total income was lower than it had been on WPA. Most of the people who did secure work got it shortly after separation and at their usual occupation.

[8] *Workers Separated from WPA Employment in Nine Areas*, 1937, WPA Division of Social Research, 1938. The nine areas were: Atlanta, Baltimore, New Bedford, St. Louis, San Francisco, Iowa counties, Mississippi counties, North Dakota counties and West Virginia counties.

Many cases could not support themselves and had to apply for direct relief. This was true of over a half of the urban and a quarter of the rural cases. On the whole, the cases in rural areas had greater success in finding jobs and suffered less reduction in income after leaving work relief. It appeared also that those workers who were most successful in maintaining their families upon their earnings from private employment were some two years younger than the rest of the group and had been unemployed for a shorter period. There were many sharp regional differences, of course, but in general the above statements seem to be characteristic of the sample.

The most recent investigation of administrative closings was made in the fall of 1939. As a result of the 18-months provision of the 1939 Relief Act, 775,000 WPA workers were dropped from the rolls in July and August.[9] More than 138,000 in 23 "large and representative cities" were interviewed twice, 3 to 4 weeks after their separation and again in November.[10] The conclusions resulting from this survey are even more depressing than those of the 1937 survey. The first interview disclosed that only 7.6 per cent were privately employed 3 to 4 weeks after the closing. The November interview with the same group indicated that 12.7 of the group (less than 100,000) had jobs in private industry. About half of the privately em-

[9] The Relief Act provided that all workers who had been on WPA continuously for 18 months must be dropped and the relief rolls investigated. If these workers were still eligible a month after the closing they could be taken back by WPA. Since appropriations were decreased at the same time, however, many persons still eligible could not be reassigned to work relief projects.

[10] *Workers Dropped from WPA in Accordance with the 18-Months Provision in the 1939 Relief Act*, mimeographed report A 658, Works Projects Administration, Division of Research, January 24, 1940. The cities included in the survey were: Boston, New Haven, Buffalo, New York, Philadelphia, Richmond, Washington, D. C., Cincinnati, Cleveland, Detroit, Indianapolis, St. Louis, Birmingham, Charleston, Jacksonville, Louisville, Nashville, Forth Worth, Milwaukee, Omaha, Denver, Los Angeles, Seattle.

ployed group were earning more than their previous WPA wage; the remainder were earning less. Some 87 per cent were unable to get jobs. A fourth of these were taken back on WPA; another fourth were found to be on local relief. The rest lived on federal surplus commodities, savings, credit; borrowed or begged. As the report puts it: "these lay-offs brought immediate and wide spread distress to thousands of workers and their families." [11]

It is of some interest for this study to examine the situation in Boston in greater detail. Out of 6,480 workers interviewed, 8.7 per cent had private employment by November, 25.9 per cent had been reassigned to WPA, 22 per cent were receiving local relief, and 43.4 per cent were without any private or relief employment or assistance. The employed workers had a median income of $16.34 per week; those not reassigned to WPA had a median weekly income of $6.82. Nearly one-quarter of the latter group in Boston had no income at all. Ranking the cities in order of the percentages given in the Report we find that Boston was next to the lowest in proportion privately employed. Jacksonville, Denver, Milwaukee, Philadelphia, and Richmond also had percentages lower than 10. As far as reassignment to WPA and local relief was concerned, the Boston proportions were in the middle, ranking as 12 in both cases. The highest employment per cents were to be found in industrial cities like Detroit, Buffalo, Cleveland, and Birmingham. New Haven, Denver, and Richmond had the largest proportions reassigned to WPA; the southern cities of Birmingham, Nashville, and Fort Worth the lowest. More than half of those who had been separated from WPA were supported by local relief in Los Angeles and Buffalo; almost none at all in the five southern cities of Birmingham, Charleston, Jacksonville, Louisville, and Nashville. Again the southern cities led in the proportion of those without any

[11] *Op. cit.*, p. 1.

known means of support, while Milwaukee, Denver, New Haven, and Los Angeles had the least who were thrown entirely on their own resources. It is evident that while private employment was low in Boston, those who had been laid off WPA were by no means in the worst straits. It was in the south that the situation of the separated cases was the worst.

This investigation is perhaps not entirely comparable with the previous ones in that all the separations were administrative. It seems to be true that those laid off work relief usually have more difficulty in securing jobs than those who leave of their own accord. Nevertheless, industrial conditions were on the upgrade in the fall of 1939 and the conclusions of the report are not conducive to optimism concerning the eventual absorption of WPA workers into private industry. A statement from the report is worth quoting on this point: "The discharged WPA workers have not benefited to any great extent from the industrial recovery this fall; they are not the first to be hired when business improves. Employers tend generally to recall workers recently laid off, most of whom have not yet been forced to seek assistance. When there are 8 to 10 million persons seeking work, WPA and relief workers, with their longer periods of unemployment, have to wait." [12]

These investigations of the WPA Division of Research indicate that up to 1937 workers who left or were dismissed from the relief rolls were, in the majority of cases, able to secure private employment. The type of employment they got, however, and the sufficiency of income attained depended upon whether they left work relief of their own accord or for administrative reasons, and upon general economic conditions. After 1937, a much smaller proportion of separated workers found private jobs. The study of general relief cases in Cincinnati shows that even direct relief cases are in some

[12] *Op. cit.* Summary, p. 1.

instances able to increase their earnings from private employment when relief is taken away but that most of them are unable to support themselves.[13] On May 31, 1936 all direct relief cases carried by the Hamilton County Department of Public Welfare were closed on account of lack of funds. These families were investigated in June to find out what had happened to them. By the time of the interviews about 20 per cent of the families had found private employment, and nearly one per cent were able to support themselves from miscellaneous sources. The rest were totally without resources, and many of them were considered by the Department as employable. Income and expenditure figures were not procured in

TABLE BB

PER CENT OF NEEDS SUPPLIED TO WHITE EMPLOYABLES, BY SOURCES, IN CINCINNATI, 1936 *

	Source	Rent	Food	Milk	Clothing	Heat and Light
Before June 1						
	County Welfare	37	97	68	37	42
	Not Provided	25	5	22	33	25
	Employment	25	.5	5	21	16
	Other Sources	14	.5	4	9	17
After June 1						
	County Welfare	10	4	4	..	10
	Not Provided	41	10	35	63	41
	Employment	36	61	45	24	42
	Other Sources	14	25	16	23	8

* *Op. cit.*, adapted from Table XII, Appendix. Tenths omitted.

this investigation but a comparison was made as to the per cent of family needs supplied by various sources before and after June 1. The figures for the white employable workers appear in Table BB.

[13] *Op. cit.* See Appendix for statistical material. The study was carried out by the Cincinnati Bureau of Governmental Research with voluntary assistance.

Before the general closing county welfare had supplied nearly all the food, two-thirds of the milk, nearly half the heat and light, and over a third of the rent and clothing for these 10,000 families. Except for food, one-quarter to one-third of their needs were not met at all, and the rest came from private employment or other sources. The financial situation was such that most of these cases could not be taken back on relief after the closing. Consequently a very small proportion of their necessary living was then provided by welfare. In all cases the per cent which was not provided for in any way went up after June 1; so also did the proportion supplied by employment and other sources after they were put off relief, whereas the greater portion had been supplied by county welfare previously. It should be remembered, however, that their needs were estimated at a minimum and that the group of white employables included those who found it least difficult to get jobs. Nearly three-quarters of the sample had no resources at all and welfare funds were not sufficient to care for them.

Although sample studies such as have been described are extremely valuable, they afford an unsatisfactory basis for estimating the extent to which relief workers who do get jobs succeed in permanently maintaining themselves and their families without relief aid. The samples are composed of all kinds of cases who left or were dismissed from relief for a variety of reasons. Their circumstances were investigated for only one month after their cases were closed. The results suggest, indeed, that private employment is secured by a select proportion of them (usually a major proportion of former work relief cases up to 1937), but that these jobs are frequently temporary or seasonal in character. They suggest, too, that a considerable number are not able to support themselves without assistance. Those who cannot get work in industry will be as much of a social problem as those who continue on work relief. But, it has been the hope of all concerned that those who leave relief for definite jobs will remove themselves permanently from the need of relief aid.

The most important information so far secured on this problem appears in the recent report on former relief cases, from which we have quoted. A sample of 1,108 families in 13 cities was investigated by the WPA Division of Research.[14] These families left relief voluntarily during the summer of 1935 because some member of the family had employment in private industry. These families were studied continuously over a period of a year, October 1935 to September 1936. Only the chief conclusions of the report can be cited here. The principal findings are as follows:

1. During the year three-fifths of the families had to ask public aid. Either their jobs were seasonal, or insufficiently paid to support their families, or they had lost their jobs.
2. Twenty per cent of the employable persons (not cases) never got a job during the entire year, although those who did averaged two jobs apiece.
3. The average annual income from private employment was $642, but this average was non-typical, as there was no concentration of cases around it.
4. The average annual income from all sources was $897, of which $200 came from relief and other sources.
5. This total income was sufficient to maintain only an emergency level of living.
6. These cases were younger than those who remained on the relief rolls, and had been unemployed about half as long. More of them were white, skilled or semi-skilled craftsmen. In every occupation experienced persons had more chance of obtaining jobs than the inexperienced.

The main conclusion of the investigators may be best stated in their own words:

[14] J. C. Bevis and S. L. Payne, *op. cit.* The cities included were: Atlanta, Baltimore, Bridgeport, Butte, Chicago, Detroit, Houston, Manchester (N. H.), Omaha, Paterson, St. Louis, San Francisco and Wilkes-Barre.

A great many of the cases leaving relief because of private employment may be expected to reappear on the public assistance rolls within a year following their separation. These cases are forced to return because of unstable employment and low earnings, occasioned by the fact that they are a part of a reserve labor supply drawn upon largely for the seasonal needs of industry. Even with the help of public funds their incomes are below any reasonably adequate level of living.[15]

The resemblance of our Cambridge sample of underemployed families to this group of former work relief cases is very striking. In nearly every respect, annual income, income from various sources, proportion on relief, inadequacy of income for decent living and so on, they are almost identical.[16] Most of them appear to be just on the edge of complete self-maintenance, and some of them have attained it. They are the upper stratum of work relief cases, who have the best chance for private employment. It is implied in the WPA report that they are the marginal workers of industry, and that many of them will continue to be at least a partial relief problem, for some time to come. That many of them have *become* marginal workers, in the sense of the least efficient or desirable from the industrial point of view, seems very probable, for reasons which will be examined.[17] That most of them were initially such marginal workers seems to me to be unproven. In fact, our evidence for Massachusetts suggests that, in that state, at any rate, the majority of them were not originally marginal workers but members of the regular self-

[15] *Op. cit.*, p. x.

[16] See especially Chapter VII and articles referred to there.

[17] The *Fortune* Survey, "Unemployment in 1937," October 1937, comes to this conclusion too. They show that many relief cases are now marginal which were not so originally. Of the 1,137 cases which they investigated, 45 per cent of those who were on the relief rolls in 1935 were supported by private employment in 1937. The others were either on relief (45 per cent) or with no resources (10 per cent). More information on this survey will be given in the next chapter.

supporting working class. It is true that marginal workers are the first to be dropped from industrial pay rolls. But economic disaster became so widespread in the past depression that entire firms and businesses were forced to shut down. Large numbers of workers who had been steadily employed for years found themselves suddenly without jobs, in addition to those who were and had always been on the margin of employment.

Drs. A. Ross Eckler and Lincoln Fairley, in an article on *Relief and Unemployment*, come to the general conclusion that ". . . so far as the solution of the unemployment relief problem is concerned, a lack of job openings is a more serious handicap than a lack of qualified applicants." [18] Their optimism is based on the fact that the relief population is constantly shifting, with separations consistently higher than accessions (by about 1 per cent), and the opinion that "the great majority of workers on relief . . . are ready and willing to take decent jobs at standard wages and will make satisfactory employees." [19] They recognize, however, that the younger workers have the best chance of re-employment and state that the rate of re-employment varies inversely with duration of unemployment. They know, too, that the average age of the relief population has increased since 1935. Nevertheless, they seem convinced of the employability of large numbers on the work relief program.

Thus far it has been assumed implicitly that the employability of those on work relief is something beyond their control; that they would work if they could. Such an assumption does not coincide with popular opinion. The statement of Dr. Eckler on this point is based on a number of WPA studies of reported

[18] *Harvard Business Review*, winter 1938, p. 153. Dr. Eckler was Assistant Director of the WPA Division of Research, and Dr. Fairley is Chief of Special Inquiries. Their conclusions are based on a large amount of information to which their official position gives them special access.

[19] *Ibid.*

job refusals in which very few were considered unjustified by the investigators. Henry B. Arthur states flatly that "these studies have conclusively shown that job refusals do not constitute a problem of major importance in the administration of relief," as a result of summarizing such studies made under the FERA.[20] Other evidence is at hand in the form of reports on the investigation of complaints, made to officials of the government and of the WPA itself in 1936 and 1937, that jobs were being refused by WPA workers, or that a labor shortage existed as a result of WPA employment. I have been permitted to read and analyze a random sample of 100 such complaints, referring to individual instances by name, and covering most of the 48 states.[21] My own analysis of the justification of these complaints, based on the statement of the complaint and the reports of the investigators, follows:

1. 58 complaints were unsubstantiated and appeared to be the result of
   a. Lack of knowledge or misrepresentation of the facts — 49 cases.

      In 14 cases investigators found no jobs available and no labor shortage.
      In 5 cases, jobs which might have been available were not, as the result of the importation of cheap labor from other states or countries.

      In one case the complainant evidently wanted an available supply of "distress labor," and in another the available jobs were not suited to WPA workers in that district.

      28 cases were completely unsubstantiated.
   b. General disapproval of the WPA and the present administration — 9 cases.
2. 17 complaints of job refusals were substantiated. Jobs were refused for the following reasons:

[20] "Summary Study of Alleged Job Refusals by Relief Persons," *FERA Monthly Report*, November 1935.

[21] Through the courtesy of the WPA Division of Research. The first 100 cases were taken at random as typical.

a. No justification — 5 cases. (They were dismissed from WPA.)

b. Sub-standard wages or working condition or employers with bad reputations — 8 cases. (They were not dismissed.)

c. Fear of losing relief status for temporary work — 4 cases. (Adjusted by WPA.)

3. 7 complaints of a labor shortage were substantiated. The WPA immediately suspended their projects in those areas.

4. 12 complaints were due to lack of knowledge of the function of the U. S. Employment Service and of the willingness of the WPA to release workers for temporary jobs. Almost all of these complaints were satisfactorily adjusted by the WPA.

5. One complaint that a WPA worker had been competing with others for private jobs in his spare time was found to be justified.

6. In two instances the evidence was confused.

If this sample of complaints is at all representative, most of them were not justified.[22] In only 25 cases, or one-quarter of the total, were the facts of job refusals or labor shortage as stated by the complainant. Many of the complaints were obviously actuated by malice or by a desire for cheap labor. Sometimes the complainant could not be found at all. Most of those who were located by the investigators were exceedingly surprised to find that their complaints were being investigated. Of course, there may have been hundreds of complaints not investigated, but in these instances the WPA instituted an immediate and thorough investigation and adjusted the situation as well as it could.

In the absence of evidence to the contrary, we shall assume that the majority of those on work relief *want* jobs and will

[22] It is, of course, possible, inasmuch as these sample cases were selected by the WPA in the first place, that they are not representative. However, most of the investigations were undertaken as a result of complaints to senators and congressmen, who requested the WPA to investigate. They were not undertaken by the WPA on its own initiative.

take them if they can get them.[23] It may be true that they are not as active in their efforts to secure them as might be wished. It is possible that removal from relief may stimulate some cases to greater effort in that direction. This seems to have been the case in Baltimore County, for instance, although there is no way of knowing to what extent private employment would have been obtained if the relief rolls had remained open.

Even if those on work relief want jobs, there appears to be no basis for optimism concerning their ability to get them. The separation studies, and particularly the analysis of those who left work relief for private employment, indicate that the employment obtained is frequently seasonal and temporary. The residue of relief workers who have been continuously on relief — and which our main sample of Massachusetts ERA workers probably typifies — are steadily becoming less employable from a business standpoint as a result of their increasing age and period of unemployment. If the demand for labor in private industry becomes sufficiently great age may become less of a handicap, as well as the reported prejudice of employers against those who have been on relief. Dr. Eckler, indeed, mentions several skilled trades where age limits have been raised as a result of labor shortage. But age remains one of the principal deterrents to the absorption of work relief recipients in private industry.

There is, in fact, a serious problem at both ends of the working span. The young and inexperienced, just out of school, have had an equally hard time in getting jobs with those who are past forty. The danger of continued idleness is greater for them than for the older workers. Their difficulties will not be

[23] I have not been able to find any factual evidence of wholesale refusals of private employment by those on relief. There are many stories of the kind floating about, which sound very like these complaints, but I should hesitate to believe them without investigating the facts in each case.

analyzed here, because they form a smaller proportion of the work relief than of the unemployed population. The NYA and the CCC programs were inaugurated to care for them. With greater employment opportunities in private industry they will probably be absorbed with less trouble than the workers at the other end of the wage scale.[24]

On the matter of age discrimination in industry, a very interesting investigation, begun in 1934, was undertaken by the Massachusetts Department of Labor and Industries.[25] The investigation was started as a result of complaints to public officials that workers of 45 or over could not find work because of their age. The results of this investigation, plus public hearings in which employers and union officials took part, substantiated the complaints. The statistical results are based on a questionnaire sent out by the Department of Labor and Industries to employers of 10 or more persons; 3,781 establishments responded with the necessary information. It was found that age discrimination existed, and to a greater extent for women of 45 or over than for men. ". . . the percentage of hiring for men dropped from 25.5 for those 24 to 29 years old to 10.1 in the age group 35 to 39. The difference for women is even greater — 31.7 to 8.1 in this 10-year interval. After the age of 45 is passed, only those who have acquired special skill not easily developed by younger rivals can hope for employment. Thus only 5 per cent of the hirings of women and 15 per cent of those of men took place in these age groups, in which, however, 20 per cent of the employable women and 36 per cent of the men were found." [26]

[24] For a comprehensive statement of the age problem, see "Young and Old Look for Work," by Corrington Gill, *American Federationist*, June 1938.

[25] Lucile Eaves, "Discrimination in the Employment of Older Workers in Massachusetts," *Monthly Labor Review*, June 1937.

[26] *Op. cit.*, pp. 24–25. The results of this study are confirmed by an analysis of hiring and firing policy made by Paul F. Lazarsfeld in an

As a result of this investigation there was passed in May 1937 "An Act Prohibiting Discrimination Against Certain Persons in Employment on Account of Their Age." [27] The act provided, among other things, for investigation of complaints of discrimination, the keeping of records on the age of employees by employers, and the punishment by fine of those employers proved to have discriminated against employees on the basis of age alone.

Another piece of evidence as to the relation of age to employment may be found in a survey of 2,485 member firms made by the National Association of Manufacturers.[28] The companies responding to the questionnaires had a total of 2,334,538 employees and covered 43 states. No indication is given of what type of manufacturing was represented, however, and all the companies did not answer all the questions. It is difficult to discover from the statistics given how representative of manufacturing or of the country as a whole the sample may be. However, for what they are worth, the following figures on hiring policy are given: of the companies who replied to the question, about 7.5 per cent reported that they had a maximum age limit for hiring new employees, 89

---

unpublished study entitled "Factors Influencing Length of Unemployment" which was made for the WPA. Mr. Lazarsfeld sets forth a rather complicated scheme for determining the hiring and firing rates from available unemployment data. The method is based on a number of assumptions which may not be correct. However, he applied the method to the data in the Massachusetts Census of Unemployment, with the result that the hiring rate was found to decrease from .34 for the 20 to 24 age group to .12 for those 45 to 50 years old. The rate sank to 0 at 60. The firing rate, on the contrary, changed very little as age increased. (I am indebted to Mr. Alexis Sommaripa, of E. I. Du Pont de Nemours & Co., for lending me his copy of the manuscript.)

[27] *Acts and Resolves of Massachusetts*, Chapter 367, 1937.

[28] *Workers over 40*, A survey by the National Association of Manufacturers.

per cent reported no such limit, and about 3 per cent did not report at all. A bare majority (50.9 per cent) stated that they gave no preference to workers under 40 in hiring new employees; 38 per cent stated that they definitely preferred the younger employees, and nearly 11 per cent did not report their company policy in hiring.[29] The companies were also asked to give the number of workers over 40 who had been hired in 1937. The 750 companies which replied to this question had added older workers to their payroll to the extent of 8 per cent of their total employment figure for 1937. This figure in itself may indicate discrimination, for although we do not know the numbers of unemployed of that age who could have been hired in these industries, the proportion was probably much greater than 8 per cent. A similar per cent was computed for six industrial states, and it is of some interest to find that Massachusetts heads the list with nearly 16 per cent of workers over 40 hired in 1937. The other states are, in order of rank: Michigan with 11 per cent, Pennsylvania with 10 per cent, Illinois with 9 per cent, Ohio with 8 per cent, New York with 7 per cent, and New Jersey with 6 per cent.[30]

It is obvious from this survey that there is considerable discrimination against hiring workers of 40 and over in industry, though that is not the conclusion arrived at by the investigators. Nearly 40 per cent of the firms canvassed admitted that this was so and others probably discriminate but won't admit it. The results of this study, therefore, are consistent with the Massachusetts investigation. Other factors besides age are operative, of course, in connection with the re-employment of workers on relief, but that is perhaps one of the most important. With a slowly ageing relief population, a definite change in industrial standards of hiring is necessary before a large number of work relief cases can be re-absorbed in pri-

[29] *Op cit.*, Tables IX and X, p. 52.
[30] *Op. cit.*, Table XIV, p. 55.

vate industry.[31] That such a change has not yet taken place seems evident from the small proportion of separated work relief cases who were able to secure private employment in the summer and fall of 1939, despite improved business conditions.

The material in this section may be briefly summarized by stating that in our Massachusetts sample of those who had left relief we found a group, differing from the continuing relief population with respect to age, economic assets, and income from private employment, most of whom were separated from the relief rolls because they could support themselves. It may be that their jobs were temporary and that many of them later returned to relief, as was often found to be true in the investigations of separated cases by the WPA. At any rate they probably represent the relief workers who have the best chance of being absorbed into regular industrial employment. Left on work relief are those still considered employable. On the whole they tend to be older, to have fewer economic resources (at least by the time they applied for relief), to be almost entirely dependent on relief. They will have some difficulty in finding jobs if they are 40, 45, or over. They are the ones who form the core of a probably permanent work relief problem in this generation.

[31] For further evidence on industrial policy as to age, see *op. cit.* by Corrington Gill, *American Federationist.*

PART IV

COMPARISONS

CHAPTER X

WORK RELIEF IN OTHER PARTS OF THE COUNTRY

IT IS PERTINENT to inquire, now that a picture of the Massachusetts work relief situation is before us, how typical the Massachusetts situation has been. In the earlier chapters, particularly Chapters I and II, evidence was given of certain peculiarities in the Massachusetts relief and industrial situation. Massachusetts was one of the first states to be federalized in the administration of work relief when the FERA was established in 1933. No state agency had been erected to handle the extraordinary relief problems which arose after 1930, except the Emergency Finance Board which was purely a financial agency. The state, indeed, all during the depression years contributed an almost infinitesimal proportion of relief expenses. The major part of the load was borne by local communities until the federal government entered into relief administration. From the beginning, too, federal funds were used exclusively for work relief in Massachusetts, although the terms of the FERA act permitted the use of funds for direct relief as well. In Massachusetts, therefore, the conduct of work relief under the ERA was far more comparable to the WPA than was true in many states, and the transition from ERA to WPA was less difficult.

Since the early 'twenties Massachusetts has been losing ground industrially with respect to her principal manufactures, such as cotton, wool, and boots and shoes. With a steadily decreasing share in the country's manufacture, unemployment and its problems had become familiar considerably before the depression. Still no attempt had been made to deal with the issue on a state rather than a local basis. The depression greatly accelerated the declining industrial trend in the state and increased unemployment to a point where localities could not longer handle it. In this respect, the Massachusetts experience was typical of the rest of the country. But the industrial situation has given rise to certain problems peculiar to regions undergoing an industrial decline, chief of which are the difficulties of re-employment, the dislocation or collapse of the manufactures of whole towns. Unemployment is more likely to be a continuing problem in regions where industrial opportunities are constantly shrinking. To the question of the rehabilitation of the employable workers on relief is added that of the establishment of new industries or possibly of the migration of groups of workers to areas where industry may be expected to expand. Massachusetts therefore takes on some of the characteristics of a depressed area. Certainly within the state there are a number of depressed towns and cities. New Bedford, for instance, is one of them. To some extent, this industrial decline is characteristic of New England as a whole. The agricultural decline began some time ago; the industrial decline is well on its way. New England in general, and Massachusetts in particular, may be looked upon as a region economically past its prime.

The difficulties engendered by the depression may thus be less easy of solution in states like Massachusetts. The problem of unemployment becomes of long time rather than of short time significance. That does not mean, however, that the impact of the depression, or the extent of unemployment, was necessarily greater than in other industrial sections of the country. Nor need it mean that those on work relief were of a different type than the unemployed in other manufacturing centers.

The 1937 Census of Unemployment has made it possible to compare the extent of unemployment in various sections of the country. The figures quoted here are those of the enumerative check census, since they seem more reliable than those of the voluntary registration.[1] The census provided for the estimate of cmployment as well as unemployment and the percentages used are based on the number considered employable [2] in each region. Judged by these figures, New England was one of three regions where the impact of unemployment was most severe. The middle Atlantic states (New York, New Jersey, and Pennsylvania) and the west south central states (Arkansas, Louisiana, Oklahoma, and Texas) were the other two sections. New England had the third greatest proportion of totally unemployed, and the highest percentage of partly unemployed in the country. New England was also the second lowest in rank with respect to the proportion of full employment and proportion of part-time employment. (See Table CC.) In evaluating the relief situation in Massachusetts, therefore, it must be remembered that the state is in a part of the country where the unemployment problem was at its height.

How do relief workers in Massachusetts compare with those in other parts of the country? The evidence on the character of the relief population is very incomplete and scattered. The data collected during the depression years are too large and too recent to have had much analysis as yet. There are a number of studies on specific parts of the problem

[1] *Census of Unemployment*, 1937, vol. IV. Comparison of the totals of the voluntary census and those derived from the check census indicate that the results of the voluntary census were too low. This would not affect the use of the figures in relative terms if the same proportion of error could be attributed to all the results. Unfortunately, however, the extent to which the voluntary registration underestimated unemployment differed markedly for geographic regions, sex, type of unemployment, and age. The state and other totals are therefore not comparable without extensive correction. The enumerative check census provided the basis for correction for age, sex, and type of unemployment by regions, but not by states.

[2] "Employed or available for employment" according to the census.

in certain localities. The most complete analyses are to be found in the reports of the WPA Division of Social Research (now the Division of Research) and monographs like the survey of the New Jersey relief situation which was sponsored by the Social Science Research Council. The *Fortune* survey presents a most interesting bird's-eye view of the situation.

TABLE CC

PER CENT OF PERSONS EMPLOYED OR AVAILABLE FOR EMPLOYMENT IN 1937

1937 Check Census of Unemployment

Vol. IV — Table 33

Region	Available or Employed	Totally Unemployed	Emergency Workers	Partly Unemployed	Part-time Workers	Fully Employed	Idle or Ill
U. S.	100	16.4	3.6	9.9	2.4	66.4	1.2
New England	100	17.5	3.4	12.9	2.0	63.1	1.1
Middle Atlantic	100	19.8	3.9	10.4	1.9	62.9	1.1
East North Central	100	15.0	3.3	10.4	2.8	67.4	1.2
West North Central	100	13.2	3.3	7.8	2.5	72.0	1.2
South Atlantic	100	14.3	2.9	10.2	2.2	69.3	1.1
East South Central	100	15.2	3.6	10.2	2.7	66.4	1.8
West South Central	100	17.8	4.0	10.3	2.9	63.5	1.7
Mountain	100	16.2	5.7	6.7	3.0	67.2	1.3
Pacific	100	15.9	3.2	7.2	3.1	69.2	1.4

The occupational census of work relief family heads which was taken by the WPA in 1935 enables us to compare the occupational distribution of those on work relief in Massachusetts with that for the whole country. The urban distribution of occupations for the United States is very similar to the Massachusetts distribution. In both cases semi-skilled, skilled, unskilled, and white collar occupations have the highest proportion of workers on relief, in the order named. In Massachusetts, however, the per cent of semi-skilled and white collar workers is about 4 per cent higher than in the United States as a whole, and the proportion of skilled craftsmen 2 per cent greater. The per cent of unskilled, domestic, and farm workers is likewise lower in Massachusetts. It can be said that the occupational distribution of those on work relief in Massachusetts was, in 1935, very like that of urban work relief people all over the country, with the possibility that white collar workers, skilled, and semi-skilled laborers were somewhat more prevalent in the state. In our own sample of continuing work relief

TABLE DD

AGE DISTRIBUTION OF UNEMPLOYED, MASSACHUSETTS AND UNITED STATES

Age	Per cent of Employable Workers* Massachusetts (1934) †	U. S. (1937)°
15–19	50.6	41.1
20–24	30.2	24.3
25–34	20.1	16.4
35–44	19.7	15.9
45–54	22.6	17.3
55–64	26.3	19.9
65–74 ‡	27.9	18.8
not reported	..	6.8
Total	24.9	20.0

* The definitions of employable workers are slightly different in the two censuses but not enough to affect the comparison. Unemployed workers are defined in Massachusetts as the totally unemployed and those temporarily employed on government or private work. It is thought that temporarily employed correspond roughly to emergency workers in the U. S. census.

† Massachusetts Census of Unemployment as of Jan. 2, 1934. Per cents are calculated from data in Table 3, p. 14.

° U. S. Census of Unemployment, 1937; vol. IV, the check enumerative census.

‡ Includes the classes 65–69, and over 70. Some of the latter may have been over 74.

cases, it will be remembered that white collar workers were represented to an even greater extent, which may be partly a result of sampling errors.

The age distribution of the unemployed (totally unemployed plus emergency workers) in Massachusetts and the United States in terms of employable workers is compared in Table DD.

Taking the figures as they stand, it is apparent that the

incidence of unemployment in Massachusetts in 1934 was relatively much greater among the very old and very young workers than was true for the whole country in 1937. Before conclusions drawn from this comparison can be considered significant, however, some account must be taken of the difference in time. Can distributions based on 1934 and 1937 age data be considered in any way comparable? One might expect that the average age of both the employable and the unemployed would tend to increase in the course of three years if the group had remained the same. There would, in that case, be a tendency for concentration in the older age groups, unless these tendencies were the same, in which case the ratios would be independent of increasing average age. Actually there is some evidence to the effect that the average age of the continuing unemployed is increasing faster than that of the employed population. This is substantiated by the growing difficulty encountered by the unemployed over 40 in finding jobs in private industry. It seems therefore that one might legitimately assume a somewhat greater concentration of relative unemployment among the older unemployed in 1937 than in 1934. However, the character of the unemployed seems to have changed with the 1937 recession, with an unusual influx of younger workers who lost their jobs. The incidence of unemployment among the young may be exaggerated by our figures, and the relative share of unemployment borne by the aged may be somewhat underestimated. Both older and younger workers suffered to a greater degree from unemployment than was true of the whole country.

A comparison between relative unemployment in New England and the United States may be made for 1937 by age groups, in terms of employable workers.[3] (See Table EE.)

These figures indicate that total unemployment was relatively

[3] Computed from tables given in vol. IV, pp. 89-91, of the Unemployment Census of 1937.

greater in New England than in the United States for workers under 25 and for those between the ages of 45 and 64. The total proportion of unemployed to employables was about the same. For New England relative unemployment among the young was more significant than that among the old, which does not entirely confirm the conclusions based on the analysis of the Massachusetts and United States figures in the preceding

TABLE EE

AGE DISTRIBUTION OF UNEMPLOYED, NEW ENGLAND AND UNITED STATES

	Per cent of Employable Workers			
	Totally Unemployed		Emergency Workers	
Age	New England	U. S.	New England	U. S.
15–19	42.7	36.5	4.6	4.7
20–24	23.4	21.3	2.6	3.0
25–34	13.6	13.6	2.6	2.8
35–44	12.3	12.4	3.6	3.6
45–54	13.5	13.0	4.1	4.3
55–64	16.6	15.1	4.5	4.8
65–74	1.8	16.2	3.4	2.7
not reported	.4	4.9	1.3	1.9
Total	10.5	10.4	2.8	2.9

table. There seems no doubt, however, that unemployment was proportionately greater in both Massachusetts and New England as a whole than in the United States, and that young and old workers suffered disproportionately.

The relief situation in New Jersey offers in many ways considerable contrast to that in Massachusetts. Since there is detailed information available concerning New Jersey relief and the people on relief,[4] whereas such material for other states

[4] Most of the data on New Jersey have been taken from four sources: (1) *Seven Years of Unemployment Relief in New Jersey, 1930–1936* by D. H. MacNeil, a report prepared for the Committee on Social Security of the Social Science Research Council; (2) *Neighbors in Need*, Report No. 1, State of New Jersey Emergency Relief Administration, 1935; (3) R. A. Lester, *Some Aspects of Unemployment Relief in New Jersey*, an unpublished thesis submitted for the doctorate at Princeton in 1936;

is not easily secured, the New Jersey experience will be used as illustrative of a region in which relief took on a character quite different from that in Massachusetts. In the first place, "New Jersey . . . established one of the first state emergency relief administrations, and constitutes an example of a state which during the depression passed from completely local control over relief to a substantial measure of state control, and back again to virtually local control." [5] The New Jersey Emergency Relief Administration was set up in 1931, originally to handle all kinds of relief, including work relief. It administered both direct and work relief until the WPA took over work relief in late 1935. From then on it had charge of direct relief only until it was discontinued in April 1936, when direct relief was handed back to the municipalities for local control. For a considerable period, then, work relief was under state control, and when the FERA was established, the state ERA continued to administer work relief, the only difference being that a large part of the expenditure was borne by the federal government. Unlike Massachusetts, the New Jersey state organization directed both direct and work relief under the FERA Act, and disbursed federal funds for both types of relief. Work relief was not federalized in New Jersey until the WPA was established in 1935. In this respect, New Jersey was more typical of the majority of states than was Massachusetts during the period of the FERA.

It is not possible to recount in detail the history of relief in New Jersey during this period. But it is of some interest to refer to the New Jersey experiment with "work-for-relief." This system was created under the state administration early in the depression (1932) to take care of work relief problems and was continued under the FERA, side by side with the

(4) Findings Resulting from Special Studies of the New Jersey Relief Census of November 30, 1937.

[5] MacNeil, p. 1.

usual form of work relief. Under "work-for-relief" an employable person would be given relief for his family, usually in kind, according to local standards. He would then be supposed to do some work for the state, or locality, in return for his assistance. It was supposed to be a reciprocal and voluntary arrangement, on the theory that the state owed it to the individual to assist him in hard times, and that the individual ought to do some work in return, and that the individual would wish to earn his assistance. It is easy to see how ineffective such a system might be — and it was in New Jersey — and how it might lead to abuse. There were no definite standards as to how much work a man who had received relief ought to do. The system was not supposed to be on a wage basis. It was difficult to carry on work projects when there was no means of forcing individuals to work regular hours or days. Some local officials actually did force people to work a stated number of hours and days by withholding their relief, although this was not supposed to be done. Some individuals flatly refused to work out their relief. The situation became even more difficult after the CWA established regular work relief, on a wage basis for certain projects. After the CWA ended, the state relief officials attempted to make the work-for-relief system more attractive by paying the men cash bonuses of 5 and 10 cents an hour in addition to their regular relief, but with little success. Under the FERA, work-for-relief and work relief, on a cash wage basis, existed simultaneously. The result was continued dissatisfaction among the workers, often culminating in riots and strikes. It seems very well agreed that work-for-relief was highly unsuccessful in New Jersey. A similar system has been utilized in Massachusetts towns, particularly in connection with work on the local roads, but it has never been adopted on a state-wide scale.[6] Work relief in this de-

[6] The system is optional with cities and towns in Massachusetts for public welfare cases. In Cambridge, for instance, in 1938, a family of 2 re-

pression has been entirely on a cash wage basis, possibly as a result of the early federalization of administrative control.

Whatever the administrative machinery, however, the problem confronting work relief officials is the same: to provide work for the unemployed in some way so as to keep up their morale, use their skill, produce results worth something to the community, and make it possible for them to get private jobs as soon as possible. We have described in some detail the kind of people who had to be taken care of by such a program in Massachusetts. Were the recipients of work relief any different in New Jersey? The New Jersey studies have dealt with relief cases in general and not with work relief recipients in particular. However, a portion of the 1934 study deals with those cases "available for employment," and it was hoped by the state administration that those cases would be taken off their hands by the federal works program, leaving the state only those who were admittedly a continuing relief responsibility.[7] Certainly WPA eligibles must have been selected from this group. Eighty per cent of the family heads studied in this 10,000 case sample were considered employable. These employable family heads were predominantly male (93.5 per cent) and one-quarter of them were Negro. One-third of them were unskilled workers, 29 per cent were semi-skilled, and 22 per cent were skilled. White collar workers composed little more than ten per cent of the sample. The majority of them were between 30 and 49 years of age, and the skilled and white collar workers tended to be concentrated to a greater degree in the higher age groups.

---

ceived a minimum of $4.50 a week from public welfare and at least 2 days' work was expected in return. There was no definite rate per hour and little was expected of the workers as long as they appeared on the job. It was the opinion of officials that they were usually grateful and did not resent being made to work. As in all such cases, the amount they accomplished depended on the foreman.

[7] *Neighbors in Need*, Introduction.

The New Jersey Relief Census of 1937 gives additional information on the character of relief cases in that state, that is, general relief cases registered with the municipalities. Nearly three-quarters of these cases (totalling approximately 48,000) were considered to have employable family members. A large majority of the family heads of such cases were between 25 and 54 years of age, and about half were between 25 and 44. Only 5 per cent were younger than 25, and 22 per cent over 55. The majority of the employable case heads were unskilled laborers, as was true in 1934, with a small proportion of white collar workers (9 per cent). Nearly one-quarter of the employable cases were Negro. Although these cases are general relief and not work relief families, the employable ones are probably comparable to work relief cases. In fact, a small proportion of them were receiving income from WPA at the time the census was taken.

Thus we see that the character of the relief population in New Jersey both in 1934 and 1937 was in several respects quite dissimilar to that in Massachusetts. In the first place, the Negro problem was relatively unimportant in Massachusetts. This was far from the case in New Jersey, especially when one considers that one-third of the male and one-half of the female employable family heads were Negroes and that they were concentrated largely in the unskilled group. The high proportion of Negroes on relief may account for the predominance of unskilled workers on relief in New Jersey. Massachusetts work relief applicants, on the other hand, had comparatively fewer unskilled (12 per cent) and more white collar workers (6 per cent). As far as age is concerned, it is probable that the average age of the work relief group was similar (around 40) in the two states. For New Jersey employables as a whole, however, there was not as high a proportion in the younger and older age classes as in Massachusetts.

It is stated that the employable group in New Jersey represents a fairly adequate cross section of the industrial population in the state. Their pre-depression median income, 1925-29, is estimated at approximately $1300. Actually median family income before the depression was probably higher, as the analysis is based only on the income of the head of the family. In other words, the employables on relief in New Jersey were no more chronic relief cases than in Massachusetts. Lester states, in fact, that two-thirds of the persons applying for relief in New Jersey in 1933 and 1934 had previously been unknown to charitable organizations.[8] One interesting result of the occupational analysis which extended to the years before the depression indicated that many individuals had shifted their occupations during the period of unemployment. There was observed a distinct tendency for the semi-skilled and others to become proprietors by starting small businesses in the hope of supporting themselves.[9] In fact, one-third of those who were listed as proprietors for 1930–34 had been unskilled or semi-skilled workers in the period 1925–29.[10]

Lester found that the New Jersey relief families were greatly in debt, principally for rent, groceries, and medical bills. He found, too, that the amount of indebtedness increased considerably between 1932 and 1934. The average family debt for groceries rose from $29 to $56; for medical care, from $7 to $24; for miscellaneous, from $52 to $175. By 1934 the indebtedness for back rent (per renting family) had increased from $58 to $185, and for back taxes (per home owning family) from $189 to $278.[11] It was estimated by the New

[8] Lester, *op. cit.*, p. 29. The 1937 relief census confirms this statement. Of the employables on general relief in 1937, only 4 per cent had any known relief record before 1931, 25 per cent before 1933. Nearly one-half had never been on relief before 1935. Twenty per cent went on relief for the first time in 1937. *Op. cit.*, Table 9–W.

[9] Lester, *op. cit.*, p. 38.

[10] *Neighbors in Need*, table on p. 42.

[11] Lester, *op. cit.*, p. 35. Based on the study of 310 families accepted for relief in New Brunswick in 1932 and 259 families on relief in Lodi Boro

Jersey ERA that more than 9 million dollars were owed in rent by relief clients by June 1934. In a sample of 5,000, nearly 84 per cent of the renting families were in debt for rent, and 50 per cent of them were in arrears for 7 or more months.[12] Lester emphasizes the points we have made in connection with the indebtedness of Massachusetts work relief families, namely, the effect on the incomes and taxpaying ability of the creditors, and the shifting of some of the incidence of unemployment to the creditor group. Before going on relief a New Jersey family went into debt, reduced its standard of living, used its savings and sold its capital assets, got assistance from relatives.[13] The same kind of procedure was followed by Massachusetts relief applicants.

Despite differences in administrative procedure the group of people who became unemployed and who needed work relief were from an economic viewpoint very similar in the two states. They had lost their jobs as the result of an economic emergency and they were not the usual relief applicant. They differed occupationally and racially as the industrial populations of the states differed, but they had been earning a reasonable income before the depression, at least in New Jersey.[14] In these states the employable relief applicants seem to be representative, for the most part, of the solid working classes of the community.

The study of 10,000 relief clients made in Hamilton County, Ohio (which includes the city of Cincinnati), in June 1937, which has been previously referred to in the section on reemployment, gives some data on the age and occupational dis-

---

in 1934. It is assumed by Lester that these two groups of families are roughly comparable.

[12] Lester, *op. cit.*, pp. 32–34. [13] Lester, *op. cit.*, pp. 29–37.

[14] We have no comparable data on pre-depression income for our main sample of work-relief applicants, but the study of 397 Cambridge families indicated that the average family income had been around $1,500 before unemployment.

tribution of 1844 white employable workers in that region.[15] The Negro problem was even more important in this vicinity, as Negroes formed 45 per cent of the total sample. Even among white employable workers, more than half belonged to the unskilled group and at least a third of them were over 45. White collar workers amounted to ten per cent of these employables, the semi-skilled and skilled about 37 per cent. A little more than a third of these employables were over 45 years of age, and some 20 per cent were under 25. It is noticeable that the white collar workers, as well as the unskilled, were heavily concentrated among the older workers. This study indicates the same disproportionate unemployment among the very young and very old employables that was evident in Massachusetts.

These examples of case studies of the relief population serve to illustrate the tremendous difficulties involved in estimating the relief situation all over the country. From an administrative standpoint there were as many systems of handling emergency unemployment, up to the establishment of the WPA, as there are states. There is observable, however, a significant tendency towards centralization of control over the various relief agencies within many states, and by 1936, 7 states had set up a permanent relief organization to deal with all relief functions.[16] We have seen how diverse was the handling of work relief, for instance, in Massachusetts and New Jersey. Only by an equally detailed study of the situation in other states would it be possible to draw any general conclusions for the country as a whole.

As far as the characteristics of the work relief population

[15] *Op. cit.*, Appendix, Table IV. The employables were selected from the total relief sample on the basis of WPA eligibility, although they were not then on WPA.

[16] See *Legislative Trends in Public Relief and Assistance*, Series III, No. 2, Division of Social Research, WPA, 1936.

are concerned, it is evident that special problems resulting from differences in occupation and age distribution, the local industrial situation, etc., arise in various sections of the country. Both Massachusetts and New Jersey are part of areas hit very severely by unemployment. Massachusetts' chief problems in the solution of unemployment lie in her declining trend of manufactures, and her age problem, the greater proportionate concentration of unemployed among the young and the old. Occupationally Massachusetts is distinguished by a large proportion of white collar and skilled workers. In New Jersey, on the other hand, it is the Negro problem and the relatively large number of unskilled which form the principal difficulties encountered among the employables. In Cincinnati, again, the age distribution (which is like that in Massachusetts), the Negro working population, and the size of the unskilled class give rise to its particular problems.

There seems to be pretty general agreement, however, in all the special studies I have examined, on several points concerning the people who went on relief, particularly on work relief, during the past nine years. Anyone who has actually studied a sample of relief cases (as opposed to individuals who have seen a few ERA or WPA workers leaning on shovels) has usually come to the conclusion that the majority of the sample were not chronic relief cases.[17] They have found, sometimes to their surprise, that many of these families had never been on relief before, that the employable members had good work histories, and that they were hard-working people who had at least managed to make ends meet up to the time they lost their

[17] Besides the special studies quoted previously, see, for example, Lundberg, E. O., "Who Are the New York Emergency Relief Families," *Social Service Review*, Dec. 1934; Wright, H. R., "The Families of the Unemployed in Chicago," *Social Service Review*, March 1934; Channing, Alice, "A Study of Unemployed Clients of Boston Family and Relief Agencies," *Bulletin of Boston Council of Social Agencies*, November 1931; *FERA Monthly Report* for May 1936, p. 2.

last job. They often discovered as well that some of these unemployed had enjoyed a much higher economic status, in the ranks of the professions, or of the very skilled, before 1930 or 1931. It seems also to be clear that most of the unemployed put off as long as they could the necessity of going on relief. This was not quite as true of work relief, for there was less stigma attached to it.[18] The first thing an unemployed worker did was to exhaust all his family resources such as savings, insurance, and property; to get help from his relatives and friends; and to go into debt. When he could get no more credit, when his relatives and friends could not or would not give him further assistance, when his assets were gone, he usually went on relief. I say usually because there were some unemployed who, even in this desperate situation, did not go on relief.[19]

One of the most comprehensive surveys of work relief was made by *Fortune* magazine in 1937.[20] Eleven communities were selected to exemplify conditions of boom and depression, and a condition in between the extremes.[21] Cases were selected at random from the January 1935 relief records and 1,137 of

[18] For instance, Lester found in his New Jersey study that many unemployed who had refused to register under the work-for-relief system registered immediately for work relief jobs under the CWA. *Op. cit.*, Ch. IX.

[19] The WPA Division of Research is now conducting a survey of such cases in order to get some idea of their numerical importance and of their means of life.

[20] "Unemployment in 1937," *Fortune*, October 1937. I attempted to get more detailed figures than those published in the Appendix from the editor, but was told that such figures could not be released. I have no information on the basic statistical method, the exact number of cases in each locality, or whether the local samples were weighted when combined, for instance.

[21] These communities were: Baltimore, San Francisco, Flint (Michigan), Beaumont (Texas), Greenville (S. C.), Adams County (Miss.), Shamokin (Pa.), Kewanee (Ill.), Thayer County (Nebraska), Scott County (Minn.), and Thomaston (Conn.).

these cases were finally interviewed to determine what had happened to them and what kind of people they were. As a group, the heads of families were, in the majority of cases, male U. S. citizens (only 3.5 per cent were aliens), over 35 years of age, married with two to four children. They had spent most of their lives in the same community. Most of them had had little education; 60 per cent had had some grammar school education. The greater portion of them had worked over five years on one job, and 50 per cent had worked from 5 to 19 years at the same job. At the time of the survey in 1937, 45 per cent were being supported by private employment, and 45 per cent by relief, including work relief. The remaining ten per cent had no source of support. Of those who were employed, 40 per cent were unskilled, 25 per cent semi-skilled, 20 per cent skilled, and 15 per cent domestic workers. Their income varied from nothing to over $40 a week, and there was no marked concentration in any income class, although nearly half had weekly incomes of $10 or below. Fifteen per cent had automobiles, 45 per cent a radio, and 60 per cent electricity.

It is difficult to be certain how typical this sample is. *Fortune*, indeed, makes no claims for representativeness, as the localities were selected to portray certain specific problems, and indicates that the south is probably overrepresented. As far as age, size of family, education, sex, and citizenship are concerned both our work relief samples are quite similar. The *Fortune* sample appears to be a combination of the type of cases included in our continuing work relief cases and those who were cancelled. As far as income is concerned, average weekly income was probably a little lower than that for both our samples in 1935. The only item of property ownership common to both investigations is automobile. Twice as many of the *Fortune* "reliefers" owned automobiles as our inactive cases, and 5 per cent less than our cancelled cases. The *Fortune* data indicate, also, considerable lag between the time at which most of the family heads lost their jobs and went on relief.

Fortune comes to conclusions very similar to ours. They believe that those on relief are not bums and that industry did not fire them because they could not do their jobs. They do not think that those on relief want or ask for too much help. They state that the WPA is not "spoiling" them and wasting the taxpayers' money. Those who have remained on relief they consider have become marginal workers, as a result of lack of skill, age, or disability, but many of them are still employable. Nevertheless, the continuing relief cases have become for the most part a permanent social problem.

Except for broad generalizations, it is not yet possible to describe accurately in economic terms the work relief population of the country. There will need to be many more studies, such as those in New Jersey, and our own in Massachusetts before adequate generalization can be made. The *Fortune* survey ought to be done on a more comprehensive scale and by methods available for critical study. I have not been able to find comparable data on property ownership, on income, on debts, or on expenditure, with a few exceptions, for other states. These data exist but have not been widely utilized up to the present. The valuable studies of the WPA Division of Research have been of great assistance, but they have not, for the most part, furnished means of analyzing local situations to any great extent.

It is not now possible to say how representative Massachusetts work relief applicants are, although they appear to have certain characteristics in common with relief recipients all over the country, nor to what extent they exemplify special local problems. One may suspect that Massachusetts is somewhat peculiar in its administrative set-up and its attitude towards those on relief; that its unemployed represent a higher occupational and economic status than could be true in many other parts of the country; and especially that its depressed industries and areas will make the problems of re-employment and rehabilitation of the unemployed markedly difficult and of longer duration. All that one can do now, however, is to present the evidence on the Massachusetts situation, without resorting to premature generalization.

CHAPTER XI

WORK RELIEF APPLICANTS AND THE EMPLOYED

IT IS OF SOME INTEREST and importance to find out in what respects the unemployed, particularly those who are employable (and by definition this includes those eligible for work relief), differ from the employed population, and those who are available for employment in general. There were many who emerged from school and college, and who would normally expect to get jobs despite their lack of experience, who found no jobs available. Also the collapse of industry in the past depression flooded the relief lists with a new type of relief applicant, people who are normally employed and who had never had to apply for relief before. The duration of the relief problem depends partly, at least, upon the economic character of those who thus lost their regular work. Are they the marginal workers, the first to be dismissed, and the last to be taken back? If so, quite apart from questions of age, occupational concentration, and length of unemployment, it will need an industrial boom of an abnormal variety, such as a war, to take them off the work relief rolls.

One would expect that the least efficient worker would be the first to be let go. But when the number of unemployed reaches the size attained in the past nine years it is at least to be questioned whether all or even most of the 10 to 11 million unemployed were marginal workers in industry. If they were, the implication is that a quarter of the normal working population form a reservoir of workers at the industrial margin. One argument against this theory that the unemployed are the least efficient workers lies in the prevalence of depressed areas. In certain regions whole industries and firms were thrown out of business in the depression. All their employees lost their jobs, the efficient along with the less efficient.[1] In such areas there is no reason to suppose that the majority of workers were marginal. The presumption is, indeed, that most of them were not. We have given some evidence to support the idea that Massachusetts is in many ways a depressed industrial area. Certainly the textile cities, the localities supported by the boot and shoe industry, form depressed areas within the state. It is thus to be anticipated that the Massachusetts unemployed contain many who are out of work for the very good reason that their factory or firm went out of business and that the contraction of Massachusetts industry offers little hope of other jobs.

In New Jersey it was stated that the unemployed in 1935 represented an adequate cross section of the industrial population.[2] Let us see if that is true for the country as a whole and for Massachusetts. As far as the occupational distribution is concerned, a comparison of the 1935 WPA census with Edwards' occupational classification of gainful workers in the 1930 census indicates that those on work relief were concentrated more heavily in certain occupations than was true of the gainful workers.[3] White collar workers were distinctly underrepresented on the work relief rolls, whereas the skilled and unskilled, and particularly the semi-skilled, were markedly overrepresented. The underrepresentation of white collar workers and the overrepresentation of the skilled and unskilled among

[1] For a description of a depressed area, in which 65 per cent of those seeking work were on WPA, 11 per cent had no work, see *Memorandum on Bush, Illinois* (mimeographed), WPA Division of Research, February 27, 1939.

[2] *Op cit.*, Report no. 1, New Jersey ERA.

[3] The classifications used by Edwards are not quite the same as those of the WPA census. They have been made as similar as possible for the purposes of this comparison. See *A Social-Economic Grouping of the Gainful Workers of the United States*, 1930, by Alba M. Edwards, U. S. Department of Commerce, Bureau of the Census, 1938.

those on work relief in 1935 was likewise the case in Massachusetts. The proportion of semi-skilled on work relief, however, was exactly the same as that among gainful workers. It cannot be said, therefore, that work relief recipients were a cross section of gainful workers either in the United States or Massachusetts. Unemployment was more prevalent among skilled and unskilled workers in Massachusetts, and in addition, among the semi-skilled throughout the country. White collar workers were less of a problem on work relief, as far as relative numbers are concerned, than any other occupational class.

There has been no such extensive survey of all unemployed as that of those on work relief, so that it is impossible to say whether the occupational distribution of all the unemployed corresponds with that for those on work relief.[4] It is possible that the extent of unemployment among the unskilled, semi-skilled, and skilled workers is exaggerated by the WPA census figures, since work relief projects have tended to be of the construction type. However, any employable person is supposed to be eligible for work relief, if family need can be proved, irrespective of occupation.

The most striking difference between the unemployed and gainful workers in the United States with respect to age is the fact that nearly 36 per cent of the unemployed in 1937 were under 25, whereas only 24 per cent of gainful workers were in that age group. (See Table FF.) The difference becomes even greater when one takes into account the fact that the Edwards compilation includes children from 10 to 15, and the unemployed census does not. The middle age groups were somewhat underrepresented among the unemployed, but the proportion

[4] The voluntary registration for the Unemployment Census of 1937 is given in occupational classes. However, as was explained before (p. 167), the error in comparisons among occupations for the voluntary registration is high, and, since occupations were not recorded in the enumerative check census, there is no satisfactory means of checking the extent of error, in the occupational classes in various regions.

of those 55 and over was almost the same for gainful workers and unemployed.

A similar comparison of ages among the unemployed and the employable (roughly equivalent to gainful workers) was made for Massachusetts. (See Table GG.) Here the most marked difference again is present among the very young. Twice as many among the unemployed were from 14 to 19 years old than among the employables. Three per cent more of the unemployed were aged 20 to 24 than of the employables, and 1½ per cent more of the unemployed were over 55. Less of the unemployed than employable workers were in the middle age groups, 25 to 54.

A most interesting study of 1992 "normal," "marginal," and relief families made in New York City in 1933 affords some significant evidence on the differences between relief and non-relief families with respect to age and occupations.[5] An analysis of the regular occupation of the family heads indicated that the proportion who were skilled, semi-skilled, and unskilled workers was very much greater among relief and marginal families than among normal families. Similarly white collar workers formed a small percentage of the relief family heads (about 11 per cent), and a much larger percentage of the normal heads of families (51 per cent).[6] The age data were very rough, but it was found that the fathers were 40 years of age or over in 30 per cent of the relief families, in 26 per cent of the marginal families, and in 22 per cent of the normal families. Here is additional evidence that the wage-earning as against the salaried workers and the older men were par-

[5] E. O. Lundberg, "Who Are the New York Emergency Relief Families," *Social Service Review*, December 1934. These families applied to temporary clinics for children's health examinations. "Normal" families were defined as those whose income was not markedly reduced by the depression; "marginal" families as those which had reduced incomes but had not gone on relief; relief families as those receiving public relief.

[6] *Ibid.*, p. 623.

ticularly important in the relief population, even as early in the depression as 1933.

Both in Massachusetts and the United States the unemployed were overweighted with workers under 25 and underweighted with those at the most effective working age, 25 to 44, compared to gainful workers as a whole. At first glance this might seem

TABLE FF

NUMBER AND PER CENT OF GAINFUL WORKERS AND UNEMPLOYED, U. S., BY AGE

Age	Gainful workers† Number	Per cent	Unemployed* Number	Per cent
15–19 } 20–24 }	11,835,225 °	24.3	1,934,000	17.6
			1,989,000	18.1
25–34	11,823,004	24.2	2,225,000	20.3
35–44	10,500,540	21.5	1,839,000	16.7
45–54	7,831,161	16.0	1,576,000	14.4
55–64	4,590,592	9.4	1,029,000	9.4
65–74	2,204,967 ‡	4.5	349,000	3.2
not reported	44,431	.1	42,000	.4
Total	48,829,920	100.0	10,983,000	100.0

† Taken from Edwards, Table 6, in his classification of the 1930 Census.

* Taken from vol. IV, the *Unemployment Census of 1937*. The figures used are those estimated from the enumerative check census. See Table 4, p. 12. Includes totally unemployed and emergency workers.

° Includes age group 10–24.

‡ Includes those over 75.

to substantiate the hypothesis that the unemployed are marginal workers. Even if it is admitted that the young and old are more apt to be the least efficient, however, it must be remembered that they make up slightly less than half of the total number of unemployed. In Massachusetts and the whole country about 52 per cent of the unemployed are between 25 and 54 years of age. There is no evidence to show that they need be marginal workers and a good deal of data to indicate the contrary. (See Chapter VII.) No one doubts, of course, that there are marginal workers among the unemployed, but to conclude that the majority of the unemployed are marginal with respect to industrial employment, is, to say the least, an unproved hypothesis. Marginal workers are most likely to be found among the continuing relief cases, and what proportion they form of the total relief load is not known. In the *Fortune* investigation they were nearly half of the original sample.

TABLE GG

NUMBER AND PER CENT OF EMPLOYABLE WORKERS AND UNEMPLOYED, MASSACHUSETTS, BY AGE *

Age	Employable Workers Number	Employable Workers Per cent	Unemployed† Number	Unemployed† Per cent
14–19	131,106	7.3	67,303	14.9
20–24	266,086	14.5	80,444	17.8
25–34	430,200	23.8	86,476	19.2
35–44	391,756	21.7	77,349	17.2
45–54	307,875	17.0	69,601	15.4
55–64	184,504	10.2	48,476	10.8
65 and over	76,104	4.2	21,206	4.7
not reported °	21,209	1.2	...	..
Total	1,808,840	100.0	450,855	100.0

* Taken from the *Massachusetts Census of Unemployment of 1934*, Table 3, p. 14.

† Includes wholly unemployed and temporary workers.

° Includes inmates and staff in institutions for which age was not ascertained.

The data are insufficient to allow any large scale comparisons between the income and expenditure of employed and unemployed groups. The data on relief families in the Consumer Purchases Study are too scattered to be of any use in estimating relief family expenditures, and their income figures had to be pieced out by estimates of the total amount of direct relief given by various government agencies by regions, since the amount of direct relief income was omitted from the questionnaire. Nevertheless, the National Resources Committee has been able to estimate roughly the broad income classes in which the relief families fell during 1935–36.[7] As might be expected, the greater part of families and single individuals on relief were to be found in the lower third of the income distribution, with incomes under $780 a year. Almost one-third of the 13 million families in this group had received relief at some time during the year. In the next "third of the nation" with income ranging between $780–1450 were another 13 million families and single persons, 13 per cent of which were classed as relief families. The upper third, in which incomes varied from $1450 to over a million dollars, included a few relief families, but no single individuals. The total number of relief families was stated as about 4,500,000; of relief individuals, 1,500,000. Nearly all the single individuals on relief, and about 56 per cent of the relief families, were in the lower third income classification. In many cases, the relief given was supplementary to family income from other sources. People on relief seem definitely to fall within the lower third of the nation as far as income is concerned.

Miss Lundberg's data show income distributions for the normal, marginal, and relief families mentioned before.[8] The skewness of the income distribution of normal families was almost the inverse of that of relief families. Approximately 58 per cent of the relief families had incomes less than $600 in 1933, and about one per cent had incomes over $1500. Among normal families, none had incomes below $400, and only one per cent were within the income range from $400 to $600, but 57 per cent had incomes of $1500 or over. The same reversal of the distribution occurs when the 1933 incomes of the relief families are compared with their pre-depression incomes. None of them had incomes of less than $300 before the depression,

[7] *Consumer Incomes in the United States*, National Resources Committee, 1938, pp. 8–10. Section 4, Appendix A, also gives the method of estimating the income of relief families and the difficulties involved.

[8] *Op. cit., Social Service Review*, December 1934, pp. 624–626.

and nearly 40 per cent had incomes of $1500 or more. In 1933, however, 13 per cent of the same families, who had had to go on relief in the meantime, had incomes of less than $300, and two-thirds of them were below the level of $700. If these data are at all accurate, the majority of these relief families dropped to a low position in the lower third of the income distribution from considerably higher economic levels.

My own study of various samples of work relief cases in Massachusetts, more completely analyzed in Part II, indicates that the usual work relief family would certainly fall within the low income group. As we have seen, average weekly income from all sources was $13.50 per family and average weekly expenditure somewhat higher. We know that these families did not secure that average continuously during the year. If they had, some of them would have been in the second third of the population, on the basis of their weekly income figures.

We have previously compared the expenditures of our work relief group with that of other relief families, as best we could with the data available. (See Chapter VII.) The figures released by the Bureau of Labor Statistics for New England cities from the Consumer Purchases Study enable us to make some comparisons between relief and non-relief expenditures. Income and expenditure are classified for three urban groups: large cities (Providence); middle-sized cities (Haverhill, Mass., and New Britain, Conn.); small cities (Greenfield, Mass.; Westbrook, Maine; Wallingford and Willimantic, Conn.). It is of interest to observe that average annual expenditure per family was greater than average annual income in all these cities for those in the lower income groups. The deficits were larger in the middle-sized and small cities, ranging from $377 to $69 for the year 1935–36. In the two middle-sized cities those families with incomes within the $250–$500 income class spent double their income, on the average. Our relief families were, therefore, when they ran into debt, as we have seen that they did, only sharing in the tendency for low-income families to live currently on credit.

On the average, a work relief family in Newton spent $20 during the week in 1935 for which we have data; in Framingham $18. If we reduce the average annual expenditure for the middle-sized cities to weekly terms, we find that the Newton and Framingham expenditures correspond most closely to the expenditure of $19 a week in the $750 to $1000 income class. But for many reasons this comparison may be quite dangerous. Not only are our figures limited by the fact that they refer to one week in the year, but the income distribution indicated that there was usually a concentration of families in a very low income group below the average. The per cent of total expenditure which went for food and housing for our relief families also suggests that they really belong to a lower income class. In Framingham, for instance, nearly 48 per cent of the weekly expenditure went for food; in Newton 44 per cent. In Haverhill and New Britain, however, the highest per cent spent for food in any income class was 41 per cent, and that was in the $500 to $750 income class. Comparison of our Somerville and Cambridge data with those for Providence gives the same results, namely that the average weekly expenditure of the relief families appears to put these families in the $750 to $1000 income class of the Providence data, but that the proportion spent on food and housing is far greater than exists in any of the Providence income classifications.

A somewhat more meaningful comparison may be made between the annual expenditure data of the first Cambridge sample (which represents an underemployed group, about half of which were on relief) and the Providence figures. Table HH lists these figures, as well as the figures for Boston from the Family Expenditure Survey.

We have the proportionate expenditure of three groups of

low income families; the underemployed in Cambridge, wage-earning families in Boston, and wage-earning and clerical families in Providence.[9] None of the families in Boston and Providence had received any relief during 1935–36. All of

TABLE HH

PER CENT SPENT BY ITEMS, CAMBRIDGE, BOSTON, AND PROVIDENCE

PER CENT OF TOTAL EXPENDITURE *

Item	Cambridge	Boston	Providence
Food	44.6	35.7	39.3
House (inc. operation and furnishings)	34.9	35.6	35.0
Clothing	5.5	9.8	7.3
Transportation (inc. auto)	2.8	5.7	5.0
Recreation (inc. tobacco and reading)	3.3	4.5	6.1
Personal Care	.7	1.7	2.1
Medical	3.2	3.1	3.3
Education	.3	.4	...
Gifts	.7	1.2	1.7
Other Expenditures	4.0	2.3	0.2
Total	100.0	100.0	100.0
Average Annual Expenditure	$955	$1571	$920

* The per cents for Boston and Cambridge have been published in the article cited previously in the *American Economic Review*, December 1938. Much of the analysis of these figures is repeated from this article. The Providence data are taken from the urban summary released by the Bureau of Labor Statistics. The comparison is rendered somewhat inaccurate because the average size of family in Providence is unknown. In Boston and Cambridge the average size of family was 4.0 and 4.2 persons respectively.

the Cambridge families had applied for work relief but only about one-half had received it during the year examined.

The Cambridge and Providence families spent about the same amount, but their expenditures were apportioned quite differently. Their relative expenditures for housing and medical care were the same, but the underemployed spent nearly

[9] The release from the Bureau of Labor Statistics states that the low income groups (the figures cited here are for the $750–1,000 income class) were composed largely of wage-earning and clerical families.

six per cent more on food, two per cent less on clothing, and about half as much, relatively, on transportation and recreation, and one-third as much on personal care, as the Providence wage earners. Evidently the Cambridge work relief applicants preferred to spend less on various "luxury" items in order to have more or better food.

Approximately the same differences in relative expenditures were found in comparing the budgets of the Boston and Cambridge families. This comparison is of particular interest because the families in the two samples are fairly homogeneous and there is adequate ground for supposing that the Boston wage-earning group represents the economic level to which the underemployed belonged before they lost their jobs. In both samples the families were mainly native-born Americans, Irish, and Italians; the majority of the family heads had been through grammar school; the chief wage earner was in his early forties. The Boston sample contained slightly more native-born Americans, included families which had had a little more schooling, and tended to be somewhat more skilled and less diverse in occupational distribution. More of the Cambridge families had unskilled laborers for the chief wage earner. Nevertheless, the Cambridge unemployed had previously had an average wage of $1500 a year which brings them within the same income class as the Boston wage earners.

It seems reasonable to assume that the Boston sample is representative of the social and economic class to which the families of the unemployed in Cambridge once belonged. They were perhaps the marginal members of that group. They were the less educated members, and more of them were foreign born. They had the less skilled jobs. Possibly they were less efficient or less essential and among the first to be let go in the depression. Perhaps they were merely the victims of business failures. At any rate, they had lost the jobs which had given them an income as high as that which the Boston families were able to maintain. One would expect the unemployed to have had a similar level of living. What happened when their incomes were almost halved?

In the first place all absolute expenditures had to be cut in amount, but food expenditure was reduced least of all, with the resulting high proportion spent for food, among the unemployed and underemployed. The expenditure for housing and medical care was reduced but remained proportionately the same. The chief economies seem to have been made in connection with clothing and transportation. Recreation and personal care were decreased but not eliminated. It looks as if the Cambridge families were trying to maintain their former level of living (as represented by the budget of the Boston wage earners), especially with respect to food and medical care. In order to do so they had to reduce certain other items such as clothing and recreation expenditures.

It is significant that when their expenditures are compared with those of a non-relief group whose annual expenditure was almost the same, their budgets still show marked differences. They continued to spend relatively more for food than the Providence families who were at that expenditure level. Perhaps if they had been accustomed to an annual expenditure of $900–$1000 they would have given up the attempt to keep a higher dietary standard (or would have learned to utilize a more economical diet), and would have diversified their expenditures to a point more in line with the Providence budget.

A high relative expenditure for food is characteristic of low income families. The Providence families, for instance, had a greater proportionate food expenditure than those in Boston. If a comparable income class had been used for Providence, however, the proportionate expenditure for food would have been much the same as that in Boston. It is interesting to observe that the expenditures for clothing and transportation were relatively lower in Providence, while those for recreation and personal care were, if anything, somewhat higher. In other words, clothing and transportation seem to be the chief economies of low income families whether or not they are on relief.[10]

A comparison of the distribution of expenditures of the relief and non-relief families in the four small towns[11] shows a situation similar to that between Boston and Cambridge, although the families are not as homogeneous in the small towns.[12] In all four towns the non-relief families spent a considerably greater proportion of their total expenditure upon commodities other than food, shelter, and clothing. Dracut is the only town in which the proportion spent for the "luxury" items was not as much as 11 per cent higher. Among the necessary expenditures, a greater proportion went for food among the relief than among non-relief cases, particularly in Gilbertville. In fact, the actual amounts spent for food by families on relief were very little less than in the case of non-relief families. What items, then, bear the brunt of enforced economy? The proportions spent for automobiles and investments (including taxes, savings, etc.) were cut drastically by the relief cases in all four towns. The clothing percentage dropped in all towns except Gilbertville, but not as much as in Cambridge. The other incidental and luxury items suffered to some extent as well. We find the unemployed in these four towns cutting down incidental and luxury expendi-

[10] This is confirmed by the income-expenditure analysis which indicated that clothing had unit elasticity or more for most of the Consumer Purchases data, and that automobile expenditure was one of the most elastic in the budget. See E. W. Gilboy, "The Propensity to Consume," *Quarterly Journal of Economics*, Nov. 1938.

[11] Gilbertville, Dracut, Marlboro, Winchester. The data were collected by Professor Carle C. Zimmerman and turned over to me.

[12] The non-relief cases were not restricted to low wage-earning families and included a considerable range of occupations and incomes.

tures, but maintaining their housing and dietary standards almost at the non-relief level. The other expenditures, however, were not abandoned, despite the existence of unpaid bills for rent, food, and medical care.

The very incomplete data available[13] suggest some significant differences between the work relief population and gainful workers generally in Massachusetts. Although half the unemployed are at the best working age, 25 to 44 years old, the very young and the older workers are greatly overrepresented. More of the work relief recipients were in the unskilled occupational class than is true of gainful workers as a whole. White collar workers were apparently less affected by unemployment and are therefore underrepresented on relief. The relief population therefore presents certain special problems with regard to age and occupations.

What data we have on the income and expenditure of relief and unemployed families in Massachusetts conform with the rough grouping of relief families in the National Resources Committee study of consumer incomes. The majority of relief cases, to which our main sample of work relief applicants belongs, are in the lower third of the income distribution. Some of them are in the second third. These are the families by whom relief is most probably used as a supplement to family income. They are underemployed, somewhat similar to our first Cambridge sample in all probability, and represent the upper fringe of the relief group.

In most cases, the circumstances of the depression have thrust the work relief population, and undoubtedly a good many of those on direct relief as well, into an economic class

[13] There are a number of studies comparing the relief and non-relief families in rural areas, such as N. L. Whetten and W. C. McKain, Jr., *A Sociological Analysis of Relief and Non-relief*, Research Mon. II, WPA Division of Social Research, which we shall not examine here, as Massachusetts presents a problem primarily urban.

to which they did not originally belong.[14] Their incomes have been reduced and their expenditures must also decrease. How do they adjust themselves to this new situation? That they do not adjust themselves immediately, and that they maintain many types of expenditure connected with their former mode of life, is only to be expected, and is suggested by a comparison of the relative distribution of their expenditures with that of the low income non-relief families in the Consumer Purchases Study. We have seen that relief families go into debt and get as much credit as they can to eke out their reduced income. But in this they are little different from non-relief families in the low income groups, at least in 1935 and 1936. Relief families apparently attempt first of all to maintain their food expenditure at its former level. Although proportionate expenditure for food increases inversely with income, our data indicate that this increase is far greater for relief families than for those not on relief. Similarly relative expenditure on clothing and transportation decreases to a greater extent than is usual at the reduced income level. This tendency of relief families to spend much more on food than is customary at that income range may be partly explained by the number of adults in relief families. But it suggests as well the maladjustment of families suddenly transferred from one economic level to another. This is another of the particular difficulties confronting those on relief and forms an additional aspect of the special problems arising in connection with the relief population.

[14] Many of them lose their capital assets, those who go on relief to a greater extent than those who do not. H. R. Wright, in comparing two groups of unemployed, those on relief and those not on relief, found little difference between them, except that the non-relief ones were able to keep their assets for a longer period and had been a little better off before the depression. This was in 1932. As the depression continued, it is more than likely that his non-relief group was also forced to resort to relief. "The Families of the Unemployed in Chicago," *Social Service Review*, March 1934.

If many of the work relief cases were not marginal workers to begin with, what has happened to them on work relief? Undoubtedly many of them have become marginal simply as a result of their increasing age and the very fact that they are unemployed. Others have entered the group of least desirable workers, from the industrial standpoint, through loss of morale and efficiency. Any prolonged period on relief, even work relief, seems to affect some workers adversely, partly because of the industrial and general public prejudice against those on relief, and partly through the inefficient management of work relief projects. Through no fault of their own, it seems probable that many on the work relief rolls, particularly those who have been there for some time, will have to accept a permanently lower level of living, and a reduction in industrial status to that of the least desirable workers in industry.

PART V

CONCLUSION

CHAPTER XII

AN EVALUATION OF WORK RELIEF

THERE ARE MANY ASPECTS of work relief which cannot be considered in one book. Perhaps the chief conclusion resulting from the investigation of any one part of the problem is a realization of the many complications involved and the tremendous ramifications of the subject. To evaluate the work relief program properly, it would be necessary to examine its administration, its costs, the efficacy of its projects in maintaining the efficiency and morale of its recipients and in producing results which add to the country's wealth, its relation to federal and local public finance, its ability to return workers to private employment, its effect upon the labor market and wage rates, its relation to labor organization, the question of its probable permanence, its efficacy as compared to direct relief, and so on. There is also the necessity for considering its place in a coordinated program dealing with all phases of unemployment. There is a great deal of scattered and uncoordinated material on all of these and many other facets of the subject. We have attempted to indicate that we are aware of these things but obviously it was impossible to deal with them all. This study is primarily an attempt to describe and analyze one basic problem of work relief in its proper economic and social setting, namely, the economic nature of those who were made eligible for work relief in Massachusetts, with some attention to their economic status before and after the provision of work relief, and their chance of re-employment.

However, in the course of research on any angle of the relief problem one cannot help being cognizant of related phases. The administration of work relief, for instance, is very closely connected with the efficiency of the work relief program. A well and efficiently administered plan of work relief would insure that the projects to be undertaken were worth while and well worked out in advance. They would be selected not merely as devices to make work but to fulfill community needs which perhaps could not be filled out of ordinary local and state budgets. Work relief recipients would be selected on the basis of employability as well as need and every effort would be made to see that the man fitted the job, that skills were utilized in the best possible way. Only thus can skill and morale be maintained and projects completed without undue waste. Frequent administrative checks would be made on the relief personnel, to be sure that the workers were still eligible for relief and that they canvassed all opportunities for private employment. Unemployables would be kept off the work relief rolls and cared for by other means, such as direct relief and the social security program. Adequate supervisors and foremen would be provided on the job.

Undoubtedly some such ideal administration was in the minds of some, at least, behind the federal relief programs. Such ideals, of course, are never attained completely in practice, but opinions differ violently as to the degree of attainment possible, and as to the actual attainments of the federal relief agencies in the present case. Charges of maladministration have been frequently made. What are the facts? It will take some years to assess the extent to which politics, local, state, and federal, affected the relief program. It would be absurd to claim that politics has not entered into relief administration, as it does, unfortunately, into all governmental business. But politics and relief have not been intertwined only in the federal agencies, but also at the local end. Projects have been selected by localities with an eye to political benefit; persons have been certified as eligibles, whose eligibility lay in political pull rather than in unemployment. The unusual rise in the work relief rolls in the summer of 1936 has already been mentioned. WPA officials deny that this increase had anything to do with the November elections. They cite the drought and various other special circumstances[1] as an explanation. Perhaps this is true of the country as a whole, but the rise was just as spectacular in Massachusetts where no such special circumstances existed. In New Jersey, it has been admitted that state and local politics played a large part in the administration of ERA and WPA funds.[2] Lester and other investigators found that New Jersey municipalities frequently used relief funds for ordinary municipal functions, thus reducing the town budget and tax rate. Former municipal employees went on relief to do their regular jobs.[3] In Massachusetts it has been intimated that towns have attempted to transfer their regular public welfare cases to the WPA in order to cut down their own relief expenses. Political scandals in connection with the WPA have made newspaper headlines all over the country. I have made no special study of the relation of politics and relief, but there seems no doubt that politics has entered into relief and affected its administration, both in the selection of personnel and of projects. The im-

[1] As a result of "numerous charges that the relief rolls have been increased in Federal election years for political purposes and allowed to decline in other years" a study was made by the WPA in 1938 of the movement of the relief load and the volume of unemployment since 1933. When drought cases are excluded from the relief estimates (direct plus work relief) in 1936, the figures move downward in June to November. Throughout the whole period the unemployment and relief series show close agreement. WPA Memorandum 2776.

[2] D. H. MacNeil, *op. cit.*

[3] Lester (*op. cit.*, p. 292) remarks, "Our narrative of relief employment in New Jersey during this depression is replete with instances in which made work also made unemployment for others. Under every one of the relief employment programs tried in New Jersey the tendency for expansion of relief employment to result in a corresponding contraction in public employment, is evident." This does not include the WPA, however, as Lester's study stopped before the WPA began.

portant question is, however, to determine how significant the political factor has been in a relative sense. Naturally, political scandals receive the most publicity. The many instances of efficient administration have far less news value.

Work relief projects have been the object of criticism on the grounds of poor planning, excessive cost, lack of efficiency of the workers and so on. These criticisms often fail to recognize the problems engendered by the very short time in which a large scale program of public work for relief had to be set up. The Federal Administration was confronted with a large and increasing body of unemployed, which it was beyond the financial power of local and state governments to handle, but which had to be taken care of in some way. Since work relief was adopted, they had to be put to work at once. It is not surprising that many projects were badly planned and carried out, even foolish, in the necessity for immediate action. It should also be remembered, as it frequently is not, that the local governments had their full share of responsibility in selecting these projects. Under the FERA, projects were selected by the community and had to be approved by the state ERA administration, except in states under direct federal control, such as Massachusetts. In such states, the procedure was similar to that made universal under the WPA, whereby local cities and towns selected the projects and voted to finance a small portion of the costs.[4] The projects had to be approved by the Washington Administration and the President before they could be carried into effect. Local communities, however, certainly shared in the responsibility for these projects. If they were absurd and a waste of money, local governments

[4] A small proportion of WPA projects were federal in nature, i.e., selected, financed, and administered entirely by the federal government. See *Hearings before the Special Committee to Investigate Unemployment and Relief*, U. S. Senate, 76th Congress, First Session on S. 1265, Feb. 24–March 10, 1939, pp. 264–292, testimony of Colonel Harrington.

were partly to blame. The waste cannot be attributed entirely to federal extravagance and maladministration. Mr. MacNeil suggests that a good deal of the public distrust of the WPA grew out of their system of marking their construction projects as solely WPA projects. Most individuals were unaware of the extent of local responsibility involved in their selection. He cites an instance, from New Jersey, in which the CCC were occupied in cutting down trees in a county park. Complaints were made as to the "vandalism" of the federal government until a sign was erected explaining that this was a part of the long-run program of the park commission in which a federal agency was participating. The complaints ceased and Mr. MacNeil feels that less antipathy to the federal government would have resulted if WPA signs had clearly stated the local agency responsible for the selection of the project instead of implying the sole responsibility of the WPA.[5] Such marking would not, of course, obviate the undesirability of wasteful projects for work relief, but it would at least make public the proper allocation of responsibility. It might, too, be one means of checking such waste, as citizens are more closely interested in the financial administration of their local communities, and more apt to do something about local extravagance.

Inefficiency of the workers is also a charge laid at the door of work relief. Everyone has heard countless jokes about WPA workers, based largely on their inability or unwillingness to move. Some of these charges are probably true, partly because some unemployables who should not be on work relief were placed there, partly because foremen and supervisors were sometimes inefficient, and partly because the best use of the available skills was not always made. There are instances of white collar workers being set to digging ditches etc. while laborers were made timekeepers and given office jobs. Under the FERA very little success was attained in

[5] *Op. cit.*, pp. 206 and 207.

placing work relief applicants in jobs for which their past occupational history and training fitted them.[6] The WPA, however, has made a distinct attempt to utilize available skill in the best way and has made progress in so doing.

Most investigators have found the majority of work relief recipients willing and even eager to work. It is difficult to evaluate their efficiency although at least one such attempt has been made. A study of 1444 skilled workers in seven cities was made in January 1937.[7] Two examiners, one sent by the international labor union of the craft[8] and one provided by the local WPA office, graded the quantity and quality of the work of the craftsmen. Almost all of the workers were from the relief rolls (95 per cent) and a small proportion were Negroes (3.8 per cent); about half had been union members at one time or another, and one-quarter actually belonged to a union at the time of the survey. The average age of the whole group was nearly 45 years, with carpenters tending to be older and painters younger. The following conclusions were reached on the basis of this investigation:

1. About three-quarters of the craftsmen were judged to be passable or better with regard to the quantity and quality of their work by both examiners.[9] Carpenters had the highest proportion of passable or better grades in both cases. Nearly 40 per cent of the work was judged excellent as to quality, nearly 30 per cent as to quantity.

[6] Lester estimates that about 80 per cent of all relief work in New Jersey under the ERA was unskilled, although unskilled laborers were only about 25 per cent of the unemployed. *Op. cit.*, Summary and Conclusions. It is also the opinion of a Massachusetts official that very little was done under the ERA to fit the worker to the job.

[7] *The Efficiency of Skilled Workers on WPA Projects*, by W. R. Curtis, W. G. Keime, & E. Berman, Bulletin of the Division of Research, Statistics, & Records, WPA. The cities were Baltimore, Birmingham, Hartford, Memphis, Minneapolis, Scranton, and Toledo.

[8] The crafts were brick and stone masons, carpenters, and painters.

[9] Although both examiners gave identical grades in 65 per cent of the cases, the union officials tended to be somewhat stricter in grading.

2. Only 9 per cent of the craftsmen were considered definitely inferior as to quality; 8 per cent as to quantity.
3. There seemed to be a direct correlation between age and the quality and quantity of work, except for the masons where inferior workers were older.
4. Union members usually were graded as more efficient and had a longer employment history at their craft than non-union members. They also tended to be older — 48 as against 41 years.
5. For the whole group, on the average, workers had spent 20.5 years at their craft.

Presumably the efficiency standard used in this investigation was that prevailing in private jobs of a similar nature. Without further studies of this sort, however, one cannot conclude that WPA workers are as efficient as those in private industry. Lester is very pessimistic about the efficiency of those on work relief in New Jersey. He thinks that efficiency was not more than 50 per cent of normal, except under the CWA.[10] No attempt was made to judge the efficiency of unskilled labor, which would undoubtedly be more difficult, but unskilled laborers are more prevalent on work relief than skilled workers.

The extent to which the morale and skill of the workers has been maintained by work relief employment is almost impossible to measure. It is being attempted, however, as an experiment on a small scale at the University of Minnesota. The continual movement between private employment and work relief which has characterized the work relief rolls from the beginning indicates that some relief recipients are able to find jobs in private industry. The implication is that this would not have been possible unless their skill and morale had been kept up. Of course, the administrative difficulties

[10] *Op. cit.*, Summary and Conclusions. Lester judges on the basis of the work relief system instituted under the N. J. ERA, which included work-for-relief. Efficiency under WPA was probably higher, as it resembled the CWA more than the FERA in that state.

which we have outlined must have a distinct effect on morale. In so far as projects are patently of little use, and supervision on the job lax, there cannot be much incentive to efficient work. Also, the inclusion of handicapped workmen and political appointees among the personnel must have a deleterious effect on the morale of those who started out with an honest desire to do their work efficiently and well.

Another form of administrative laxness may have succeeded in some cases in keeping on the relief rolls those who, from the point of family need, should not have been there and excluding eligible workers who did need assistance. I refer to the administrative check on the eligibility of those certified for work relief.[11] In the examination of cases separated from WPA, from which our second sample (analyzed in Chapter VII) was selected, it appeared that a considerable period of time elapsed between certification of eligibility and the checking process. In a few instances, concealment of assets or income of other members of the family had enabled a case to obtain an original certification of eligibility which should never have been given. In more instances, family circumstances had changed since certification, usually by other members of the family securing work in the interim. It was often some months before family eligibility was rechecked and during this period the family head was being employed on work relief. Of course, it is a tremendous task to maintain a continuous check of this sort on the relief rolls and frequently the staff was inadequate for this purpose. In Massachusetts certified cases submitted by local agencies are checked by the Intake and Certification Section of the state administration. A staff of 107 social workers is maintained for this purpose, with 67 visitors working in the field and 40 in state and branch offices. The visitors average 30 completed investigations a week, a small

[11] The new WPA appropriation act requires a complete review of the relief load every six months.

number in comparison with the total cases. In some places, it was not attempted. For instance in Cincinnati the WPA simply stated that such checking was not its job and that it would have to be done, if at all, by the referral agency.[12] Probably the slowness or lack of such checking has been another factor in prejudicing public opinion against federal work relief. Naturally when individuals know or hear of others on work relief who have an adequate income (according to relief standards) they feel that work relief is not fulfilling its purpose and that public money is being deflected to the pockets of those who ought not to have it.

Another policy of the FERA and WPA which has occasioned criticism, rather from professionals than the general public, is their insistence that the major portion of their funds should be spent directly in paying labor. Their construction work, which is fully 70 per cent of the work relief program, has been operated on "force account," or by day labor, and not by the usual contract system. Contractors have protested against this,[13] partly because it obviously takes work away from them, but to a considerable extent because it seems to them an almost archaic method of handling construction. In some cases it has seemed like setting the clock back to an era of hand labor, when many of the operations which would normally be done by machines were, under the WPA, carried out by manual labor. From the point of view of efficiency it would undoubtedly be more effective to use the machines. The point of view of those behind the work relief program, however, has been that the first concern of the FERA and WPA should

[12] See *op. cit.* The referral agency, in this case the Hamilton County Department of Public Welfare, had not the staff or means to do the job either, although they were certain that eligibility had changed for many of those still on WPA.

[13] See the testimony of Mr. B. L. Knowles, Field Engineer of the Associated General Contractors of America in the *Hearings before the Byrnes Committee*, on S. 1265, February 24 to March 10, 1939, pp. 300 ff.

be to get money directly into the hands of those who need it. And from this point of view, they have succeeded. Ninety per cent of WPA funds have been paid directly to WPA workers by check. In so doing the administration has been influenced not only by the desire to aid employable persons in need of relief as quickly as possible, but by the monetary theory now prevalent in Washington. We shall not examine this theory or attempt to evaluate it. But it should be stated that the relief program has been tied up from the beginning with the idea that relief expenditures, if paid directly to labor, would increase consumption expenditures and stimulate business recovery.

This brief statement of the administrative difficulties involved in the work relief program and the criticisms engendered thereby may lead one to a pessimistic view of the accomplishments of work relief. Such is not my intention. When the immensity of the problem of setting to work some 5 million unemployed is taken into account, along with the relatively short period of time in which this had to be done, and the nature of American political system, it is my considered opinion that the federal work relief program, particularly under the WPA, has justified itself indeed. Despite its inadequacies, it has put millions of people to work and enabled them to earn some kind of livelihood, when private industry was unable to keep them at work. It has completed many valuable additions to the country's wealth.[14] Even if many of these projects were erected at high cost, possibly they would not have existed at all without some such program. Even most of the bitterest critics of the work relief program admit now the necessity for some kind of work relief program.[15] Their criticism centers

[14] See list of projects completed in Massachusetts and Connecticut, for instance, and the reports of the WPA on projects throughout the country.

[15] As evidence of the acceptance of the work relief principle it may be noted that nearly one-quarter of the states have recently passed legislation enabling a state work relief program.

rather upon the inadequacies and inefficiencies of the program of this Administration. They claim that another administration or political party could have handled the thing more effectively. Whether this is true we shall never know. But many of the inadequacies of the program seem to me to have resulted from the emergency nature of unemployment in this depression, the size of the problem, the immediate necessity for action, the lack of time for adequate planning, and the nature of our political system. In other words the deficiencies of the relief program have been determined to a marked degree by difficulties inherent in our economic and political system in time of emergency. Now, however, we have surely passed the emergency stage and the experience of the past six years should provide the data for an efficiently planned program.

Let us return to the basic problem of this study, namely, the economic character of applicants for work relief. What may we conclude? Our evidence supports the idea that the majority of work relief applicants were not, in Massachusetts, at least, ne'er-do-wells or "paupers," [16] who looked upon work relief as a way to get a living with less effort than in private industry. They were responsible citizens who had lost their jobs as a result of economic circumstance before which they were powerless.[17] The analysis which we have presented makes it clear that our sample contained many types of relief applicants, farmers, professional men, inexperienced youths and women,

[16] The word is used here in the sense of New England poor relief tradition, in which "pauper" implies a chronic relief case.

[17] This opinion is also supported by Mrs. Armstrong's evidence. She estimates that about 50 per cent of the relief workers who came under her jurisdiction in a Michigan county during the FERA "were sufficiently capable, steady workers to be considered satisfactory employees in factories or in any other employment for which they were fitted. Had there been plenty of jobs they would never have needed public aid." L. V. Armstrong, *op. cit.*, p. 153.

unskilled laborers, domestic servants, and so on. We have also gone into the difficulties of selecting an average, or typical case. However, we may say that most of them were men in their early forties, with families of 4 or 5 persons to support, who had had jobs as white collar or skilled workers, or as semi-skilled factory operatives before the depression. They applied for work relief because they could exist no longer on their assets. Many of them had cashed in their insurance, sold their cars, let their homes be taken over by the mortgagee, used their savings, or lived on credit. Still about one-third of them had managed to retain one or more of these assets at the time of relief application, although the income from such assets was usually negligible. Nearly all of them were considerably in debt. They had belonged, for the most part, to the great wage-earning population, who manage to live without outside aid in normal times. Their resources, however, are totally inadequate to sustain them in any long-continued emergency, such as serious illness or unemployment.

How did they fare on work relief? Were they pampered and given relatively high incomes? A very large majority were entirely dependent on relief, either work relief alone or work relief supplemented by public welfare. Some of them were able to supplement relief with private employment or other non-relief sources of income. A few subsisted on private employment or non-relief income entirely. Some had no income at all. This applies to the cross section week in 1935 after application. Those who were not on work relief during that week were probably assigned to projects later on. But in any one week the sources of income of work relief recipients would probably be similar to the above.

Their average family income was about $13.50 during this week, although there was a considerable number who were in the lowest income class of zero to $4 a week. Most of them spent more than their income for the necessities of life such as food, rent and fuel, clothing, and miscellaneous, thus adding to the debts they already owed. They could scarcely live in luxury on such a figure, particularly as they did not get this every week. The annual income of our main sample is unknown, but that of the underemployed Cambridge group was, for 1935, around $850. Our sample of those mainly dependent on relief probably netted considerably less during the year. For most of them such an income meant a distinct lowering of their former level of living and an inability to sustain more than an emergency standard. In Cambridge the average incomes of the underemployed were almost halved. Part of this reduction in living standards was shifted to other groups in the community who gave them credit, mainly landlords, doctors, and grocers, but a great deal of it was undoubtedly borne by the unemployed themselves.

The economic situation of the unemployed varied, of course, within the state. In wealthy metropolitan suburbs such as Newton, relief was such a relatively small problem that the relief client fared far better, both as to the adequacy of relief income and opportunities for private employment. In rural towns and villages relief, again, was more of a minor problem, and most of the relief applicants could at least feed their families from their land. It is in the large cities, in an urban state like Massachusetts, where the relief problem is most pressing. And in really depressed industrial centers like New Bedford the situation becomes extremely serious.

This main sample of work relief applicants consisted of unemployed who were certified as eligible for the ERA in 1935 and had been continued on work relief as active cases until 1937, when their records were used for this study. Thus they were continuing work relief cases for at least three years and as such probably exemplify those least likely to return to private employment in any normal economic situation. They form part of what WPA officials call the "hard core" of unemployment. Another sample of cases was also investigated, of those who were admitted to work relief in 1935 and were subsequently separated from the work relief rolls. This sample represents the portion of WPA workers who can get some kind of private employment. Two-thirds of our sample were cancelled from work relief as a result of the return to private employment of some member of the family. How permanent this employment was, it is not possible to say. The WPA policy of urging workers to take private jobs, even if temporary, and guaranteeing that they will be taken back on work relief if the jobs end, may mean that we have here the group representing the turnover on the relief rolls. As a whole this group was a little younger, had had more income from private employment while on relief, was in debt to a greater extent. Undoubtedly they are the ones with the greatest chance of getting off and remaining off relief.

Evidence on the question of re-employment and the permanence of the relief problem was discussed in Chapter IX. It seems clear that we have a permanent relief problem, whether we like it or not, for a number of reasons. In the first place, the chances of re-employment for those on the relief rolls who are 40 years of age or over are small, unless the preference in private industry for hiring younger men changes. Although older men are not usually discriminated against in firing, once they have lost their jobs, it becomes almost impossible for them to be re-hired.[18] Most of those over 40 now on the relief rolls, and many of them have been on work relief for several years, will continue to be a problem, until they reach the age when old age pensions can apply to them. Second, there appears to be a distinct prejudice against hiring workers who have been on relief, on the part of managers of private industry.

[18] Such individuals are among those forming a new chronic relief class, according to an editorial in *Connecticut Social Trends*, November 1935, which has been created by the past depression.

This prejudice may be attributed to some extent to the idea, which still persists, that there is something wrong with anyone who applies for relief. But it is partly due as well to the belief (and in some cases the actual experience) that work relief affects adversely the skill and morale of its recipients. Consequently, the third reason lies in the administrative defects of the work relief program. There are undoubtedly cases where the poor management of relief projects, the bad use of skills, political maneuvering etc. have had the reverse effect of that intended and have led to the deterioration of workmen on relief. How prevalent this is, I do not know, and I have no doubt that it is greatly exaggerated by the adherents of the Elizabethan attitude towards relief. But where such deterioration has occurred, the people who have been affected by it will tend to become unemployable.

A fourth very cogent reason lies in the short-period contraction of employment opportunities in industry. In a state like Massachusetts, where a declining industrial tendency was observed early in the 'twenties, there is very little hope of reabsorbing the unemployed, even if they were all considered desirable workers and industry wished to hire them. The general conclusion of Dr. Davenport's careful study of unemployment in Massachusetts is extremely pessimistic. He sees no solution for the unemployed in this state, except possibly migration.[19] This is a special Massachusetts, and to some extent, a New England problem. But the improvements in industrial technique, which characterize an extended depression, have succeeded in cutting down available jobs all over the country. Now the short-time effect of such technical changes has always been technological unemployment. Ever since the "industrial revolution," history has been replete with instances

[19] *Op. cit.*, p. 68. The growth of new industries or trades may assist in the solution but even that necessitates the transfer of workers from one occupation to another.

of workmen displaced by machines. In the past the long period effect of such technical improvements has been to increase employment opportunities, by the growth of new industries or the expansion of those already in existence. The short period effect has always been to create a very difficult period of unemployment and even misery for the generation of workers displaced. I see no evidence to support the conclusions of some who believe that we have reached the end of industrial expansion and the growth of new industries.[20] Nevertheless, our generation will certainly have to deal with the effects of technological unemployment as an additional deterrent to reducing the number on relief.

Another reason why the relief problem is likely to become permanent lies in the increased social consciousness of the general public and the growing belief that unemployment and other such social problems are the concern of the government. The present depression has been compared with past depressions, particularly the long decline in the 'seventies, and it has been said that unemployment is relatively no more of a problem than it was then. Perhaps that is so. But the public conscience can no longer dismiss unemployment as an inevitable industrial occurrence for which no one has any responsibility. In fact, the belief is increasing that such occurrences are a general social responsibility, not of individual business men or local governments primarily, but of the government of the whole country. The present Administration may have hastened the growth of government responsibility, particularly that of the federal government, for such social problems, but it is part of a long-observed change in social attitude which has been prevalent in other countries for some time.

Certain policies of the WPA itself may affect the permanence of the present relief personnel. In response to criticism

[20] For instance, the 7 Harvard and Tufts economists, in *An Economic Program for American Democracy*, 1938.

that many on relief have refused private jobs, the ERA and WPA have investigated a number of areas where such criticism was most outspoken. Their general conclusion has been that, except for a few instances, such criticism has been quite wrong. In nearly all the cases where jobs were refused it was for what they considered adequate reasons.[21] Ordinarily, too, the opportunities for private employment were found to be greatly overrepresented. Two types of reasons for "job refusal," however, raise somewhat controversial issues. A number of such refusals seem to have been caused by administrative deficiencies; the relief person did not get the notice, or the office did not have his address, and so on. Undoubtedly such refusals are no reflection upon the relief worker. but a considerable reflection on the efficiency of the relief administration. An experience of this sort is not likely to create a desire to hire relief workers in the minds of private employers. The other adequate reason upon which I wish to comment is that of refusing a job with inadequate wages or working conditions. It has been a frankly stated policy of the WPA not to force those on work relief (by taking them off the relief rolls) to accept jobs which are underpaid or which provide bad working conditions. This policy has given rise to considerable criticism. Many think that *any* job is preferable to a relief job and that relief recipients should be forced to take such jobs. Others object to the government's attempt to raise standards of wages and working conditions in this way. On the other hand, it is obvious that there are employers who would take advantage of those on relief, if they could, to offer them subnormal wages and conditions of work. The whole question of the interaction of relief wages and working conditions upon private employment is a very complicated one and offers a new and important field for investigation. One school of thought considers that relief wages should be below the prevailing wage level, so

[21] See summary of job refusal investigations in Chapter IX.

that there can be no possible inducement to stay on relief. Against this opinion are presented the arguments of union officials who see the rates they have established through the years being undermined, and of those who think that relief jobs should be considered comparable to other jobs and the work paid for at the customary rates. There is no doubt that relief wages do affect industrial wages and vice versa.[22] Whatever one's opinion is on this matter, the fact that the relief administration allows workers to select jobs in any way may have the effect of making some of those on work relief prefer to stay there.[23]

For these and other reasons it will be impossible to discontinue relief of some sort to a number of people now on work relief. Many of them are not likely to be placed in private employment, even in an industrial upswing, unless it is a war boom. They will be in need of assistance during their lives. The hearings before the Byrnes Committee on the bill for the reorganization of WPA, PWA, and Social Security indicate that this view is becoming generally accepted. Controversy centers now about the means of providing these people with some kind of livelihood. Despite the admittedly greater cost of work relief and the criticisms of WPA, there seems to be a general opinion, also, that work relief should be continued

[22] See Lester, *op. cit.*, Summary and Conclusions. In New Jersey industrial wage rates were lowered as a result of relief wages, and raised when the CWA was operating. In regions such as Massachusetts, where the WPA wage rate is set at the union rate it was often higher than prevailing non-union wages in various localities. The new relief act which specifies that 130 hours must be worked each month has changed this situation.

[23] According to *Connecticut Social Trends*, another addition to the permanent relief class will be made by those "who have achieved through relief a standard of living, (and) are not likely to make the extra effort to get and hold unattractive jobs." (Nov. 1935, p. 2.) I do not believe that many work relief recipients have achieved a very high level of living. On the other hand, the government's refusal to force them to take unattractive jobs may tend to increase the permanent elements on the relief rolls.

and that it is preferable to direct relief for those considered employable. The proposed Byrnes bill provided for the grouping of all construction work done by the WPA, PWA, and CCC under one government department or agency, and for the extension of Social Security jurisdiction over the handicapped, etc., and a more comprehensive system of unemployment compensation. This plan omitted all non-construction activities of WPA, such as the white collar projects in art, music, historical records, etc. Money was to be granted to the states for construction projects on the basis of a formula which took into account population and unemployment. This particular bill has not gone through as proposed, but the new relief bill provides for the combination of WPA and PWA under one agency and for some white collar projects. The bill also provides for rechecking the rolls every six months and for a greater number of hours' work per month for approximately the same wages.[24]

It is interesting, however, that the Byrnes Committee came to the conclusion that work relief should be handled by the federal government rather than by the states. Many of the critics of the WPA have insisted that work relief would have been much better handled by the states and should be returned to their control at the earliest possible moment. Their main argument lies in the greater familiarity with local conditions which the state and local administrations have. They claim also that federal administration is too standardized, too political, and too inefficient. I see no reason to suppose that state administration is, *per se*, any more efficient or less political than the federal. In fact, under the FERA, in which the federal government had supervisory powers only and the states were, with six exceptions, in control of work relief, there is considerable evidence on the inefficiency of state and local organiza-

[24] This provision called forth strikes of WPA workers all over the country in the summer of 1939, when the Relief Act was put into effect.

tions.[25] As for politics, there unfortunately seems to be little difference between the state and federal variety. If anything, federal politics may be less petty and local. The same argument as to the importance of local knowledge of local conditions has been used in Massachusetts in opposition to more direct state control of local welfare boards. There is no doubt that knowledge of local conditions is essential, but it is equally important to have some outside agency set up general standards of administration and relief, and to have some outside agency, not concerned with local issues, political or otherwise, determine broad policy. Unemployment is not a local problem. It is of national concern and can only be handled effectively and fairly by some central organization. At the same time, local conditions vary and must also be taken into account. The WPA has attempted to do this by using local welfare agencies as referral agencies for work relief applicants, by insisting that projects be initiated by the towns and cities concerned, and by varying the security wage with regional wage conditions, for example. Some nice balance must be struck in utilizing federal, state, and local administrations and facilities to the best advantage. But unless there is some federal control, the relief situation may well become chaotic under present economic circumstances.

Far less criticism has been heard of local administration of relief than of federal. In the recent controversy concerning the reorganization of relief many voices have been heard to proclaim that if relief were only returned to state and local governments, maladministration would practically disappear. In Massachusetts, however, there is dissatisfaction with the local administration of relief among some informed persons and even some charges that the use of local individuals or public

[25] The only way in which such maladministration can be controlled under a grant-in-aid system is by withholding funds, and that works hardship on those who need relief, for administrative defects which are in no way their fault.

welfare boards as referral agencies for WPA is undesirable because of local politics.[26] The *Fortune* investigators of 1937 came to the conclusion that in the localities they studied, local governments had made a far worse job of administering direct relief than the FERA, with the exception of Baltimore. *Fortune* also concluded that the administration of work relief by the WPA was, contrary to public opinion, very efficient. They state: — "This impartial and wholly unbiased survey gave strongest support to the feeling that the *machinery* (as opposed to the laborer cared for) of the damned and despised WPA functions with an efficiency of which any industrialist would be proud." [27] My own investigation, since it was not primarily administrative, does not enable me to say whether such an extreme statement is accurate. I can say, however, that many of the records which I examined gave evidence of careful investigation on the part of state and federal administrations. In some cases, the investigation was too long delayed; in others it appeared to be very prompt.

Efficiency of administration will depend largely on the individuals in charge, whether it be local, state, or federal. It is too much to hope that politics will be "taken out of relief" entirely but it should be minimized. I should expect that there would be a greater chance of securing disinterested administrators in a federal system. But if administrative efficiency were equal, unemployment and relief is still a national rather than a local problem. Without some federal control of standards and finances there is no way of insuring equality of treatment of the unemployed all over the country. Financial resources vary with states and within states. Paul Edwards,

[26] Mrs. Armstrong gives a vivid account of the difficulties of local politics which, in Michigan, were in the hands of county officials. Her experience was that local politics were far worse than state politics under the FERA, and that county officials fought state or federal control of relief at every step. L. V. Armstrong, *op. cit.*

[27] *Op cit.*, November 1937.

Acting Administrator of the Massachusetts WPA in 1936, gave some very interesting figures as to the uneven increases in local taxes which would have been required to handle relief locally, if the federal government had not stepped in. In some towns where unemployment was not much of a problem, local taxes would not have risen greatly; but in industrial towns with a great many unemployed relief simply could not have been given adequately if local finances had had to carry the burden.[28] Aside from the financial aspects, rehabilitation of the unemployed cannot be carried on entirely within state or local boundaries. The existence of depressed areas, of technological unemployment, necessitates a radical transfer of employable persons either from one region to another or from one industry to another. Many work relief projects themselves transcend state boundaries.

The greater cost of work relief as compared with direct relief has been mentioned. There are many who believe that work relief is not worth this greater expenditure and advocate a return to direct relief for all the unemployed. As a result of his investigation Lester is very cautious about recommending work relief as a solution to unemployment. He believes that the burden of proof is on the adherent of work relief in any particular situation. He also considers that certain economic assumptions commonly made by those in favor of work relief are incorrect, namely, that work relief projects can be "non-competitive" with private industry; that work relief wages need not affect normal industrial wage rates; that the use of the unemployed will save the community "considerable ultimate expense"; that such work will leave the worker as well if not better able to do his regular work than before he went on relief.[29] Unless exceptionally well managed, Lester thinks

[28] *Report of the Proceedings of the Statewide Coordination Meeting of Federal Agencies Operating in Massachusetts*, April 23, 1936.

[29] Lester, *op. cit.*, Summary and Conclusions.

that relief work may be detrimental to the unemployed. If work relief is to be continued Lester advises that projects should be selected which will raise the community's standard of living and which are more like normal work. He also recommends that the production and distribution of goods needed by those on relief be carried on. A good deal has been done on those lines by the WPA and the Federal Surplus Commodities Corporation in recent years.

Early in the depression three members of the Russell Sage Foundation undertook to survey emergency work relief.[30] They had at that time no concept of a nationally administered program of work relief and examined the programs put into effect by cities and counties throughout the country. They state that "work relief is certainly no solution for the problem of *unemployment*; it remains to determine how effective it may become in offering a solution for some of the problems of *unemployed individuals*." [31] They recommend that work relief should be voluntary and assume that the best of the unemployed will choose it. All the rest should be given direct relief. We have seen that voluntary work relief worked poorly in New Jersey and has not been very effective when used by local towns in Massachusetts. It seems dubious that it could have become an effective program for millions of unemployed.

It is true that work relief is not a solution of unemployment. At its best it is an expedient for providing work, useful both to the individual and the community, for those who are temporarily out of work in private industry. If the economic system functioned perfectly, work relief would not be needed. A real solution would involve the elimination of business cycles, of seasonal fluctuations in employment at the very least. Plans to insure an annual wage, methods of eliminating seasonal

[30] Colcord, J. C., Koplovitz, W. C., Kurtz, R. H., *Emergency Work Relief*, Russell Sage Foundation, 1932.

[31] *Idem*, p. 250.

unemployment which a few industrial firms have instituted, are all means of attacking the bases of unemployment. Technological unemployment necessitates the transfer of displaced workers into other types of work. A system of unemployment exchanges is one method of attempting to secure greater mobility in labor. The system of unemployment services set up by the Wagner-Peyser Act proceeds in this direction.

Since the problem of unemployment is one of the fundamental difficulties of the economic system, it does not seem probable that it will be solved easily or quickly. In the meantime the fact of unemployment and its results must somehow be met. Work relief is one way of taking care of the employable portion of those out of work and can be made effective, as the experience of Sweden shows. It can only be used, however, in conjunction with other forms of public assistance, as it should be limited to those who can work efficiently. With the inauguration of a program of social insurance, including unemployment compensation, under the Social Security Board, the United States is beginning to put into effect a coordinated scheme for dealing with all phases of unemployment. For the able-bodied unemployed, unemployment compensation will take care of short-period loss of work, or the first few weeks of long-continued unemployment. After that recourse must be had to relief of some sort, either direct or work relief.

The FERA and the WPA were the answer to an emergency situation, in which thousands of people, hitherto self-sustaining members of the wage-earning and salary-earning class, found themselves out of work, with their resources either entirely gone or rapidly disappearing. On the whole, those federal work relief organizations were a good answer to the emergency. Now, however, the emergency, if not over, has changed in character. Work relief must be effectively planned and taken out of politics. Administrative efficiency should be improved. Projects should be planned well in advance of the next crisis.

They should be carefully selected for their value to the community and to the country. There are many public improvements which town, city, and state governments cannot afford out of their regular budgets, which could be undertaken by the Federal Works Agency in periods of unemployment. There are certain types of projects, such as flood control, which affect a number of states, and can only be satisfactorily handled by the federal government. The difficulty lies in introducing sufficient elasticity into such a public works program so that public works may expand and contract with unemployment. Both short-time and long-time projects would be necessary for that and very careful administration of them. The idea of dovetailing employment in public works inversely with private employment is not new, and it has been tried in other countries.[32] Such programs have usually been insufficiently well planned in advance, with resulting waste and inefficiency.

The suggestion has been made that such a public works program should not be handled as work relief, that is, that eligibility for relief based on statement of family need should not be required of applicants for work. Employees would presumably be selected only on the basis of their ability to do the work and none of the social stigma attached to relief would fall upon them. In many ways this seems very desirable.

[32] For a detailed summary of methods of handling unemployment in other countries, see *Aiding the Unemployed*, by Hertha Kraus, a study made for the Temporary Emergency Relief Administration of New York, published in 1935. All the various systems used may be roughly divided into social insurance and relief (either direct or work relief). Social insurance, especially unemployment insurance, has been the most popular, as being to some extent a method of self-help, and one involving no relief stigma. In any long depression, however, such insurance has had to be supplemented by relief by most countries, and direct relief is most usual. Work relief has and is being used in some countries but is not ordinarily well planned in advance. Sweden is one of the few countries with a well planned public works program which is coordinated with fluctuations in employment.

Selection of workers on the basis of family need is not the best method of securing the most efficient workers. Deterioration of morale and skill should be less under such a system. It is necessary to set up some means, however, whereby such a system would really benefit the unemployed and not simply mean the transfer of employees from private employment to the public works program. Under the present philosophy of work relief, the aim is to return the workers to private industry as soon as possible. If that philosophy is to continue, some means must be found of making employment on public works less attractive than that in private industry. A wage differential may be the answer, or the same wage rate as in private industry but with less total wages. Under the present relief bill hourly rates have been reduced by increasing hours to be worked, with resulting protests from organized labor. The Committee of Mayors is strongly opposed to the abolition of the family need criterion, as evidenced by their letter to the Byrnes Committee.[33] Their chief objection lies in the cost of such a program unless it is restricted to those who really need it.

This brief summary of the various aspects of the work relief question will, it is hoped, make evident how complicated a problem it is and how wide are its ramifications. It is difficult to see the problem as a whole, both because of the lack of factual data, the recency of the experience in this country, and the emotional factors involved. It is too often forgotten that judgments cannot be made on the basis of a few instances. That the general public should judge the work relief program by a few projects or a few stories heard is perhaps to be expected but that such judgments should be carried over into the testimony of experts is surprising. The two sets of hearings before the Byrnes Committee are full of individual instances related by the experts as proof of their points. Such instances

[33] See Hearings, *op. cit.*, p. 328.

may be valuable as illustrations but one must be very careful in using them as a basis to judge the whole system.

Whatever is to be done about it, we have on our hands a number of unemployment victims, some of whom may never be re-employed in private industry again. Most of these unemployed were really victims of economic circumstances, who applied for relief of any kind only as a last resort. They cannot be allowed to starve — not under our present social philosophy. They are not paupers and should not be treated as such. Their skill and self-respect should be preserved. It is difficult to see how this can be done by direct relief, with its greater stigma, its less adequate maintenance, its dole based entirely on need. The greater monetary cost of work relief must be balanced against the loss which would result from any system which permitted the unemployed to sink irretrievably into the chronic relief class. Critics of work relief contend that this has happened with work relief, but their criticism is aimed at the administration of the present program rather than at the principle of work relief itself. Congress has maintained on the whole that work relief is desirable for employables but that it must be more efficiently administered.

Conclusion

A brief summary of conclusions in rather more definite form may be of some use at this point to those concerned with the relief problem. One cannot go through a mass of data such as those forming the basis of this investigation without coming to some quite definite conclusions. Qualifications, contradictory evidence, and so on, have received considerable attention throughout the book, and must not be neglected. Here, however, they will not be restated.

Unlike Lester, I have emerged from this study with a positive opinion in favor of work relief. It seems to me desirable that the able-bodied unemployed should be given work and not forced to depend upon public welfare or other forms of direct relief for the maintenance of themselves or their families. The undesirable aspects of work relief as it has actually existed in this country appear to be the result of administrative defects rather than inherent in work relief itself.

As to the system by which work for the unemployed should be carried out, it seems clear to me that it should be a federally controlled system, with cooperation from state and local agencies. I do not believe that a nation-wide problem such as unemployment can be successfully handled by regional agencies. There should be direct federal control of the administration, of the personnel, of the selection of projects, and federal standards should be set up and maintained. Of course, local sources of information, local personnel, local organizations should be utilized as much as possible, and the federal system should be sufficiently flexible to take advantage of their assistance. From the financial end, it is desirable for localities to make some contribution, and for federal funds to be allocated with some regard for the extent of unemployment and the economic resources of the regions concerned. The original Byrnes bill proposed to accomplish this purpose through a formula based on unemployment and population figures.

Two alternatives deserve particular consideration as far as the work to be provided for the unemployed is concerned. The first would entail a system of public work which would expand at periods when private industry was unable to give sufficient employment and contract at other periods, and from which the stigma of relief would be removed. Public employment would take the place of private employment in periods of depression. The only requirement for eligibility as far as a worker is concerned would be unemployment, a good occupational record, and ability to do the work. I am not unaware of the difficulties of such a program but I should like to see it tried. To some extent the PWA has done this for heavy construction work, but the program I have in mind would be much more extensive and would include all kinds of work: white collar projects, heavy and light construction, — anything which could be economically and socially justified at the periods when it was needed. Such a program would necessitate very careful planning in advance, with both long time and short time projects, extremely efficient management, and a far better liaison between the government and private industry than now exists. If the criterion of employability were strictly adhered to, without reference to individual and family need, a great many of those who have been included in the ERA and WPA programs would undoubtedly be excluded. A larger direct relief program would be necessary at the same time. The Mayors Committee has objected to the elimination of the means' test on grounds of cost. Possibly the increased cost of such a program for the cream of work relief applicants would be balanced by the lesser cost of the direct relief maintenance of the remainder. The advantage of such a program would lie in the removal of the relief stigma for those who are really employable, the provision of work for them which would be comparable in all respects to that which they had had before (including wages, hours of work, efficiency of management etc.) except that it would be run by the government instead of private industry. Maintenance of morale and skill should be far more successful than under a system such as the WPA. One of the distinct disadvantages of such a system, in addition to questions of cost and administration, lies in its condemnation of those on the margin of employment to direct relief. Yet the question may well be asked whether it is not better to do a really good job for those who are definitely employable than a half way job for a more inclusive group.

The other alternative is the one which has been selected by those who have put into effect the work relief program in the United States, namely, a system of work relief which takes in a wide range of employables, whose eligibility depends upon family need. Employability, although of increasing importance under the WPA, has been secondary to the criterion of need. If this system is to be continued, and there is every indication that it will be, emphasis on employability should be increased and the means test should be made more effective. That this is the attitude of Congress is attested by certain provisions in the new relief bill which call for re-checking the work relief rolls every six months and for separating from the rolls every eighteen months those who have been on work relief continuously for that period. Since such a system is a relief system and its avowed purpose is to provide work which will enable the unemployed to maintain a certain minimum level of living until they can re-enter private industry, marked effort ought to be made to see that those on work relief canvass all private employment opportunities. There should be no inducement for them to remain on relief if there are jobs available. Relief wages should therefore be determined in relation to the minimum level of living for the region rather than by industrial wage standards. This is a difficult question and there are arguments on both sides. I am inclined to think, however, that there should be some differential in wages between the industrial and relief work rates, in favor of the industrial rates. Again, Congress has adopted this view by extending the hours to be worked by those on WPA so that local rates, either union or non-union as the case may be, are now not ordinarily met by the WPA rates.

Cooperation between the National Employment Service and the WPA should be made more effective. Information as to jobs which do exist should be readily available to relief workers. Administrative procedure should be such that there are no technical difficulties in the way of transferring workers from the work relief rolls to private industry.

A more efficient administration of work relief and better

selected and better planned work relief projects would probably assist in dissipating the prejudice of private employers against those on work relief. The question of age, however, cannot be so easily disposed of. If private industry refuses to re-employ those above a certain age and if these workers are employable, apart from the question of age, the government will have to provide work for them. I do not think that they should be forced upon public welfare if they are able to perform useful work. They will form the basis of a permanent work relief program which must expand to take in other age groups in time of depression.

I am heartily in favor of abandoning any make-work aspects of work relief. There are plenty of jobs to be done which are really needed. Although those which have not been done and perhaps could not be done by industry and local governments should be given preference, the idea that all work relief projects must be non-competitive with private industry should be abolished. If the work relief program is economically justifiable it probably will be competitive in this sense, and it has been found that there has been such competition. I agree with Lester that it is practically inevitable.

Projects should be conducted in the most efficient manner. Labor should not be given preference over machines if this means a less efficient job. Projects may be selected which legitimately call for more labor than machinery, but to attempt to conduct large construction and engineering projects by hand, when any ordinary contractor would use machinery, seems frankly ridiculous.

The work relief system as set up in this country was the answer to an emergency situation. On the whole it has functioned adequately. A more coordinated, more flexible, and better planned system is now necessary in order to take care of the permanent residue of work relief applicants and to handle the able-bodied unemployed in future depressions.

The 1939 relief act, which set up the Federal Works Agency, has made some advance in that direction, particularly towards greater administrative efficiency. It is doubtful, however, if the decrease of administrative and research staffs and the exclusion of many white collar projects are desirable. Nevertheless, the Federal Works Agency has the opportunity to develop a really efficient system of federal work relief, which will be part of the general program of alleviating the effects of widespread unemployment.

The opinion that the continuance of work relief is desirable must be based on the assumption that applicants for work relief are employable, and that they became unemployed as a result of economic and social forces beyond their control. That this is true of a great many of the work relief applicants in the last few years, probably a majority of them, seems to me to be indicated not only by the Massachusetts data which form the basis of this study, but by the scattered evidence on the nature of work relief applicants in other states. These workers, who may be found in all occupational classes but who are more concentrated in the ordinary working classes, are able to support themselves in times of prosperity but cannot withstand long periods of unemployment. The provision of work relief is not a solution of their problem but an expedient which will be necessary until cyclical and technological unemployment can be controlled. It does not seem probable that this will happen in the near future. Some means of maintaining these unemployed in periods of industrial crisis will be essential for some time to come. At present work relief seems to be the best answer.

APPENDIX A

STATISTICAL METHOD

APPENDIX A: STATISTICAL METHOD

Selection of Sample

The 2180 active relief cases were taken from records in the active file in the district office of the Works Progress Administration in Cambridge (later transferred to Boston while the copying was in progress). The twenty towns and cities included in the sample had been selected in advance to represent economic conditions in Massachusetts. The records used were the ERA application blank (form 15A) and the Home Visit Report (form 25A). The latter was given preference wherever possible as being more accurate. It was the opinion of the administrative staff and my own opinion, as a result of inspection of both types of records, that the Home Visit Report was more likely to give a correct picture of family circumstances. In some cases, 25A was lacking and 15A had to be used. When both forms were present both were copied and it was later decided which information was more accurate.

The sample was further restricted by using only those on the A list who had applied for ERA work in 1935. In the smaller towns and cities all such cases for which there were records were used. In Cambridge, Somerville, and New Bedford where there were over 2000 active cases for each city at the time, every other letter of the alphabet was used, beginning with A.

The sample therefore consists of work relief cases which had applied for ERA and been declared eligible in 1935. They had been transferred to WPA and were in the active file in 1937 when the records were copied. The chances are that they had been continuously on and off work relief from 1935 through 1937.

Since the above sample tends to represent work relief cases

continuing on the rolls over several years, it was decided to take another sample representative of cases which had been separated from work relief within this period. These cases were taken from the inactive work relief file during 1938 (the records were kept at the Army Base in Boston). Only those cases which had applied for ERA in 1935, and had been removed from or left work relief subsequently were utilized. The same rules for the selection of the cases as for the previous sample were used for four cities and the Small Town group: Newton, New Bedford, Framingham, Somerville, and the Small Towns. The same information was collected for both samples, and, in addition, all data given in the case file on the reason why the case was removed from work relief were secured. This information was not always given, since form 403, the official dismissal slip, was sometimes not filed with the case. However, in about 70 per cent of the cases, it was possible to secure the reason for leaving relief and the means of support between the original loss of job and application for ERA work. This second sample consisted of 408 cases.

Accuracy of Records

It was apparent from the records themselves that the care with which they had been kept varied from city to city. The best records were those of Newton, Brookline, and Somerville; those of Cambridge, Framingham, and Hudson were fairly well kept; and the others showed considerable evidence of carelessness. This was particularly true of form 15A which was ordinarily filled out in the ERA offices from information given by the applicant in person. One of the officials on the district staff estimated that approximately one-third of the applicants were or tried to be deliberately dishonest in stating their income, expenditure, debts and so on. Since form 25A was the report of the ERA social worker sent to check the information given by the applicant, it was obviously more accurate and it was used for this study in preference to 15A.

Such records as these are never precise and the fact that they were kept by an administrative staff working under great pressure means a somewhat greater possibility of inaccuracy. Only an approximate validity can be expected from them but, if used with care, they are of great value. The results, checked against information secured by personal interview in connection with my study of Cambridge ERA families, with Professor Zimmerman's investigation of five rural towns, and with information secured from the WPA Division of Research, indicate that they can be relied upon in rough fashion. The schedules were edited very carefully and whenever there was any doubt as to the reasonableness of the information, that case was discarded.

Nature of data secured

1. Occupation of economic head of case
2. Citizenship
3. Education (not given in many instances)
4. Size of family (lodgers and members of family away from home not included)
5. Union membership (not given in many instances)
6. Age (for New Bedford only in active case sample; for all cases in cancelled case sample)
7. Sex of economic head of case
8. Ownership of property, including real estate, cash (readily marketable) securities, insurance, automobile and other property
9. Debts or liabilities, including taxes owed, mortgages, and other obligations (usually specified)
10. Total income per family for week following application, including income from
    a. earnings from private employment of any member of family

b. rentals (used only if paid, and not in arrears)
c. lodgers
d. ERA
e. Public welfare (food and fuel donations used only if cash equivalent given)
f. Other relief, including soldier's relief, old age pensions, CCC wage etc.
g. All other sources

11. Total expenditure per family for week following application, including
a. Rent (carrying charges on house used if home owned)
b. Food (tended to be overestimated)
c. Light
d. Heat
e. Clothing
f. Debts (not usually included)
g. Carfare
h. Insurance
i. Miscellaneous

In tabulating this information, rent, light, and heat were lumped under *House*; carfare, debts, and, occasionally, medical, telephone, and laundry were grouped under *Other*.

The weekly expenditure information was supposed to refer to the *actual* expenditure of the family. In many instances it was apparent that the expenditure data referred to the ERA standard budget set up for the family. In Newton the actual expenditures and the standard budget were both given. The former were used. In Somerville, Framingham, and Brookline it seemed evident that the attempt was made to estimate actual family expenditures. But in the other towns and cities the standard budget was recorded, except for rent and insurance. Thus, the expenditure data are very dubious as an actual record of what the family spent. They have been used for this purpose only in the case of Newton, Framingham, Somerville, and Brookline and even here with many reservations.

12. Other information. Some figures on the assessed value of homes owned, mortgages, and value of insurance were given, but they were so scattered, and so obviously guesses on the part of interviewer or applicant, that they were not used at all.

Statistical Method

The data were tabulated and classified and the very simplest statistical methods used. The arithmetic mean was used throughout, except in the case of income, for which the median was computed as well. In the case of income, it was felt that the mean was a better measure of average income than the median inasmuch as the median tended to reflect only the prevalent ERA wage and to underrepresent the extremes which were affected by other sources of income. Frequency distributions were used to indicate the grouping of the cases with respect to income and the representative nature of the average. Percentage distributions were utilized in many instances to show the comparative distribution of the cases with respect to various characteristics. Probable errors and standard deviations were not calculated, as it was felt that the data were too inaccurate statistically to warrant the time and money involved in such computations.

Most of the methods used and the validity of the averages and percentages calculated are discussed in the text as they come up. The principal tables are reproduced in Appendix B. Further details as to the data and the methods used may be secured on application to the author.

APPENDIX B

STATISTICAL TABLES

TABLE 1

Massachusetts Relief Case Load

Direct Relief — May 1934–May 1938
ERA — May 1934–November 1935
WPA — December 1935–July 1939

	Direct Relief	Number of Cases Work Relief	Direct Relief & ERA
1934			
May	90,286	64,238	8,038
June	81,930	75,002	7,324
July	80,680	78,285	6,759
August	80,526	79,238	7,056
September	84,230	85,499	7,969
October	85,686	89,689	8,988
November	90,277	91,321	11,875
December	95,898	99,613	14,727
1935			
January	103,547	101,346	19,213
February	102,222	108,327	21,732
March	98,871	116,084	22,411
April	91,807	119,115	22,173
May	86,648	117,648	14,080
June	81,665	116,275	14,361
July	79,311	115,022	12,965
August	85,797	110,119	18,969
September	80,941	103,693	15,618
October	79,789	100,997 †	20,641
November	85,194	86,731 †	20,222
December	93,239	109,833 †	7,245
1936			
January	88,306	107,259	
February	82,428	114,660	
March	77,223	119,164	
April	67,909	119,349	
May	60,238	112,400	
June	64,946	102,242	
July	63,196	97,829	
August	61,357	95,067	
September	59,068	103,202	
*October	55,436	110,251	
November	57,069	109,969	
December	61,849	95,861	

*† For these footnotes, see p. 246.

Note: The Direct Relief and ERA figures were taken from data at the Massachusetts WPA office. The figures for WPA were supplied by Mr. C. O. Littlefield, Assistant Director. They do not include those working on Federal Agency Projects prior to July 1937.

TABLE 1 (*continued*)

	Direct Relief	Number of Cases Work Relief	Direct Relief & ERA
1937			
January	65,580	92,360	
February	65,120	91,419	
March	62,843	90,407	
April	57,787	89,014	
May	51,938	88,849	
June	51,283	75,252	
July	54,368	59,780	
August	56,115	60,896	
September	57,349	61,422	
October	59,511	61,332	
November	69,250	62,955	
December	81,660	77,419	
1938			
January	88,077	83,134	
February	85,010	86,828	
March	83,779	108,313	
April	78,046	112,159	
May	72,600	112,826	
June		119,080	
July		121,258	
August		128,538	
September		130,008	
October		133,039	
November		135,179	
December		129,786	
1939			
January		127,011	
February		125,834	
March		128,401	
April		124,146	
May		112,939	
June		106,265	
July		104,389	

* Slight change in Direct Relief series.

† During these three months ERA workers were gradually being transferred to the WPA, so that the ERA figures do not give a complete total for those on work relief. The Massachusetts WPA office informs me that it is not possible to get a total of those on ERA and WPA from their records for these months without duplication of cases. By the end of December, however, the transfer had been completed and during the week of December 28, 111,060 workers were on WPA. The December figure used here is the average of the weekly WPA payroll figures.

TABLE 2

Case Load — ERA — By Towns, May 1934–Dec. 1935

	Somerville	Cambridge	New Bedford	Brookline	Newton	Framingham & Ashland	Maynard	Hudson	Small Towns	Total No. of Cases
1934										
May	1025	1534	1873	285	391	293	156	148	252	5957
June	1450	1441	2076	284	632	360	170	176	292	6881
July	1525	1641	2337	279	455	366	181	191	272	7247
August	1649	1656	2251	370	435	447	202	175	289	7474
September	1868	1770	1985	397	492	525	230	233	357	7857
October	2001	1694	1973	477	528	500	232	231	409	8045
November	2016	1741	2204	566	669	538	183	233	488	8638
December	2236	1764	2117	610	688	593	242	225	564	9039
1935										
January	2289	1822	2128	620	659	620	235	225	627	9225
February	2356	1816	2345	637	652	595	233	278	626	9538
March	2754	1799	2342	672	632	611	223	278	646	9957
April	2706	2040	2493	599	630	635	231	313	659	10306
May	2734	2269	2584	594	591	622	206	277	588	10465
June	2636	2324	2724	620	588	586	206	306	573	10563
July	2631	2374	2475	553	582	585	207	312	568	10287
August	2525	2177	2320	542	567	539	194	243	547	9654
September	2487	2085	2274	501	548	569	184	207	492	9347
October	2498	2026	2170	472	533	493	167	201	478	9038
November	2333	1888	1871	417	531	431	127	184	378	8160
December	103	476	728	..	101	32	..	..	26	1466

TABLE 3

Case Load — By Towns; Direct Relief (Public Welfare & Soldiers' Relief Combined)

	Somerville	Cambridge	New Bedford	Brookline	Newton	Framingham & Ashland	Maynard	Hudson	Small Towns	Total No. of Cases
1934										
May	1676	2123	1606	429	682	636	89	131	240	7612
June	1328	1568	1585	415	875	634	57	128	258	6848
July	1373	1502	1559	395	594	562	53	131	252	6421
August	1251	1420	1564	435	566	536	65	129	240	6206
September	1189	1495	2037	342	495	504	97	145	223	6527
October	1027	1498	1826	416	573	535	126	168	225	6394
November	1048	1605	1737	397	655	564	115	204	217	6542
December	1052	1800	1798	384	715	712	100	205	263	7029
1935										
January	1079	2656	1993	383	718	649	95	225	317	8115
February	1106	2806	2009	435	703	669	108	224	311	8371
March	1136	2700	1942	468	744	633	109	250	286	8268
April	963	2065	1915	466	687	602	103	249	267	7317
May	979	1635	2008	477	610	458	95	234	207	6703
June	998	1629	1974	452	583	423	87	156	191	6493
July	1096	1620	1881	435	569	397	77	133	190	6398
August	1927	3121	2013	470	633	394	71	97	183	8909
September	869	1816	1965	431	570	398	75	105	189	6418
October	1346	3320	1893	497	644	391	80	120	189	8480
November	1455	3452	1894	504	708	314	90	144	219	8780
December	1625	3785	1584	445	840	316	77	134	262	9068
1936										
January	1746	2840	1034	444	849	346	75	131	249	7714
February	1419	3802	1110	481	952	347	70	187	236	8604
March	1268	3568	1117	525	927	293	70	250	236	8254
April	1170	3238	1099	488	864	220	71	270	187	7607
May	1065	2529	1123	385	808	251	63	272	172	6668
June	1271	1676	1236	349	510	312	64	279	145	6142
*July	1411	2169	1695	479	660	299	69	271	215	7268
August	1489	2212	1729	449	671	295	75	242	205	7367
September	1483	2064	1644	424	706	255	75	214	185	7050
October	1477	1968	1593	405	694	230	78	196	180	6821
November	1341	2685	1608	429	710	256	85	187	208	7509
December	1389	2744	1707	489	807	321	87	211	244	7999
1937										
January	1497	2894	1800	528	861	396	86	223	254	8539
February	1593	2949	1763	504	883	372	85	211	258	8618
March	1533	2965	1531	481	911	369	82	189	261	8322
April	1441	2396	1411	464	826	323	74	172	214	7321
May	1381	1980	1370	430	698	250	71	147	181	6508

* From this point "unemployables" (not previously included in Direct Relief) are included.

TABLE 4

Active Cases

OCCUPATIONS (Per cent of Total)

Occupation	Somerville	Cambridge	New Bedford	Brookline	Newton	Framingham [1]	Maynard	Hudson	Small Towns [2]	Total
No. of cases	502	306	497	122	241	237	39	131	146	2221
White collar	33.0	17.6	16.7	39.4	23.6	18.6	10.5	11.4	13.0	22.0
Professional	7.0	2.6	3.2	4.9	2.9	1.3	..	1.5	2.0	3.6
Proprietors	4.8	4.9	3.2	4.1	8.3	3.4	..	3.8	.7	4.2
Office workers	12.9	5.9	6.3	19.7	6.6	5.9	8.0	2.3	5.5	8.2
Salesmen	8.3	4.2	4.0	10.7	5.8	8.0	2.5	3.8	4.8	6.0
Skilled	21.7	19.6	18.1	8.2	31.1	28.7	23.0	15.3	17.1	21.0
Semi-skilled	20.1	24.5	36.2	27.1	15.8	23.6	30.7	55.7	23.3	27.1
Unskilled	11.3	22.8	13.5	8.2	21.2	15.2	17.9	6.9	15.1	14.8
Domestic	4.8	6.5	6.3	6.5	1.2	2.9	2.6	1.5	10.3	5.0
Farm	1.0	.7	1.0	4.1	3.7	2.9	7.7	5.3	11.6	2.7
Inexperienced	7.2	4.9	7.0	6.5	3.3	4.6	7.7	3.0	8.2	4.5
Unknown	.8	3.2	1.2	..	..	3.4	..	.8	1.4	1.4

[1] Includes 11 Ashland cases.
[2] Eleven rural and residential towns.

TABLE 5

Cancelled Cases

SOURCE OF SUPPORT BETWEEN LOSS OF JOB AND CERTIFICATION FOR ERA

Towns	No. of Sources *	Savings	Insurance & Loans	Friends & Relatives	Credit	Public Welfare	Other Relief Agencies	Went on ERA at once	Odd Jobs Temporary Work
New Bedford	32	2	..	11	3	8	3	2	3
Newton	95	17	7	18	..	12	12	4	25
Framingham	23	2	1	4	1	12	1	..	2
Somerville	113	24	7	25	..	23	9	3	22
Small Towns	27	..	..	2	..	1	4	12	8
Total	290	45	15	60	4	56	29	21	60
Per cent	..	15.5	5.2	20.7	1.4	19.3	10.0	7.2	20.7

* The number of sources is not equal to the number of cases (279) since some families received support from more than one source.

TABLE 6

Active Cases

MEAN INCOME, EXPENDITURE, AND DEBTS, BY SOURCES, TOWNS, AND SIZE OF FAMILY

No. of Cases	Towns	Average Size of Family	Total Weekly Income	Total Weekly Expenditure	Difference	Total Debts	SOURCES OF INCOME: Private Employment	Rents	Lodgers and Boarders	ERA	Public Welfare	Other Relief	Other Income
492	Somerville	3.9	$14.27	$19.11	$−4.84	$303.92	$1.33	$.90	$.09	$11.07	$.28	$.34	$.26
303	Cambridge	4.9	12.81	16.79	−3.98	116.31	1.45	.41	.10	9.88	.52	.43	.02
494	New Bedford	4.2	11.81	16.24	−4.43	257.49	.70	.18	.01	9.95	.38	.51	.08
120	Brookline	3.1	11.32	15.13	−3.81	133.42	2.05	.17	.44	7.30	.98	.14	.23
235	Newton	5.0	18.11	20.34	−2.23	392.66	2.80	.58	.36	12.95	.83	.52	.08
230	Framingham & Ashland	4.8	15.77	17.79	−2.02	201.51	1.55	.35	.55	11.63	.04	.40	1.25
34	Maynard	3.1	12.89	12.58	.31	162.29	.53	.34	..	11.23	.16	.63	..
128	Hudson	4.0	12.81	19.05	−6.24	87.77	1.93	.12	.35	9.63	.36	.32	.10
144	Small Towns	3.9	9.62	15.75	−6.13	165.69	.69	.14	.27	7.65	.30	.34	.23
	Total	4.3	$13.50	$17.58	$−4.08	$232.67	$1.41	$.43	$.19	$10.40	$.41	$.41	$.25

MEANS BY SIZE OF FAMILY GROUPS

No. of Cases	Size of Family	Total Weekly Income	Total Weekly Expenditure	Difference	Total Debts	Private Employment	Rents	Lodgers and Boarders	ERA	Public Welfare	Other Relief	Other Income
165	One in family	$ 7.81	$ 9.76	$−1.95	$149.26	$ .06	$.06	$.06	$ 7.15	$.33	$.15	..
341	Two in family	10.13	13.40	−3.27	209.92	.40	.55	.16	8.17	.38	.24	$.23
448	Three in family	12.45	15.95	−3.50	225.14	.63	.39	.20	10.31	.28	.28	.36
383	Four in family	13.92	17.75	−3.83	236.90	1.43	.49	.20	10.95	.27	.43	.15
307	Five in family	14.74	19.06	−4.32	269.48	1.52	.50	.17	11.36	.47	.45	.28
181	Six in family	15.82	20.61	−4.79	260.81	2.19	.56	.27	11.50	.51	.35	.44
139	Seven in family	16.57	22.06	−5.49	255.96	3.19	.38	.24	11.49	.44	.61	.22
97	Eight in family	17.58	23.55	−5.97	228.33	2.68	.23	.35	12.85	.65	.72	.10
119	Nine in family or more	20.11	27.54	−7.43	266.79	4.42	.40	.22	12.43	1.06	1.13	.45

		EXPENDITURES					DEBTS								
No. of Cases	Towns	House	Food	Clothing	Insurance	Other	Food	Rent	Taxes	Personal Loans	Indus. Loans	Furniture	Medical	Unspecified	Mortgage
492	Somerville	$7.76	$8.51	$1.54	$.39	$.91	$11.92	$69.69	$23.40	$96.21	$ 9.31	$15.61	$41.99	$26.74	$ 9.05
303	Cambridge	6.25	8.88	.66	.45	.56	7.05	41.37	7.80	16.96	4.15	13.06	15.89	9.64	.39
494	New Bedford	4.79	7.51	2.12	..	1.82	21.00	34.78	4.68	17.68	3.95	11.70	16.58	146.45	.67
120	Brookline	7.17	7.01	.17	.30	.49	5.32	26.79	2.58	34.21	4.29	4.29	9.85	41.93	4.17
235	Newton	8.82	9.04	1.16	.55	.76	48.47	86.72	33.16	67.64	58.96	4.86	32.27	26.93	33.66
230	Framingham & Ashland	6.71	8.47	1.58	.53	.50	28.12	39.11	30.15	11.28	17.37	14.94	31.24	29.30	...
34	Maynard	4.46	6.90	.57	.37	.26	.35	2.48	32.53	38.24	.89	...	25.91	61.90	...
128	Hudson	5.78	9.67	2.77	.62	.21	9.26	5.90	5.05	13.48	7.43	5.48	6.71	32.11	2.34
144	Small Towns	5.55	7.01	2.70	.05	.44	18.85	7.35	41.78	10.71	3.46	2.24	25.32	48.46	7.52
	Total	$6.53	$8.25	$1.57	$.33	$.90	$18.71	$45.18	$17.89	$40.50	$12.67	$10.80	$25.23	$54.91	$ 6.74

MEANS BY SIZE OF FAMILY GROUPS

165	One in family	$4.23	$3.85	$ .56	$.10	$1.02	$13.65	$31.70	$ 3.40	$22.12	$ 2.43	$ 1.20	$14.39	$60.37	...
341	Two in family ...	6.17	5.17	.95	.29	.82	10.48	36.74	16.30	47.75	5.11	10.12	22.05	61.26	$ .12
448	Three in family ..	6.61	6.91	1.29	.28	.86	9.83	43.93	14.72	44.37	15.12	10.53	22.26	50.98	13.40
383	Four in family ...	6.86	8.21	1.51	.34	.83	17.03	53.54	16.03	39.74	16.87	13.66	23.72	48.67	7.64
307	Five in family ...	6.83	9.11	1.76	.40	.96	18.58	44.28	21.19	53.85	8.72	12.11	33.53	66.49	10.73
181	Six in family	7.25	10.21	1.83	.40	.93	36.42	44.05	27.56	26.76	28.94	12.32	37.67	43.14	3.95
139	Seven in family ..	6.89	11.38	2.24	.40	1.15	27.50	47.60	31.27	16.75	19.15	13.91	32.53	58.41	8.84
97	Eight in family ..	6.74	13.02	2.53	.33	.91	34.20	59.49	18.07	37.39	5.36	10.87	16.53	44.89	1.53
119	Nine in family or more	6.98	15.56	3.55	.50	.95	38.62	55.40	21.44	50.51	9.76	8.41	23.61	56.23	2.81

TABLE 7

PER CENT OF TOTAL EMPLOYED AND UNEMPLOYED BY AGE *

UNEMPLOYED (as of Jan. 2, 1934)

Years	New Bedford Total Unemployed	New Bedford Temporarily Employed on Gov. Work	Somerville Total Unemployed	Somerville Temporarily Employed on Gov. Work	Cambridge Total Unemployed	Cambridge Temporarily Employed on Gov. Work	Brookline Total Unemployed	Brookline Temporarily Employed on Gov. Work	Newton Total Unemployed	Newton Temporarily Employed on Gov. Work
14–24	33.9%	19.4%	34.5%	17.9%	32.3%	17.2%	31.5%	20.7%	30.2%	18.8%
25–34	18.3	21.9	21.1	24.4	21.9	25.2	25.1	32.9	21.8	25.1
35–44	18.0	29.1	16.8	29.2	17.7	27.3	16.6	21.5	17.3	27.9
45 and over ..	29.6	29.6	29.3	28.5	28.3	30.2	26.7	24.8	30.3	28.2

FULL TIME EMPLOYED

Years	New Bedford	Somerville	Cambridge	Brookline	Newton
14–24	20.9%	18.2%	16.6%	13.2%	13.8%
25–34	25.4	29.2	29.8	26.3	26.1
35–44	24.3	22.6	23.2	24.2	24.9
45 and over	29.3	30.0	30.3	36.2	35.2

* From Massachusetts Census of Unemployment, 1934.

TABLE 8

Active Cases

PROPERTY OWNED (Per cent of Total)

Property	Somer-ville	Cam-bridge	New Bedford	Newton	Brook-line	Framing-ham **	Hudson	Maynard	Small Towns °	Total
No. of cases	502	306	497	241	122	237	131	39	146	2221
Telephone †	2.4	..	..	7.1	..	..	..	..	..	1.3
Home owned	19.5	7.5	11.9	36.9	8.2	25.7	32.0	20.5	47.2	20.7
Home mortgaged *	87.8	91.2	79.6	88.7	90.0	84.0	78.6	87.5	68.1	82.6
Other real estate	.2	..	1.4	.8	..	..	..	..	..	.5
Insurance	32.5	46.1	18.9	53.9	45.1	51.8	52.7	41.0	9.6	36.2
Automobile	2.8	1.0	5.0	12.0	2.5	16.0	11.4	7.7	23.3	7.4
Cash securities	.2	..	.6	.8	..	..	..	..	..	.3
Savings	1.0	2.0	1.2	3.7	1.6	3.8	.8	2.6	4.8	2.1
Other property	..	..	1.2	..	..	.8	..	..	3.4	.6

** Includes 11 cases for Ashland.
° Acton, Concord, Holliston, Hopkinton, Lincoln, Littleton, Sherborn, Stow, Sudbury, Weston, Wayland.
† Not property, but used as indicative of economic status.
* Per cent of homes owned.

TABLE 9

Sources of Income (Active Cases)

(NUMBER)

Sources of Income	Somerville	Cambridge	New Bedford	Brookline	Newton	Framingham	Maynard	Hudson	Small Towns	Total
Total number of cases	492	303	494	120	235	230	34	128	144	2180
Non-supplemented income										
Relief only	316	211	377	72	111	144	27	81	17	1416
ERA only	281	166	303	50	74	130	20	68	60	1152
Other relief	35	45	74	22	37	14	7	13	17	264
Supplemented income										
Relief and non-relief	99	31	43	15	91	53	4	17	18	371
Relief and private employment	41	20	32	10	64	19	2	12	11	211
ERA and private employment	38	18	30	7	62	18	2	11	11	197
Other relief and private employment	3	2	2	3	2	1	0	1	0	14
Relief and other non-relief	58	11	11	5	27	34	2	5	7	160
Private employment only	10	21	11	12	9	7	0	6	5	81
Other non-relief	19	7	11	9	8	9	0	4	4	71
No income	48	33	52	12	16	17	3	20	40	241

(PERCENTAGES OF TOTAL NO. OF CASES)

Sources of Income	Somerville	Cambridge	New Bedford	Brookline	Newton	Framingham	Maynard	Hudson	Small Towns	Total	WPA * March 1936
Total number of cases	100%	100%	100%	100%	100%	100%	100%	100%	100%	100%	100%
Non-supplemented income											
Relief only	64.2	69.6	76.4	60.0	47.2	62.6	79.4	63.2	53.4	65.0	67.0
ERA only	57.1	54.8	61.3	41.7	31.5	56.5	58.8	53.1	41.6	52.8	52.0
Other relief	7.1	14.8	15.0	18.3	15.7	6.1	20.6	10.1	11.8	12.2	15.0
Supplemented income											
Relief and non-relief	20.1	10.2	8.7	12.5	38.7	23.0	11.8	13.3	12.5	17.0	16.0
Relief and private employment	8.3	6.6	6.5	8.3	27.2	8.2	5.9	9.4	7.6	9.7	11.0
ERA and private employment	7.7	5.9	6.1	5.8	26.4	7.8	5.9	8.6	7.6	9.0	8.0
Other relief and private employment	0.6	0.7	0.4	2.5	0.8	0.4	0.0	0.8	0.0	0.7	3.9
Relief and other non-relief	11.8	3.6	2.2	4.2	11.5	14.8	5.9	3.9	4.9	7.3	5.0
Private employment only	2.0	7.0	2.2	10.0	3.9	3.1	0.0	4.7	3.5	3.7	11.0
Other non-relief	3.9	2.3	2.2	7.5	3.4	3.9	0.0	3.2	2.8	3.2	4.0
No income	9.8	10.9	10.5	10.0	6.8	7.4	8.8	15.6	27.8	11.1	2.0

* WPA figures from "Survey of Cases Certified for WPA Employment in 13 Cities," Series IV, No. 2, Division of Social Research, Washington 1937, Table 26, p. 43. The categories are not quite comparable to mine, but are combined as well as possible to correspond. Reference to ERA in my data is, of course, WPA for this study.

TABLE 10

Active Cases

AVERAGE WEEKLY INCOME BY SOURCE

(dollars)

Town	Relief Only		Relief plus Non-relief: Total		Relief plus Non-relief: Relief		Relief plus Non-relief: Supplemented		Private Employment Only		All Sources *	
	Mean	No. Cases	Mean	No. Cases	Mean	No. Cases	Mean	No. Cases	Mean	No. Cases	Mean	No. Cases
Somerville	$13.89	316	$22.53	99	$13.76	99	$ 8.77	99	$15.15	10	$14.27	492
Cambridge	13.53	211	25.00	31	14.45	31	10.55	31	8.52	21	12.81	303
New Bedford	12.73	377	20.15	43	12.87	43	7.28	43	7.71	11	11.81	494
Brookline	11.72	72	18.07	15	11.13	15	6.94	15	14.08	12	11.32	120
Newton	17.83	111	22.94	91	15.14	91	7.79	91	14.97	9	18.11	235
Framingham & Ashland	14.30	144	25.28	53	13.56	53	11.72	53	10.14	7	15.77	230
Maynard	13.14	27	20.88	4	13.50	4	7.38	4	..	..	12.89	34
Hudson	13.57	81	25.30	17	12.97	17	12.33	17	10.33	6	12.81	128
Small Towns	12.30	77	19.03	18	13.67	18	5.36	18	9.90	5	9.62	144
Whole Sample	13.65	1416	22.71	371	13.88	371	8.83	371	11.13	81	13.50	2180
MEDIAN WEEKLY INCOME BY SOURCE												
Somerville	$12.00	316	$22.00	99	$12.00	99	$ 7.00	99	$15.00	10	$13.50	492
Cambridge	12.00	211	23.18	31	12.00	31	10.00	31	6.00	21	12.00	303
New Bedford	12.00	377	20.00	43	12.00	43	6.83	43	8.00	11	12.00	494
Brookline	12.00	72	18.00	15	12.00	15	6.00	15	13.50	12	12.00	120
Newton	17.59	111	22.00	91	12.00	91	6.00	91	10.00	9	18.00	235
Framingham & Ashland	12.00	144	22.45	53	12.00	53	8.00	53	8.00	7	12.00	230
Maynard	12.00	27	20.75	4	12.00	4	8.25	4	..	..	12.00	34
Hudson	12.00	81	22.00	17	12.00	17	9.00	17	7.00	6	12.00	128
Small Towns	12.00	77	17.00	18	12.00	18	5.00	18	4.00	5	12.00	144
Whole Sample	12.00	1416	21.47	371	12.00	371	7.00	371	10.00	81	12.00	2180

* Including "other non-relief only" and "no income."

TABLE 11

ACTIVE CASES

PROPORTION OF INCOME FROM VARIOUS SOURCES

Town	Average Income	Private Employment	Rents	Boarders	Relief: ERA	Relief: Pub. Wel.	Relief: Other	Relief: Total	Misc.	Total
Newton	$18.11	15.5%	3.2%	2.0%	71.4%	4.6%	2.9%	78.9%	.4%	100%
Somerville	14.27	9.3	6.3	.6	77.5	2.0	2.4	81.9	1.8	100%
Framingham	15.77	9.8	2.2	3.5	73.8	.3	2.5	76.6	7.9	100%
Hudson	12.81	15.1	.9	2.7	75.1	2.8	2.5	80.4	.8	100%
Maynard	12.89	4.1	2.6	..	87.2	1.2	4.9	93.3	..	100%
Brookline	11.32	18.1	1.5	3.9	64.4	8.7	1.2	74.3	2.0	100%
Cambridge	12.81	11.3	3.2	.8	77.1	4.1	3.3	84.5	.2	100%
New Bedford	11.81	5.9	1.5	.1	84.2	3.2	4.3	91.7	.7	100%
Small Towns	9.62	7.2	1.5	2.8	79.5	3.1	3.5	86.1	2.4	100%

TABLE 12

ACTIVE CASES

AVERAGE INCOME BY SIZE OF FAMILY AND TOWNS

Size of Family	Newton	Somerville	Framing-ham	Hudson	Maynard	Brookline	Cambridge	New Bedford	Small Towns
One	$ 9.00	$ 8.91	$ 6.18	$ 7.55	$10.63	$ 6.59	$ 4.47	$ 8.70	$ 5.27
Two	7.38	12.90	10.47	7.77	11.16	10.95	6.45	10.28	5.62
Three	14.97	14.00	14.90	13.64	15.62	12.12	10.27	10.44	9.95
Four	18.10	15.00	14.16	13.90	12.30	14.34	11.73	12.79	10.49
Five	19.38	15.53	17.29	13.35	15.60	12.45	13.02	12.36	10.04
Six	18.28	17.41	15.48	15.76	12.00	21.00	14.94	12.93	14.18
Seven	20.39	15.54	22.13	13.93	20.50	19.90	15.19	13.75	14.26
Eight	24.49	16.25	20.88	16.51	...	15.33	14.59	17.02	13.69
Nine & over	26.46	18.68	21.10	24.84	19.30	...	23.32	14.56	18.50

TABLE 13

Active Cases

PROPORTION OF DEBT OWED FOR

Town	Average Debt	Food	Rent	Taxes	Bus. Loans	Ind. Loans	Furniture	Medical	Mortgage	Misc.
Somerville	$303.92	3.9%	22.9%	7.7%	31.7%	3.1%	5.1%	13.8%	3.0%	8.8%
Framingham	201.51	13.9	19.4	15.0	5.6	8.6	7.4	15.5	..	14.5
Hudson	87.77	10.6	6.7	5.8	15.3	8.4	6.2	7.7	2.7	36.6
Maynard	161.41	0.2	1.5	20.2	23.7	..	3.0	13.0	..	38.2
Brookline	133.42	4.0	20.1	1.9	25.7	3.2	3.2	26.8	12.0	3.1
Cambridge	116.31	6.1	35.5	6.7	14.6	3.6	10.2	13.6	.3	8.2
Newton	392.66	12.3	22.1	8.4	17.2	15.0	1.2	8.2	8.6	6.9
Small Towns	165.69	11.4	4.4	25.2	6.5	2.1	1.4	15.3	4.5	29.2
New Bedford	257.49	8.2	13.5	1.8	6.9	1.5	4.5	6.4	.3	56.8

TABLE 14

Average Expenditure by Income Groups

Cambridge 1935 (397 Cases)

PER CENT OF TOTAL EXPENDITURE

Income Class	Cases No.	Food	Cloth-ing	Hous-ing	Tobacco	Recrea-tion	Books	Medical	Travel	Per-sonal Care	Alco-hol	Auto	Other	Sav-ings & Insur-ance
$ 200–399	11	49.6	2.5	38.9	.5	.2	1.6	.1	2.4	.5	..	..	1.6	2.1
400–599	51	43.4	3.4	44.0	1.6	.6	1.1	1.6	1.3	.4	..	..	.8	2.0
600–799	92	43.4	4.0	41.8	2.0	.4	.7	1.5	1.7	.8	.1	..	.6	3.0
800–999	83	47.0	4.8	36.4	1.8	.5	.7	2.7	1.6	.7	..	.3	.6	2.7
1000–1199	75	45.0	5.6	34.3	2.1	.5	.7	3.4	1.8	.8	.2	.5	1.5	3.5
1200–1399	38	44.7	6.4	30.7	2.2	.6	.8	4.0	1.9	.9	.1	1.7	1.3	4.7
1400 & over	47	42.3	6.8	28.2	2.1	.9	.6	4.7	2.3	.7	.3	3.0	1.8	6.1
Average Expenditure						AMOUNT (dollars)								
$ 312	11	152	7	125	2	..	6	..	7	2	..	..	5	7
500	51	217	16	220	8	3	4	8	6	2	..	..	4	10
716	92	311	29	297	15	3	5	11	12	5	1	..	4	22
906	83	426	44	329	16	5	6	25	15	6	..	3	6	25
1081	75	489	61	371	23	5	7	37	19	9	2	6	16	38
1293	38	578	83	395	29	8	10	52	25	11	2	22	17	61
1698	47	712	119	471	37	16	10	87	38	12	6	53	33	103

TABLE 15

SHIPMENTS OF COMMODITIES PURCHASED BY THE FEDERAL SURPLUS COMMODITIES CORPORATION TO THE STATE OF MASSACHUSETTS FOR DISTRIBUTION TO NEEDY PERSONS

OCTOBER 4, 1933 TO DECEMBER 31, 1938

Commodity	Unit	October 4, 1933 to December 31, 1934	Calendar Year 1935	Calendar Year 1936	Calendar Year 1937	Calendar Year 1938
Canned Beef	Pounds	4,321,944	14,188,829	1,985,049	...	...
Fresh Beef	Pounds	12,513	...	...	...	...
Canned Mutton	Pounds	...	695,353	...	...	...
Salt Pork	Pounds	2,349,217	...	...	...	...
Smoked Pork	Pounds	3,503,673	...	...	...	...
Canned Veal	Pounds	...	693,648	...	...	...
Fresh Veal	Pounds	1,934,688	...	...	...	...
Vegetable Soup	Pounds	...	...	242,100	...	...
Lard	Pounds	476,850	...	...	...	...
Fresh Frozen Fish	Pounds	...	...	...	1,129,446	1,036,327
Butter	Pounds	2,046,330	480,000	512,406	645,158	4,641,984
Cheese	Pounds	199,413	360,138	...	68,500	...
Dry Skim Milk	Pounds	...	...	...	880,900	1,480,000
Fluid Milk	Quarts	...	...	...	2,502,453	25,420,057
Evaporated Milk	Cases	...	29,600	10,400	41,800	39,000
Eggs	Dozens	...	...	275,760	1,030,860	73,650
Cereal Foods	Pounds	520,416	...	1,200,288	399,840	1,423,940
Wheat Flour	Pounds	3,161,088	...	6,098,540	...	27,988,800
Rice	Pounds	920,544	239,616	...	800,000	3,800,000
Dried Apples	Pounds	...	...	...	...	1,036,000
Fresh Apples	Bushels	...	...	85,500	91,583	183,172
Dried Beans	Pounds	150,000	...	650,000	...	5,380,000
Cabbage	Pounds	5,472,000	688,750	...	...	13,066,072
Carrots	Bushels	...	...	9,600	...	43,783
Celery	Crates	...	...	...	...	29,688
Citrus Fruits	Pounds	190,400	...	7,704,000	12,070,000	18,338,904

Grapefruit Juice	Cases	...	...	...	22,774	116,200
Grapes	Pounds	...	...	...	1,187,280	...
Onions	Pounds	...	...	2,664,000	...	...
Pears	Boxes	...	...	...	5,086	17,370
Canned Peas	Cases	...	...	...	...	86,643
Dried Peas	Pounds	...	...	1,140,075	...	600,000
White Potatoes	Pounds	10,760,000	5,907,500	...	11,174,235	17,852,125
Sweet Potatoes	Pounds	...	...	...	3,389,694	4,887,866
Dried Prunes	Pounds	...	900,000	2,820,000	180,000	6,120,000
Turnips	Bushels	...	...	17,880	...	...
Snap Beans	Bushels	...	...	...	...	8,198
Shortening	Pounds	...	...	...	214,720	775,170
Sugar	Pounds	300,000	...	...	...	...
Grass Seed	Pounds	30,000	...	...	...	...
Sheepskins	Pelts	...	2,400	...	...	...
Sheepskin Coats	Pelts	...	16,629	...	...	...
Blankets	Pairs	23,600	...	...	...	...
Cotton	Pounds	2,045,709	1,191,877	250,000	...	...
Comforter Covering	Yards	946,900	195,590	...	...	...
Sheeting	Yards	712,714	9,694	...	...	...
Ticking	Yards	389,500	338,170	...	...	...
Toweling	Yards	761,464	142,393	...	...	...
Wool	Pounds	...	273,097	...	...	...
Paper Bags	Each	...	...	...	924,000	2,017,200
Dried Peaches	Pounds	...	...	...	...	398,600
Fresh Prunes	½ bu. bas.	...	...	...	...	11,536
Dried Raisins	Pounds	...	...	...	...	3,540,000
Beets	Bushels	...	...	...	...	48,986
Potato Starch	Pounds	...	...	...	...	560,000
Graham Flour	Pounds	...	...	...	...	3,675,000
Cornmeal	Pounds	...	...	...	...	600,000
Fresh Tomatoes	Bushels	...	...	...	...	19,482

TABLE 16

Cancelled Cases

Average Income, Expenditure, and Debts by Towns

No. of Cases	Towns	Total Weekly Income	Total Weekly Expend.	Difference	Total Debts	Sources of Income: Private Employment	Rents	Lodgers and Boarders	ERA	Public Welfare	Other Relief	Other Income
20	Framingham	$11.93	$16.23	$−4.30	$163.33	$3.72	$.52	$.70	$4.98	$1.70	$.31	...
99	New Bedford	12.13	18.15	−6.02	261.84	1.52	.61	...	8.87	.21	.18	$.74
100	Newton	17.35	21.24	−3.89	395.94	5.40	.79	.07	9.89	.47	.73	...
85	Small Towns	8.73	...	...	268.87	1.66	.34	.20	5.81	.10	.48	.14
76	Cases having expenditure data	8.93	15.56	−6.63	...	1.59	.12	.12	6.50	.11	.33	.16
104	Somerville	16.99	21.77	−4.78	381.29	3.97	.90	.10	11.30	.18	.31	.23
408	Whole Sample	13.93	...	...	321.79	3.28	.62	.12	8.91	.32	.41	.27
399	Cases having expenditure data	14.09	19.28	−5.19	...	3.30	.59	.10	9.11	.33	.38	.27

No. of Cases	Towns	Expenditures: House	Food	Clothing	Insurance	Other	Debts: Food	Rent	Taxes	Personal Loans	Industrial Loans	Furniture	Medical	Other Unspecified	Mortgage	Average Size of Family
20	Framingham	$5.80	$8.45	$1.08	$.44	$ .46	$ 7.00	$13.30	$24.20	$ 5.00	$43.25	...	$23.15	$ 47.42	...	4.1
99	New Bedford	4.86	8.95	2.44	..	1.90	25.07	25.58	1.33	10.44	5.15	$3.99	13.70	176.58	...	4.9
100	Newton	9.05	9.15	1.16	.83	1.05	26.64	85.68	33.01	124.28	48.13	9.54	24.08	28.39	$16.19	4.7
85	Small Towns	..	..	..	..	..	3.49	16.17	46.76	14.94	18.22	1.18	2.46	158.60	7.05	3.5
76	Cases having expenditure data	5.92	6.78	2.35	.03	.48	...	...	...	...	...	...	...	...	...	...
104	Somerville	8.40	10.24	1.84	.45	.84	17.02	54.94	38.84	106.38	5.63	9.47	53.17	86.42	9.42	4.7
408	Whole Sample	..	..	..	..	..	18.02	45.23	29.24	63.47	20.40	5.97	24.42	107.20	7.84	4.4
399	Cases having expenditure data	7.08	8.90	1.88	.35	1.07	...	...	...	...	...	...	...	...	...	...

TABLE 17

Cancelled Cases

SOURCES OF INCOME BY TOWNS

(Percentages of total no. of cases)

Towns	Framingham	New Bedford	Newton	Small Towns	Somerville	Whole Sample
No. of cases	20	99	100	85	104	408
Non-supplemented income						
1. Relief only	50.0	61.6	40.0	41.2	53.8	49.5
a. ERA only	25.0	52.5	29.0	36.5	50.0	41.4
b. Other relief	25.0	9.1	11.0	4.7	3.8	8.1
Supplemented income						
2. Relief & non-relief	15.0	13.2	35.0	11.7	30.7	22.8
a. Relief & private employment	10.0	7.1	27.0	8.2	19.2	15.4
(1) ERA & private employment	10.0	7.1	25.0	7.0	19.2	14.7
(2) Other relief & private employment	..	..	2.0	1.2	..	0.7
b. Relief & other non-relief	5.0	6.1	8.0	3.5	11.5	7.4
3. Private employment only	20.0	8.1	11.0	5.9	2.9	7.6
4. Other non-relief	10.0	5.0	2.0	5.9	3.9	4.4
5. No income	5.0	12.1	12.0	35.3	8.7	15.7
Total	100.0	100.0	100.0	100.0	100.0	100.0

TABLE 18

CANCELLED CASES

MEDIAN AND AVERAGE WEEKLY INCOME BY SOURCE

(dollars)

	All Sources		Relief Only		Relief and Non-relief				Priv. Empl. Only		Other Non-relief		No. of Cases having No Income
	Cases	Mean	Cases	Mean	Cases	Total Mean	Relief Mean	Non-relief Mean	Cases	Mean	Cases	Mean	
Framingham	20	$11.93	10	$ 9.79	3	$24.30	$14.00	$10.30	4	$13.58	2	$ 6.75	1
New Bedford	99	12.13	61	12.20	13	21.71	13.29	8.42	8	11.88	5	15.95	12
Newton	100	17.35	40	14.83	35	26.41	14.70	11.71	11	16.74	2	16.31	12
Small Towns	85	8.73	35	12.27	10	21.91	11.41	10.50	5	9.22	5	9.58	30
Somerville	104	16.99	56	14.00	32	27.29	13.81	13.47	3	9.67	4	20.23	9
Whole sample	408	13.93	202	13.11	93	25.50	13.82	11.68	31	13.18	18	14.15	64
MEDIANS													
Framingham	20	$11.00	10	$10.80	3	$24.00	$12.00	$ 9.00	4	$11.00	2	$ 6.75	1
New Bedford	99	12.00	61	12.00	13	21.68	12.00	9.23	8	10.00	5	21.17	12
Newton	100	16.18	40	13.07	35	22.50	12.00	7.00	11	17.00	2	16.31	12
Small Towns	85	9.60	35	12.00	10	18.50	12.00	5.50	5	6.00	5	7.00	30
Somerville	104	15.00	56	14.10	32	23.75	12.00	10.00	3	7.00	4	20.58	9
Whole Sample	408	12.00	202	12.00	93	22.00	12.00	8.07	31	12.00	18	17.00	64

TABLE 19

Cancelled Cases

INCOME FREQUENCY DISTRIBUTION

(Per cents)

Income Groups	Framingham	New Bedford	Newton	Small Towns	Somerville	Whole Sample
$ 0– 3.99	5.0	15.1	12.0	40.0	8.6	17.4
4– 7.99	25.0	8.1	5.0	4.7	2.9	6.1
8–11.99	20.0	2.0	2.0	8.2	1.9	4.2
12–15.99	30.0	52.4	31.0	29.4	41.3	38.5
16–19.99	..	8.1	18.0	9.4	20.2	13.5
20–23.99	5.0	7.1	11.0	3.5	8.6	7.6
24–27.99	10.0	6.1	6.0	1.2	6.7	5.4
28–31.99	5.0	..	2.0	..	2.9	1.5
32–35.99	..	1.1	5.0	2.4	2.9	2.7
36–39.99	..	..	3.0	..	1.0	1.0
40–43.99	..	..	2.0	1.2	1.0	1.0
44–47.99	..	..	1.0	..	..	.2
48–51.99	..	..	..	..	..	..
52–55.99	..	..	2.0	..	..	.5
56–59.99	..	..	..	..	1.0	.2
60 & over	..	..	..	..	1.0	.2
Total	100.0	100.0	100.0	100.0	100.0	100.0
No. of cases	20	99	100	85	104	408

TABLE 20

Active Cases

INCOME FREQUENCY DISTRIBUTION

(Per cents)

Income Groups	Framing-ham & Ashland	Maynard	Hudson	Wayland & Small Towns	Somer-ville	Cam-bridge	New Bedford	Brook-line	Newton	Whole Sample
$ 0– 3.99	7.8	8.8	16.4	30.6	10.6	12.9	14.8	12.5	7.3	12.9
4– 7.99	2.2	5.9	5.5	5.5	3.5	8.2	8.5	9.2	3.4	5.7
8–11.99	3.0	..	3.1	12.5	2.8	3.6	5.1	22.5	3.0	5.2
12–15.99	48.2	58.8	50.0	33.3	50.6	48.5	51.4	35.8	23.8	45.5
16–19.99	15.2	11.8	9.4	9.7	16.3	11.9	9.7	12.5	22.1	13.6
20–23.99	7.0	14.7	7.0	3.5	6.3	6.3	4.2	3.3	13.6	6.5
24–27.99	7.0	..	3.9	2.8	4.9	4.0	4.1	2.5	15.3	5.5
28–31.99	2.2	..	2.3	..	2.8	3.0	1.6	1.7	6.4	2.6
32–35.99	1.3	..	.8	1.4	.8	.6	.4	..	1.7	.8
36–39.99	4.4	..	..	.7	.4	1.0	.2	..	2.1	1.0
40–43.99	.9	..	.8	..	.6	..	..	..	.9	.4
44–47.99	.4	..	..	..	.2	..	..	..	..	.1
48–51.99	.4	..	..	..	.2	..	..	..	.4	.1
52–55.99	..	..	.8	..	..	..	..	..	..	.1
No. of cases	230	34	128	144	492	303	494	120	235	2180

TABLE 21

Active Cases

AVERAGE SIZE OF FAMILY, BY TOWNS, ACCORDING TO SOURCES OF INCOME

(Unit: persons per family)

Town	All Sources	Relief Only	Relief and Non-relief	Private Employment	Other Non-relief
Somerville	3.9	3.7	4.6	5.2	4.8
Cambridge	4.9	4.8	7.2	4.5	5.0
New Bedford	4.2	4.5	4.0	4.8	3.7
Brookline	3.1	2.7	4.3	4.2	3.1
Newton	5.0	4.9	5.3	5.8	3.0
Framingham	4.8	4.7	5.5	3.1	6.0
Maynard	3.1	3.4	2.3	..	..
Hudson	4.0	4.1	5.9	3.6	4.3
Small Towns	3.9	4.2	4.1	3.2	5.0
Whole Sample	4.3	4.3	4.9	4.4	4.2

INDEX

INDEX

FSC
www.fsc.org
MIX
Papier | Fördert
gute Waldnutzung
FSC® C083411

Kolibri 360 GmbH
Ferdinand-Jühlke-Straße 7
99095 Erfurt, Deutschland
produktsicherheit@kolibri360.de

VOLUME ONE HUNDRED AND NINETEEN

ADVANCES IN PROTEIN CHEMISTRY AND STRUCTURAL BIOLOGY

Inflammatory Disorders, Part A

VOLUME ONE HUNDRED AND NINETEEN

ADVANCES IN PROTEIN CHEMISTRY AND STRUCTURAL BIOLOGY

Inflammatory Disorders, Part A

Edited by

Rossen Donev
Head of Research
MicroPharm Ltd
Newcastle Emlyn, Carmarthenshire
United Kingdom

ELSEVIER

ACADEMIC PRESS
An imprint of Elsevier

Academic Press is an imprint of Elsevier
125 London Wall, London EC2Y 5AS, United Kingdom
525 B Street, Suite 1650, San Diego, CA 92101, United States
50 Hampshire Street, 5th Floor, Cambridge, MA 02139, United States
The Boulevard, Langford Lane, Kidlington, Oxford OX5 1GB, United Kingdom

First edition 2020

ISBN: 978-0-12-816844-8
ISSN: 1876-1623

Publisher: Zoe Kruze
Acquisition Editor: Ashlie Jackman
Editorial Project Manager: Leticia M. Lima
Production Project Manager: Abdulla Sait
Cover Designer: Greg Harris
Typeset by TNQ Technologies

Contents

Contributors

Rachel Adams
School of Health Sciences, Cardiff Metropolitan University, Cardiff, United Kingdom

Fabrice Allain
University Lille, CNRS, UMR 8576 - UGSF - Unite de Glycobiologie Structurale et Fonctionnelle, F-59000 Lille, France

Fatin Atrooz
Department of Pharmacological and Pharmaceutical Sciences, College of Pharmacy, University of Houston, Houston, TX, United States

Shoumo Bhattacharya
RDM Division of Cardiovascular Medicine, University of Oxford, Oxford, United Kingdom

Sumeyye Cavdarli
University Lille, CNRS, UMR 8576 - UGSF - Unite de Glycobiologie Structurale et Fonctionnelle, F-59000 Lille, France

Ruth E. Coxon
Micropharm Ltd, Carmarthenshire, United Kingdom

Philippe Delannoy
University Lille, CNRS, UMR 8576 - UGSF - Unite de Glycobiologie Structurale et Fonctionnelle, F-59000 Lille, France

Yun Ge
Department of General Intensive Care Unit, The Second Affiliated Hospital of Zhejiang University School of Medicine, Hangzhou 310052, China

Kursad Genc
Department of Neuroscience, Institute of Health and Science, Dokuz Eylul University Health Campus, Balcova, Izmir, Turkey

Sermin Genc
Izmir Biomedicine and Genome Center, Dokuz Eylul University Health Campus Balcova, Izmir, Turkey; Izmir International Biomedicine and Genome Institute (iBG-Izmir), Dokuz Eylul University Health Campus, Balcova, Izmir, Turkey; Department of Neuroscience, Institute of Health and Science, Dokuz Eylul University Health Campus, Balcova, Izmir, Turkey

Owen R. Griffiths
Micropharm Ltd, Carmarthenshire, United Kingdom; School of Health Sciences, Cardiff Metropolitan University, Cardiff, United Kingdom

Sophie Groux-Degroote
University Lille, CNRS, UMR 8576 - UGSF - Unite de Glycobiologie Structurale et Fonctionnelle, F-59000 Lille, France

Man Huang
Department of General Intensive Care Unit, The Second Affiliated Hospital of Zhejiang University School of Medicine, Hangzhou 310052, China

Philip James
School of Health Sciences, Cardiff Metropolitan University, Cardiff, United Kingdom

Akane Kawamura
RDM Division of Cardiovascular Medicine, University of Oxford, Oxford, United Kingdom

Rekha Khandia
Department of Genetics, Barkatullah University, Bhopal, Madhya Pradesh, India

Cagla Kiser
Izmir Biomedicine and Genome Center, Dokuz Eylul University Health Campus Balcova, Izmir, Turkey; Izmir International Biomedicine and Genome Institute (iBG-Izmir), Dokuz Eylul University Health Campus, Balcova, Izmir, Turkey

John Landon
Micropharm Ltd, Carmarthenshire, United Kingdom

Declan P. McKernan
Pharmacology & Therapeutics School of Medicine, Galway, Ireland

Keith Morris
School of Health Sciences, Cardiff Metropolitan University, Cardiff, United Kingdom

Ashok Munjal
Department of Genetics, Barkatullah University, Bhopal, Madhya Pradesh, India

Melis Olcum
Izmir Biomedicine and Genome Center, Dokuz Eylul University Health Campus Balcova, Izmir, Turkey

Samina Salim
Department of Pharmacological and Pharmaceutical Sciences, College of Pharmacy, University of Houston, Houston, TX, United States

Bora Tastan
Izmir Biomedicine and Genome Center, Dokuz Eylul University Health Campus Balcova, Izmir, Turkey; Izmir International Biomedicine and Genome Institute (iBG-Izmir), Dokuz Eylul University Health Campus, Balcova, Izmir, Turkey

Kenji Uchimura
University Lille, CNRS, UMR 8576 - UGSF - Unite de Glycobiologie Structurale et Fonctionnelle, F-59000 Lille, France

Yong-ming Yao
Trauma Research Center, Fourth Medical Center of the Chinese PLA General Hospital, Beijing 100048, China

Xiao-mei Zhu
Trauma Research Center, Fourth Medical Center of the Chinese PLA General Hospital, Beijing 100048, China

CHAPTER ONE

Using evasins to target the chemokine network in inflammation

Shoumo Bhattacharya* and Akane Kawamura
RDM Division of Cardiovascular Medicine, University of Oxford, Oxford, United Kingdom
*Corresponding author: E-mail: sbhattac@well.ox.ac.uk

Contents

Advances in Protein Chemistry and Structural Biology, Volume 119
ISSN 1876-1623
https://doi.org/10.1016/bs.apcsb.2019.09.003

Abstract

Inflammation, is driven by a network comprising cytokines, chemokines, their target receptors and leukocytes, and is a major pathologic mechanism that adversely affects organ function in diverse human diseases. Despite being supported by substantial target validation, no successful anti-chemokine therapeutic to treat inflammatory disease has yet been developed. This is in part because of the robustness of the chemokine network, which emerges from a large total chemokine load in disease, promiscuous expression of receptors on leukocytes, promiscuous and synergistic interactions between chemokines and receptors, and feedforward loops created by secretion of chemokines by leukocytes themselves. Many parasites, including viruses, helminths and ticks, evade the chemokine network by producing proteins that bind promiscuously to chemokines or their receptors. Evasins - three small glycoproteins identified in the saliva of the brown dog tick - bind multiple chemokines, and are active in several animal models of inflammatory disease. Over 50 evasin homologs have recently been identified from diverse tick species. Characterization of the chemokine binding patterns of evasins show that several have anti-chemokine activities that extend substantially beyond those previously described. These studies indicate that evasins function at the site of the tick bite by reducing total chemokine load. This not only reduces chemokine signaling to receptors, but also interrupts feedforward loops, thus disabling the chemokine network. Taking the lead from nature, a goal for the development of new anti-chemokine therapeutics would be to reduce the total chemokine load in disease. This could be achieved by administering appropriate evasin combinations or by smaller peptides that mimic evasin action.

1. Inflammation and disease

Although inflammation is a fundamental host-defense response that serves to rid the body of the causes and consequences of infection and tissue injury, it is also a pathologic mechanism that can adversely affect organ function (Kumar, Abbas, & Aster, 2015). Indeed, inflammation is thought to contribute to a variety of cardiovascular, pulmonary neurological, gastrointestinal, musculoskeletal, cutaneous, renal and hepatic disorders, creating substantial disease burden. Inflammation is driven by a network including secreted cytokines and chemokines, cellular receptors and leukocytes. The leukocytes include neutrophils, eosinophils, basophils, monocytes, macrophages, T and B-lymphocytes and dendritic cells (Kumar et al., 2015). Cytokines and chemokines are secreted proteins, and are produced by damaged tissues in response to damage-associated molecular patterns (DAMPs) or pathogen-associated molecular patterns (PAMPs) which signal through pattern-recognition receptors to activate gene transcription. In broad terms, cytokines function in immune cell proliferation and maturation, and include molecules such as TNF and interleukins. Cytokines and their receptors have been successful as therapeutic targets for drug development in inflammatory diseases (Rodgers & Chou, 2016). Chemokines cause directed leukocyte migration to sites of inflammation. Despite having a well-documented mechanistic role in this process, and despite being supported by substantial target validation, no successful anti-chemokine therapeutic to treat inflammatory disease has yet been developed. We suggest that the reason for this lies in the inherent robustness of the chemokine network.

2. The chemokine network in inflammation

2.1 Overview

Chemo-attractant cyto*kines* or *chemokines* are a group of small structurally related proteins that are present in all vertebrates (Bachelerie et al., 2014). Based on the arrangement of the cysteine residues at their N-termini they are classified as CC, CXC, CX3C or XC. Of these, the CC and CXC chemokines are the most numerous. Their chemoattractant functions are mediated by binding to a family of structurally related G-protein coupled receptors which are classified as CCR, CXCR, CX3CR and XCR based on the main chemokines that they bind. The structural mechanisms of these interactions have been recently reviewed (Kufareva, Gustavsson, Zheng, Stephens, & Handel, 2017). Briefly, chemokines engage G-protein coupled receptors through at least four distinct sites on the receptor, termed *chemokine-recognition sites*. Certain CXC-chemokines contain a characteristic Glu-Leu-Arg motif ("ELR"), in the N-terminal region. This motif binds CXCR1 and CXCR2 receptors on neutrophils (Bachelerie et al., 2014). Binding of chemokines to their receptors leads to activation of leukocyte responses including directed migration or chemotaxis. Distinct leukocyte subtypes respond to different chemokines. CC chemokines function in recruitment of leukocytes including monocyte/macrophages, dendritic cells, eosinophils, and in Th2 immune responses. CXC chemokines play major roles in neutrophil trafficking and in Th1 immune responses (Bachelerie et al., 2014).

2.2 Target validation in inflammatory disease

Genome-wide association studies (GWAS) and gene expression data support the role of chemokines and receptors in diseases where inflammation plays a significant role. Chemokine or receptor genes identified within GWAS loci include:

- CXCL12 in atherosclerosis (Kathiresan et al., 2009; Schunkert et al., 2011);
- CCL7, CCL11, CCL8, CCL1, CCL13, CCL1, CCL2, CCL7, CCR6, CXCR5 and GPR35 in inflammatory bowel disease (Jostins et al., 2012; Kenny et al., 2012);
- CCL21, CCR6 and CXCR5 in rheumatoid arthritis (Okada et al., 2014; Stahl et al., 2010);
- CCR4 in atopic dermatitis (Hirota et al., 2012);
- CXCR5 in multiple sclerosis (Beecham et al., 2013);
- and CCL21, CXCR2 and GPR35 in chronic inflammatory diseases comprising ankylosing spondylitis, inflammatory bowel disease, psoriasis, and primary sclerosing cholangitis (Ellinghaus et al., 2016).

Systematic literature searches of chemokine expression in 24 inflammatory disease conditions, covering major organ systems (Fig. 1A), indicate that multiple chemokines are typically expressed in human inflammatory disease (see references in Appendix). Extensive genetic data from mouse models of human disease fuwrther support the role of chemokines and their receptors in driving inflammation (see Appendix).

2.3 Structure of the chemokine network

The chemokine network consists of chemokines produced by damaged tissues and leukocytes, their target receptors, and leukocytes expressing these receptors. Key features of the network that contribute to robustness include: the total chemokine load; promiscuity in receptor expression and chemokine-receptor interactions; synergistic mechanisms; and feedforward loops. These features are considered individually below.

2.4 Total chemokine load in human disease

The secretion of multiple chemokines by damaged tissues, and also by leukocytes themselves, is a fundamental feature of the network. The *total chemokine load* (here defined as the total number of different chemokines expressed in a disease) can range up to 15 or over in conditions such as rheumatoid arthritis, atherosclerosis, idiopathic pulmonary fibrosis, vasculitis, psoriasis, inflammatory bowel disease, and influenza (Fig. 1A). Many of these chemokines are actually produced by leukocytes themselves (Fig. 1B), and contribute to the total chemokine load (see column FF in Fig. 1A). For instance, neutrophils, the first leukocyte class typically recruited in acute

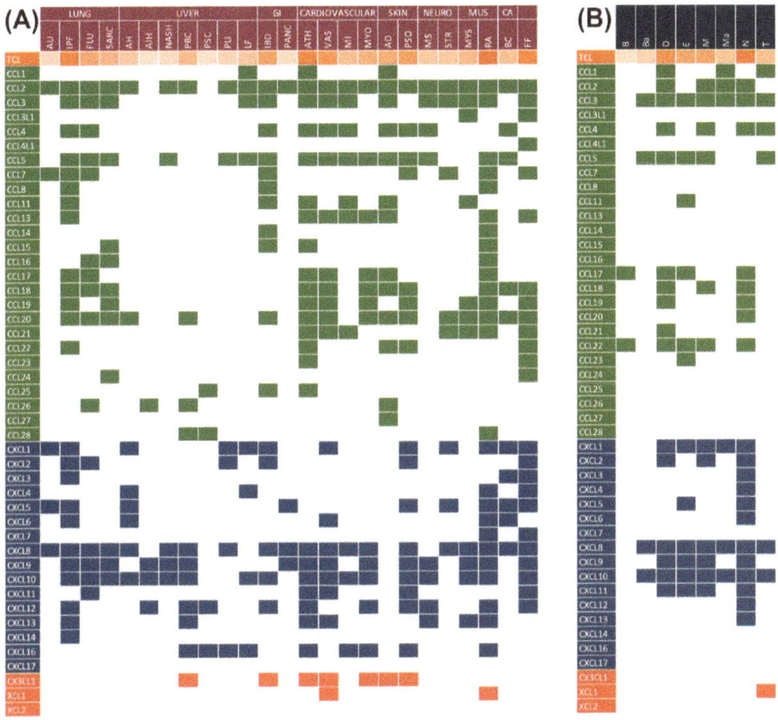

Fig. 1 ***Chemokine expression patterns. (A) Chemokine expression patterns in human inflammatory diseases are shown as filled rectangles at the intersection of chemokine (left column) and disease (top row). CC chemokines are colored in green, CXC in blue, CX3C and XC in red.*** The total chemokine load in a given disease (TCL) is colored orange with darker shades indicating higher load. Abbreviations: ALI – acute lung injury, IPF – idiopathic pulmonary fibrosis, FLU – influenza, SARC – sarcoidosis, AH – alcoholic hepatitis, AIH – autoimmune hepatitis, NASH – non-alcoholic steatohepatitis, PBC – primary biliary cirrhosis, PSC – primary sclerosing cholangitis, PLI – paracetamol liver injury, LF – liver fibrosis, IBD – inflammatory bowel disease, PANC – pancreatitis, ATH – atherosclerosis, VAS – vasculitis, MI – myocardial infarction, MYO – myocarditis, AD – atopic dermatitis, PSO – psoriasis, MS – multiple sclerosis, STR – stroke, MYS- myositis, RA – rheumatoid arthritis, BC – breast cancer, FF – feed-forward (see Fig. 1B), CA – cancer. References are listed in the Appendix. (B) Chemokines (left column) expressed by human leukocyte types (top row) are shown as filled rectangles at the intersection of chemokine and leukocyte type. The total chemokine load (TCL) produced by leukocyte type is color-coded in orange with darker shades indicating higher load. CC chemokines are coded in green, CXC in blue, CX3C and XC in red. Abbreviations: B – B cells, Ba – basophils, D – dendritic cells, E – eosinophils, M – monocytes/macrophages, Ma – mast cells, N – neutrophils, T – T cells. References are listed in the Appendix.

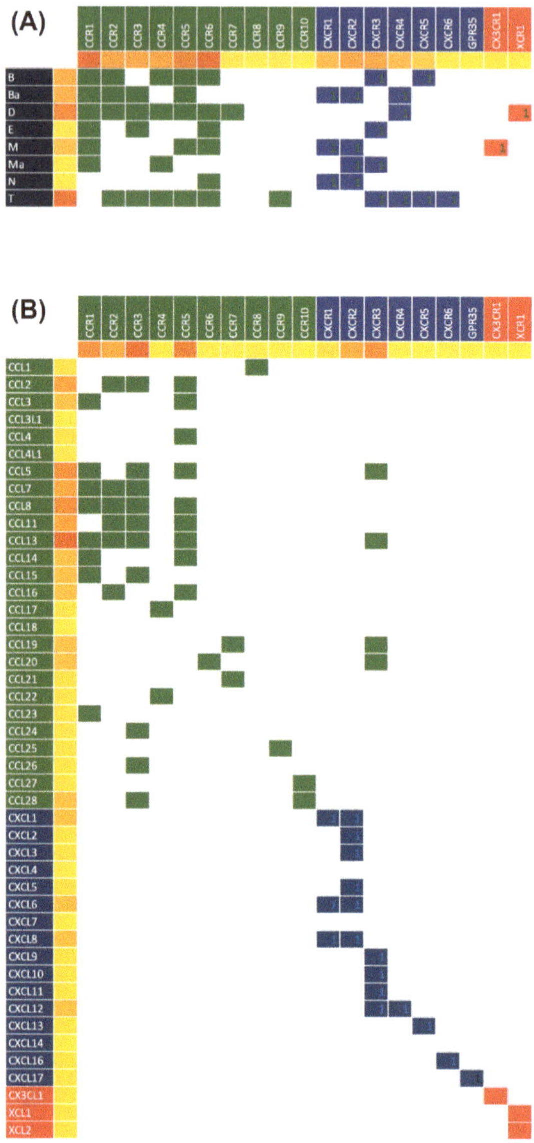

Fig. 2 Chemokine receptor expression and interactions. (A) Expression of receptors (top row) by human leukocyte type (left column) are shown as filled rectangles at the intersection of receptor and leukocyte type. Receptor and leukocyte promiscuity (number of receptors expressed by a leukocyte, or number of leukocytes that express a receptor) is indicated in the immediately adjacent row and column respectively, and is color-coded with low promiscuity in yellow and high in orange. CC receptors are coded in green, CXC and GPR35 in blue, CX3C and XC in red. Abbreviations: B – B cells, Ba – basophils, D – dendritic cells, E – eosinophils, M– monocytes/macrophages,

inflammation, are known to secrete up to 20 chemokines, which recruit not only more neutrophils but also other cell classes (Tecchio, Micheletti, & Cassatella, 2014). Chemokines produced by recruited leukocytes thus have the potential to create feedforward amplification loops (*see below*).

2.5 Promiscuity

Data from the *Guides to Pharmacology and Immunopharmacology* (Harding et al., 2018) indicate that promiscuity in leukocyte receptor expression, and in interactions between chemokines and receptors are key features of the network. Multiple receptors are typically expressed on leukocytes (Fig. 2A). Receptor numbers expressed on leukocytes range from three (neutrophils) to six or more (T helper, dendritic cells, monocytes and basophils). Several human chemokines can agonistically bind multiple receptors, and conversely, several receptors can bind multiple agonist chemokines (Fig. 2B). Receptors such as CCR3, CCR5, CCR1, CXCR3, CCR2 and CXCR2 are promiscuous, binding over five different chemokines. Chemokines such as CCL13, CCL5, CCL8, CCL19, CCL11, CCL2, and CCL7 are also promiscuous, binding three or more receptors. The mechanisms underlying promiscuous chemokine-receptor interactions likely arise, in part, from the structural similarities between chemokines and also between chemokine receptors, both of which protein classes have arisen by gene duplication and divergence (DeVries et al., 2006; Zlotnik, Yoshie, & Nomiyama, 2006).

2.6 Synergy

Synergism in the chemokine response has been shown to occur at the level of the chemokine receptor, when two receptors are activated simultaneously or sequentially by their agonists. Synergism also occurs at the level of the chemokine, when certain chemokines form heteromeric complexes (Proudfoot & Uguccioni, 2016). Examples of the latter include the synergistic activation of CCR7 by CXCL13/CCL19 and CXCL13/CCL21, of CCR4 by CXCL10/CCL22, of CCR2 by CCL19 and CCL21 interacting

Ma — mast cells, N — neutrophils, T — T cells. (B) Agonistic interactions between human chemokines (left column) and receptors (top row) are shown as filled rectangles at the intersection of chemokine and receptor. Receptor and chemokine promiscuity is indicated in the immediately adjacent row and column respectively, and is color-coded with low promiscuity in yellow and high in orange. CC chemokines and receptors are coded in green, CXC in blue, CX3C and XC in red.

with CCR2 ligands, and of CXCR4 by CXCL9/CXCL12. Other chemokine heterodimers that synergise agonistically include CCL5/CCL17, CCL5/CXCL4 and CCL5/CCL2 (von Hundelshausen et al., 2017). Importantly, low affinity interactions between chemokines and glycosaminoglycans has been shown to induce cooperativity between different chemokines (Proudfoot & Uguccioni, 2016).

2.7 Feedforward loops

As discussed above, leukocytes recruited to damaged tissues are themselves capable of producing chemokines. These chemokines can recruit further leukocytes of the same or of different classes thus creating feedforward loops that amplify the inflammatory response. The major feedforward chemokines include CXCL1, CXCL2, CXCL8, CXCL9, CXCL10, CXCL11, and CCL2, CCL3, CCL4, CCL5, CCL17, and CCL22 (Fig. 1B). The importance of chemokine feedforward loops has been experimentally demonstrated in influenza-induced lung inflammation (Brandes, Klauschen, Kuchen, & Germain, 2013) and in inflammatory breast cancer (Valeta-Magara et al., 2019).

2.8 Robustness

The chemokine network functions as a hierarchy, with information being relayed from chemokines via their receptors to the leukocytes. Leukocytes integrate the chemokine signals which induce their directional migration or *chemotaxis* toward damaged tissues (Fig. 3A). As discussed above, leukocytes arriving at damaged tissues produce more chemokines, creating feedforward loops that amplify the inflammatory response (Fig. 3B). The ability of a network to function despite perturbations (*e.g.* failure of individual components) is referred to as its *robustness* (Kitano, 2004). The robustness of a network can be inferred by the impact of interference with one or more "nodes" in the network (Scardoni, Montresor, Tosadori, & Laudanna, 2014). This is seen in Fig. 4A, where the impact of removal of two receptor nodes (CCR5 and CCR2) on chemokine signaling to leukocytes, and on the associated feedforward loops (Fig. 4B) is seen to be minimal. This analysis predicts that the chemokine network in inflammatory diseases cannot be effectively targeted by therapeutics that neutralize just one or even two chemokine or receptor nodes in the network. In accordance with this prediction, targeting individual chemokines or receptors has repeatedly failed as a pharmacological strategy in inflammatory disease (Pease & Horuk, 2010; Szekanecz & Koch, 2016). This prediction is also supported by data from

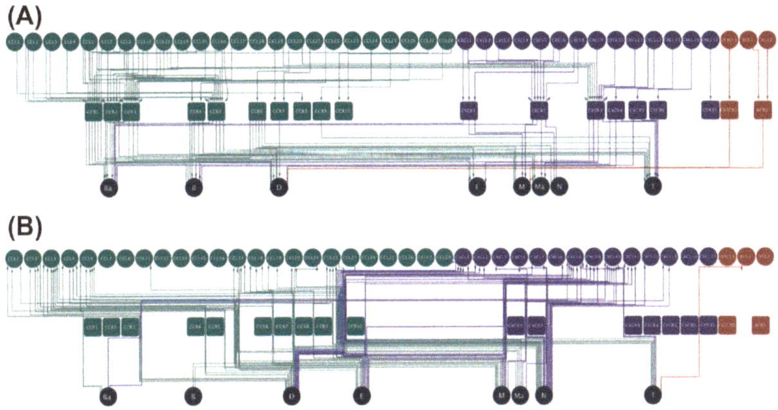

Fig. 3 The human chemokine network. (A) Hierarchical representation of the chemokine network, showing chemokine nodes at the top (blue, green, and red circles), receptors in the middle (blue, green and red squares) and leukocytes at the bottom (black circles). Arrows connecting chemokines to receptors and receptors to cells indicate agonistic interactions and cellular expression respectively, and are colored according to the originating node. CC chemokines and receptors are shown in green, CXC in blue, CX3C and XC in red. Leukocytes (T, T helper cells, B - B cells, Ba – basophils, N - neutrophils, E – eosinophils, Ma – mast cells, M – monocytes/macrophages) are in black. (B) Hierarchical representation of the chemokine network as above showing feedforward loops. Arrows connect leukocytes to chemokines that they secrete, and are colored according to the target node.

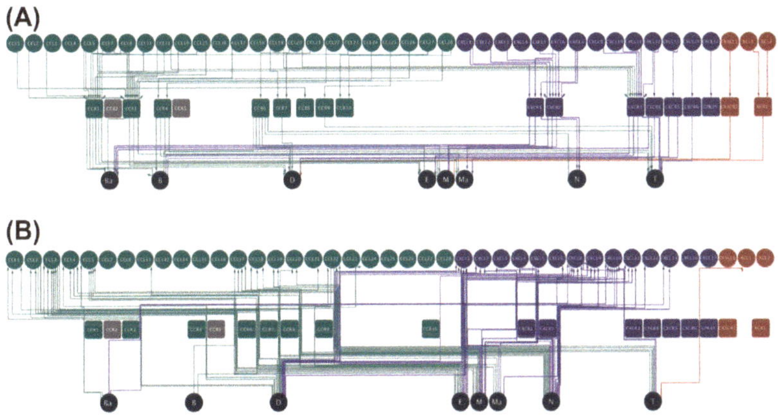

Fig. 4 Impact of receptor node deletion on the human chemokine network. (A) Impact of receptor node deletion on chemokine signaling to leukocytes. The chemokine network is represented as in Fig. 3A, but with CCR5 and CCR2 receptors (indicated in gray) and their connections removed from the network. (B) Impact of receptor node deletion on feedforward loops. The chemokine network is represented as in Fig. 3B, but with CCR5 and CCR2 receptors (indicated in gray) and their connections removed from the network.

mouse models, where it is seen that combinatorial knockout or depletion of chemokines and/or chemokine receptors is more effective than single knockout or depletion in preventing inflammation in diverse mouse models. These models include atherosclerosis (Combadière et al., 2008; Saederup, Chan, Lira, & Charo, 2008), asthma (Mattes et al., 2002), contact dermatitis (Mirshahpanah, Li, Burkhardt, Asadullah, & Zollner, 2008), response to influenza (Rangel-Moreno, Moyron-Quiroz, Hartson, Kusser, & Randall, 2007), experimental autoimmune encephalomyelitis (Moriguchi, Miyamoto, Tanaka, Yoshie, & Kusunoki, 2013) and pulmonary eosinophilia (Pope, Zimmermann, Stringer, Karow, & Rothenberg, 2005).

3. Evasins: tick proteins targeting the chemokine network

3.1 Overview

Parasitic organisms, including viruses, helminths and ticks, necessarily adapt through natural selection to survive in their hosts. One aspect of such adaptation is the ability to neutralize or evade the host's defense mechanisms. Examination of the host-parasite protein interactome thus provides an opportunity to understand how a robust host-defense network can be overcome, and thus identify the critical nodes in the host-defense network. Many parasites produce proteins that bind, in a promiscuous fashion, to multiple chemokines or receptors, and are thus able to disable the chemokine network (reviewed in (Gonzalez-Motos, Kropp, & Viejo-Borbolla, 2016; Heidarieh, Hernaez, & Alcami, 2015; Proudfoot, Bonvin, & Power, 2015)). Here we will focus on reviewing recent advances in tick chemokine binding proteins.

3.2 Tick chemokine binding proteins

Ticks draw blood for days to weeks without eliciting significant inflammation and their saliva has been shown to contain a veritable goldmine of proteins that block pain, itching, blood coagulation, and inflammation (Kazimírová; Štibrániová, 2013). Investigation of the saliva of the brown dog tick *Rhipicephalus sanguineus* led to the cloning of two classes of chemokine-binding proteins which were termed *evasins* (Deruaz et al., 2008; Frauenschuh et al., 2007; Hajnická et al., 2001). The first class, consisting of proteins with eight conserved Cys residues (EVA-1 and EVA-4), exclusively bound CC chemokines. The second class, consisting of a single member with six Cys residues (EVA-3), exclusively bound CXC chemokines. The predicted molecular weight of these proteins was between 7 and 12 KDa. When expressed in mammalian cells, these evasins were found to be highly glycosylated. A remarkable property of evasins was their ability to bind multiple chemokines, yet retain chemokine-class binding specificity (reviewed in (Bonvin, Power, & Proudfoot, 2016)). When administered parenterally, evasins were shown to be potently active in a number of animal models of inflammatory disease suggesting their utility as therapeutic agents. These models included myocardial ischemia and reperfusion injury, plaque inflammation, colitis, acute pancreatitis, lung inflammation, arthritis, graft-versus-host disease, psoriasis, and intestinal ischemia (Bonvin et al., 2014, 2016; Braunersreuther et al., 2013; Castor et al., 2010; Copin et al., 2013; Déruaz et al., 2013; Dias et al., 2009; Frauenschuh et al., 2007; Krohn, Garin, Gabay, & Proudfoot, 2013; Mohs et al., 2016; Montecucco et al., 2010, 2014; Russo et al., 2011; Vieira et al., 2009).

3.3 Identification of putative novel evasins using bioinformatics

A limitation of evasins as therapeutic agents was their inability to target chemokines such as CCL2, CCL13, CXCL9, 10 and 11, which are not only expressed in human disease (Fig. 1A), but are also produced as feedforward chemokines (Fig. 1B). To discover new evasins that could have potential in inhibiting chemokine function, we (Singh et al., 2017) and others (Hayward et al., 2017) undertook bioinformatic searches of tick salivary gland transcriptome datasets, and identified over 350 putative sequences that resembled EVA-1/EVA-4 or EVA-3.

3.4 Yeast surface display

To rapidly identify novel evasins that bound with high-affinity to target chemokines we used yeast surface display. We expressed the putative evasins using yeast surface display vectors, and screened the resulting yeast libraries systematically with fluorescent chemokines. We used several rounds of fluorescent assisted cell sorting to enrich for high-affinity binding yeast cells. Plasmids from the identified yeast clones were sequenced to identify the evasin sequences, which were then expressed in mammalian cells as secreted glycosylated proteins. Using this approach, we cloned 12 new CC-chemokine binding evasins and 28 new CXC-chemokine binding evasins (Alenazi et al., 2018; Eaton et al., 2018; Lee et al., 2019; Singh et al., 2017). Sequence analysis revealed that the CC-chemokine binding evasins had eight Cys

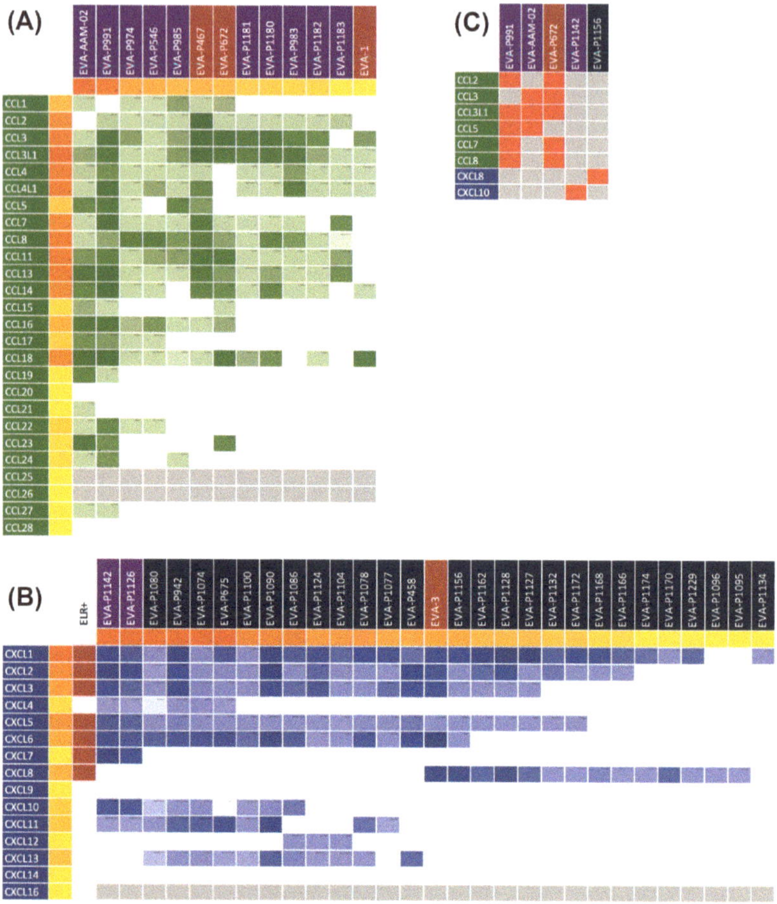

Fig. 5 Interactions of tick evasins with human chemokines. (A) Interactions between CC chemokines (left column) and class A evasins (top row) are shown as filled green rectangles at the intersection of chemokine and evasin and are shaded darker where the binding occurs at higher affinity. Evasin and chemokine promiscuity (number of partners) is indicated in the immediately adjacent row and column respectively, and is color-coded with low promiscuity in yellow and high in orange. CC chemokines are color-coded in green. Evasins are color-coded by genus, *Amblyomma* in purple and *Rhipicephalus* in dark red. Empty rectangles indicate that no binding was detected. Gray rectangles indicate where binding assays could not be performed either because of background binding to the sensor or because of lack of chemokine availability. (B) Interactions between CXC chemokines (left column) and class B evasins (top row) are shown as filled blue rectangles at the intersection of chemokine and evasin and are shaded darker where the binding occurs at higher affinity. Evasin and chemokine promiscuity (number of partners) is indicated in the immediately adjacent row and column respectively, and is color-coded with low promiscuity in yellow and high in orange. CXC chemokines are color-coded in blue. Evasins are color-coded by genus, *Amblyomma* in

residues, conserved with EVA-1 and EVA-4, whereas the CXC-chemokine binding evasins had six Cys residues, conserved with EVA-3. The predicted molecular weights ranged from 9 to 12 KDa for the EVA-1/EVA4 homologs, and 6−12 kDa for EVA-3 homologs. When expressed in mammalian cells, these evasins were found to be highly glycosylated. During this period, Hayward et al. (Hayward et al., 2017) also characterized eight new CC-chemokine binding evasins, some of which overlapped with the ones we had identified. The aligned sequences of all evasins, and a revised unifying nomenclature have recently been described (Bhusal et al., 2019). Based on sequence homology, evasins are divided into class A, or EVA-1/EVA-4 homologs, and class B, or EVA-3 homologs (Bhusal et al., 2019).

3.5 Characterization of evasin promiscuity and specificity

The yeast surface display experiments showed that certain evasins, such as EVA-P991, were recovered in screens performed with several different chemokine probes (Singh et al., 2017). This suggested a high level of promiscuity. To investigate this, we studied the binding of purified evasins, expressed from mammalian cells, to commercially available human chemokines. The results of these systematic binding experiments (Alenazi et al., 2018; Eaton et al., 2018; Lee et al., 2019; Singh et al., 2017) are summarized in Fig. 5. Class A evasins exclusively bound CC chemokines, with several binding CCL2 and CCL13 (Fig. 5A). Certain class A evasins such as EVA-AAM-02 (reported by us as P1243), and EVA-P991 had broad-spectrum chemokine binding activity (with K_D values in the low nM range), whereas others had a much narrower set of binding partners. Class B evasins (Lee et al., 2019) exclusively bound CXC chemokines, with several binding CXCL10, CXCL11, CXCL12 and CXCL13 (Fig. 5B). Two distinct subclasses of class B evasins were thus defined. The first, which included the class founder EVA-3 (to the right of EVA-3 in Fig. 5B), bound ELR + CXC-chemokines including CXCL1 and/or CXCL8. The second class (to the left of EVA-3 in Fig. 5B) had broad-spectrum activity, with members

purple, *Ixodes* in black, *Rhipicephalus* in dark red. ELR + chemokines are indicated by dark red rectangles. Empty rectangles indicate that no binding was detected. Gray rectangles indicate where binding assays could not be performed either because of background binding to the sensor or because of lack of chemokine availability. (C) Neutralization of chemokine (left column) activity by selected evasins (top row) is indicated by red filled rectangles at the at the intersection of chemokine and evasin. Gray filled rectangles indicate where neutralization assays have not been performed.

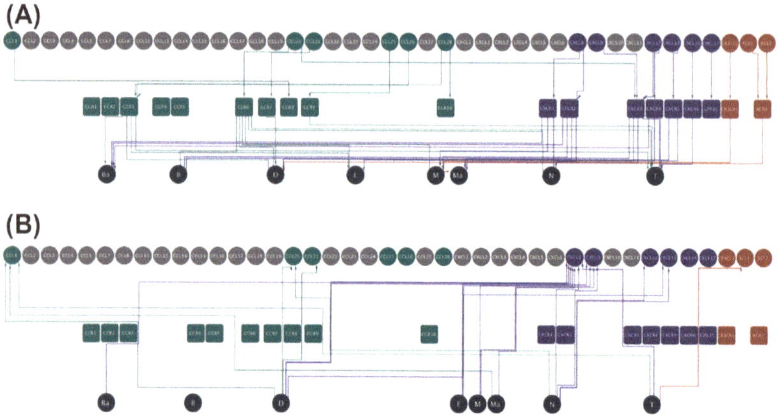

Fig. 6 Impact of *Amblyomma cajennense* evasins EVA-P991 and EVA-P1142 on the human chemokine network. (A) Impact of EVA-P991 and EVA-P1142 on chemokine signaling to leukocytes. The chemokine network is represented as in Fig. 3A, but with the chemokine targets of EVA-P991 and EVA-P1142 (indicated in gray) and their connections removed from the network. (B) Impact of EVA-P991 and EVA-P1142 on feedforward loops. The chemokine network is represented as in Fig. 3B, but with the chemokine targets of EVA-P991 and EVA-P1142 (indicated in gray) and their connections removed from the network.

binding both ELR+ and ELR-chemokines. The most promiscuous class B evasins were EVA-P1142 and EVA-P1126, both from *Amblyomma cajenennse*. Neither class A or class B evasins bound CX3CL or XCL chemokines. While extensive neutralization studies have not been conducted, we have found that where tested, evasin binding invariably predicts neutralization of chemokine activity (Fig. 5C). The spectrum of chemokine binding observed indicates that evasins function to inhibit inflammation at the site of tick bite by reducing not only chemokine signaling to receptors (Fig. 6A) but also by interrupting the feedforward loops (Fig. 6B), thus disabling the chemokine network.

3.6 Molecular mechanism of evasin-chemokine interactions

The mechanisms of evasin binding, elucidated by structural studies of evasin – chemokine complexes, have recently been reviewed (Bhusal et al., 2019). Both evasin classes have disulfide bonded cores, with EVA1 having four, between the eight conserved Cys residues, and EVA-3 having three disulfide bonds between the six conserved Cys residues that forms an inhibitory-cystine knot or "knottin" scaffold. A concave surface in EVA-1 created by N and C-terminal regions together with the first beta-sheet binds the chemokine CCL3 through regions that interact with the receptor (Dias et al., 2009). In EVA-3, the "knottin" scaffold interacts with CXCL8 to inhibit dimerization and interaction with glycosaminoglycans, causing structural rearrangement of CXCL8 regions that are thought to inhibit receptor binding (Denisov et al., 2019).

3.7 Mechanisms underlying evasin promiscuity

The mechanisms underlying evasin promiscuity are not clearly understood. One potential mechanism is differential ligand positioning (Sethi, Agarwal, Manivel, Rao, & Salunke, 2006), where different chemokines bind different parts of the evasin molecule. An alternative mechanism is conformational structural plasticity (Aharoni et al., 2005; James, Roversi, & Tawfik, 2003), where different chemokines bind the same part of the evasin but which adopts different conformations. Using domain swapping approaches to create hybrid evasins, we have shown that a linear segment from the N-terminus of EVA-P672 when transferred to EVA-1, transfers CCL8 binding activity. Likewise, a linear segment from the knottin scaffold of EVA-P1142 when transferred to EVA-3, also transfers CXCL10 binding activity (Eaton et al., 2018; Lee et al., 2019). These studies indicate that differential ligand positioning may, at least in part, explain evasin promiscuity.

4. Outlook: developing evasins as therapeutics

4.1 Combinatorial action of evasins in human disease

A considerable body of evidence thus indicates that natural selection in parasites such as viruses, helminths and ticks has resulted in a formidable array of proteins that target multiple nodes in the chemokine network. The extensive examples from tick evasins indicate that they function at the site of tick bite by reducing total chemokine load, which not only reduces chemokine signaling to receptors but also interrupts feedforward loops, thus disabling the chemokine network. Taking the lead from nature, a goal for the development of new anti-chemokine therapeutics would be to reduce the total chemokine load in disease. Certain broad-spectrum evasins such as EVA-P991 and EVA-P1142, which block multiple CC and CXC chemokines respectively, together with EVA-3 which blocks CXCL8, if used in appropriate combinations, may substantially lower the total chemokine load in a number of human diseases, and also disable feedforward loops that amplify the inflammatory response (Fig. 7).

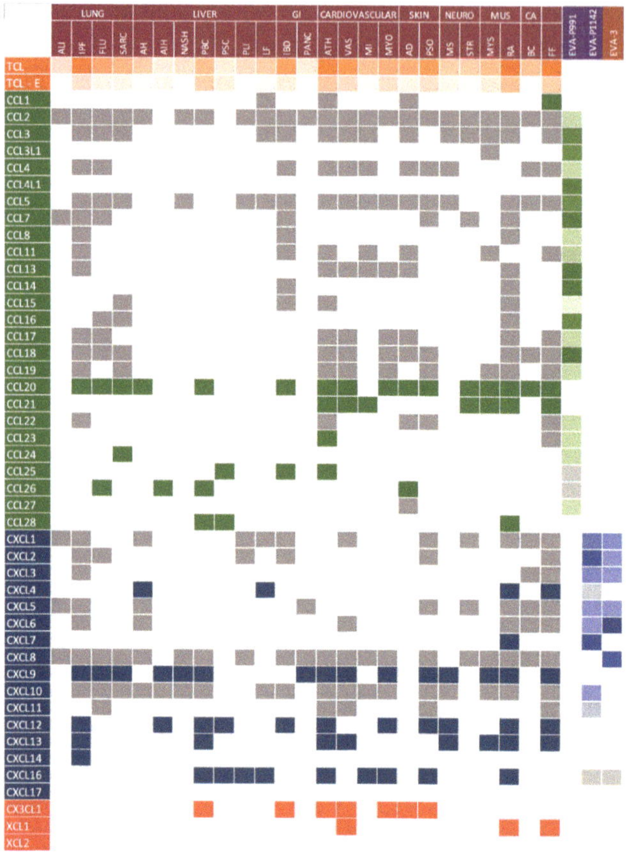

Fig. 7 The impact of evasins on total chemokine load in human disease. Chemokine expression patterns in human inflammatory diseases and feedforward chemokines are shown as filled rectangles at the intersection of chemokine (left column) and disease (top row). The chemokine binding patterns of EVA-P991, EVA-P1142, and EVA-3 are shown in adjacent columns. CC chemokine patterns are colored green, CXC in blue, CX3C and XC in red, and where expected to be neutralized by the evasins are shown in gray. The total chemokine load in individual diseases (TCL) and effect of evasin on total chemokine load (TCL-E) are color-coded in orange with darker shades indicating higher load. Abbreviations as in Fig. 1.

4.2 Two-warhead evasins

Ticks inject a cocktail of evasins at the site of attachment. Practical considerations currently limit the clinical development of therapeutic cocktails, as each component of a cocktail needs to be independently validated for safety and efficacy(Woodcock, Griffin, & Behrman, 2011). One possible approach to overcome these hurdles is the development and application of "two-warhead" or even "multi-warhead" evasins where CC and CXC-chemokine binding evasins are physically linked together to create a single agent. We have shown that such an approach creates novel bioactive agents that neutralize both CC and CXC chemokines (Alenazi et al., 2018). Such agents could potentially be applicable to the therapy of a large number of inflammatory diseases. Importantly, selecting appropriate tick evasin combinations should make it possible to develop agents that specifically target only those chemokines that are important in disease pathophysiology, thus allowing precision targeting of disease-relevant CC and CXC chemokine subsets by a single agent.

4.3 Prospects for the development of peptidomimetics

Key limitations of biologicals are the possibility of immunogenicity and the requirement for parenteral delivery, which hinder their application in chronic diseases where long term therapy is required. These limitations have been overcome in several instances by the development of peptidomimetic therapeutics, which are derived from biologicals and mimic their activity. Small molecules have the advantage that they can be administered orally. Examples of small molecule peptidomimetics include ACE inhibitors, tirofiban and eptifibatide, which were developed from snake venom through the deconvolution of a protein-protein interaction, via a protein-peptide interaction and then finally to a peptidomimetic (small molecule)-protein interaction (Koh & Kini, 2012). Denisov et al. recently reported the development of synthetic EVA-3 variants that bind and neutralize CXCL8 (Denisov et al., 2019). These results suggest that by identifying evasin regions that independently bind chemokines, we can identify smaller peptides, and ultimately small molecule therapeutics, that inhibit chemokine function.

5. Appendix

5.1 Chemokine expression patterns in human disease

Alcoholic liver injury: (Marra & Tacke, 2014). *Atherosclerosis:* (Abd Alla et al., 2010; Abi-Younes et al., 2000; Calvayrac et al., 2011; Erbel et al., 2007; Haley et al., 2000; Haque et al., 2000; Kim, Kang, et al., 2011; Kimura et al., 2012; Mach et al., 1999; Minami et al., 2001; Reape & Groot, 1999; Smedbakken et al., 2012; Weber et al., 2011; Yu et al., 2004). *Atopic dermatitis:* (Echigo, Hasegawa, Shimada, Takehara, & Sato, 2004; Hijnen et al., 2004; Kakinuma et al., 2003; Nomura et al., 2003; Owczarek et al., 2010; Park et al., 2008; Pivarcsi et al., 2004) (Homey, Steinhoff, Ruzicka, & Leung, 2006). *Autoimmune hepatitis:* (Czaja, 2014). Breast cancer: (Bell et al., 1999; Bieche et al., 2007; Chavey et al., 2007; Chen et al., 2011; Luboshits et al., 1999; Soria et al., 2008; Ueno et al., 2000). *Idiopathic pulmonary fibrosis:* (Antoniou et al., 2006; Belperio et al., 2004; Capelli, Di Stefano, Gnemmi, & Donner, 2005; DePianto et al., 2015; Hartl et al., 2005; Petrek et al., 1997; Schmidt et al., 2009; Schupp et al., 2015; Vasakova et al., 2009; Vuga et al., 2014; Willems et al., 2013). *Inflammatory bowel disease:* (Ahrens et al., 2008; Banks, Bateman, Payne, Johnson, & Sheron, 2003; Dotan et al., 2010; Izzo et al., 1993; Kotarsky et al., 2010; Mahida et al., 1992; Mazzucchelli et al., 1996; Papadakis et al., 2001; Puleston et al., 2005; Reinecker et al., 1995; Sans et al., 2007; Uguccioni et al., 1999). *Influenza:* (Bian et al., 2014; de Jong et al., 2006; Gao et al., 2013; Hagau et al., 2010; Kim, Kim, & Hyun, 2011; Lee et al., 2007, 2011; Marion et al., 2016; Takano, Tajiri, Kashiwagi, Kimura, & Kawashima, 2011; Wang et al., 2014; Zeng et al., 2015). *Liver fibrosis:* (Czaja, 2014; Sahin & Wasmuth, 2013). *Multiple sclerosis:* (Krumbholz et al., 2006; Miyagishi, Kikuchi, Fukazawa, & Tashiro, 1995; Simpson, Newcombe, Cuzner, & Woodroofe, 2000). *Myocardial infarction:* (de Lemos et al., 2007; Orn et al., 2009). *Myocarditis:* (Borst et al., 2014; Escher et al., 2011; Fahmy et al., 2003; Fuse et al., 2001; Kittleson et al., 2005; Lassner et al., 2014; Lehmann, Kuhnert, Muller, & Sigusch, 1998; Nogueira et al., 2012; Satoh et al., 1996; Zuern et al., 2015). *Myositis:* (De Paepe, Creus, & De Bleecker, 2009; Szodoray et al., 2010; Tateyama et al., 2006). *Non-alcoholic steatohepatitis:* (Braunersreuther, Viviani, Mach, & Montecucco, 2012; Xu, Zhang, Lau, & Yu, 2016). *Pancreatitis:* (Rau, Baumgart, Kruger, Schilling, & Beger, 2003; Saurer et al., 2000). *Paracetamol liver injury:* (Krenkel, Mossanen, & Tacke, 2014). *Primary biliary cirrhosis:*(Borchers, Shimoda, Bowlus, Keen, & Gershwin, 2009; Dyson et al., 2015; Heydtmann et al., 2005; Hirschfield & Gershwin, 2013; Landi et al., 2014; Li et al., 2015; Sasaki, Miyakoshi, Sato, & Nakanuma, 2014). *Primary sclerosing cholangitis:* (Borchers et al., 2009; Eksteen et al., 2004). *Psoriasis:* (Brunner et al., 2015; Congjun, Yanmei, Huiling, Zhen, & Shuo, 2015; Ferrari et al., 2015; Fukuoka et al., 1998; Nomura et al., 2003; Zhou et al., 2003). *Rheumatoid arthritis:* (Szekanecz & Koch, 2016): *Sarcoidosis:* (Agostini et al., 1998; Arakelyan et al., 2009; Cai et al., 2013; Facco et al., 2007; Gibejova et al., 2003; Palchevskiy et al., 2011; Petrek, Kolek,

Szotkowska, & du Bois, 2002). Stroke: (Mirabelli-Badenier et al., 2011). *Vasculitis:*(Blaschke, Brandt, Wessels, & Muller, 2009; Brix et al., 2015; Bruhl, 2005; Corbera-Bellalta et al., 2016; Dallos et al., 2010; Deng et al., 2009; Dhawan, Mahajan, & Jain, 2006; Eardley, Smith, & Cockwell, 2009; Eriksson, Andersson, Cassel, Nystrom, & Ernerudh, 2015; Freire Ade, Bertolo, de Pinho, Samara, & Fernandes, 2004; Noris, Daina, Gamba, Bonazzola, & Remuzzi, 1999).

5.2 Chemokine expression by human leukocytes

B cells: (Vazquez, Catalan-Dibene, & Zlotnik, 2015). *Basophils:* (Varricchi, Raap, Rivellese, Marone, & Gibbs, 2018). *Dendritic cells:* (Lebre et al., 2005). Eosinophils: (Davoine & Lacy, 2014). *Monocytes/macrophages:* (Arango Duque & Descoteaux, 2014; Fantuzzi, Belardelli, & Gessani, 2003; Ferrara et al., 2008). *Mast cells:* (Varricchi et al., 2018). *Neutrophils:* (Tecchio et al., 2014). *T cells* (Cristillo, Macri, & Bierer, 2003; Miller & Krangel, 1992; Ward & Westwick, 1998):

5.3 Target validation using mouse models

Atherosclerosis: CX3CL1, CCL2, CCL3, CCL17, CCL5, CXCL4, CXCL10, (Gu et al., 1998; Heller et al., 2006; Kennedy et al., 2012; King et al., 2009; Koenen et al., 2009; Saederup et al., 2008; Teupser et al., 2004; Weber et al., 2011). *Atopic dermatitis:* CCR4, CCR10, (Mirshahpanah et al., 2008). *Bleomycin lung injury:* CCL3, CCL6, CXCL2, CXCL6, CXCL12, CCL12, CCR2, CCR1, CCR7, CXCR2 (Belperio et al., 2002; Besnard et al., 2013; Keane et al., 1999; Moore et al., 2001, 2006; Phillips et al., 2004; Russo et al., 2009; Smith et al., 1994; Tokuda et al., 2000; Trujillo, Hartigan, & Hogaboam, 2010)). *Inflammatory bowel disease:* CCL2, CCL3, CCR1, CCR2, CCR5, (Andres et al., 2000; Khan et al., 2006; Morteau et al., 2002; Platt, Bain, Bordon, Sester, & Mowat, 2010). Influenza pneumonitis: CCL2, CCL3, CCL7, CCR2, (Cook et al., 1995; Dawson, Beck, Kuziel, Henderson, & Maeda, 2000; Ellis et al., 2015; Herold et al., 2008). *Rheumatoid arthritis:* CXCR2, CXCR4, (Chung et al., 2010; Shin et al., 2009).

Acknowledgments

This work was supported by a Chair Award (CH/09/003/26631), a Project Grant (PG/16/100/32632) and a Program Grant (RG/18/1/33351) from the British Heart Foundation. The authors are grateful to Richard Williams and Garrett Morris for their most helpful and detailed comments on the manuscript.

References

Abd Alla, J., Langer, A., Elzahwy, S. S., Arman-Kalcek, G., Streichert, T., & Quitterer, U. (2010). Angiotensin-converting enzyme inhibition down-regulates the pro-atherogenic chemokine receptor 9 (CCR9)-chemokine ligand 25 (CCL25) axis. *Journal of Biological Chemistry, 285*(30), 23496–23505. Retrieved from http://eutils.ncbi.nlm.nih.gov/entrez/eutils/elink.fcgi?dbfrom=pubmed&id=20504763&retmode=ref&cmd=prlinks http://www.jbc.org/content/285/30/23496.full.pdf.

Abi-Younes, S., Sauty, A., Mach, F., Sukhova, G. K., Libby, P., & Luster, A. D. (2000). The stromal cell-derived factor-1 chemokine is a potent platelet agonist highly expressed in atherosclerotic plaques. *Circulation Research, 86*(2), 131–138. Retrieved from http://eutils.ncbi.nlm.nih.gov/entrez/eutils/elink.fcgi?dbfrom=pubmed&id=10666407&retmode=ref&cmd=prlinks http://circres.ahajournals.org/content/86/2/131.full.pdf.

Agostini, C., Cassatella, M., Zambello, R., Trentin, L., Gasperini, S., Perin, A., et al. (1998). Involvement of the IP-10 chemokine in sarcoid granulomatous reactions. *The Journal of Immunology, 161*(11), 6413–6420. Retrieved from http://www.ncbi.nlm.nih.gov/pubmed/9834133.

Aharoni, A., Gaidukov, L., Khersonsky, O., Mc, Q. G. S., Roodveldt, C., & Tawfik, D. S. (2005). The 'evolvability' of promiscuous protein functions. *Nature Genetics, 37*(1), 73–76. http://dx.doi.org/10.1038/ng1482.

Ahrens, R., Waddell, A., Seidu, L., Blanchard, C., Carey, R., Forbes, E., et al. (2008). Intestinal macrophage/epithelial cell-derived CCL11/eotaxin-1 mediates eosinophil recruitment and function in pediatric ulcerative colitis. *The Journal of Immunology, 181*(10), 7390–7399. Retrieved from http://www.ncbi.nlm.nih.gov/pubmed/18981162 http://www.jimmunol.org/content/jimmunol/181/10/7390.full.pdf.

Alenazi, Y., Singh, K., Davies, G., Eaton, J. R. O., Elders, P., Kawamura, A., et al. (2018). Genetically engineered two-warhead evasins provide a method to achieve precision targeting of disease-relevant chemokine subsets. *Scientific Reports, 8*(1), 6333. http://dx.doi.org/10.1038/s41598-018-24568-9.

Andres, P. G., Beck, P. L., Mizoguchi, E., Mizoguchi, A., Bhan, A. K., Dawson, T., et al. (2000). Mice with a selective deletion of the CC chemokine receptors 5 or 2 are protected from dextran sodium sulfate-mediated colitis: Lack of CC chemokine receptor 5 expression results in a NK1.1+ lymphocyte-associated Th2-type immune response in the intestine. *The Journal of Immunology, 164*(12), 6303–6312. Retrieved from http://www.ncbi.nlm.nih.gov/pubmed/10843684.

Antoniou, K. M., Tzouvelekis, A., Alexandrakis, M. G., Sfiridaki, K., Tsiligianni, I., Rachiotis, G., et al. (2006). Different angiogenic activity in pulmonary sarcoidosis and idiopathic pulmonary fibrosis. *Chest, 130*(4), 982–988. http://dx.doi.org/10.1378/chest.130.4.982.

Arakelyan, A., Kriegova, E., Kubistova, Z., Mrazek, F., Kverka, M., du Bois, R. M., et al. (2009). Protein levels of CC chemokine ligand (CCL)15, CCL16 and macrophage stimulating protein in patients with sarcoidosis. *Clinical and Experimental Immunology, 155*(3), 457–465. http://dx.doi.org/10.1111/j.1365-2249.2008.03832.x.

Arango Duque, G., & Descoteaux, A. (2014). Macrophage cytokines: Involvement in immunity and infectious diseases. *Frontiers in Immunology, 5*, 491. http://dx.doi.org/10.3389/fimmu.2014.00491.

Bachelerie, F., Ben-Baruch, A., Burkhardt, A. M., Combadiere, C., Farber, J. M., Graham, G. J., et al. (2014). International Union of Basic and Clinical Pharmacology. LXXXIX. Update on the extended family of chemokine receptors and introducing a new nomenclature for atypical chemokine receptors. *Pharmacological Reviews, 66*(1), 1–79. http://dx.doi.org/10.1124/pr.113.007724.

Banks, C., Bateman, A., Payne, R., Johnson, P., & Sheron, N. (2003). Chemokine expression in IBD. Mucosal chemokine expression is unselectively increased in both ulcerative colitis and Crohn's disease. *The Journal of Pathology, 199*(1), 28–35. http://dx.doi.org/10.1002/path.1245.

Beecham, A. H., Patsopoulos, N. A., Xifara, D. K., Davis, M. F., Kemppinen, A., Cotsapas, C., et al. (2013) Analysis of immune-related loci identifies 48 new susceptibility variants for multiple sclerosis. *Nature Genetics, 45*(11), 1353–1360. http://dx.doi.org/10.1038/ng.2770.

Bell, D., Chomarat, P., Broyles, D., Netto, G., Harb, G. M., Lebecque, S., et al. (1999). In breast carcinoma tissue, immature dendritic cells reside within the tumor, whereas mature dendritic cells are located in peritumoral areas. *Journal of Experimental Medicine, 190*(10), 1417–1426. Retrieved from http://www.ncbi.nlm.nih.gov/pubmed/10562317 https://www.ncbi.nlm.nih.gov/pmc/articles/PMC2195690/pdf/99-1248.pdf.

Belperio, J. A., Dy, M., Burdick, M. D., Xue, Y. Y., Li, K., Elias, J. A., et al. (2002). Interaction of IL-13 and C10 in the pathogenesis of bleomycin-induced pulmonary fibrosis. *American Journal of Respiratory Cell and Molecular Biology, 27*(4), 419–427. http://dx.doi.org/10.1165/rcmb.2002-0009OC.

Belperio, J. A., Dy, M., Murray, L., Burdick, M. D., Xue, Y. Y., Strieter, R. M., et al. (2004). The role of the Th2 CC chemokine ligand CCL17 in pulmonary fibrosis. *The Journal of Immunology, 173*(7), 4692–4698. http://dx.doi.org/10.4049/jimmunol.173.7.4692.

Besnard, A. G., Struyf, S., Guabiraba, R., Fauconnier, L., Rouxel, N., Proost, P., et al. (2013). CXCL6 antibody neutralization prevents lung inflammation and fibrosis in mice in the bleomycin model. *Journal of Leukocyte Biology, 94*(6), 1317–1323. http://dx.doi.org/10.1189/jlb.0313140.

Bhusal, R. P., Eaton, J. R. O., Chowdhury, S. T., Power, C. A., Proudfoot, A. E. I., Stone, M. J., & Bhattacharya, S. (2019). Evasins: Tick salivary proteins that inhibit mammalian chemokines. *Trends in Biochemical Science.* pii: S0968-0004(19)30204-X. https://doi.org/10.1016/j.tibs.2019.10.003. [Epub ahead of print] Review. PMID: 31679840

Bian, J. R., Nie, W., Zang, Y. S., Fang, Z., Xiu, Q. Y., & Xu, X. X. (2014). Clinical aspects and cytokine response in adults with seasonal influenza infection. *International Journal of Clinical and Experimental Medicine,* 7(12), 5593–5602. Retrieved from http://www.ncbi.nlm.nih.gov/pubmed/25664078.

Bieche, I., Chavey, C., Andrieu, C., Busson, M., Vacher, S., Le Corre, L., et al. (2007). CXC chemokines located in the 4q21 region are up-regulated in breast cancer. *Endocrine-Related Cancer, 14*(4), 1039–1052. http://dx.doi.org/10.1677/erc.1.01301.

Blaschke, S., Brandt, P., Wessels, J. T., & Muller, G. A. (2009). Expression and function of the C-class chemokine lymphotactin (XCL1) in Wegener's granulomatosis. *Journal of Rheumatology, 36*(11), 2491–2500. http://dx.doi.org/10.3899/jrheum.090244.

Bonvin, P., Dunn, S. M., Rousseau, F., Dyer, D. P., Shaw, J., Power, C. A., et al. (2014). Identification of the pharmacophore of the CC chemokine-binding proteins evasin-1 and-4 using phage display. *Journal of Biological Chemistry, 289*(46), 31846–31855. http://dx.doi.org/10.1074/jbc.M114.599233.

Bonvin, P., Power, C. A., & Proudfoot, A. E. (2016). Evasins: Therapeutic potential of a new family of chemokine-binding proteins from ticks. *Frontiers in Immunology,* 7(208), 208. http://dx.doi.org/10.3389/fimmu.2016.00208.

Borchers, A. T., Shimoda, S., Bowlus, C., Keen, C. L., & Gershwin, M. E. (2009). Lymphocyte recruitment and homing to the liver in primary biliary cirrhosis and primary sclerosing cholangitis. *Seminars in Immunopathology, 31*(3), 309–322. http://dx.doi.org/10.1007/s00281-009-0167-2.

Borst, O., Schaub, M., Walker, B., Sauter, M., Muenzer, P., Gramlich, M., et al. (2014). CXCL16 is a novel diagnostic marker and predictor of mortality in inflammatory cardiomyopathy and heart failure. *International Journal of Cardiology, 176*(3), 896–903. http://dx.doi.org/10.1016/j.ijcard.2014.08.033.

Brandes, M., Klauschen, F., Kuchen, S., & Germain, R. N. (2013). A systems analysis identifies a feedforward inflammatory circuit leading to lethal influenza infection. *Cell, 154*(1), 197–212. http://dx.doi.org/10.1016/j.cell.2013.06.013.

Braunersreuther, V., Montecucco, F., Pelli, G., Galan, K., Proudfoot, A. E., Belin, A., et al. (2013). Treatment with the CC chemokine-binding protein Evasin-4 improves post-infarction myocardial injury and survival in mice. *Thrombosis & Haemostasis, 110*(4), 807–825. Retrieved from http://eutils.ncbi.nlm.nih.gov/entrez/eutils/elink.fcgi?dbfrom=pubmed&id=23925450&retmode=ref&cmd=prlinks http://th.schattauer.de/en/contents/archive/issue/1791/manuscript/20025/download.html.

Braunersreuther, V., Viviani, G. L., Mach, F., & Montecucco, F. (2012). Role of cytokines and chemokines in non-alcoholic fatty liver disease. *World Journal of Gastroenterology, 18*(8), 727–735. http://dx.doi.org/10.3748/wjg.v18.i8.727.

Brix, S. R., Stege, G., Disteldorf, E., Hoxha, E., Krebs, C., Krohn, S., et al. (2015). CC chemokine ligand 18 in ANCA-associated crescentic GN. *Journal of the American Society of Nephrology, 26*(9), 2105–2117. http://dx.doi.org/10.1681/ASN.2014040407.

Bruhl, H. (2005). Expression of DARC, CXCR3 and CCR5 in giant cell arteritis. *Rheumatology, 44*(3), 309–313. http://dx.doi.org/10.1093/rheumatology/keh485.

Brunner, P. M., Glitzner, E., Reininger, B., Klein, I., Stary, G., Mildner, M., et al. (2015). CCL7 contributes to the TNF-alpha-dependent inflammation of lesional psoriatic skin. *Experimental Dermatology, 24*(7), 522–528. http://dx.doi.org/10.1111/exd.12709.

Cai, M., Bonella, F., He, X., Sixt, S. U., Sarria, R., Guzman, J., et al. (2013). CCL18 in serum, BAL fluid and alveolar macrophage culture supernatant in interstitial lung diseases. *Respiratory Medicine, 107*(9), 1444–1452. http://dx.doi.org/10.1016/j.rmed.2013.06.004.

Calvayrac, O., Rodríguez-Calvo, R., Alonso, J., Orbe, J., Martín-Ventura, J. L., Guadall, A., et al. (2011). CCL20 is increased in hypercholesterolemic subjects and is upregulated by LDL in vascular smooth muscle cells: Role of NF-κB. *Arteriosclerosis, Thrombosis, and Vascular Biology, 31*(11), 2733–2741. Retrieved from http://eutils.ncbi.nlm.nih.gov/entrez/eutils/elink.fcgi?dbfrom=pubmed&id=21852561&retmode=ref&cmd=prlinks http://atvb.ahajournals.org/content/31/11/2733.full.pdf.

Capelli, A., Di Stefano, A., Gnemmi, I., & Donner, C. F. (2005). CCR5 expression and CC chemokine levels in idiopathic pulmonary fibrosis. *European Respiratory Journal, 25*(4), 701–707. http://dx.doi.org/10.1183/09031936.05.00082604.

Castor, M. G. M., Rezende, B., Resende, C. B., Alessandri, A. L., Fagundes, C. T., Sousa, L. P., et al. (2010). The CCL3/macrophage inflammatory protein-1alpha-binding protein evasin-1 protects from graft-versus-host disease but does not modify graft-versus-leukemia in mice. *The Journal of Immunology, 184*(5), 2646–2654. Retrieved from http://eutils.ncbi.nlm.nih.gov/entrez/eutils/elink.fcgi?dbfrom=pubmed&id=20100934&retmode=ref&cmd=prlinks http://www.jimmunol.org/content/184/5/2646.full.pdf.

Chavey, C., Bibeau, F., Gourgou-Bourgade, S., Burlinchon, S., Boissiere, F., Laune, D., et al. (2007). Oestrogen receptor negative breast cancers exhibit high cytokine content. *Breast Cancer Research: BCR, 9*(1), R15. http://dx.doi.org/10.1186/bcr1648.

Chen, J., Yao, Y., Gong, C., Yu, F., Su, S., Chen, J., et al. (2011). CCL18 from tumor-associated macrophages promotes breast cancer metastasis via PITPNM3. *Cancer Cell, 19*(4), 541–555. http://dx.doi.org/10.1016/j.ccr.2011.02.006.

Chung, S. H., Seki, K., Choi, B. I., Kimura, K. B., Ito, A., Fujikado, N., et al. (2010). CXC chemokine receptor 4 expressed in T cells plays an important role in the development of collagen-induced arthritis. *Arthritis Research and Therapy, 12*(5), R188. http://dx.doi.org/10.1186/ar3158.

Combadière, C., Potteaux, S., Rodero, M., Simon, T., Pezard, A., Esposito, B., et al. (2008). Combined inhibition of CCL2, CX3CR1, and CCR5 abrogates Ly6C(hi) and Ly6C(lo) monocytosis and almost abolishes atherosclerosis in hypercholesterolemic mice. *Circulation, 117*(13), 1649–1657. Retrieved from http://eutils.ncbi.nlm.nih.gov/entrez/eutils/elink.fcgi?dbfrom=pubmed&id=18347211&retmode=ref&cmd=prlinks http://circ.ahajournals.org/content/117/13/1649.full.pdf.

Congjun, J., Yanmei, Z., Huiling, J., Zhen, Y., & Shuo, L. (2015). Elevated local and serum CX3CL1(fractalkine) expression and its association with disease severity in patients with psoriasis. *Annals of Clinical & Laboratory Science, 45*(5), 556–561. Retrieved from http://www.ncbi.nlm.nih.gov/pubmed/26586708 http://www.annclinlabsci.org/content/45/5/556.full.pdf.

Cook, D. N., Beck, M. A., Coffman, T. M., Kirby, S. L., Sheridan, J. F., Pragnell, I. B., et al. (1995). Requirement of MIP-1 alpha for an inflammatory response to viral infection. *Science, 269*(5230), 1583–1585. Retrieved from http://www.ncbi.nlm.nih.gov/pubmed/7667639 http://science.sciencemag.org/content/sci/269/5230/1583.full.pdf.

Copin, J.-C., da Silva, R. F., Fraga-Silva, R. A., Capettini, L., Quintao, S., Lenglet, S., et al. (2013). Treatment with Evasin-3 reduces atherosclerotic vulnerability for ischemic stroke, but not brain injury in mice. *Journal of Cerebral Blood Flow and Metabolism, 33*(4), 490–498. Retrieved from http://eutils.ncbi.nlm.nih.gov/entrez/eutils/elink.fcgi?dbfrom=pubmed&id=23250107&retmode=ref&cmd=prlinks http://www.ncbi.nlm.nih.gov/pmc/articles/PMC3618389/pdf/jcbfm2012198a.pdf.

Corbera-Bellalta, M., Planas-Rigol, E., Lozano, E., Terrades-García, N., Alba, M. A., Prieto-González, S., et al. (2016). Blocking interferon γ reduces expression of chemokines CXCL9, CXCL10 and CXCL11 and decreases macrophage infiltration in ex vivo cultured arteries from patients with giant cell arteritis. *Annals of the Rheumatic Diseases, 75*(6), 1177–1186. http://dx.doi.org/10.1136/annrheumdis-2015-208371.

Cristillo, A. D., Macri, M. J., & Bierer, B. E. (2003). Differential chemokine expression profiles in human peripheral blood T lymphocytes: Dependence on T-cell coreceptor and calcineurin signaling. *Blood, 101*(1), 216–225. http://dx.doi.org/10.1182/blood-2002-03-0697.

Czaja, A. J. (2014). Review article: Chemokines as orchestrators of autoimmune hepatitis and potential therapeutic targets. *Alimentary Pharmacology & Therapeutics, 40*(3), 261–279. http://dx.doi.org/10.1111/apt.12825.

Dallos, T., Heiland, G. R., Strehl, J., Karonitsch, T., Gross, W. L., Moosig, F., et al. (2010). CCL17/thymus and activation-related chemokine in Churg-Strauss syndrome. *Arthritis & Rheumatism, 62*(11), 3496–3503. http://dx.doi.org/10.1002/art.27678.

Davoine, F., & Lacy, P. (2014). Eosinophil cytokines, chemokines, and growth factors: Emerging roles in immunity. *Frontiers in Immunology, 5*, 570. http://dx.doi.org/10.3389/fimmu.2014.00570.

Dawson, T. C., Beck, M. A., Kuziel, W. A., Henderson, F., & Maeda, N. (2000). Contrasting effects of CCR5 and CCR2 deficiency in the pulmonary inflammatory response to influenza a virus. *American Journal of Pathology, 156*(6), 1951–1959. http://dx.doi.org/10.1016/s0002-9440(10)65068-7.

De Paepe, B., Creus, K. K., & De Bleecker, J. L. (2009). Role of cytokines and chemokines in idiopathic inflammatory myopathies. *Current Opinion in Rheumatology, 21*(6), 610–616. http://dx.doi.org/10.1097/BOR.0b013e3283317b31.

Deng, J., Ma-Krupa, W., Gewirtz, A. T., Younge, B. R., Goronzy, J. J., & Weyand, C. M. (2009). Toll-like receptors 4 and 5 induce distinct types of vasculitis. *Circulation Research, 104*(4), 488–495. http://dx.doi.org/10.1161/CIRCRESAHA.108.185777.

Denisov, S. S., Ippel, J. H., Heinzmann, A. C. A., Koenen, R. R., Ortega-Gomez, A., Soehnlein, O., et al. (2019). Tick saliva protein Evasin-3 modulates chemotaxis by disrupting CXCL8 interactions with glycosaminoglycans and CXCR2. *Journal of Biological Chemistry*. http://dx.doi.org/10.1074/jbc.RA119.008902.

DePianto, D. J., Chandriani, S., Abbas, A. R., Jia, G., N'Diaye, E. N., Caplazi, P., et al. (2015). Heterogeneous gene expression signatures correspond to distinct lung pathologies and biomarkers of disease severity in idiopathic pulmonary fibrosis. *Thorax, 70*(1), 48–56. http://dx.doi.org/10.1136/thoraxjnl-2013-204596.

Déruaz, M., Bonvin, P., Severin, I. C., Johnson, Z., Krohn, S., Power, C. A., et al. (2013). Evasin-4, a tick-derived chemokine-binding protein with broad selectivity can be modified for use in preclinical disease models. *FEBS Journal, 280*(19), 4876–4887. Retrieved from http://doi.wiley.com/10.1111/febs.12463 http://www.ncbi.nlm.nih.gov/pmc/articles/PMC4240464/pdf/febs0280-4876.pdf.

Deruaz, M., Frauenschuh, A., Alessandri, A. L., Dias, J. M., Coelho, F. M., Russo, R. C., et al. (2008). Ticks produce highly selective chemokine binding proteins with antiinflammatory activity. *Journal of Experimental Medicine, 205*(9), 2019–2031. http://dx.doi.org/10.1084/jem.20072689.

DeVries, M. E., Kelvin, A. A., Xu, L., Ran, L., Robinson, J., & Kelvin, D. J. (2006). Defining the origins and evolution of the chemokine/chemokine receptor system. *The Journal of Immunology, 176*(1), 401–415. Retrieved from http://eutils.ncbi.nlm.nih.gov/entrez/eutils/elink.fcgi?dbfrom=pubmed&id=16365434&retmode=ref&cmd=prlinks http://www.jimmunol.org/content/176/1/401.full.pdf.

Dhawan, V., Mahajan, N., & Jain, S. (2006). Role of C-C chemokines in Takayasu's arteritis disease. *International Journal of Cardiology, 112*(1), 105–111. http://dx.doi.org/10.1016/j.ijcard.2005.11.101.

Dias, J. M., Losberger, C., Déruaz, M., Power, C. A., Proudfoot, A. E. I., & Shaw, J. P. (2009). Structural basis of chemokine sequestration by a tick chemokine binding protein: The crystal structure of the complex between evasin-1 and CCL3. *PLoS One, 4*(12), e8514. Retrieved from http://dx.plos.org/10.1371/journal.pone.0008514.s004 http://www.ncbi.nlm.nih.gov/pmc/articles/PMC2796168/pdf/pone.0008514.pdf.

Dotan, I., Werner, L., Vigodman, S., Weiss, S., Brazowski, E., Maharshak, N., et al. (2010). CXCL12 is a constitutive and inflammatory chemokine in the intestinal immune system. *Inflammatory Bowel Diseases, 16*(4), 583–592. http://dx.doi.org/10.1002/ibd.21106.

Dyson, J. K., Hirschfield, G. M., Adams, D. H., Beuers, U., Mann, D. A., Lindor, K. D., et al. (2015). Novel therapeutic targets in primary biliary cirrhosis. *Nature Reviews Gastroenterology & Hepatology, 12*(3), 147–158. http://dx.doi.org/10.1038/nrgastro.2015.12.

Eardley, K. S., Smith, S. W., & Cockwell, P. (2009). Chemokines in vasculitis. *Frontiers in Bioscience, 1*, 26–35. Retrieved from https://www.ncbi.nlm.nih.gov/pubmed/19482621.

Eaton, J. R. O., Alenazi, Y., Singh, K., Davies, G., Geis-Asteggiante, L., Kessler, B., et al. (2018). The N-terminal domain of a tick evasin is critical for chemokine binding and neutralization and confers specific binding activity to other evasins. *Journal of Biological Chemistry, 293*(16), 6134–6146. http://dx.doi.org/10.1074/jbc.RA117.000487.

Echigo, T., Hasegawa, M., Shimada, Y., Takehara, K., & Sato, S. (2004). Expression of fractalkine and its receptor, CX3CR1, in atopic dermatitis: Possible contribution to skin inflammation. *The Journal of Allergy and Clinical Immunology, 113*(5), 940–948. http://dx.doi.org/10.1016/j.jaci.2004.02.030.

Eksteen, B., Grant, A. J., Miles, A., Curbishley, S. M., Lalor, P. F., Hubscher, S. G., et al. (2004). Hepatic endothelial CCL25 mediates the recruitment of CCR9+ gut-homing lymphocytes to the liver in primary sclerosing cholangitis. *Journal of Experimental Medicine, 200*(11), 1511–1517. http://dx.doi.org/10.1084/jem.20041035.

Ellinghaus, D., Jostins, L., Spain, S. L., Cortes, A., Bethune, J., Han, B., et al. (2016). Analysis of five chronic inflammatory diseases identifies 27 new associations and highlights disease-specific patterns at shared loci. *Nature Genetics, 48*(5), 510–518. http://dx.doi.org/10.1038/ng.3528.

Ellis, G. T., Davidson, S., Crotta, S., Branzk, N., Papayannopoulos, V., & Wack, A. (2015). TRAIL+ monocytes and monocyte-related cells cause lung damage and thereby increase susceptibility to influenza-Streptococcus pneumoniae coinfection. *EMBO Reports, 16*(9), 1203–1218. http://dx.doi.org/10.15252/embr.201540473.

Erbel, C., Sato, K., Meyer, F. B., Kopecky, S. L., Frye, R. L., Goronzy, J. J., et al. (2007). Functional profile of activated dendritic cells in unstable atherosclerotic plaque. *Basic Research in Cardiology, 102*(2), 123–132. Retrieved from http://eutils.ncbi.nlm.nih.gov/entrez/eutils/elink.fcgi?dbfrom=pubmed&id=17136419&retmode=ref&cmd=prlinks http://link.springer.com/article/10.1007%2Fs00395-006-0636-x http://download.springer.com/static/pdf/531/art%253A10.1007%252Fs00395-006-0636-x.pdf?originUrl=http%3A%2F%2Flink.springer.com%2Farticle%2F10.1007%2Fs00395-006-0636-x&token2=exp=1437488789~acl=%2Fstatic%2Fpdf%2F531%2Fart%25253A10.1007%25252Fs00395-006-0636-x.pdf%3ForiginUrl%3Dhttp%253A%252F%252Flink.springer.com, %252Farticle%252F10.1007%252Fs00395-006-0636-x*~hmac=e07785bafe4376ebfe62090b0336165b76d671dab3f9128667d290244d1794ae.

Eriksson, P., Andersson, C., Cassel, P., Nystrom, S., & Ernerudh, J. (2015). Increase in Th17-associated CCL20 and decrease in Th2-associated CCL22 plasma chemokines in active ANCA-associated vasculitis. *Scandinavian Journal of Rheumatology, 44*(1), 80–83. http://dx.doi.org/10.3109/03009742.2014.952332.

Escher, F., Vetter, R., Kuhl, U., Westermann, D., Schultheiss, H. P., & Tschope, C. (2011). Fractalkine in human inflammatory cardiomyopathy. *Heart, 97*(9), 733–739. http://dx.doi.org/10.1136/hrt.2010.205716.

Facco, M., Baesso, I., Miorin, M., Bortoli, M., Cabrelle, A., Boscaro, E., et al. (2007). Expression and role of CCR6/CCL20 chemokine axis in pulmonary sarcoidosis. *Journal of Leukocyte Biology, 82*(4), 946–955. http://dx.doi.org/10.1189/jlb.0307133.

Fahmy, N. M., Yamani, M. H., Starling, R. C., Ratliff, N. B., Young, J. B., McCarthy, P. M., et al. (2003). Chemokine and receptor-gene expression during early and late acute rejection episodes in human cardiac allografts. *Transplantation, 75*(12), 2044–2047. http://dx.doi.org/10.1097/01.TP.0000069601.73079.94.

Fantuzzi, L., Belardelli, F., & Gessani, S. (2003). Monocyte/macrophage-derived CC chemokines and their modulation by HIV-1 and cytokines: A complex network of interactions influencing viral replication and AIDS pathogenesis. *Journal of Leukocyte Biology, 74*(5), 719–725. http://dx.doi.org/10.1189/jlb.0403175.

Ferrara, G., Bleck, B., Richeldi, L., Reibman, J., Fabbri, L. M., Rom, W. N., et al. (2008). *Mycobacterium tuberculosis* induces CCL18 expression in human macrophages. *Scandinavian Journal of Immunology, 68*(6), 668–674. http://dx.doi.org/10.1111/j.1365-3083.2008.02182.x.

Ferrari, S. M., Ruffilli, I., Colaci, M., Antonelli, A., Ferri, C., & Fallahi, P. (2015). CXCL10 in psoriasis. *Advances in Medical Sciences, 60*(2), 349–354. http://dx.doi.org/10.1016/j.advms.2015.07.011.

Frauenschuh, A., Power, C. A., Déruaz, M., Ferreira, B. R., Silva, J. S., Teixeira, M. M., et al. (2007). Molecular cloning and characterization of a highly selective chemokine-binding protein from the tick Rhipicephalus sanguineus. *Journal of Biological Chemistry, 282*(37), 27250–27258. Retrieved from http://eutils.ncbi.nlm.nih.gov/entrez/eutils/elink.fcgi?dbfrom=pubmed&id=17640866&retmode=ref&cmd=prlinks.

Freire Ade, L., Bertolo, M. B., de Pinho, A. J., Jr., Samara, A. M., & Fernandes, S. R. (2004). Increased serum levels of interleukin-8 in polyarteritis nodosa and Behcet's disease. *Clinical Rheumatology, 23*(3), 203–205. http://dx.doi.org/10.1007/s10067-003-0851-x.

Fukuoka, M., Ogino, Y., Sato, H., Ohta, T., Komoriya, K., Nishioka, K., et al. (1998). RANTES expression in psoriatic skin, and regulation of RANTES and IL-8 production in cultured epidermal keratinocytes by active vitamin D3 (tacalcitol). *British Journal of Dermatology, 138*(1), 63–70. http://dx.doi.org/10.1046/j.1365-2133.1998.02027.x.

Fuse, K., Kodama, M., Hanawa, H., Okura, Y., Ito, M., Shiono, T., et al. (2001). Enhanced expression and production of monocyte chemoattractant protein-1 in myocarditis. *Clinical and Experimental Immunology, 124*(3), 346–352. Retrieved from http://www.ncbi.nlm.nih.gov/pubmed/11472393.

Gao, R., Bhatnagar, J., Blau, D. M., Greer, P., Rollin, D. C., Denison, A. M., et al. (2013). Cytokine and chemokine profiles in lung tissues from fatal cases of 2009 pandemic influenza A (H1N1): Role of the host immune response in pathogenesis. *American Journal of Pathology, 183*(4), 1258–1268. http://dx.doi.org/10.1016/j.ajpath.2013.06.023.

Gibejova, A., Mrazek, F., Subrtova, D., Sekerova, V., Szotkowska, J., Kolek, V., et al. (2003). Expression of macrophage inflammatory protein-3 beta/CCL19 in pulmonary sarcoidosis. *American Journal of Respiratory and Critical Care Medicine, 167*(12), 1695–1703. http://dx.doi.org/10.1164/rccm.200205-487OC.

Gonzalez-Motos, V., Kropp, K. A., & Viejo-Borbolla, A. (2016). Chemokine binding proteins: An immunomodulatory strategy going viral. *Cytokine & Growth Factor Reviews, 30*, 71–80. http://dx.doi.org/10.1016/j.cytogfr.2016.02.007.

Gu, L., Okada, Y., Clinton, S. K., Gerard, C., Sukhova, G. K., Libby, P., et al. (1998). Absence of monocyte chemoattractant protein-1 reduces atherosclerosis in low density lipoprotein receptor-deficient mice. *Molecular Cell, 2*(2), 275–281. Retrieved from http://eutils.ncbi.nlm.nih.gov/entrez/eutils/elink.fcgi?dbfrom=pubmed&id=9734366&retmode=ref&cmd=prlinks http://ac.els-cdn.com/S1097276500801392/1-s2.0-S1097276500801392-main.pdf?_tid=43c0b0e0-2f81-11e5-a677-00000aab0f02&acdnat=1437466973_5dfa98a5f7ac92e5c49741e57672b83d.

Hagau, N., Slavcovici, A., Gonganau, D. N., Oltean, S., Dirzu, D. S., Brezoszki, E. S., et al. (2010). Clinical aspects and cytokine response in severe H1N1 influenza A virus infection. *Critical Care, 14*(6), R203. http://dx.doi.org/10.1186/cc9324.

Hajnická, V., Kocáková, P., Sláviková, M., Slovák, M., Gasperík, J., Fuchsberger, N., et al. (2001). Anti-interleukin-8 activity of tick salivary gland extracts. *Parasite Immunology, 23*(9), 483–489. Retrieved from http://eutils.ncbi.nlm.nih.gov/entrez/eutils/elink.fcgi?dbfrom=pubmed&id=11589777&retmode=ref&cmd=prlinks http://onlinelibrary.wiley.com/store/10.1046/j.1365-3024.2001.00403.x/asset/j.1365-3024.2001.00403.x.pdf?v=1&t=icd2i67p&s=f27dcd4bebbc62050993ca744dc8635511300c61.

Haley, K. J., Lilly, C. M., Yang, J. H., Feng, Y., Kennedy, S. P., Turi, T. G., et al. (2000). Overexpression of eotaxin and the CCR3 receptor in human atherosclerosis: Using genomic technology to identify a potential novel pathway of vascular inflammation. *Circulation, 102*(18), 2185–2189. Retrieved from http://eutils.ncbi.nlm.nih.gov/entrez/eutils/elink.fcgi?dbfrom=pubmed&id=11056090&retmode=ref&cmd=prlinks http://circ.ahajournals.org/content/102/18/2185.full.pdf.

Haque, N. S., Zhang, X., French, D. L., Li, J., Poon, M., Fallon, J. T., et al. (2000). CC chemokine I-309 is the principal monocyte chemoattractant induced by apolipoprotein(a) in human vascular endothelial cells. *Circulation, 102*(7), 786–792. Retrieved from http://eutils.ncbi.nlm.nih.gov/entrez/eutils/elink.fcgi?dbfrom=pubmed&id=10942748&retmode=ref&cmd=prlinks http://circ.ahajournals.org/content/102/7/786.full.pdf.

Harding, S. D., Sharman, J. L., Faccenda, E., Southan, C., Pawson, A. J., Ireland, S., et al. (2018). The IUPHAR/BPS guide to Pharmacology in 2018: Updates and expansion to encompass the new guide to Immunopharmacology. *Nucleic Acids Research, 46*(D1), D1091–D1106. http://dx.doi.org/10.1093/nar/gkx1121.

Hartl, D., Griese, M., Nicolai, T., Zissel, G., Prell, C., Reinhardt, D., et al. (2005). A role for MCP-1/CCR2 in interstitial lung disease in children. *Respiratory Research, 6*, 93. http://dx.doi.org/10.1186/1465-9921-6-93.

Hayward, J., Sanchez, J., Perry, A., Huang, C., Rodriguez Valle, M., Canals, M., et al. (2017). Ticks from diverse genera encode chemokine-inhibitory evasin proteins. *Journal of Biological Chemistry, 292*(38), 15670–15680. http://dx.doi.org/10.1074/jbc.M117.807255.

Heidarieh, H., Hernaez, B., & Alcami, A. (2015). Immune modulation by virus-encoded secreted chemokine binding proteins. *Virus Research, 209*, 67–75. http://dx.doi.org/10.1016/j.virusres.2015.02.028.

Heller, E. A., Liu, E., Tager, A. M., Yuan, Q., Lin, A. Y., Ahluwalia, N., et al. (2006). Chemokine CXCL10 promotes atherogenesis by modulating the local balance of effector and regulatory T cells. *Circulation, 113*(19), 2301–2312. Retrieved from http://eutils.ncbi.nlm.nih.gov/entrez/eutils/elink.fcgi?dbfrom=pubmed&id=16682613&retmode=ref&cmd=prlinks http://circ.ahajournals.org/content/113/19/2301.full.pdf.

Herold, S., Steinmueller, M., von Wulffen, W., Cakarova, L., Pinto, R., Pleschka, S., et al. (2008). Lung epithelial apoptosis in influenza virus pneumonia: The role of macrophage-expressed TNF-related apoptosis-inducing ligand. *Journal of Experimental Medicine, 205*(13), 3065–3077. http://dx.doi.org/10.1084/jem.20080201.

Heydtmann, M., Lalor, P. F., Eksteen, J. A., Hubscher, S. G., Briskin, M., & Adams, D. H. (2005). CXC chemokine ligand 16 promotes integrin-mediated adhesion of liver-infiltrating lymphocytes to cholangiocytes and hepatocytes within the inflamed human liver. *The Journal of Immunology, 174*(2), 1055–1062. http://dx.doi.org/10.4049/jimmunol.174.2.1055.

Hijnen, D., De Bruin-Weller, M., Oosting, B., Lebre, C., De Jong, E., Bruijnzeel-Koomen, C., et al. (2004). Serum thymus and activation-regulated chemokine (TARC) and cutaneous T cell- attracting chemokine (CTACK) levels in allergic diseases: TARC and CTACK are disease-specific markers for atopic dermatitis. *The Journal of Allergy and Clinical Immunology, 113*(2), 334–340. http://dx.doi.org/10.1016/j.jaci.2003.12.007.

Hirota, T., Takahashi, A., Kubo, M., Tsunoda, T., Tomita, K., Sakashita, M., et al. (2012). Genome-wide association study identifies eight new susceptibility loci for atopic dermatitis in the Japanese population. *Nature Genetics, 44*(11), 1222–1226. Retrieved from http://eutils.ncbi.nlm.nih.gov/entrez/eutils/elink.fcgi?dbfrom=pubmed&id=23042114&retmode=ref&cmd=prlinks.

Hirschfield, G. M., & Gershwin, M. E. (2013). The immunobiology and pathophysiology of primary biliary cirrhosis. *Annual Review of Pathology: Mechanisms of Disease, 8*, 303–330. http://dx.doi.org/10.1146/annurev-pathol-020712-164014.

Homey, B., Steinhoff, M., Ruzicka, T., & Leung, D. Y. (2006). Cytokines and chemokines orchestrate atopic skin inflammation. *The Journal of Allergy and Clinical Immunology, 118*(1), 178–189. http://dx.doi.org/10.1016/j.jaci.2006.03.047.

von Hundelshausen, P., Agten, S. M., Eckardt, V., Blanchet, X., Schmitt, M. M., Ippel, H., et al. (2017). Chemokine interactome mapping enables tailored intervention in acute and chronic inflammation. *Science Translational Medicine, 9*(384). http://dx.doi.org/10.1126/scitranslmed.aah6650.

Izzo, R. S., Witkon, K., Chen, A. I., Hadjiyane, C., Weinstein, M. I., & Pellecchia, C. (1993). Neutrophil-activating peptide (interleukin-8) in colonic mucosa from patients with Crohn's disease. *Scandinavian Journal of Gastroenterology, 28*(4), 296–300. Retrieved from http://www.ncbi.nlm.nih.gov/pubmed/8387693.

James, L. C., Roversi, P., & Tawfik, D. S. (2003). Antibody multispecificity mediated by conformational diversity. *Science, 299*(5611), 1362–1367. http://dx.doi.org/10.1126/science.1079731.

de Jong, M. D., Simmons, C. P., Thanh, T. T., Hien, V. M., Smith, G. J., Chau, T. N., et al. (2006). Fatal outcome of human influenza A (H5N1) is associated with high viral load and hypercytokinemia. *Nature Medicine, 12*(10), 1203–1207. http://dx.doi.org/10.1038/nm1477.

Jostins, L., Ripke, S., Weersma, R. K., Duerr, R. H., McGovern, D. P., Hui, K. Y., et al. (2012). Host-microbe interactions have shaped the genetic architecture of inflammatory bowel disease. *Nature, 491*(7422), 119–124. http://dx.doi.org/10.1038/nature11582.

Kakinuma, T., Saeki, H., Tsunemi, Y., Fujita, H., Asano, N., Mitsui, H., et al. (2003). Increased serum cutaneous T cell-attracting chemokine (CCL27) levels in patients with atopic dermatitis and psoriasis vulgaris. *The Journal of Allergy and Clinical Immunology, 111*(3), 592–597. Retrieved from http://www.ncbi.nlm.nih.gov/pubmed/12642842 https://www.jacionline.org/article/S0091-6749(02)91376-X/pdf.

Kathiresan, S., Voight, B. F., Purcell, S., Musunuru, K., Ardissino, D., Mannucci, P. M., et al. (2009). Genome-wide association of early-onset myocardial infarction with single nucleotide polymorphisms and copy number variants. *Nature Genetics, 41*(3), 334–341. Retrieved from http://eutils.ncbi.nlm.nih.gov/entrez/eutils/elink.fcgi?dbfrom=pubmed&id=19198609&retmode=ref&cmd=prlinks.

Kazimírová, M., & Štibrániová, I. (2013). Tick salivary compounds: Their role in modulation of host defences and pathogen transmission. *Frontiers in Cellular Infection Microbiology, 3*, 1–19. Retrieved from http://journal.frontiersin.org/Journal/10.3389/fcimb.2013.00043/full.

Keane, M. P., Belperio, J. A., Moore, T. A., Moore, B. B., Arenberg, D. A., Smith, R. E., et al. (1999). Neutralization of the CXC chemokine, macrophage inflammatory protein-2, attenuates bleomycin-induced pulmonary fibrosis. *The Journal of Immunology, 162*(9), 5511–5518. Retrieved from http://www.ncbi.nlm.nih.gov/pubmed/10228032.

Kennedy, A., Gruen, M. L., Gutierrez, D. A., Surmi, B. K., Orr, J. S., Webb, C. D., et al. (2012). Impact of macrophage inflammatory protein-1α deficiency on atherosclerotic lesion formation, hepatic steatosis, and adipose tissue expansion. *PLoS One, 7*(2), e31508. Retrieved from http://eutils.ncbi.nlm.nih.gov/entrez/eutils/elink.fcgi?dbfrom=pubmed&id=22359597&retmode=ref&cmd=prlinks http://www.ncbi.nlm.nih.gov/pmc/articles/PMC3281060/pdf/pone.0031508.pdf.

Kenny, E. E., Pe'er, I., Karban, A., Ozelius, L., Mitchell, A. A., Ng, S. M., et al. (2012). A genome-wide scan of Ashkenazi Jewish Crohn's disease suggests novel susceptibility loci. *PLoS Genetics, 8*(3), e1002559. http://dx.doi.org/10.1371/journal.pgen.1002559.

Khan, W. I., Motomura, Y., Wang, H., El-Sharkawy, R. T., Verdu, E. F., Verma-Gandhu, M., et al. (2006). Critical role of MCP-1 in the pathogenesis of experimental colitis in the context of immune and enterochromaffin cells. *American Journal of Physiology - Gastrointestinal and Liver Physiology, 291*(5), G803–G811. http://dx.doi.org/10.1152/ajpgi.00069.2006.

Kim, C.-S., Kang, J.-H., Cho, H.-R., Blankenship, T. N., Erickson, K. L., Kawada, T., et al. (2011). Potential involvement of CCL23 in atherosclerotic lesion formation/progression by the enhancement of chemotaxis, adhesion molecule expression, and MMP-2 release from monocytes. *Inflammation Research, 60*(9), 889–895. Retrieved from: http://eutils.ncbi.nlm.nih.gov/entrez/eutils/elink.fcgi?dbfrom=pubmed&id=21656154&retmode=ref&cmd=prlinkshttp://link.springer.com/article/10.1007%2Fs00011-011-0350-5http://download.springer.com/static/pdf/6/art%253A10.1007%252Fs00011-011-0350-5.pdf?originUrl=http%3A%2F%2Flink.springer.com%2Farticle%2F10.1007%2Fs00011-011-0350-5&token2=exp=1437488835~acl=%2Fstatic%2Fpdf%2F6%2Fart%25253A10.1007%25252Fs00011-011-0350-5.pdf%3ForiginUrl%3Dhttp%253A%252F%252Flink.springer.com%252Farticle%252F10.1007%252Fs00011-011-0350-5*~hmac=6534b2453eea8b50494c85bf0c28952c30f1b1ea1f4db234f5572dcf15cb8768.

Kim, Y. H., Kim, J. E., & Hyun, M. C. (2011). Cytokine response in pediatric patients with pandemic influenza H1N1 2009 virus infection and pneumonia: Comparison with pediatric pneumonia without H1N1 2009 infection. *Pediatric Pulmonology, 46*(12), 1233–1239. http://dx.doi.org/10.1002/ppul.21496.

Kimura, S., Tanimoto, A., Wang, K.-Y., Shimajiri, S., Guo, X., Tasaki, T., et al. (2012). Expression of macrophage-derived chemokine (CCL22) in atherosclerosis and regulation by histamine via the H2 receptor. *Pathology International, 62*(10), 675–683. Retrieved from http://eutils.ncbi.nlm.nih.gov/entrez/eutils/elink.fcgi?dbfrom=pubmed&id=23005594&retmode=ref&cmd=prlinks http://onlinelibrary.wiley.com/doi/10.1111/j.1440-1827.2012.02854.x/abstract http://onlinelibrary.wiley.com/store/10.1111/j.1440-1827.2012.02854.x/asset/j.1440-1827.2012.02854.x.pdf?v=1&t=icdf10oz&s=990cf7cdc164275e44d0db983d5e7831dc7363d8.

King, V. L., Lin, A. Y., Kristo, F., Anderson, T. J. T., Ahluwalia, N., Hardy, G. J., et al. (2009). Interferon-gamma and the interferon-inducible chemokine CXCL10 protect against aneurysm formation and rupture. *Circulation, 119*(3), 426–435. Retrieved from http://eutils.ncbi.nlm.nih.gov/entrez/eutils/elink.fcgi?dbfrom=pubmed&id=19139386&retmode=ref&cmd=prlinks http://circ.ahajournals.org/content/119/3/426.full.pdf.

Kitano, H. (2004). Biological robustness. *Nature Reviews Genetics, 5*(11), 826–837. http://dx.doi.org/10.1038/nrg1471.

Kittleson, M. M., Minhas, K. M., Irizarry, R. A., Ye, S. Q., Edness, G., Breton, E., et al. (2005). Gene expression in giant cell myocarditis: Altered expression of immune response genes. *International Journal of Cardiology, 102*(2), 333–340. http://dx.doi.org/10.1016/j.ijcard.2005.03.075.

Koenen, R. R., von Hundelshausen, P., Nesmelova, I. V., Zernecke, A., Liehn, E. A., Sarabi, A., et al. (2009). Disrupting functional interactions between platelet chemokines inhibits atherosclerosis in hyperlipidemic mice. *Nature Medicine, 15*(1), 97–103. Retrieved from http://eutils.ncbi.nlm.nih.gov/entrez/eutils/elink.fcgi?dbfrom=pubmed&id=19122657&retmode=ref&cmd=prlinks http://www.nature.com/nm/journal/v15/n1/pdf/nm.1898.pdf.

Koh, C. Y., & Kini, R. M. (2012). From snake venom toxins to therapeutics–cardiovascular examples. *Toxicon, 59*(4), 497–506. http://dx.doi.org/10.1016/j.toxicon.2011.03.017.

Kotarsky, K., Sitnik, K. M., Stenstad, H., Kotarsky, H., Schmidtchen, A., Koslowski, M., et al. (2010). A novel role for constitutively expressed epithelial-derived chemokines as antibacterial peptides in the intestinal mucosa. *Mucosal Immunology, 3*(1), 40–48. http://dx.doi.org/10.1038/mi.2009.115.

Krenkel, O., Mossanen, J. C., & Tacke, F. (2014). Immune mechanisms in acetaminophen-induced acute liver failure. *Hepatobiliary Surgery and Nutrition, 3*(6), 331–343. http://dx.doi.org/10.3978/j.issn.2304-3881.2014.11.01.

Krohn, S., Garin, A., Gabay, C., & Proudfoot, A. E. I. (2013). The activity of CCL18 is principally mediated through interaction with glycosaminoglycans. *Frontiers in Immunology, 4*, 193. Retrieved from http://eutils.ncbi.nlm.nih.gov/entrez/eutils/elink.fcgi?dbfrom=pubmed&id=23874339&retmode=ref&cmd=prlinks.

Krumbholz, M., Theil, D., Cepok, S., Hemmer, B., Kivisakk, P., Ransohoff, R. M., et al. (2006). Chemokines in multiple sclerosis: CXCL12 and CXCL13 up-regulation is differentially linked to CNS immune cell recruitment. *Brain, 129*(Pt 1), 200–211. http://dx.doi.org/10.1093/brain/awh680.

Kufareva, I., Gustavsson, M., Zheng, Y., Stephens, B. S., & Handel, T. M. (2017). What do structures tell us about chemokine receptor function and antagonism? *Annual Review of Biophysics, 46*, 175–198. http://dx.doi.org/10.1146/annurev-biophys-051013-022942.

Kumar, V., Abbas, A. K., & Aster, J. C. (2015). *Robbins and Cotran pathologic basis of disease* (9th ed.). Philadelphia, PA: Elsevier/Saunders.

Landi, A., Weismuller, T. J., Lankisch, T. O., Santer, D. M., Tyrrell, D. L., Manns, M. P., et al. (2014). Differential serum levels of eosinophilic eotaxins in primary sclerosing cholangitis, primary biliary cirrhosis, and autoimmune hepatitis. *Journal of Interferon and Cytokine Research, 34*(3), 204–214. http://dx.doi.org/10.1089/jir.2013.0075.

Lassner, D., Kuhl, U., Siegismund, C. S., Rohde, M., Elezkurtaj, S., Escher, F., et al. (2014). Improved diagnosis of idiopathic giant cell myocarditis and cardiac sarcoidosis by myocardial gene expression profiling. *European Heart Journal, 35*(32), 2186–2195. http://dx.doi.org/10.1093/eurheartj/ehu101.

Lebre, M. C., Burwell, T., Vieira, P. L., Lora, J., Coyle, A. J., Kapsenberg, M. L., et al. (2005). Differential expression of inflammatory chemokines by Th1- and Th2-cell promoting dendritic cells: A role for different mature dendritic cell populations in attracting appropriate effector cells to peripheral sites of inflammation. *Immunology & Cell Biology, 83*(5), 525–535. http://dx.doi.org/10.1111/j.1440-1711.2005.01365.x.

Lee, A. W., Deruaz, M., Lynch, C., Davies, G., Singh, K., Alenazi, Y., et al. (2019). A knottin scaffold directs the CXC-chemokine-binding specificity of tick evasins. *Journal of Biological Chemistry, 294*(29), 11199–11212. http://dx.doi.org/10.1074/jbc.RA119.008817.

Lee, N., Wong, C. K., Chan, P. K., Chan, M. C., Wong, R. Y., Lun, S. W., et al. (2011). Cytokine response patterns in severe pandemic 2009 H1N1 and seasonal influenza among hospitalized adults. *PLoS One, 6*(10), e26050. http://dx.doi.org/10.1371/journal.pone.0026050.

Lee, N., Wong, C. K., Chan, P. K., Lun, S. W., Lui, G., Wong, B., et al. (2007). Hypercytokinemia and hyperactivation of phospho-p38 mitogen-activated protein kinase in severe human influenza A virus infection. *Clinical Infectious Diseases, 45*(6), 723–731. http://dx.doi.org/10.1086/520981.

Lehmann, M. H., Kuhnert, H., Muller, S., & Sigusch, H. H. (1998). Monocyte chemoattractant protein 1 (MCP-1) gene expression in dilated cardiomyopathy. *Cytokine, 10*(10), 739–746. http://dx.doi.org/10.1006/cyto.1998.0354.

de Lemos, J. A., Morrow, D. A., Blazing, M. A., Jarolim, P., Wiviott, S. D., Sabatine, M. S., et al. (2007). Serial measurement of monocyte chemoattractant protein-1 after acute coronary syndromes: Results from the A to Z trial. *Journal of the American College of Cardiology, 50*(22), 2117–2124. http://dx.doi.org/10.1016/j.jacc.2007.06.057.

Li, Y., Wang, W., Tang, L., He, X., Yan, X., Zhang, X., et al. (2015). Chemokine (C-X-C motif) ligand 13 promotes intrahepatic chemokine (C-X-C motif) receptor 5+ lymphocyte homing and aberrant B-cell immune responses in primary biliary cirrhosis. *Hepatology, 61*(6), 1998–2007. http://dx.doi.org/10.1002/hep.27725.

Luboshits, G., Shina, S., Kaplan, O., Engelberg, S., Nass, D., Lifshitz-Mercer, B., et al. (1999). Elevated expression of the CC chemokine regulated on activation, normal T cell expressed and secreted (RANTES) in advanced breast carcinoma. *Cancer Research, 59*(18), 4681–4687. Retrieved from http://www.ncbi.nlm.nih.gov/pubmed/10493525 http://cancerres.aacrjournals.org/content/canres/59/18/4681.full.pdf.

Mach, F., Sauty, A., Iarossi, A. S., Sukhova, G. K., Neote, K., Libby, P., et al. (1999). Differential expression of three T lymphocyte-activating CXC chemokines by human atheroma-associated cells. *Journal of Clinical Investigation, 104*(8), 1041–1050. Retrieved from http://eutils.ncbi.nlm.nih.gov/entrez/eutils/elink.fcgi?dbfrom=pubmed&id=10525042&retmode=ref&cmd=prlinks http://www.ncbi.nlm.nih.gov/pmc/articles/PMC408576/pdf/JCI9906993.pdf.

Mahida, Y. R., Ceska, M., Effenberger, F., Kurlak, L., Lindley, I., & Hawkey, C. J. (1992). Enhanced synthesis of neutrophil-activating peptide-1/interleukin-8 in active ulcerative colitis. *Clinical Science, 82*(3), 273–275. Retrieved from http://www.ncbi.nlm.nih.gov/pubmed/1312411 http://www.clinsci.org/content/ppclinsci/82/3/273.full.pdf.

Marion, T., Elbahesh, H., Thomas, P. G., DeVincenzo, J. P., Webby, R., & Schughart, K. (2016). Respiratory mucosal proteome quantification in human influenza infections. *PLoS One, 11*(4), e0153674. http://dx.doi.org/10.1371/journal.pone.0153674.

Marra, F., & Tacke, F. (2014). Roles for chemokines in liver disease. *Gastroenterology, 147*(3), 577–594 e571. http://dx.doi.org/10.1053/j.gastro.2014.06.043.

Mattes, J., Yang, M., Mahalingam, S., Kuehr, J., Webb, D. C., Simson, L., et al. (2002). Intrinsic defect in T cell production of interleukin (IL)-13 in the absence of both IL-5 and eotaxin precludes the development of eosinophilia and airways hyperreactivity in experimental asthma. *Journal of Experimental Medicine, 195*(11), 1433–1444. Retrieved from http://eutils.ncbi.nlm.nih.gov/entrez/eutils/elink.fcgi?dbfrom=pubmed&id=12045241&retmode=ref&cmd=prlinks http://www.ncbi.nlm.nih.gov/pmc/articles/PMC2193548/pdf/020009.pdf.

Mazzucchelli, L., Hauser, C., Zgraggen, K., Wagner, H. E., Hess, M. W., Laissue, J. A., et al. (1996). Differential in situ expression of the genes encoding the chemokines MCP-1 and RANTES in human inflammatory bowel disease. *The Journal of Pathology, 178*(2), 201–206. http://dx.doi.org/10.1002/(SICI)1096-9896(199602)178:2<201::AID-PATH440>3.0.CO;2-4.

Miller, M. D., & Krangel, M. S. (1992). The human cytokine I-309 is a monocyte chemoattractant. *Proceedings of the National Academy of Sciences of the United States of America, 89*(7), 2950–2954. http://dx.doi.org/10.1073/pnas.89.7.2950.

Minami, M., Kume, N., Shimaoka, T., Kataoka, H., Hayashida, K., Akiyama, Y., et al. (2001). Expression of SR-PSOX, a novel cell-surface scavenger receptor for phosphatidylserine and oxidized LDL in human atherosclerotic lesions. *Arteriosclerosis, Thrombosis, and Vascular Biology, 21*(11), 1796–1800. Retrieved from http://eutils.ncbi.nlm.nih.gov/entrez/eutils/elink.fcgi?dbfrom=pubmed&id=11701468&retmode=ref&cmd=prlinks http://atvb.ahajournals.org/content/21/11/1796.full.pdf.

Mirabelli-Badenier, M., Braunersreuther, V., Viviani, G. L., Dallegri, F., Quercioli, A., Veneselli, E., et al. (2011). CC and CXC chemokines are pivotal mediators of cerebral injury in ischaemic stroke. *Thrombosis & Haemostasis, 105*(3), 409–420. http://dx.doi.org/10.1160/TH10-10-0662.

Mirshahpanah, P., Li, Y. Y., Burkhardt, N., Asadullah, K., & Zollner, T. M. (2008). CCR4 and CCR10 ligands play additive roles in mouse contact hypersensitivity. *Experimental Dermatology, 17*(1), 30–34. http://dx.doi.org/10.1111/j.1600-0625.2007.00630.x.

Miyagishi, R., Kikuchi, S., Fukazawa, T., & Tashiro, K. (1995). Macrophage inflammatory protein-1 alpha in the cerebrospinal fluid of patients with multiple sclerosis and other inflammatory neurological diseases. *Journal of the Neurological Sciences, 129*(2), 223–227. Retrieved from http://www.ncbi.nlm.nih.gov/pubmed/7608739 https://www.jns-journal.com/article/0022-510X(95)00004-L/pdf.

Mohs, A., Kuttkat, N., Reissing, J., Wolfgang Zimmermann, H., Sonntag, R., Proudfoot, A., et al. (2016). Functional role of CCL5/RANTES for HCC progression during chronic liver disease. *Journal of Hepatology*. http://dx.doi.org/10.1016/j.jhep.2016.12.011.

Montecucco, F., Lenglet, S., Braunersreuther, V., Pelli, G., Pellieux, C., Montessuit, C., et al. (2010). Single administration of the CXC chemokine-binding protein evasin-3 during ischemia prevents myocardial reperfusion injury in mice. *Arteriosclerosis, Thrombosis, and Vascular Biology, 30*(7), 1371–1377. Retrieved from http://atvb.ahajournals.org/cgi/doi/10.1161/ATVBAHA.110.206011 http://atvb.ahajournals.org/content/30/7/1371.full.pdf.

Montecucco, F., Mach, F., Lenglet, S., Vonlaufen, A., Gomes Quinderé, A. L., Pelli, G., et al. (2014). Treatment with Evasin-3 abrogates neutrophil-mediated inflammation in mouse acute pancreatitis. *European Journal of Clinical Investigation, 44*(10), 940–950. Retrieved from http://doi.wiley.com/10.1111/eci.12327 http://onlinelibrary.wiley.com/doi/10.1111/eci.12327/abstract http://onlinelibrary.wiley.com/store/10.1111/

eci.12327/asset/eci12327.pdf?v=1&t=icdf1wfz&s=bb1dca07f4361a611a06e135e7073 303bb20b7a9.
Moore, B. B., Murray, L., Das, A., Wilke, C. A., Herrygers, A. B., & Toews, G. B. (2006). The role of CCL12 in the recruitment of fibrocytes and lung fibrosis. *American Journal of Respiratory Cell and Molecular Biology, 35*(2), 175–181. http://dx.doi.org/10.1165/rcmb.2005-0239OC.
Moore, B. B., Paine, R., 3rd, Christensen, P. J., Moore, T. A., Sitterding, S., Ngan, R., et al. (2001). Protection from pulmonary fibrosis in the absence of CCR2 signaling. *The Journal of Immunology, 167*(8), 4368–4377. Retrieved from http://www.ncbi.nlm.nih.gov/pubmed/11591761.
Moriguchi, K., Miyamoto, K., Tanaka, N., Yoshie, O., & Kusunoki, S. (2013). The importance of CCR4 and CCR6 in experimental autoimmune encephalomyelitis. *Journal of Neuroimmunology, 257*(1–2), 53–58. Retrieved from http://eutils.ncbi.nlm.nih.gov/entrez/eutils/elink.fcgi?dbfrom=pubmed&id=23477966&retmode=ref&cmd=prlinks http://www.jni-journal.com/article/S0165-5728(13)00029-5/abstract http://ac.els-cdn.com/S0165572813000295/1-s2.0-S0165572813000295-main.pdf?_tid=e841b314-2fb1-11e5-ba4d-00000aacb35e&acdnat=1437487865_006b1f8812f56b681649abf001b168b2.
Morteau, O., Castagliuolo, I., Mykoniatis, A., Zacks, J., Wlk, M., Lu, B., et al. (2002). Genetic deficiency in the chemokine receptor CCR1 protects against acute *Clostridium difficile* toxin A enteritis in mice. *Gastroenterology, 122*(3), 725–733. Retrieved from http://www.ncbi.nlm.nih.gov/pubmed/11875005.
Nogueira, L. G., Santos, R. H., Ianni, B. M., Fiorelli, A. I., Mairena, E. C., Benvenuti, L. A., et al. (2012). Myocardial chemokine expression and intensity of myocarditis in Chagas cardiomyopathy are controlled by polymorphisms in CXCL9 and CXCL10. *PLOS Neglected Tropical Diseases, 6*(10), e1867. http://dx.doi.org/10.1371/journal.pntd.0001867.
Nomura, I., Gao, B., Boguniewicz, M., Darst, M. A., Travers, J. B., & Leung, D. Y. (2003). Distinct patterns of gene expression in the skin lesions of atopic dermatitis and psoriasis: A gene microarray analysis. *The Journal of Allergy and Clinical Immunology, 112*(6), 1195–1202. http://dx.doi.org/10.1016/j.jaci.2003.08.049.
Noris, M., Daina, E., Gamba, S., Bonazzola, S., & Remuzzi, G. (1999). Interleukin-6 and RANTES in *Takayasu arteritis*: A guide for therapeutic decisions? *Circulation, 100*(1), 55–60. Retrieved from https://www.ncbi.nlm.nih.gov/pubmed/10393681.
Okada, Y., Wu, D., Trynka, G., Raj, T., Terao, C., Ikari, K., et al. (2014). Genetics of rheumatoid arthritis contributes to biology and drug discovery. *Nature, 506*(7488), 376–381. Retrieved from http://eutils.ncbi.nlm.nih.gov/entrez/eutils/elink.fcgi?dbfrom=pubmed&id=24390342&retmode=ref&cmd=prlinks http://www.nature.com/nature/journal/v506/n7488/pdf/nature12873.pdf.
Orn, S., Breland, U. M., Mollnes, T. E., Manhenke, C., Dickstein, K., Aukrust, P., et al. (2009). The chemokine network in relation to infarct size and left ventricular remodeling following acute myocardial infarction. *The American Journal of Cardiology, 104*(9), 1179–1183. http://dx.doi.org/10.1016/j.amjcard.2009.06.028.
Owczarek, W., Paplinska, M., Targowski, T., Jahnz-Rozyk, K., Paluchowska, E., Kucharczyk, A., et al. (2010). Analysis of eotaxin 1/CCL11, eotaxin 2/CCL24 and eotaxin 3/CCL26 expression in lesional and non-lesional skin of patients with atopic dermatitis. *Cytokine, 50*(2), 181–185. http://dx.doi.org/10.1016/j.cyto.2010.02.016.
Palchevskiy, V., Hashemi, N., Weigt, S. S., Xue, Y. Y., Derhovanessian, A., Keane, M. P., et al. (2011). Immune response CC chemokines CCL2 and CCL5 are associated with pulmonary sarcoidosis. *Fibrogenesis & Tissue Repair, 4*, 10. http://dx.doi.org/10.1186/1755-1536-4-10.

Papadakis, K. A., Prehn, J., Moreno, S. T., Cheng, L., Kouroumalis, E. A., Deem, R., et al. (2001). CCR9-positive lymphocytes and thymus-expressed chemokine distinguish small bowel from colonic Crohn's disease. *Gastroenterology, 121*(2), 246–254. Retrieved from http://www.ncbi.nlm.nih.gov/pubmed/11487533 https://www.gastrojournal.org/article/S0016-5085(01)44948-1/pdf.

Park, C. O., Lee, H. J., Lee, J. H., Wu, W. H., Chang, N. S., Hua, L., et al. (2008). Increased expression of CC chemokine ligand 18 in extrinsic atopic dermatitis patients. *Experimental Dermatology, 17*(1), 24–29. http://dx.doi.org/10.1111/j.1600-0625.2007.00634.x.

Pease, J. E., & Horuk, R. (2010). Small molecule antagonists of chemokine receptors–is promiscuity a virtue? *Current Topics in Medicinal Chemistry, 10*(13), 1351–1358. Retrieved from https://www.ncbi.nlm.nih.gov/pubmed/20536423.

Petrek, M., Kolek, V., Szotkowska, J., & du Bois, R. M. (2002). CC and C chemokine expression in pulmonary sarcoidosis. *European Respiratory Journal, 20*(5), 1206–1212. http://dx.doi.org/10.1183/09031936.02.00289902.

Petrek, M., Pantelidis, P., Southcott, A. M., Lympany, P., Safranek, P., Black, C. M., et al. (1997). The source and role of RANTES in interstitial lung disease. *European Respiratory Journal, 10*(6), 1207–1216. Retrieved from http://www.ncbi.nlm.nih.gov/pubmed/9192918 http://erj.ersjournals.com/content/erj/10/6/1207.full.pdf.

Phillips, R. J., Burdick, M. D., Hong, K., Lutz, M. A., Murray, L. A., Xue, Y. Y., et al. (2004). Circulating fibrocytes traffic to the lungs in response to CXCL12 and mediate fibrosis. *Journal of Clinical Investigation, 114*(3), 438–446. http://dx.doi.org/10.1172/JCI20997.

Pivarcsi, A., Gombert, M., Dieu-Nosjean, M. C., Lauerma, A., Kubitza, R., Meller, S., et al. (2004). CC chemokine ligand 18, an atopic dermatitis-associated and dendritic cell-derived chemokine, is regulated by staphylococcal products and allergen exposure. *The Journal of Immunology, 173*(9), 5810–5817. Retrieved from http://www.ncbi.nlm.nih.gov/pubmed/15494534 http://www.jimmunol.org/content/jimmunol/173/9/5810.full.pdf.

Platt, A. M., Bain, C. C., Bordon, Y., Sester, D. P., & Mowat, A. M. (2010). An independent subset of TLR expressing CCR2-dependent macrophages promotes colonic inflammation. *The Journal of Immunology, 184*(12), 6843–6854. http://dx.doi.org/10.4049/jimmunol.0903987.

Pope, S. M., Zimmermann, N., Stringer, K. F., Karow, M. L., & Rothenberg, M. E. (2005). The eotaxin chemokines and CCR3 are fundamental regulators of allergen-induced pulmonary eosinophilia. *The Journal of Immunology, 175*(8), 5341–5350. Retrieved from http://eutils.ncbi.nlm.nih.gov/entrez/eutils/elink.fcgi?dbfrom=pubmed&id=16210640&retmode=ref&cmd=prlinks http://www.jimmunol.org/content/175/8/5341.full.pdf.

Proudfoot, A. E., Bonvin, P., & Power, C. A. (2015). Targeting chemokines: Pathogens can, why can't we? *Cytokine, 74*(2), 259–267. http://dx.doi.org/10.1016/j.cyto.2015.02.011.

Proudfoot, A. E., & Uguccioni, M. (2016). Modulation of chemokine responses: Synergy and cooperativity. *Frontiers in Immunology, 7*, 183. http://dx.doi.org/10.3389/fimmu.2016.00183.

Puleston, J., Cooper, M., Murch, S., Bid, K., Makh, S., Ashwood, P., et al. (2005). A distinct subset of chemokines dominates the mucosal chemokine response in inflammatory bowel disease. *Alimentary Pharmacology & Therapeutics, 21*(2), 109–120. http://dx.doi.org/10.1111/j.1365-2036.2004.02262.x.

Rangel-Moreno, J., Moyron-Quiroz, J. E., Hartson, L., Kusser, K., & Randall, T. D. (2007). Pulmonary expression of CXC chemokine ligand 13, CC chemokine ligand 19, and CC chemokine ligand 21 is essential for local immunity to influenza. *Proceedings of the National Academy of Sciences of the United States of America, 104*(25), 10577–10582. Retrieved from http://eutils.ncbi.nlm.nih.gov/entrez/eutils/elink.fcgi?dbfrom=pubmed&id=17563386&retmode=ref&cmd=prlinks http://www.ncbi.nlm.nih.gov/pmc/articles/PMC1965555/pdf/zpq10577.pdf.

Rau, B., Baumgart, K., Kruger, C. M., Schilling, M., & Beger, H. G. (2003). CC-chemokine activation in acute pancreatitis: Enhanced release of monocyte chemoattractant protein-1 in patients with local and systemic complications. *Intensive Care Medicine, 29*(4), 622–629. http://dx.doi.org/10.1007/s00134-003-1668-4.

Reape, T. J., & Groot, P. H. (1999). Chemokines and atherosclerosis. *Atherosclerosis, 147*(2), 213–225. Retrieved from http://eutils.ncbi.nlm.nih.gov/entrez/eutils/elink.fcgi?dbfrom=pubmed&id=10559506&retmode=ref&cmd=prlinks http://www.atherosclerosis-journal.com/article/S0021-9150(99)00346-9/abstract http://ac.els-cdn.com/S0021915099003469/1-s2.0-S0021915099003469-main.pdf?_tid=fab1bc06-2fb1-11e5-b12e-00000aab0f01&acdnat=1437487896_e96c65b5733959c224f9a08e27d7115c.

Reinecker, H. C., Loh, E. Y., Ringler, D. J., Mehta, A., Rombeau, J. L., & MacDermott, R. P. (1995). Monocyte-chemoattractant protein 1 gene expression in intestinal epithelial cells and inflammatory bowel disease mucosa. *Gastroenterology, 108*(1), 40–50. Retrieved from http://www.ncbi.nlm.nih.gov/pubmed/7806062.

Rodgers, K. R., & Chou, R. C. (2016). Therapeutic monoclonal antibodies and derivatives: Historical perspectives and future directions. *Biotechnology Advances, 34*(6), 1149–1158. http://dx.doi.org/10.1016/j.biotechadv.2016.07.004.

Russo, R. C., Alessandri, A. L., Garcia, C. C., Cordeiro, B. F., Pinho, V., Cassali, G. D., et al. (2011). Therapeutic effects of evasin-1, a chemokine binding protein, in bleomycin-induced pulmonary fibrosis. *American Journal of Respiratory Cell and Molecular Biology, 45*(1), 72–80. Retrieved from http://www.atsjournals.org/doi/abs/10.1165/rcmb.2009-0406OC http://www.atsjournals.org/doi/pdf/10.1165/rcmb.2009-0406OC.

Russo, R. C., Guabiraba, R., Garcia, C. C., Barcelos, L. S., Roffe, E., Souza, A. L., et al. (2009). Role of the chemokine receptor CXCR2 in bleomycin-induced pulmonary inflammation and fibrosis. *American Journal of Respiratory Cell and Molecular Biology, 40*(4), 410–421. http://dx.doi.org/10.1165/rcmb.2007-0364OC.

Saederup, N., Chan, L., Lira, S. A., & Charo, I. F. (2008). Fractalkine deficiency markedly reduces macrophage accumulation and atherosclerotic lesion formation in CCR2-/- mice: Evidence for independent chemokine functions in atherogenesis. *Circulation, 117*(13), 1642–1648. Retrieved from http://eutils.ncbi.nlm.nih.gov/entrez/eutils/elink.fcgi?dbfrom=pubmed&id=18165355&retmode=ref&cmd=prlinks http://circ.ahajournals.org/content/117/13/1642.full.pdf.

Sahin, H., & Wasmuth, H. E. (2013). Chemokines in tissue fibrosis. *Biochimica et Biophysica Acta, 1832*(7), 1041–1048. Retrieved from http://eutils.ncbi.nlm.nih.gov/entrez/eutils/elink.fcgi?dbfrom=pubmed&id=23159607&amp.

Sans, M., Danese, S., de la Motte, C., de Souza, H. S., Rivera-Reyes, B. M., West, G. A., et al. (2007). Enhanced recruitment of CX3CR1+ T cells by mucosal endothelial cell-derived fractalkine in inflammatory bowel disease. *Gastroenterology, 132*(1), 139–153. http://dx.doi.org/10.1053/j.gastro.2006.10.010.

Sasaki, M., Miyakoshi, M., Sato, Y., & Nakanuma, Y. (2014). Chemokine-chemokine receptor CCL2-CCR2 and CX3CL1-CX3CR1 axis may play a role in the aggravated inflammation in primary biliary cirrhosis. *Digestive Diseases and Sciences, 59*(2), 358–364. http://dx.doi.org/10.1007/s10620-013-2920-6.

Satoh, M., Tamura, G., Segawa, I., Tashiro, A., Hiramori, K., & Satodate, R. (1996). Expression of cytokine genes and presence of enteroviral genomic RNA in endomyocardial biopsy tissues of myocarditis and dilated cardiomyopathy. *Virchows Archiv, 427*(5), 503–509. Retrieved from http://www.ncbi.nlm.nih.gov/pubmed/8624580.

Saurer, L., Reber, P., Schaffner, T., Buchler, M. W., Buri, C., Kappeler, A., et al. (2000). Differential expression of chemokines in normal pancreas and in chronic pancreatitis.

Gastroenterology, 118(2), 356–367. Retrieved from https://www.ncbi.nlm.nih.gov/pubmed/10648464.

Scardoni, G., Montresor, A., Tosadori, G., & Laudanna, C. (2014). Node interference and robustness: Performing virtual knock-out experiments on biological networks: The case of leukocyte integrin activation network. *PLoS One, 9*(2), e88938. http://dx.doi.org/10.1371/journal.pone.0088938.

Schmidt, K., Martinez-Gamboa, L., Meier, S., Witt, C., Meisel, C., Hanitsch, L. G., et al. (2009). Bronchoalveoloar lavage fluid cytokines and chemokines as markers and predictors for the outcome of interstitial lung disease in systemic sclerosis patients. *Arthritis Research and Therapy, 11*(4), R111. http://dx.doi.org/10.1186/ar2766.

Schunkert, H., König, I. R., Kathiresan, S., Reilly, M. P., Assimes, T. L., Holm, H., et al. (2011). Large-scale association analysis identifies 13 new susceptibility loci for coronary artery disease. *Nature Genetics, 43*(4), 333–338. Retrieved from http://eutils.ncbi.nlm.nih.gov/entrez/eutils/elink.fcgi?dbfrom=pubmed&id=21378990&retmode=ref&cmd=prlinks http://www.ncbi.nlm.nih.gov/pmc/articles/PMC3119261/pdf/nihms287053.pdf.

Schupp, J. C., Binder, H., Jager, B., Cillis, G., Zissel, G., Muller-Quernheim, J., et al. (2015). Macrophage activation in acute exacerbation of idiopathic pulmonary fibrosis. *PLoS One, 10*(1), e0116775. http://dx.doi.org/10.1371/journal.pone.0116775.

Sethi, D. K., Agarwal, A., Manivel, V., Rao, K. V., & Salunke, D. M. (2006). Differential epitope positioning within the germline antibody paratope enhances promiscuity in the primary immune response. *Immunity, 24*(4), 429–438. http://dx.doi.org/10.1016/j.immuni.2006.02.010.

Shin, K., Nigrovic, P. A., Crish, J., Boilard, E., McNeil, H. P., Larabee, K. S., et al. (2009). Mast cells contribute to autoimmune inflammatory arthritis via their tryptase/heparin complexes. *The Journal of Immunology, 182*(1), 647–656. Retrieved from http://www.ncbi.nlm.nih.gov/pubmed/19109198.

Simpson, J. E., Newcombe, J., Cuzner, M. L., & Woodroofe, M. N. (2000). Expression of the interferon-gamma-inducible chemokines IP-10 and Mig and their receptor, CXCR3, in multiple sclerosis lesions. *Neuropathology and Applied Neurobiology, 26*(2), 133–142. Retrieved from http://www.ncbi.nlm.nih.gov/pubmed/10840276 https://onlinelibrary.wiley.com/doi/full/10.1046/j.1365-2990.2000.026002133.x.

Singh, K., Davies, G., Alenazi, Y., Eaton, J. R. O., Kawamura, A., & Bhattacharya, S. (2017). Yeast surface display identifies a family of evasins from ticks with novel polyvalent CC chemokine-binding activities. *Scientific Reports,* 7(1), 4267. http://dx.doi.org/10.1038/s41598-017-04378-1.

Smedbakken, L. M., Halvorsen, B., Daissormont, I., Ranheim, T., Michelsen, A. E., Skjelland, M., et al. (2012). Increased levels of the homeostatic chemokine CXCL13 in human atherosclerosis - potential role in plaque stabilization. *Atherosclerosis, 224*(1), 266–273. Retrieved from http://eutils.ncbi.nlm.nih.gov/entrez/eutils/elink.fcgi?dbfrom=pubmed&id=22840692&retmode=ref&cmd=prlinks http://www.atherosclerosis-journal.com/article/S0021-9150(12)00461-3/abstract http://ac.els-cdn.com/S0021915012004613/1-s2.0-S0021915012004613-main.pdf?_tid=06a37392-2fb2-11e5-b5c7-00000aab0f02&acdnat=1437487916_db7e11637f4088ce4ac9f8fde86be2e6.

Smith, R. E., Strieter, R. M., Phan, S. H., Lukacs, N. W., Huffnagle, G. B., Wilke, C. A., et al. (1994). Production and function of murine macrophage inflammatory protein-1 alpha in bleomycin-induced lung injury. *The Journal of Immunology, 153*(10), 4704–4712. Retrieved from http://www.ncbi.nlm.nih.gov/pubmed/7525712.

Soria, G., Yaal-Hahoshen, N., Azenshtein, E., Shina, S., Leider-Trejo, L., Ryvo, L., et al. (2008). Concomitant expression of the chemokines RANTES and MCP-1 in human breast cancer: A basis for tumor-promoting interactions. *Cytokine, 44*(1), 191–200. http://dx.doi.org/10.1016/j.cyto.2008.08.002.

Stahl, E. A., Raychaudhuri, S., Remmers, E. F., Xie, G., Eyre, S., Thomson, B. P., et al. (2010). Genome-wide association study meta-analysis identifies seven new rheumatoid arthritis risk loci. *Nature Genetics, 42*(6), 508–514. http://dx.doi.org/10.1038/ng.582.

Szekanecz, Z., & Koch, A. E. (2016). Successes and failures of chemokine-pathway targeting in rheumatoid arthritis. *Nature Reviews Rheumatology, 12*(1), 5–13. http://dx.doi.org/10.1038/nrrheum.2015.157.

Szodoray, P., Alex, P., Knowlton, N., Centola, M., Dozmorov, I., Csipo, I., et al. (2010). Idiopathic inflammatory myopathies, signified by distinctive peripheral cytokines, chemokines and the TNF family members B-cell activating factor and a proliferation inducing ligand. *Rheumatology (Oxford), 49*(10), 1867–1877. http://dx.doi.org/10.1093/rheumatology/keq151.

Takano, T., Tajiri, H., Kashiwagi, Y., Kimura, S., & Kawashima, H. (2011). Cytokine and chemokine response in children with the 2009 pandemic influenza A (H1N1) virus infection. *European Journal of Clinical Microbiology & Infectious Diseases, 30*(1), 117–120. http://dx.doi.org/10.1007/s10096-010-1041-9.

Tateyama, M., Fujihara, K., Misu, T., Feng, J., Onodera, Y., & Itoyama, Y. (2006). Expression of CCR7 and its ligands CCL19/CCL21 in muscles of polymyositis. *Journal of the Neurological Sciences, 249*(2), 158–165. http://dx.doi.org/10.1016/j.jns.2006.06.021.

Tecchio, C., Micheletti, A., & Cassatella, M. A. (2014). Neutrophil-derived cytokines: Facts beyond expression. *Frontiers in Immunology, 5*, 508. http://dx.doi.org/10.3389/fimmu.2014.00508.

Teupser, D., Pavlides, S., Tan, M., Gutierrez-Ramos, J.-C., Kolbeck, R., & Breslow, J. L. (2004). Major reduction of atherosclerosis in fractalkine (CX3CL1)-deficient mice is at the brachiocephalic artery, not the aortic root. *Proceedings of the National Academy of Sciences of the United States of America, 101*(51), 17795–17800. Retrieved from http://eutils.ncbi.nlm.nih.gov/entrez/eutils/elink.fcgi?dbfrom=pubmed&id=15596719&retmode=ref&cmd=prlinks http://www.ncbi.nlm.nih.gov/pmc/articles/PMC539720/pdf/pnas-0408096101.pdf.

Tokuda, A., Itakura, M., Onai, N., Kimura, H., Kuriyama, T., & Matsushima, K. (2000). Pivotal role of CCR1-positive leukocytes in bleomycin-induced lung fibrosis in mice. *The Journal of Immunology, 164*(5), 2745–2751. Retrieved from http://www.ncbi.nlm.nih.gov/pubmed/10679116.

Trujillo, G., Hartigan, A. J., & Hogaboam, C. M. (2010). T regulatory cells and attenuated bleomycin-induced fibrosis in lungs of CCR7-/- mice. *Fibrogenesis & Tissue Repair, 3*, 18. http://dx.doi.org/10.1186/1755-1536-3-18.

Ueno, T., Toi, M., Saji, H., Muta, M., Bando, H., Kuroi, K., et al. (2000). Significance of macrophage chemoattractant protein-1 in macrophage recruitment, angiogenesis, and survival in human breast cancer. *Clinical Cancer Research, 6*(8), 3282–3289. Retrieved from http://www.ncbi.nlm.nih.gov/pubmed/10955814 http://clincancerres.aacrjournals.org/content/clincanres/6/8/3282.full.pdf.

Uguccioni, M., Gionchetti, P., Robbiani, D. F., Rizzello, F., Peruzzo, S., Campieri, M., et al. (1999). Increased expression of IP-10, IL-8, MCP-1, and MCP-3 in ulcerative colitis. *American Journal of Pathology, 155*(2), 331–336. http://dx.doi.org/10.1016/S0002-9440(10)65128-0.

Valeta-Magara, A., Gadi, A., Volta, V., Walters, B., Arju, R., Giashuddin, S., et al. (2019). Inflammatory breast cancer promotes development of M2 tumor-associated macrophages and cancer mesenchymal cells through a complex chemokine network. *Cancer Research, 79*(13), 3360–3371. http://dx.doi.org/10.1158/0008-5472.CAN-17-2158.

Varricchi, G., Raap, U., Rivellese, F., Marone, G., & Gibbs, B. F. (2018). Human mast cells and basophils-How are they similar how are they different? *Immunological Reviews, 282*(1), 8–34. http://dx.doi.org/10.1111/imr.12627.

Vasakova, M., Sterclova, M., Kolesar, L., Slavcev, A., Pohunek, P., Sulc, J., et al. (2009). Bronchoalveolar lavage fluid cellular characteristics, functional parameters and cytokine and chemokine levels in interstitial lung diseases. *Scandinavian Journal of Immunology, 69*(3), 268–274. http://dx.doi.org/10.1111/j.1365-3083.2008.02222.x.

Vazquez, M. I., Catalan-Dibene, J., & Zlotnik, A. (2015). B cells responses and cytokine production are regulated by their immune microenvironment. *Cytokine, 74*(2), 318–326. http://dx.doi.org/10.1016/j.cyto.2015.02.007.

Vieira, A. T., Fagundes, C. T., Alessandri, A. L., Castor, M. G., Guabiraba, R., Borges, V. O., et al. (2009). Treatment with a novel chemokine-binding protein or eosinophil lineage-ablation protects mice from experimental colitis. *American Journal of Pathology, 175*(6), 2382–2391. http://dx.doi.org/10.2353/ajpath.2009.090093.

Vuga, L. J., Tedrow, J. R., Pandit, K. V., Tan, J., Kass, D. J., Xue, J., et al. (2014). C-X-C motif chemokine 13 (CXCL13) is a prognostic biomarker of idiopathic pulmonary fibrosis. *American Journal of Respiratory and Critical Care Medicine, 189*(8), 966–974. http://dx.doi.org/10.1164/rccm.201309-1592OC.

Wang, Z., Zhang, A., Wan, Y., Liu, X., Qiu, C., Xi, X., et al. (2014). Early hypercytokinemia is associated with interferon-induced transmembrane protein-3 dysfunction and predictive of fatal H7N9 infection. *Proc Natl Acad Sci U S A, 111*(2), 769–774. http://dx.doi.org/10.1073/pnas.1321748111.

Ward, S. G., & Westwick, J. (1998). Chemokines: Understanding their role in T-lymphocyte biology. *Biochemical Journal, 333*(Pt 3), 457–470. http://dx.doi.org/10.1042/bj3330457.

Weber, C., Meiler, S., Döring, Y., Koch, M., Drechsler, M., Megens, R. T. A., et al. (2011). CCL17-expressing dendritic cells drive atherosclerosis by restraining regulatory T cell homeostasis in mice. *Journal of Clinical Investigation, 121*(7), 2898–2910. Retrieved from http://eutils.ncbi.nlm.nih.gov/entrez/eutils/elink.fcgi?dbfrom=pubmed&id=21633167&retmode=ref&cmd=prlinks http://www.ncbi.nlm.nih.gov/pmc/articles/PMC3223829/pdf/JCI44925.pdf.

Willems, S., Verleden, S. E., Vanaudenaerde, B. M., Wynants, M., Dooms, C., Yserbyt, J., et al. (2013). Multiplex protein profiling of bronchoalveolar lavage in idiopathic pulmonary fibrosis and hypersensitivity pneumonitis. *Annals of Thoracic Medicine, 8*(1), 38–45. http://dx.doi.org/10.4103/1817-1737.105718.

Woodcock, J., Griffin, J. P., & Behrman, R. E. (2011). Development of novel combination therapies. *New England Journal of Medicine, 364*(11), 985–987. http://dx.doi.org/10.1056/NEJMp1101548.

Xu, Z., Zhang, X., Lau, J., & Yu, J. (2016). C-X-C motif chemokine 10 in non-alcoholic steatohepatitis: Role as a pro-inflammatory factor and clinical implication. *Expert Reviews in Molecular Medicine, 18*, e16. http://dx.doi.org/10.1017/erm.2016.16.

Yu, R., Kim, C.-S., Kawada, T., Kwon, T.-W., Lim, T.-H., Kim, Y.-W., et al. (2004). Involvement of leukotactin-1, a novel CC chemokine, in human atherosclerosis. *Atherosclerosis, 174*(1), 35–42. Retrieved from http://eutils.ncbi.nlm.nih.gov/entrez/eutils/elink.fcgi?dbfrom=pubmed&id=15135248&retmode=ref&cmd=prlinks http://www.atherosclerosis-journal.com/article/S0021-9150(04)00006-1/abstract http://ac.els-cdn.com/S0021915004000061/1-s2.0-S0021915004000061-main.pdf?_tid=26085ca2-2fb2-11e5-b38c-00000aab0f26&acdnat=1437487969_5a33c444311d13364917a39d23bb76cf.

Zeng, H., Belser, J. A., Goldsmith, C. S., Gustin, K. M., Veguilla, V., Katz, J. M., et al. (2015). A(H7N9) virus results in early induction of proinflammatory cytokine responses in both human lung epithelial and endothelial cells and shows increased human adaptation compared with avian H5N1 virus. *Journal of Virology, 89*(8), 4655–4667. http://dx.doi.org/10.1128/JVI.03095-14.

Zhou, X., Krueger, J. G., Kao, M. C., Lee, E., Du, F., Menter, A., et al. (2003). Novel mechanisms of T-cell and dendritic cell activation revealed by profiling of psoriasis on the

63,100-element oligonucleotide array. *Physiological Genomics, 13*(1), 69–78. http://dx.doi.org/10.1152/physiolgenomics.00157.2002.

Zlotnik, A., Yoshie, O., & Nomiyama, H. (2006). The chemokine and chemokine receptor superfamilies and their molecular evolution. *Genome Biology,* 7(12), 243. Retrieved from http://genomebiology.com/2006/7/12/243 http://www.ncbi.nlm.nih.gov/pmc/articles/PMC1794421/pdf/gb-2006-7-12-243.pdf.

Zuern, C. S., Walker, B., Sauter, M., Schaub, M., Chatterjee, M., Mueller, K., et al. (2015). Endomyocardial expression of SDF-1 predicts mortality in patients with suspected myocarditis. *Clinical Research in Cardiology, 104*(12), 1033–1043. http://dx.doi.org/10.1007/s00392-015-0871-y.

CHAPTER TWO

Biological functions and clinical implications of interleukin-34 in inflammatory diseases

Yun Ge[a,1], Man Huang[a,1], Xiao-mei Zhu[b] and Yong-ming Yao[b,*]

[a]Department of General Intensive Care Unit, The Second Affiliated Hospital of Zhejiang University School of Medicine, Hangzhou 310052, China

[b]Trauma Research Center, Fourth Medical Center of the Chinese PLA General Hospital, Beijing 100048, China

*Corresponding author: E-mail: c_ff@sina.com

Contents

Abstract

Interleukin (IL)-34 is a recently discovered cytokine and ligand of the colony-stimulating factor (CSF)-1 receptor. Although CSF-1 and IL-34 share similar biological properties,

[1] Contributed equally to this work.

Advances in Protein Chemistry and Structural Biology, Volume 119
ISSN 1876-1623
https://doi.org/10.1016/bs.apcsb.2019.02.003

their expression patterns and downstream signaling pathways are distinct. IL-34 can influence differentiation and has functions in multiple cell types (e.g., dendritic cells, monocytes, macrophages). In the pathological conditions, IL-34 is induced by proinflammatory stimuli (e.g., cytokines, pathogen-associated molecular patterns, and infection). Current evidence shows that IL-34 is a critical player in inflammatory response and is involved in the pathogenesis of inflammatory autoimmune dysfunction. Therefore, IL-34 may be a promising clinical biomarker and therapeutic target for treating inflammatory related disorders. In this article, we review the advances in biological functions of IL-34 and our understanding of its role in the development of inflammatory diseases as well as therapeutic applications.

Abbreviations

AKI acute kidney injury
CCL-20 chemokine ligand 20
CD Crohn's disease
HBV hepatitis B virus
IBD inflammatory bowel disease
MAPK mitogen-activated protein kinases
NF-κB nuclear factor of kappa B
PTP-ζ protein-tyrosine phosphatase ζ
RA rheumatoid arthritis
SLE systemic lupus erythematosus
UC ulcerative colitis

1. Introduction

Interleukin (IL)-34 was identified in 2008 as a ligand of the colony-stimulating factor-1 (CSF-1) receptor and is known to promote proliferation, differentiation, and survival in hematopoietic cells such as macrophages, osteoclasts, and monocytes (Chow, Brown, & Merad, 2011; Droin & Solary, 2010). Prior to the discovery of IL-34, CSF-1 was thought to be the sole ligand of CSF-1 receptor. However, studies showed that while CSF-1 receptor-deficient mice exhibited severe systemic depletion of macrophages and osteopetrosis (Dai et al., 2002), CSF-1 deficient mice had relatively normal Langerhans and microglia cells and recovered from osteopetrosis with age (Nakamichi, Udagawa, & Takahashi, 2013). This discrepancy suggested the possibility of another CSF-1 receptor ligand. Subsequent studies identified IL-34 as a novel protein that could activate monocytes *via* the CSF-1 receptor and rescue the defects of CSF-1-deficient mice (Lin et al., 2008). IL-34 deficiency also dramatically decreased the number of Langerhans and microglia cells (Grayfer & Robert, 2015; Wang et al., 2013). These findings have been demonstrated that IL-34 acts as a tissue-specific ligand of the CSF-1 receptor.

IL-34 is normally expressed in the skin and the brain, but it can also be induced in stressed cells by inflammatory pathways such as nuclear factor kappaB (NF-κB) signaling. IL-34 may therefore promote an inflammatory microenvironment (Barve et al., 2013; Uhlen et al., 2015). There is growing evidence that IL-34 is involved in the development of inflammatory diseases, and may be useful as a potential prognostic biomarker and therapeutic target (Tables 1 and 2) (Baghdadi, Endo, Tanaka, Wada, & Seino, 2017). In this review, we discuss the biological functions of IL-34, its downstream signaling cascade, and potential implications in inflammatory diseases.

Table 1 Interleukin (IL)-34 in various inflammatory diseases.

Diseases	Year	Authors	Clinical implications
HBV infection	2017	Cheng et al.	IL-34 was decreased in the serum and PBMCs of patients with chronic HBV infection, and it was negatively correlated with parameters reflecting disease activity.
	2018	Wang et al.	Serum IL-34 was elevated in HBV infection and correlated with liver inflammation and fibrosis in patients with chronic HBV infection.
HCV infection	2014	Preisser et al.	High levels of serum IL-34 were associated with advanced liver fibrosis stage.
Influenza A viral infection	2015	Yu et al.	High levels of IL-34 were found in PBMCs and serum.
Sepsis	2018	Lin et al.	Serum IL-34 levels were increased in sepsis.
IBD	2015 2015	Franzè et al. Zwicker et al.	IL-34 expression was enhanced in the epithelial layer and infiltrating immune cells in the inflamed mucosa.

(Continued)

Table 1 Interleukin (IL)-34 in various inflammatory diseases.—cont'd

Diseases	Year	Authors	Clinical implications
RA	2012	Hwang et al.	High levels of serum IL-34 were correlated with disease activity.
	2013	Moon et al.	
	2013	Tian et al.	
	2015	Chang et al.	
	2015	Zhang et al.	
	2017	Wang et al.	High levels of IL-34 in synovial fluid were correlated with the disease activity.
	2012	Cheme et al.	
	2012	Hwang et al.	
	2013	Moon et al.	
	2013	Tian et al.	
	2015	Chang et al.	
	2016	Yang et al.	High levels of IL-34 in the synovial lining and sibling layer were correlated with total leukocyte counts and severity of synovitis.
	2017	Cheme et al.	
	2012	Cheme et al.	
	2015	Chang et al.	
	2016	Garcia et al.	IL-34 levels in serum predicted response to TNF-α antagonist therapy.
	2015	Ding et al.	
SS	2013	Ciccia et al.	High expression of IL-34 was present in ductal epithelial cells and infiltrating mononuclear cells of the inflamed salivary gland, and it was correlated with pro-inflammatory cytokines and local expansion of pro-inflammatory $CD14^{bright}$ $CD16^{+}$ monocytes.
SLE	2016	Wang et al.	Elevated levels of serum IL-34 were positively correlated with the disease activity of SLE.
	2018	Xie et al.	
AD	2015	Esaki et al.	Low expression of IL-34 was noted in lesional epidermis.
Chronic apical periodontitis	2016	Ma et al.	IL-34 was over-expressed in lymphocytes, plasma cells, and macrophages in chronic periapical lesions.
T2DM	2011	Below et al.	Serum IL-34 predicted the risk of vascular diabetic complications.
	2016	Zorena et al.	IL-34 was located within characteristic risk loci of T2DM.

Table 1 Interleukin (IL)-34 in various inflammatory diseases.—cont'd

Diseases	Year	Authors	Clinical implications
Tumors	2017	Raggi et al.	Elevated serum IL-34 was observed in cholangiocarcinoma.
	2010	Baud'huin et al.	Expression of IL-34 was enhanced in giant cell tumors.
	2016	Zhou et al.	Elevated levels of IL-34 were correlated with poor prognosis in hepatocellular carcinoma.
	2018	Han et al.	IL-34 was strongly expressed in melanoma and correlated with $CD163^+$ cell counts in nivolumab-resistant metastatic melanoma.
	2018	Baghdadi et al.	IL-34 levels were associated with tumor progression in lung cancer.
	2015	Rietkötter et al.	IL-34 mRNA expression was upregulated in breast cancer and lung cancer with brain metastasis.
	2015	Ségaliny et al.	Heterogeneous expression of IL-34 was shown in human osteosarcomas.
	2017	Franzè et al.	Over-expression of IL-34 was evident in sporadic colorectal cancer.
	2014	Cioce et al.	IL-34 was released from malignant pleural mesothelioma cells and induced chemoresistance.
Heart failure	2016	Fan et al.	Elevated serum IL-34 level was correlated with risk of renal dysfunction, cardiovascular death, and mortality.

AD, atopic dermatitis; *HBV*, hepatitis B virus; *HCV*, hepatitis C virus; *IBD*, inflammatory bowel disease; *PBMCs*, peripheral blood mononuclear cells; *RA*, rheumatoid arthritis; *SLE*, systemic lupus erythematosus; *T2DM*, type II diabetes mellitus.

Table 2 Therapeutic applications of interleukin (IL)-34 in inflammatory responses.

Disease	Year	Authors	Therapeutic applications
HBV infection	2017	Cheng et al.	Treatment of HBV transgenic mice with IL-34 effectively reduced serum levels of HBV DNA.
Sepsis	2018	Lin et al.	IL-34 administration improved survival and bacterial clearance in a mouse model of polymicrobial sepsis.
Atopic dermatitis	2015	Esaki et al.	IL-34 inhibited propagation of inflammatory cascades in the development of active skin lesions.
IBD	2016	Franze et al.	Blockade of IL-34 attenuated inflammatory responses by suppressing TNF-α, IL-6, and CCL20.
Kidney injury	2015	Baek et al.	IL-34 mediated acute kidney injury and exacerbated chronic kidney disease
RA	2013 2016 2016	Bostrom et al. Yang et al. Zhou et al.	Neutralizing IL-34 blocked inflammatory lesions, reduced pathogenic immune cell subsets, sensitized synovial fibroblasts to apoptosis, and reduced bone erosion as well as cartilage destruction in RA
Sjogren's syndrome	2013	Ciccia et al.	Targeting IL-34 suppressed expansion of pro-inflammatory $CD14^{bright}$ $CD16^{+}$ monocytes in inflamed salivary glands.
HIV infection	2010	Chihara et al.	Neutralizing IL-34 suppressed HIV replication.
IAV infection	2015	Yu et al.	Neutralizing IL-34 inhibited the inflammatory cascade in IAV infection.

HBV, hepatitis B virus; *HCV*, hepatitis C virus; *IAV*, influenza A virus; *IBD*, inflammatory bowel disease; *RA*, rheumatoid arthritis.

2. Biological functions of IL-34

2.1 The IL-34 gene and protein structure

The human *IL-34* gene is located on chromosome 16q22.1 and is highly conserved, with>70% sequence similarity to the rat, chimpanzee, and mouse orthologs (Garceauet al., 2010). IL-34 is a secreted homodimeric protein of 235 amino acids in mouse and 242 amino acids in humans, with a molecular mass of 39 kDa. The IL-34 protein contains an antiparallel four-helix core and comprises two β strands (β1, β2), four short helices (α1-4), and four long helices (αA-D) (Fig. 1) (Ma et al., 2012). IL-34 has

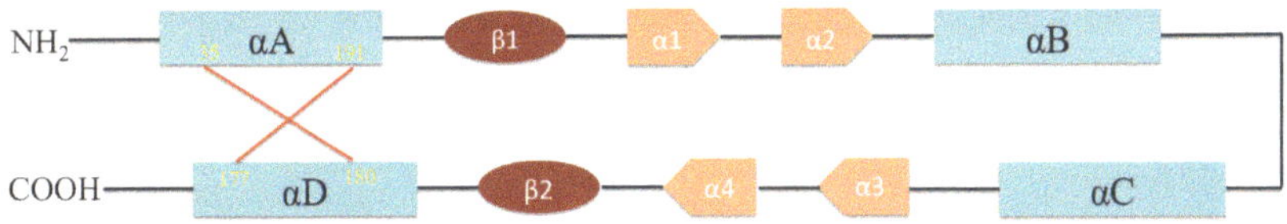

Fig. 1 ***Schematic structure of interleukin-34.*** IL-34 is comprised of an antiparallel 4 helix core, with four additional helices and two short β strands. The helices are connected by α strands. Disulfide bridges between C177-C191 and C35-C180 link the helix bundle.

the smallest dimerization interface of all short-chain helical hematopoietic cytokines (Felix et al., 2013, 2015). The glutamine residue at position 81 (Q81) is thought to be essential for IL-34, as removal disrupts the four α-helices and changes the coiled-coil into an α-helix, thereby altering the biological property of IL-34.

2.2 Expression and production of IL-34

IL-34 mRNA is highly expressed in the embryonic brain and neural tube of chicken embryos (Garceau et al., 2015). Particularly, it was more highly expressed in the hippocampus and cerebral cortex than cerebellum (Zhang et al., 2017). In humans, IL-34 mRNA is present in a wide range of tissues including brain, spleen, ovary, prostate, colon, thymus, testis, small intestine, kidney, liver, lung, and heart. However, IL-34 protein is most strongly expressed in the brain and skin (Wang et al., 2012). Intracellular IL-34 expression has been reported in neurons, seminiferous tubule germ cells, proximal renal tubule cells, hair follicles, and keratinocytes (Gao et al., 2017; Gow et al., 2012; Wang & Colonna, 2014).

Recent studied have been documented that IL-34 can be secreted into the extracellular fluid where it functions as an endocrine regulator. For example, IL-34 is detectable in saliva, cerebral spinal fluid, synovial fluid, serum, and the human fetal-maternal interface (Garceau et al., 2015; Kawabe et al., 2015; Lindau et al., 2018; Schuster et al., 2014). However, IL-34 may also function differently depending on cell type, e.g., it can be detectable in total lysates of epidermal cells but not in supernatants, indicating it might be associated with larger structures or membrane-associated proteins.

Many reports have been shown that IL-34 expressions are positively correlated with severity and progression of various diseases including cancer, inflammatory and autoimmune disorders, and metabolic as well as neurological diseases. These diseases have been associated with increased secretion of IL-34 in immune cells, cancer cells, endothelial cells, epithelial cells, adipocytes, and synovial fibroblasts (Baghdadi, Endo et al., 2018,

Baghdadi, Ishikawa et al., 2018; Baudhuin et al., 2010; Bostrom & Lundberg, 2013; Chemel et al., 2012; Han et al., 2018; Nakamichi et al., 2012). In addition, decreased IL-34 expression was reported in Alzheimer's disease (Walker, Tang, & Lue, 2017). The mechanisms that alter the secretion and expression of IL-34 in diseases are not yet understood.

2.3 Biological functions of IL-34

Like CSF-1, IL-34 is known to induce activated/regenerative (M2) macrophages, $CD11b^+$ cells, and osteoclasts. IL-34- and CSF-1-induced macrophages can then switch from memory T cells to helper T cell (Th) 17 cells in a membrane-bound IL-1α-dependent manner (Foucher et al., 2015). Moreover, IL-34 promotes proliferation of human $CD14^+$ monocytes, endothelial cells, macrophages, and microglial cells *via* the CSF-1 receptor; it acts as a critical regulator to increase adhesion of macrophage and osteoclast progenitors; and it promotes migration of THP-1 and M2a macrophages *via* syndecan-1 signaling (Galligan & Fish, 2017).

It should be noticed that the expression pattern of IL-34 differs remarkably from that of CSF-1. CSF-1 expression is relatively broad, while IL-34 expression is limited primarily to the neurons and epidermis (Greter et al., 2012). IL-34 deficiency has been reported to decrease the number of microglia and Langerhans cells (Fig. 2A) as well as influence other cells (e.g. dendritic cells, tissue macrophages, monocytes). IL-34 mRNA is detectable in the testes, kidney, and spleen, where it plays a critical role in maintaining the splenic reservoir of osteoclast precursor cells (Wei et al., 2010). Thus, IL-34 signaling may have more tissue-specific regulatory roles than CSF-1.

2.4 IL-34 signaling pathways

The CSF-1 receptor is thought to be the primary receptor of IL-34, as blocking the CSF-1 receptor with neutralizing antibodies or specific inhibitors dramatically reduces IL-34 downstream signaling (Ségaliny, Brion, et al., 2015, Ségaliny, Mohamati, et al., 2015; Gow et al., 2013; Yamane et al., 2014). IL-34 binds to the CSF-1 receptor at the cleft between the immunoglobulin-like domain (D)2 and D3 and activates numerous downstream pathways, including signal transducer and activator of transcription (STAT)3, Janus kinase (JAK), phosphoinositide 3-kinase (PI3K)/AKT, NF-κB, p38 mitogen-activated protein kinase (MAPK), c-Jun N-terminal kinase (JNK), and extracellular signal-regulated protein kinases 1 and 2

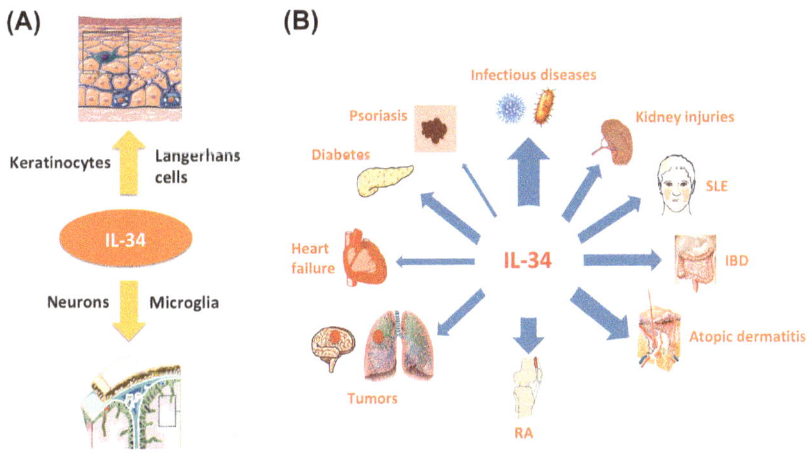

Fig. 2 ***Physical and pathological roles of interleukin-34.*** **(A) Physiological functions of IL-34.** IL-34 is expressed mainly in keratinocytes and neurons. It is also known to play a crucial role in regulatory functions of Langerhans cells and microglia. **(B) The role of IL-34 in inflammatory diseases.** The expression and secretion of IL-34 is induced in the inflammatory milieu and contributes to the development of numerous inflammatory diseases, including infectious diseases, kidney injuries, inflammatory bowel disease (IBD), rheumatoid arthritis (RA), systemic lupus erythematous (SLE), atopic dermatitis, psoriasis, heart failure, diabetes, and tumors.

(ERK1/2) (Fig. 3) (Chihara et al., 2010; Eda, Shimada, Beidler, & Monahan, 2011; Liu et al., 2012; Yu et al., 2014; Zhou et al., 2018). A recent study suggested that IL-34 binding induced AKT and caspase 3/8 and activated cellular autophagy *via* the AMP-activated protein kinase (AMPK)-UNC-51-Like Kinase (ULK)1 pathway (Boulakirba et al., 2018). These signaling pathways are known to be essential for differentiation, migration, proliferation, spreading, and survival in microglia, osteoclasts, and macrophages (Cannarile, Weisser, Jacob, Jegg, Ries, & Ruttinger, 2017; Cioce et al., 2014; Kumari, Silakari, & Singh, 2018; Peyraud, Cousin, & Italiano, 2017; Stanley & Chitu, 2014; Zelante & Ricciardi-Castagnoli, 2012).

It was reported that IL-34 was positively expressed in regions together with minimal expression of the CSF-1 receptor (Nandi et al., 2013), implying that IL-34 might have alternative receptors. Protein-tyrosine phosphatase ζ (PTP-ζ) was subsequently identified as a novel receptor of IL-34 (Nandi et al., 2013). PTP-ζ is a chondroitin sulfate proteoglycan that is strongly expressed in neuronal progenitors and glial cells (Zwicker et al., 2016). IL-34/PTP-ζ interactions are thought to induce

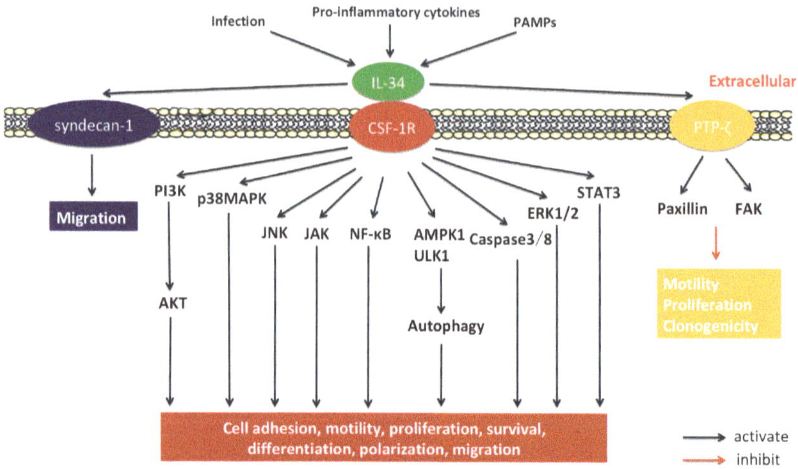

Fig. 3 ***The signaling pathways of interleukin-34.*** IL-34 can be induced by various inflammatory stimuli such as pro-inflammatory cytokines, pathogen-associated molecular patterns (PAMPs), and pathogens. Typically, IL-34 binds to the CSF-1 receptor (CSF-1R) and then triggers several signaling networks, including signal transducer and activator of transcription (STAT)-3, Janus kinase (JAK), phosphoinositide 3-kinase (PI3K)/AKT, nuclear factor-kappaB (NF-κB), p38 mitogen-activated protein kinase (p38 MAPK), c-Jun N-terminal kinase (JNK), extracellular signal-regulated protein kinases 1 and 2 (ERK1/2), caspase-3/8, and AMP-activated protein kinase (AMPK)-UNC-51-like kinase (ULK)1. IL-34 can activate focal adhesion kinase (FAK) and paxillin by binding the novel receptor protein-tyrosine phosphatase ζ (PTP-ζ). Activation of these signaling pathways regulates multiple cellular functions including cellular adhesion, motility, proliferation, differentiation, metabolism, survival. Syndecan-1 can regulate IL-34-mediated CSF-1R activation and may act as a critical modulator of IL-34 biology. However, the signaling pathways induced by IL-34/syndecan-1 interaction are unclear.

phosphorylation of focal adhesion kinase and paxillin, which dampen motility and proliferation in U251 human glioblastoma cells (Nandi et al., 2013). IL-34 may therefore have additional roles independent of the CSF-1 receptor.

Recently, syndecan-1 has been reported to regulate signaling mediated by IL-34 and the CSF-1 receptor. Low or moderate expression of syndecan-1 resulted in limited interaction between the CSF-1 receptor and IL-34, whereas over-expression of syndecan-1 promoted signaling mediated by IL-34 and the CSF-1 receptor (Segaliny et al., 2015). Taken together, IL-34 can bind to several different receptors, each of which activates different signaling cascades with distinct cellular functions.

3. IL-34 in mediated inflammatory response

IL-34 is known to modulate the inflammatory response and is involved in the pathogenesis of inflammatory diseases (Guillonneau, Bézie, & Anegon, 2017; Boulakirba et al., 2018; Eda et al., 2010). IL-34 levels were found to be elevated in experimental colitis and in patients with inflammatory bowel disease (Zwicker et al., 2015). In inflammatory bowel disease, IL-34 markedly accelerated release of chemokine ligands (CCL)-20, IL-6, and tumor necrosis factor (TNF)-α in lamina propria mononuclear cells *via* ERK1/2 signaling (Franzè et al., 2016). Likewise, IL-34 was found to induce production of IL-8/CXCL8, interferon-inducible protein 10/ CXCL10, and monocyte chemotactic protein-1 (MCP)-1/CCL2 in the blood of patients with inflammatory disorders (Franzè et al., 2015; Zwicker et al., 2015).

Paradoxically, IL-34 was reported to inhibit TNF-α production in M1 macrophages by suppressing Dectin-1 and Toll-like receptor (TLR)2 (Xu et al., 2015). The effects of IL-34 on inflammation may therefore vary depending on the signaling microenvironment. Alternatively, it is possible that increased IL-34 signaling may activate a negative feedback mechanism in response to inflammation, rather than being a direct cause of inflammatory disease. In support of this notion, high levels of IL-34 expressions were observed to overlap with anti-inflammatory IL-10-secreting macrophages, suggesting that IL-34 might play a protective role in inflammatory bowel disease (Zwicker et al., 2015).

4. Potential role and its significance of IL-34 in inflammatory diseases

Enhanced IL-34 expression has been found in animal models and patients with inflammatory diseases such as infectious disease, kidney injury, skin disease, inflammatory bowel disease, rheumatoid arthritis, and cancer (Fig. 2B and Table 1). Up-regulation of IL-34 can be triggered by inflammatory stimuli including infectious pathogens, pathogen-associated molecular patterns, and pro-inflammatory cytokines (e.g., TNF-α, IL-1β) (Eda et al., 2011; Masteller & Wong, 2014; Franzè et al., 2015; Yu et al., 2015). Suppression of NF-κB (a critical regulator of inflammatory responses) can reduce IL-34 levels after stimulation (Yu et al., 2014). More importantly, IL-34 secretion is tightly correlated with the pathogenesis, progression, and severity of inflammatory disease. Treatment of rheumatoid arthritis with TNF-α antagonist therapy returned IL-34 levels to normal range (Chang et al., 2015; Tian, Shen, Xia, & Lu, 2013). Thus, IL-34 may be a useful biomarker for predicting disease prognosis and responsiveness to treatment.

4.1 IL-34 in infectious disease

Inflammation plays a key role in host defense against invading pathogens, nevertheless, it accompanied by dysregulated chemokines and cytokines can exacerbate tissue and organ damage. IL-34 up-regulation in infectious disease was first reported in macrophages in response to infection with equine infectious anemia virus (Covaleda, Fuller, & Payne, 2010). Macrophages are thought to be a natural target for viral replication, as they are known to act as viral reservoirs and vectors. In human immunodeficiency virus (HIV) infection, IL-34-differentiated macrophages showed high levels of HIV-1 replication *via* signaling mediated by MAPK and the CSF-1 receptor (Chihara et al., 2010), indicating that such signaling might be required for the development of HIV-infected macrophage reservoirs. In support of this concept, IL-34 was found to facilitate expansion of IL-10^{+} monocytes and HIV-1 production in microglia by a mechanism dependent on the CSF-1 receptor (Gerngross & Fischer, 2015; Gerngross, Lehmicke, Belkadi, & Fischer, 2015). IL-34-deficient mice revealed reduced synaptic terminal loss upon West Nile virus infection (Vasek et al., 2016). Therefore, IL-34 signaling may promote survival of infected macrophages/microglia, contributing to neuro-cognitive impairment.

In contrast, other studies have been documented that IL-34 may play beneficial roles in infectious diseases. For instance, IL-34 administration significantly inhibited replication of the hepatitis B virus (Cheng et al., 2017), and IL-34-expressing macrophages displayed strong antiviral activity and improved survival of ranavirus-infected tadpoles (Grayfer & Robert, 2014; Grayfer & Robert, 2015). Likely, IL-34 was reported to recruit neutrophils and macrophages by inducing release of chemokines as well as cytokines, which improved bacterial clearance. Treatment with IL-34 markedly protected against sepsis, while neutralization of IL-34 activity reduced the survival rate (Lin et al., 2018). In addition, IL-34 was implicated in immune tolerance to *Candida albicans* fungal infection (Xu et al., 2015) and prevented *Enteromyxumleei* parasitic infection (Mo, Li, Zhou, Li, Luo, & Dan, 2015). How does IL-34 improve the outcomes in infectious disease is unclear, though IL-34 has been reported to block TNF-α release in M1-polarized macrophages. Thus, IL-34 may have both adverse and protective effects in infectious diseases and it appears to be a useful marker for screening anti-inflammatory medicine.

4.2 IL-34 in inflammatory bowel disease

The IL-34 receptor PTP-ζ is highly expressed in the colon but weakly expressed in monocytes and mononuclear cells of peripheral blood. In contrast, the CSF-1 receptor is expressed primarily in monocytes and intestinal epithelial cells.

Inflammatory bowel diseases such as ulcerative colitis (UC) and Crohn's disease (CD) are characterized by chronic inflammation of the colonic mucosa. Increased expression of IL-34 was observed in the inflamed colon of patients with UC or CD (Guillonneau et al., 2017; Franzè et al., 2015). TNF-α stimulation induced high expression of IL-34 in colon epithelial cells *via* an NF-κB-dependent mechanism (Franzè et al., 2015), while IL-34 in turn enhanced the release of CCL20, IL-6, and TNF-α in an ERK-dependent manner (Franzè et al., 2015). In animal models of UC, IL-34 mediated Th2 inflammatory response and induced inflammatory remodeling with fibrosis and epithelial hyperplasia. In patients with inflammatory bowel diseases, neutralizing TNF-α weakened the expression of IL-34, while neutralizing IL-34 decreased TNF-α level in mucosal explants (Franzè et al., 2016; Zwicker et al., 2015). Taken together, IL-34 appears to be involved in the development of gut inflammation, and it might be a useful biomarker for predicting severity of inflammatory bowel diseases and is a promising therapeutic target.

4.3 IL-34 in acute kidney injury

Acute kidney injury (AKI) is caused by exposure to harmful substances, kidney ischemia or obstructions of the urinary tract. In the AKI, activated macrophages mediate an inflammatory response that leads to kidney repair or destruction (Lee et al., 2011).

Proliferation, activation, and survival of macrophages in the kidney are regulated by cytokines. CSF-1 is secreted from tubular cells and mediates kidney repair *via* a macrophage-dependent pattern (Baek et al., 2015). It has been demonstrated that IL-34 plays a pathological role during inflammation in kidney disease. IL-34 levels were elevated following ischemia-reperfusion kidney injury in a murine model (Sanchez-Niño, Sanz, & Ortiz, 2016), and IL-34-mediated inflammation resulted in tubule destruction *via* a neutrophil- and macrophage-dependent response. In chronic inflammation, IL-34 activated myeloid cells and augmented infiltration of intrarenal macrophages, which exacerbated the development of kidney inflammation (Liao et al., 2014; Zorena, Jachimowicz-Duda, & Waż, 2016).

4.4 IL-34 in skin disease

It has been documented that IL-34 is strongly expressed in the epidermis and is implicated in the proliferation, differentiation, and maintenance of Langerhans cells (Wang, Bugatti, Ulland, Vermi, Gilfillan, & Colonna, 2016). Abnormal up-regulation of IL-34 is thought to be involved in several skin diseases. For example, atopic dermatitis is characterized by inflammatory lesions (Esaki et al., 2015) together with decreased IL-34 expression. As IL-34 is a negative regulator of inflammatory response, it may be a potential therapeutic target for preventing inflammation in skin lesions (Li et al., 2017; Ma, Qu, Xu, Yu, & Qiu, 2016).

4.5 IL-34 in inflammatory autoimmune diseases

IL-34 has been implicated in several inflammatory autoimmune disorders including rheumatoid arthritis (RA), systemic lupus erythematosus (SLE), Sjogren's syndrome, psoriasis and psoriatic arthritis. RA is an inflammatory autoimmune disease characterized by progressive inflammation of the joints and surrounding tissues, resulting in irreversible joint destruction. Many studies indicate that IL-34 can serve as an important mediator of inflammation in RA (Clavel, Thiolat, & Boissier, 2013; Hwang et al., 2012). High levels of IL-34 were measured in synovial fluid and serum in animal models and patients with active RA (Chemel et al., 2017; Ding, Li, Song, Zhang, & Bi, 2015; Moon et al., 2013; Wang et al., 2017, 2018; Yang et al., 2016; Zhou, Hu, et al., 2016, Zhou, Wu, et al., 2016). IL-34 could be released from synovial fibroblasts stimulated by IL-1β or TNF-α, in turn amplifying the inflammatory response. Several studies reported that IL-34 levels were significantly correlated with autoimmune disease severity as measured by leukocyte counts, pro-inflammatory cytokine concentrations, synovial hyperplasia, histological severity of synovitis, disease activity index, inflammation parameters, and auto-antibody production (Chang et al., 2015; Tian et al., 2013). Furthermore, IL-34 levels in serum were observed to decrease sharply after treatment with TNF-α antagonist or disease-modifying anti-rheumatic drugs (Zhang et al., 2018, Zhang et al., 2015), and neutralizing IL-34 activity with monoclonal antibodies was shown to attenuate inflammatory arthritis (Garcia et al., 2016).

As we known, SLE is a systemic autoimmune disease caused by production of immune complexes, auto-antibodies, and polyclonal activation of B and T lymphocytes, leading to organ damage. Serum IL-34 was increased in SLE patients and correlated with disease activity, as measured by clinical symptoms and physiological parameters such as C-reactive protein levels, SLE disease activity index, and antibody titer (Wang, Cao, & Lai, 2016; Bethunaickan et al., 2013). IL-34 levels declined after SLE patients were treated with corticosteroid or immunosuppressive drugs (Xie et al., 2018).

Sjogren's syndrome is a chronic immune disease characterized by macrophage-induced inflammation of the salivary glands. IL-34 was known to regulate macrophage activity and was found to be positively associated with pro-inflammatory cytokine levels (IL-1β, TNF-α, IL-17) in Sjogren's lesions (Ciccia et al., 2013; Martinez, Majster, Bjurshammar, Johannsen, Figueredo, & Bostrom, 2017).

Psoriasis is a chronic autoimmune disease that can lead to psoriatic arthritis with prolonged inflammation. Psoriatic arthritis is characterized by osteoclastogenesis, bone erosion, and progressive joint injury. High levels of serum IL-34 were noted in psoriasis patients, particularly psoriatic arthritis, and they were positively correlated with circulating osteoclast precursor counts, implicating a possible role for IL-34 in the pathogenesis of osteoclastogenesis (Li et al., 2017; Ma et al., 2016).

IL-34 has been widely implicated in numerous autoimmune inflammatory diseases, and it may be useful as a novel predictive marker to evaluate autoimmune disease progression and treatment response. Inhibition of IL-34 signaling may be a promising therapeutic target for treating autoimmune diseases.

4.6 IL-34 and tumors

"Smouldering" inflammation is known to be a pivotal part of tumor pathogenesis. Tumor-associated inflammatory responses are regulated by inflammatory cells such as tumor-associated macrophages (TAMs), which act as immunosuppressive leukocytes. TAMs are essential for the growth, invasion, and metastasis of tumors (Rietkotter et al., 2015; Baghdadi, Endo et al., 2018, Baghdadi, Ishikawa et al., 2018; Ségaliny, Brion, et al., 2015, Ségaliny, Mohamati, et al., 2015), and a high TAM intensity correlates with adverse outcomes in cancer (Qian & Pollard, 2010).

Signaling *via* the CSF-1 receptor has been shown to affect activity and survival of TAMs. Surprisingly, studies suggested that IL-34 might have pro-tumorigenic effects on myeloid and tumor cells (Cannarile, Weisser,

Jacob, Jegg, Ries, & Ruttinger, 2017; Peyraud et al., 2017). For instance, IL-34 was released from cholangiocarcinoma stem-like subsets and reprogrammed TAMs, resulting in a beneficial immunological milieu for tumor cells (Raggi et al., 2017). Also, IL-34 could improve tumor survival in an autocrine manner: tumor-derived IL-34 triggered ERK1/2 and AKT signaling, which protected tumor cells from death and chemotherapy (Cioce et al., 2014). IL-34 was shown to promote chemoresistance in cancer treatment (Baghdadi et al., 2016; Franzè et al., 2017). However, the precise mechanisms underlying the pro-tumorigenic effects of IL-34 remain unclear. Further studies are required to investigate the impact of IL-34 on tumor associated-neutrophils, dendritic cells, and regulatory T cells in tumors.

There is increasing evidence that IL-34 modifies macrophages into TAMs, which is critical for tumor progression. IL-34-derived macrophages and TAMs then switch non-Th17 committed memory $CD4^+$ T cells into Th17 cells in a membrane-IL-1α (mIL-1α)-dependent manner. In addition, mIL-1α can display pro-inflammatory and pro-angiogenetic abilities and allow IL-34-modified macrophages and TAMs to maintain locally restrained and smoldering inflammation, which is required for the growth and metastasis of tumors (Foucher et al., 2015). Moreover, it was reported that IL-34 accelerated TGF-1β release from TAMs in hepatocellular carcinoma cells, and TGF-1β in turn augmented production of IL-34 *via* down-regulation of miR-28-5p. This feedback loop was shown to increase tumor metastasis (Zhou, Hu, et al., 2016, Zhou, Wu, et al., 2016). IL-34 level was increased in brain metastatic tumors, and it might therefore be useful as a marker of poor prognosis.

4.7 IL-34 in other diseases

IL-34-associated inflammation is involved in metabolic, cardiovascular, and neurological diseases. Type II diabetes is characterized by chronic inflammation, metabolic dysfunction, and cellular stress. High IL-34 expression was evident in adipose tissues and strongly correlated with insulin resistance and metabolic parameters associated with obesity (Chang et al., 2014), and increased serum IL-34 was observed in patients with obesity and type II diabetes mellitus (Below et al., 2011; Chang et al., 2014; Guruprasad & Pradeep, 2018).

Inflammation is associated with initiation and progression of heart failure. IL-34 can regulate NF-κB-mediated inflammation and has been proposed to play a role in heart failure (Fan et al., 2016). In particular, IL-34 was positively associated with C-reactive protein in patients with coronary artery disease, implying that IL-34 might be useful as an independent predictor of heart failure prognosis (Li et al., 2012; Tao et al., 2017).

Blood-brain barrier disruption occurs in several neurological disorders including Alzheimer disease, Parkinson's disease, and multiple sclerosis (Amos et al., 2017; Bohlen et al., 2017; Chitu, Gokhan, Nandi, Mehler, & Stanley, 2016; Luo et al., 2013; Nandi et al., 2012; Ohgidani et al., 2014; Ohgidani, Kato, & Kanba, 2015; Okubo et al., 2016; Xing & Lo, 2017; Zhu et al., 2016). Interestingly, IL-34 was noticed to exert a neuroprotective effect by improving tight junction molecules in blood-brain barrier endothelial cells (Jin et al., 2014). Thus, IL-34 could be a helpful biomarker to monitor disease progression in neurological diseases.

5. Discussion and outlook

IL-34 is a multifunctional cytokine that plays crucial roles in numerous cellular processes including migration, adhesion, differentiation, angiogenesis, and inflammation. Like its twin cytokine CSF-1, IL-34 binds the CSF-1 receptor and initiates downstream molecular signaling to impact monocyte/macrophage activity. IL-34 has been recently found to bind PTP-ζ and syndecan-1, and may therefore exert additional biological functions through these receptors. The molecular mechanisms that regulate IL-34 expression under normal and pathological situations remain obscure. Future investigations should identify novel receptors or modulators of IL-34, to explore the enigmatic role of IL-34 in health and disease.

Evidence accumulated over the past ten years indicates that IL-34 appears to be critically involved in various inflammatory diseases. Increased IL-34 release is thought to act as an "alarm signal" that amplifies inflammatory responses or exerts protective effects. IL-34 may therefore be useful as a novel biomarker to evaluate progression of numerous inflammatory diseases.

Recently, there has been great interest in using or targeting IL-34 as a treatment in inflammatory disorders. IL-34 can augment inflammation by accelerating metalloprotease, chemokine, and pro-inflammatory cytokine secretion. Blocking IL-34 signaling therefore mitigate inflammatory cascades. For example, neutralization of IL-34 obviously dampened IL-6 and TNF-α production in mucosal explants from patients with inflammatory bowel disease. Blocking IL-34 activity might have potential benefits for anti-tumor treatment as IL-34 is a key pro-tumorigenic regulator of TAMs. Additionally, neutralizing IL-34 signaling has potential in the treatment of many other diseases associated with inflammation, including viral infection, RA, kidney injury, and Sjogren's syndrome.

IL-34 signaling has been demonstrated to be associated with the survival of endothelial cells of the blood-brain barrier, microglia, and neurons, and may mitigate inflammatory response by down-regulating pro-inflammatory mediators and promoting expansion of immunosuppressive immune cells such as regulatory T cells and M2-polarized macrophages. It is evident that IL-34 could prevent HBV viral replication in mice, and replenishing IL-34 reduced mortality and enhanced bacterial clearance in a murine model of polymicrobial sepsis. Therefore, increasing expression of IL-34 might serve as a promising therapeutic tool in infectious complications and inflammatory disorders.

In conclusion, IL-34 orchestrates the initiation and development of many inflammatory diseases through numerous molecular and cellular mechanisms. Elucidating the beneficial and adverse effects of IL-34 in the inflammatory microenvironment may be of importance to understand and treat inflammatory diseases.

Acknowledgments

This work was supported by grants from the National Natural Science Foundation (81873946, 81730057, 81842025) and the National Key Research and Development Program of China (2017YFC1103302).

References

Amos, P. J., Fung, S., Case, A., Kifelew, J., Osnis, L., Smith, C. L., et al. (2017). Modulation of hematopoietic lineage specification impacts TREM2 expression in microglia-like cells derived from human stem cells. *ASN Neuro, 9*, 1759091417716610.

Baek, J. H., Zeng, R., Weinmann-Menke, J., Valerius, M. T., Wada, Y., Ajay, A. K., et al. (2015). IL-34 mediates acute kidney injury and worsens subsequent chronic kidney disease. *Journal of Clinical Investigation, 125*, 3198–3214.

Baghdadi, M., Wada, H., Nakanishi, S., Abe, H., Han, N., & Putra, W. E. (2016). Chemotherapy-induced IL34 enhances immunosuppression by tumor-associated macrophages and mediates survival of chemoresistant lung cancer cells. *Cancer Research, 76*, 6030–6042.

Baghdadi, M., Endo, H., Tanaka, Y., Wada, H., & Seino, K. I. (2017). Interleukin 34, from pathogenesis to clinical applications. *Cytokine, 99*, 139–147.

Baghdadi, M., Endo, H., Takano, A., Ishikawa, K., Kameda, Y., Wada, H., et al. (2018). High co-expression of IL-34 and M-CSF correlates with tumor progression and poor survival in lung cancers. *Scientific Reports, 8*, 418.

Baghdadi, M., Ishikawa, K., Endo, H., Umeyama, Y., Ataka, T., Wada, H., et al. (2018). Enhanced expression of IL-34 in an inflammatory cyst of the submandibular gland: A case report. *Inflammation and Regeneration, 38*, 12.

Barve, R. A., Zack, M. D., Weiss, D., Song, R. H., Beidler, D., & Head, R. D. (2013). Transcriptional profiling and pathway analysis of CSF-1 and IL-34 effects on human monocyte differentiation. *Cytokine, 63*, 10–17.

Baudhuin, M., Renault, R., Charrier, C., Riet, A., Moreau, A., Brion, R., et al. (2010). Interleukin-34 is expressed by giant cell tumours of bone and plays a key role in RANKL induced osteoclastogenesis. *The Journal of Pathology, 221*, 77–86.

Below, J. E., Gamazon, E. R., Morrison, J. V., Konkashbaev, A., Pluzhnikov, A., McKeigue, P. M., et al. (2011). Genome-wide association and meta-analysis in populations from Starr County, Texas, and Mexico City identify type 2 diabetes susceptibility loci and enrichment for expression quantitative trait loci in top signals. *Diabetologia, 54*, 2047–2055.

Bethunaickan, R., Berthier, C. C., Zhang, W., Kretzler, M., & Davidson, A. (2013). Comparative transcriptional profiling of 3 murine models of SLE nephritis reveals both unique and shared regulatory networks. *PLoS One, 8*, e77489.

Bohlen, C. J., Bennett, F. C., Tucker, A. F., Collins, H. Y., Mulinyawe, S. B., & Barres, B. A. (2017). Diverse requirements for microglial survival, specification, and function revealed by defined-medium cultures. *Neuron, 94*, 759–773.

Böstrom, E. A., & Lundberg, P. (2013). The newly discovered cytokine IL-34 is expressed in gingival fibroblasts, shows enhanced expression by pro-inflammatory cytokines, and stimulates osteoclast differentiation. *PLoS One, 8*, e81665.

Boulakirba, S., Pfeifer, A., Mhaidly, R., Obba, S., Goulard, M., Schmitt, T., et al. (2018). IL-34 and CSF-1 display an equivalent macrophage differentiation ability but a different polarization potential. *Scientific Reports, 8*, 256.

Cannarile, M. A., Weisser, M., Jacob, W., Jegg, A. M., Ries, C. H., & Rüttinger, D. (2017). Colony-stimulating factor 1 receptor (CSF1R) inhibitors in cancer therapy. *Journal for ImmunoTherapy of Cancer, 5*, 53.

Chang, S. H., Choi, B. Y., Choi, J., Yoo, J. J., Ha, Y. J., Cho, H. J., et al. (2015). Baseline serum interleukin-34 levels independently predict radiographic progression in patients with rheumatoid arthritis. *Rheumatology International, 35*, 71–79.

Chang, E. J., Lee, S. K., Song, Y. S., Jang, Y. J., Park, H. S., Hong, J. P., et al. (2014). IL-34 is associated with obesity, chronic inflammation, and insulin resistance. *Journal of Clinical Endocrinology & Metabolism, 99*, E1263–E1271.

Chemel, M., Brion, R., Segaliny, A. I., Lamora, A., Charrier, C., Brulin, B., et al. (2017). Bone morphogenetic protein 2 and transforming growth factor β1 inhibit the expression of the proinflammatory cytokine IL-34 in rheumatoid arthritis synovial fibroblasts. *American Journal of Pathology, 187*, 156–162.

Chemel, M., LeGoff, B., Brion, R., Cozic, C., Berreur, M., Amiaud, J., et al. (2012). Interleukin 34 expression is associated with synovitis severity in rheumatoid arthritis patients. *Annals of the Rheumatic Diseases, 71*, 150–154.

Cheng, S. T., Tang, H., Ren, J. H., Chen, X., Huang, A. L., & Chen, J. (2017). Interleukin-34 inhibits hepatitis B virus replication in vitro and in vivo. *PLoS One, 12*, e0179605.

Chihara, T., Suzu, S., Hassan, R., Chutiwitoonchai, N., Hiyoshi, M., Motoyoshi, K., et al. (2010). IL-34 and M-CSF share the receptor FMS but are not identical in biological activity and signal activation. *Cell Death & Differentiation, 17*, 1917–1927.

Chitu, V., Gokhan, S., Nandi, S., Mehler, M. F., & Stanley, E. R. (2016). Emerging roles for CSF-1 receptor and its ligands in the nervous system. *Trends in Neurosciences, 39*, 378–393.

Chow, V., Brown, B. D., & Merad, M. (2011). Studying the mononuclear phagocyte system in the molecular age. *Nature Reviews Immunology, 11*, 788–798.

Ciccia, F., Alessandro, R., Rodolico, V., Guggino, G., Raimondo, S., Guarnotta, C., et al. (2013). IL-34 is overexpressed in the inflamed salivary glands of patients with Sjogren's

syndrome and is associated with the local expansion of pro-inflammatory CD14 (bright) $CD16^+$ monocytes. *Rheumatology, 52*, 1009–1017.
Cioce, M., Canino, C., Goparaju, C., Yang, H., Carbone, M., & Pass, H. I. (2014). Autocrine CSF-1R signaling drives mesothelioma chemoresistance via AKT activation. *Cell Death & Disease, 5*, e1167.
Clavel, G., Thiolat, A., & Boissier, M. C. (2013). Interleukin newcomers creating new numbers in rheumatology: IL-34 to IL-38. *Joint Bone Spine, 80*, 449–453.
Covaleda, L., Fuller, F. J., & Payne, S. L. (2010). EIAVS2 enhances pro-inflammatory cytokine and chemokine response in infected macrophages. *Virology, 397*, 217–223.
Dai, X. M., Ryan, G. R., Hapel, A. J., Dominguez, M. G., Russell, R. G., Kapp, S., et al. (2002). Targeted disruption of the mouse colony-stimulating factor 1 receptor gene results in osteopetrosis, mononuclear phagocyte deficiency, increased primitive progenitor cell frequencies, and reproductive defects. *Blood, 99*, 111–120.
Ding, R., Li, P., Song, D., Zhang, X., & Bi, L. (2015). Predictors of response to TNF-α antagonist therapy in Chinese rheumatoid arthritis. *Clinical Rheumatology, 34*, 1203–1210.
Droin, N., & Solary, E. (2010). Editorial: cSF1R, CSF-1, and IL-34, a "ménage à trois" conserved across vertebrates. *Journal of Leukocyte Biology, 87*, 745–747.
Eda, H., Shimada, H., Beidler, D. R., & Monahan, J. B. (2011). Proinflammatory cytokines, IL-1β and TNF-α, induce expression of interleukin-34 mRNA via JNK- and p44/42 MAPK-NF-κB pathway but not p38 pathway in osteoblasts. *Rheumatology International, 31*, 1525–1530.
Eda, H., Zhang, J., Keith, R. H., Michener, M., Beidler, D. R., & Monahan, J. B. (2010). Macrophage-colony stimulating factor and interleukin-34 induce chemokines in human whole blood. *Cytokine, 52*, 215–220.
Esaki, H., Ewald, D. A., Ungar, B., Rozenblit, M., Zheng, X., Xu, H., et al. (2015). Identification of novel immune and barrier genes in atopic dermatitis by means of laser capture microdissection. *The Journal of Allergy and Clinical Immunology, 135*, 153–163.
Fan, Q., Yan, X., Zhang, H., Lu, L., Zhang, Q., Wang, F., et al. (2016). IL-34 is associated with the presence and severity of renal dysfunction and coronary artery disease in patients with heart failure. *Scientific Reports, 6*, 39324.
Felix, J., DeMunck, S., Verstraete, K., Meuris, L., Callewaert, N., Elegheert, J., et al. (2015). Structure and assembly mechanism of the signaling complex mediated by human CSF-1. *Structure, 23*, 1621–1631.
Felix, J., Elegheert, J., Gutsche, I., Shkumatov, A. V., Wen, Y., Bracke, N., et al. (2013). Human IL-34 and CSF-1 establish structurally similar extracellular assemblies with their common hematopoietic receptor. *Structure, 21*, 528–539.
Foucher, E. D., Blanchard, S., Preisser, L., Descamps, P., Ifrah, N., Delneste, Y., et al. (2015). IL-34- and M-CSF-induced macrophages switch memory T cells into Th17 cells via membrane IL-1α. *European Journal of Immunology, 45*, 1092–1102.
Franzè, E., Dinallo, V., Rizzo, A., Di Giovangiulio, M., Bevivino, G., Stolfi, C., et al. (2017). Interleukin-34 sustains pro-tumorigenic signals in colon cancer tissue. *Oncotarget, 9*, 3432–3445.
Franzè, E., Marafini, I., De Simone, V., Monteleone, I., Caprioli, F., Colantoni, A., et al. (2016). Interleukin-34 induces cc-chemokine ligand 20 in gut epithelial cells. *Journal of Crohns & Colitis, 10*, 87–94.
Franzè, E., Monteleone, I., Cupi, M. L., Mancia, P., Caprioli, F., Marafini, I., et al. (2015). Interluekin-34 sustains inflammatory pathways in the gut. *Clinical Science, 129*, 271–280.
Galligan, C. L., & Fish, E. N. (2017). Interleukin-34 promotes fibrocyte proliferation. *Journal of Interferon and Cytokine Research, 37*, 440–448.

Gao, X., Zhang, S., Xu, Z., Shan, Y., Wang, Z., Cai, T., et al. (2017). Effects of interleukin-34 expressed by human bone marrow derived mesenchymal stem cells on THP-1 cells. *Sheng Wu Gong Cheng Xue Bao, 33*, 642–652.

Garceau, V., Balic, A., Garcia-Morales, C., Sauter, K. A., McGrew, M. J., Smith, J., et al. (2015). The development and maintenance of the mononuclear phagocyte system of the chick is controlled by signals from the macrophage colony-stimulating factor receptor. *BMC Biology, 13*, 12.

Garceau, V., Smith, J., Paton, I. R., Davey, M., Fares, M. A., Sester, D. P., et al. (2010). Pivotal advance: Avian colony-stimulating factor 1 (CSF-1), interleukin-34 (IL-34), and CSF-1 receptor genes and gene products. *Journal of Leukocyte Biology, 87*, 753–764.

Garcia, S., Hartkamp, L. M., Malvar-Fernandez, B., van Es, I. E., Lin, H., Wong, J., et al. (2016). Colony-stimulating factor (CSF) 1 receptor blockade reduces inflammation in human and murine models of rheumatoid arthritis. *Arthritis Research and Therapy, 18*, 75.

Gerngross, L., & Fischer, T. (2015). Evidence for cFMS signaling in HIV production by brain macrophages and microglia. *Journal of Neurovirology, 21*, 249–256.

Gerngross, L., Lehmicke, G., Belkadi, A., & Fischer, T. (2015). Role for cFMS in maintaining alternative macrophage polarization in SIV infection: Implications for HIV neuropathogenesis. *Journal of Neuroinflammation, 12*, 58.

Gow, D. J., Garceau, V., Kapetanovic, R., Sester, D. P., Fici, G. J., Shelly, J. A., et al. (2012). Cloning and expression of porcine colony stimulating factor-1 (CSF-1) and colony stimulating factor-1 receptor (CSF-1R) and analysis of the species specificity of stimulation by CSF-1 and interleukin 34. *Cytokine, 60*, 793–805.

Gow, D. J., Garceau, V., Pridans, C., Gow, A. G., Simpson, K. E., Gunn-Moore, D., et al. (2013). Cloning and expression of feline colony stimulating factor receptor (CSF-1R) and analysis of the species specificity of stimulation by colony stimulating factor-1 (CSF-1) and interleukin-34 (IL-34). *Cytokine, 61*, 630–638.

Grayfer, L., & Robert, J. (2014). Divergent antiviral roles of amphibian (*Xenopus laevis*) macrophages elicited by colony-stimulating factor-1 and interleukin-34. *Journal of Leukocyte Biology, 96*, 1143–1153.

Grayfer, L., & Robert, J. (2015). Distinct functional roles of amphibian (*Xenopus laevis*) colony-stimulating factor-1- and interleukin-34-derived macrophages. *Journal of Leukocyte Biology, 98*, 641–649.

Greter, M., Lelios, I., Pelczar, P., Hoeffel, G., Price, J., Leboeuf, M., et al. (2012). Stroma-derived interleukin-34 controls the development and maintenance of Langerhans cells and the maintenance of microglia. *Immunity, 37*, 1050–1060.

Guillonneau, C., Bézie, S., & Anegon, I. (2017). Immunoregulatory properties of the cytokine IL-34. *Cellular and Molecular Life Sciences, 74*, 2569–2586.

Guruprasad, C. N., & Pradeep, A. R. (2018). Interleukin-34 levels in gingival crevicular fluid and plasma in periodontal health and disease with and without type-2 diabetes mellitus. *Journal of Investigative and Clinical Dentistry, 9*, e12317.

Han, N., Baghdadi, M., Ishikawa, K., Endo, H., Kobayashi, T., Wada, H., et al. (2018). Enhanced IL-34 expression in Nivolumab-resistant metastatic melanoma. *Inflammation and Regeneration, 38*, 3.

Hwang, S. J., Choi, B., Kang, S. S., Chang, J. H., Kim, Y. G., Chung, Y. H., et al. (2012). Interleukin-34 produced by human fibroblast-like synovial cells in rheumatoid arthritis supports osteoclastogenesis. *Arthritis Research and Therapy, 14*, R14.

Jin, S., Sonobe, Y., Kawanokuchi, J., Horiuchi, H., Cheng, Y., Wang, Y., et al. (2014). Interleukin-34 restores blood-brain barrier integrity by upregulating tight junction proteins in endothelial cells. *PLoS One, 9*, e115981.

Kawabe, M., Ohyama, H., Kato-Kogoe, N., Yamada, N., Yamanegi, K., Nishiura, H., et al. (2015). Expression of interleukin-34 and colony stimulating factor-1 in the stimulated periodontal ligament cells with tumor necrosis factor-α. *Medical Molecular Morphology, 48*, 169–176.

Kumari, A., Silakari, O., & Singh, R. K. (2018). Recent advances in colony stimulating factor-1 receptor/c-FMS as an emerging target for various therapeutic implications. *Biomedicine & Pharmacotherapy, 103*, 662–679.

Lee, S., Huen, S., Nishio, H., Nishio, S., Lee, H. K., Choi, B. S., et al. (2011). Distinct macrophage phenotypes contribute to kidney injury and repair. *Journal of the American Society of Nephrology, 2*, 317–326.

Liao, L. N., Chen, C. C., Wu, F. Y., Lin, C. C., Hsiao, J. H., Chang, C. T., et al. (2014). Identified single-nucleotide polymorphisms and haplotypes at 16q22.1 increase diabetic nephropathy risk in Han Chinese population. *BMC Genetics, 15*, 113.

Li, Z., Jin, D., Wu, Y., Zhang, K., Hu, P., Cao, X., et al. (2012). Increased serum interleukin-34 in patients with coronary artery disease. *Journal of International Medical Research, 40*, 1866–1870.

Li, J., Liu, L., Rui, W., Li, X., Xuan, D., Zheng, S., et al. (2017). New interleukins in psoriasis and psoriatic arthritis patients: The possible roles of interleukin-33 to interleukin-38 in disease activities and bone erosions. *Journal of Dermatology, 233*, 37–46.

Lindau, R., Mehta, R. B., Lash, G. E., Papapavlou, G., Boij, R., Berg, G., et al. (2018). Interleukin-34 is present at the fetal-maternal interface and induces immunoregulatory macrophages of a decidual phenotype in vitro. *Human Reproduction, 33*, 588–599.

Lin, H., Lee, E., Hestir, K., Leo, C., Huang, M., Bosch, E., et al. (2008). Discovery of a cytokine and its receptor by functional screening of the extracellular proteome. *Science, 320*, 807–811.

Lin, X., Luo, H., Yan, X., Song, Z., Gao, X., Xia, Y., et al. (2018). Interleukin-34 ameliorates survival and bacterial clearance in polymicrobial sepsis. *Critical Care Medicine, 46*, e584–e590.

Liu, H., Leo, C., Chen, X., Wong, B. R., William, L. T., Lin, H., et al. (2012). The mechanism of shared but distinct CSF-1R signaling by the non-homologous cytokines IL-34 and CSF-1. *Biochimica et Biophysica Acta - Molecular Basis of Disease, 1824*, 938–945.

Luo, J., Elwood, F., Britschgi, M., Villeda, S., Zhang, H., Ding, Z., et al. (2013). Colony-stimulating factor 1 receptor (CSF1R) signaling in injured neurons facilitates protection and survival. *Journal of Experimental Medicine, 210*, 157–172.

Ma, X., Lin, W. Y., Chen, Y., Stawicki, S., Mukhyala, K., Wu, Y., et al. (2012). Structural basis for the dual recognition of helical cytokines IL-34 and CSF-1 by CSF-1R. *Structure, 20*, 676–687.

Ma, N., Qu, L., Xu, L. Y., Yu, Y. Q., & Qiu, L. H. (2016). Expression of IL-34 in chronic periapical lesions and its clinical significance. *Shang Hai Kou Qiang Yi Xue, 25*, 53–57.

Martinez, G. L., Majster, M., Bjurshammar, N., Johannsen, A., Figueredo, C. M., & Boström, E. A. (2017). Salivary colony stimulating factor-1 and interleukin-34 in periodontal disease. *Journal of Periodontology, 8*, e140–e149.

Masteller, E. L., & Wong, B. R. (2014). Targeting IL-34 in chronic inflammation. *Drug Discovery Today, 19*, 1212–1216.

Mo, Z. Q., Li, Y. W., Zhou, L., Li, A. X., Luo, X. C., & Dan, X. M. (2015). Grouper (Epinepheluscoioides) IL-34/MCSF2 and MCSFR1/MCSFR2 were involved in mononuclear phagocytes activation against Cryptocaryonirritans infection. *Fish & Shellfish Immunology, 43*, 142–149.

Moon, S. J., Hong, Y. S., Ju, J. H., Kwok, S. K., Park, S. H., & Min, J. K. (2013). Increased levels of interleukin 34 in serum and synovial fluid are associated with rheumatoid factor and anticyclic citrullinated peptide antibody titers in patients with rheumatoid arthritis. *Journal of Rheumatology, 40*, 1842–1849.

Nakamichi, Y., Mizoguchi, T., Arai, A., Kobayashi, Y., Sato, M., Penninger, J. M., et al. (2012). Spleen serves as a reservoir of osteoclast precursors through vitamin D-induced

IL-34 expression in osteopetrotic op/op mice. *Proceedings of the National Academy of Sciences of the United States of America, 109*, 10006–10011.
Nakamichi, Y., Udagawa, N., & Takahashi, N. (2013). IL-34 and CSF-1: Similarities and differences. *Journal of Bone and Mineral Metabolism, 31*, 486–495.
Nandi, S., Cioce, M., Yeung, Y. G., Nieves, E., Tesfa, L., Lin, H., et al. (2013). Receptor-type protein-tyrosine phosphatase ζ is a functional receptor for interleukin-34. *Journal of Biological Chemistry, 288*, 21972–21986.
Nandi, S., Gokhan, S., Dai, X. M., Wei, S., Enikolopov, G., Lin, H., et al. (2012). The CSF-1 receptor ligands IL-34 and CSF-1 exhibit distinct developmental brain expression patterns and regulate neural progenitor cell maintenance and maturation. *Developmental Biology, 367*, 100–113.
Ohgidani, M., Kato, T. A., & Kanba, S. (2015). Introducing directly induced microglia-like (iMG) cells from fresh human monocytes: A novel translational research tool for psychiatric disorders. *Frontiers in Cellular Neuroscience, 9*, 184.
Ohgidani, M., Kato, T. A., Setoyama, D., Sagata, N., Hashimoto, R., Shigenobu, K., et al. (2014). Direct induction of ramified microglia-like cells from human monocytes: Dynamic microglial dysfunction in Nasu-Hakola disease. *Scientific Reports, 4*, 4957.
Okubo, M., Yamanaka, H., Kobayashi, K., Dai, Y., Kanda, H., Yagi, H., et al. (2016). Macrophage colony stimulating factor derived from injured primary afferent induces proliferation of spinal microglia and neuropathic pain in rats. *PLoS One, 11*, e0153375.
Peyraud, F., Cousin, S., & Italiano, A. (2017). CSF-1R inhibitor development: Current clinical status. *Current Oncology Reports, 19*, 70.
Qian, B. Z., & Pollard, J. W. (2010). Macrophage diversity enhances tumor progression and metastasis. *Cell, 141*, 39–51.
Raggi, C., Correnti, M., Sica, A., Andersen, J. B., Cardinale, V., Alvaro, D., et al. (2017). Cholangiocarcinoma stem-like subset shapes tumor-initiating niche by educating associated macrophages. *Journal of Hepatology, 66*, 102–115.
Rietkotter, E., Bleckmann, A., Bayerlová, M., Menck, K., Chuang, H. N., Wenske, B., et al. (2015). Anti-CSF-1 treatment is effective to prevent carcinoma invasion induced by monocyte-derived cells but scarcely by microglia. *Oncotarget, 6*, 15482–15493.
Sanchez-Niño, M. D., Sanz, A. B., & Ortiz, A. (2016). Chronicity following ischaemia-reperfusion injury depends on tubular-macrophage crosstalk involving two tubular cell-derived CSF-1R activators: CSF-1 and IL-34. *Nephrology Dialysis Transplantation, 31*, 1409–1416.
Schuster, C., Mildner, M., Mairhofer, M., Bauer, W., Fiala, C., Prior, M., et al. (2014). Human embryonic epidermis contains a diverse Langerhans cell precursor pool. *Development, 141*, 807–815.
Segaliny, A. I., Brion, R., Mortier, E., Maillasson, M., Cherel, M., Jacques, Y., et al. (2015). Syndecan-1 regulates the biological activities of interleukin-34. *Biochimica et Biophysica Acta - Molecular Basis of Disease, 1853*, 1010–1021.
Ségaliny, A. I., Brion, R., Brulin, B., Maillasson, M., Charrier, C., Téletchéa, S., et al. (2015). IL-34 and M-CSF form a novel heteromeric cytokine and regulate the M-CSF receptor activation and localization. *Cytokine, 76*, 170–181.
Ségaliny, A. I., Mohamadi, A., Dizier, B., Lokajczyk, A., Brion, R., Lanel, R., et al. (2015). Interleukin-34 promotes tumor progression and metastatic process in osteosarcoma through induction of angiogenesis and macrophage recruitment. *International Journal of Cancer, 137*, 73–85.
Stanley, E. R., & Chitu, V. (2014). CSF-1 receptor signaling in myeloid cells. *Cold Spring Harbor Perspectives in Biology, 6*, a021857.
Tao, R., Fan, Q., Zhang, H., Xie, H., Lu, L., Gu, G., et al. (2017). Prognostic significance of interleukin-34 (IL-34) in patients with chronic heart failure with or without renal insufficiency. *Journal of American Heart Association, 6*, e004911.

Tian, Y., Shen, H., Xia, L., & Lu, J. (2013). Elevated serum and synovial fluid levels of interleukin-34 in rheumatoid arthritis: Possible association with disease progression via interleukin-17 production. *Journal of Interferon and Cytokine Research, 33*, 398–401.

Uhlén, M., Fagerberg, L., Hallström, B. M., Lindskog, C., Oksvold, P., Mardinoglu, A., et al. (2015). Tissue-based map of the human proteome. *Science, 347*, 1260419.

Vasek, M. J., Garber, C., Dorsey, D., Durrant, D. M., Bollman, B., Soung, A., et al. (2016). A complement-microglial axis drives synapse loss during virus-induced memory impairment. *Nature, 534*, 538–543.

Walker, D. G., Tang, T. M., & Lue, L. F. (2017). Studies on colony stimulating factor receptor-1 and ligands colony stimulating factor-1 and interleukin- 34 in Alzheimer's disease brains and human microglia. *Frontiers in Aging Neuroscience, 9*, 244.

Wang, Y., Bugatti, M., Ulland, T. K., Vermi, W., Gilfillan, S., & Colonna, M. (2016). Nonredundant roles of keratinocyte-derived IL-34 and neutrophil-derived CSF1 in Langerhans cell renewal in the steady state and during inflammation. *European Journal of Immunology, 46*, 552–559.

Wang, H., Cao, J., & Lai, X. (2016). Serum interleukin-34 levels are elevated in patients with systemic lupus erythematosus. *Molecules, 22*, E35.

Wang, Y., & Colonna, M. (2014). Interleukin-34, a cytokine crucial for the differentiation and maintenance of tissue resident macrophages and Langerhans cells. *European Journal of Immunology, 44*, 1575–1581.

Wang, T., Kono, T., Monte, M. M., Kuse, H., Costa, M. M., Korenaga, H., et al. (2013). Identification of IL-34 in teleost fish: Differential expression of rainbow trout IL-34, MCSF1 and MCSF2, ligands of the MCSF receptor. *Molecular Immunology, 53*, 398–409.

Wang, B., Ma, Z., Wang, M., Sun, X. T., Tang, Y. W., Li, M., et al. (2017). IL-34 upregulated Th17 production through increased IL-6 expression by rheumatoid fibroblast-like synoviocytes. *Mediators of Inflammation, 2017*, 1567120.

Wang, Y., Szretter, K. J., Vermi, W., Gilfillan, S., Rossini, C., Cella, M., et al. (2012). IL-34 is a tissue-restricted ligand of CSF1R required for the development of Langerhans cells and microglia. *Nature Immunology, 13*, 753–760.

Wang, B., Tang, Y., Sun, X., Ouyang, X., Li, H., Wei, J., et al. (2018). Increased IL-6 expression on THP-1 by IL-34 stimulation up-regulated rheumatoid arthritis Th17 cells. *Clinical Rheumatology, 37*, 127–137.

Wei, S., Nandi, S., Chitu, V., Yeung, Y. G., Yu, W., Huang, M., et al. (2010). Functional overlap but differential expression of CSF-1 and IL-34 in their CSF-1 receptor-mediated regulation of myeloid cells. *Journal of Leukocyte Biology, 88*, 495–505.

Xie, H. H., Shen, H., Zhang, L., Cui, M. Y., Xia, L. P., & Lu, J. (2018). Elevated serum interleukin-34 level in patients with systemic lupus erythematosus is associated with disease activity. *Scientific Reports, 8*, 3462.

Xing, C., & Lo, E. H. (2017). Help-me signaling: Non-cell autonomous mechanisms of neuroprotection and neurorecovery. *Progress in Neurobiology, 152*, 181–199.

Xu, R., Sun, H. F., Williams, D. W., Jones, A. V., Hussaini, A. A., Song, B., et al. (2015). IL-34 suppresses Candida albicans induced TNFα production in M1 macrophages by downregulating expression of Dectin-1 and TLR2. *Journal of Immunology Research, 2015*, 328146.

Yamane, F., Nishikawa, Y., Matsui, K., Asakura, M., Iwasaki, E., Watanabe, K., et al. (2014). CSF-1 receptor-mediated differentiation of a new type of monocytic cell with B cell-stimulating activity: Its selective dependence on IL-34. *Journal of Leukocyte Biology, 95*, 19–31.

Yang, S., Jiang, S., Wang, Y., Tu, S., Wang, Z., & Chen, Z. (2016). Interleukin 34 upregulation contributes to the increment of MicroRNA 21 expression through STAT3 activation associated with disease activity in rheumatoid arthritis. *Journal of Rheumatology, 43*, 1312–1319.

Yu, Y., Yang, D., Qiu, L., Okamura, H., Guo, J., & Haneji, T. (2014). Tumor necrosis factor-α induces interleukin-34 expression through nuclear factor-κB activation in MC3T3-E1 osteoblastic cells. *Molecular Medicine Reports, 10*, 1371–1376.

Yu, G., Bing, Y., Zhu, S., Li, W., Xia, L., Li, Y., et al. (2015). Activation of the interleukin-34 inflammatory pathway in response to influenza A virus infection. *The American Journal of the Medical Sciences, 349*, 145–150.

Zelante, T., & Ricciardi-Castagnoli, P. (2012). The yin-yang nature of CSF1R-binding cytokines. *Nature Immunology, 13*, 717–719.

Zhang, L., Cui, M., Ding, L., Xia, L., Lu, J., & Shen, H. (2018). Interleukin-34 aggravates the severity of arthritis in collagen-induced arthritis collagen-induced arthritis mice by inducing interleukin-17 production. *Journal of Interferon and Cytokine Research, 38*, 221–225.

Zhang, F., Ding, R., Li, P., Ma, C., Song, D., Wang, X., et al. (2015). Interleukin-34 in rheumatoid arthritis: Potential role in clinical therapy. *International Journal of Clinical and Experimental Medicine, 8*, 7809–7815.

Zhang, D., Li, M., Dong, Y., Zhang, X., Liu, X., Chen, Z., et al. (2017). 1α, 25-Dihydroxyvitamin D3 up-regulates IL-34 expression in SH-SY5Y neural cells. *Innate Immunity, 23*, 584–591.

Zhou, S. L., Hu, Z. Q., Zhou, Z. J., Dai, Z., Wang, Z., Cao, Y., et al. (2016). miR-28-5p-IL-34-macrophage feed-back loop modulates hepatocellular carcinoma metastasis. *Hepatology, 63*, 1560–1575.

Zhou, R. P., Wu, X. S., Xie, Y. Y., Dai, B. B., Hu, W., Ge, J. F., et al. (2016). Functions of interleukin-34 and its emerging association with rheumatoid arthritis. *Immunology, 149*, 362–373.

Zhou, J., Sun, X., Zhang, J., Yang, Y., Chen, D., & Cao, J. (2018). IL-34 regulates IL-6 and IL-8 production in human lung fibroblasts via MAPK, PI3K-Akt, JAK and NF-κB signaling pathways. *International Immunopharmacology, 61*, 119–125.

Zhu, C., Herrmann, U. S., Falsig, J., Abakumova, I., Nuvolone, M., Schwarz, P., et al. (2016). A neuroprotective role for microglia in prion diseases. *Journal of Experimental Medicine, 213*, 1047–1059.

Zorena, K., Jachimowicz-Duda, O., & Waż, P. (2016). The cut-off value for interleukin 34 as an additional potential inflammatory biomarker for the prediction of the risk of diabetic complications. *Biomarkers, 21*, 276–282.

Zwicker, S., Bureik, D., Bosma, M., Martinez, G. L., Almer, S., & Boström, E. A. (2016). Receptor-type protein-tyrosine phosphatase ζ and colony stimulating factor-1 receptor in the intestine: Cellular expression and cytokine- and chemokine responses by interleukin-34 and colony stimulating factor-1. *PLoS One, 11*, e0167324.

Zwicker, S., Martinez, G. L., Bosma, M., Gerling, M., Clark, R., Majster, M., et al. (2015). Interleukin 34: A new modulator of human and experimental inflammatory bowel disease. *Clinical Science, 129*, 281–290.

CHAPTER THREE

Pattern recognition receptors as potential drug targets in inflammatory disorders

Declan P. McKernan*
Pharmacology & Therapeutics School of Medicine, Galway, Ireland
*Corresponding author: E-mail: declan.mckernan@nuigalway.ie

Contents

Abstract

Pattern recognition receptors (PRRs) are a key part of the innate immune system, the body's first line of defense against infection and tissue damage. This superfamily of receptors including Toll-like receptors (TLRs), NOD-like receptors (NLRs), C-type lectin-like receptors (CLRs) and RIG-like receptors (RLRs) are responsible for initiation of the inflammatory response by their recognition of molecular patterns present in invading microorganisms (such as bacteria, viruses or fungi) during infection or in molecules released following tissue damage during acute or chronic disease states (such as sepsis or arthritis). These receptors are widely expressed and located on the cell surface, in intracellular compartments or in the cytoplasm can detect a single or subset of molecules

Advances in Protein Chemistry and Structural Biology, Volume 119
ISSN 1876-1623
https://doi.org/10.1016/bs.apcsb.2019.09.001

including lipoproteins, carbohydrates or nucleic acids. In response, they initiate an intracellular signaling cascade that culminates in the synthesis and release of cytokines, chemokines and vasoactive molecules. These steps are necessary to maintain tissue homeostasis and remove potentially dangerous pathogens. However, during extreme or acute responses or during chronic disease, this can be damaging and even lead to death. Therefore, it is thought that targeting such receptors may offer a therapeutic approach in chronic inflammatory diseases or in cases of acute infection leading to sepsis. Herein, the current knowledge on the molecular biology of PRRs is reviewed along with their association with inflammatory and infectious diseases. Finally, the testing of therapeutic compounds and their future merit as targets is discussed.

1. Introduction

Inflammation is usually initiated as a result of infection, tissue injury or tissue stress and malfunction. Once initiated by one or more of these triggers, inflammation involves the delivery of cellular and molecular components to the site of the noxious insult or infection by the circulatory system (Medzhitov, 2008). Whether the insult is biological or physical, the response involves the production of inflammatory mediators such as chemokines, cytokines, eicosanoids and vasoactive amines. These are produced by cells which are resident in the injured or infected tissue and consist of cell types such as macrophages, dendritic cells, lymphocytes, endothelial cells, epithelial cells, fibroblasts and mast cells (Fullerton & Gilroy, 2016). One of the main effects of these mediators is they allow the entry of immune cells, such as neutrophils, into the inflamed or infected tissue. These immune cells are normally restricted to the vasculature, but components of the mediators produced upon the initiation of the immune response allow the entry of these immune cells into the extravascular spaces (Friedl & Weigelin, 2008). The cardinal signs of inflammation which are fever, redness, swelling and edema, pain and loss of function (Taylor, 1997). These hallmarks of inflammation are a means to an end, the end being the removal of the source of the noxious insult, the protection of the affected tissues, and ultimately the restoration of hemostasis. Pattern recognition receptors play an essential role in the recognition of and response to such insults. They mediate a response accordingly to neutralize and eliminate these invaders. The PRRs consist of four families of receptors, namely the RIG-like receptors (RLRs), the NOD-like receptors (NLRs), the C-type lectin receptors, and finally the Toll-like Receptors (TLRs). PRR signaling can become dysregulated in a number of disease states and therefore are good potential candidates for therapy such diseases. Herein, I will review the current knowledge on pattern recognition receptors, their potential as drug targets in inflammatory and infectious diseases and also review molecules that target them that have recently been tested in clinical trials (Table 1).

2. Pattern-recognition receptors

2.1 Toll-like receptors

Toll-like receptors (TLRs) are a family of membrane-bound receptors, of which 10 are present in humans. These receptors are located in intracellular and extracellular compartments (Blasius & Beutler, 2010). TLRs recognize structurally conserved molecules present in bacteria and viruses as well as products released from damaged or dying cells. These structurally conserved molecules are known as pathogen associated molecular patterns (PAMPs) or damage associated molecular patterns (DAMPs) and activate TLRs (Akira, Uematsu, & Takeuchi, 2006). This results in a signal transduction cascade that leads to the cytoplasmic activation of transcription factors such as nuclear factor kappa-light-chain-enhancer of activated B cells (NF-κB), or interferon regulatory factors (IRFs) 3/5/7, which, upon activation translocate to the nucleus of the cell and alter transcription of proinflammatory cytokines such as interleukin 6 (IL6) and tumor necrosis factor α (TNF α) as well as type I interferons (Akira et al., 2006). Toll-like receptors on the cell surface recognize bacterial and fungal PAMPs and intracellular TLRs recognize viral or microbial PAMPs (Akira et al., 2006). TLRs possess two key domains, the extracellular domain, which consists of leucine rich repeats (LRRs), whose function is ligand binding, and the intracellular Toll-Interleukin-1 resistance domain (TIR), which is involved in intracellular signaling (Akira & Takeda, 2004). It allows the recruitment of adapter molecules such as Myeloid differentiation primary response gene 88 (MyD88) or MyD88 adapter-like (Mal) which are essential in the TLR signaling (O'Neill, Fitzgerald, & Bowie, 2003).

TLRs have been shown to have different basal expression levels in different tissues with certain TLRs having higher levels in certain organs (Hennessy & McKernan, 2016; Nishimura & Naito, 2005). Cell surface Toll like receptors consist of TLRs 1, 2, 4, 5, and 6 and the intracellular Toll-like receptors consist of TLRs 2, 7, 8, 9 and 10 (in humans). The first TLR discovered was TLR4 and was described as the receptor which responds to lipopolysaccharide (LPS), the component of Gram-negative

Table 1 Clinical testing of compounds targeting pattern recognition receptors.

Disease	Drug	Type	PRR	Trial #	Phase	References
Ulcerative colitis	DIMS015	Agonist	TLR9	NCT03178669	IIb	
				NCT01493960	III	Atreya et al., 2016; Atreya et al., 2018
Rheumatoid Arthritis	NI-0101	Antibody	TLR4	NCT03241108	II	
Asthma/Allergic rhinitis	GSK2245035	Agonist	TLR7	NCT01480271	I	Biggadike et al., 2016; Tsitoura et al., 2015; Ellis et al., 2017
				NCT02833974	II	
	AZD8848	Agonist	TLR7	NCT00688779	I	
				NCT00770003	IIa	Greiff et al., 2012; Greiff et al., 2015
	VTX1463	Agonist	TLR8	VRXP-B101/B102		Horak, 2011
	MPLA	Agonist	TLR4	EudraCT 2012-004336-28	II	
				EudraCT 2015-000984-15	II	Scihichilone et al., 2011; Worm et al., 2018; Zielen et al., 2018
	AZD1419	Agonist	TLR9	DV8-AST-01	I	
				NCT02898662	IIa	Jackson et al., 2018
	QbG10	Agonist	TLR9	NCT00800332	IIb	
				NCT00890734		Klimek et al., 2011; Beeh et al., 2013
	CYT003	Agonist	TLR9	NCT01673672	IIb	Casale et al., 2015
	CNTO3157	Antibody	TLR3	NCT01195207	I	
				NCT01704040	II	Silkoff et al., 2018

Psoriasis	IMO-8400	Antagonist	TLR7/8/9	NCT01899729	IIa	Balak et al., 2017
	IMO-3100	Antagonist	TLR7/9	NCT01622348	II	Kimball et al., 2013
	VB-102	Antagonist	TLR2	NCT01001468	II	
				NCT01837420	II	
Systemic Lupus Erythematosus	CPG-52364	Antagonist	TLR7/8/9	NCT00547014	I	Shereen et al., 22016
	RSLV-132	Antagonist	TLR3/7/8	NCT02194400	Ib	Burge et al., 2017
				NCT02660944	II	
Sepsis	E5564	Antagonist	TLR4		II	Tidswell et al., 2010
				NCT00334828	III	Opal et al., 2013
	TAK-242	Antagonist	TLR4	NCT00334828	III	
				NCT00633477	III	Rice et al., 2010
Infection						
Hepatitis B	GS-9620	Agonist	TLR7	NCT02166047	II	Janssen e: al.,. 2018
	SB9200	Agonist	RIG-I/ NOD2	NCT01803308	I	Korolowicz et al., 2016; Suresh et al., 2017
				NCT0343453	II	Thompson et al., 2015; Walsh et al., 2018
				NCT03932513	II	
Hepatitis C	ANA773	Agonist	TLR7	NCT01211626	I	Bergman et al., 2011
	GS-9620	Agonist	TLR7	NCT01591668	I	Lopatin et al., 2013; Lawitz et al., 2015
	RO7020531	Agonist	TLR7	NCT02956850	I	
				NCT03530917	I	Gane et al., 2018
	IMO-2125	Agonist	TLR9	NCT00728936	I	
				NCT00990938	I	Muir et al., 2010
	SD-101	Agonist	TLR9	NCT00823862	Ib	Cianciara et al., 2010

(*Continued*)

Table 1 Clinical testing of compounds targeting pattern recognition receptors.—cont'd

Disease	Drug	Type	PRR	Trial #	Phase	References
HIV	MGN1703	Agonist	TLR9	NCT02443935	Ib/Iia	Vibholm et al., 2017; Vibholm et al., 2019
HPV	Imiquimod	Agonist	TLR7	NCT00761371	IV	Saiag et al., 2009
				CTRI/2009/091/000055		Kumar et al., 2014
Vaccine/drug adjuvant						
Hepatitis	Heplisav	Agonist	TLR9	NCT00435812	III	
				NCT01005407	III	
				NCT02117934	III	Hyer et al., 2018; Jackson et al., 2018
Anthrax	CpG7909	agonist	TLR9	NCT01263691	Ib	
				NCT01770743	III	Hopkins et al., 2013; Minang et al., 2014; Hopkins et al., 2016
HIV	Rintatolimod	Agonist	TLR3	NCT00000735	I	
				NCT00001000	I	
				NCT00035893	II	
				NCT02071095	I	Armstrong et al., 1992; Hendrix et al., 1993; Saxena et al., 2019

	Poly ICLC	Agonist	TLR3	NCT01127464	I	Overton et al., 2014
Influenza	Rintatolimod	Agonist	TLR3	NCT01591473	I/II	Overton et al., 2014
	VAX125	Agonist	TLR5	NCT00730457	I	
				NCT00966238	I	Treanor et al., 2010; Taylor et al., 2011; Taylor et al., 2012
	VAX128	Agonist	TLR5	NCT01172054	I	Taylor et al., 2012
	VAX102	Agonist	TLR5	NCT00603811	I	Turley et al., 2011
	Imiquimod	Agonist	TLR7	NCT01508884	I	
				NCT02103023	III	Hung et al., 2016

Shown in this table is a list of compounds used in various inflammatory or infectious diseases. Alongside these are the names of the specific targets, the type of drug, the clinical trial information and the references of the published data.

bacteria known for inducing septic shock (Poltorak et al., 1998). TLR4 forms a complex with MD2 on the cell surface and the complex binds to LPS (Shimazu et al., 1999). Binding to LPS causes the recruitment of intracellular adapters such as MyD88 and TIR-domain-containing adapter-inducing interferon-β (TRIF) which initiate the transduction cascade (Tanimura, Saitoh, Matsumoto, Akashi-Takamura, & Miyake, 2008). TLR4 has been shown to be essential for defense against Gram-negative bacteria, with mutations in *tlr4* resulting in the development of Gram-negative induced sepsis while other immune function remain intact (Poltorak et al., 1998). Furthermore, in studies using C3H/HeJ and C57BL/10ScCr mice, both of which possess mutations in *tlr4* that confer hypo-responsiveness to LPS, it was shown that following challenge with LPS they produced a much weaker immune response when compared to control mice (Qureshi, Gros, & Malo, 1999).

Toll-like receptor 2 responds mostly to a range of structurally conserved motifs in lipopeptides from bacteria, fungi and viruses (Akira et al., 2006). It forms heterodimers with other TLRs, namely TLR1 and TLR6, with each combination recognizing different structural motifs. When TLR1/2 form a heterodimer, the complex responds to triacylated lipopeptides from Gram-positive bacteria and mycoplasma whereas when TLR1/TLR6 heterodimers are formed it instead recognizes diacylated lipopeptides from Gram-negative bacteria and mycoplasma (Kang et al., 2009).

TLR5 was initially identified by the presence of the Toll/interleukin (IL-1) receptor homology domain (TIR) (Rock, Hardiman, Timans, Kastelein, & Bazan, 1998) which is a conserved signaling domain considered to be a defining trait of the Toll-like receptor family (Medzhitov et al., 1998). TLR5 recognizes the flagellin protein which is the structurally conserved component of bacterial flagella (Akira et al., 2006). Studies have shown that there is high TLR5 expression in the lamina propria dendritic cells (DCs) of the small intestine. Lamina propria DCs promote the differentiation of interleukin 17 producing T helper cells (Th17) and T helper 1 (Th1) cells as well as the differentiation of naive B cells into immunoglobulin A producing cells in response to challenge by flagellin (Uematsu et al., 2008). TLR5 has also been shown to be expressed on monocytes as well as epithelial cells (Cario & Podolsky, 2000). Studies have identified its action to be proinflammatory, acting via MyD88 to activate TNF-α which in turn stimulates cytokine production (Hayashi et al., 2001).

The intracellular TLRs evolved to detect intracellular foreign nucleic acids, generated mostly from invading viruses. In order to better distinguish foreign DNA from that of the host, the intracellular TLRs act within the endosomal compartment, a compartment which generally excludes host DNA (Blasius & Beutler, 2010). The intracellular TLR, TLR3 was originally identified as recognizing the structure of a synthetic analog of double stranded RNA (dsRNA) known as polyinosinic-polycytidylic acid (poly (I: C)) (Alexopoulou, Holt, Medzhitov, & Flavell, 2001). Poly I:C is a synthetic compound that mimics a viral infection and induces the production of type I interferon as well as other inflammatory cytokines. TLR3 interactions with dsRNA were determined by analysis of the domain of TLR3 which was bound to the dsRNA (Bell, Askins, Hall, Davies, & Segal, 2006). TLR3 is important in the immune response due to its role in recognizing ssRNA viruses such as Respiratory Syncytial Virus (RSV), encephalomyocarditis virus, West Nile virus and certain small interfering RNAs (Akira et al., 2006). The importance of TLR3 function has been shown in animal studies wherein *tlr3* deficient mice are susceptible to lethal infection by murine cytomegalovirus (MCMV). *Tlr3* knockout mice infected with MCMV possessed a much higher viral titer when compared to controls. Furthermore, although there was no significant increase in death when compared to controls the authors remarked that the $tlr3^{-/-}$ mice appeared to be sicker and trended toward higher mortality (Tabeta et al., 2004).

TLR7 was first described as recognizing imidazoquinolinone derivatives such as imiquimod and resiquimod as well as guanine analogs such as loxoribine. Its purpose in host defense is its recognition of ssRNA from viruses such as Vesicular stomatitis virus (VSV), influenza type A and human immunodeficiency virus (HIV) (Akira et al., 2006; Kawai & Akira, 2006). Plasmacytoid dendritic cells (pDCs) show a relatively high expression of TLR7, and in response to viral challenge produce an immune response by releasing type I interferon as well as other inflammatory cytokines. It has been shown that TLR7 is necessary for the immune response of pDCs to viral challenge, and in the absence of TLR7 no release of interferon or cytokines occurs. TLR8 is similar phylogenetically to TLR7, and it also recognizes ssRNA. However it was determined that ssRNA sensing in mice is not dependent on TLR8 and that ssRNA sensing was normal even in the absence of TLR8 (Akira et al., 2006; Kawai & Akira, 2006). A recent study has determined the mechanism behind the activation of RNA sensing by TLR8 has been implicated in the development of many autoimmune conditions, leading to suggestions that inhibiting it in humans may be beneficial in treating certain autoimmune conditions (Guiducci et al., 2013).

TLR9 recognizes the unmethylated CpG motifs that are present in bacterial and viral genomes but are rarely seen in mammalian cells. Their activation by these motifs results in activation of dendritic cells, B cells and also initiates a T_H1 response (Bafica et al., 2005). Studies have also shown that in certain cases TLR9 can recognize self CpG-DNA which can lead to the development of autoantibodies and has been implicated in the development of certain autoimmune condition (Bauer et al., 2001). Until recently, the structure and function of TLR10 were unknown, however, recent research has illuminated its potential importance in the immune system. The study showed that blocking TLR10 led to increased production of proinflammatory cytokines, including IL1β, following TLR2 stimulation. The study also noted that in humans with polymorphisms in *tlr10*, there was documented increases in IL-1β, TNF-α, and IL6 upon ligation of TLR2 (Oosting et al., 2014).

TLR signaling pathways share many common features (illustrated in Fig. 1). For example, upon ligand binding of a TLR dimer complexes are formed and MyD88 will be recruited to the cytoplasmic TIR domain of the TLR. MyD88 will then recruit IRAK4, which then results in IRAK 4 phosphorylation of IRAK1. This event allows for TRAF6 to then bind

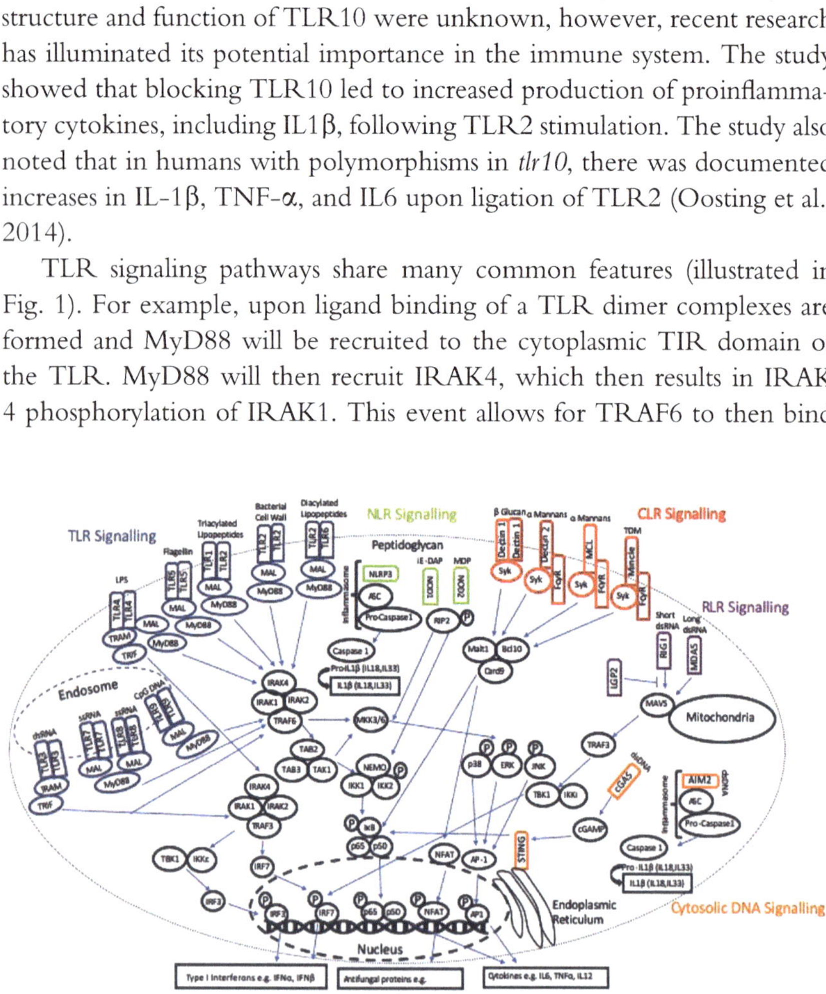

Fig. 1 ***Pattern recognition receptor signaling pathways.*** Shown above in figure are the signaling pathways of each of the pattern recognition receptors mentioned in the text as well as their cellular location, their specific ligands, adapters and effector molecules. Each PRR specific group is highlighted in a specific color, while shared signaling molecules are identified in black.

to IRAK1 in its phosphorylated state, and generates the TRAF6-IRAK1 complex, which then interacts with a TAK1/TAB1-3 complex. TAK1 phosphorylates IKKs, which then phosphorylate the IκB (which forms an inhibitory complex with NFκB). This IκB phosphorylation leads to the degradation of IκB and the release of NFκB. Phosphorylated NFκB is released from its inhibitory partner and translocates to the nucleus to initiate transcription of inflammatory cytokines such as IL1, IL6, IL8, and TNFα (Akira & Takeda, 2004). Activation of TAK1 can also result in the activation of the mitogen-activated protein kinases (MAPKs) such as p38, ERK and JNK, which initiate further downstream signaling events (Arthur & Ley, 2013).

In addition to the MyD88 signaling, an alternative pathway was also identified in stimulation studies in MyD88 deficient mice. This was observed in the TLR3/4 transduction cascades and used another adapter called TRIF. It was subsequently shown that in TRIF deficient mice there was impaired phosphorylation of IRF3 and decreased expression of IFN inducible genes in response to stimulation with TLR3/4 ligands (Yamamoto et al., 2003). Further research demonstrated that TRIF interacted with both TRAF6 and TRAF3. TRAF6 acts to recruit RIP1, which activates the TAK1 complex, leading to phosphorylation of NF-κB and MAPKs, and the induction of inflammatory cytokines. However, in contrast to the MyD88 pathway, TRAF3 activates the IKKs and TANK-binding kinase (TBK1) which results in IRF3 phosphorylation, which ultimately results in the transcription of type I interferons (Kawai & Akira, 2010).

2.2 NOD-like receptors

Similar to TLRs, Nucleotide-binding oligomerization domain (NOD)-like receptors (NLRs) play a crucial role in the innate immune response through recognition of specific PAMPs and DAMPs, leading to activation of adapters and effectors required to induce an inflammatory response. NLRs are a family of 22 intracellular PRRs that mostly recognize invading bacteria (Franchi, Warner, Viani, & Nuñez, 2009; Kanneganti, Lamkanfi, & Núñez, 2007). NLRs have a similar structure consisting of a C-terminal leucine-rich repeat (LRR) domain, a central nucleotide-binding domain (NACHT domain), and a variable N-terminal domain. PAMP/DAMP recognition and binding is mediated by the LRR domain which initiates the receptor activation process. Ligand sensing leads to oligomerisation and is mediated by the NACHT domain. Finally, effector functions such as recruiting and interacting with signal transduction proteins required to trigger cellular responses to pathogen invasion or tissue damage is mediated by the N-terminal domain (Y. K. Kim, Shin, & Nahm, 2016).

The NLR family fall into one of four subfamilies; NLRA, NLRB, NLRC and NLRP and are classified according to their N-terminal domain. These subfamilies contain either an acidic transactivation domain, baculovirus inhibitor of apoptosis repeat (BIR), caspase recruitment domain (CARD) or pyrin domain (PYD), respectively (Ting et al., 2008; Zhong, Kinio, & Saleh, 2013). The LRR domain holds the NLRs in a state of auto-inhibition by binding to the N-terminal, thereby preventing signaling transduction. Once the LRR domain encounters a receptor ligand a conformational change occurs, causing the LRR domain to release the N-terminal from its auto-inhibition. The exposed N-terminal can subsequently bind and activate different downstream signaling adapters and effectors, depending on which NLR it is. NLRP1, NLRP3, NLRP6, NLRP7, NLRP12, NLRC4, and NAIP, are known to form inflammasome complexes which activate caspase-1 and subsequently cleave inflammatory cytokines such as IL1β, IL18 and IL33. NOD1, NOD2, NLRP10, NLRX1, NLRC5 and CITTA have been found to activate MAPKs, nuclear factor-κB (NF- κB) and interferon regulatory factors (IRFs) (Zhong et al., 2013). NOD1 (CARD4) and NOD2 (CARD15) receptors, which are both NLRC proteins, were the first of the NLRs to be identified and so are the most extensively studied members of the family (N. Inohara, Ogura, Chen, Muto, & Nuñez, 2001; Ogura et al., 2001).

While NOD2 receptors are found mostly in macrophages, monocytes, Paneth intestinal cells and dendritic cells, NOD1 receptors are expressed ubiquitously (Inohara, Chamaillard, McDonald, & Nuñez, 2005). Both receptors recognize different components of the bacterial cell wall known as peptidoglycan (PGN). PGN is made up of alternating N-acetylmuramic acid (NAM) and N-acetylglucosamine (NAG) residues, which are cross-linked by short peptides (Chen, Shaw, Kim, & Nuñez, 2009; Kersse, Bertrand, Lamkanfi, & Vandenabeele, 2011). Bacteria that are Gram-negative have a thin peptidoglycan cell wall, whereas the wall of Gram-positive cells is much thicker due to the presence of many peptidoglycan layers (Silhavy, Kahne, & Walker, 2010). The minimal motif detected by NOD1 is the dipeptide; γ-D-glutamyl-mesodiaminopimelic acid (iE-DAP) but give stronger responses in the presence of a tripeptide from peptidoglycan called L-Ala-γ-D-glutamyl-mesodiaminopimelic acid (TRI-DAP) (Girardin et al., 2003). Both iE-DAP and TRI-DAP are found in some Gram-positive bacteria, such as *Listeria monocytogenes* (Opitz et al.,

2006), and all Gram-negative bacteria including; *Escherichia coli* (J. G. Kim, Lee, & Kagnoff, 2004), *Shigella flexneri* (Girardin et al., 2001), and *Helicobacter pylori* (Watanabe et al., 2011).

NOD1/2 are able to correctly assemble by forming complexes with chaperones such as heat-shock proteins, e.g. Hsp70 or Hsp90, and avoid premature degradation (J. S. Hahn, 2005; Lee, Biswas, Liu, & Kobayashi, 2012; Mohanan & Grimes, 2014). These complexes are thought to contribute to bacterial tolerance, preventing an excessive inflammatory response in regions where lots of bacteria reside such as the intestine (Lee et al., 2012). NOD1/2 receptors recognize and bind specific components of peptidoglycan (iE-DAP/Tri-DAP or MDP) via their LRR domains (Boyle, Mayle, Parkhouse, & Monie, 2013) (summarized in Fig. 1). The monomeric receptors subsequently translocate to the plasma membrane and undergo a conformational change, allowing the NOD1/2 receptors to homo-oligomerise via their central NACHT domains (Franchi et al., 2009; Hsu et al., 2008). These NACHT domains possess ATPase activity, which accommodates oligomerisation and activation of the receptors (Zurek, Proell, Wagner, Schwarzenbacher, & Kufer, 2012).

The activated receptors recruit and bind receptor-interacting protein 2 (RIP2) kinase, a serine-threonine kinase (Park et al., 2007) (He & Wang, 2018). RIP2 binds to NOD1/2 via a CARD-CARD interaction and is activated by auto-phosphorylation at tyrosine 474 (Manon, Favier, Núñez, Simorre, & Cusack, 2007; Tigno-Aranjuez, Asara, & Abbott, 2010). RIP2 oligomerizes and then conjugates with K63-linked polyubiquitin chains at K209 residues positioned in their kinase domain (Hasegawa et al., 2008). RIP2 then binds three E3 ubiquitin ligases; X-chromosome-linked inhibitor of apoptosis (XIAP), cellular inhibitors of apoptosis proteins (cIAP1/cIAP2) and linear ubiquitin chain assembly complex (LUBAC). These E3 ubiquitin ligases further polyubiquitinate RIP2 at K63, assisting the binding and activation of the TAK1 complex containing transforming growth factor β-activated kinase 1 (TAK1) – TAK1 binding protein 2 (TAB 2) – TAK1 binding protein 3 (TAB 3) (Hasegawa et al., 2008). The TAK1 kinase becomes highly active when associated with its complex components. Active TAK1 subsequently recruits the IKK complex (discussed above) for activation. Phosphorylation of IKKβ renders it active so that it can phosphorylate the NF-κB inhibitor; inhibitor of κBα (IκBα) (Akira & Takeda, 2004).

Due to its newly acquired phosphorylated status, IκBα can be polyubiquitinated at K48 causing it to dissociate from the NF-κB transcription factor heterodimer (p50–p65), before then traveling to the proteasome for proteolytic degradation (Hasegawa et al., 2008). The NF-κB p50–p65 heterodimer translocates to the nucleus where it promotes expression of pro-inflammatory mediators such as cytokines and anti-microbial peptides (Chen et al., 2009; Shaw, Reimer, Kim, & Nuñez, 2008). Phosphorylated TAK1 kinase also phosphorylates the MAPKs; p38, extracellular signal-regulated kinase (ERK), and c-Jun N-terminal kinase (JNK), which are upstream promoters of the activator protein-1 (AP1) transcription factor. Activated activator protein-1 subsequently translocates to the nucleus in the same manner as NF-κB, where it promotes the expression of pro-inflammatory mediators (Chen et al., 2009; Vandenabeele & Bertrand, 2012). Activation of other NLRs, such as NLRP3, by PGN components initiates inflammasome assembly. For example, active NLRP3 oligomers recruit apoptosis-associated speck-like protein containing CARD (ASC) and pro-caspase-1, with subsequent maturation of pro-caspase-1 to caspase-1. Caspase-1 has the capacity to cleave inactive pro-inflammatory cytokines to their active counterparts, such as pro-interleukin-1 (pro-IL-1) to IL-1 (Martinon & Tschopp, 2005). Therefore, although NLRs may react differently upon stimulation they have co-operative effects essential for an innate immune response. Signaling is tightly regulated in healthy cells and a number of positive and negative regulators enhance or inhibit signaling when required in specific cell types (Feerick & McKernan, 2017). This potentially offers a number of therapeutic targets in chronic inflammatory diseases.

2.3 Cytoplasmic nucleic acid sensors

As mentioned above, microbial nucleic acids can be detected by Toll-like receptors, in particular TLR3, 7, 8 & 9. However, there are a number of receptor families that can also do this which can be categorized according to their cellular location and environment. The two major classes of nucleic acid receptors include endosomal or cytosolic. This allows for the detection of nucleic acids from viruses that uncoat in the endosomes as well when the virus enters the cytoplasm. This results in the release of type I interferons as well as inflammatory cytokines such as IL1β, IL6 & TNFα. TLRs fall into the first category, those that are associated with the endosomes. The second class comprises those receptor that can detect RNA or DNA (Bryant et al., 2015; Junt & Barchet, 2015).

The retinoic acid inducible gene (RIG)-like receptors detect RNA and consists of three members that are DExD/H box helicases (DHXs). These receptors are widely expressed across many tissues and cell types. RIG-I and melanoma differentiation associated antigen 5 (MDA5) appear to be the members primarily involved in the recognition of RNA viruses whereas laboratory of genetics and physiology 2 (LGP2) lacks an N-terminal CARD domain and may be involved in regulating MDA5 and RIG-I signaling. RIG-I recognizes 5′ diphosphates in short RNA molecules as well as uncapped RNA which is 5′-triphosphorylated. MDA5 recognizes long dsRNA as well as high molecular weight branched RNAs. Both receptors proceed to signal via the mitochondrial protein mitochondrial antiviral signaling protein (MAVS) leading to activation of the IKK related kinases TBK1 and IKKi which then activate the transcription factors IRF3 and IRF7 which will induce type I interferon production (illustrated in Fig. 1) (Barrat, Elkon, & Fitzgerald, 2016; Junt & Barchet, 2015).

There are several cytosolic receptors that have now been identified that recognize microbial DNA. These include DNA activator of interferon regulatory factors (DAIs), absent in melanoma 2 (AIM2), RNA Polymerase III, DHX9, DHX36, DDX41, DNA dependent protein kinase (DNA-PK) and cyclic GMP-AMP (cGAMP) synthase (cGAS) among others. These receptors can in turn activate the endoplasmic reticulum bound molecule stimulator of interferon genes (STING) which leads to type I interferon production via TBK1 activation and IRF3 (described above) (Bryant et al., 2015; Motwani, Pesiridis, & Fitzgerald, 2019).

2.4 C-type lectin receptors

C-type lectins were initially described as such due to their calcium-dependent carbohydrate binding of lectins. CLRs are glycosylated type II transmembrane receptors that recognize self- or non-self-carbohydrates via their carbohydrate recognition domains (CRDs). They are expressed in myeloid cells and play a key role in defense against fungal infections commonly encountered on the skin and mucosal surfaces. The CLR family consist of at least 17 subgroups and over 1000 proteins. They are highly conserved in vertebrates but their ligands vary a lot across different species. They can synergies with other PRRs such as TLRs to promote anti-fungal responses (Bryant et al., 2015; Shiokawa, Yamasaki, & Saijo, 2017). They can signal either directly through integral signal domains or indirectly by associating with adaptation molecules. Many CLRs share signaling pathways including the phosphorylation of spleen tyrosine kinase (Syk), recruitment of CARD9, B-cell lymphoma (Bcl10) and mucosa associated lymphoid tissue 1 (MALT1) forming a complex (illustrated in Fig. 1). These can occur directly via activation of immune-receptor tyrosine-based activation motif

(ITAM) or via adapter proteins such as fragment crystallizable gamma receptor (FcγR). The resulting CBM complex was found to activate NF-κB. In addition, Syk activation was found to activate MAP kinase signaling pathways involving p38, JNK and ERK. Recently, there have been reports of Syk-independent signaling via Raf 1, a serine-threonine kinase, that can regulate Th differentiation. Alternatively, activation of immune-receptor tyrosine-based inhibition motif (ITIM) induces recruitment of phosphatases SHP-1 and SHP-2 that can subsequently inhibit cell activation (Hardison & Brown, 2012).

Notable members of this family include dendritic cell associated C-type lectin 1 (Dectin 1), Dectin 2, macrophage inducible C-type lectin (Mincle) and macrophage C-type lectin (MCL), all of whom play a key role in antifungal immunity. Dectin 1 is predominantly expressed in innate immune cells such as macrophages, dendritic cells and neutrophils as well as microglia. Its major ligand is Beta glucans, which are components of fungal cell walls found in yeasts, mushrooms and seaweeds. It was originally thought to be a DC specific CLR that stimulated T cell proliferation. Dectin 1 signaling also induces interferon beta via IRF5 activation (Lepenies, Lee, & Sonkaria, 2013). Dectin 1 knockout mice die due to infections with several fungi such as *C. albicans, A. fumigatus, P. carinii* and *C. podasii*. Genetic studies have indicated SNPs in intronic regions that confer susceptibility to fungal infections and in some cases familial chronic mucocutaneous candidiasis and inflammatory bowel diseases. Recent studies suggest a necessary role for Dectin 1 in the maintenance of the intestinal microbiome and so are thought to be important in the maintenance of gut homeostasis (Shiokawa et al., 2017).

Similar to Dectin 1, Dectin 2 was originally cloned as a DC specific CLR but is also expressed in macrophages and monocytes. Dectin 2 is known to bind alpha mannans. Fungi, parasites, bacteria and some mammals can contain high mannose structures. Fungi in particular contain polycarbohydrate backbones of alpha 1,6-linked mannose units with polymannose side chains. These are expressed in the outermost parts of cell walls in species such as C. albicans. Mice lacking Dectin 2 have been shown to succumb easily to *C. albicans, Malassezia, A. fumigatus* and *C. glabrata* infections. Signaling following Dectin 2 stimulation has been shown to lead to Th17 polarization which thought to be essential to mount an anti-fungal response (Hardison & Brown, 2012; Shiokawa et al., 2017).

Mincle is lowly expressed during homeostasis but strongly induced in myeloid cells following exposure to classic inflammatory stimuli such as TNFα, IL6, IFNγ and LPS under the control of C/EBPB. It is capable of recognizing and responding to many fungal species including *C. albicans* and *Malassezia* as well as the mycobacterial ligand trehalose dimycolate (TDM). It has been shown myeloid cells lacking Mincle fail to induce TNFα expression upon stimulation with *C. albicans* (Shiokawa et al., 2017). Mincle is associated with FcγR chains and acts as an ITAM-coupled activated receptor. Mcl (also known as Dectin 3), initially thought to be a phagocytic receptor is expressed on myeloid cells is also linked with FcγR. It is able to interact with other CLRs to affect their activity and expression. Mcl has been shown to form heterodimers with Dectin 2 allowing recognition of alpha mannans from *C. albicans*. It also forms heterodimers with Mincle leading to a stabilization of its expression. It has been shown to interact with commensal fungi such as *C. tropicalis* as well as pathogens and the IL6 response is significantly reduced in Mincle knockout mice suggesting a role in homeostasis (Hardison & Brown, 2012).

Dendritic cell-specific intracellular cell adhesion molecule 3 grabbing nonintegrin (DC-SIGN) has two family members DC-SIGN and L-SIGN. DC-SIGN is expressed on dendritic cells and macrophages and recognizes mannose and fucosylated proteins. It is therefore capable of detecting the presence of fungi, mycobacterium and helminths. It is different from the other members mentioned this far as it signals independently of both ITAM and ITIM. It internalizes immediately after ligand binding and aids in processing of antigens for presentation to T cells. It can activate Raf 1 and subsequently NF-κB and modulate the expression of several cytokines including IL6, IL12 and IL10. There have been some studies that suggest DC-SIGN signaling can interact with pathways from other PRRs such as TLRs by regulating signaling by the p65 subunit of NF-κB. DC-SIGN has been associated with viral infections, in particular HIV and Dengue virus as well as with tuberculosis. A particular variant found in the promoter region which alters the expression of the transcript has been associated with these infections (Bryant et al., 2015).

3. Pharmacological targeting of PRRs

From a pharmacological point of view, PRR signaling could be targeted at a number of different points in the pathway. These include the receptors themselves, which as described above can be located at the cell surface or intracellularly in endosomal compartments. Molecules have also been designed to interfere with many of the signaling molecules (often kinases) however these are very often shared between the PRR pathways as well as some other signaling pathways (Bryant et al., 2015). This review will focus specifically on the receptors as targets rather than discussing molecules targeting proteins further downstream. To date both agonists and antagonists as well as antagonistic antibodies have been designed for PRRs (mostly TLRs) and these have been tested in animal models as well as in clinical trials for many indications including acute and chronic inflammatory diseases, neurological conditions as well as cancer. This review will focus on those tested for inflammatory and infectious diseases, there are many other reviews pertaining to PRRs as targets in cancer and other conditions (Bourquin, Pommier, & Hotz, 2019).

3.1 Inflammatory bowel diseases

Inflammatory bowel diseases (IBD) is a group of disorders known to cause chronic inflammation within varying segments of the digestive tract. These disorders are thought to be caused by excessive activation of the innate immune response in the mucosal cell lining (Maloy & Powrie, 2011). The primary subtypes of IBD, Crohn's disease (CD) and ulcerative colitis (UC) share similarities in pathologies but differ in the location within the gastrointestinal tract in which they manifest. Ulcerative colitis is characterized by chronic inflammation localized to the colon and rectum (Maloy & Powrie, 2011). NOD expression has been reported to be altered in these conditions. Analysis of colon mucosal biopsies from patients with UC revealed an eightfold increase in NOD1 expression relative to control biopsies. Analysis of biopsies from the same cohort of UC patients during remission revealed a reduction in NOD1 expression relative to control biopsy levels. These findings suggest heightened NOD1 expression as a contributing factor behind the UC chronic inflammatory state (Verma, Verma, & Paul, 2013).

Crohn's Disease can manifest across any region of the gastrointestinal tract and can be further classified according to the region affected and its clinical presentation (Maglinte, Gourtsoyiannis, Rex, Howard, & Kelvin, 2003). Three polymorphisms within or neighboring the LRR region of the NOD2 gene have been directly associated with the disease. One of these is a frame-shift mutation (L1007fs) whereas the other two are missense mutations (R702W and G908R) (Hugot et al., 2001; Ogura et al., 2001; Russell, Nimmo, & Satsangi, 2004). Individuals who are heterozygous for NOD2 variants have a 2- to 4-fold increased risk of developing CD, whereas homozygous variants have an additional risk of 20–to 40-fold (Hugot et al., 2001, 2007; Ogura et al., 2001). These polymorphisms have been regarded as loss-of-function, with NOD2 variants having diminished responsiveness to MDP. NOD2 has been found to maintain the intestinal epithelial barrier by regulating antimicrobial agent release and sustaining bacterial levels and population types. NOD2 variants may lose this protective function, providing insufficient bacterial clearance and allowing excessive bacterial invasion, resulting in augmented inflammation through NOD2-independent proinflammatory pathways (N. Inohara et al., 2003; Y. G. Kim et al., 2011).

The NOD2 receptor is highly expressed within Paneth cells, which are specialized cells located at the base of the intestinal crypts of Lieberkühn. These cells are most numerous in the terminal ileum of the small intestine, which is interestingly the most commonly affected site in CD sufferers. These cells release antimicrobial agents, such as α-defensin, collectively referred to as cryptidins (Frank et al., 2011; Ogura et al., 2003). Disruption of Paneth cell function (and α-defensin release), potentially as a result of NOD2 deficiency, could alter the load and composition of the intestinal flora, an attribute of IBD (Frank et al., 2011). Early studies investigating the effect of NOD2 polymorphisms on release of α-defensin from Paneth cells recorded reduced release in patients with ileal CD holding the NOD2 L1007fs polymorphism (Wehkamp et al., 2004, 2005). However, more recent data imply that the reduction recorded is in fact a secondary effect of the NOD2 knock-down, whereby defective NOD2 results in excessive inflammation, which in turn blocks the release of α-defensin (Simms et al., 2008). Despite their association, there have not been any successes to date with molecules targeting NLRs.

Both TLR4 and TLR3 dysregulation has also been implicated in the development of intestinal inflammatory conditions. However in contrast to TLR4, TLR3 was significantly downregulated in intestinal epithelial cells (IECs) in CD but not in UC (Cario, 2010; Cario & Podolsky, 2000). Similarly, to TLR3/4, TLR9 has also been shown to be dysregulated in IBD, with peripheral B cells taken from patients with IBD patients shown to have significantly higher expression of TLR9. The study also showed a positive correlation between TLR9 expression and IBD severity (Berkowitz, Peri, Lavy, & Kessel, 2013). A TLR9 agonist, which is a modified single stranded DNA-based oligonucleotide, DIMS015 (cobitolimod, Kappaproct), had been tested (by rectal administration) in a randomized, dose optimization phase IIb trial (NCT03178669) to evaluate safety and efficacy in patients ($n = 213$) with moderate to severe ulcerative colitis prompting further evaluation in phase III trials. In this placebo controlled double blind RCT phase III trial (NCT01493960) cobitolimod was assessed as an add-on therapy in chronic treatment refractory ulcerative colitis patients (n = 131). Results showed that the drug was well tolerated and that more patients on cobitolimod had mucosal healing and histological improvement as well as a higher proportion achieving symptomatic remission (Atreya et al., 2016, 2018). It was also reported that certain biomarkers (CD163, TSP1 and IL1RII) may be able to predict responders to such therapy (Kuznetsov et al., 2014).

3.2 Arthritis

Rheumatoid arthritis is an autoimmune disease that is characterized by synovial inflammation and swelling, progressive bone and cartilage destruction, autoantibody production as well as associated cardiopulmonary problems (McInnes & Schett, 2011). Recent clinical studies have underlined the importance of TLRs in the propagation of the disease. TLR5 has been shown to play a role in the development of inflammatory conditions such as rheumatoid arthritis (RA) and osteoarthritis (OA). TLR5 expression has been shown to be elevated in synovial tissue, macrophages and endothelial cells in these conditions. TLR5 was shown to be instrumental in the development of RA pathogenesis, as there was a direct correlation between TLR5 expression, levels of TNFα in the synovial fluid and the disease activity score. The importance of TLR5 in disease development was determined when TLR5 was blocked and there was a resultant 80% decrease in synovial TNFα as well as a decrease in disease activity (Chamberlain et al., 2012). To date however, TLR5 molecules have not made it to the clinic.

TLR5 is not the only TLR to be implicated in the pathophysiology of RA. Recently, a clinical study identified a TLR7 ligand which is present in the synovial fluid of RA patients and is thought to provoke joint inflammation (S. J. Kim et al., 2016). It is also thought that TLR4 may play a key role in amplifying elements of the illness and as such has been identified as a potential target. NI-0101 is a recently described antagonistic antibody that is capable of binding an epitope on TLR4 and thereby prevent dimerization and subsequent pro inflammatory cytokine release. This has been tested for tolerability in healthy volunteers and also shown to prevent LPS induced cytokine increases in such participants. It has recently been administered via multiple intravenous infusion in a Phase II RCT proof of concept trial with rheumatoid arthritis patients, but no results are available as of writing (NCT03241108).

Other pattern recognition receptors have also been identified as targets for arthritis. Several Nod-like receptor inhibitors pertaining to inflammasomes have recently been developed (Guo, Callaway, & Ting, 2015), including OLT1177 (dapansutrile) which inhibits the NRLP3 inflammasome (Marchetti, Swartzwelter, Gamboni, et al., 2018). There has already been two randomized dose escalation phase I studies (NCT02134964 & NCT0163141) undertaken to evaluate its safety as a topical gel for single and multiple use in healthy volunteers (n = 35 & n = 36) and it has been reported to be safe at oral doses with no organ toxicities observed (Marchetti, Swartzwelter, Gamboni, et al., 2018). Having already demonstrated efficacy in animal models (Marchetti, Swartzwelter, Koenders, et al., 2018), it has since been evaluated in two randomized double blind phase II trials (NCT02104050 & NCT01768975) for knee pain in osteoarthritis patients (n = 79 & n = 202) but results are not available as of writing. It has also been evaluated in a phase II proof of concept trial (EudraCT 2016-000943-14) for the oral version of the drug in patients with acute gout flare (n = 29). Initial results suggest that it can inhibit acute joint inflammation and circulating IL1β during gout flares (Klück et al., 2020).

3.3 Asthma/allergic rhinitis

Asthma is a chronic inflammatory airway disease associated with overproduction of mucus, bronchial hyper-responsiveness and overproduction of Th2 cytokines. It is a highly prevalent disorder affecting the nasal cavity following exposure to common allergens such as pollen, dust, mold spores or animal dander (Lambrecht, Hammad, & Fahy, 2019). Studies have suggested that altered NOD1 and/or NOD2 expression may contribute to allergic rhinitis, but further investigations are needed to clarify their role in this disorder (Bogefors et al., 2010; Hu, You, Cao, Liu, & Cui, 2013). TLRs have also been associated with asthma in many human populations as well in various animal models (reviewed in (Zakeri & Russo, 2018)). Targeting TLRs is a potential route for therapies as their stimulation is thought to alter the Th1/Th2 cytokine profile (Aryan, Holgate, Radzioch, & Rezaei, 2014; Aryan & Rezaei, 2015).

Recently, a selective TLR7 agonist GSK2245035 has been developed for respiratory diseases such as asthma as well as allergic rhinitis. It has been evaluated for safety and tolerability in participants (n = 61) a double-blind RCT phase I trial (NCT01480271) as well for efficacy in phase II trial (NCT02833974) in subjects (n = 36) with mild allergic asthmatic.

It was shown to modulate Th2 cytokines *ex vivo* (Biggadike et al., 2016) and was well tolerated up to 100 ng when administered intranasally in healthy volunteers (Ellis, Tsitoura, Quint, Powley, & Lee, 2017; Tsitoura et al., 2015). This was also the case with another TLR7 agonist, AZD8848 which showed tolerability and also sustained reduction in the responsiveness to allergen in allergic rhinitis patients in a small placebo-controlled trial (NCT00688779 and NCT00770003) when administered intranasally once weekly for five weeks (Greiff et al., 2012). A subsequent phase IIa trial (NCT00770003) of AZD8848 for seasonal allergic rhinitis patients ($n = 83$) challenged with grass pollen showed symptoms reduced up to eight days after the final dose as well as significant changes in levels of cytokines (Greiff et al., 2015).

TLR8 has also been a notable target with asthma and allergic rhinitis, this is not surprising given the similarities between TLR7 and TLR8. VTX1463 is a selective TLR8 agonist that has also been formulated as a nasal spray and has shown to attenuate nasal congestion after ragweed challenge in beagle dogs (Royer, Rudolph, Dietsch, Hershberg, & Barrett, 2016). It was found to be safe and tolerable in human healthy volunteers (VRXP-B101) and reduced the total nasal symptom score in sufferers of allergic rhinitis ($n = 70$; VRXP-B102) exposed to grass pollen as well (Horak, 2011).

As with TLR7/8 agonists, a number of attempts using TLR4 agonists have been tried based on the evidence that switching the T cell profile from Th2 to Th1 will be of benefit to patients suffering from allergic asthma/rhinitis. Initial studies using monophosphoryl lipid (A MPL) adjuvant were shown to be well tolerated and gave a significant reduction in both nasal and ocular symptoms following grass pollen sensitization (Drachenberg, Wheeler, Stuebner, & Horak, 2001). Administering MPL (derived from *Salmonella minnesota*) by four subcutaneous injection, known as Pollinex Quattro, is also an effective vaccine for allergic asthma sufferer showing reductions in the degree of airway inflammation and markers of oxidative stress (Scichilone et al., 2011). In two separate phase II studies (PQBirch203 & PQBirch204) conducted in Europe (EudraCT 2012-004336-28 & 2015-000984-15) using a range of doses there was a statistically significant response to injection as determined by total symptom scores (Worm et al., 2018). Further studies have shown this was not just a short-term effect and may actually have long-term efficacy ($n = 68$) (Zielen et al., 2018).

A TLR9 agonist named AZD1419 (a C type CpG) has been formulated for inhalation to induce type I interferon in the lung. It has already shown efficacy in rat models of allergen challenge and has recently shown safety and tolerability in monkeys and in phase I human trials (DV8-AST-01) via this route (Jackson, Candia, et al., 2018). A phase 2a randomized placebo-controlled double-blind human trial has been undertaken in four EU countries (NCT02898662) enrolling 81 patients with eosinophilic, moderate to severe asthma. No results are available as of writing. Other TLR9 agonists have also been tested including QbG10 and CYT003 in patients with allergic rhino-conjunctivitis and mild to moderate persistent allergic asthma. Nanoparticles (virus-like particles) containing both agonists were used in a phase 2b trial (NCT00800332). Patients with house dust mite allergy were injected six times at weekly intervals over a duration of nine weeks. Average symptom as well as quality of life scores improved in the high dose group (Klimek et al., 2011). A proof of concept randomized double-blind trial (NCT00890734; n = 63) showed improvement (symptom score and FEV1) in those injected with the QbG10 agonist (0.9 mg 7 times) over 12 weeks (Beeh et al., 2013).

More recently, CYT003 (also a TLR9 agonist) was used in a Phase 2b RCT (NCT01673672) with 365 patients receiving 7 doses over 12 weeks. In this case however, there was no statistically significant difference between the treated and placebo groups with regards to their symptom scores and quality of life even though it was well tolerated (Casale et al., 2015). Finally, TLR3 has been suggested as a potential target for allergic asthma and antagonistic antibodies have been developed. One inhibitory monoclonal antibody CNTO3157 has been tested as an infusion in healthy volunteers and patients in a phase I RCT trial (NCT01195207). It was reported that no serious adverse events were recorded (Silkoff et al., 2018). It was subsequently tested in a multi-center double-blind RCT trial (NCT01704040) in patients inoculated with human rhinovirus but CNTO3157 was not found to be effective in attenuating the response to this challenge, as determined by symptom score and FEV_1 (Silkoff et al., 2018).

3.4 Psoriasis/inflammatory skin disorders

Psoriasis (or psoriasis vulgaris) is a chronic skin disease which is usually manifested as raised oval plaques with silvery scales, often caused by hyperproliferation of the epidermal layer. It also is noted for redness of lesions due to increased numbers of capillaries near the surface as well as inflammatory cells includes macrophages, DCs and neutrophils as well as T cells of varying types (Nestle, Kaplan, & Barker, 2009). Many studies suggest that TLRs contribute to the initiation and maintenance of psoriasis and that TLR antagonists (TLR7,8,9) have benefit in animal models of the disease (Jiang et al., 2013; Suárez-Fariñas et al., 2013). To date, a mixed TLR7,8,9 antagonist IMO-8400 has been developed and tested in a phase IIa RCT (NCT01899729) in patients with moderate to severe plaque psoriasis (n = 46). Here, it was demonstrated that all four doses tested (by subcutaneous injection) showed clinical improvement with a clear dose-response relationship as well as no serious adverse events (Balak et al., 2017). A TLR7/9 antagonist, IMO-3100, has also been tested in a RCT double blind phase II trial (NCT01622348) in patients with moderate to severe plaque psoriasis (n = 44) at two different doses (also by s.c. injection) and was associated with a reduction in the psoriasis area severity index score (Kimball, Krueger, Sullivan, & Arbeit, 2013). There have also been two phase II double-blind RCT trials, NCT01001468 (n = 185) and NCT01837420 (n = 194) conducted with a TLR2 antagonist, VB-102. Although the drug was safe and well tolerated in both trials, there was no significant improvement in either primary or secondary outcome measures according to a company press release.

AC-203 (CCP-020, diacerein), as well as being an inhibitor of IL-1B production was also found to inhibit the formation of the NLRP3 inflammasome. It has recently been tested as a topical ointment (1%) in two proof of concept trials for rare skin disorders. One was an intra-individual trial (NCT03468322) in epidermolysis bullosa (EB) patients (n = 9). EB is a rare genetic skin disorder with recurrent blisters and skin fragility, the notable symptoms (Prodinger, Reichelt, Bauer, & Laimer, 2019). Trial results are not yet available. A recent randomized double-blind phase II trial (NCT03154333) with EB patients (n = 80) was conducted to study safety and efficacy There is also a longer-term trial (NCT03389308) in progress to assess the long-term safety and tolerability of the drug in such patients. Results to date indicate that the drug has an acceptable safety profile and that those patients receiving the drug see a reduction in absolute blister numbers (Ablinger et al., 2018; Wally et al., 2013, 2018). AC-203 has also been evaluated in another cohort of patients with a rare skin condition. A randomized open label phase II trial (NCT03286582) in patients with bullous pemphigoid (estimated n = 40), which is a chronic, inflammatory, sub-epidermal autoimmune blistering disease which mainly develops in elderly patients (Genovese et al., 2019), is still in the recruitment phase as of writing.

3.5 Lupus

Systemic lupus erythematosus (SLE) is a systemic autoimmune condition that affects a variety of organs where patients present with a variety of symptoms including rash, ulcers, a, kidney dysfunction, neurological disorders as well as alterations in blood counts and immune parameters such as anti nuclear antibodies (Tsokos, 2011). There has been a number of studies suggesting genetic associations with Toll-like receptors, in particular TLR7 & TLR9 with others suggesting increased expression of these receptors in SLE (Lyn-Cook et al., 2014). Patients with systemic lupus erythematosus (SLE) have antibodies against endogenous antigens, including nucleic acids (B. H. Hahn, 1998). It has been shown that signaling via TLR9 can occur when the DNA is present in DNA-immune complexes (Leadbetter et al., 2002; Viglianti et al., 2003) although under normal circumstances mammalian DNA is usually inert or inhibitory to signaling via TLR9 (Gursel et al., 2003). DNA recognized by the TLR9 receptor, could potentially lead to the development of antibodies to one's own DNA prior to SLE pathophysiology.

Antagonists of TLR7,8,9 have been tested in animal models of the disease and show suppression of lupus associated parameters in a genetic (lupus-prone) mouse model (Barrat, Meeker, Chan, Guiducci, & Coffman, 2007; Zhu et al., 2013). A small molecule inhibitor of TLR7,8,9 (CPG-52364) was shown to be safe and effective in animal studies and although there was a first in human safety trial conducted (NCT00547014), no results were reported (Oon, Wilson, & Wicks, 2016). A TLR3/7/8 antagonist called RSLV-132 was tested by intravenous infusion in a phase 1b double blind randomized dose escalation study (NCT02194400) with SLE patients ($n = 32$) and found to be well tolerated (Burge et al., 2017). There is a subsequent phase 2a study (NCT02660944) with SLE patients ($n = 64$) that is still active and so as of writing no results have been published.

3.6 Sepsis

TLRs have been a target for infections and related sepsis since early in their discovery due to their biological roles. Given the key role of Toll-likes receptors in recognizing components of bacteria and viruses, it has long been a strategy to find ways of interfering with TLR signaling to prevent hyper-responsiveness to infection leading to death. One of the most prominent targets for this has been TLR4 and sepsis. Mutations in the *tlr4* gene have been implicated in the development of sepsis. The D299G *tlr4* mutation has been shown to increase the risk of infection in patients and sepsis development, with studies in particular linking this polymorphism to the increased susceptibility to gram negative infections (Agnese et al., 2002; Lorenz, Patel, Hartung, & Schwartz, 2002). LPS hypersensitivity which leads to the development of these inflammatory conditions via increase cytokine production due to higher levels of TLR4 has also been linked to the D299G mutation (Ohto, Yamakawa, Akashi-Takamura, Miyake, & Shimizu, 2012).

One of the earliest molecules to be tested was the TLR4 antagonist E5564 (later eritoran), which showed efficacy first *in vitro* (Mullarkey et al., 2003) and later *in vivo* animal models by reducing cytokines responses preventing loss of cardiovascular pressure (Barochia, Solomon, Cui, Natanson, & Eichacker, 2011). This molecule is a synthetic lipid A antagonist that blocks LPS from biding at the cell surface MD2-TLR4 receptor. It has since been tested in humans with severe sepsis (n = 300) and both doses used appeared to be well tolerated when administered intravenously in a phase 2 RCT trial. There was a trend toward lower mortality after 28 days in those receiving the higher dose (105 mg) compared to the lower dose (45 mg) or placebo (Tidswell et al., 2010). However, in the most recent multinational phase 3 trial (ACCESS Randomized Trial - NCT00334828) the use of eritoran (105 mg) did not result in a reduced 28-day mortality in patients given the drug (n = 1304) compared to those who were given placebo (n = 657). The authors also found no differences in secondary endpoints including 1-year mortality between any of the subgroups (Opal et al., 2013). While not strictly a TLR4 antagonist, TAK-242 (resatorvid) inhibits TLR4 protein interactions with its adapters and therefore disrupts downstream signaling (Matsunaga, Tsuchimori, Matsumoto, & Ii, 2011). It has also been evaluated by infusion in randomized, placebo-controlled, multicenter phase III trials using patients with sepsis (NCT00143611; n = 277) and sepsis related cardiovascular and respiratory failure (NCT00633477; n = 18). Like eritoran, however, it failed to significantly improve mortality rates or cytokine levels in these patients (Rice et al., 2010).

3.7 Viral infections

Viral infections of many tissues have long been associated with TLR pathways. Respiratory syncytial virus (RSV), which is the leading cause of lower respiratory tract infections in young children has been linked to TLR3, leading to exacerbation of symptoms (Shay, Holman, Roosevelt, Clarke, & Anderson, 2001). Activation of TLR3 by RSV leads to the production of cytokines and chemokines which serve to propagate the immune response and pathogenesis of the disease (Rudd, Burstein, Duckett, Li, & Lukacs, 2005). In addition, a study investigating responses to *vaccinia* infection showed that *tlr3−/−* mice had much lower viral replication in the respiratory tract when compared to WT animals. It also showed that TLR3 is linked to increased morbidity and mortality with this infection. Furthermore there were significantly lower levels of cytokines, specifically IL6, MCP-1, and TNF-alpha, present in the knockout mice when compared to their WT counterparts. All of which suggest a role for TLR3 in the pathogenesis of *vaccinia* infection.

Hepatitis C viral (HCV) infection is a major cause of liver cirrhosis and hepatocellular carcinoma and majority of those infected develop chronic symptoms (Rosen, 2011). Toll-like receptors have been identified as a potential target for future therapies given their key role in viral recognition (Soriano, Barreiro, Benitez, Peña, & de Mendoza, 2017). In a phase I RCT (NCT01211626) ascending and multiple dose study in healthy volunteers and patients with hepatitis C ($n = 34$), the TLR7 agonist ANA773 was administered orally. There were no serious adverse events reported and there were dose-related interferon responses leading to a significant decrease in serum HCV RNA levels in the highest dose group (2000 mg) (Bergmann et al., 2011). Other TLR7 agonists tested include GS-9620 (vesatolimod), which is orally available. In a phase I dose escalation RCT trial it was shown to be safe, well absorbed and tolerated in health volunteers ($n = 75$) (Lopatin et al., 2013) as well as in a phase 1 double blind RCT trial (NCT01591668) with treatment naïve HCV patients ($n = 51$) (Lawitz et al., 2015). However, in a recent phase II double-blind RCT trial (NCT02166047) in virally suppressed patients with hepatitis B ($n = 162$) it did not show any significant induction of interferon expression or significant declines in hepatitis B surface antigen (Janssen et al., 2018). Finally, in phase I trials (NCT02956850 & NCT03530917) in healthy volunteers and patients with chronic hepatitis B ($n = 140$), the TLR7 agonist, RO7020531 was shown to be safe, well tolerated and activated TLR signaling (Gane et al., 2018). To date, there have been no further trials evaluating efficacy at the time of writing.

TLR9 agonists tested to date include IMO-2125 which was evaluated in a phase I placebo-controlled (NCT00728936) dose escalation study in hepatitis C infected patients unresponsive to standard therapy as well as in a combination treatment with ribavirin (NCT00990938) with no treatment related serious adverse events observed (Muir et al., 2010). SD-101 has also been tested in a phase 1b dose escalation study (NCT00823862) in treatment naïve chronic hepatitis C patients (n = 34) and was generally well tolerated and found to be safe (Cianciara, Martin, & Spellman, 2010). There have not been any further reports on testing and the extent of their efficacy is not known in these patients.

Given the now recognized role of cytoplasmic nucleic acid sensors in mediating anti-viral responses, recent research has focused on the role the non-endosomal pattern recognition receptors, in particular RIG-I. A RIG-I/NOD 2 agonist, SB9200, which is an oral prodrug (composed of a small molecule nucleic acid) has recently been tested based on the validation of its anti-viral activity in an animal model of chronic hepatitis B (Korolowicz et al., 2016; Suresh et al., 2017) as well as activity against resistant hepatitis C variants (Jones et al., 2017). A randomized phase I placebo controlled ascending dose trial (NCT01803308) in chronic hepatitis C patients (n = 37) has shown that SB9200 was safe, well tolerated and reduced viral replication (Thompson et al., 2015). At the time of writing, there is an ongoing randomized open label phase II trial (NCT0343453) in chronic hepatitis C patients (estimated n = 120) to evaluate safety and antiviral activity when combined with tenofovir (Walsh et al., 2018) and also a trial (NCT03932513) in chronic hepatitis B patients (n = 16).

TLR9 agonists have also been tested in HIV patients. In a phase Ib/IIa open label trial (NCT02443935) to investigate if TLR9 agonist could enhance immune responses and reactivate viral transcription HIV patients (n = 15) were given MGN1703 (lefitolimod) subcutaneously for four weeks which led to activation of plasmacytoid dendritic cells, activated cytotoxic natural killer cells and $CD8^+$ T cells as well as increased plasma HIV1 RNA levels in a proportion of patients (L. Vibholm et al., 2017). Furthermore, in a separate arm of the study conducted over 24 weeks, it was reported that MGN1073 treatment was safe and increased HIV1 T cell specific responses (L. K. Vibholm et al., 2019).

Finally, the TLR7 agonist imiquimod has been evaluated in human papillomavirus infection for the treatment of anogenital warts. Imiquimod cream (5%) given to patients with genital warts (n = 16) was associated with increases in IFN, TNF and IL12 mRNA as well as decreases in in viral load as measured by HPV DNA (Arany et al., 1999). It has also been tested on HIV + patients (who have a higher risk of anogenital warts). In a open label phase 4 trial (NCT00761371) in HIV patients treated with HAART (n = 52), it was shown to be safe and effective at achieving total wart clearance and decreasing HPV viral load in a large percentage of patients (Saiag et al., 2009). In subsequent double blind RCT trials (CTRI/2009/091/000055) patients with anogenital warts treated with imiquimod ($n = 44$) showed clinical and virologist clearance for HPV6 and a significant decline in HPV11 viral load (Kumar et al., 2014).

3.8 Adjuvant

There have a number of studies which have shown the benefits of using TLR agonists as adjuvants. In many cases these agonists have improved efficacy and also safety profiles of drugs and vaccines with TLR3/5/7/8/9 agonists proving the most effective. In one case, a combination of the TLR9 agonist CpG DNA as an adjuvant with the Hepatitis B surface antigen 1018 as a vaccine known as Heplisav (Cooper & Mackie, 2011). Three phase 3 trials (NCT00435812, NCT01005407, NCT02117934) concluded that the combination improves immunogenicity and allows for fewer doses over a shorter period of time (Hyer, McGuire, Xing, Jackson, & Janssen, 2018; Jackson, Lentino, et al., 2018). A similar outcome was reported when another TLR agonist, CpG 7909 was combined with the anthrax vaccine. A phase Ib trial (NCT01263691) and a phase II RCT (NCT01770743) demonstrated safety, immunogenicity with increased T cell effects and required fewer doses relative to vaccine alone (Hopkins et al., 2013) (Hopkins et al., 2016; Minang et al., 2014).

The TLR3 agonist Poly I:C or Rintatolimod (Ampligen) has been used as an adjuvant for the HIV treatment highly active anti-retroviral therapy (HAART) as well as with HIV and influenza vaccines. In initial phase I trials in HIV infected patients with AIDS (NCT00000735) as well as in healthy controls (NCT00001000), it showed no significant effects on HIV p24 levels but an increase in $CD4^+$ cell counts in patients as well as only minimal toxic effects was reported (Armstrong et al., 1992; Hendrix et al., 1993). A phase 2 RCT trial (NCT00035893) was conducted to evaluate the potential effectiveness of Rintatolimod to increase the HAART-free time interval before HIV rebound during the STI of HAART but no results have been posted to date. Recently, data was published from a phase I RCT trial (NCT02071095) showing that Poly ICLC given subcutaneously could be used safely for inducing transient immune responses in aviremic, combination anti-retroviral (cART)-treated HIV patients (Saxena et al., 2019). Poly I:C or its different forms has been combined with viral antigens to enhance immunogenicity of vaccines. Poly ICLC has been combined in a phase I RCT trial (NCT01127464) with DCVax (a vaccine composed of a fusion protein containing a human antibody to the dendritic cell receptor

CD205 and HIV gag p24 protein) using healthy volunteers (n = 43) but results have not been published as of writing.

Rintatolimod (Ampligen) has also been combined with the intranasal quadrivalent flu vaccine FluMist in a phase I/II RCT trial (NCT01591473) but this was terminated despite being reported to be well tolerated and showing higher increases in antibody titers as well as cross-reactivity to avian flu strains in published studies (Overton et al., 2014). Recently, the TLR5 agonist flagellin has been used as an adjuvant in combination with flu vaccines. The ligand has been fused to the HA1 domain of the H1N1 influenza virus to generate VAX125. This was shown to be safe and well tolerated when give as a single dose intramuscularly to participants (n = 128) in a phase I randomized open label trial (NCT00730457) (Treanor et al., 2010) and also found to induce a potent antibody immune response (10-fold over baseline) in elderly subjects (n = 120) (NCT00966238) (D. N. Taylor et al., 2011). Alternative versions of this vaccine with different domains of flagellin fused to the vaccine (VAX128A/B/C) have also been tested in healthy subjects (n = 112) in dose escalation trials (NCT01172054) and found to be safe and still retain immunogenicity (D. N. Taylor et al., 2012). An alternative fusion protein has been generated with flagellin and flu vaccine targeting the ectodomain of matrix protein 2 (VAX102) and this has been tested in phase I trials (NCT00603811) and found to be safe and induced a high antibody level to M2E (four-fold over baseline) (Turley et al., 2011).

Finally, the TLR7 agonist imiquimod has also been evaluated in trials to test if it improves the immunogenicity of the influenza vaccine. In a double-blind RCT trial (NCT01508884) where imiquimod was given topically with an intradermal trivalent influenza vaccine to participants (n = 93), it was found to be safe, well tolerated and it significantly increased, prolonged and expedited the immunogenicity of the vaccine (Hung et al., 2016). This was also confirmed in a double blind RCT phase III (NCT02103023) trial with young healthy volunteers (n = 160) as well as showing increased immunogenicity against non-vaccine strains such as H3N2 where there is often antigenic drift (Hung et al., 2016).

4. Perspectives/Conclusions

As highlighted above, there are many diseases that show an over activation of and genetic links to specific PRRs. However, as many of these receptors converge on NF-κB and IRF activation similar to other PRRs, there is potential issue with safety as shutting down all signaling pathways would prevent immunity to infection. Therefore, it is sensible to investigate some targets upstream of this event which would potentially reduce specific PRR activity but still allow other PRRs to respond to infection. There is also the possibility that inhibitors of PRR signaling could interfere with the cross talk between TLRs and NLRs or RLRs for example. There are a number of approaches that could be taken such as targeting specific domains in the PRR structure such as the LRR domain involved in ligand recognition, targeting the ATP binding sites or the NOD oligomerisation domain/NACHT domain in NLRs, targeting the TIR domain or recruitment of adapters like Mal or RIP2, targeting kinase activity or targeting some of the regulatory proteins involved in signaling. This review has focused specifically on those molecules that act as agonist or antagonists at the receptor itself. The compounds reviewed here have already made it to clinical trials and are predominantly targeting TLRs. Development of molecules targeting the other PRRs seems to be further behind but research is still active in this field particularly targeting NLRs, given the genetic evidence linking them to a number of disorders.

A number of different approaches have been taken to identify such molecules, some are endogenous while others were found in natural or synthetic libraries. Groups have already begun to investigate the potential of NOD1 and NOD2 inhibitors without inhibiting RIP2 kinase, for example (Rickard et al., 2013, 2014). The benzimidazole compounds tested for NOD2 by Rickard et al., 2013 compete with MDP for binding of NOD2 and reduce NOD2 activity *in vitro* as assessed by IL8 secretion but not TLR or RIP2 activity. They do not directly interfere with MDP internalization, but data suggest that they interfere somewhere between MDP processing and NOD2 oligomerisation (Rickard et al., 2013). In a similar manner, NOD1 inhibitors seem to antagonize Tri-DAP induced IL8 secretion in intestinal epithelial cells *in vitro* (Rickard et al., 2014). Recently, compounds such as curcumin, parthenolide, helenalin, pseudopterosin A, docosahexaenoic acid and eicosapentaenoic acid have been tested for their ability to inhibit NOD1 and NOD2 signaling (Jakopin, 2014). There is also considerable promise in compounds targeting inflammasomes such as NLRP3 (Guo et al., 2015; Shao, Xu, Han, Su, & Liu, 2015). One molecule, MCC950, has already shown efficacy in animal models of inflammatory disease such as experimental autoimmune encephalomyelitis (a model of multiple sclerosis) (Coll et al., 2015) and steroid resistant asthma (R. Y. Kim et al., 2017).

There is also thought to be potential for NLR agonists to be used as adjuvants and for treating acute infections (Geddes, Magalhães, & Girardin, 2009).

Although there has not been the same progress made as TLR compounds, targeting CLRs is thought to be a promising strategy for managing certain diseases. There is still a need to identifying more specific endogenous ligands, further elucidate signaling and to investigate their role in sterile inflammation (similar to other PRRs). To date, there has been an emphasis on using ligands in cancer therapy (Chiffoleau, 2018). While there has been over two decades of compound discovery and development, there have still been very few successes. This may, as discussed above, be due to shared components and crossover in signaling pathways, which is why unique features of each pathway need to be identified. Overall, these receptors still hold a lot of promise as targets in inflammatory and infectious diseases.

References

Ablinger, M., Felder, T. K., Wimmer, M., Zauner, R., Hofbauer, P., Lettner, T., et al. (2018). Basal pharmacokinetic parameters of topically applied diacerein in pediatric patients with generalized severe epidermolysis bullosa simplex. *Orphanet Journal of Rare Diseases, 13*(1), 193. http://dx.doi.org/10.1186/s13023-018-0940-1.

Agnese, D. M., Calvano, J. E., Hahm, S. J., Coyle, S. M., Corbett, S. A., Calvano, S. E., et al. (2002). Human toll-like receptor 4 mutations but not CD14 polymorphisms are associated with an increased risk of gram-negative infections. *The Journal of Infectious Diseases, 186*(10), 1522–1525. http://dx.doi.org/10.1086/344893.

Akira, S., & Takeda, K. (2004). Toll-like receptor signalling. *Nature Reviews Immunology, 4*(7), 499–511. http://dx.doi.org/10.1038/nri1391.

Akira, S., Uematsu, S., & Takeuchi, O. (2006). Pathogen recognition and innate immunity. *Cell, 124*(4), 783–801. http://dx.doi.org/10.1016/j.cell.2006.02.015.

Alexopoulou, L., Holt, A. C., Medzhitov, R., & Flavell, R. A. (2001). Recognition of double-stranded RNA and activation of NF-kappaB by Toll-like receptor 3. *Nature, 413*(6857), 732–738. http://dx.doi.org/10.1038/35099560.

Arany, I., Tyring, S. K., Stanley, M. A., Tomai, M. A., Miller, R. L., Smith, M. H., McDermott, D. J., & Slade, H. B. (1999). Enhancement of the innate and cellular immune response in patients with genital warts treated with topical imiquimod cream 5%. *Antiviral Research, 43*(1), 55–63.

Armstrong, J. A., McMahon, D., Huang, X. L., Pazin, G. J., Gupta, P., Rinaldo, C. R., et al. (1992). A phase I study of ampligen in human immunodeficiency virus-infected subjects. *The Journal of Infectious Diseases, 166*(4), 717–722. http://dx.doi.org/10.1093/infdis/166.4.717.

Arthur, J. S., & Ley, S. C. (2013). Mitogen-activated protein kinases in innate immunity. *Nature Reviews Immunology, 13*(9), 679–692. http://dx.doi.org/10.1038/nri3495.

Aryan, Z., Holgate, S. T., Radzioch, D., & Rezaei, N. (2014). A new era of targeting the ancient gatekeepers of the immune system: Toll-like agonists in the treatment of allergic rhinitis and asthma. *International Archives of Allergy and Immunology, 164*(1), 46–63. http://dx.doi.org/10.1159/000362553.

Aryan, Z., & Rezaei, N. (2015). Toll-like receptors as targets for allergen immunotherapy. *Current Opinion in Allergy and Clinical Immunology, 15*(6), 568–574. http://dx.doi.org/10.1097/ACI.0000000000000212.

Atreya, R., Bloom, S., Scaldaferri, F., Gerardi, V., Admyre, C., Karlsson, Å., et al. (2016). Clinical effects of a topically applied toll-like receptor 9 agonist in active moderate-to-severe ulcerative colitis. *Journal of Crohn's and Colitis, 10*(11), 1294–1302. http://dx.doi.org/10.1093/ecco-jcc/jjw103.

Atreya, R., Reinisch, W., Peyrin-Biroulet, L., Scaldaferri, F., Admyre, C., Knittel, T., et al. (2018). Clinical efficacy of the Toll-like receptor 9 agonist cobitolimod using patient-reported-outcomes defined clinical endpoints in patients with ulcerative colitis. *Digestive and Liver Disease, 50*(10), 1019–1029. http://dx.doi.org/10.1016/j.dld.2018.06.010.

Bafica, A., Scanga, C. A., Feng, C. G., Leifer, C., Cheever, A., & Sher, A. (2005). TLR9 regulates Th1 responses and cooperates with TLR2 in mediating optimal resistance to *Mycobacterium tuberculosis*. *Journal of Experimental Medicine, 202*(12), 1715–1724. http://dx.doi.org/10.1084/jem.20051782.

Balak, D. M., van Doorn, M. B., Arbeit, R. D., Rijneveld, R., Klaassen, E., Sullivan, T., et al. (2017). IMO-8400, a toll-like receptor 7, 8, and 9 antagonist, demonstrates clinical activity in a phase 2a, randomized, placebo-controlled trial in patients with moderate-to-severe plaque psoriasis. *Clinical Immunology, 174*, 63–72. http://dx.doi.org/10.1016/j.clim.2016.09.015.

Barochia, A., Solomon, S., Cui, X., Natanson, C., & Eichacker, P. Q. (2011). Eritoran tetrasodium (E5564) treatment for sepsis: Review of preclinical and clinical studies. *Expert Opinion on Drug Metabolism and Toxicology, 7*(4), 479–494. http://dx.doi.org/10.1517/17425255.2011.558190.

Barrat, F. J., Elkon, K. B., & Fitzgerald, K. A. (2016). Importance of nucleic acid recognition in inflammation and autoimmunity. *Annual Review of Medicine, 67*, 323–336. http://dx.doi.org/10.1146/annurev-med-052814-023338.

Barrat, F. J., Meeker, T., Chan, J. H., Guiducci, C., & Coffman, R. L. (2007). Treatment of lupus-prone mice with a dual inhibitor of TLR7 and TLR9 leads to reduction of autoantibody production and amelioration of disease symptoms. *European Journal of Immunology, 37*(12), 3582–3586. http://dx.doi.org/10.1002/eji.200737815.

Bauer, S., Kirschning, C. J., Häcker, H., Redecke, V., Hausmann, S., Akira, S., et al. (2001). Human TLR9 confers responsiveness to bacterial DNA via species-specific CpG motif recognition. *Proceedings of the National Academy of Sciences of the United States of America, 98*(16), 9237–9242. http://dx.doi.org/10.1073/pnas.161293498.

Beeh, K. M., Kanniess, F., Wagner, F., Schilder, C., Naudts, I., Hammann-Haenni, A., et al. (2013). The novel TLR-9 agonist QbG10 shows clinical efficacy in persistent allergic asthma. *The Journal of Allergy and Clinical Immunology, 131*(3), 866–874. http://dx.doi.org/10.1016/j.jaci.2012.12.1561.

Bell, J. K., Askins, J., Hall, P. R., Davies, D. R., & Segal, D. M. (2006). The dsRNA binding site of human Toll-like receptor 3. *Proceedings of the National Academy of Sciences of the United States of America, 103*(23), 8792–8797. http://dx.doi.org/10.1073/pnas.0603245103.

Bergmann, J. F., de Bruijne, J., Hotho, D. M., de Knegt, R. J., Boonstra, A., Weegink, C. J., et al. (2011). Randomised clinical trial: Anti-viral activity of ANA773, an oral inducer of endogenous interferons acting via TLR7, in chronic HCV. *Alimentary Pharmacology & Therapeutics, 34*(4), 443–453. http://dx.doi.org/10.1111/j.1365-2036.2011.04745.x.

Berkowitz, D., Peri, R., Lavy, A., & Kessel, A. (2013). Increased Toll-like receptor 9 expression by B cells from inflammatory bowel disease patients. *Human Immunology, 74*(12), 1519–1523. http://dx.doi.org/10.1016/j.humimm.2013.08.285.

Biggadike, K., Ahmed, M., Ball, D. I., Coe, D. M., Dalmas Wilk, D. A., Edwards, C. D., et al. (2016). Discovery of 6-amino-2-{[(1S)-1-methylbutyl]oxy}-9-[5-(1-piperidinyl) pentyl]-7,9-dihydro-8H-purin-8-one (GSK2245035), a highly potent and selective intranasal toll-like receptor 7 agonist for the treatment of asthma. *Journal of Medicinal Chemistry, 59*(5), 1711–1726. http://dx.doi.org/10.1021/acs.jmedchem.5b01647.

Blasius, A. L., & Beutler, B. (2010). Intracellular toll-like receptors. *Immunity, 32*(3), 305–315. http://dx.doi.org/10.1016/j.immuni.2010.03.012.

Bogefors, J., Rydberg, C., Uddman, R., Fransson, M., Månsson, A., Benson, M., et al. (2010). Nod1, Nod2 and Nalp3 receptors, new potential targets in treatment of allergic rhinitis? *Allergy, 65*(10), 1222–1226. http://dx.doi.org/10.1111/j.1398-9995.2009.02315.x.

Bourquin, C., Pommier, A., & Hotz, C. (2019). Harnessing the immune system to fight cancer with Toll-like receptor and RIG-I-like receptor agonists. *Pharmacological Research*, 104192. http://dx.doi.org/10.1016/j.phrs.2019.03.001.

Boyle, J. P., Mayle, S., Parkhouse, R., & Monie, T. P. (2013). Comparative genomic and sequence analysis provides insight into the molecular functionality of NOD1 and NOD2. *Frontiers in Immunology, 4*, 317. http://dx.doi.org/10.3389/fimmu.2013.00317.

Bryant, C. E., Orr, S., Ferguson, B., Symmons, M. F., Boyle, J. P., & Monie, T. P. (2015). International union of basic and clinical pharmacology. XCVI. Pattern recognition receptors in health and disease. *Pharmacological Reviews, 67*(2), 462–504. http://dx.doi.org/10.1124/pr.114.009928.

Burge, D. J., Eisenman, J., Byrnes-Blake, K., Smolak, P., Lau, K., Cohen, S. B., et al. (2017). Safety, pharmacokinetics, and pharmacodynamics of RSLV-132, an RNase-fc fusion protein in systemic lupus erythematosus: A randomized, double-blind, placebo-controlled study. *Lupus, 26*(8), 825–834. http://dx.doi.org/10.1177/0961203316678675.

Cario, E. (2010). Toll-like receptors in inflammatory bowel diseases: A decade later. *Inflammatory Bowel Diseases, 16*(9), 1583–1597. http://dx.doi.org/10.1002/ibd.21282.

Cario, E., & Podolsky, D. K. (2000). Differential alteration in intestinal epithelial cell expression of toll-like receptor 3 (TLR3) and TLR4 in inflammatory bowel disease. *Infection and Immunity, 68*(12), 7010–7017.

Casale, T. B., Cole, J., Beck, E., Vogelmeier, C. F., Willers, J., Lassen, C., et al. (2015). CYT003, a TLR9 agonist, in persistent allergic asthma - a randomized placebo-controlled Phase 2b study. *Allergy, 70*(9), 1160–1168. http://dx.doi.org/10.1111/all.12663.

Chamberlain, N. D., Vila, O. M., Volin, M. V., Volkov, S., Pope, R. M., Swedler, W., et al. (2012). TLR5, a novel and unidentified inflammatory mediator in rheumatoid arthritis that correlates with disease activity score and joint TNF-α levels. *The Journal of Immunology, 189*(1), 475–483. http://dx.doi.org/10.4049/jimmunol.1102977.

Chen, G., Shaw, M. H., Kim, Y. G., & Nuñez, G. (2009). NOD-like receptors: Role in innate immunity and inflammatory disease. *Annual Review of Pathology: Mechanisms of Disease, 4*, 365–398. http://dx.doi.org/10.1146/annurev.pathol.4.110807.092239.

Chiffoleau, E. (2018). C-type lectin-like receptors as emerging Orchestrators of sterile inflammation represent potential therapeutic targets. *Frontiers in Immunology, 9*, 227. http://dx.doi.org/10.3389/fimmu.2018.00227.

Cianciara, J., Martin, J. T., & Spellman, M. C. (2010). *Phase 1B dose-escalation study OF SD-101, a novel therapeutic TLR-9 agonist, IN treatment-naive chronic hepatitis C patients*. Vienna: Paper presented at the International Liver Congress.

Coll, R. C., Robertson, A. A., Chae, J. J., Higgins, S. C., Muñoz-Planillo, R., Inserra, M. C., et al. (2015). A small-molecule inhibitor of the NLRP3 inflammasome for the treatment of inflammatory diseases. *Nature Medicine, 21*(3), 248–255. http://dx.doi.org/10.1038/nm.3806.

Cooper, C., & Mackie, D. (2011). Hepatitis B surface antigen-1018 ISS adjuvant-containing vaccine: A review of HEPLISAV™ safety and efficacy. *Expert Rev Vaccines, 10*(4), 417–427. http://dx.doi.org/10.1586/erv.10.162.

Drachenberg, K. J., Wheeler, A. W., Stuebner, P., & Horak, F. (2001). A well-tolerated grass pollen-specific allergy vaccine containing a novel adjuvant, monophosphoryl lipid A, reduces allergic symptoms after only four preseasonal injections. *Allergy, 56*(6), 498–505.

Ellis, A. K., Tsitoura, D. C., Quint, D., Powley, W., & Lee, L. A. (2017). Safety and pharmacodynamics of intranasal GSK2245035, a TLR7 agonist for allergic rhinitis: A randomized trial. *Clinical and Experimental Allergy, 47*(9), 1193–1203. http://dx.doi.org/10.1111/cea.12974.

Feerick, C. L., & McKernan, D. P. (2017). Understanding the regulation of pattern recognition receptors in inflammatory diseases - a 'Nod' in the right direction. *Immunology, 150*(3), 237–247. http://dx.doi.org/10.1111/imm.12677.

Franchi, L., Warner, N., Viani, K., & Nuñez, G. (2009). Function of Nod-like receptors in microbial recognition and host defense. *Immunological Reviews, 227*(1), 106–128. http://dx.doi.org/10.1111/j.1600-065X.2008.00734.x.

Frank, D. N., Robertson, C. E., Hamm, C. M., Kpadeh, Z., Zhang, T., Chen, H., et al. (2011). Disease phenotype and genotype are associated with shifts in intestinal-associated microbiota in inflammatory bowel diseases. *Inflammatory Bowel Diseases, 17*(1), 179–184. http://dx.doi.org/10.1002/ibd.21339.

Friedl, P., & Weigelin, B. (2008). Interstitial leukocyte migration and immune function. *Nature Immunology, 9*(9), 960–969. http://dx.doi.org/10.1038/ni.f.212.

Fullerton, J. N., & Gilroy, D. W. (2016). Resolution of inflammation: A new therapeutic frontier. *Nature Reviews Drug Discovery, 15*(8), 551–567. http://dx.doi.org/10.1038/nrd.2016.39.

Gane, E., Folitar, I., Schwabe, C., Rodriguez, I., Gao, L., Calleja, E., et al. (2018). *RO7020531, a novel prodrug of a toll-like receptor 7 agonist, is safe, well tolerated and activates TLR signaling in healthy volunteers.* Paris: Paper presented at the The International Liver Congress.

Geddes, K., Magalhães, J. G., & Girardin, S. E. (2009). Unleashing the therapeutic potential of NOD-like receptors. *Nature Reviews Drug Discovery, 8*(6), 465–479. http://dx.doi.org/10.1038/nrd2783.

Genovese, G., Di Zenzo, G., Cozzani, E., Berti, E., Cugno, M., & Marzano, A. V. (2019). New insights into the pathogenesis of bullous pemphigoid: 2019 update. *Frontiers in Immunology, 10,* 1506. http://dx.doi.org/10.3389/fimmu.2019.01506.

Girardin, S. E., Tournebize, R., Mavris, M., Page, A. L., Li, X., Stark, G. R., et al. (2001). CARD4/Nod1 mediates NF-kappaB and JNK activation by invasive Shigella flexneri. *EMBO Reports, 2*(8), 736–742. http://dx.doi.org/10.1093/embo-reports/kve155.

Girardin, S. E., Travassos, L. H., Hervé, M., Blanot, D., Boneca, I. G., Philpott, D. J., et al. (2003). Peptidoglycan molecular requirements allowing detection by Nod1 and Nod2. *Journal of Biological Chemistry, 278*(43), 41702–41708. http://dx.doi.org/10.1074/jbc.M307198200.

Greiff, L., Ahlström-Emanuelsson, C., Alenäs, M., Almqvist, G., Andersson, M., Cervin, A., et al. (2015). Biological effects and clinical efficacy of a topical toll-like receptor 7 agonist in seasonal allergic rhinitis: A parallel group controlled phase IIa study. *Inflammation Research, 64*(11), 903–915. http://dx.doi.org/10.1007/s00011-015-0873-2.

Greiff, L., Cervin, A., Ahlström-Emanuelsson, C., Almqvist, G., Andersson, M., Dolata, J., et al. (2012). Repeated intranasal TLR7 stimulation reduces allergen responsiveness in allergic rhinitis. *Respiratory Research, 13,* 53. http://dx.doi.org/10.1186/1465-9921-13-53.

Guiducci, C., Gong, M., Cepika, A. M., Xu, Z., Tripodo, C., Bennett, L., et al. (2013). RNA recognition by human TLR8 can lead to autoimmune inflammation. *Journal of Experimental Medicine, 210*(13), 2903–2919. http://dx.doi.org/10.1084/jem.20131044.

Guo, H., Callaway, J. B., & Ting, J. P. (2015). Inflammasomes: Mechanism of action, role in disease, and therapeutics. *Nature Medicine, 21*(7), 677–687. http://dx.doi.org/10.1038/nm.3893.

Gursel, I., Gursel, M., Yamada, H., Ishii, K. J., Takeshita, F., & Klinman, D. M. (2003). Repetitive elements in mammalian telomeres suppress bacterial DNA-induced immune activation. *The Journal of Immunology, 171*(3), 1393–1400. http://dx.doi.org/10.4049/jimmunol.171.3.1393.

Hahn, B. H. (1998). Antibodies to DNA. *New England Journal of Medicine, 338*(19), 1359–1368. http://dx.doi.org/10.1056/NEJM199805073381906.

Hahn, J. S. (2005). Regulation of Nod1 by Hsp90 chaperone complex. *FEBS Letters, 579*(20), 4513–4519. http://dx.doi.org/10.1016/j.febslet.2005.07.024.

Hardison, S. E., & Brown, G. D. (2012). C-type lectin receptors orchestrate antifungal immunity. *Nature Immunology, 13*(9), 817–822. http://dx.doi.org/10.1038/ni.2369.

Hasegawa, M., Fujimoto, Y., Lucas, P. C., Nakano, H., Fukase, K., Núñez, G., et al. (2008). A critical role of RICK/RIP2 polyubiquitination in Nod-induced NF-kappaB activation. *The EMBO Journal, 27*(2), 373–383. http://dx.doi.org/10.1038/sj.emboj.7601962.

Hayashi, F., Smith, K. D., Ozinsky, A., Hawn, T. R., Yi, E. C., Goodlett, D. R., et al. (2001). The innate immune response to bacterial flagellin is mediated by Toll-like receptor 5. *Nature, 410*(6832), 1099–1103. http://dx.doi.org/10.1038/35074106.

He, S., & Wang, X. (2018). RIP kinases as modulators of inflammation and immunity. *Nature Immunology, 19*(9), 912–922. http://dx.doi.org/10.1038/s41590-018-0188-x.

Hendrix, C. W., Margolick, J. B., Petty, B. G., Markham, R. B., Nerhood, L., Farzadegan, H., et al. (1993). Biologic effects after a single dose of poly(I):poly(C12U) in healthy volunteers. *Antimicrobial Agents and Chemotherapy, 37*(3), 429–435. http://dx.doi.org/10.1128/aac.37.3.429.

Hennessy, C., & McKernan, D. P. (2016). Epigenetics and innate immunity: The 'unTolld' story. *Immunology & Cell Biology, 94*(7), 631–639. http://dx.doi.org/10.1038/icb.2016.24.

Hopkins, R. J., Daczkowski, N. F., Kaptur, P. E., Muse, D., Sheldon, E., LaForce, C., et al. (2013). Randomized, double-blind, placebo-controlled, safety and immunogenicity study of 4 formulations of Anthrax Vaccine Adsorbed plus CPG 7909 (AV7909) in healthy adult volunteers. *Vaccine, 31*(30), 3051–3058. http://dx.doi.org/10.1016/j.vaccine.2013.04.063.

Hopkins, R. J., Kalsi, G., Montalvo-Lugo, V. M., Sharma, M., Wu, Y., Muse, D. D., et al. (2016). Randomized, double-blind, active-controlled study evaluating the safety and immunogenicity of three vaccination schedules and two dose levels of AV7909 vaccine for anthrax post-exposure prophylaxis in healthy adults. *Vaccine, 34*(18), 2096–2105. http://dx.doi.org/10.1016/j.vaccine.2016.03.006.

Horak, F. (2011). VTX-1463, a novel TLR8 agonist for the treatment of allergic rhinitis. *Expert Opinion on Investigational Drugs, 20*(7), 981–986. http://dx.doi.org/10.1517/13543784.2011.583237.

Hsu, L. C., Ali, S. R., McGillivray, S., Tseng, P. H., Mariathasan, S., Humke, E. W., et al. (2008). A NOD2-NALP1 complex mediates caspase-1-dependent IL-1beta secretion in response to Bacillus anthracis infection and muramyl dipeptide. *Proceedings of the National Academy of Sciences of the United States of America, 105*(22), 7803–7808. http://dx.doi.org/10.1073/pnas.0802726105.

Hu, S., You, X., Cao, P., Liu, Z., & Cui, Y. (2013). [The expression of NOD1 and NOD2 and the regulation of glucocorticoids on them in allergic rhinitis]. *Lin Chung Er Bi Yan Hou Tou Jing Wai Ke Za Zhi, 27*(8), 393–396.

Hugot, J. P., Chamaillard, M., Zouali, H., Lesage, S., Cézard, J. P., Belaiche, J., et al. (2001). Association of NOD2 leucine-rich repeat variants with susceptibility to Crohn's disease. *Nature, 411*(6837), 599–603. http://dx.doi.org/10.1038/35079107.

Hugot, J. P., Zaccaria, I., Cavanaugh, J., Yang, H., Vermeire, S., Lappalainen, M., et al. (2007). Prevalence of CARD15/NOD2 mutations in Caucasian healthy people. *American Journal of Gastroenterology, 102*(6), 1259–1267. http://dx.doi.org/10.1111/j.1572-0241.2007.01149.x.

Hung, I. F., Zhang, A. J., To, K. K., Chan, J. F., Li, P., Wong, T. L., et al. (2016). Topical imiquimod before intradermal trivalent influenza vaccine for protection against heterologous non-vaccine and antigenically drifted viruses: A single-centre, double-blind, randomised, controlled phase 2b/3 trial. *The Lancet Infectious Diseases, 16*(2), 209–218. http://dx.doi.org/10.1016/S1473-3099(15)00354-0.

Hyer, R., McGuire, D. K., Xing, B., Jackson, S., & Janssen, R. (2018). Safety of a two-dose investigational hepatitis B vaccine, HBsAg-1018, using a toll-like receptor 9 agonist adjuvant in adults. *Vaccine, 36*(19), 2604–2611. http://dx.doi.org/10.1016/j.vaccine.2018.03.067.

Inohara, Chamaillard, McDonald, C., & Nuñez, G. (2005). NOD-LRR proteins: Role in host-microbial interactions and inflammatory disease. *Annual Review of Biochemistry, 74*, 355–383. http://dx.doi.org/10.1146/annurev.biochem.74.082803.133347.

Inohara, N., Ogura, Y., Chen, F. F., Muto, A., & Nuñez, G. (2001). Human Nod1 confers responsiveness to bacterial lipopolysaccharides. *Journal of Biological Chemistry, 276*(4), 2551–2554. http://dx.doi.org/10.1074/jbc.M009728200.

Inohara, N., Ogura, Y., Fontalba, A., Gutierrez, O., Pons, F., Crespo, J., et al. (2003). Host recognition of bacterial muramyl dipeptide mediated through NOD2. Implications for Crohn's disease. *Journal of Biological Chemistry, 278*(8), 5509–5512. http://dx.doi.org/10.1074/jbc.C200673200.

Jackson, S., Candia, A. F., Delaney, S., Floettmann, S., Wong, C., Campbell, J. D., et al. (2018). First-in-Human study with the inhaled TLR9 oligonucleotide agonist AZD1419 results in interferon responses in the lung, and is safe and well-tolerated. *Clinical Pharmacology & Therapeutics, 104*(2), 335–345. http://dx.doi.org/10.1002/cpt.938.

Jackson, S., Lentino, J., Kopp, J., Murray, L., Ellison, W., Rhee, M., et al. (2018). Immunogenicity of a two-dose investigational hepatitis B vaccine, HBsAg-1018, using a toll-like receptor 9 agonist adjuvant compared with a licensed hepatitis B vaccine in adults. *Vaccine, 36*(5), 668–674. http://dx.doi.org/10.1016/j.vaccine.2017.12.038.

Jakopin, Ž. (2014). Nucleotide-binding oligomerization domain (NOD) inhibitors: A rational approach toward inhibition of NOD signaling pathway. *Journal of Medicinal Chemistry, 57*(16), 6897–6918. http://dx.doi.org/10.1021/jm401841p.

Janssen, H. L. A., Brunetto, M. R., Kim, Y. J., Ferrari, C., Massetto, B., Nguyen, A. H., et al. (2018). Safety, efficacy and pharmacodynamics of vesatolimod (GS-9620) in virally suppressed patients with chronic hepatitis B. *Journal of Hepatology, 68*(3), 431–440. http://dx.doi.org/10.1016/j.jhep.2017.10.027.

Jiang, W., Zhu, F. G., Bhagat, L., Yu, D., Tang, J. X., Kandimalla, E. R., et al. (2013). A Toll-like receptor 7, 8, and 9 antagonist inhibits Th1 and Th17 responses and inflammasome activation in a model of IL-23-induced psoriasis. *Journal of Investigative Dermatology, 133*(7), 1777–1784. http://dx.doi.org/10.1038/jid.2013.57.

Jones, M., Cunningham, M. E., Wing, P., DeSilva, S., Challa, R., Sheri, A., Padmanabhan, S., Iyer, R.p., Korba, B. E., Afdhal, N., & Foster, G. R. (2017). SB9200, a novel agonist of innate immunity, shows potent antiviral activity against resistant HCV variants. *Journal of Medical Virology, 89*(9), 1620–1628.

Junt, T., & Barchet, W. (2015). Translating nucleic acid-sensing pathways into therapies. *Nature Reviews Immunology, 15*(9), 529–544. http://dx.doi.org/10.1038/nri3875.

Kang, J. Y., Nan, X., Jin, M. S., Youn, S. J., Ryu, Y. H., Mah, S., et al. (2009). Recognition of lipopeptide patterns by Toll-like receptor 2-Toll-like receptor 6 heterodimer. *Immunity, 31*(6), 873–884. http://dx.doi.org/10.1016/j.immuni.2009.09.018.

Kanneganti, T. D., Lamkanfi, M., & Núñez, G. (2007). Intracellular NOD-like receptors in host defense and disease. *Immunity, 27*(4), 549–559. http://dx.doi.org/10.1016/j.immuni.2007.10.002.

Kawai, T., & Akira, S. (2006). Innate immune recognition of viral infection. *Nature Immunology, 7*(2), 131–137. http://dx.doi.org/10.1038/ni1303.

Kawai, T., & Akira, S. (2010). The role of pattern-recognition receptors in innate immunity: Update on toll-like receptors. *Nature Immunology, 11*(5), 373–384. http://dx.doi.org/10.1038/ni.1863.

Kersse, K., Bertrand, M. J., Lamkanfi, M., & Vandenabeele, P. (2011). NOD-like receptors and the innate immune system: Coping with danger, damage and death. *Cytokine & Growth Factor Reviews, 22*(5–6), 257–276. http://dx.doi.org/10.1016/j.cytogfr.2011.09.003.

Kim, J. G., Lee, S. J., & Kagnoff, M. F. (2004). Nod1 is an essential signal transducer in intestinal epithelial cells infected with bacteria that avoid recognition by toll-like receptors. *Infection and Immunity, 72*(3), 1487–1495. http://dx.doi.org/10.1128/iai.72.3.1487-1495.2004.

Kim, R. Y., Pinkerton, J. W., Essilfie, A. T., Robertson, A. A. B., Baines, K. J., Brown, A. C., et al. (2017). Role for NLRP3 inflammasome-mediated, IL-1β-dependent responses in severe, steroid-resistant asthma. *American Journal of Respiratory and Critical Care Medicine, 196*(3), 283–297. http://dx.doi.org/10.1164/rccm.201609-1830OC.

Kim, S. J., Chen, Z., Essani, A. B., Elshabrawy, H. A., Volin, M. V., Volkov, S., et al. (2016). Identification of a novel toll-like receptor 7 endogenous ligand in rheumatoid arthritis synovial fluid that can provoke arthritic joint inflammation. *Arthritis & Rheumatism, 68*(5), 1099–1110. http://dx.doi.org/10.1002/art.39544.

Kim, Y. G., Shaw, M. H., Warner, N., Park, J. H., Chen, F., Ogura, Y., et al. (2011). Cutting edge: Crohn's disease-associated Nod2 mutation limits production of proinflammatory cytokines to protect the host from Enterococcus faecalis-induced lethality. *The Journal of Immunology, 187*(6), 2849–2852. http://dx.doi.org/10.4049/jimmunol.1001854.

Kim, Y. K., Shin, J. S., & Nahm, M. H. (2016). NOD-like receptors in infection, immunity, and diseases. *Yonsei Medical Journal, 57*(1), 5–14. http://dx.doi.org/10.3349/ymj.2016.57.1.5.

Kimball, A. B., Krueger, J., Sullivan, T., & Arbeit, R. D. (2013). *IMO-3100, an antagonist of Toll-like receptor (TLR) 7 and TLR9, demonstrates clinical activity in psoriasis patients with 4 weeks of treatment in a phase 2a trials*. Paper presented at the International Investigative Dermatology Meeting, Edinburgh.

Klimek, L., Willers, J., Hammann-Haenni, A., Pfaar, O., Stocker, H., Mueller, P., et al. (2011). Assessment of clinical efficacy of CYT003-QbG10 in patients with allergic rhinoconjunctivitis: A phase IIb study. *Clinical and Experimental Allergy, 41*(9), 1305–1312. http://dx.doi.org/10.1111/j.1365-2222.2011.03783.x.

Klück, V., Jansen, T., Janssen, M., Tengesdal, I. W., Schraa, K., Skouras, D. B., et al. (2020). *olt1177™, an oral nlrp3 inflammasome inhibitor, inhibits acute joint inflammation and circulating il-1β during gout flares in humans*. Paper presented at the European Crystal Network, Paris.

Korolowicz, K. E., Iyer, R. P., Czerwinski, S., Suresh, M., Yang, J., Padmanabhan, S., et al. (2016). Antiviral efficacy and host innate immunity associated with SB 9200 treatment in the Woodchuck model of chronic hepatitis B. *PLoS One, 11*(8), e0161313. http://dx.doi.org/10.1371/journal.pone.0161313.

Kumar, P., Dar, L., Saldiwal, S., Varma, S., Datt Upadhyay, A., Talwar, D., et al. (2014). Intralesional injection of Mycobacterium w vaccine vs imiquimod, 5%, cream in patients with anogenital warts: A randomized clinical trial. *JAMA Dermatology, 150*(10), 1072–1078. http://dx.doi.org/10.1001/jamadermatol.2014.794.

Kuznetsov, N. V., Zargari, A., Gielen, A. W., von Stein, O. D., Musch, E., Befrits, R., et al. (2014). Biomarkers can predict potential clinical responders to DIMS0150 a toll-like receptor 9 agonist in ulcerative colitis patients. *BMC Gastroenterology, 14*, 79. http://dx.doi.org/10.1186/1471-230X-14-79.

Lambrecht, B. N., Hammad, H., & Fahy, J. V. (2019). The cytokines of asthma. *Immunity, 50*(4), 975–991. http://dx.doi.org/10.1016/j.immuni.2019.03.018.

Lawitz, E., Gruener, D., Marbury, T., Hill, J., Webster, L., Hassman, D., et al. (2015). Safety, pharmacokinetics and pharmacodynamics of the oral toll-like receptor 7 agonist GS-9620 in treatment-naive patients with chronic hepatitis C. *Antiviral Therapy, 20*(7), 699–708. http://dx.doi.org/10.3851/IMP2845.

Leadbetter, E. A., Rifkin, I. R., Hohlbaum, A. M., Beaudette, B. C., Shlomchik, M. J., & Marshak-Rothstein, A. (2002). Chromatin-IgG complexes activate B cells by dual engagement of IgM and Toll-like receptors. *Nature, 416*(6881), 603–607. http://dx.doi.org/10.1038/416603a.

Lee, K. H., Biswas, A., Liu, Y. J., & Kobayashi, K. S. (2012). Proteasomal degradation of Nod2 protein mediates tolerance to bacterial cell wall components. *Journal of Biological Chemistry, 287*(47), 39800–39811. http://dx.doi.org/10.1074/jbc.M112.410027.

Lepenies, B., Lee, J., & Sonkaria, S. (2013). Targeting C-type lectin receptors with multivalent carbohydrate ligands. *Advanced Drug Delivery Reviews, 65*(9), 1271–1281. http://dx.doi.org/10.1016/j.addr.2013.05.007.

Lopatin, U., Wolfgang, G., Tumas, D., Frey, C. R., Ohmstede, C., Hesselgesser, J., et al. (2013). Safety, pharmacokinetics and pharmacodynamics of GS-9620, an oral Toll-like receptor 7 agonist. *Antiviral Therapy, 18*(3), 409–418. http://dx.doi.org/10.3851/IMP2548.

Lorenz, E., Patel, D. D., Hartung, T., & Schwartz, D. A. (2002). Toll-like receptor 4 (TLR4)-deficient murine macrophage cell line as an in vitro assay system to show TLR4-independent signaling of Bacteroides fragilis lipopolysaccharide. *Infection and Immunity, 70*(9), 4892–4896. http://dx.doi.org/10.1128/iai.70.9.4892-4896.2002.

Lyn-Cook, B. D., Xie, C., Oates, J., Treadwell, E., Word, B., Hammons, G., et al. (2014). Increased expression of toll-like receptors (TLRs) 7 and 9 and other cytokines in systemic lupus erythematosus (SLE) patients: Ethnic differences and potential new targets for therapeutic drugs. *Molecular Immunology, 61*(1), 38–43. http://dx.doi.org/10.1016/j.molimm.2014.05.001.

Maglinte, D. D., Gourtsoyiannis, N., Rex, D., Howard, T. J., & Kelvin, F. M. (2003). Classification of small bowel Crohn's subtypes based on multimodality imaging. *Radiologic Clinics of North America, 41*(2), 285–303.

Maloy, K. J., & Powrie, F. (2011). Intestinal homeostasis and its breakdown in inflammatory bowel disease. *Nature, 474*(7351), 298–306. http://dx.doi.org/10.1038/nature10208.

Manon, F., Favier, A., Núñez, G., Simorre, J. P., & Cusack, S. (2007). Solution structure of NOD1 CARD and mutational analysis of its interaction with the CARD of downstream kinase RICK. *Journal of Molecular Biology, 365*(1), 160–174. http://dx.doi.org/10.1016/j.jmb.2006.09.067.

Marchetti, C., Swartzwelter, B., Gamboni, F., Neff, C. P., Richter, K., Azam, T., et al. (2018). OLT1177, a β-sulfonyl nitrile compound, safe in humans, inhibits the NLRP3 inflammasome and reverses the metabolic cost of inflammation. *Proceedings of the National Academy of Sciences of the United States of America, 115*(7), E1530–E1539. http://dx.doi.org/10.1073/pnas.1716095115.

Marchetti, C., Swartzwelter, B., Koenders, M. I., Azam, T., Tengesdal, I. W., Powers, N., et al. (2018). NLRP3 inflammasome inhibitor OLT1177 suppresses joint inflammation

in murine models of acute arthritis. *Arthritis Research and Therapy, 20*(1), 169. http://dx.doi.org/10.1186/s13075-018-1664-2.
Martinon, F., & Tschopp, J. (2005). NLRs join TLRs as innate sensors of pathogens. *Trends in Immunology, 26*(8), 447–454. http://dx.doi.org/10.1016/j.it.2005.06.004.
Matsunaga, N., Tsuchimori, N., Matsumoto, T., & Ii, M. (2011). TAK-242 (resatorvid), a small-molecule inhibitor of Toll-like receptor (TLR) 4 signaling, binds selectively to TLR4 and interferes with interactions between TLR4 and its adaptor molecules. *Molecular Pharmacology, 79*(1), 34–41. http://dx.doi.org/10.1124/mol.110.068064.
McInnes, I. B., & Schett, G. (2011). The pathogenesis of rheumatoid arthritis. *New England Journal of Medicine, 365*(23), 2205–2219. http://dx.doi.org/10.1056/NEJMra1004965.
Medzhitov, R. (2008). Origin and physiological roles of inflammation. *Nature, 454*(7203), 428–435. http://dx.doi.org/10.1038/nature07201.
Medzhitov, R., Preston-Hurlburt, P., Kopp, E., Stadlen, A., Chen, C., Ghosh, S., et al. (1998). MyD88 is an adaptor protein in the hToll/IL-1 receptor family signaling pathways. *Molecular Cell, 2*(2), 253–258.
Minang, J. T., Inglefield, J. R., Harris, A. M., Lathey, J. L., Alleva, D. G., Sweeney, D. L., et al. (2014). Enhanced early innate and T cell-mediated responses in subjects immunized with Anthrax Vaccine Adsorbed Plus CPG 7909 (AV7909). *Vaccine, 32*(50), 6847–6854. http://dx.doi.org/10.1016/j.vaccine.2014.01.096.
Mohanan, V., & Grimes, C. L. (2014). The molecular chaperone HSP70 binds to and stabilizes NOD2, an important protein involved in Crohn disease. *Journal of Biological Chemistry, 289*(27), 18987–18998. http://dx.doi.org/10.1074/jbc.M114.557686.
Motwani, M., Pesiridis, S., & Fitzgerald, K. A. (2019). DNA sensing by the cGAS-STING pathway in health and disease. *Nature Reviews Genetics*. http://dx.doi.org/10.1038/s41576-019-0151-1.
Muir, A., Ghalib, R., Lawitz, E., Patel, K., Rodriguez-Torres, M., Sheikh, A., et al. (2010). *A phase 1, multi-center, randomized, placebo-controlled, dose-escalation study OF IMO-2125, a TLR9 agonist, IN hepatitis C-nonresponders*. Paper presented at the International Liver Congress, Vienna.
Mullarkey, M., Rose, J. R., Bristol, J., Kawata, T., Kimura, A., Kobayashi, S., et al. (2003). Inhibition of endotoxin response by e5564, a novel Toll-like receptor 4-directed endotoxin antagonist. *Journal of Pharmacology and Experimental Therapeutics, 304*(3), 1093–1102. http://dx.doi.org/10.1124/jpet.102.044487.
Nestle, F. O., Kaplan, D. H., & Barker, J. (2009). Psoriasis. *New England Journal of Medicine, 361*(5), 496–509. http://dx.doi.org/10.1056/NEJMra0804595.
Nishimura, M., & Naito, S. (2005). Tissue-specific mRNA expression profiles of human toll-like receptors and related genes. *Biological & Pharmaceutical Bulletin, 28*(5), 886–892. http://dx.doi.org/10.1248/bpb.28.886.
O'Neill, L. A., Fitzgerald, K. A., & Bowie, A. G. (2003). The Toll-IL-1 receptor adaptor family grows to five members. *Trends in Immunology, 24*(6), 286–290.
Ogura, Y., Inohara, N., Benito, A., Chen, F. F., Yamaoka, S., & Nunez, G. (2001). Nod2, a Nod1/Apaf-1 family member that is restricted to monocytes and activates NF-kappaB. *Journal of Biological Chemistry, 276*(7), 4812–4818. http://dx.doi.org/10.1074/jbc.M008072200.
Ogura, Y., Lala, S., Xin, W., Smith, E., Dowds, T. A., Chen, F. F., et al. (2003). Expression of NOD2 in Paneth cells: A possible link to Crohn's ileitis. *Gut, 52*(11), 1591–1597. http://dx.doi.org/10.1136/gut.52.11.1591.
Ohto, U., Yamakawa, N., Akashi-Takamura, S., Miyake, K., & Shimizu, T. (2012). Structural analyses of human Toll-like receptor 4 polymorphisms D299G and T399I. *Journal of Biological Chemistry, 287*(48), 40611–40617. http://dx.doi.org/10.1074/jbc.M112.404608.

Oon, S., Wilson, N. J., & Wicks, I. (2016). Targeted therapeutics in SLE: Emerging strategies to modulate the interferon pathway. *Clin Transl Immunology, 5*(5), e79. http://dx.doi.org/10.1038/cti.2016.26.

Oosting, M., Cheng, S. C., Bolscher, J. M., Vestering-Stenger, R., Plantinga, T. S., Verschueren, I. C., et al. (2014). Human TLR10 is an anti-inflammatory pattern-recognition receptor. *Proceedings of the National Academy of Sciences of the United States of America, 111*(42), E4478–E4484. http://dx.doi.org/10.1073/pnas.1410293111.

Opal, S. M., Laterre, P. F., Francois, B., LaRosa, S. P., Angus, D. C., Mira, J. P., et al. (2013). Effect of eritoran, an antagonist of MD2-TLR4, on mortality in patients with severe sepsis: The ACCESS randomized trial. *Journal of the American Medical Association, 309*(11), 1154–1162. http://dx.doi.org/10.1001/jama.2013.2194.

Opitz, B., Püschel, A., Beermann, W., Hocke, A. C., Förster, S., Schmeck, B., et al. (2006). Listeria monocytogenes activated p38 MAPK and induced IL-8 secretion in a nucleotide-binding oligomerization domain 1-dependent manner in endothelial cells. *The Journal of Immunology, 176*(1), 484–490. http://dx.doi.org/10.4049/jimmunol.176.1.484.

Overton, E. T., Goepfert, P. A., Cunningham, P., Carter, W. A., Horvath, J., Young, D., et al. (2014). Intranasal seasonal influenza vaccine and a TLR-3 agonist, rintatolimod, induced cross-reactive IgA antibody formation against avian H5N1 and H7N9 influenza HA in humans. *Vaccine, 32*(42), 5490–5495. http://dx.doi.org/10.1016/j.vaccine.2014.07.078.

Park, J. H., Kim, Y. G., McDonald, C., Kanneganti, T. D., Hasegawa, M., Body-Malapel, M., et al. (2007). RICK/RIP2 mediates innate immune responses induced through Nod1 and Nod2 but not TLRs. *The Journal of Immunology, 178*(4), 2380–2386. http://dx.doi.org/10.4049/jimmunol.178.4.2380.

Poltorak, A., He, X., Smirnova, I., Liu, M. Y., Van Huffel, C., Du, X., et al. (1998). Defective LPS signaling in C3H/HeJ and C57BL/10ScCr mice: Mutations in Tlr4 gene. *Science, 282*(5396), 2085–2088. http://dx.doi.org/10.1126/science.282.5396.2085.

Prodinger, C., Reichelt, J., Bauer, J. W., & Laimer, M. (2019). Epidermolysis bullosa: Advances in research and treatment. *Experimental Dermatology*. http://dx.doi.org/10.1111/exd.13979.

Qureshi, S. T., Gros, P., & Malo, D. (1999). The lps locus: Genetic regulation of host responses to bacterial lipopolysaccharide. *Inflammation Research, 48*(12), 613–620. http://dx.doi.org/10.1007/s000110050511.

Rice, T. W., Wheeler, A. P., Bernard, G. R., Vincent, J. L., Angus, D. C., Aikawa, N., et al. (2010). A randomized, double-blind, placebo-controlled trial of TAK-242 for the treatment of severe sepsis. *Critical Care Medicine, 38*(8), 1685–1694. http://dx.doi.org/10.1097/CCM.0b013e3181e7c5c9.

Rickard, D. J., Sehon, C. A., Kasparcova, V., Kallal, L. A., Haile, P. A., Zeng, X., et al. (2014). Identification of selective small molecule inhibitors of the nucleotide-binding oligomerization domain 1 (NOD1) signaling pathway. *PLoS One, 9*(5), e96737. http://dx.doi.org/10.1371/journal.pone.0096737.

Rickard, D. J., Sehon, C. A., Kasparcova, V., Kallal, L. A., Zeng, X., Montoute, M. N., et al. (2013). Identification of benzimidazole diamides as selective inhibitors of the nucleotide-binding oligomerization domain 2 (NOD2) signaling pathway. *PLoS One, 8*(8), e69619. http://dx.doi.org/10.1371/journal.pone.0069619.

Rock, F. L., Hardiman, G., Timans, J. C., Kastelein, R. A., & Bazan, J. F. (1998). A family of human receptors structurally related to Drosophila Toll. *Proceedings of the National Academy of Sciences of the United States of America, 95*(2), 588–593. http://dx.doi.org/10.1073/pnas.95.2.588.

Rosen, H. R. (2011). Clinical practice. Chronic hepatitis C infection. *New England Journal of Medicine, 364*(25), 2429–2438. http://dx.doi.org/10.1056/NEJMcp1006613.

Royer, C. M., Rudolph, K., Dietsch, G. N., Hershberg, R. M., & Barrett, E. G. (2016). VTX-1463, a novel TLR-8 agonist, attenuates nasal congestion after ragweed challenge in sensitized beagle dogs. *Immunity, Inflammation and Disease, 4*(1), 45–51. http://dx.doi.org/10.1002/iid3.91.

Rudd, B. D., Burstein, E., Duckett, C. S., Li, X., & Lukacs, N. W. (2005). Differential role for TLR3 in respiratory syncytial virus-induced chemokine expression. *Journal of Virology, 79*(6), 3350–3357. http://dx.doi.org/10.1128/JVI.79.6.3350-3357.2005.

Russell, R. K., Nimmo, E. R., & Satsangi, J. (2004). Molecular genetics of Crohn's disease. *Current Opinion in Genetics & Development, 14*(3), 264–270. http://dx.doi.org/10.1016/j.gde.2004.04.004.

Saiag, P., Bauhofer, A., Bouscarat, F., Aquilina, C., Ortonne, J. P., Dupin, N., et al. (2009). Imiquimod 5% cream for external genital or perianal warts in human immunodeficiency virus-positive patients treated with highly active antiretroviral therapy: An open-label, noncomparative study. *British Journal of Dermatology, 161*(4), 904–909. http://dx.doi.org/10.1111/j.1365-2133.2009.09210.x.

Saxena, M., Sabado, R. L., La Mar, M., Mohri, H., Salazar, A. M., Dong, H., et al. (2019). Poly-iclc, a TLR3 agonist, induces transient innate immune responses in patients with treated HIV-infection: A randomized double-blinded placebo controlled trial. *Frontiers in Immunology, 10*, 725. http://dx.doi.org/10.3389/fimmu.2019.00725.

Scichilone, N., Minaldi, C., Santagata, R., Battaglia, S., Camarda, G., & Bellia, V. (2011). Anti-inflammatory effects of pre-seasonal Th1-adjuvant vaccine to Parietaria judaica in asthmatics. *Journal of Asthma and Allergy, 4*, 19–25. http://dx.doi.org/10.2147/JAA.S17784.

Shao, B. Z., Xu, Z. Q., Han, B. Z., Su, D. F., & Liu, C. (2015). NLRP3 inflammasome and its inhibitors: A review. *Frontiers in Pharmacology, 6*, 262. http://dx.doi.org/10.3389/fphar.2015.00262.

Shaw, M. H., Reimer, T., Kim, Y. G., & Nuñez, G. (2008). NOD-like receptors (NLRs): Bona fide intracellular microbial sensors. *Current Opinion in Immunology, 20*(4), 377–382. http://dx.doi.org/10.1016/j.coi.2008.06.001.

Shay, D. K., Holman, R. C., Roosevelt, G. E., Clarke, M. J., & Anderson, L. J. (2001). Bronchiolitis-associated mortality and estimates of respiratory syncytial virus-associated deaths among US children, 1979-1997. *The Journal of Infectious Diseases, 183*(1), 16–22. http://dx.doi.org/10.1086/317655.

Shimazu, R., Akashi, S., Ogata, H., Nagai, Y., Fukudome, K., Miyake, K., et al. (1999). MD-2, a molecule that confers lipopolysaccharide responsiveness on Toll-like receptor 4. *Journal of Experimental Medicine, 189*(11), 1777–1782. http://dx.doi.org/10.1084/jem.189.11.1777.

Shiokawa, M., Yamasaki, S., & Saijo, S. (2017). C-type lectin receptors in anti-fungal immunity. *Current Opinion in Microbiology, 40*, 123–130. http://dx.doi.org/10.1016/j.mib.2017.11.004.

Silhavy, T. J., Kahne, D., & Walker, S. (2010). The bacterial cell envelope. *Cold Spring Harbor Perspectives in Biology, 2*(5), a000414. http://dx.doi.org/10.1101/cshperspect.a000414.

Silkoff, P. E., Flavin, S., Gordon, R., Loza, M. J., Sterk, P. J., Lutter, R., et al. (2018). Toll-like receptor 3 blockade in rhinovirus-induced experimental asthma exacerbations: A randomized controlled study. *The Journal of Allergy and Clinical Immunology, 141*(4), 1220–1230. http://dx.doi.org/10.1016/j.jaci.2017.06.027.

Simms, L. A., Doecke, J. D., Walsh, M. D., Huang, N., Fowler, E. V., & Radford-Smith, G. L. (2008). Reduced alpha-defensin expression is associated with inflammation and not NOD2 mutation status in ileal Crohn's disease. *Gut, 57*(7), 903–910. http://dx.doi.org/10.1136/gut.2007.142588.

Soriano, V., Barreiro, P., Benitez, L., Peña, J. M., & de Mendoza, C. (2017). New antivirals for the treatment of chronic hepatitis B. *Expert Opinion on Investigational Drugs, 26*(7), 843–851. http://dx.doi.org/10.1080/13543784.2017.1333105.

Suárez-Fariñas, M., Arbeit, R., Jiang, W., Ortenzio, F. S., Sullivan, T., & Krueger, J. G. (2013). Suppression of molecular inflammatory pathways by Toll-like receptor 7, 8, and 9 antagonists in a model of IL-23-induced skin inflammation. *PLoS One, 8*(12), e84634. http://dx.doi.org/10.1371/journal.pone.0084634.

Suresh, M., Korolowicz, K. E., Balarezo, M., Iyer, R. P., Padmanabhan, S., Cleary, D., et al. (2017). Antiviral efficacy and host immune response induction during sequential treatment with SB 9200 followed by entecavir in Woodchucks. *PLoS One, 12*(1), e0169631. http://dx.doi.org/10.1371/journal.pone.0169631.

Tabeta, K., Georgel, P., Janssen, E., Du, X., Hoebe, K., Crozat, K., et al. (2004). Toll-like receptors 9 and 3 as essential components of innate immune defense against mouse cytomegalovirus infection. *Proceedings of the National Academy of Sciences of the United States of America, 101*(10), 3516–3521. http://dx.doi.org/10.1073/pnas.0400525101.

Tanimura, N., Saitoh, S., Matsumoto, F., Akashi-Takamura, S., & Miyake, K. (2008). Roles for LPS-dependent interaction and relocation of TLR4 and TRAM in TRIF-signaling. *Biochemical and Biophysical Research Communications, 368*(1), 94–99. http://dx.doi.org/10.1016/j.bbrc.2008.01.061.

Taylor, D. N., Treanor, J. J., Sheldon, E. A., Johnson, C., Umlauf, S., Song, L., et al. (2012). Development of VAX128, a recombinant hemagglutinin (HA) influenza-flagellin fusion vaccine with improved safety and immune response. *Vaccine, 30*(39), 5761–5769. http://dx.doi.org/10.1016/j.vaccine.2012.06.086.

Taylor, D. N., Treanor, J. J., Strout, C., Johnson, C., Fitzgerald, T., Kavita, U., et al. (2011). Induction of a potent immune response in the elderly using the TLR-5 agonist, flagellin, with a recombinant hemagglutinin influenza-flagellin fusion vaccine (VAX125, STF2.HA1 SI). *Vaccine, 29*(31), 4897–4902. http://dx.doi.org/10.1016/j.vaccine.2011.05.001.

Taylor, F. B. (1997). Tissue factor and thrombin in posttraumatic systemic inflammatory response syndrome. *Critical Care Medicine, 25*(11), 1774–1775. http://dx.doi.org/10.1097/00003246-199711000-00006.

Thompson, A., Roberts, S., Cheng, W., Angus, P., Visvanathan, K., Iyer, R., et al. (2015). *SB 9200, A novel immunomodulator for patients with viral hepatitis: Phase 1 mad study in patients with hepatitis c virus (HCV) infection.*

Tidswell, M., Tillis, W., Larosa, S. P., Lynn, M., Wittek, A. E., Kao, R., et al. (2010). Phase 2 trial of eritoran tetrasodium (E5564), a toll-like receptor 4 antagonist, in patients with severe sepsis. *Critical Care Medicine, 38*(1), 72–83. http://dx.doi.org/10.1097/CCM.0b013e3181b07b78.

Tigno-Aranjuez, J. T., Asara, J. M., & Abbott, D. W. (2010). Inhibition of RIP2's tyrosine kinase activity limits NOD2-driven cytokine responses. *Genes & Development, 24*(23), 2666–2677. http://dx.doi.org/10.1101/gad.1964410.

Ting, J. P., Lovering, R. C., Alnemri, E. S., Bertin, J., Boss, J. M., Davis, B. K., et al. (2008). The NLR gene family: A standard nomenclature. *Immunity, 28*(3), 285–287. http://dx.doi.org/10.1016/j.immuni.2008.02.005.

Treanor, J. J., Taylor, D. N., Tussey, L., Hay, C., Nolan, C., Fitzgerald, T., et al. (2010). Safety and immunogenicity of a recombinant hemagglutinin influenza-flagellin fusion vaccine (VAX125) in healthy young adults. *Vaccine, 28*(52), 8268–8274. http://dx.doi.org/10.1016/j.vaccine.2010.10.009.

Tsitoura, D., Ambery, C., Price, M., Powley, W., Garthside, S., Biggadike, K., et al. (2015). Early clinical evaluation of the intranasal TLR7 agonist GSK2245035: Use of translational biomarkers to guide dosing and confirm target engagement. *Clinical Pharmacology & Therapeutics, 98*(4), 369–380. http://dx.doi.org/10.1002/cpt.157.

Tsokos, G. C. (2011). Systemic lupus erythematosus. *New England Journal of Medicine, 365*(22), 2110–2121. http://dx.doi.org/10.1056/NEJMra1100359.
Turley, C. B., Rupp, R. E., Johnson, C., Taylor, D. N., Wolfson, J., Tussey, L., et al. (2011). Safety and immunogenicity of a recombinant M2e-flagellin influenza vaccine (STF2.4xM2e) in healthy adults. *Vaccine, 29*(32), 5145–5152. http://dx.doi.org/10.1016/j.vaccine.2011.05.041.
Uematsu, S., Fujimoto, K., Jang, M. H., Yang, B. G., Jung, Y. J., Nishiyama, M., et al. (2008). Regulation of humoral and cellular gut immunity by lamina propria dendritic cells expressing Toll-like receptor 5. *Nature Immunology, 9*(7), 769–776. http://dx.doi.org/10.1038/ni.1622.
Vandenabeele, P., & Bertrand, M. J. (2012). The role of the IAP E3 ubiquitin ligases in regulating pattern-recognition receptor signalling. *Nature Reviews Immunology, 12*(12), 833–844. http://dx.doi.org/10.1038/nri3325.
Verma, R., Verma, N., & Paul, J. (2013). Expression of inflammatory genes in the colon of ulcerative colitis patients varies with activity both at the mRNA and protein level. *European Cytokine Network, 24*(3), 130–138. http://dx.doi.org/10.1684/ecn.2013.0343.
Vibholm, L., Schleimann, M. H., Højen, J. F., Benfield, T., Offersen, R., Rasmussen, K., et al. (2017). Short-course toll-like receptor 9 agonist treatment impacts innate immunity and plasma viremia in individuals with human immunodeficiency virus infection. *Clinical Infectious Diseases, 64*(12), 1686–1695. http://dx.doi.org/10.1093/cid/cix201.
Vibholm, L. K., Konrad, C. V., Schleimann, M. H., Frattari, G., Winckelmann, A., Klastrup, V., et al. (2019). Effects of 24-week Toll-like receptor 9 agonist treatment in HIV type 1+ individuals. *AIDS, 33*(8), 1315–1325. http://dx.doi.org/10.1097/QAD.0000000000002213.
Viglianti, G. A., Lau, C. M., Hanley, T. M., Miko, B. A., Shlomchik, M. J., & Marshak-Rothstein, A. (2003). Activation of autoreactive B cells by CpG dsDNA. *Immunity, 19*(6), 837–847.
Wally, V., Hovnanian, A., Ly, J., Buckova, H., Brunner, V., Lettner, T., et al. (2018). Diacerein orphan drug development for epidermolysis bullosa simplex: A phase 2/3 randomized, placebo-controlled, double-blind clinical trial. *Journal of the American Academy of Dermatology, 78*(5). http://dx.doi.org/10.1016/j.jaad.2018.01.019, 892-901.e897.
Wally, V., Kitzmueller, S., Lagler, F., Moder, A., Hitzl, W., Wolkersdorfer, M., et al. (2013). Topical diacerein for epidermolysis bullosa: A randomized controlled pilot study. *Orphanet Journal of Rare Diseases, 8*, 69. http://dx.doi.org/10.1186/1750-1172-8-69.
Walsh, R., Hammond, R., Jackson, K., Edwards, R., Macfarlane, C., Iyer, R., et al. (2018). *Effects of SB9200 (Inarigivir) therapy on immune responses in patients with chronic hepatitis B.* Paper presented at the International Liver Congress, Paris.
Watanabe, T., Asano, N., Kitani, A., Fuss, I. J., Chiba, T., & Strober, W. (2011). Activation of type I IFN signaling by NOD1 mediates mucosal host defense against *Helicobacter pylori* infection. *Gut Microbes, 2*(1), 61–65. http://dx.doi.org/10.4161/gmic.2.1.15162.
Wehkamp, J., Harder, J., Weichenthal, M., Schwab, M., Schäffeler, E., Schlee, M., et al. (2004). NOD2 (CARD15) mutations in Crohn's disease are associated with diminished mucosal alpha-defensin expression. *Gut, 53*(11), 1658–1664. http://dx.doi.org/10.1136/gut.2003.032805.
Wehkamp, J., Salzman, N. H., Porter, E., Nuding, S., Weichenthal, M., Petras, R. E., et al. (2005). Reduced Paneth cell alpha-defensins in ileal Crohn's disease. *Proceedings of the National Academy of Sciences of the United States of America, 102*(50), 18129–18134. http://dx.doi.org/10.1073/pnas.0505256102.
Worm, M., Higenbottam, T., Pfaar, O., Mösges, R., Aberer, W., Gunawardena, K., et al. (2018). Randomized controlled trials define shape of dose response for Pollinex Quattro Birch allergoid immunotherapy. *Allergy, 73*(9), 1812–1822. http://dx.doi.org/10.1111/all.13478.

Yamamoto, M., Sato, S., Hemmi, H., Hoshino, K., Kaisho, T., Sanjo, H., et al. (2003). Role of adaptor TRIF in the MyD88-independent toll-like receptor signaling pathway. *Science, 301*(5633), 640–643. http://dx.doi.org/10.1126/science.1087262.

Zakeri, A., & Russo, M. (2018). Dual role of toll-like receptors in human and experimental asthma models. *Frontiers in Immunology, 9*, 1027. http://dx.doi.org/10.3389/fimmu.2018.01027.

Zhong, Y., Kinio, A., & Saleh, M. (2013). Functions of NOD-like receptors in human diseases. *Frontiers in Immunology, 4*, 333. http://dx.doi.org/10.3389/fimmu.2013.00333.

Zhu, F. G., Jiang, W., Bhagat, L., Wang, D., Yu, D., Tang, J. X., et al. (2013). A novel antagonist of Toll-like receptors 7, 8 and 9 suppresses lupus disease-associated parameters in NZBW/F1 mice. *Autoimmunity, 46*(7), 419–428. http://dx.doi.org/10.3109/08916934.2013.798651.

Zielen, S., Gabrielpillai, J., Herrmann, E., Schulze, J., Schubert, R., & Rosewich, M. (2018). Long-term effect of monophosphoryl lipid A adjuvanted specific immunotherapy in patients with grass pollen allergy. *Immunotherapy, 10*(7), 529–536. http://dx.doi.org/10.2217/imt-2018-0004.

Zurek, B., Proell, M., Wagner, R. N., Schwarzenbacher, R., & Kufer, T. A. (2012). Mutational analysis of human NOD1 and NOD2 NACHT domains reveals different modes of activation. *Innate Immunity, 18*(1), 100–111. http://dx.doi.org/10.1177/1753425910394002.

CHAPTER FOUR

Glycosylation changes in inflammatory diseases

Sophie Groux-Degroote, Sumeyye Cavdarli, Kenji Uchimura, Fabrice Allain and Philippe Delannoy*

University Lille, CNRS, UMR 8576 - UGSF - Unite de Glycobiologie Structurale et Fonctionnelle, F-59000 Lille, France

*Corresponding author: E-mail: philippe.delannoy@univ-lille.fr

Contents

Advances in Protein Chemistry and Structural Biology, Volume 119
ISSN 1876-1623
https://doi.org/10.1016/bs.apcsb.2019.08.008

Abstract

Glycosylation is one of the most important modifications of proteins and lipids, and cell surface glycoconjugates are thought to play important roles in a variety of biological functions including cell-cell and cell-substrate interactions, bacterial adhesion, cell immunogenicity and cell signaling. Alterations of glycosylation are observed in a number of inflammatory diseases. Pro-inflammatory cytokines have been shown to modulate cell surface glycosylation by regulating the expression of glycosyltransferases and sulfotransferases involved in the biosynthesis of glycan chains, inducing the expression of specific carbohydrate antigens at the cell surface that can be recognized by different types of lectins or by bacterial adhesins, contributing to the development of diseases. Glycosylation can also regulate biological functions of immune cells by recruiting leukocytes to inflammation sites with pro- or anti-inflammatory effects. Cell surface proteoglycans provide a large panel of binding sites for many mediators of inflammation, and regulate their bio-availability and functions. In this review, we summarize the current knowledge of the glycosylation changes occurring in mucin type O-linked glycans, glycosaminoglycans, as well as in glycosphingolipids, with a particular focus on cystic fibrosis and neurodegenerative diseases, and their consequences on cell interactions and disease progression.

1. Introduction

Glycosylation is one of the most important modifications of proteins and lipids, and cell surface glycoconjugates are known to play important roles in a variety of biological functions including cell-cell and cell-substrate interactions, viruses and bacterial adhesion, cell immunogenicity and cell signaling.

The biosynthesis of the glycan moiety of glycoconjugates is a dynamic process that starts in the endoplasmic reticulum and carries on in the Golgi apparatus. Glycosylation process involves a large number of specific glycosyltransferases, glycosidases, sugar-nucleotide transporters and protein chaperones; the final glycan structures depend on the level of expression of these different enzymes/transporters/chaperones, which is mainly regulated at the transcriptional level. The glycan structures are highly diversified and the glycans can be further modified by the addition of functional groups such as sulfate or acetyl groups, increasing again the diversity of structures exposed at the cell surface or secreted in the extracellular medium. The periphery of *N*– and *O*-glycan chains are usually substituted by blood group related carbohydrate antigens, the structures of which depend largely on the cell type, differentiation and developmental stage. The specific carbohydrate epitopes expressed at the cell surface can serve as ligands for different types of proteins including lectins, antibodies or bacterial adhesins, and regulate the biological functions of the cells.

Glycan structures can be modified in pathologic conditions such as cancers or inflammatory diseases. These changes of cell glycosylation are mainly supported by the deregulation of the expression of glycosyltransferase genes and pro-inflammatory cytokines have been shown to modulate cell surface glycosylation by regulating the expression of glycosyltransferases and sulfotransferases involved in the biosynthesis of glycan chains. These changes of glycan structures expressed at the cell surface modulate the interactions of the cells with the environment (immune cells, pathogens) and contribute to the development of the disease. Structural modifications of glycosaminoglycans (GAGs) are observed in a number of several inflammatory diseases. GAGs are ubiquitously found on the cell surface as well as in the extracellular matrices (ECM) as negatively charged linear polysaccharides. Their anionic properties and the diversity of structures provide a large panel of binding sites for different kinds of molecules including mediators of inflammation, regulating their bio-availability and functions. Finally, gangliosides, a subclass of glycosphingolipids carrying one or more sialic acid residues, are also modified in their structure and composition in inflammatory diseases. Gangliosides are located in the outer leaflet of the plasma membrane, forming lipid rafts together with cholesterol, phospholipids, interacting with transmembrane proteins and regulating major cell signaling pathways. The biosynthesis of gangliosides can be also impaired in inflammatory conditions, especially in neurodegenerative disorders, with consequences on the regulation of receptor tyrosine kinases (RTKs) signaling.

2. *O*-glycosylation changes in chronic inflammation

2.1 Cystic fibrosis airways: how inflammation modifies O-glycosylation and paves the way to chronic bacterial infections

Cystic fibrosis (CF) is the most common autosomal recessive genetic disease among Caucasians. This disease is linked to defects in the gene that encodes the cystic fibrosis transmembrane conductance regulator (CFTR) protein, which serves as a cAMP-regulated chloride ion transmembrane channel (Riordan et al., 1989). Defects in CFTR result in general exocrinopathy, and affect numerous tissues and organs, including gastrointestinal, airway, hepatobiliary, pancreas, reproductive, salivary tissues, but the major cause of death in most CF patients is the devastating lung disease.

Lung pathology is characterized by early inflammation and infection by pathogens such as *Staphylococcus aureus* and *Hemophilus influenzae*. As the disease progresses, chronic and vigorous inflammation combined with airways plugging by thick and infected mucus, lead to progressive lung damage and failure. Chronic lung infection in CF patients usually involves multiple bacterial species but is frequently dominated by *Pseudomonas aeruginosa*. There is growing evidence that the preferential infection by *P. aeruginosa* could be linked to the sustained inflammation in CF lungs. Pro-inflammatory mediators present in the respiratory tract of CF patients can modulate the expression of specific carbohydrate epitopes present on bronchial mucins that are preferential receptors for *P. aeruginosa* (Colomb et al., 2012; 2014).

2.1.1 Mucin type bronchial O-glycan alterations in cystic fibrosis

2.1.1.1 Biosynthesis of bronchial mucins

Bronchial mucins are the major component of the bronchial mucus that protects the underlying mucosa from inhaled particles and pathogens, and constitutes an important part of the innate immune system. Mucins are a family of high molecular weight heavily *O*-glycosylated glycoproteins, which fulfill multiple biological functions. Because of their rheological properties, they serve as a protective barrier for the underlying bronchial epithelium, but also fulfill signaling functions (Lakshmanan et al., 2015).

The human *MUC* gene family encodes 21 mucin-type glycoproteins, which are recognized by the Human Genome Organization gene nomenclature committee (http://www.genenames.org). The protein backbone of the mucin molecule, also called apomucin, is composed of a variable number of tandem repeats rich in proline and hydroxylated amino acids (threonine and/or serine) (PTS domains), as well as cysteine-rich regions at the N— and C-termini, but also interspersed between the PTS domains (Dekker, Rossen, Buller, & Einerhand, 2002). Mucins can be divided into two major subgroups: secreted mucins and tethered membrane-bound mucins. The subgroup of secreted mucins gathers five oligomeric gel-forming mucins (MUC2, MUC5AC, MUC5B, MUC6, and MUC19) as well as two non-polymeric mucin-type glycoproteins (MUC7 and MUC8) (Thornton, Rousseau, & McGuckin, 2008). The mucin genes mostly expressed in the respiratory tract encode membrane-bound MUC1 and MUC4, and secreted MUC5AC, MUC5B, MUC19, MUC2, MUC7. In normal conditions, the secreted polymeric mucins MUC5AC and MUC5B provide the organizing framework of the airways mucus gel. They are the major contributors to its rheological properties and to an optimal defense of the respiratory tract toward aggressions.

MUC5AC and MUC5B synthesis and secretion are modulated by inflammatory factors such as neutrophil elastase, bacteria, and cytokines (Hauber, Foley, & Hamid, 2006). Modifications in bronchial mucin biosynthesis, secretion or O-glycosylation have been demonstrated in several pathologies, including lung cancer, but also chronic obstructive bronchial diseases (COPD), asthma and CF (Voynow, Gendler, & Rose, 2006). In most cases, these changes induce unfavorable modifications of bronchial mucus viscosity, resulting in impaired mucociliary clearance and increased infection by viruses and bacteria, which use modified sugar chains as receptors.

Mucin carbohydrate chains are synthesized by the sequential action of Golgi-localized glycosyltransferases. The first step of mucin O-glycosylation is the transfer of the first N– acetylgalactosamine (GalNAc) residue to the hydroxyl group of a serine or threonine from the apomucin, catalyzed by one of 20 UDP-GalNAc: polypeptide N-acetylgalactosaminyltransferases (ppGalNAcT) characterized in humans (Schjoldager & Clausen, 2012). This GalNAc-*O*-Ser/Thr linkage provides the starting point for the elongation of the oligosaccharide chains, leading to numerous and various linear or branched glycans that can contain galactose (Gal), N-acetylglucosamine (GlcNAc), fucose (Fuc), sialic acids (*N*-acetylneuraminic acid, Neu5Ac) residues and also sulfate groups. Terminal structures corresponding to histo-blood groups H/A/B determinants, and to Lewis type structures (Lewis^a, Lewis^b, Lewis^x or Lewis^y) and their sialylated and/or sulfated derivatives, have been characterized in bronchial mucins (Degroote et al., 2003; Lo-Guidice et al., 1994) (Fig. 1).

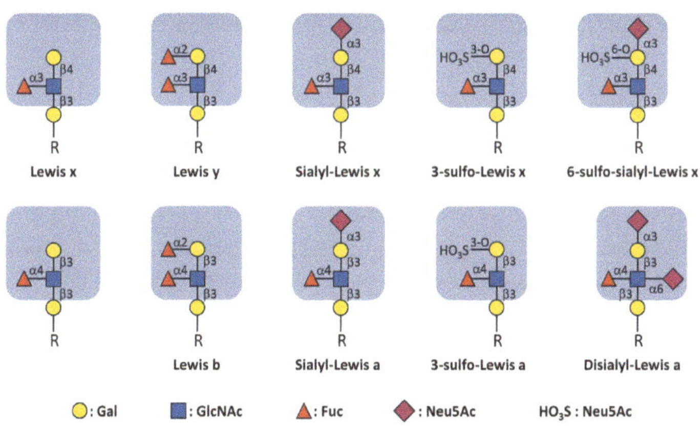

Fig. 1 ***Major types of carbohydrate structures present at the periphery of bronchial mucin O– glycan chains.*** Sialylated and/or sulfated derivatives of the Lewis epitope can be present on terminal type 1 (Galβ1-3GlcNAc) or type 2 (Galβ1-4GlcNAc) disaccharides.

2.1.1.2 Alteration of glycosylation and sulfation of CF glycoconjugates influences *P. aeruginosa*

Defects in glycosylation and sulfation of glycoconjugates from CF cells or CF patients have been described for decades. Notably, bronchial mucins purified from the sputum of CF patients are more sulfated, sialylated and fucosylated than those from non-CF individuals. Increased sulfation has also been described in salivary and intestinal mucins from CF patients (Boat, Cheng, & Wood, 1977; Carnoy et al., 1993; Wesley, Forstner, Qureshi, Mantle, & Forstner, 1983). Mass spectrometry and NMR analysis of purified carbohydrate chains from CF and non CF patients has shown that CF bronchial mucins contained more sialylated and sulfated *O*-glycans than non CF mucins, with increased amounts of sialyl Lewis x (sLe^x) and 6-sulfo- sialyl Lewis x (6-sulfo-sLe^x) structures (Lo-Guidice et al., 1994; Degroote et al., 2003; Xia, Royall, Damera, Sachdev, & Cummings, 2005). Interestingly, studies regarding the glycosylation of bronchial mucins purified from infected versus Non infected patients suffering from CF or other lung pathologies, showed that the sLe^x structure was over-expressed on bronchial mucins from all severely infected patients, regardless of the nature of the disease (Davril et al., 1999). In other studies, the sLe^x and 6-sulfo-sLe^x determinants have been described as preferential ligands for *P. aeruginosa,* and their over-expression in CF bronchial mucins could therefore contribute to the specificity and the chronicity of CF airways infection by these bacteria (Scharfman et al., 1999, 2000).

Interestingly, it seems that glycosylation of membrane-bound CF glycoconjugates and secreted glycoconjugates are differently affected. In particular, membrane glycoconjugates from CF epithelial cells are less sialylated compared to wild-type (WT) cells (Rhim, Stoykova, Glick, & Scanlin, 2001). Since CFTR is not expressed by mucin-secreting cells, defects in *CFTR* expression cannot be directly responsible for the glycosylation modifications of secreted bronchial mucins. The chronic and unresolved lung inflammation that characterizes CF and the abundant literature on the effects of inflammation on glycosylation, especially sialylation, was the starting point to various studies regarding the influence of lung inflammation in CF patients on glycosylation and sulfation of bronchial mucins (Van Dijk & Mackiewicz, 1995).

2.1.2 CF airways inflammation

2.1.2.1 Inflammation and its genesis in CF

In CF airways, mutations in *CFTR* induce defects in ion transport across the epithelium, leading to a decrease in airway surface liquid (ASL) hydration

(Boucher, 2007). This altered ASL composition impairs mucociliary clearance, which is one of the basic innate immune defense mechanism in airways. This disruption of respiratory host defenses increases the susceptibility of CF patients to bacterial infection, subsequent inflammation, and mucus accumulation that will progressively alter lung function and be the major cause of mortality in patients. In early life, repeated infections, mainly by *Haemophilus influenza* and *S. aureus,* pave the way to chronic *P. aeruginosa* infections, reducing the quality and expectancy of life.

However, the lung pathology in CF patients is characterized by an exaggerated inflammatory response, with a large infiltration of neutrophils aiways (Elizur, Cannon, & Ferkol, 2008). These neutrophils are unable to completely clear bacteria, and at the same time they secrete proteases, reactive oxygen species (ROS) and form neutrophil extracellular traps (NET), leading to progressive alteration of lung function and tissue destruction. The concept has emerged that the early and progressive uncontrolled inflammatory response in CF airway is excessive relative to the bacterial burden, worsens host defenses and airway obstruction, and contributes to progressive loss in lung function instead of improving it (Roesch, Nichols, & Chmiel, 2018).

Numerous defects in the inflammatory response have been associated with CFTR deficiency, including dysregulation in innate and acquired immunity, abnormalities in various transcription factors signaling, in lipid expression and signaling, as well as altered kinase and Toll-like receptor (TLR) responses (Cantin, Hartl, Konstan, & Chmiel, 2015). Increased neutrophils, as well as increased concentrations of neutrophil elastase and pro-inflammatory cytokines (TNF, IL-6) were reported in the bronchoalveolar fluid (BAL) of very young children with CF, in the absence of any detectable pathogen (Khan et al., 1995), suggesting that inflammation occurs very early in life and does not necessarily result from bacterial infection. CF airways contain increased amounts of pro-inflammatory mediators, such as TNF, IL-1β, IL-6, IL-8, IL-17, IL-33, GM-CSF, G-CSF (Nichols & Chmiel, 2015). IL-17 is markedly increased in the CF lung and promotes inflammatory cell signaling in response to noxious stimuli (Dubin, McAllister, & Kolls, 2007). Moreover, CF mice had greater concentrations of IL-17, pro-inflammatory cytokines, and neutrophils isolated from BAL than did WT mice despite similar bacterial burdens (Bayes, Ritchie, & Evans, 2016). IL-17 present in excessive amounts, particularly in the context of chronic infection in CF respiratory tract, could contribute to chronic inflammation through its ability to promote neutrophil influx.

This imbalance between pro- and anti-inflammatory cytokines is largely linked to their altered secretion by CF cells: different types of cells with defective CFTR were shown to secrete increased amounts of pro-inflammatory cytokines (IL-1β, IL-6, IL-8), as well as decreased anti-inflammatory cytokines, such as IL-10 (Bonfield, Konstan, & Berger, 1999). For example, blood and lung neutrophils from CF patients synthesize high levels of IL-8 compared to controls, which are even increased by lipopolysaccharide (LPS) treatment, suggesting that infection can contribute to perpetuating the "vicious circle of inflammation" in CF (Conese Assael, 2006; Corvol et al., 2008). In conclusion, there is more and more evidence that the exaggerated/deregulated inflammatory response in CF patients/cells is at least partially directly linked to CFTR deficiency, although the mechanisms involved are not fully understood.

Why a defective CFTR protein can induce an exaggerated and uncontrolled inflammatory response in CF patients, especially in the respiratory tract, is still not well understood, but it is now accepted that CFTR mutation can be considered *per se* as a real cause of inflammatory disease. Weber et al. suggest that AF^{508}CFTR with impaired folding and activity accumulates in the ER, resulting in NFκB activation and increased IL-8 synthesis, even in the absence of bacteria (Weber, Soong, Bryan, Saba, & Prince, 2001). Another study suggests that mutations in *CFTR* can affect the antioxidant defenses in the lung, creating an antioxidant imbalance and contributing to the exaggerated inflammatory response observed in CF (Velsor, van Heeckeren, & Day, 2001). Levels of ROS are also affected in CFTR defective cells or organs and could be involved in the initiation or the chronicity of inflammation. Defects in CFTR lead to increased ROS and to mitochondrial oxidative stress in the lungs of CF mice. Increased ROS levels in CF cells could activate the MAPK pathway and induce the expression of inflammation-related genes (Velsor, Kariya, Kachadourian, & Day, 2006).

Many reports indicate that ceramide accumulation in CF significantly contributes to sustaining hyperinflammation and inability to fight lung infection (Ghidoni, Caretti, & Signorelli, 2015). The synthesis of ceramide or its metabolites (sphingosine-1-phosphate) can result from the activation of different pathways. These molecules subsequently act as second messengers: they can activate the apoptotic cascade, the NFκB pathway, as well as pro-inflammatory cytokines up-regulation, and modulate immune cells functions. Ceramides and their derivatives contribute therefore to chronic inflammation and increased neutrophils and macrophages in the lungs (Xu, Krause, Limberis, Worgall, & Worgall, 2013).

2.1.2.2 Influence of pro-inflammatory cytokines on the expression and activity of glycosyltransferases and sulfotransferases

Several studies have shown that the pro-inflammatory cytokine TNF, which is notably increased is CF aiways, can up-regulate the expression and activities of several sialyl-, fucosyl- and sulfotransferases in different cultures bronchial cell or tissues (Delmotte et al., 2001). TNF increased the expression of α2,3-sialyltransferase *ST3GAL3* and *ST3GAL4* genes and the overall α2,3-sialyltransferase activity, which could explain the over-sialylation and sLe^x over-expression on human airway mucins of patients with severe lung infection such as those with CF (Delmotte et al., 2002). TNF also increased GlcNAc-6-*O*-sulfotransferase and Gal-3-*O*-sulfotransferase activities in human bronchial mucosa, contributing to the increased sulfate content in mucins observed in CF.

Other inflammatory mediators present in CF airways could also modulate glycosyltransferase and sulfotransferase genes expression, thereby contributing to the altered glycosylation and sulfation of CF bronchial mucins. In a model of bronchial explants, interleukins IL-6 and IL-8 increase the expression of several α1,3/4-fucosyltransferases genes, α2,3-sialyltransferases genes (notably *ST3GAL4)* and GlcNAc-6-*O*-sulfotransferases genes. In parallel, IL-6 and IL-8 treatment induced the over-expression of sLe^x and 6-sulfo-sLe^x epitopes on bronchial high-molecular-mass proteins, including membrane bound mucin MUC4 (Groux-Degroote et al., 2008). These results indicate that multiple inflammatory mediators, including TNF, IL-6 and IL-8, may contribute to over-expression of the sLe^x and 6-sulfo-sLe^x epitopes on CF bronchial mucins, and to increased *P. aeruginosa* adhesion.

2.1.3 Signaling pathways involved in the regulation of sialyl Lewis^x biosynthesis by TNF in the human bronchial mucosa

The molecular mechanisms and signaling pathways involved in the regulation of glycosyltransferase genes by inflammatory mediators are largely unknown, but seem to occur mostly at the transcriptional level. Several studies have been performed to unravel the mechanisms underlying sLe^x over-expression in CF airways, focusing on TNF-induced up-regulation of glycosyltransferase genes in the bronchial mucosa.

TNF binding to its receptor is known to activate of different signaling pathways, including the NFκB and MAPK pathways (Baud & Karin, 2001). In NCI—H292 human pulmonary carcinoma cells, the inhibition of the phosphoinositide-phospholipase C (PI-PLC) pathway represses TNF-induced over-expression of several glycosyltransferase genes involved in sLe^x biosynthesis on mucin-type *O*– glycans: the α2,3-sialyltransferase gene *ST3GAL4*, the α1,3-fucosyltransferase gene *FUT3* and core 2/4 synthase gene *GCNT4* (Ishibashi, Inouye, Okano, & Taniguchi, 2005). It is likely that in NCI–H292 cells, a common signaling pathway, which depends on the PI-PLC pathway rather than the NFκB pathway, is involved in the regulation of these three genes and of sLe^x expression.

TNF was also shown to up-regulate the sialyltransferase gene *ST3GAL4* in A549 human lung epithelial cells and in human bronchial explants, *via* other signaling pathways. In these models, TNF activates the p38/ERK and downstream MSK1/2 pathways, increasing the expression of *ST3GAL4* transcript isoform BX, and of the sLe^x epitope on glycoproteins (Colomb et al., 2012; 2014). An intronic ATF2-responsive element present in *ST3GAL4* gene mediates TNF-induced *ST3GAL4* over-expression, which results in sLe^x increase on human bronchial mucins (Colomb et al., 2016).

Moreover, TNF treatment was able to modify *P. aeruginosa* adhesion to lung cancer cells. The FliD/sLe^x-dependent adhesion of two strains of *P. aeruginosa* was increased after TNF treatment in a sialic acid-dependent manner, demonstrating the relationship between *ST3GAL4* over-expression and bacterial adhesion (Colomb et al., 2014). *P. aeruginosa* toxin pyocyanin itself is able to modulate sLe^x expression on mucins from NCI–H292 cells, *via* a TNF-mediated PI-PLC-dependent pathway, leading to an increased binding of *P. aeruginosa* (Jeffries et al., 2016).

2.2 Mucins in inflammatory bowel diseases

Crohn's disease and ulcerative colitis (UC), the two forms of chronic human inflammatory bowel diseases (IBD), are both characterized by a chronic inflammation of parts of the gastrointestinal (GI) mucosa. Multiple factors are involved in the development of Crohn's disease and UC, such as genetic and epigenetic factors, immunological, environmental, but also alterations in the gut microbiote.

In both diseases, cytokines play a major role in the pathogenesis, and the imbalance between pro- and anti-inflammatory cytokines may contribute to unresolved inflammation, disease progression and progressive tissue destruction (Neurath, 2014). In IBD, microbial dysbiosis results in uncontrolled bowel inflammation, partially because the barrier formed by the intestinal mucus and the innate immune system is compromised. The main function of the intestinal mucus is to form a protective barrier between the epithelium and the intestinal lumen. The major intestinal mucin is gel-forming MUC2. The intestinal mucus is composed of two layers: an inner attached stratified mucus layer, and a nonattached outer mucus layer. In healthy individuals, the inner mucus layer is impermeable to bacteria, whereas the outer layer contains commensal bacteria (Hansson, 2019). Another element of the gut defense system is the sentinel goblet cells, which are activated when bacteria come in close contact. Abnormalities in the inner mucus layer that allow bacteria to reach the underlying epithelium are an early event in the pathogenesis of IBD. Analysis of the mucus proteome in patients with active/non active UC versus controls showed that in active UC, major structural mucus components including MUC2 were reduced, both in inflamed and non-inflamed segments. The mucus gel layer is thinner than normal, and the number of sentinel goblet cells was decreased, as well as their response to bacterial challenge (van der Post et al., 2019).

As mucins are the main components of both mucus layers that are present between the intestinal mucosa and the content of the bowel, modifications in mucin expression, organization and/or glycosylation are likely to influence the protection of the intestinal mucosa, bacterial adhesion, and may therefore constitute important factors in the pathogenesis of IBD.

The dysregulated balance between pro-inflammatory cytokines (TNF, IL-1β, IL-8, IL-17), anti-inflammatory cytokines (IL-4, IL-13), and immuno-regulatory cytokines described in IBD is likely to modify mucin expression and glycosylation, as described for other inflammatory diseases such as CF discussed above (Guan & Zhang, 2017). Multiple studies show the beneficial effects of anti-cytokine treatments for IBD patients (Powrie et al., 1994; van Dullemen et al., 1995) The most common treatments for Crohn's disease are based on the use of anti-TNF antibodies, but antibodies against specific interleukins of the pro-inflammatory cascade, such as IL-12, IL-17, or IL-23, are also tested in ongoing clinical trials (Li et al., 2019).

Cytokines such as TNF, but also bacterial components have been shown to influence mucin gene and protein expression in intestinal cell lines, as well as in animal models (Elson, Sartor, Tennyson, & Riddell, 1995; Maerten et al., 2004) and also induce mucin glycosylation changes.

Alterations in O-glycosylation of mucins, especially sialylation and sulfation, have been reported in UC (Raouf et al., 1992). Detailed studies by mass spectroscopy studies have shown a MUC2- associated increase in small glycans, notably the Tn (GalNAc-S/T) and sialyl-Tn (Neu5Acα2-6GalNAc- S/T) antigens, with concomitant lower amounts of larger glycans in patients with active UC (Larsson et al., 2011). Patients whose mucins exhibited strong glycosylation alterations usually had a more severe disease course. Interestingly, Tn and sialy-Tn antigens are also known as tumor-associated carbohydrate antigens (Harduin-Lepers et al., 2012).

Other glycosylation modifications, which are not MUC2 associated, were described such as increased levels of the TF antigen Galβ1-3GalNAc-S/T in UC, with a concomitant NFκB activation at epithelial cell surface, indicating a connection between inflammation and the aberrant expression of the TF antigen (Bodger et al., 2006). Although inflammation seems largely involved in the altered glycosylation observed on mucins from patients with active UC, the molecular mechanisms involved in cytokine-induced glycosylation and sulfation changes are not described yet. Their precise significance on IBD pathogenesis is currently investigated: altered glycosylation and sulfation of colonic mucins could alter the protective properties of the colonic mucus barrier observed in IBD. Accordingly, Muc2-deficient mice spontaneously develop colitis and colorectal cancer (Velcich et al., 2002). Other mouse models deficient in *O*-glycan synthesizing enzymes have been used to decipher the importance of mucin O-glycosylation on the development of UC and colorectal cancer. Colonic MUC2 carries mostly core 1 (Galβl -3GalNAc-S/T) and core 3 (GlcNAcβl -3GalNAc-S/T) based *O*-glycans. Mutant mice with intestinal deficiency of core 1-derived *O*-glycans developed spontaneous colitis (Bergstrom et al., 2016). Intestinal tissues from core1/core3 DKO mice exhibited altered glycosylation, with increased levels of Tn antigen. These DKO mice had more severe spontaneous chronic colitis than core 1 KO mice, whereas core 3 KO and control mice did not develop chronic colitis. In addition, core 1 KO and core 1/core 3 DKO mice developed spontaneous colorectal tumors. Properties of mucins from DKO mice were altered, with increased sensitivity to proteolysis compared to mucins from WT mice, suggesting that both core 1 and core 3 derived *O*-glycans on colonic mucins are necessary to maintain the efficiency of the colonic mucus barrier and protect against spontaneous colitis in mice (Bergstrom et al., 2017).

3. Glycosaminoglycans in inflammation

GAGs are linear polysaccharides that are ubiquitously found on the cell surface as well as in the ECM. Their anionic properties and variable structures enable them to provide a large panel of binding sites for numerous protein ligands, including many mediators of inflammation, for which they regulate bio-availability and functions (Collins & Troeberg, 2019; Mikami & Kitagawa, 2013; Parish, 2006; Petrey & de la Motte, 2014; Taylor & Gallo, 2006; Zhang, 2010).

3.1 Structure of glycosaminoglycans

Structurally, GAGs are linear polysaccharides consisting of the polymerization of repeat disaccharide units. Depending on the structure of these units, GAGs are made up of four families: hyaluronan, heparan sulfates (HS)/heparin, chondroitin/dermatan sulfate (CS/DS), and keratan sulfate (KS). With the exception of hyaluronan, GAGs are sulfated at various positions of the glycan backbone (Fig. 2), and covalently attached to core proteins, thus forming proteoglycans (Taylor & Gallo, 2006; Zhang, 2010).

The first step that occurs during the synthesis of HS and CS/DS is the assembly of the tetrasaccharide linker GlcAβ1-3Galβ1-3Galβ1-4Xylβ1-, which is covalently attached to specific serine residues in different core proteins. Thereafter, the following step determines the type of GAG chain that will be polymerized (Zhang, 2010). In the case of HS, a GlcNAc is first added and the HS polysaccharide backbone is then elongated by the addition of alternating GlcUA and GlcNAc residues, catalyzed by enzymes of the exostosin (EXT) family. Thereafter, the HS precursor undergoes sequential enzymatic modifications, beginning with N-deacetylation/N-sulfation of GlcNAc residues and C5-epimerization of some GlcUA into L-IdoUA residues. Structural complexity is then increased by sulfation at various positions by 2-*O*—, 3-*O*— and 6-*O*-sulfotransferases. The glycan backbone of HS and heparin are similar in structure, but heparin contains higher levels of sulfation and epimerization when compared with HS

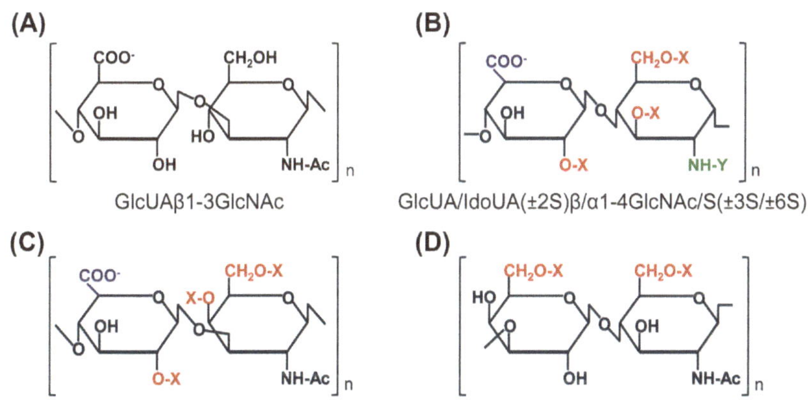

Fig. 2 ***Typical disaccharide units found in hyaluronan (A), HS/heparin (B), CS/DS (C) and KS (D) chains.*** Modifications of hydroxyl and amino groups by sulfate are indicated by "X" and "Y", respectively. Gal, galactose; GalNAc, N-acetyl-galactosamine; GlcNAc, N-acetyl-glucosamine; GlcUA, glucuronic acid; IdoUA, L-iduronic acid.

(Carlsson, Presto, Spillmann, Lindahl, & Kjellen, 2008; Kreuger & Kjellén, 2012; Zhang, 2010). All these modifications take place in the Golgi apparatus. Extracellularly, HS chains can undergo a last modification by the endosulfatases Sulfs, which specifically cleave 6-*O*-sulfate groups (Morimoto-Tomita, Uchimura, Werb, Hemmerich, & Rosen, 2002). In the case of CS/DS, a GalNAc is first added to the tetrasaccharide linker, which is the prerequisite for the assembly of repeat units containing one GalNAc and one GlcUA residue. Then, the growing CS chain can undergo modifications by 2-*O*–, 4-*O*– and/or 6-*O*-sulfotransferases. DS, also called CS-B, is often regarded as a separate class of CS. The difference between DS and other CS chains is the epimerization of some GlcUA into L-IdoUA in DS, which has important functional consequences (Mikami & Kitagawa, 2013; Zhang, 2010) (Fig. 3).

KS is extended from the linkage oligosaccharides that are N-linked, *O*-GalNAc linked, or *O*– Mannose linked to the core protein. The building blocks of KS are repeating disaccharides of Gal and.

GlcNAc. C-6 sulfation modifications of the vast majority of GlcNAc residues and a significant proportion of adjacent Gal residues are observed in KS. These modifications are mediated by GlcNAc- 6-O-sulfotransferases and Gal-6-*O*-sulfotranserases, respectively (Caterson & Melrose, 2018; Uchimura, 2015). KS can be modified at their non-reducing termini with various types of monosaccharides including sialic acids conferring possible interactions with Siglecs (Gonzalez-Gil et al., 2018; Zhang et al., 2017).

Hyaluronan is composed of repeat units consisting of GlcUA linked to GlcNAc residues. It differs from the other GAGs in that it is assembled at the cytosolic side of the cell membrane by the hyaluronan synthases HAS1, HAS2 and HAS3 (Petrey & de la Motte, 2014; Weigel, 2015).

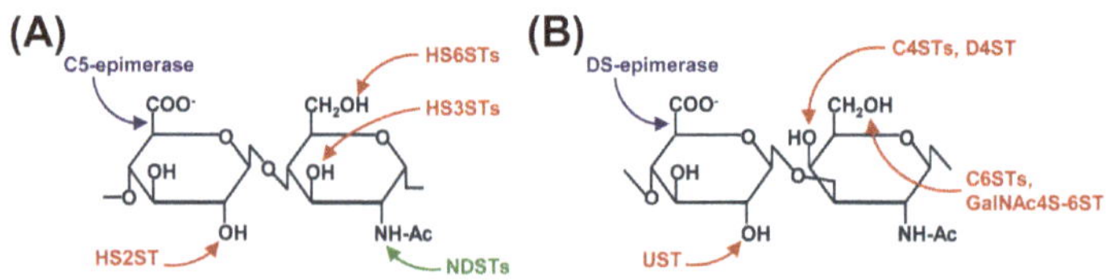

Fig. 3 ***Schematic representation of the maturation of HS (A) and CS/DS (B) precursors.*** The sites of modification of the backbones of HS and CS/DS by specific sulfotransferases and C5- epimerases are indicated: *NDST*, N-deacetylases/N-sulfotransferases; *HS2ST*, HS 2-O– sulfotransferase; *HS3STs*, HS 3-O-sulfotransferases; *HS6STs*, HS 6-O-sulfotransferases; *C4STs*, chondroitin 4-O-sulfotransferases; *C6STs*, chondroitin 6-O-sulfotransferase; *D4ST*, dermatan 4-O– sulfotransferase; *UST*, uronyl 2-O-sulfotransferase; *GalNAc4S-6ST*, GalNAc 4-sulfate 6-O– sulfotransferase.

3.2 Glycosaminoglycans of the endothelium glycocalyx as regulators in inflammation

Leukocyte infiltration during the inflammatory response involves sequential steps of rolling, adhesion and crawling over the endothelium, followed by transmigration into injured tissue. These events are tightly regulated by a number of soluble mediators and cell surface molecules, including chemokines, selectins and integrins, and by the interactions they have with the endothelium glycocalyx that coats the luminal surface of blood vessels (Ley, Laudanna, Cybulsky, & Nourshargh, 2007; Parish, 2006; Reitsma, Slaaf, Vink, van Zandvoort, & oude Egbrink, 2007; Weninger, Biro, & Jain, 2014).

Proteoglycans, which contribute mainly to the structural organization and functions of the glycocalyx, are either membrane-bound to the endothelial cells, such as syndecans and glypicans, or secreted after their assembly, such as perlecan and biglycan. Besides CS/DS and hyaluronan, HS is predominantly involved in blood cell-endothelium interactions. In normal conditions, the endothelium glycocalyx is required to regulate vascular permeability and to maintain tissue homeostasis, repulsing blood cells and platelets from the endothelium. On the other hand, it plays a key role in the orchestration of wound healing by controlling the recruitment of leukocytes (Collins & Troeberg, 2019; Kumar, Katakam, Urbanowitz, & Gotte, 2015; Reitsma et al., 2007). Following inflammatory stimulation, rolling of leukocytes requires interactions that occur between P-selectin on endothelial cells and P-selectin glycoprotein ligand (PSGL)-1 on the surface of leukocytes. Migration of leukocytes is then driven by a chemokine gradient, wherein chemokines are presented by endothelial HS to their G-protein-coupled receptors on the surface of leukocytes. Many chemokines also form oligomers on HS, which is critical to achieve maximal local concentration and haptotactic property. Concomitantly, the interactions of chemokines with their receptors result in the activation of leukocyte integrins, which in turn bind to their cell surface ligands on endothelial cells. This is followed by transmigration of leukocytes to the site of inflammation (Ley et al., 2007; Parish, 2006; Weninger et al., 2014).

Structural modifications of the endothelium glycocalyx have been incriminated in several human pathologies. The thickness of this compartment is profoundly altered upon inflammatory stimulation. This alteration modifies the vascular permeability and uncovers adhesion molecules, which was proved to play a fundamental role in the recruitment of immune cells during acute inflammation. Experimental studies have provided evidence of a prominent role for endothelial HS in this process (Collins & Troeberg, 2019; Kumar et al., 2015; Reitsma et al., 2007). For example, removal of cell surface HS with heparinase reduced the rolling and firm adhesion of granulocytes to an endothelial cell monolayer (Rops et al., 2007a). Radiation therapy is currently used as an anti-cancer treatment. Exposure to ionizing radiation induces an inflammatory response and consequent immune cell infiltration (Halle et al., 2010; Rannou et al., 2015). While the recruitment of leukocytes can be beneficial in the control of tumor cells, it becomes detrimental to surrounding healthy tissues, with the emergence of chronic and unresolved inflammation (Zitvogel & Kroemer, 2015). Exposure of endothelial cells to ionizing radiation dramatically reduced the thickness of the glycocalyx by decreasing the level of GAGs, which was related to an exacerbated monocyte adhesion under flow (Jaillet et al., 2017). Interestingly, these findings share similarities with other experimental works showing that inflammatory stimuli induce shedding of GAGs from the endothelium and greater accessibility of adhesion proteins to circulating leukocytes, thus reinforcing the idea that alteration of the endothelium glycocalyx is a central mechanism of the inflammatory response (Reitsma et al., 2007; Rops et al., 2014; Schmidt et al., 2012).

3.3 Glycosaminoglycans of the ECM as regulators in inflammation

The ECM not only provides structural support for tissue resident cells, but is also a major effector of cell behavior. One compartment of the ECM is the basement membrane, which is the substratum on which endothelial and epithelial cells reside. HS is a major component of this compartment, wherein it participates in cell-matrix interactions and regulates the functions of many soluble proteins, including cytokines, enzymes and growth factors. The other compartments have connective tissue properties and are enriched in structural macromolecules, such as fibrillar collagens, hyaluronan, and proteoglycans of the hyalectan family. A number of cytokines, chemokines and growth factors can be immobilized within the ECM through interactions with the GAG moieties of proteoglycans, forming local reservoirs that protect them from degradation and ensure their localization close to their target cells. Upon an inflammatory stimulation, these soluble mediators are released at high concentrations locally to ensure a rapid and efficient activation of immune cells. On the other hand, there is now evidence that aberrant expression of the ECM components and/or fragments that are derived from ECM degradation can directly influence immune cell activation (Cheng et al., 2011; Collins & Troeberg, 2019; Sorokin, 2010; Taylor & Gallo, 2006; Vaday & Lider, 2000).

Increased concentrations of GAGs have been found in bronchial tissues and bronchoalveolar lavage fluids from patients with CF and HS was found to be increased in epithelial and endothelial basement membranes in samples from CF patients (Hilliard et al., 2007; Rahmoune et al., 1991; Reeves, et al., 2011). Moreover, high concentration of the chemokine IL-8 was incriminated in the sustained inflammation observed in CF bronchial tissue. Thus, it was suggested that high levels of HS in the CF airway may enhance the stability and activity of IL-8 and consequent neutrophil recruitment, thus contributing to the chronic airway inflammation and fibrosis (Solic, Wilson, Wilson, & Shute, 2005).

Heparanase is an endo-p-glucuronidase that degrades HS chains at sites of low sulfation. Apart from its extensively studied role in cancer progression, there is a growing body of evidence that heparanase also affects a variety of inflammatory processes (Meirovitz et al., 2013). Up-regulation of heparanase was indeed observed in various mouse models of inflammation, including vascular injury (Baker et al., 2009), delayed hypersensitivity (Edovitsky et al., 2006), chronic colitis (Lerner et al., lung injury (Schmidt et al., 2012), as well as in several auto-immune and inflammatory human disorders, such as in psoriasis (Lerner et al., 2014), rheumatoid arthritis (Li et al., 2008), atherosclerosis (Osterholm et al., 2013; Rao et al., 2011), inflammatory lung disease (Schmidt et al.,2012), ulcerative colitis and Crohn's disease (Waterman et al., 2007). In response to inflammatory stimuli, heparanase is produced by various cell types and releases HS fragments from cell-surface and ECM proteoglycans. These HS fragments can still associate with cytokines, chemokines and growth factors, and facilitate their biological activity. Accordingly, heparanase activity was found to contribute to leukocyte activation and accumulation in inflamed tissues (Lider et al., 1990; Matzner et al., 1985; Meirovitz et al., 2013) Besides its role in releasing HS-immobilized protein ligands heparanase was shown to increase the activation of macrophages by LPS, suggesting that it could be involved in the persistence of an unresolved and chronic inflammation (Lerner et al., 2011).

A number of studies have reported the importance of hyaluronan during tissue inflammation in many chronic and fibrotic diseases and across many tissues, including the lung (Ayars et al., 2013; Teder et al., 2002), colon (De la Motte, Hascall, Calabro, Yen-Lieberman, & Strong, 1999; De la Motte, Hascall, Drazba, Bandyopadhyay, & Strong, 2003), kidney (Wang

& Hascall, 2007), and skin (Milinkovic, Antin, Hergrueter, Underhill, & Sackstein, 2004). In non-inflamed tissue, the turn-over of hyaluronan involves its degradation into smaller fragments by hyaluronidases and internalization by receptors such as CD44. Moreover, binding of hyaluronan to macrophages contributes to the maintenance of an anti-inflammatory environment. Upon inflammatory stimulation, hyaluronan synthesis is rapidly upregulated, which is associated with leukocyte infiltration at the site of injury. Final resolution of the inflammatory response requires the return of hyaluronan to baseline level, meaning that its clearance is essential for the restoration of tissue homeostasis (Aya & Stern, 2014; Bourguignon & Flamion, 2016; Lee- Sayer et al., 2015; Petrey & de la Motte, 2014). Consistently, high levels of hyaluronan fragments were observed during a persistent inflammatory response, which was related to a reduced efficiency of CD44 to clear them. As detrimental consequences, these fragments promote the expression of inflammatory cytokines, which in turn leads to the maintenance of immune cells and an inability to resolve the inflammatory response (Cheng et al., 2011; Johnson, Arif, Lee-Sayer, & Dong, 2018; Liang et al., 2011; McKee et al., 1996; Taylor et al., 2007).

Aggrecan is a member of the hyalectan family, which interacts with hyaluronan and forms large multimolecular complexes in cartilaginous tissue. One of the earliest modifications observed in rheumatoid arthritis is the degradation of aggrecan and consequent breakdown of the cartilage network, which is due to increased proteolytic cleavage (Ishiguro et al., 2001). Like other members of this proteoglycan family, versican is capable of forming large aggregates *via* interactions with hyaluronan. It can also interact with CD44, suggesting that the functions of both versican and hyaluronan may be regulated by CD44-dependent interactions (Kawashima et al., 2000; Wight, Kang, & Merrilees, 2014). This CS/DS proteoglycan is normally present in low amounts in the ECM, but its expression level increases dramatically in inflamed tissues. Its accumulation was observed in the lung of mouse models of acute lung injury (Xu, Xue, Zhang, & Qu, 2016) and allergen-induced airway inflammation (Reeves et al., 2016). Similarly, high expression of versican has been reported in human lung diseases, such acute respiratory distress syndrome (Morales et al., 2011), severe asthma (Ayars et al., 2013; Weitoft et al., 2014), and chronic obstructive pulmonary disease (COPD) (Andersson-Sjoland et al., 2015; Merrilees et al., 2008). Versican-enriched structures are observed in tissues with leukocyte enrichment, such as in atherosclerosis and IBD (De la Motte et al., 2003; Wight et al., 2014). However, published results show that versican may exhibit either pro- or anti-inflammatory activities, and it is still unclear how this proteoglycan, alone or in combination with other components of the ECM, influences the inflammatory response.

3.4 GAG fragments as danger signals in inflammation

There is growing evidence indicating that GAG fragments released upon tissue injury from cell membrane or the ECM are capable of activating the immune system, acting as damage-associated molecular patterns (DAMPs). Such a mechanism of sterile inflammation has been suggested to occur in a number of pathologies, including inflammatory disorders, atherosclerosis, myocardial infarction, Alzheimer's disease and tumorigenesis. Among the different pattern recognition receptors (PRRs), TLR2 and TLR4 have been recognized as key players in sensing soluble GAG fragments originating from injured tissues (Chen; Nunez, 2010; Erridge, 2010).

Evidence arising from study on the role of heparanase in inflammation has demonstrated that soluble HS fragments can directly trigger TLR4-dependent responses (Johnson, Brunn, Kodaira, & Platt, 2002; Goodall, Poon, Phipps, & Hulett, 2014). In support to this assumption, injection of HS oligosaccharides was described to induce neutrophil tissue infiltration in WT but not in TLR4-null mice (Akbarshahi et al., 2011). Mucopolysaccharidoses (MPS) are inheritable diseases that result from deficiencies or loss of functions of the enzymes involved in GAG lysosomal degradation. In the Sanfilippo syndrome of MPS- III, the defect of lysosomal hydrolysis of HS causes progressive abnormal accumulation of HS oligosaccharides, which triggers inflammation and oxidative stress affecting multiple organ systems and neurodegenerative disorders (Zelei, Csetneki, Vokó, & Siffel, 2018). In experimental models, HS oligosaccharides isolated from MPS-III patients urine were shown to activate directly mouse microglial cells through TLR-4 and to trigger inflammation in the mouse brain. Structural analysis of these HS fragments revealed a variety of sizes comprised between di-to dodecasaccharides, but hexasaccharides were found as the most pathogenic HS fragments involved in microglia activation (Ausseil et al., 2008; Mason, Meikle, Hopwood, & Fuller, 2006; Puy et al., 2018).

Besides soluble HS oligosaccharides, hyaluronan has been also described as an endogenous TLR agonist. However, the inflammatory outcomes of these interactions appeared to be dependent on the molecular weight of the glycan chain. The native form of hyaluronan, which exhibits a high molecular weight of up to 10^7 Da, exerts protective and anti-inflammatory functions. Upon inflammation, hyaluronan fragments are generated by the actions of hyaluronidases or reactive oxygen species. These small hyaluronan fragments target TLR2/4 in monocytes, macrophages and dendritic cells, inducing downstream signaling and expression of pro-inflammatory factors as well as ECM modifying enzymes (Jiang et al., 2005, 2011; Scheibner et al., 2006; Taylor et al., 2007; Termeer et al., 2002). However, the absence of evidence showing a direct binding to TLRs has questioned whether hyaluronan fragments can be considered as DAMPs. An alternative explanation is that these small hyaluronan derivatives can be inhibitory for the interaction between native hyaluronan and CD44, thus disrupting its anti-inflammatory effect (Dong et al., 2016; Johnson et al., 2018).

Proteoglycans of the ECM do not interact with TLRs under physiological conditions. However, some of them have been described as potent danger signaling molecules in soluble and/or degraded forms. For example, versican was reported to interact with TLR2 and to modulate the responses of macrophages and dendritic cells (Kim et al., 2009; Wang et al., 2009). Structurally different from versican, biglycan and decorin are two members of the small leucine-rich proteoglycan (SLRPs) family. These CS/DS proteoglycans are crucial regulators of collagen fibrillogenesis and ECM assembly. Originally present in the ECM under immobilized forms, they can be released by partial proteolysis under inflammatory conditions and act as endogenous ligands for TLR2 and TLR4 other CS/DS proteoglycans (Merline, Schaefer, & Schaefer, 2009; Nastase, Iozzo, & Schaefer, 2014; Schaefer et al., 2005). Unlike what has been suggested for HS and hyaluronan, CS/DS fragments alone were however not capable of triggering TLR signaling. Instead, the CS/DS chains would have to be attached to the protein core of these proteoglycans to evoke TLR signaling (Frey, Schroeder, Manon-Jensen, Iozzo, & Schaefer, 2013).

3.5 GAGs in neuroinflammation and neurodegeneration

About 20% of the total volume of adult central nervous system (CNS) is filled with interstitial extracellular components (Nicholson & Rice, 1996). The ECM composition in the CNS is remarkably different from most of peripheral tissues, in that interstitial ECM is enriched in collagen, laminin, and fibronectin. The ECM of adult CNS consists primarily of HA, sulfated GAG/proteoglycans, and tenascin (Lau, Cua, Keough, Haylock-Jacobs, & Yong, 2013). It is clear that sulfated GAGs and proteoglycans restrict synaptic plasticity and axonal regrowth/sprouting (Fawcett, 2015; Silver, Schwab, & Popovich, 2014). Recent reports also present that GAGs regulate biological functions of microglia and macrophages in the CNS inflammation

(Bartus et al., 2014; O'Callaghan, Li, Lannfelt, Lindahl, & Zhang, 2015; Zhang et al., 2017; Dyck et al., 2018). Multiple sclerosis (MS) is a chronic disorder of the CNS characterized by neuroinflammation and demyelination. Dynamic ECM changes occur in brain tissues of MS patients. Expression level of CS/DS proteoglycans is decreased in active and chronically active MS lesions that are characterized by large influx of inflammatory cells (Sobel & Ahmed, 2001). Conversely, HS proteoglycans are upregulated in active lesions that show accumulation of CD45 $^{+}$ leukocytes and macrophages. It was suggested that excessive production and deposition of these molecules in active MS lesions may be caused by increased production of TGF-β1 (van Horssen, Bö, Dijkstra, & de Vries, 2006), and that HS may be involved in signaling of cytokine/chemokine in recruited leukocytes and resident microglia within the lesion. On the other hand, intravenous delivery of chondroitinase ABC-degraded products of CS showed crucial implications of CS for infiltration and activation of inflammatory cells in experimental autoimmune encephalomyelitis (EAE), a rodent model of MS (Rolls et al., 2006; Zhou, Nagarkatti, Zhong, & Nagarkatti, 2010). Recent reports clearly showed that CS-A and versican V1 are accumulated in perivascular spaces of regions of inflammation in MS and peak phase EAE, and that inhibition of the CS synthesis attenuated EAE disease severity (Keough et al., 2016; Stephenson et al., 2018). It is probable that the perivascular CS proteoglycans enhance the production of matrix metalloproteinases and transmigratory ability of detrimental leukocytes into the CNS parenchyma. Intriguingly, inhibition of CS proteoglycan-receptor signaling facilitates remyelination (Luo et al., 2018). A number of studies have demonstrated useful strategies to attenuate adverse effects of CS proteoglycans on recovery from MS and EAE.

Injury to the adult CNS also causes neuroinflammation. Damage to the CNS tissue triggers degradation of the ECM components eliciting an inflammatory response that is similar to that caused by injury in peripheral tissues *(see above sections)*. Fragments of sulfated GAGs and HA may directly activate PRRs and regulate inflammatory cell responses. Tenascin acts as a DAMP by binding to TLR4 and activates innate immune cells in an autocrine loop (Goh, Piccinini, Krausgruber, Udalova, & Midwood, 2010). It is suggested that these bindings of ECM components of CNS to PRRs could propagate chronic neuroinflammation after the CNS injury (Gaudet & Popovich, 2014). In a transgenic mouse model of heparanase, HS was also shown to facilitate CD14-dependent TLR4 signaling of LPS in microglia (O'Callaghan et al., 2015). It has been reported that LAR and PTP-σ are specific CSPG receptors and that perturbation of signaling through these receptors promoted microglial phagocytosis and migration, showing a potential way to modulate neuroinflammation after CNS injury (Dyck et al., 2018).

Neurodegenerative disorders are caused by progressive loss of neurons and neurodegeneration. Many neurodegenerative diseases including Alzheimer's disease (AD), Parkinson's disease (PD), and amyotrophic lateral sclerosis (ALS), are associated with abnormal protein aggregation and deposition in CNS and also called protein aggregation diseases. GAGs affect the pathogenesis and progression of certain neurodegenerative diseases at various steps that include regulation of protein aggregation and neuroinflammation. Amyloidosis is a common type of these diseases and is a pathological condition that is accompanied by the formation of extracellular amyloid fibrils or intracellular inclusions with amyloid-like characters (Chiti & Dobson, 2017). Sulfated GAGs especially HS are known to be involved in amyloidosis as a cofactor *in vivo* (Liu et al., 2016). Critical roles of HS on the cell surface in cellular uptake, cellular interaction, cytotoxicity, or transcellular propagation of various protein aggregates, i.e., amyloid β, tau, and α-synuclein (αsyn), have been reported (Nishitsuji & Uchimura, 2017). Neuroinflammation is a prominent feature of these diseases (Heneka et al., 2015; Ransohoff, 2016). As described above, HS may also be involved in regulation of microglial functions in progression of these neurodegenerative diseases. Sialylated KS-like structure is upregulated in microglia of AD and ALS, and is shown to regulate microglial phagocytosis and sensitivity to anti-inflammatory cytokine IL-4 (Foyez et al., 2015; Zhang et al., 2017). It is proposed that inhibition of GlcNAc-6-sulfotransferase 1 that transfers sulfate to the sialylated KS-like structure in microglia may be a therapeutic target in AD (Zhang et al., 2017).

3.6 Impact of GAG structure remodeling in inflammation

Various inflammatory stimuli have been reported to affect GAG biosynthesis and structure (Asplund, Ostergren-Lundén, Camejo, Stillemark-Billton, & Bondjers, 2009; Krenn et al., 2008; Martinez et al., 2015; Sikora et al., 2016; Wegrowski et al., 1995). In view of its large structural and functional diversity, it may be expected that HS structure remodeling can profoundly affect a variety of pathophysiological processes, either by inducing the release of immobilized inflammatory factors, or by modulating their binding to cognate receptors at the membrane of target cells (Collins & Troeberg, 2019). Accordingly, it was reported that polarization of macrophages to a

M2 phenotype resulted in the synthesis of more cell-surface HS with a higher degree of 2-*O*-sulfation (Martinez et al., 2015). In contrast to M1 macrophages that exhibit pro-inflammatory properties, M2 macrophages are preferentially involved in the resolution phase of inflammation, scavenging cell debris, promoting angiogenesis and repairing damaged tissues (Martinez & Gordon, 2014). HS remodeling in M2 macrophages was found accompanied with an increased binding of FGF-2, suggesting that the production of highly sulfated HS may be important for the role of M2 macrophages during the phase of tissue repair (Martinez et al., 2015). It is of note that macrophages from the synovial fluids of patients with rheumatoid arthritis or systemic lupus erythematosus also showed high FGF-2 binding properties. Thus, the excessive growth factor activity observed during these chronic inflammatory disorders may be partly related to an aberrant HS sulfation in pathogenic macrophages (Clasper et al., 1999).

An increase in the levels of *N*– and 6-*O*-sulfated HS domains was observed on the glomerular endothelium of kidney sections from systemic lupus erythematosus patients and lupus mouse models, highlighting the functional importance of *N*– and 6-*O*-sulfation (Rops et al., 2007b). In line with this assumption, knockdown of the enzyme NDST1, which results in a dramatic reduction in N-sulfation within endothelial HS chains, inhibited leukocyte infiltration in mouse models of glomerular injury (Rops et al., 2014) and allergen-induced airway inflammation (Zuberi et al., 2009). On the other hand, the ability of endothelial HS to bind L-selectin and the chemokine CCL2 was found increased in an experimental model of renal ischemia/reperfusion and in human renal allograft biopsies. These higher binding properties were not related to an increase in the activity of HS sulfotransferases but rather to a loss of the expression of Sulf-1, which in turn resulted in an increase in the level of 6-*O*-sulfated HS domains (Celie et al., 2007). These results are in line with the findings that Sulf-induced HS 6-*O*– desulfation destabilized the chemotactic gradients for migrating leukocytes by reducing the interactions between HS and chemokines (Pempe, Burch, Law, & Liu, 2012; Uchimura et al., 2006). Sulfs also impair the activity of FGFs by preventing the formation of functional ternary complexes between the growth factor, its signaling receptor and 6-*O*-sulfated HS domains (Wang et al., 2004). Interestingly, human lung fibroblasts exposed to TNF or TGF-β were found to release high amounts of Sulf-1. Silencing the expression of the sulfatase enhanced the activation of fibroblasts, suggesting that Sulf-1 may function as an autocrine regulator of fibroblast expansion and fibrogenesis in the course of an inflammatory response (Sikora et al., 2016; Yue et al., 2008). Similarly, the expression level of Sulf-2 was increased in epithelial cells from lung tissues with idiopathic pulmonary fibrosis (Yue, Lu, Auduong, Sides, & Lasky, 2013) and in bronchoalveolar lavage fluid from a murine model of bleomycin-induced lung inflammation (Yue, 2017). Sulf-2 knock-out induced an enhanced neutrophil infiltration, which further supports the idea that these HS sulfatases play a protective role in inflammation (Yue, 2017).

Whether GAG structure remodeling in inflammatory disorders is a cause or consequence is of potential importance. If the former, then normal GAG structure and function could be recovered after an anti-inflammatory treatment; conversely, if dysregulated GAG biosynthesis is directly related to the pathology, targeting the modified GAG structures or the enzymes required for their production may be a potential way to develop new therapeutic approaches. Besides its wide use as an anticoagulant drug, there is a strong evidence that heparin is capable of interfering within the interactions between HS and a number of inflammatory mediators. These findings have highlighted the potential of heparin derivatives as anti-inflammatory drugs (Farrugia, Lord, Melrose, & Whitelock, 2018; Johnson, Proudfoot, & Handel, 2005; Mohamed & Coombe, 2017).

4. Crosstalk between gangliosides and inflammation in neurodegenerative diseases

Neurodegeneration is a long term process that leads to gradual or progressive loss of neural cells in the brain or spinal cords, generating the chronic inflammation characteristic of neurodegenerative diseases (ND). Alzheimer's disease (AD) and Parkinson's disease (PD) are the most prevalent ND. Despite AD mostly occurs in the elderly, after the age of 65, a small proportion called early onset AD (AD I) occurs in younger individuals and is considered to have a more aggressive course and shorter relative survival time. The late onset of AD (AD II) occurs at 85, affecting largest number of individuals, and is often considered by acting in pair with aging (Pierce, Bullain, & Kawas, 2017). AD is mainly characterized by the formation of extracellular amyloid plaques produced by the aggregation of β-amyloid peptide (Aβ) and the presence of intracellular neurofibrillary tangles (NFTs). PD is a dementia characterized by the death of dopaminergic neurons in *substantia nigra pars compacta,* resulting in motor disabilities, as well as in cognitive, emotional and behavioral symptoms (Poewe et al., 2017). PD can be divided into idiopathic PD for 85–90% and familial PD for 15%

(Bonifati et al., 2008). It is mainly characterized by the presence of αsyn as a major component of Lewy bodies that are considered as a marker of neuron degeneration. In both diseases, microglial activation is part of the neurodegenerative process, but it remains unclear whether this activation plays a role at the initiation step of the disease, or rather as a response to neuronal death.

The key points of neurodegeneration are inflammation, amyloid protein aggregation and apoptosis of neuronal cells. The two last points underline the role of cellular membranes in ND. In cell membranes, lipid raft domains, alternatively named glycolipid enriched microdomains (GEM), play essential roles in the maintenance of cell physiology and cell biological properties. Rafts are microdomains from which major cellular pathways are engaged under physiological conditions. They are composed of cholesterol, sphingomyelin, glycosphingolipids and specific raft-associated proteins, and the alteration of one of these compounds may induce the disruption and alteration of cell signaling pathways, especially when the ganglioside content of raft domains is altered. Gangliosides are a subclass of glycosphingolipids carrying one or more sialic acid residues, interacting in *cis* or *trans* with membrane proteins and lipids, engaging major cell signaling pathways. In this part, we will focus on the intricate relationships between inflammation, tissues homeostasis and raft domains in order to decipher their involvement (causes or consequences) in ND.

4.1 Lipid rafts: composition and biological consequences of disruption

Ganglioside composition of brain tissues plays a role in the exacerbation of inflammation process and neurodegeneration. The global content of gangliosides in brain is usually decreased in the aging process and ND, and ganglioside composition is differentially altered depending on the area of the brain and the age at the onset in AD (Sarbu, Dehelean, Munteanu, Vukelic, & Zamfir, 2017) (Table 1). Different studies have also shown that increased levels of gangliosides are found in the plasma of PD patients and ganglioside expression can be differentially altered in PD brain (Valdes-Gonzalez et al., 2011). For example, decreased levels of GM1, GD1a, GD1b, and GT1b have been described in dopaminergic neurons in human as well as in mouse PD brain (Wu, Lu, Kulkarni, & Ledeen, 2012). Schneider and co-workers demonstrated a decreased expression of glycosyltransferase genes *B3GALT4* and *ST3GAL2* involved in GD1b and GT1b biosynthesis in the central nervous system of PD patients compared to controls, which could explain the variations in ganglioside composition (Schneider, 2018). In the early onset of

Table 1 Main changes in gangliosides composition observed in ND.

Disease	Increased ganglioside expression	Decreased ganglioside expression	References
Parkinson	–	GM1, GD1a, GD1 b, GT1b	Valdes-Gonzalez et al., 2011; Wu et al., 2012
Alzheimer early onset	GM1	GD1b, GT1b	Svennerholm & Gottfries, 1994
Alzheimer late onset	GM2	GM1	Svennerholm & Gottfries, 1994

AD (AD I), the ganglioside content was reduced by 60–70% in the gray matter area, and by 80% in the white matter area, compared to age-matched controls. A 50% decrease in phospholipid content and cholesterol in cell membrane was also observed, inducing the loss of nerves ending in brain. In AD II, the total ganglioside content decreased in white matter tissue, especially in the temporal, hippocampal and frontal lobes (Svennerholm & Gottfries, 1994). Similarly, Svennerholm and coworkers demonstrated changes in ganglioside content in different areas of the brain, which are more severe in AD I than in AD II (Svennerholm & Gottfries, 1994). in AD II, GM1 levels decreased to the benefit of increased GM2 levels. In AD I, complex gangliosides with at least 2 sialic acid residues tend to decrease, whereas more simple gangliosides are increased. In that way, GM1 expression increases in frontal and temporal lobes, while GD1b and GT1b tend to decrease in AD I brains compared to control.

Different mutant mice KO for specific glycosyltransferases and deficient in ganglioside biosynthesis have been shown to exhibit inflammation in nervous tissues, leading to progressive neurodegeneration. GM3 synthase deficient mice expressing 0-series gangliosides do not show any inflammation, whereas GD3 synthase KO mice that express 0- and a-series gangliosides have mild brain inflammation. Double KO-mice (DKO) for GM2/GD2 synthase expression exhibit progressive neurodegenerative disorders and moderate inflammation by the remaining expression of neutral glycolipids (Ohmi et al., 2011). Furthermore, complement-related gene expression is increased in the spinal cord of DKO mice for GM2/GD2 synthase. In parallel, specific pro-inflammatory cytokines such as IL-1 or TNF, are highly expressed in these mouse models. On the other hand, mature T cells from GM2/GD2 synthase DKO mice do not respond to IL-2/IL-2 receptor due to alterations of lipid composition the cell membrane (Zhao et al., 1999). Interestingly, Wu and collaborators have demonstrated that ganglioside depletion in DKO GM2/GD2 synthase mice induces Parkinson's disease symptoms such as motor disabilities and impairment (Wu, Lu, Kulkarni, Amin, & Ledeen, 2011). However, the defect or disruption of ganglioside expression in raft domains is not the only way to exacerbate inflammation: the formation of insoluble aggregates of amyloid protein also exhibits pro-inflammatory effects, and Aβ oligomerization in AD induces classical C1 complement activation, leading to initial damage for neuronal loss (McGeer & McGeer, 1998).

4.2 Deposition of protein fibrils on membrane

The formation of αsyn fibrils in PD and amyloid plaques in AD share related mechanisms involving two common structural motifs: a Glycosphingolipid Binding Domain (GBD) and a Cholesterol Binding Domain (CBD). Although the precise role of cholesterol in PD patients remains uncertain, the generation of glucosylcerebrosidase 1 *(GBA1)* KO mice induces cholesterol accumulation in lysosomes, showing a link between glycolipids and cholesterol metabolism (Magalhaes et al., 2016). Gangliosides and cholesterol are the two partners involved in the aggregation amyloid peptides. In the first step, αsyn and Aβ peptides bind to GM1 or GM3 on a portion of twelve amino acids (AA) residues corresponding to the GBD motif (Di Scala et al., 2016) (Fig. 4). In PD, αsyn preferentially binds to GM3 and this interaction requires AA residues 35–47 (Yahi & Fantini, 2014). Lipid monolayer experiments showed that αsyn-GM3 binding involves interactions between the K34, Y39, K35 residues of asyn, and the glucose and sialic acid residues of GM3, respectively, but only Y39 residue is critical for αsyn

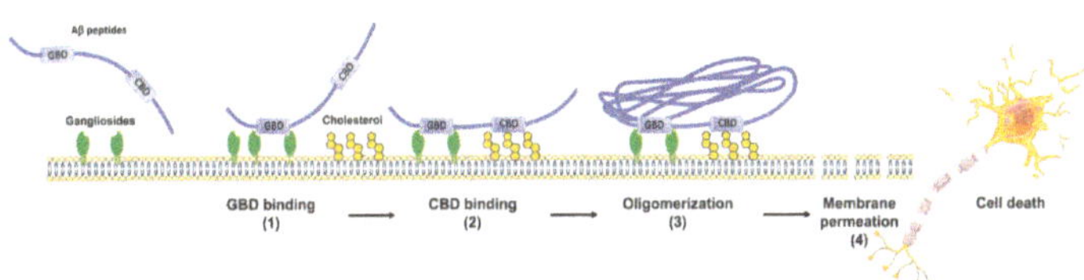

Fig. 4 ***Schematic representation of the role of gangliosides and cholesterol in amyloid peptides oligomerization and membrane permeation.*** (1) GBD motif of Aβ peptides binds to gangliosides, mainly GM3 and GM1. (2) Ganglioside-bound peptides bind to cholesterol *via* the CBD motif. (3) Conformational changes trigger the oligomerization of amyloid peptides. (4) Integration in cell membrane induces membrane permeation (Williams et al., 2011).

binding In AD, Aβ peptides bind to GM1 on AA residues 5–16 (Yahi & Fantini, 2014) to form GAβ, specifically involving H13, H14 and K16 residues of Aβ peptides (Fantini & Yahi, 2011). In a second step, ganglioside-bound peptides will bind to cholesterol *via* the CBD motif, which leads to the membrane insertion of the amyloid protein (Di Scala et al., 2016). Subsequently, conformational changes of amyloid proteins trigger the oligomerization process. GAβ forms the a helix seed for Aβ oligomerization with conformational changes in β-sheets. 40-residues Aβ monomers ($A\beta_{40}$) that naturally assemble in anti-parallel β-sheets, form parallel β-sheets with GAβ, inducing the acceleration of the oligomerization process in raft domains (Matsubara et al., 2018; Okada, Ikeda, Wakabayashi, Ogawa, & Matsuzaki, 2008; Yanagisawa, 2007). Furthermore, $A\beta_{40}$ form hydrogen bounds with Neu5Ac or Gal residues of raft-localized GM1, more efficiently than with other membrane lipids such as palmitoyl-oleoyl-phosphatidylcholine (POPC) or palmitoyl-oleoyl-phosphatidylethanolamine (POPE) (Lemkul & Bevan, 2011). Following to the Aβ binding on GM1, Aβ integration in cell membrane is facilitated inducing membrane permeation leading to cytotoxicity process and AD progression (Williams et al., 2011).

In PD, αsyn dimerization in helical bound structures on exosomes has been demonstrated on isolated neuronal cells. The aggregation occurs in the form of proteinase K resistant β-sheets. Gray and coworkers showed that αsyn binding to GM3 accelerates the oligomerization process (Grey et al., 2015). Furthermore αsyn-GM3 binding induced channel formation in cholesterol containing membranes, forming cation permeable amyloid pores. The final step of amyloid protein aggregation is therefore the formation of amyloid pores in the plasma of cell membranes, leading to the entry of calcium and sodium (Mironov, 2015). As a consequence, the disturbance of calcium homeostasis generates progressive induction of inflammation and neuronal loss.

4.3 Gangliosides and protein aggregation: intricate relationships with inflammation

The data presented in sections 4.1. and 4.2. clearly suggest a connection between gangliosides and amyloid protein aggregation in ND. Gangliosides themselves are implicated in many cellular functions and could bear different roles in ND. In AD, Herzer and collaborators showed that GM1 expression on cell membrane activates Caveolin-1 dependent-insulin receptor internalization and degradation, inhibiting insulin signaling and inducing neuronal loss (Herzer, Meldner, Rehder, Gröne, & Nordström, 2016). The crossing of st3gal5-deficient mice ($ST3^{-/-}$) exhibiting lack of GM1, GD1a, GD3, GT1b, and GQ1b expression with 5XFAD transgenic mice mutated in amyloid protein AP695 or presenilin PS1 genes, generated $ST3^{-/-}$ 5XFAD mice. These mice exhibit low level of burden deposition of Ap peptides as well as a low level of neuroinflammation. They also showed neither neuronal loss nor synaptic dysfunction (Dukhinova et al., 2019), suggesting that GM3 increases neurotoxicity in AD. Newburn and coworkers showed tripartite binding of glial cell line derived neurotrophic factor (GDNF), GPI-linked co-receptor 1α (GFR1α) and RET tyrosine kinase receptor inducing RET phosphorylation on Y1062, causing its redistribution into lipid rafts. Activated RET subsequently induces the phosphorylation of MAPK and PI3K/Akt, promoting neuroprotection of dopaminergic neurons in PD brain (Hadaczek et al., 2015; Newburn, Duchemin, Neff, & Hadjiconstantinou, 2014).

Aggregation and deposition of amyloid protein are the singular characteristics of ND. This burden promotes neurotoxicity. In PD, imaging in live neuronal cells and electrophysiology on artificial membranes showed that αsyn in either monomeric or oligomeric states increase the basal levels of intracellular calcium (Angelova et al., 2016). Similar results have been obtained on transgenic mice expressing human asyn (Reznichenko et al., 2012). Furthermore, asyn aggregation is involved in microglial activation, ROS production, and cytokine/chemokine secretion (Béraud et al., 2013). In AD, Ap oligomerization induces classical complement activation (promoted by C1 activation), leading to the initial damage that induces progressive neuronal loss (McGeer & McGeer, 1998).

Still, the precise role of amyloid protein binding to gangliosides is not well understood. PD is often linked to glucosylcerebrosidase 1 *GBA1* gene, which is essential for the hydrolysis of glucosylceramide (GlcCer). Depletion of *GBA1* in drosophila induces GlcCer accumulation and increases asyn fibrils toxicity (Suzuki & Cheung, 2015; Suzuki et al., 2015). In PD, lipidomic studies have revealed that GM3 levels are increased (Chan et al., 2017). GlcCer is the precursor of GM3, and increased levels of GlcCer could be responsible for the increased GM3 levels, which promote the formation of αsyn-GM3 complexes in membranes. The role of GM1 is still controversial: on the one hand, GM1 is involved in the internalization and clearance of αsyn aggregates on microglia (Park et al., 2009) and it has a neuroprotective role by the inhibition of inflammatory response induced by MPTP (1-methyl-4-phenyl-1,2,3,6-tetrahydropyridine) or 6-OHDA (6-hydroxydopamine) chemical treatments (Schneider

& Yuwiler, 1989; Gupta et al., 1990; Hadjiconstantinou et al., 1989). Martinez and coworkers showed that αsyn-GM1 inhibits fibrillation and αsyn-GM3 interferes with amyloid channel function in membrane (Martinez, Zhu, Han, & Fink, 2007; Yahi & Fantini, 2014). On the other hand, Gray and collaborators have shown that GM1 and GM3 expression on membranes promotes aggregation of αsyn in Lewy bodies, increasing their toxic effects on neuronal cells (Gray et al., 2015).

5. Perspectives in therapeutic applications

Whether glycan structure remodeling is a cause or a consequence of inflammatory disorders is of potential importance. If the former, normal glycan structures and functions could be recovered after an anti-inflammatory treatment. Conversely, if dysregulated glycan biosynthesis is directly related to the pathology, targeting the modified glycan structures or biosynthetic enzymes may be a potential way to develop new therapeutic approaches.

In CF, CFTR-deficient airway epithelial cells display intrinsic abnormalities in intracellular signaling and in the synthesis of pro-inflammatory factors, which further increase the synthesis of inflammatory mediators, but also cellular stress and apoptosis, leading to exaggerated and ineffective airway inflammation (Verhaeghe et al., 2007). The sustained and chronic inflammation is responsible for modifications of glycosylation and sulfation exhibited by CF bronchial mucins, leading to an increased and specific *P. aeruginosa* infection. In NCI–H292 cells, mAbs against sLe^x and against TNF decreased *P. aeruginosa* binding (Jeffries et al., 2016). Thus, treatment aiming at specifically interfering with inflammatory mediators/signaling pathways in CF aiways, or aiming at blocking the binding of *P. aeruginosa* to sialylated mucins may help to decrease recurring infection in CF. In the same way, interfering with chronic inflammation-induced glycosylation changes of mucins observed in IBD could provide new therapeutic targets to improve intestinal mucus barrier function in patients.

There are close relationships between gangliosides present in raft domains, inflammation, and the maintenance of cell homeostasis. Data indicate that gangliosides induce inflammation and neurodegeneration, but neurodegeneration could also generate ganglioside defects. Establishing cause - consequence relationships between the different partners seems difficult for a given neurodegenerative disease for the moment, but gangliosides could be promising therapeutic targets for these diseases.

Extensive studies have been carried out to produce heparin-based HS mimetics (Farrugia et al., 2018; Johnson et al., 2005; Mohamed & Coombe, 2017). However, it is still difficult to synthesize oligosaccharides with complex sulfation patterns. A seducing alternative is the use of a chemo-enzymatic approach, in which controlled sulfation could be achieved by recombinant enzymes (Chen et al., 2005; Kuberan, Lech, Beeler, Wu, & Rosenberg, 2003). Finally, there has been a recent interest in the identification of inhibitors of GAG-modifying enzymes (Byrne et al., 2018). These last findings suggest that designing specific inhibitors of GAG biosynthesis *via* high-throughput screening of bio-active molecules might be a future strategy to control the functions of GAGs in inflammatory disorders.

References

Akbarshahi, H., Axelsson, J. B., Said, K., Malmström, A., Fischer, H., & Andersson, R. (2011). TLR4 dependent heparan sulphate-induced pancreatic inflammatory response is IRF3-mediated. *Journal of Translational Medicine, 9*, 219. http://dx.doi.org/10.1186/1479-5876-9-219.

Andersson-Sjoland, A., Hallgren, O., Rolandsson, S., Weitoft, M., Tykesson, E., Larsson-Callerfelt, A. K., et al. (2015). Versican in inflammation and tissue remodeling: The impact on lung disorders. *Glycobiology, 25*, 243–251. http://dx.doi.org/10.1093/glycob/cwu120.

Angelova, P. R., Ludtmann, M. H., Horrocks, M. H., Negoda, A., Cremades, N., Klenerman, D., et al. (2016). Ca^{2+} is a key factor in a-synuclein-induced neurotoxicity. *Journal of Cell Science, 129*, 1792–1801. http://dx.doi.org/10.1242/jcs.180737.

Asplund, A., Ostergren-Lundén, G., Camejo, G., Stillemark-Billton, P., & Bondjers, G. (2009). Hypoxia increases macrophage motility, possibly by decreasing the heparan sulfate proteoglycan biosynthesis. *Journal of Leukocyte Biology, 86*, 381–388. http://dx.doi.org/10.1189/jlb.0908536.

Ausseil, J., Desmaris, N., Bigou, S., Attali, R., Corbineau, S., Vitry, S., et al. (2008). Early neurodegeneration progresses independently of microglial activation by heparan sulfate in the brain of mucopolysaccharidosis IIIB mice. *PLoS One, 3*, e2296. http://dx.doi.org/10.1371/journal.pone.0002296.

Ayars, A. G., Altman, L. C., Potter-Perigo, S., Radford, K., Wight, T. N., & Nair, P. (2013). Sputum hyaluronan and versican in severe eosinophilic asthma. *International Archives of Allergy and Immunology, 161*, 65–73. http://dx.doi.org/10.1159/000343031.

Aya, K. L., & Stern, R. (2014). Hyaluronan in wound healing: Rediscovering a major player. *Wound Repair and Regeneration, 22*, 579–593. http://dx.doi.org/10.1111/wrr.12214.

Baker, A. B., Groothuis, A., Jonas, M., Ettenson, D. S., Shazly, T., Zcharia, E., et al. (2009). Heparanase alters arterial structure, mechanics, and repair following endovascular stenting in mice. *Circulation Research, 104*, 380–387. http://dx.doi.org/10.1161/CIRCRESAHA.108.180695.

Bartus, K., James, N. D., Didangelos, A., Bosch, K. D., Verhaagen, J., Yáñez-Muñoz, R. J., et al. (2014). Large-scale chondroitin sulfate proteoglycan digestion with chondroitinase gene therapy leads to reduced pathology and modulates macrophage phenotype

following spinal cord contusion injury. *Journal of Neuroscience, 34*, 4822–4836. http://dx.doi.org/10.1523/JNEUROSCI.4369-13.2014.
Baud, V., & Karin, M. (2001). Signal transduction by tumor necrosis factor and its relatives. *Trends in Cell Biology, 11*, 372–377. http://dx.doi.org/10.1016/S0962-8924(01)02064-5.
Bayes, H. K., Ritchie, N. D., & Evans, T. J. (2016). Interleukin-17 is required for control of chronic lung infection caused by *Pseudomonas aeruginosa. Infection and Immunity, 84*, 3507–3516. http://dx.doi.org/10.1128/IAI.00717-16.
Béraud, D., Hathaway, H. A., Trecki, J., Chasovskikh, S., Johnson, D. A., Johnson, J. A., et al. (2013). Microglial activation and antioxidant responses induced by the Parkinson's disease protein a- synuclein. *Journal of Neuroimmune Pharmacology, 8*, 94–117. http://dx.doi.org/10.1007/s11481-012-9401-0.
Bergstrom, K., Fu, J., Johansson, M. E., Liu, X., Gao, N., Wu, Q., et al. (2017). Core 1- and 3- derived O-glycans collectively maintain the colonic mucus barrier and protect against spontaneous colitis in mice. *Mucosal Immunology, 10*, 91–103. http://dx.doi.org/10.1038/mi.2016.45.
Bergstrom, K., Liu, X., Zhao, Y., Gao, N., Wu, Q., Song, K., et al. (2016). Defective Intestinal Mucin-type O-glycosylation causes spontaneous colitis-associated cancer in mice. *Gastroenterology, 151*, 152–164. http://dx.doi.org/10.1053/j.gastro.2016.03.039.
Boat, T. F., Cheng, P. W., & Wood, R. E. (1977). Tracheobronchial mucus secretion *in vivo* and *in vitro* by epithelial tissues from CF and control subjects. *Modern Problems in Paediatrics, 19*, 141–152. PMID:1031903.
Bodger, K., Halfvarson, J., Dodson, A. R., Campbell, F., Wilson, S., Lee, R., et al. (2006). Altered colonic glycoprotein expression in unaffected monozygotic twins of inflammatory bowel disease patients. *Gut, 55*, 973–977. http://dx.doi.org/10.1136/gut.2005.086413.
Bonfield, T. L., Konstan, M. W., & Berger, M. (1999). Altered respiratory epithelial cell cytokine production in cystic fibrosis. *The Journal of Allergy and Clinical Immunology, 104*, 72–78. PMID: 10400842.
Bonifati, V., Wu-Chou, Y. H., Schweiger, D., Fonzo, A. D., Lu, C. S., & Oostra, B. (2008). Re: LRRK2 mutation analysis in Parkinson disease families with evidence of linkage to PARK8. *Neurology, 70*, 2348–2349. http://dx.doi.org/10.1212/01.wnl.0000317005.06662.01.
Boucher, R. C. (2007). Evidence for airway surface dehydration as the initiating event in CF airway disease. *Journal of Internal Medicine, 261*, 5–16. http://dx.doi.org/10.1111/j.1365-2796.2006.01744.x.
Bourguignon, V., & Flamion, B. (2016). Respective roles of hyaluronidases 1 and 2 in endogenous hyaluronan turnover. *Federation of American Societies for Experimental Biology Journal, 30*, 2108–2114. http://dx.doi.org/10.1096/fj.201500178R.
Byrne, D. P., Li, Y., Ramakrishnan, K., Barsukov, I. L., Yates, E. A., Eyers, C. E., et al. (2018). New tools for carbohydrate sulfation analysis: Heparan sulfate 2-O-sulfotransferase (HS2ST) is a target for small-molecule protein kinase inhibitors. *Biochemical Journal, 475*, 2417–2433. http://dx.doi.org/10.1042/BCJ20180265.
Cantin, A. M., Hartl, D., Konstan, M. W., & Chmiel, J. F. (2015). Inflammation in cystic fibrosis lung disease: Pathogenesis and therapy. *Journal of Cystic Fibrosis, 14*, 419–430. http://dx.doi.org/10.1016/j.jcf.2015.03.003.
Carlsson, P., Presto, J., Spillmann, D., Lindahl, U., & Kjellen, L. (2008). Heparin/heparan sulfate biosynthesis. *Journal of Biological Chemistry, 283*, 20008–20014. http://dx.doi.org/10.1074/jbc.M801652200.
Carnoy, C., Ramphal, R., Scharfman, A., Lo-Guidice, J. M., Houdret, N., Klein, A., et al. (1993). Altered carbohydrate composition of salivary mucins from patients with cystic

fibrosis and the adhesion of *Pseudomonas aeruginosa*. *American Journal of Respiratory Cell and Molecular Biology, 9*, 323–334. http://dx.doi.org/10.1165/ajrcmb/9.3.323.

Caterson, B., & Melrose, J. (2018). Keratan sulfate, a complex glycosaminoglycan with unique functional capability. *Glycobiology, 28*, 182–206. http://dx.doi.org/10.1093/glycob/cwy003.

Celie, J. W., Rutjes, N. W., Keuning, E. D., Soininen, R., Heljasvaara, R., Pihlajaniemi, T., et al. (2007). Subendothelial heparan sulfate proteoglycans become major L-selectin and monocyte chemoattractant protein-1 ligands upon renal ischemia/reperfusion. *American Journal Of Pathology, 170*, 1865–1878. http://dx.doi.org/10.2353/ajpath.2007.070061.

Chan, R. B., Perotte, A. J., Zhou, B., Liong, C., Shorr, E. J., Marder, K. S., et al. (2017). Elevated GM3 plasma concentration in idiopathic Parkinson's disease: A lipidomic analysis. *PLoS One, 12*, e0172348. http://dx.doi.org/10.1371/journal.pone.0172348.

Chen, J., Avci, F. Y., Muñoz, E. M., McDowell, L. M., Chen, M., Pedersen, L. C., et al. (2005). Enzymatic redesigning of biologically active heparan sulfate. *Journal of Biological Chemistry, 280*, 42817–42825. http://dx.doi.org/10.1074/jbc.M504338200.

Cheng, G., Swaidani, S., Sharma, M., Lauer, M. E., Hascall, V. C., & Aronica, M. A. (2011). Hyaluronan deposition and correlation with inflammation in a murine ovalbumin model of asthma. *Matrix Biology, 30*, 126–134. http://dx.doi.org/10.1016/j.matbio.2010.12.003.

Chen, G. Y., & Nunez, G. (2010). Sterile inflammation: Sensing and reacting to damage. *Nature Reviews Immunology, 10*, 826–837. http://dx.doi.org/10.1038/nri2873.

Chiti, F., & Dobson, C. M. (2017). Protein misfolding, amyloid formation, and human disease: A summary of progress over the last decade. *Annual Review of Biochemistry, 86*, 27–68. http://dx.doi.org/10.1146/annurev-biochem-061516-045115.

Clasper, S., Vekemans, S., Fiore, M., Plebanski, M., Wordsworth, P., David, G., et al. (1999). Inducible expression of the cell surface heparan sulfate proteoglycan syndecan-2 (fibroglycan) on human activated macrophages can regulate fibroblast growth factor action. *Journal of Biological Chemistry, 274*, 24113–24123. http://dx.doi.org/10.1074/jbc.274.34.24113.

Collins, L. E., & Troeberg, L. (2019). Heparan sulfate as a regulator of inflammation and immunity. *Journal of Leukocyte Biology, 105*, 81–92. http://dx.doi.org/10.1002/JLB.3RU0618-246R.

Colomb, F., Krzewinski-Recchi, M. A., El Machhour, F., Mensier, E., Jaillard, S., Steenackers, A., et al. (2012). TNF regulates sialyl-Lewis^x and 6-sulfo-sialyl-Lewis^x expression in human lung through up-regulation of *ST3GAL4* transcript isoform BX. *Biochimie, 94*, 2045–2053. http://dx.doi.org/10.1016/j.biochi.2012.05.030.

Colomb, F., Krzewinski-Recchi, M. A., Steenackers, A., Vincent, A., Harduin-Lepers, A., Delannoy, P., et al. (2016). TNF up-regulates ST3GAL4 and sialyl-Lewis^x expression in lung epithelial cells through an intronic ATF2-responsive element. *Biochemical Journal, 474*, 65–78. http://dx.doi.org/10.1042/BCJ20160602.

Colomb, F., Vidal, O., Bobowski, M., Krzewinski-Recchi, M. A., Harduin-Lepers, A., Mensier, E., et al. (2014). TNF induces the expression of the sialyltransferase ST3Gal IV in human bronchial mucosa via MSK1/2 protein kinases and increases FliD/sialyl-Lewis^x-mediated adhesion of *Pseudomonas aeruginosa*. *Biochemical Journal, 457*, 79–87. http://dx.doi.org/10.1042/BJ20130989.

Conese, M., & Assael, B. M. (2001). Bacterial infections and inflammation in the lungs of cystic fibrosis patients. *The Pediatric Infectious Disease Journal, 20*, 207–213. PMID: 11224844.

Corvol, H., Fitting, C., Chadelat, K., Jacquot, J., Tabary, O., Boule, M., et al. (2008). Distinct cytokine production by lung and blood neutrophils from children with cystic fibrosis. *American Journal of Physiology - Lung Cellular and Molecular Physiology, 284*, L997–L1003. http://dx.doi.org/10.1152/ajplung.00156.2002.

Davril, M., Degroote, S., Humbert, P., Galabert, C., Dumur, V., Lafitte, J. J., et al. (1999). The sialylation of bronchial mucins secreted by patients suffering from cystic fibrosis or from chronic bronchitis is related to the severity of airway infection. *Glycobiology, 9*, 311–321. PMID: 10024669.

Degroote, S., Maes, E., Humbert, P., Delmotte, P., Lamblin, G., & Roussel, P. (2003). Sulfated oligosaccharides isolated from the respiratory mucins of a secretor patient suffering from chronic bronchitis. *Biochimie, 85*, 369–379. PMID: 12770775.

Dekker, J., Rossen, J.W., Buller, H. A., & Einerhand, A. W. (2002). The MUC family: An obituary. *Trends in Biochemical Sciences, 27*, 126–131. PMID: 11893509.

Delmotte, P., Degroote, S., Lafitte, J. J., Lamblin, G., Perini, J. M., & Roussel, P. (2002). TNFa increases the expression of glycosyltransferases and sulfotransferases responsible for the biosynthesis of sialylated and/or sulfated Lewis^{x} epitopes in the human bronchial mucosa. *Journal of Biological Chemistry, 277*, 424–431. http://dx.doi.org/10.1074/jbc.M109958200.

Delmotte, P., Degroote, S., Merten, M. D., Van Seuningen, I., Bernigaud, A., Figarella, C., et al. (2001). Influence of TNFa on the sialylation of mucins produced by a transformed cell line MM-39 derived from human tracheal gland cells. *Glycoconjugate Journal, 18*, 487–497. http://dx.doi.org/10.1074/jbc.M109958200.

De la Motte, C. A., Hascall, V. C., Calabro, A., Yen-Lieberman, B., & Strong, S. A. (1999). Mononuclear leukocytes preferentially bind *via* CD44 to hyaluronan on human intestinal mucosal smooth muscle cells after virus infection or treatment with poly(I.C). *Journal of Biological Chemistry, 274*, 30747–30755. http://dx.doi.org/10.1074/jbc.274.43.30747.

De la Motte, C. A., Hascall, V. C., Drazba, J., Bandyopadhyay, S. K., & Strong, S. A. (2003). Mononuclear leukocytes bind to specific hyaluronan structures on colon mucosal smooth muscle cells treated with polyinosinic acid:polycytidylic acid: Inter-α -trypsin inhibitor is crucial to structure and function. *American Journal of Pathology, 163*, 121–133. http://dx.doi.org/10.1016/s0002-9440(10)63636-x.

Di Scala, C., Yahi, N., Boutemeur, S., Flores, A., Rodriguez, L., Chahinian, H., et al. (2016). Common molecular mechanism of amyloid pore formation by Alzheimer's p-amyloid peptide and a- synuclein. *Scientific Reports, 6*, 28781. http://dx.doi.org/10.1038/srep28781.

Dong, Y., Arif, A., Olsson, M., Cali, V., Hardman, B., Dosanjh, M., et al. (2016). Endotoxin free hyaluronan and hyaluronan fragments do not stimulate TNFa, interleukin-12 or upregulate co- stimulatory molecules in dendritic cells or macrophages. *Scientific Reports, 6*, 36928. http://dx.doi.org/10.1038/srep36928.

Dubin, P. J., McAllister, F., & Kolls, J. K. (2007). Is cystic fibrosis a TH17 disease? *Inflammation Research, 56*, 221–227. http://dx.doi.org/10.1007/s00011-007-6187-2.

Dukhinova, M., Veremeyko, T., Yung, A. W. Y., Kuznetsova, I. S., Lau, T. Y. B., Kopeikina, E., et al. (2019). Fresh evidence for major brain gangliosides as a target for the treatment of Alzheimer's disease. *Neurobiology of Aging, 77*, 128–143. http://dx.doi.org/10.1016/j.neurobiolaging.2019.01.020.

van Dullemen, H. M., van Deventer, S. J., Hommes, D. W., Bijl, H. A., Jansen, J., Tytgat, G. N., et al. (1995). Treatment of Crohn's disease with anti-tumor necrosis factor chimeric monoclonal antibody (cA2). *Gastroenterology, 109*, 129–135. PMID: 7797011.

Dyck, S., Kataria, H., Alizadeh, A., Santhosh, K. T., Lang, B., Silver, J., et al. (2018). Perturbing chondroitin sulfate proteoglycan signaling through LAR and PTPa receptors promotes a beneficial inflammatory response following spinal cord injury. *Journal of Neuroinflammation, 15*, 90. http://dx.doi.org/10.1186/s12974-018-1128-2.

Edovitsky, E., Lerner, I., Zcharia, E., Peretz, T., Vlodavsky, I., & Elkin, M. (2006). Role of endothelial heparanase in delayed-type hypersensitivity. *Blood, 107*, 3609–3616. http://dx.doi.org/10.1182/blood- 2005-08-3301.

Elizur, A., Cannon, C. L., & Ferkol, T. W. (2008). Airway inflammation in cystic fibrosis. *Chest, 133*, 489–495. http://dx.doi.org/10.1378/chest.07-1631.

Elson, C. O., Sartor, R. B., Tennyson, G. S., & Riddell, R. H. (1995). Experimental models of inflammatory bowel disease. *Gastroenterology, 109*, 1344–1367. http://dx.doi.org/10.1016/0016-5085(95)90599-5.

Erridge, C. (2010). Endogenous ligands of TLR2 and TLR4: Agonists or assistants? *Journal of Leukocyte Biology, 87*, 989–999. http://dx.doi.org/10.1189/jlb.1209775.

Fantini, J., & Yahi, N. (2011). Molecular basis for the glycosphingolipid-binding specificity of a- synuclein: Key role of tyrosine 39 in membrane insertion. *Journal of Molecular Biology, 408*, 654–669. http://dx.doi.org/10.1016/j.jmb.2011.03.009.

Farrugia, B. L., Lord, M. S., Melrose, J., & Whitelock, J. M. (2018). The role of heparan sulfate in inflammation, and the development of biomimetics as anti-inflammatory strategies. *Journal of Histochemistry and Cytochemistry, 66*, 321–336. http://dx.doi.org/10.1369/0022155417740881.

Fawcett, J. W. (2015). The extracellular matrix in plasticity and regeneration after CNS injury and neurodegenerative disease. *Progress in Brain Research, 218*, 213–226. http://dx.doi.org/10.1016/bs.pbr.2015.02.001.

Foyez, T., Takeda-Uchimura, Y., Ishigaki, S., Narentuya, Zhang, Z., Sobue, G., et al. (2015). Microglial keratan sulfate epitope elicits in central nervous tissues of transgenic model mice and patients with amyotrophic lateral sclerosis. *American Journal of Pathology, 185*, 3053–3065. http://dx.doi.org/10.1016/j.ajpath.2015.07.016.

Frey, H., Schroeder, N., Manon-Jensen, T., Iozzo, R. V., & Schaefer, L. (2013). Biological interplay between proteoglycans and their innate immune receptors in inflammation. *FEBS Journal, 280*, 2165–2179. http://dx.doi.org/10.1111/febs.12145.

Gaudet, A. D., & Popovich, P. G. (2014). Extracellular matrix regulation of inflammation in the healthy and injured spinal cord. *Experimental Neurology, 258*, 24–34. http://dx.doi.org/10.1016/j.expneurol.2013.11.020.

Ghidoni, R., Caretti, A., & Signorelli, P. (2015). Role of sphingolipids in the pathobiology of lung inflammation. *Mediators of Inflammation*, 487–508. http://dx.doi.org/10.1155/2015/487508.

Goh, F. G., Piccinini, A. M., Krausgruber, T., Udalova, I. A., & Midwood, K. S. (2010). Transcriptional regulation of the endogenous danger signal tenascin-C: A novel autocrine loop in inflammation. *The Journal of Immunology, 184*, 2655–2662. http://dx.doi.org/10.4049/jimmunol.0903359.

Gonzalez-Gil, A., Porell, R. N., Fernandes, S. M., Wei, Y., Yu, H., Carroll, D. J., et al. (2018). Sialylated keratan sulfate proteoglycans are Siglec-8 ligands in human airways. *Glycobiology, 28*, 786–801. http://dx.doi.org/10.1093/glycob/cwy057.

Goodall, K. J., Poon, I. K., Phipps, S., & Hulett, M. D. (2014). Soluble heparan sulfate fragments generated by heparanase trigger the release of pro-inflammatory cytokines through TLR-4. *PLoS One, 9*, e109596. http://dx.doi.org/10.1371/journal.pone.0109596.

Grey, M., Dunning, C. J., Gaspar, R., Grey, C., Brundin, P., Sparr, E., et al. (2015). Acceleration of a-synuclein aggregation by exosomes. *Journal of Biological Chemistry, 290*, 2969–2982. http://dx.doi.org/10.1074/jbc.M114.585703.

Groux-Degroote, S., Krzewinski-Recchi, M. A., Cazet, A., Vincent, A., Lehoux, S., Lafitte, J. J., et al. (2008). IL-6 and IL-8 increase the expression of glycosyltransferases and sulfotransferases involved in the biosynthesis of sialylated and/or sulfated Lewis^{x} epitopes in the human bronchial mucosa. *Biochemical Journal, 410*, 213–223. http://dx.doi.org/10.1042/BJ20070958.

Guan, Q., & Zhang, J. (2017). Recent advances: The imbalance of cytokines in the pathogenesis of inflammatory bowel disease. *Mediators of Inflammation*, 4810258. http://dx.doi.org/10.1155/2017/4810258.

Gupta, M., Schwarz, J., Chen, X. L., & Roisen, F. J. (1990). Gangliosides prevent MPTP toxicity in mice - an immunocytochemical study. *Brain Research, 527*, 330–334. http://dx.doi.org/10.1016/0006- 8993(90)91154-9.

Hadaczek, P., Wu, G., Sharma, N., Ciesielska, A., Bankiewicz, K., Davidow, A. L., et al. (2015). GDNF signaling implemented by GM1 ganglioside; failure in Parkinson's disease and GM1-deficient murine model. *Experimental Neurology, 263*, 177–189. http://dx.doi.org/10.1016/j.expneurol.2014.10.010.

Hadjiconstantinou, M., Mariani, A. P., & Neff, N. H. (1989). GM1 ganglioside-induced recovery of nigrostriatal dopaminergic neurons after MPTP: An immunohistochemical study. *Brain Research, 484*, 297–303. http://dx.doi.org/10.1016/0006-8993(89)90373-9.

Halle, M., Gabrielsen, A., Paulsson-Berne, G., Gahm, C., Agardh, H. E., Farnebo, F., et al. (2010). Sustained inflammation due to nuclear factor-kappa B activation in irradiated human arteries. *Journal of the American College of Cardiology, 55*, 1227–1236. http://dx.doi.org/10.1016/j.jacc.2009.10.047.

Hansson, G. C. (2019). Mucus and mucins in diseases of the intestinal and respiratory tracts. *Journal of Internal Medicine, 285*, 479–490. http://dx.doi.org/10.1111/joim.12910.

Harduin-Lepers, A., Krzewinski-Recchi, M. A., Colomb, F., Foulquier, F., Groux-Degroote, S., & Delannoy, P. (2012). Sialyltransferases functions in cancers. *Frontiers in Bioscience, 4*, 499–515. PMID: 22201891.

Hauber, H. P., Foley, S. C., & Hamid, Q. (2006). Mucin overproduction in chronic inflammatory lung disease. *Canadian Respiratory Journal, 13*, 327–335. http://dx.doi.org/10.1155/2006/901417.

Heneka, M. T., Carson, M. J., El Khoury, J., Landreth, G. E., Brosseron, F., Feinstein, D. L., et al. (2015). Neuroinflammation in Alzheimer's disease. *The Lancet Neurology, 14*, 388–405. http://dx.doi.org/10.1016/S1474-4422(15)70016-5.

Herzer, S., Meldner, S., Rehder, K., Gröne, H. J., & Nordström, V. (2016). Lipid microdomain modification sustains neuronal viability in models of Alzheimer's disease. *Acta Neuropathologica Communications, 4*, 103. http://dx.doi.org/10.1186/s40478-016-0354-z.

Hilliard, T. N., Regamey, N., Shute, J. K., Nicholson, A. G., Alton, E. W., Bush, A., et al. (2007). Airway remodelling in children with cystic fibrosis. *Thorax, 62*, 1074–1080. http://dx.doi.org/10.1136/thx.2006.074641.

van Horssen, J., Bö, L., Dijkstra, C. D., & de Vries, H. E. (2006). Extensive extracellular matrix depositions in active multiple sclerosis lesions. *Neurobiology of Disease, 24*, 484–491. http://dx.doi.org/10.1016/j.nbd.2006.08.005.

Ishibashi, Y., Inouye, Y., Okano, T., & Taniguchi, A. (2005). Regulation of sialyl-Lewis^x epitope expression by TNFa and EGF in an airway carcinoma cell line. *Glycoconjugate Journal, 22*, 53–62. http://dx.doi.org/10.1007/s10719-005-0292-7.

Ishiguro, N., Ito, T., Oguchi, T., Kojima, T., Iwata, H., Ionescu, M., et al. (2001). Relationships of matrix metalloproteinases and their inhibitors to cartilage proteoglycan and collagen turnover and inflammation as revealed by analyses of synovial fluids from patients with rheumatoid arthritis. *Arthritis & Rheumatology, 44*, 2503–2511. PMID: 11710706.

Jaillet, C., Morelle, W., Slomianny, M. C., Paget, V., Tarlet, G., Buard, V., et al. (2017). Radiation- induced changes in the glycome of endothelial cells with functional consequences. *Scientific Reports, 7*, 5290. http://dx.doi.org/10.1038/s41598-017-05563-y.

Jeffries, J. L., Jia, J., Choi, W., Choe, S., Miao, J., Xu, Y., et al. (2016). *Pseudomonas aeruginosa* pyocyanin modulates mucin glycosylation with sialyl-Lewis^x to increase binding to airway epithelial cells. *Mucosal Immunology, 9*, 1039–1050. http://dx.doi.org/10.1038/mi.2015.119.

Jiang, D., Liang, J., Fan, J., Yu, S., Chen, S., Luo, Y., et al. (2005). Regulation of lung injury and repair by Toll-like receptors and hyaluronan. *Nature Medicine, 11*, 1173–1179. http://dx.doi.org/10.1038/nm1315.

Jiang, D., Liang, J., & Noble, P. W. (2011). Hyaluronan as an immune regulator in human diseases. *Physiological Reviews, 91*, 221–264. http://dx.doi.org/10.1152/physrev.00052.2009.

Johnson, P., Arif, A. A., Lee-Sayer, S. S. M., & Dong, Y. (2018). Hyaluronan and its interactions with immune cells in the healthy and inflamed lung. *Frontiers in Immunology, 9*, 2787. http://dx.doi.org/10.3389/fimmu.2018.02787.

Johnson, G. B., Brunn, G. J., Kodaira, Y., & Platt, J. L. (2002). Receptor-mediated monitoring of tissue well-being *via* detection of soluble heparan sulfate by Toll-like receptor 4. *The Journal of Immunology, 168*, 5233–5239. http://dx.doi.org/10.4049/jimmunol.168.10.5233.

Johnson, Z., Proudfoot, A. E., & Handel, T. M. (2005). Interaction of chemokines and glycosaminoglycans: A new twist in the regulation of chemokine function with opportunities for therapeutic intervention. *Cytokine & Growth Factor Reviews, 16*, 625–636. http://dx.doi.org/10.1016/j.cytogfr.2005.04.006.

Kawashima, H., Hirose, M., Hirose, J., Nagakubo, D., Plaas, A. H., & Miyasaka, M. (2000). Binding of a large chondroitin sulfate/dermatan sulfate proteoglycan, versican, to L-selectin, P-selectin, and CD44. *Journal of Biological Chemistry, 275*, 35448–35456. http://dx.doi.org/10.1074/jbc.M003387200.

Keough, M. B., Rogers, J. A., Zhang, P., Jensen, S. K., Stephenson, E. L., Chen, T., et al. (2016). An inhibitor of chondroitin sulfate proteoglycan synthesis promotes central nervous system remyelination. *Nature Communications, 7*, 11312. http://dx.doi.org/10.1038/ncomms11312.

Khan, T. Z., Wagener, J. S., Bost, T., Martinez, J., Accurso, F. J., & Riches, D. W. (1995). Early pulmonary inflammation in infants with cystic fibrosis. *American Journal of Respiratory and Critical Care Medicine, 151*, 1075–1082. http://dx.doi.org/10.1164/ajrccm.151.4.7697234.

Kim, S., Takahashi, H., Lin, W. W., Descargues, P., Grivennikov, S., Kim, Y., et al. (2009). Carcinoma-produced factors activate myeloid cells through TLR2 to stimulate metastasis. *Nature, 457*, 102–106. http://dx.doi.org/10.1038/nature07623.

Krenn, E. C., Wille, I., Gesslbauer, B., Poteser, M., van Kuppevelt, T. H., & Kungl, A. J. (2008). Glycanogenomics: A qPCR-approach to investigate biological glycan function. *Biochemical and Biophysical Research Communications, 375*, 297–302. http://dx.doi.org/10.1016/j.bbrc.2008.07.144.

Kreuger, J., & Kjellén, L. (2012). Heparan sulfate biosynthesis: Regulation and variability. *Journal of Histochemistry and Cytochemistry, 60*, 898–907. http://dx.doi.org/10.1369/0022155412464972.

Kuberan, B., Lech, M. Z., Beeler, D. L., Wu, Z. L., & Rosenberg, R. D. (2003). Enzymatic synthesis of antithrombin III-binding heparan sulfate pentasaccharide. *Nature Biotechnology, 21*, 1343–1346. http://dx.doi.org/10.1038/nbt885.

Kumar, A. V., Katakam, S. K., Urbanowitz, A. K., & Gotte, M. (2015). Heparan sulphate as a regulator of leukocyte recruitment in inflammation. *Current Protein & Peptide Science, 16*, 77–86. PMID: 25692849.

Lakshmanan, I., Seshacharyulu, P., Haridas, D., Rachagani, S., Gupta, S., Joshi, S., et al. (2015). Novel HER3/MUC4 oncogenic signaling aggravates the tumorigenic phenotypes of pancreatic cancer cells. *Oncotarget, 6*, 21085–21099. http://dx.doi.org/10.18632/oncotarget.3912.

Larsson, J. M., Karlsson, H., Crespo, J. G., Johansson, M. E., Eklund, L., Sjovall, H., et al. (2011). Altered O-glycosylation profile of MUC2 mucin occurs in active ulcerative

colitis and is associated with increased inflammation. *Inflammatory Bowel Diseases, 17,* 2299–2307. http://dx.doi.org/10.1002/ibd.21625.
Lau, L. W., Cua, R., Keough, M. B., Haylock-Jacobs, S., & Yong, V. W. (2013). Pathophysiology of the brain extracellular matrix: A new target for remyelination. *Nature Reviews Neuroscience, 14,* 722–729. http://dx.doi.org/10.1038/nrn3550.
Lee-Sayer, S. S., Dong, Y., Arif, A. A., Olsson, M., Brown, K. L., & Johnson, P. (2015). The where, when, how, and why of hyaluronan binding by immune cells. *Frontiers in Immunology, 6,* 150. http://dx.doi.org/10.3389/fimmu.2015.00150.
Lemkul, J. A., & Bevan, D. R. (2011). Lipid composition influences the release of Alzheimer's amyloid p-peptide from membranes. *Protein Science, 20,* 1530–1545. http://dx.doi.org/10.1002/pro.678.
Lerner, I., Hermano, E., Zcharia, E., Rodkin, D., Bulvik, R., Doviner, V., et al. (2011). Heparanase powers a chronic inflammatory circuit that promotes colitis-associated tumorigenesis in mice. *Journal of Clinical Investigation, 121,* 1709–1721. http://dx.doi.org/10.1172/JCI43792.
Lerner, I., Zcharia, E., Neuman, T., Hermano, E., Rubinstein, A. M., Vlodavsky, I., et al. (2014). Heparanase is preferentially expressed in human psoriatic lesions and induces development of psoriasiform skin inflammation in mice. *Cellular and Molecular Life Sciences, 71,* 2347–2357. http://dx.doi.org/10.1007/s00018-013-1496-9.
Ley, K., Laudanna, C., Cybulsky, M. I., & Nourshargh, S. (2007). Getting to the site of inflammation: The leukocyte adhesion cascade updated. *Nature Reviews Immunology, 7,* 678–689. http://dx.doi.org/10.1038/nri2156.
Liang, J., Jiang, D., Jung, Y., Xie, T., Ingram, J., Church, T., et al. (2011). Role of hyaluronan and hyaluronan-binding proteins in human asthma. *The Journal of Allergy and Clinical Immunology, 128,* 403–411 e3. http://dx.doi.org/10.1016/j.jaci.2011.04.006.
Lider, O., Mekori, Y. A., Miller, T., Bar-Tana, R., Vlodavsky, I., Baharav, E., et al. (1990). Inhibition of T lymphocyte heparanase by heparin prevents T cell migration and T cell-mediated immunity. *European Journal of Immunology, 20,* 493–499. http://dx.doi.org/10.1002/eji.1830200306.
Li, R. W., Freeman, C., Yu, D., Hindmarsh, E. J., Tymms, K. E., Parish, C. R., et al. (2008). Dramatic regulation of heparanase activity and angiogenesis gene expression in synovium from patients with rheumatoid arthritis. *Arthritis & Rheumatology, 58,* 1590–1600. http://dx.doi.org/10.1002/art.23489.
Li, K., Friedman, J. R., Chan, D., Pollack, P., Yang, F., Jacobstein, D., et al. (2019). Effects of Ustekinumab on histologic disease activity in patients with Crohn's disease. *Gastroenterology, 19,* 41079–41082. http://dx.doi.org/10.1053/j.gastro.2019.06.037. pii: S0016-5085([Epub ahead of print]).
Liu, C. C., Zhao, N., Yamaguchi, Y., Cirrito, J. R., Kanekiyo, T., Holtzman, D. M., et al. (2016). Neuronal heparan sulfates promote amyloid pathology by modulating brain amyloid-p clearance and aggregation in Alzheimer's disease. *Science Translational Medicine, 8,* 332ra44. http://dx.doi.org/10.1126/scitranslmed.aad3650.
Lo-Guidice, J. M., Wieruszeski, J. M., Lemoine, J., Verbert, A., Roussel, P., & Lamblin, G. (1994). Sialylation and sulfation of the carbohydrate chains in respiratory mucins from a patient with cystic fibrosis. *Journal of Biological Chemistry, 269,* 18794–18813. PMID: 8034632.
Luo, F., Tran, A. P., Xin, L., Sanapala, C., Lang, B. T., Silver, J., et al. (2018). Modulation of proteoglycan receptor PTPa enhances MMP-2 activity to promote recovery from multiple sclerosis. *Nature Communications, 9,* 4126. http://dx.doi.org/10.1038/s41467-018-06505-6.
Maerten, P., Shen, C., Colpaert, S., Liu, Z., Bullens, D. A., van Assche, G., et al. (2004). Involvement of interleukin 18 in Crohn's disease: Evidence from *in vitro* analysis of human gut inflammatory cells and from experimental colitis models. *Clinical and*

Experimental Immunology, 135, 310–317. http://dx.doi.org/10.1111/j.1365-2249.2004.02362.x.

Magalhaes, J., Gegg, M. E., Migdalska-Richards, A., Doherty, M. K., Whitfield, P. D., & Schapira, A. H. (2016). Autophagic lysosome reformation dysfunction in glucocerebrosidase deficient cells: Relevance to Parkinson disease. *Human Molecular Genetics, 25*, 3432–3445. http://dx.doi.org/10.1093/hmg/ddw185.

Martinez, P., Denys, A., Delos, M., Sikora, A. S., Carpentier, M., Julien, S., et al. (2015). Macrophage polarization alters the expression and sulfation pattern of glycosaminoglycans. *Glycobiology, 25*, 502–513. http://dx.doi.org/10.1093/glycob/cwu137.

Martinez, F. O., & Gordon, S. (2014). The M1 and M2 paradigm of macrophage activation: Time for reassessment. *F1000Prime Reports, 6*, 13. http://dx.doi.org/10.12703/P6-13.

Martinez, Z., Zhu, M., Han, S., & Fink, A. L. (2007). GM1 specifically interacts with a-synuclein and inhibits fibrillation. *Biochemistry, 46*, 1868–1877. http://dx.doi.org/10.1021/bi061749a.

Mason, K. E., Meikle, P. J., Hopwood, J. J., & Fuller, M. (2006). Characterization of sulfated oligosaccharides in mucopolysaccharidosis type IIIA by electrospray ionization mass spectrometry. *Analytical Chemistry, 78*, 4534–4542. http://dx.doi.org/10.1021/ac052083d.

Matsubara, T., Yasumori, H., Ito, K., Shimoaka, T., Hasegawa, T., & Sato, T. (2018). Amyloid-p fibrils assembled on ganglioside-enriched membranes contain both parallel p-sheets and turns. *Journal of Biological Chemistry, 293*, 14146–14154. http://dx.doi.org/10.1074/jbc.RA118.002787.

Matzner, Y., Bar-Ner, M., Yahalom, J., Ishai-Michaeli, R., Fuks, Z., & Vlodavsky, I. (1985). Degradation of heparan sulfate in the subendothelial extracellular matrix by a readily released heparanase from human neutrophils. Possible role in invasion through basement membranes. *Journal of Clinical Investigation, 76*, 1306–1313. http://dx.doi.org/10.1172/JCI112104.

McGeer, E. G., & McGeer, P. L. (1998). The importance of inflammatory mechanisms in Alzheimer disease. *Experimental Gerontology, 33*, 371–378. PMID: 9762518.

McKee, C. M., Penno, M. B., Cowman, M., Burdick, M. D., Strieter, R. M., Bao, C., et al. (1996). Hyaluronan (HA) fragments induce chemokine gene expression in alveolar macrophages. The role of HA size and CD44. *Journal of Clinical Investigation, 98*, 2403–2413. http://dx.doi.org/10.1172/JCI119054.

Meirovitz, A., Goldberg, R., Binder, A., Rubinstein, A. M., Hermano, E., & Elkin, M. (2013). Heparanase in inflammation and inflammation-associated cancer. *FEBS Journal, 280*, 2307–2319. http://dx.doi.org/10.1111/febs.

Merline, R., Schaefer, R. M., & Schaefer, L. (2009). The matricellular functions of small leucine-rich proteoglycans (SLRPs). *Journal of Cell Communication and Signaling, 3*, 323–335. http://dx.doi.org/10.1007/s12079-009-0066-2.

Merrilees, M. J., Ching, P. S. T., Beaumont, B., Hinek, A., Wight, T. N., & Black, P. N. (2008). Changes in elastin, elastin binding protein and versican in alveoli in chronic obstructive pulmonary disease. *Respiratory Research, 18*, 41–50. http://dx.doi.org/10.1186/1465-9921-9-41.

Mikami, T., & Kitagawa, H. (2013). Biosynthesis and function of chondroitin sulfate. *Biochimica et Biophysica Acta, 1830*, 4719–4733. http://dx.doi.org/10.1016/j.bbagen.2013.06.006.

Milinkovic, M., Antin, J. H., Hergrueter, C. A., Underhill, C. B., & Sackstein, R. (2004). CD44- hyaluronic acid interactions mediate shear-resistant binding of lymphocytes to dermal endothelium in acute cutaneous GVHD. *Blood, 103*, 740–742. http://dx.doi.org/10.1182/blood-2003-05-1500.

Mironov, S. L. (2015). a-synuclein forms non-selective cation channels and stimulates ATP-sensitive potassium channels in hippocampal neurons. *Journal of Physiology, 593*, 145–159. http://dx.doi.org/10.1113/jphysiol.2014.280974.

Mohamed, S., & Coombe, D. R. (2017). Heparin mimetics: Their therapeutic potential. *Pharmaceuticals, 10*. http://dx.doi.org/10.3390/ph10040078. pii: E78.

Morales, M. M., Pires-Neto, R. C., Inforsato, N., Lancas, T., da Silva, L. F., Saldiva, P. H., et al. (2011). Small airway remodeling in acute respiratory distress syndrome: A study in autopsy lung tissue. *Critical Care, 15*, R4. http://dx.doi.org/10.1186/cc9401.

Morimoto-Tomita, M., Uchimura, K., Werb, Z., Hemmerich, S., & Rosen, S. D. (2002). Cloning and characterization of two extracellular heparin-degrading endosulfatases in mice and humans. *Journal of Biological Chemistry, 277*, 49175–49185. http://dx.doi.org/10.1074/jbc.M205131200.

Nastase, M. V., Iozzo, R. V., & Schaefer, L. (2014). Key roles for the small leucine-rich proteoglycans in renal and pulmonary pathophysiology. *Biochimica et Biophysica Acta, 1840*, 2460–2470. http://dx.doi.org/10.1016/j.bbagen.2014.01.035.

Neurath, M. F. (2014). Cytokines in inflammatory bowel disease. *Nature Reviews Immunology, 14*, 329–342. http://dx.doi.org/10.1038/nri3661.

Newburn, E. N., Duchemin, A. M., Neff, N. H., & Hadjiconstantinou, M. (2014). GM1 ganglioside enhances ret signaling in striatum. *Journal of Neurochemistry, 130*, 541–554. http://dx.doi.org/10.1111/jnc.12760.

Nichols, D. P., & Chmiel, J. F. (2015). Inflammation and its genesis in cystic fibrosis. *Pediatric Pulmonology, 50*(Suppl. 40), S39–S56. http://dx.doi.org/10.1002/ppul.23242.

Nicholson, C., & Rice, M. E. (1996). The migration of substances in the neuronal microenvironment. *Annals of the New York Academy of Sciences, 481*, 55–71. http://dx.doi.org/10.1111/j.1749- 6632.1986.tb27139.x.

Nishitsuji, K., & Uchimura, K. (2017). Sulfated glycosaminoglycans in protein aggregation diseases. *Glycoconjugate Journal, 34*, 453–466. http://dx.doi.org/10.1007/s10719-017-9769-4.

O'Callaghan, P., Li, J. P., Lannfelt, L., Lindahl, U., & Zhang, X. (2015). Microglial heparan sulfate proteoglycans facilitate the Cluster-of-Differentiation 14 (CD14)/Toll-like Receptor 4 (TLR4)-dependent inflammatory response. *Journal of Biological Chemistry, 290*, 14904–14914. http://dx.doi.org/10.1074/jbc.M114.634337.

Ohmi, Y., Tajima, O., Ohkawa, Y., Yamauchi, Y., Sugiura, Y., Furukawa, K., et al. (2011). Gangliosides are essential in the protection of inflammation and neurodegeneration *via* maintenance of lipid rafts: Elucidation by a series of ganglioside-deficient mutant mice. *Journal of Neurochemistry, 116*, 926–935. http://dx.doi.org/10.1111/j.1471-4159.2010.07067.x.

Okada, T., Ikeda, K., Wakabayashi, M., Ogawa, M., & Matsuzaki, K. (2008). formation of toxic Ap(1-40) fibrils on GM1 ganglioside-containing membranes mimicking lipid rafts: Polymorphisms in Ap(1-40) fibrils. *Journal of Molecular Biology, 382*, 1066–1074. http://dx.doi.org/10.1016/j.jmb.2008.07.072.

Osterholm, C., Folkersen, L., Lengquist, M., Ponten, F., Renne, T., Li, J., et al. (2013). Increased expression of heparanase in symptomatic carotid atherosclerosis. *Atherosclerosis, 226*, 67–73. http://dx.doi.org/10.1016/j.atherosclerosis.2012.09.030.

Parish, C. R. (2006). The role of heparan sulphate in inflammation. *Nature Reviews Immunology, 6*, 633–643. http://dx.doi.org/10.1038/nri1918.

Park, J. Y., Kim, K. S., Lee, S. B., Ryu, J. S., Chung, K. C., Choo, Y. K., et al. (2009). On the mechanism of internalization of a-synuclein into microglia: Roles of ganglioside GM1 and lipid raft. *Journal of Neurochemistry, 110*, 400–411. http://dx.doi.org/10.1111/j.1471-4159.2009.06150.x.

Pempe, E. H., Burch, T. C., Law, C. J., & Liu, J. (2012). Substrate specificity of 6-O-endo-sulfatase (Sulf-2) and its implications in synthesizing anticoagulant heparan sulfate. *Glycobiology, 22,* 1353–1362. http://dx.doi.org/10.1093/glycob/cws092.

Petrey, A. C., & de la Motte, C. A. (2014). Hyaluronan, a crucial regulator of inflammation. *Frontiers in Immunology, 5,* 101. http://dx.doi.org/10.3389/fimmu.2014.00101.

Pierce, A. L., Bullain, S. S., & Kawas, C. H. (2017). Late-onset Alzheimer disease. *Neurologic Clinics, 35,* 283–293. http://dx.doi.org/10.1016/j.ncl.2017.01.006.

Poewe, W., Seppi, K., Tanner, C. M., Halliday, G. M., Brundin, P., Volkmann, J., et al. (2017). Parkinson disease. *Nature Reviews. Disease Primers, 3,* 17013. http://dx.doi.org/10.1038/nrdp.2017.13.

van der Post, S., Jabbar, K. S., Birchenough, G., Arike, L., Akhtar, N., Sjovall, H., et al. (2019). Structural weakening of the colonic mucus barrier is an early event in ulcerative colitis pathogenesis. *Gut.* http://dx.doi.org/10.1136/gutjnl-2018-317571. Mar 26. pii: gutjnl-2018-317571([Epub ahead of print]).

Powrie, F., Leach, M. W., Mauze, S., Menon, S., Caddle, L. B., & Coffman, R. L. (1994). Inhibition of Th1 responses prevents inflammatory bowel disease in SCID mice reconstituted with CD45RBhi CD4+ T cells. *Immunity, 1,* 553–562. PMID: 7600284.

Puy, V., Darwiche, W., Trudel, S., Gomila, C., Lony, C., Puy, L., et al. (2018). Predominant role of microglia in brain iron retention in Sanfilippo syndrome, a pediatric neurodegenerative disease. *Glia, 66,* 1709–1723. http://dx.doi.org/10.1002/glia.23335.

Rahmoune, H., Lamblin, G., Lafitte, J. J., Galabert, C., Filliat, M., & Roussel, P. (1991). Chondroitin sulfate in sputum from patients with cystic fibrosis and chronic bronchitis. *American Journal of Respiratory Cell and Molecular Biology, 5,* 315–320. http://dx.doi.org/10.1165/ajrcmb/5.4.315.

Rannou, E., Francois, A., Toullec, A., Guipaud, O., Buard, V., Tarlet, G., et al. (2015). *In vivo* evidence for an endothelium-dependent mechanism in radiation-induced normal tissue injury. *Scientific Reports, 5,* 15738. http://dx.doi.org/10.1038/srep15738.

Ransohoff, R. M. (2016). How neuroinflammation contributes to neurodegeneration. *Science, 353,* 777–783. http://dx.doi.org/10.1126/science.aag2590.

Rao, G., Ding, H. G., Huang, W., Le, D., Maxhimer, J. B., Oosterhof, A., et al. (2011). Reactive oxygen species mediate high glucose-induced heparanase-1 production and heparan sulphate proteoglycan degradation in human and rat endothelial cells: A potential role in the pathogenesis of atherosclerosis. *Diabetologia, 54,* 1527–1538. http://dx.doi.org/10.1007/s00125-011-2110-z.

Raouf, A. H., Tsai, H. H., Parker, N., Hoffman, J., Walker, R. J., & Rhodes, J. M. (1992). Sulfation of colonic mucin in ulcerative colitis and Crohn's disease. *Clinical Science, 83,* 623–626. PMID: 1335401.

Reeves, E. P., Bergin, D. A., Murray, M. A., & McElvaney, N. G. (2011). The involvement of glycosaminoglycans in airway disease associated with cystic fibrosis. *Science World Journal, 11,* 959–971. http://dx.doi.org/10.1100/tsw.2011.81.

Reeves, S. R., Kaber, G., Sheih, A., Cheng, G., Aronica, M. A., Merrilees, M. J., et al. (2016). Subepithelial accumulation of versican in a cockroach antigen-induced murine model of allerigic asthma. *Journal of Histochemistry and Cytochemistry, 64,* 364–380. http://dx.doi.org/10.1369/0022155416642989.

Reitsma, S., Slaaf, D. W., Vink, H., van Zandvoort, M. A., & oude Egbrink, M. G. (2007). The endothelial glycocalyx: Composition, functions, and visualization. *Pfluegers Archiv European Journal of Physiology, 454,* 345–359. http://dx.doi.org/10.1007/s00424-007-0212-8.

Reznichenko, L., Cheng, Q., Nizar, K., Gratiy, S. L., Saisan, P. A., Rockenstein, E. M., et al. (2012). *In vivo* alterations in calcium buffering capacity in transgenic mouse model of synucleinopathy. *Journal of Neuroscience, 32,* 9992–9998. http://dx.doi.org/10.1523/JNEUROSCI.1270-12.2012.

Rhim, A. D., Stoykova, L., Glick, M. C., & Scanlin, T. F. (2001). Terminal glycosylation in cystic fibrosis (CF): A review emphasizing the airway epithelial cell. *Glycoconjugate Journal, 18*, 649–659. PMID: 12386452.

Riordan, J. R., Rommens, J. M., Kerem, B., Alon, N., Rozmahel, R., Grzelczak, Z., et al. (1989). Identification of the cystic fibrosis gene: Cloning and characterization of complementary DNA. *Science, 245*, 1066–1073. PMID: 2475911.

Roesch, E. A., Nichols, D. P., & Chmiel, J. F. (2018). Inflammation in cystic fibrosis: An update. *Pediatric Pulmonology, 53*, S30–S50. http://dx.doi.org/10.1002/ppul.24129.

Rolls, A., Cahalon, L., Bakalash, S., Avidan, H., Lider, O., & Schwartz, M. (2006). A sulfated disaccharide derived from chondroitin sulfate proteoglycan protects against inflammation-associated neurodegeneration. *Federation of American Societies for Experimental Biology Journal, 20*, 547–549. http://dx.doi.org/10.1096/fj.05-4540fje.

Rops, A. L., Jacobs, C. W., Linssen, P. C., Boezeman, J. B., Lensen, J. F., Wijnhoven, T. J., et al. (2007a). Heparan sulfate on activated glomerular endothelial cells and exogenous heparinoids influence the rolling and adhesion of leucocytes. *Nephrology Dialysis Transplantation, 22*, 1070–1077. http://dx.doi.org/10.1093/ndt/gfl801.

Rops, A. L., Loeven, M. A., van Gemst, J. J., Eversen, I., Van Wijk, X. M., Dijkman, H. B., et al. (2014). Modulation of heparan sulfate in the glomerular endothelial glycocalyx decreases leukocyte influx during experimental glomerulonephritis. *Kidney International, 86*, 932–942. http://dx.doi.org/10.1038/ki.2014.115.

Rops, A. L., van den Hoven, M. J., Bakker, M. A., Lensen, J. F., Wijnhoven, T. J., van den Heuvel, L. P., et al. (2007b). Expression of glomerular heparan sulphate domains in murine and human lupus nephritis. *Nephrology Dialysis Transplantation, 22*, 1891–1902. http://dx.doi.org/10.1093/ndt/gfm194.

Sarbu, M., Dehelean, L., Munteanu, C. V. A., Vukelic, Ž., & Zamfir, A. D. (2017). Assessment of ganglioside age-related and topographic specificity in human brain by orbitrap mass spectrometry. *Analytical Biochemistry, 521*, 40–54. http://dx.doi.org/10.1016/j.ab.2017.01.010.

Schaefer, L., Babelova, A., Kiss, E., Hausser, H. J., Baliova, M., Krzyzankova, M., et al. (2005). The matrix component biglycan is proinflammatory and signals through Toll-like receptors 4 and 2 in macrophages. *Journal of Clinical Investigation, 115*, 2223–2233. http://dx.doi.org/10.1172/JCI23755.

Scharfman, A., Degroote, S., Beau, J., Lamblin, G., Roussel, P., & Mazurier, J. (1999). *Pseudomonas aeruginosa* binds to neoglycoconjugates bearing mucin carbohydrate determinants and predominantly to sialyl-Lewis^{x} conjugates. *Glycobiology, 9*, 757–764. http://dx.doi.org/10.1093/glycob/9.8.757.

Scharfman, A., Delmotte, P., Beau, J., Lamblin, G., Roussel, P., & Mazurier, J. (2000). Sialyl-Le^{x} and sulfo-sialyl-Le^{x} determinants are receptors for *P. aeruginosa*. *Glycoconjugate Journal, 17*, 735–740. PMID: 11425194.

Scheibner, K. A., Lutz, M. A., Boodoo, S., Fenton, M. J., Powell, J. D., & Horton, M. R. (2006). Hyaluronan fragments act as an endogenous danger signal by engaging TLR2. *The Journal of Immunology, 177*, 1272–1281. http://dx.doi.org/10.4049/jimmunol.177.2.1272.

Schjoldager, K. T., & Clausen, H. (2012). Site-specific protein O-glycosylation modulates proprotein processing - deciphering specific functions of the large polypeptide GalNAc-transferase gene family. *Biochimica et Biophysica Acta, 1820*, 2079–2094. PMID: 23022508.

Schmidt, E. P., Yang, Y., Janssen, W. J., Gandjeva, A., Perez, M. J., Barthel, L., et al. (2012). The pulmonary endothelial glycocalyx regulates neutrophil adhesion and lung injury during experimental sepsis. *Nature Medicine, 18*, 1217–1223. http://dx.doi.org/10.1038/nm.2843.

Schneider, J. S. (2018). Altered expression of genes involved in ganglioside biosynthesis in *substantia nigra* neurons in Parkinson's disease. *PLoS One, 13*, e0199189. http://dx.doi.org/10.1371/journal.pone.0199189.

Schneider, J. S., & Yuwiler, A. (1989). GM1 ganglioside treatment promotes recovery of striatal dopamine concentrations in the mouse model of MPTP-induced parkinsonism. *Experimental Neurology, 105*, 177–183. PMID: 2568945.

Sikora, A. S., Hellec, C., Carpentier, M., Martinez, P., Delos, M., Denys, A., et al. (2016). Tumour- necrosis factor-a induces heparan sulfate 6-O-endosulfatase 1 (Sulf-1) expression in fibroblasts. *The International Journal of Biochemistry & Cell Biology, 80*, 57–65. http://dx.doi.org/10.1016/j.biocel.2016.09.021.

Silver, J., Schwab, M. E., & Popovich, P. G. (2014). Central nervous system regenerative failure: Role of oligodendrocytes, astrocytes, and microglia. *Cold Spring Harbor Perspectives in Biology, 7*, a020602. http://dx.doi.org/10.1101/cshperspect.a020602.

Sobel, R. A., & Ahmed, A. S. (2001). White matter extracellular matrix chondroitin sulfate/dermatan sulfate proteoglycans in multiple sclerosis. *Journal of Neuropathology & Experimental Neurology, 60*, 1198–1207. http://dx.doi.org/10.1093/jnen/60.12.1198.

Solic, N., Wilson, J., Wilson, S. J., & Shute, J. K. (2005). Endothelial activation and increased heparan sulfate expression in cystic fibrosis. *American Journal of Respiratory and Critical Care Medicine, 172*, 892–898. http://dx.doi.org/10.1164/rccm.200409-1207OC.

Sorokin, L. (2010). The impact of the extracellular matrix on inflammation. *Nature Reviews Immunology, 10*, 712–723. http://dx.doi.org/10.1038/nri2852.

Stephenson, E. L., Mishra, M. K., Moussienko, D., Laflamme, N., Rivest, S., Ling, C. C., et al. (2018). Chondroitin sulfate proteoglycans as novel drivers of leucocyte infiltration in multiple sclerosis. *Brain, 141*, 1094–1110. http://dx.doi.org/10.1093/brain/awy033.

Suzuki, M., & Cheung, N. K. (2015). Disialoganglioside GD2 as a therapeutic target for human diseases. *Expert Opinion on Therapeutic Targets, 19*, 349–362. http://dx.doi.org/10.1517/14728222.2014.986459.

Suzuki, M., Fujikake, N., Takeuchi, T., Kohyama-Koganeya, A., Nakajima, K., Hirabayashi, Y., et al. (2015). Glucocerebrosidase deficiency accelerates the accumulation of proteinase K-resistant a- synuclein and aggravates neurodegeneration in a drosophila model of Parkinson's disease. *Human Molecular Genetics, 24*, 6675–6686. http://dx.doi.org/10.1093/hmg/ddv372.

Svennerholm, L., & Gottfries, C. G. (1994). Membrane lipids, selectively diminished in Alzheimer brains, suggest synapse loss as a primary event in early-onset form (type I) and demyelination in late- onset form (type II). *Journal of Neurochemistry, 62*, 1039–1047. http://dx.doi.org/10.1046/j.1471- 4159.1994.62031039.x.

Taylor, K. R., & Gallo, R. L. (2006). Glycosaminoglycans and their proteoglycans: Host-associated molecular patterns for initiation and modulation of inflammation. *Federation of American Societies for Experimental Biology Journal, 20*, 9–22. http://dx.doi.org/10.1096/fj.05-4682rev.

Taylor, K. R., Yamasaki, K., Radek, K. A., Di Nardo, A., Goodarzi, H., Golenbock, D., et al. (2007). Recognition of hyaluronan released in sterile injury inolves a unique receptor complex dependent on Toll-like receptor 4, CD44, and MD-2. *Journal of Biological Chemistry, 282*, 18265–18275. http://dx.doi.org/10.1074/jbc.M606352200.

Teder, P., Vandivier, R. W., Jiang, D., Liang, J., Cohn, L., Pure, E., et al. (2002). Resolution of lung inflammation by CD44. *Science, 296*, 155–158. http://dx.doi.org/10.1126/science.1069659.

Termeer, C., Benedix, F., Sleeman, J., Fieber, C., Voith, U., Ahrens, T., et al. (2002). Oligosaccharides of hyaluronan activate dendritic cells via toll-like receptor 4. *Journal of Experimental Medicine, 195*, 99–111. http://dx.doi.org/10.1084/jem.20001858.

Thornton, D. J., Rousseau, K., & McGuckin, M. A. (2008). Structure and function of the polymeric mucins in airways mucus. *Annual Review of Physiology, 70*, 459–486. http://dx.doi.org/10.1146/annurev.physiol.70.113006.100702.

Uchimura, K. (2015). Keratan sulfate: Biosynthesis, structures, and biological functions. *Methods in Molecular Biology, 1229*, 389–400. http://dx.doi.org/10.1007/978-1-4939-1714-3_30.

Uchimura, K., Morimoto-Tomita, M., Bistrup, A., Li, J., Lyon, M., Gallagher, J., et al. (2006). HSulf- 2, an extracellular endoglucosamine-6-sulfatase, selectively mobilizes heparin-bound growth factors and chemokines: Effects on VEGF, FGF-1, and SDF-1. *BMC Biochemistry, 7*, 2. http://dx.doi.org/10.1186/1471-2091-7-2.

Vaday, G. G., & Lider, O. (2000). Extracellular matrix moieties, cytokines, and enzymes: Dynamic effects on immune cell behavior and inflammation. *Journal of Leukocyte Biology, 67*, 149–159. http://dx.doi.org/10.1002/jlb.67.2.149.

Valdes-Gonzalez, T., Goto-Inoue, N., Hirano, W., Ishiyama, H., Hayasaka, T., Setou, M., et al. (2011). New Approach for glyco- and lipidomics - molecular scanning of human brain gangliosides by TLC-Blot and MALDI-QIT-TOF MS. *Journal of Neurochemistry, 116*, 678–683. http://dx.doi.org/10.1111/j.1471- 4159.2010.07152.x.

Van Dijk, W., & Mackiewicz, A. (1995). Interleukin-6-type cytokine-induced changes in acute phase protein glycosylation. *Annals of the New York Academy of Sciences, 762*, 319–330. PMID: 7545370.

Velcich, A., Yang, W., Heyer, J., Fragale, A., Nicholas, C., Viani, S., et al. (2002). Colorectal cancer in mice genetically deficient in the mucin Muc2. *Science, 295*, 1726–1729. http://dx.doi.org/10.1126/science.1069094.

Velsor, L. W., Kariya, C., Kachadourian, R., & Day, B. J. (2006). Mitochondrial oxidative stress in the lungs of cystic fibrosis transmembrane conductance regulator protein mutant mice. *American Journal of Respiratory Cell and Molecular Biology, 35*, 579–586. http://dx.doi.org/10.1165/rcmb.2005-0473OC.

Velsor, L. W., van Heeckeren, A., & Day, B. J. (2001). Antioxidant imbalance in the lungs of cystic fibrosis transmembrane conductance regulator protein mutant mice. *American Journal of Physiology - Lung Cellular and Molecular Physiology, 281*, L31–L38. http://dx.doi.org/10.1152/ajplung.2001.281.1.L31.

Verhaeghe, C., Remouchamps, C., Hennuy, B., Vanderplasschen, A., Chariot, A., Tabruyn, S. P., et al. (2007). Role of IKK and ERK pathways in intrinsic inflammation of cystic fibrosis airways. *Biochemical Pharmacology, 73*, 1982–1994. http://dx.doi.org/10.1016/j.bcp.2007.03.019.

Voynow, J. A., Gendler, S. J., & Rose, M. C. (2006). Regulation of mucin genes in chronic inflammatory airway diseases. *American Journal of Respiratory Cell and Molecular Biology, 34*, 661–665. http://dx.doi.org/10.1165/rcmb.2006-0035SF.

Wang, S., Ai, X., Freeman, S. D., Pownall, M. E., Lu, Q., Kessler, D. S., et al. (2004). QSulf1, a heparan sulfate 6-O-endosulfatase, inhibits fibroblast growth factor signaling in mesoderm induction and angiogenesis. *Proceedings of the National Academy of Sciences, 101*, 4833–4838. http://dx.doi.org/10.1073/pnas.0401028101.

Wang, A., & Hascall, V. C. (2007). Hyaluronan structures synthesized by rat mesangial cells in response to hyperglycemia induce monocyte adhesion. *Journal of Biological Chemistry, 279*, 10279–10285. http://dx.doi.org/10.1074/jbc.M312045200.

Wang, W., Xu, G. L., Jia, W. D., Ma, J. L., Li, J. S., Ge, Y. S., et al. (2009). Ligation of TLR2 by versican: A link between inflammation and metastasis. *Archives of Medical Research, 40*, 321–323. http://dx.doi.org/10.1016/j.arcmed.2009.04.005.

Waterman, M., Ben-Izhak, O., Eliakim, R., Groisman, G., Vlodavsky, I., & Ilan, N. (2007). Heparanase upregulation by colonic epithelium in inflammatory bowel disease. *Modern Pathology, 20*, 8–14. http://dx.doi.org/10.1038/modpathol.3800710.

Weber, A. J., Soong, G., Bryan, R., Saba, S., & Prince, A. (2001). Activation of NFkB in airway epithelial cells is dependent on CFTR trafficking and Cl⁻ channel function. *American Journal of Physiology - Lung Cellular and Molecular Physiology, 281*, L71–L78. http://dx.doi.org/10.1152/ajplung.2001.281.1.L71.

Wegrowski, Y., Paltot, V., Gillery, P., Kalis, B., Randoux, A., & Maquart, F. X. (1995). Stimulation of sulphated glycosaminoglycan and decorin production in adult dermal fibroblasts by recombinant human interleukin-4. *Biochemical Journal, 307*, 673–678. http://dx.doi.org/10.1042/bj3070673.

Weigel, P. H. (2015). Hyaluronan synthase: The mechanism of initiation at the reducing end and a pendulum model for polysaccharide translocation to the cell exterior. *International Journal of Cell Biology*, 367579. http://dx.doi.org/10.1155/2015/367579.

Weitoft, M., Andersson, C., Andersson-Sjoland, A., Tufvesson, E., Bjermer, L., Erjefalt, J., et al. (2014). Controlled and uncontrolled asthma display distinct alveolar tissue matrix compositions. *Respiratory Research, 15*, 67. http://dx.doi.org/10.1186/1465-9921-15-67.

Weninger, W., Biro, M., & Jain, R. (2014). Leukocyte migration in the interstitial space of non- lymphoid organs. *Nature Reviews Immunology, 14*, 232–246. http://dx.doi.org/10.1038/nri3641.

Wesley, A., Forstner, J., Qureshi, R., Mantle, M., & Forstner, G. (1983). Human intestinal mucins in cystic fibrosis. *Pediatric Research, 17*, 65–69. PMID: 6835717.

Wight, T. N., Kang, I., & Merrilees, M. J. (2014). Versican and the control of inflammation. *Matrix Biology, 35*, 152–161. http://dx.doi.org/10.1016/j.matbio.2014.01.015.

Williams, T. L., Johnson, B. R., Urbanc, B., Jenkins, A. T., Connell, S. D., & Serpell, L. C. (2011). Ap42 oligomers, but not fibrils, simultaneously bind to and cause damage to ganglioside-containing lipid membranes. *Biochemical Journal, 439*, 67–77. http://dx.doi.org/10.1042/BJ20110750.

Wu, G., Lu, Z. H., Kulkarni, N., Amin, R., & Ledeen, R. W. (2011). Mice lacking major brain gangliosides develop parkinsonism. *Neurochemical Research, 36*, 1706–1714. http://dx.doi.org/10.1007/s11064- 011-0437-y.

Wu, G., Lu, Z. H., Kulkarni, N., & Ledeen, R. W. (2012). Deficiency of ganglioside GM1 correlates with Parkinson's disease in mice and humans. *Journal of Neuroscience Research, 90*, 1997–2008. http://dx.doi.org/10.1002/jnr.23090.

Xia, B., Royall, J. A., Damera, G., Sachdev, G. P., & Cummings, R. D. (2005). Altered O-glycosylation and sulfation of airway mucins associated with cystic fibrosis. *Glycobiology, 15*, 747–775. PMID: 15994837.

Xu, Y., Krause, A., Limberis, M., Worgall, T. S., & Worgall, S. (2013). Low sphingosine-1-phosphate impairs lung dendritic cells in cystic fibrosis. *American Journal of Respiratory Cell and Molecular Biology, 48*, 250–257. http://dx.doi.org/10.1165/rcmb.2012-0021OC.

Xu, L., Xue, T., Zhang, J., & Qu, J. (2016). Knockdown of versican V1 induces a severe inflammatory response in LPS-induced acute lung injury *via* the TLR2-NF-kappaB signaling pathway in C57BL/6J mice. *Molecular Medicine Reports, 13*, 5005–5012. http://dx.doi.org/10.3892/mmr.2016.5168.

Yahi, N., & Fantini, J. (2014). Deciphering the glycolipid code of Alzheimer's and Parkinson's amyloid proteins allowed the creation of a universal ganglioside-binding peptide. *PLoS One, 9*, e104751. http://dx.doi.org/10.1371/journal.pone.0104751.

Yanagisawa, K. (2007). Role of gangliosides in Alzheimer's disease. *Biochimica et Biophysica Acta, 1768*, 1943–1951. http://dx.doi.org/10.1016/j.bbamem.2007.01.018.

Yue, X. (2017). Epithelial deletion of Sulf2 exacerbates bleomycin-induced lung injury, inflammation, and mortality. *American Journal of Respiratory Cell and Molecular Biology, 57*, 560–569. http://dx.doi.org/10.1165/rcmb.2016-0367OC.

Yue, X., Li, X., Nguyen, H. T., Chin, D. R., Sullivan, D. E., & Lasky, J. A. (2008). Transforming growth factor-p1 induces heparan sulfate 6-O-endosulfatase 1 expression in vitro and in vivo. *Journal of Biological Chemistry, 283*, 20397–20407. http://dx.doi.org/10.1074/jbc.M802850200.

Yue, X., Lu, J., Auduong, L., Sides, M. D., & Lasky, J. A. (2013). Overexpression of Sulf2 in idiopathic pulmonary fibrosis. *Glycobiology, 23*, 709–719. http://dx.doi.org/10.1093/glycob/cwt010.

Zelei, T., Csetneki, K., Vokó, Z., & Siffel, C. (2018). Epidemiology of Sanfilippo syndrome: Results of a systematic literature review. *Orphanet Journal of Rare Diseases, 13*, 53. http://dx.doi.org/10.1186/s13023-018- 0796-4.

Zhang, L. (2010). Glycosaminoglycan (GAG) biosynthesis and GAG-binding proteins. *Progress in Molecular Biology and Translational Science, 93*, 1–17. http://dx.doi.org/10.1016/S1877-1173(10)93001-9.

Zhang, Z., Takeda-Uchimura, Y., Foyez, T., Ohtake-Niimi, S., Narentuya, Akatsu, H., et al. (2017). Deficiency of a sulfotransferase for sialic acid-modified glycans mitigates Alzheimer's pathology. *Proceedings of the National Academy of Sciences, 114*, E2947–E2954. http://dx.doi.org/10.1073/pnas.1615036114.

Zhao, J., Furukawa, K., Fukumoto, S., Okada, M., Furugen, R., Miyazaki, H., et al. (1999). Attenuation of interleukin 2 signal in the spleen cells of complex ganglioside-lacking mice. *Journal of Biological Chemistry, 274*, 13744–13747. http://dx.doi.org/10.1074/jbc.274.20.13744.

Zhou, J., Nagarkatti, P., Zhong, Y., & Nagarkatti, M. (2010). Immune modulation by chondroitin sulfate and its degraded disaccharide product in the development of an experimental model of multiple sclerosis. *Journal of Neuroimmunology, 223*, 55–64. http://dx.doi.org/10.1016/j.jneuroim.2010.04.002.

Zitvogel, L., & Kroemer, G. (2015). Subversion of anticancer immunosurveillance by radiotherapy. *Nature Immunology, 16*, 1005–1007. http://dx.doi.org/10.1038/ni.3236.

Zuberi, R. I., Ge, X. N., Jiang, S., Bahaie, N. S., Kang, B. N., Hosseinkhani, R. M., et al. (2009). Deficiency of endothelial heparan sulfates attenuates allergic airway inflammation. *The Journal of Immunology, 183*, 3971–3979. http://dx.doi.org/10.4049/jimmunol.0901604.

CHAPTER FIVE

Inflammatory bowel disease and targeted oral anti-TNFα therapy

Owen R. Griffiths[a,b,*], John Landon[a], Ruth E. Coxon[a], Keith Morris[b], Philip James[b] and Rachel Adams[b]
[a]Micropharm Ltd, Carmarthenshire, United Kingdom
[b]School of Health Sciences, Cardiff Metropolitan University, Cardiff, United Kingdom
*Corresponding author: E-mail: Owen.Griffiths@micropharm.co.uk

Contents

Advances in Protein Chemistry and Structural Biology, Volume 119
ISSN 1876-1623
https://doi.org/10.1016/bs.apcsb.2019.08.009

Abstract

Antibodies have provided invaluable treatment options for many diseases, with immunotherapy revolutionising the treatment of several inflammatory disorders including inflammatory bowel disease (IBD). Accumulating evidence suggests that IBD results from an inappropriate response to intestinal microbes and environmental factors in genetically susceptible individuals, with overactivity of the pro-inflammatory pathways. On a pathophysiological level, IBD is a complex disease with intestinal fibrosis, stenosis and an increased incidence of cancer observed in those whose disease is inadequately controlled over time.

Regulating the actions of the pro-inflammatory cytokine human tumor necrosis factor-alpha (hTNFα) through the use of anti-TNFα monoclonal antibodies (e.g. infliximab, certolizumab, adalimumab and golimumab) has proven an effective intervention for IBD with their increased use a testament of their effectiveness. These agents are administered systemically thereby causing their distribution throughout the body in a condition that is localised to the gastrointestinal (GI) tract. Immunogenicity, the induction of anti-drug antibodies (ADAs), serum sickness and other undesirable side effects limit their use, whilst up to 50% of patients do not respond to initial therapy.

Diseases confined to the GI tract are ideal for targeting by oral therapy which mitigates side effects and allows for lower doses to be administered. Several oral anti-TNFα agents have been investigated with success but are not yet in general clinical use. This partially reflects the fact that the oral administration of antibodies has many barriers including the harsh environment of the GI tract and the presence of enzymes including pepsin, trypsin and chymotrypsin in the intestine which provide significant challenges to targeted oral therapy.

1. Immunotherapy

Antibodies are glycoproteins that are members of the immunoglobulin superfamily of molecules. They have been utilised for over a century for diagnostic, therapeutic and scientific purposes. Antibodies are host proteins found in serum and extracellular fluid that recognise specific regions (epitopes) on target proteins (antigens) to which they bind with high strength to modulate the activity of their target molecules. Immunotherapy, which is also called biological therapy, is a broad term that involves the treatment or prevention of conditions or diseases through the use of substances derived from living organisms or containing components of living organisms. Antibody-based immunotherapy is one type of biological therapy that can be further divided into active or passive immunotherapy:

- Active immunotherapy involves stimulating the body's own immune system by the introduction of trace amounts of an antigen(s), which activates the adaptive immune system to fight against, for example, a pathogen, and also creates immunological memory. This provides immunity (or protection) for a prolonged period but may require a booster dose to ensure an adequate response toward the antigen if re-challenged. An example would be vaccination against the influenza virus.

- Passive immunotherapy is the administration of exogenous antibodies to treat a myriad of medical conditions by, for example, neutralising toxin(s) or the clearance of endogenous cytokines. One successful application is the systemic administration of antibodies that bind to and clear snake venom constituents following envenomation (Gerardo et al., 2017).

The earliest records of active immunotherapy date back to the fifteenth century when the Chinese applied dried crusts from smallpox pustules into small cuts in the skin to elicit an immune response (Newcombe & Newcombe, 2007). In 1901 Emil von Behring was awarded the Nobel prize for his introduction of the administration of anti-diphtheria serum, making passive immunotherapy an innovative approach to medicine (von Behring, 1901).

Antibodies can be divided into monoclonal or polyclonal. Monoclonal antibodies (McAb) bind to a single epitope on an antigen with equal strength. They are produced by a single clone of B cells, meaning that all of the antibodies produced are identical in their specificity and binding strength. Alternatively, polyclonal antibodies (PcAb) are produced by several different B cells and represent a heterogenous cocktail, capable of recognising and binding to several different epitopes on an antigen with different affinities. Whereas affinity is the binding strength of a single (monovalent) interaction between an antibody and epitope, avidity reflects the average binding intensity between multivalent antibodies and antigens. For instance, IgM is decavalent whilst IgG is bivalent; a higher valency means that IgM can bind several epitopes and has a higher avidity. Similarly, several PcAb may bind to an antigen to form large, stable structures with high avidity.

Whereas a McAb targets a single epitope on an antigen, PcAb target multiple epitopes, which augments the likelihood of neutralisation. For this reason, PcAb could be considered more efficacious, especially as they bind with higher numbers. Antibodies can also activate cells via the Fc region leading to the effective elimination of micro-organisms, viruses and toxic molecules via phagocytosis.

Antibodies can be processed into fragments allowing for deeper tissue penetration and a lowered protein-load, thus reducing the likelihood of mounting a humoral immune response and serum sickness when administered. For deep-seated applications such as digoxin toxicity, where the drug is small and able to penetrate deeply, Fab fragments are considered

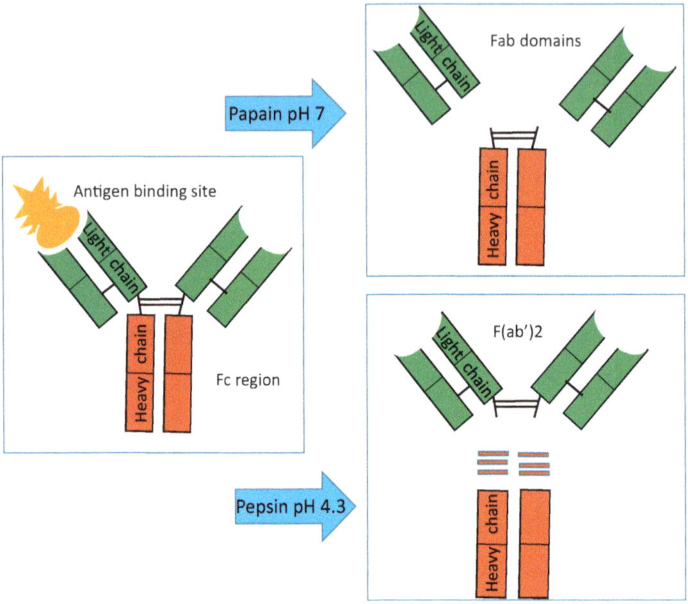

Fig. 1 Papain cleaves an antibody into three domains: two Fabs (monovalent for antigen binding) and one Fc (effector) by cleaving above the disulphide bond of the heavy chain. Pepsin cleaves below the disulphide bond giving rise to one F(ab')$_2$ (bivalent for antigen binding) and Fc fragments of various size. *(Adapted from: Lipman, Jackson, Trudel, & Weis-Garcia, 2005).*

better than intact immunoglobulins (Ig) (see Fig. 1). However, in lowering the molecular weight and size, the antibody's systemic half-life is reduced and may necessitate more frequent or repeated antibody dosing.

2. Inflammatory bowel disease

Inflammatory bowel disease (IBD) is a collective term for the autoimmune inflammatory disorders ulcerative colitis (UC), Crohn's disease (CD) and the less common phenotype, indeterminate colitis, which accounts for 10%–15% of cases (Clarke & Chintanaboina, 2018; Wu, Wei, Wang, Qi, & Wang, 2018). These distinct disorders are lifelong conditions associated with mucosal inflammation of the GI tract (Coskun, 2014).

IBD arises from an unrestrained and inappropriately activated immune system and is perpetuated through the continuous release and actions of pro-inflammatory cytokines. It is a highly destructive condition that leads to an altered architecture of the GI tract and culminates in complications such as stenosis, abscesses, fistulae, extraintestinal manifestations and colitis-associated neoplasia (Baumgart & Sandborn, 2012; Chelakkot, Ghim, & Ryu, 2018; Danese & Fiocchi, 2011; Neurath, 2017). Being chronic, relapsing and incurable, it carries significant morbidity. IBD has a substantial impact on quality of life, with personal, emotional and social burdens affecting general wellbeing and mental health (Jones et al., 2019). Therefore, there is an urgent need for novel, clinically efficacious agents to improve the quality of life of patients with IBD.

2.1 Etiology

The etiology of IBD remains idiopathic, but evidence suggests that it is multifactorial: an interplay between genetic, microbial and environmental factors that together trigger an inappropriate mucosal immune response (Coskun, 2014; Miyoshi & Chang, 2017). Two reviews in the Lancet examined the etiology, pathology, diagnosis and management of both CD and UC (Torres, Mehandru, Colombel, & Peyrin-Biroulet, 2017; Ungaro, Mehandru, Allen, Peyrin-Biroulet, & Colombel, 2017). Accumulating evidence suggests that IBD results from an inappropriate response to intestinal microbes and environmental factors in genetically susceptible individuals (Wilhelm & Love, 2017), with a growing body of evidence reporting smoking, antibiotics, oral contraceptives, appendectomy and diet as being contributory to its increasing prevalence (Ng et al., 2013; Wilhelm & Love, 2017). There are several hypotheses around the pathophysiology of IBD including an impaired mucosal barrier, dysbiosis, persistent pathogenic infection and immune dysregulation (Silva, Rodrigues, Ayrizono, & Leal, 2016). IBD pathogenesis arises from genetic susceptibility and environmental impact on the microbiome that through a weakened intestinal barrier leads to the inappropriate activation of intestinal immune cells (Ramos & Papadakis, 2019), giving rise to a pro-inflammatory cytokine loop that overrides anti-inflammatory signals and causes chronic intestinal inflammation (Neurath, 2019).

2.2 Incidence and prevalence

The incidence and prevalence of IBD is increasing worldwide, being most common in the Western world with approximately 2.5−3.0 million affected in Europe (Burisch, Jess, Martinato, Lakatos, & ECCO -EpiCom, 2013) (see Fig. 2). The highest incidence is found in Scandinavia and the UK (Burisch et al., 2013). In Europe, as many as 1 in 198 persons have UC and 1 in 310 have CD (Wehkamp, Götz, Herrlinger, Steurer, & Stange, 2016), while in the UK, 0.5%−1% of the population have IBD (Ghosh & Premchand, 2015). All age groups can be affected, but usually there is a bimodal age

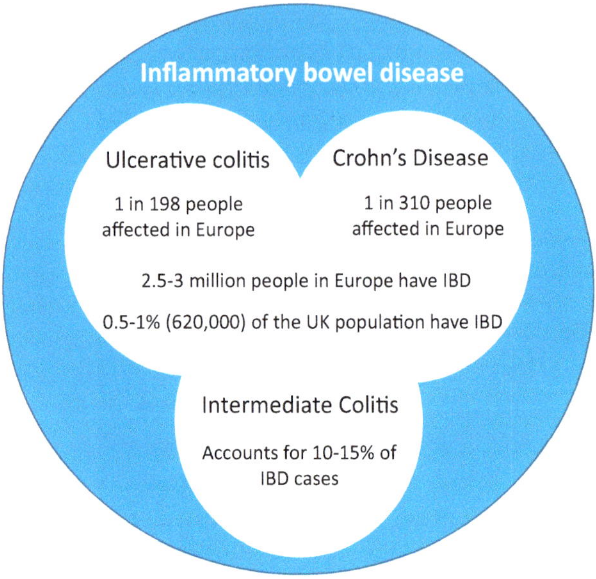

Fig. 2 The incidence and prevalence of IBD.

of presentation, mainly in the 20–40 and 60–80 age groups (Ghosh & Premchand, 2015; Wilhelm & Love, 2017).

2.3 Symptoms

A typical presentation of IBD includes diarrhea, weight loss, abdominal pain and, in UC, perianal bleeding (Wehkamp et al., 2016). CD generally involves the ileum and/or colon, is usually transmural and can be associated with granulomas, strictures and fistulae. In contrast, UC is typically confined to the mucosa, is continuous and involves all or parts of the colon and rectum. Patients with IBD also have a higher incidence of other autoimmune inflammatory disorders such as asthma, rheumatoid arthritis, type 1 diabetes, celiac disease, primary sclerosing cholangitis, pyoderma gangrenosum, sarcoidosis, iridocyclitis, psoriasis and ankylosing spondylitis (Halling, Kjeldsen, Knudsen, Nielsen, & Hansen, 2017).

2.4 Diagnosis

Diagnosis of IBD is based on clinical symptoms followed by a sigmoidoscopy or colonoscopy to provide the most accurate confirmation of disease. The diagnosis of a chronic condition carries, in the immediate phase, psychological and physical challenges that have an impact on morbidity and quality of life (Wilhelm, & Love, 2017). The stigma and challenges can continue beyond the initial flare-up phase when, owing to the condition's sporadic or unrelenting nature, impact on social and sexual aspects of life and body image, together affects quality of life (Umanskiy & Fichera, 2010).

2.5 Current management

Current management includes treatment with aminosalicylates (e.g. 5-aminosalicylic acid) (Wang, Parker, Feagan, & MacDonald, 2016), glucocorticosteroids (Ford et al., 2011), immunomodulators (e.g. azathioprine and 6-mercaptopurine) (Chande, Townsend, Parker, & MacDonald, 2016; Timmer, Patton, Chande, McDonald, & MacDonald, 2016), anti-TNFα biological agents (Hanauer et al., 2002; Sandborn et al., 2014, 2007, 2012) and inhibitors of other molecular pathways, such as leukocyte adhesion inhibitors (Cherry, Yunker, Lambert, Vaughan, & Lowe, 2015), introduced in a stepwise manner (Torres et al., 2017; Ungaro et al., 2017). Therapy aims to induce and then maintain remission, improve quality of life, avoid or delay the need for surgery and prevent complications such as perforation, strictures, toxic megacolon or colitis-associated cancer (Khajah, 2017). However, no pharmacological treatment is curative, with a third of IBD patients requiring surgical intervention (Coskun, 2014), thus highlighting the limitations of current pharmacological therapies. Current therapies are limited by their cost, undesirable side effects, including the reactivation of latent tuberculosis and non-Hodgkin's lymphoma, and reduced efficacy over time. Thus, there exists an urgent, unmet, medical need for more effective agents, with acceptable tolerability profiles that can be used indefinitely without their efficacy diminishing.

3. The gastrointestinal tract

The human intestine forms the fundamental barrier between the harmful luminal contents of the gut and the host, being home to trillions of commensal and pathogenic bacteria (see Fig. 3). The intestinal epithelium is strategically positioned as a protective physical barrier, dividing the luminal microbiota from the mucosal immune cells found in the lamina propria and the rest of the body. This barrier comprises a monolayer of specialised intestinal epithelial cells (IEC) that are coated in a layer of mucus and are crucial in maintaining intestinal homeostasis (Coskun, 2014; Wu et al., 2018). A breakdown in this barrier leads to increased intestinal permeability culminating in the interaction between microbial contents of the gut, the IEC

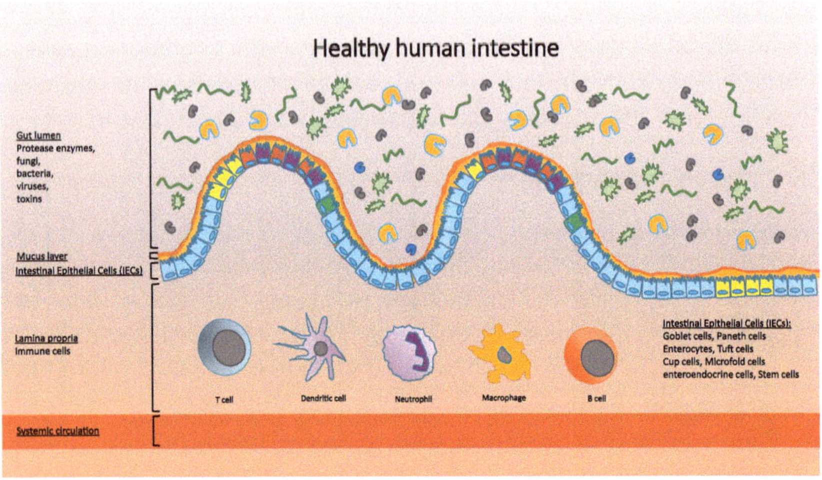

Fig. 3 A schematic diagram showing the 'ideal' physiology of a healthy human gut. Intestinal epithelial cells (IEC) provide a protective barrier that prevents noxious luminal contents from coming into contact with immune cells situated in the lamina propria. A layer of mucus sits on top of the IEC acts as a protective barrier, preventing commensal bacteria, microbial peptides and protease enzymes from translocating beyond the lumen of the intestine.

and immune cells in the underlying lamina propria, thereby disturbing intestinal immune homeostasis (Coskun, 2014) (see Fig. 4). The mucus contains antimicrobial peptides called defensins that prevent cross-talk between the microbial contents and the immune cells of the gut. The epithelial barrier divides the lamina propria - which contains cells such as dendritic cells, T cells, B cells and macrophages - from the lumen of the gut that contains micro-organisms and protease enzymes (Chelakkot et al., 2018; Eri & Chieppa, 2013; Saenz, Taylor, & Artis, 2008). The selective absorption of nutrients, ions and water is carefully regulated while the passage of foreign proteins is occluded (Clayburgh, Shen, & Turner, 2004; Eutamene, Beaufrand, Harkat, & Theodorou, 2018).

3.1 Pathophysiology of inflammatory bowel disease (IBD)

3.1.1 Intestinal epithelial barrier

The luminal surface of the gut contains a monolayer of several specialised cells including absorptive and secretory cells (e.g. goblet cells, enteroendocrine cells, Paneth cells), all of which are derived from epithelial stem cells (Coskun, 2014; Wu et al., 2018). Goblet cells secrete mucus while Paneth

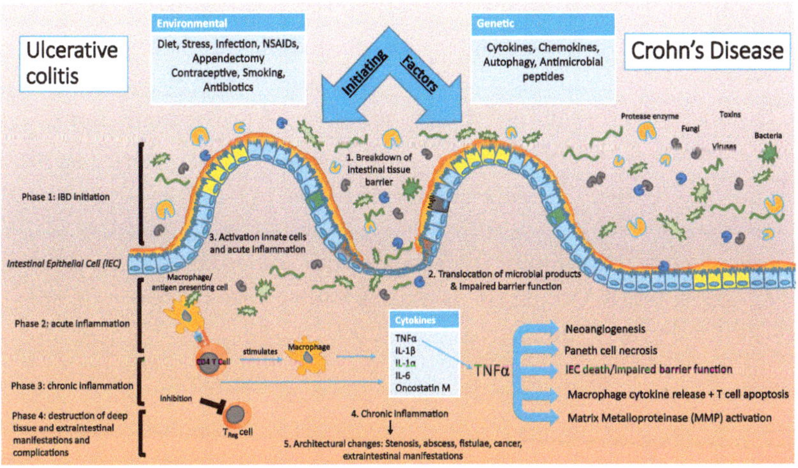

Fig. 4 A schematic diagram showing the pathophysiology of IBD. Environmental and genetic factors predispose and trigger inflammatory bowel disease (IBD). A breakdown in the intestinal epithelial cell (IEC) barrier leads to the translocation of commensal bacteria and microbial products that come into contact with immune cells in the lamina propria and activate immune cells. The activation of pro-inflammatory immune cells and the inhibition of anti-inflammatory pathways leads to chronic inflammation and structural changes resulting in disease complications such as intestinal fibrosis, stenosis and cancer. Several cytokines and immune cells are involved but tumor necrosis factor alpha is considered a major player in driving inflammation in IBD.

cells produce antimicrobial peptides. Together, these cells maintain homeostasis, forming the division between the noxious contents of the lumen and the lamina propria, a thin layer of connective tissue that is home to immune cells. This protective barrier becomes compromised and 'leaky' in inflammatory bowel disease, often orchestrated by cytokines released by immune cells in response to bacteria in the intestinal lumen. It has been shown that the dysregulated differentiation of these specialised cells plays a significant role in the pathogenesis of IBD, with several of the encoding genes overexpressed (Ahn et al., 2008; Coskun et al., 2012; Zheng et al., 2011). The impaired mucosal barrier allows entry of harmful luminal pathogens which elicits an immune response and, in a genetically susceptible individual, leads to IBD. The intestinal epithelial cells also contain toll-like receptors (TLR) and nucleotide oligomerization domain (NOOD) receptors that are pathogen-sensitive innate immune receptors (Coskun, 2014). Upon activation by pathogens, chemokines and cytokines are produced to recruit immune cells (Hisamatsu et al., 2013; Silva et al., 2016).

3.1.2 Lamina propria

The hallmark of IBD is the pronounced infiltration of both innate and adaptive immune cells (including macrophages, dendritic cells, B and T cells) into the lamina propria, resulting in elevated levels of pro-inflammatory cytokines including TNFα, IL-1α, IL-1β, IL-6 and oncostatin M (West et al., 2017). The cytokine oncostatin M (OSM) and its receptor, which is found on stromal cells in the lamina propria, is increased in the intestine of IBD patients and has been shown to correlate with disease severity (West et al., 2017). High OSM expression is strongly linked to treatment failure of anti-TNFα therapy (Abraham & Cho, 2009).

3.1.3 Intestinal microbiota

The commensal microbiota, with its varied function and composition, has been reported to be involved in IBD (Khajah, 2017; Sartor, 2008; Tannock, 2008) with a disrupted intestinal barrier being the entry port for pathogenic bacteria (Nell, Suerbaum, & Josenhans, 2010), although this evidence is limited. Among several factors, it has also been proposed that minor variances in the host's genetics can influence the gut's microbiota and consequently an individual's susceptibility to IBD (Spor, Koren, & Ley, 2011), with diet and lifestyle also affecting the intestinal microbiota leading to an impaired mucosal barrier (Devkota et al., 2012; Hisamatsu et al., 2013; Silva et al., 2016; Ward et al., 2016). It has been shown that a constant diet that keeps the microbiota constant can be a preventative measure for IBD (Devkota et al., 2012; Silva et al., 2016).

The gut contains approximately 10^{11}-10^{12} micro-organisms per gram of intestinal lumen content that are essential to protect the gut epithelium (Silva et al., 2016). To date, no single bacterium has been proven responsible for causing IBD. Dysbiosis, the imbalance of gut micro-organisms disrupting gut immune homeostasis, is considered causative (Miyoshi & Chang, 2017; Silva et al., 2016). Antibiotics, for instance, are known to affect commensal gut bacteria, causing dysbiosis. There exists substantial evidence that antibiotic exposure in childhood increases the risk of IBD (Hviid, Svanström, & Frisch, 2011; Kronman, Zaoutis, Haynes, Feng, & Coffin, 2012; Miyoshi & Chang, 2017; Ungaro et al., 2014), with an even higher incidence correlating with the number of antibiotic prescriptions issued (Miyoshi & Chang, 2017; Virta, Auvinen, Helenius, Huovinen, & Kolho, 2012). Conversely, childhood exposure to commensal bacteria has been proposed to protect against IBD by stabilising immune tolerance (Silva et al., 2016; von Mutius, 2007).

The concept behind fecal microbiota transplantation is to restore commensal bacteria to their normal state. In IBD, the levels of protective bacteria (clostridia and bacteroid) are lowered, while pathogenic bacteria (e.g. adhesive invasive *Escherichia coli* and *Mycobacterium avium paratuberculosis*) are increased (Khajah, 2017). However, this method poses risks with the potential for transferring diseases and infectious organisms.

3.1.4 Mucus layer

A mucus layer lines the top of the intestinal epithelial cell monolayer and coats the entire surface of the digestive tract. Produced by goblet cells, mucus is the defense wall protecting the immune system of the gut from commensal microbiota and helps provide a division between the host and the outside world. It also protects the epithelial layer against protease and other enzymes (Qin, 2017; Wu et al., 2018), microbial pathogens and toxins. The mucus layer is divided into a sterile inner layer and a non-sterile outer layer which is in contact with the lumen (Johansson et al., 2014; Wu et al., 2018). The inner layer is very dense, sterile and difficult to remove, while the outer layer is hydrolyzed by glycosidases into a looser structure that is occupied by commensal bacteria and is continuously being removed by the movement of the luminal contents (Wu et al., 2018). Owing to the regeneration of mucus, bacteria are pushed outwards to the lumen. Once homeostasis is lost, this barrier becomes compromised leading to the entry of bacteria and toxins that come into contact and activate the immune system (Wu et al., 2018). IEC provide the barrier that separates the host and the environment and is crucial in ensuring that microbes and toxins do not enter the systemic circulation.

It has been shown that the thickness of the mucus layer and the population of goblet cells is reduced in UC patients (Fyderek et al., 2009; Schultsz, Van Den Berg, Ten Kate, Tytgat, & Dankert, 1999; Steck, Mueller, Schemann, & Haller, 2012; Strugala, Dettmar, & Pearson, 2008; Wu et al., 2018). Also observed was that MUC2 deficient mice spontaneously developed colitis, which highlights the protective role it plays (Van der Sluis et al., 2006; Wu et al., 2018). Fecal supernatants from UC patients were shown to break down mucus (Dwarakanath et al., 1995; Wu et al., 2018).

3.1.5 Digestive enzymes

Pancreas-derived serine protease enzymes such as trypsin, chymotrypsin and elastase are powerful hydrolyzing enzymes found in the gut that are essential for the breakdown of proteins duringdigestion (Wu et al., 2018). It is well established that the levels of fecal protease enzymes in feces are raised in UC (Bustos et al., 1998; Róka et al., 2007; Steck et al., 2012; Van Spaendonk et al., 2017). In the event of the mucus layer becoming compromised, the epithelial layer becomes exposed to self-digestion, which inflicts tissue damage and ulceration. In IBD patients, protease enzymes are elevated to three times the level found in healthy individuals (Gecse et al., 2008; Wu et al., 2018). Furthermore, an established colitis mouse model of IBD (Galphai2−/− mice) showed elevated levels of fecal peptidase D, an intracellular protease enzyme, compared to control (Bergemalm, Kruse, Sapnara, Halfvarson, & Hörnquist, 2017). All these findings, and the "Bacteria-Protease-Mucus-Barrier hypothesis" (Qin, 2012), demonstrate the role of protease enzymes in IBD pathogenesis. Although the focus has been on host-derived proteases, those released by bacteria have received less attention (Steck et al., 2012; Van Spaendonk et al., 2017). However, mice administered antibiotics saw a reduction in colonic microbiota and serine protease activity, suggesting that bacteria also contribute (Róka et al., 2007).

3.1.6 Tight junction proteins

The intestinal epithelial monolayer is connected by tight junction proteins (TJP) which are the gatekeepers of paracellular permeability (Van Spaendonk et al., 2017; Wu et al., 2018), as well as adherens junctions and desmosomes (Van Spaendonk et al., 2017). TJP include the adhesive transmembrane proteins occludin, claudins, and the cytoplasmic proteins zonula occludens (Zos) (Van Spaendonk et al., 2017). Nutrients, ions and water are selectively allowed passage, whereas bacterial toxins and pathogens are occluded (Rescigno, 2011). TJP are crucial for barrier integrity and an impaired system can be detrimental to gut homeostasis. The expression and structure of these proteins are altered in IBD (Coskun, 2014; Heller et al., 2005; Schmitz et al., 1999; Zeissig et al., 2007), with increased levels of IFNγ, TNFα and other cytokines augmenting TJP permeability and the apoptosis of intestinal epithelial cells (Chelakkot et al., 2018; Coskun, 2014; Marini et al., 2003; Nava et al., 2010; Su et al., 2013). A link has been demonstrated between cellular permeability and mucosal inflammation in CD and UC (Coskun, 2014; Mankertz & Schulzke, 2007) and it has been proposed that evaluating TJP expression may prove a potential marker for mucosal healing.

3.1.7 Cytokines

Cytokines control the initiation, evolution and resolution of all inflammatory states. The role of cytokines in IBD was first described by Ebert et al. and Mitsuyama et al. in the mid-1980s and early 1990s (Ebert, Wright, Lipshutz, & Hauptman, 1984; Mitsuyama, Sata, & Tanikawa, 1991). They described the pro-inflammatory roles of IL-2 and IL-6, respectively, and observed a change in cytokine levels produced by immune cells in the periphery and lamina propria of IBD patients. Owing to differences in the pathological and clinical features of CD and UC, at the time it seemed that different cytokines were involved for each condition.

Initial research concentrated on treating IBD by administering anti-inflammatory cytokines (e.g. IFNβ, IL-10 and IL-11) but the outcomes proved disappointing (Herrlinger et al., 2006; Musch et al., 2005; Neurath, 2014; Tilg, Ulmer, Kaser, & Weiss, 2002). Focus then turned to targeting pro-inflammatory cytokines, or more specifically, the neutralisation of TNFα using a chimeric monoclonal antibody (infliximab). This proved a significant success in initiating and maintaining disease remission through the blockade of TNFα alone (Hanauer et al., 2002; Kornbluth, 1998; van Dullemen et al., 1995). TNFα blockade has since become the cornerstone of clinical intervention and revolutionised the treatment of IBD.

Cytokines not only drive inflammation but also give rise to extraintestinal disease manifestations (e.g. arthritis and arthralgia) and disease symptoms (e.g. diarrhea). For instance, TNFα has been the driving cytokine in arthritis and cachexia, whereas IL-6 is known to induce acute-phase proteins by the liver (Neurath, 2014).

The drive of cytokines in IBD cannot be underestimated. Modulating cytokine levels in mouse models of IBD has helped identify cytokines as targets for therapy (Neurath, Finotto, & Glimcher, 2002; Powrie et al., 1994). For example, gene knock-out mice deficient of the regulatory cytokines IL-2 & IL-10 were found to spontaneously develop colitis (Strober, Fuss, & Blumberg, 2002). Furthermore, out of 66 children with early-onset severe IBD (all aged below 5), 16 patients had loss in function mutations: three in IL-10, and 13 in the IL-10 receptor. Remission could be induced in the IL10R patients through allogenic haematopoietic stem cell transplantation (Kotlarz et al., 2012). However, the neutralisation of the pro-inflammatory cytokine interferon γ (IFN-γ) with fontolizumab proved disappointing (Reinisch et al., 2006), with the anti-IL-17A agents, secukinumab and ixekizumab, aggravating IBD (Hueber et al., 2012; Philipose, Ahmed, Idiculla, Mulrooney, & Gumaste, 2018).

A correlation has been shown between the genetic make-up of individuals and several cytokine and chemokine receptor signaling proteins that they encode for (Jostins et al., 2012), thus highlighting the significance of specific cytokines in IBD pathogenesis. IL-2, IL-21, IFNγ, IL-10 and IL-27 were identified as IBD risk loci (Jostins et al., 2012; Neurath, 2014). The Genome Wide Association Studies (GWASs) and subsequent meta-analysis has also identified a crossover of several gene loci between IBD and other immune-mediated disorders including ankylosing spondylitis and psoriasis (Jostins et al., 2012). A total of 163 IBD associated gene loci have been identified, with 110 associated with CD and UC, suggesting shared pathology (Jostins et al., 2012). However, not all patients with genetic susceptibility genes develop IBD which suggests that other factors such as diet, smoking, drugs, infections, geography and stress play a role (Abraham & Cho, 2009; Coskun, 2014). With cytokines playing such a significant role in IBD, and with our understanding improving, focus may be moving toward individualised therapy based on genetic make-up.

A detailed review of cytokines in IBD identified TNFα, IFNγ, IL-6, IL-12, IL-17A, IL-17F, IL-23 and IL-21 as potential pro-inflammatory cytokines with IL-10, IL-33, IL-35, and IL-37 as anti-inflammatory cytokine targets (M. F. Neurath, 2014). Despite several attempts at targeting different cytokines and proteins in the inflammatory pathway to manage IBD, few agents have provided promise. TNFα, most likely due to its early position in the inflammatory cascade, has shown the most significant benefit for managing IBD (Hanauer et al., 2002; Sandborn et al., 2014, 2007, 2012).

4. Tumor necrosis factor-alpha (TNFα)

TNFα is a potent, pleiotropic, pro-inflammatory cytokine involved in the pathogenesis of several inflammatory disorders (Netea et al., 2017). It is produced by various immune and non-immune cells in the inflamed gut of patients with IBD including activated macrophages, T cells, dendritic cells, fibroblasts, smooth muscle and fat cells (Atzeni et al., 2015; Horiuchi, Mitoma, Harashima, Tsukamoto, & Shimoda, 2010; Neurath, 2014).

The increased number of TNFα-producing cells present in intestinal specimens from IBD patients (Breese et al., 1994) explains why the introduction of agents that neutralise its effects, when administered systemically over prolonged periods of time, has proven beneficial (Parameswaran & Patial, 2010). TNFα's early on position in the inflammatory pathway makes it the ideal target for therapy. It is therefore no surprise that TNFα is referred to as "the master regulator of inflammatory cytokines" considering its pivotal role in orchestrating the cytokine cascade in several inflammatory conditions, including IBD (Parameswaran & Patial, 2010). It is one of the first cytokines to appear at the site of injury or stress to trigger inflammation, presenting within minutes (Monaco, Nanchahal, Taylor, & Feldmann, 2015). It can be imagined as the body's 'fire alarm system' in response to a stress stimuli, recruiting 'firefighters' which are the leukocytes that arrive from the bloodstream to the site of inflammation, infection or injury (Feldmann & Pusey, 2006). For instance, the pro-inflammatory cytokines IL-1β and IL-6 present later, with evidence supporting the need for TNFα to induce their synthesis and secretion (Fong et al., 1989). It is therefore unsurprising that TNFα has become such a desirable target for inflammatory conditions (Parameswaran & Patial, 2010).

The name tumor necrosis factor (previously cachectin) suggests anti-cancer properties which were observed initially when necrosis of subcutaneous tumors in mice resulted from TNFα exposure, leading to vascular activation and thrombosis[9]. However, such anti-tumour activity appears atypical in most human cancers and, to date, there has not been any substantial role for TNFα in cancer.

In inflammation, TNFα causes vasodilation, oedema formation, leukocyte adhesion to epithelial cells through the expression of adhesion molecules, the regulation of blood coagulation, oxidative stress at sites of inflammation and indirectly induces fever (Zelová & Hošek, 2013). In the bowel wall, TNFα induces neoangiogenesis, activates macrophages to produce inflammatory cytokines, leads to Paneth cell death, increases epithelial cell death, regulates T-cell apoptosis and interferes with tissue inhibitor matrix metalloproteinases (MMPs) by fibroblasts, resulting in tissue injury via activated MMPs (Neurath, 2017).

One form of TNFα is bound to the cell membrane as a polypeptide (mTNFα) of 233 amino acids with a molecular weight of 26 kDa. A metalloproteinase TNFα converting enzyme (TACE) cleaves it between alanine^{76} and valine^{77} to release soluble TNFα (sTNFα) comprising 157 amino acids with a molecular weight of 17 kDa (Horiuchi et al., 2010). Once released, the unglycosylated polypeptide associates non-covalently to form a homo-trimer. Evidence suggests that TNFα acts as a bi-functional molecule where both the soluble and membrane bound TNFα can interact in a cell-to-cell fashion with its receptors, resulting in the activation of an inflammatory response (Horiuchi et al., 2010). Effective TNFα blocking agents must therefore target both membrane and soluble TNFα.

Membrane TNFα and soluble TNFα cause their effects by binding with high affinity to one of two receptors, TNF-R1 and TNF-R2 (McCann et al., 2014). TNFR1, known as p55, is found on all nucleated cells and its binding with soluble TNFα causes activation of the inflammatory cascade through nuclear factor kappa-light-chain-enhancer of activated B cells (NF-κB), mitogen-activated protein kinases as well as anti-apoptotic responses and the generation of other pro-inflammatory cytokines such as IL-1, IL-6 and GM-CSF (Monaco et al., 2015). TNFR1 knockout mice have reduced inflammatory responses (Monaco et al., 2015).

TNFR2, referred to as p75, is believed to have an immunoregulatory role and is found mostly on the surface of regulatory T cells (Monaco et al., 2015). Its actions are mostly involved in repair and homeostasis (Monaco et al., 2015), with receptor activation resulting in immunosuppression and the resolution of inflammation (McCann et al., 2014). This suggests that selective antagonism of TNFR1 while sparing TNFR2 may be a better approach to targeting inflammation.

4.1 TNFα blockade

Intravenous and subcutaneous biologics that target TNFα have revolutionised the treatment of IBD; they have become the best agents available for inducing and maintaining IBD remission and form the fundamental backbone of present therapy (Paramsothy, Cleveland, Zmeter, & Rubin, 2016). They bind and remove TNFα, thus inhibiting its inflammatory actions in the gut (Horiuchi et al., 2010) and allowing healing to occur. However, the actions of a drug administered intravenously cannot be confined to an area such as the gut and fundamentally treats the entire body; this has been responsible for many of its major side effects, including the reactivation of latent tuberculosis and non-Hodgkin's lymphoma.

In 1998, the chimeric monoclonal anti-TNFα agent infliximab was approved by the FDA for the treatment of moderate to severe Crohn's disease (Kornbluth, 1998). The ACCENT I trial evaluated 335 patients and reported that infliximab improved CD remission rates at week 30 compared to placebo (45% vs. 21%; $p = 0.002$) (Hanauer et al., 2002). At week 54, these effects were maintained, highlighting TNFα blockade as a means of inducing and, most importantly, maintaining remission. It is administered intravenously at a dose of 5 mg/kg at 0, 2 and 6 weeks, and then continued every 8 weeks thereafter.

Since Infliximab was approved, other McAb have become available: adalimumab, certolizumab and golimumab (see Table 1). These are fully humanised McAb that are usually reserved for people who cannot tolerate or who have developed resistance to infliximab (Hanauer et al., 2006; Sandborn et al., 2014, 2007, 2012). Whereas infliximab is given as an intravenous infusion, these agents have the benefit of being administered subcutaneously which allows administration outside of a hospital setting. Upcoming biosimilar agents offer cheaper alternatives to the branded equivalents.

A substantial proportion of total IBD expenditure is on TNFα blockers that are very expensive. The 2017 top drug by sales was adalimumab, reaching 18.4 US $ billion (Urquhart, 2018). Moreover, six of the top eight drugs by sales in 2017 were monoclonal antibodies, with the anti-TNFα agents Remicade® (infliximab) (5.8 US $ billion) sixth and Enbrel® (etanercept) (5.4 US $ billion) eighth (Urquhart, 2018). The UK National IBD audit estimated NHS IBD expenditure to be £1 billion in 2010, with an average spend of £3000 per patient per annum (Ghosh & Premchand, 2015). With inflation, this figure will have risen annually.

Etanercept, an anti-TNFα receptor used for rheumatoid arthritis, has proven disappointing in Crohn's disease (Sandborn et al., 2001). This may be explained by its structure, where a soluble TNFα receptor fusion protein blocks soluble TNFα but not the membrane bound form (Almon et al., 2017).

4.2 Response to systemic anti-TNFα therapy

Approximately 40–50% of the population with IBD will not respond to anti TNFα therapy (Strober & Fuss, 2011; West et al., 2017), with one-third of patients requiring surgery as a result of complete non-responsiveness to conventional therapy (Coskun, 2014). Although the reason is not known, it has been proposed that failure to cause T cell apoptosis is the predominant cause (Mitoma et al., 2005; Strober & Fuss, 2011; Tilg, Moschen, & Kaser, 2007). The population receiving anti-TNFα therapy who fail to benefit fully can be categorised into primary non-responders or secondary non-responders (Ben-Horin, Kopylov, & Chowers, 2014). It is currently unknown whether those patients who do not respond to intravenous anti-TNFα therapy will respond to anti-TNFα therapy administered orally, where the antibodies will not be exposed to the systemic circulation.

Table 1 Currently approved anti-TNFα therapy and licensed UK indications.

Drug name	Brand name	Biosimilar	Route of administration	Licensed UK indication(s)	Structure
Infliximab	Remicade®	Inflectra® Flixabi®, Remsima®, Zessly®	Intravenous	Severe active UC, severe active CD and fistulating CD, rheumatoid arthritis (in combination with methotrexate), ankylosing spondylitis, psoriatic arthritis, plaque psoriasis	Chimeric McAb. The Fab fragments are murine and the rest of human origin
Adalimumab	Humira®	Amgevita®, Hulio®, Hyrimoz®, Imraldi®	Subcutaneous	UC, CD plaque psoriasis, rheumatoid arthritis, psoriatic arthritis, ankylosing spondylitis, axial spondylarthritis, hidradenitis suppurativa, uveitis	Fully humanised McAb
Golimumab	Simponi®	–	Subcutaneous	UC, rheumatoid arthritis, psoriatic arthritis, ankylosing spondylitis, non-radiographic axial spondylarthritis	Fully humanised McAb

Certolizumab pegol	Cimzia®	—	Subcutaneous	Not licensed for IBD. Rheumatoid arthritis, axial spondyloarthritis, psoriatic arthritis and plaque psoriasis	Human Fab-fragments covalently linked to polyethylene glycol (PEG). No Fc present
Etanercept	Enbrel®	Benepali®, Erelzi®	Subcutaneous	Not licensed for IBD, Rheumatoid arthritis, juvenile idiopathic arthritis, psoriatic arthritis, axial spondyloarthritis, ankylosing spondylitis, non-radiographic axial spondylarthritis and plaque psoriasis.	Human TNF-R2 covalently coupled to the heavy chain of human IgG1

4.2.1 Primary non-responders

About 10–20% of patients with IBD fail to respond to infliximab therapy. However, by switching to another agent (e.g. Adalimumab, Golimumab or Certolizumab) 50% of these patients subsequently respond, which implies it is not a class effect (Ben-Horin et al., 2014). For the remaining non-responders, it seems that immune dysregulation is driven by a different cytokine - possibly Oncostatin M, an interleukin-6 family member (West et al., 2017). It is also plausible that the TNFα is situated in regions where the McAb cannot penetrate, or TNFα levels are too high for the McAb to neutralise.

4.2.2 Secondary non-responders

Another group of patients with IBD have an excellent initial response to systemically administered McAb followed by a progressive failure in response (secondary non-responders). This is seen in 23–46% of patients at 12 months after anti-TNFα initiation (Ben-Horin et al., 2014). It has been proposed that this is due to the recipients mounting a humoral immune response to the anti-TNFα antibodies, which is recognised as a foreign protein and results in the generation of anti-drug antibodies (ADAs) (Farrell et al., 2003). The development of ADAs is believed to be the principal reason for treatment failure. The measurement of drug levels to detect the presence of antibodies has been proposed as a therapy optimisation strategy (Weisshof & Chowers, 2017).

4.3 Limitations of current anti-TNFα therapy

The occurrence of allergic reactions following parenteral immune therapy is well documented (O'Meara, Nanda, & Moss, 2014). These include a flu-like infusion reaction that can be managed by premedication with an antihistamine such as chlorphenamine and paracetamol, with or without a corticosteroid (Wilhelm & Love, 2017). With systemic antibody therapy, the toxic side effects associated with exposure of a host to a foreign protein can lead to serum sickness that includes fever, rash and joint pains (Llewelyn, Hawkins, & Russell, 1992). At worst, an anaphylactic reaction can happen. There have also been reports of patients developing psoriasis or psoriasiform skin lesions (Angelucci, Cocco, Viscido, Vernia, & Caprilli, 2007), lymphomas, infections, congestive heart failure, demyelinating disease, a lupus-like syndrome, induction of autoantibodies and systemic side effects (Scheinfeld, 2004). All patients, before therapy with an anti-TNFα agent, undergo tuberculosis and hepatitis B screening, counseling regarding the risk of lymphoma as well as hepatitis C and HIV screening (Wilhelm, Sheila & Love, Bryan, 2017). Their highly undesirable side effects can hinder their use in patients with opportunistic and non-opportunistic infections (Minozzi et al., 2016), haematological and neurological complications, hepatotoxicity and malignancies (Atzeni et al., 2015; Marino, Giani, & Cimaz, 2018). Also, with the development of a humoral immune response and the development of ADAs (Weisshof & Chowers, 2017), their clinical use and potential can be limited.

5. Future therapy

5.1 Targeted antibody therapy

The notion of delivering antibodies locally to the target site to neutralise toxins, cytokines or viruses is not novel (Hilpert et al., 1987; Kink & Williams, 1998; Worledge, Godiska, Barrett, & Kink, 2000). Doing so allows the administered systemic dose to be reduced, thus lowering cost and the incidence of side effects. In the field of ophthalmology, the treatment of age-related macular degeneration and diabetic retinopathy of the eye has been revolutionised by the local injection of vascular endothelial growth factor (VEGF) inhibitor antibodies, using only one hundredth of the systemic dose (Jones & Martino, 2016).

Anti-TNFα therapeutics have been administered via the systemic route for over 20 years when the oral route could have offered a markedly superior alternative.

5.1.1 Peroral antibody therapy

The use of oral serum dates back to the early twentieth century when diphtheria antiserum was administered orally at regular intervals with clinical benefit, requiring only a fraction of the dose needed systemically (Cumberlege, 1911). In 1906 Paton documented the use of oral serum produced from ox, sheep and horse to treat influenza and other conditions, describing it as being "treated on nature's own lines" (Paton, 1906).

Immunoglobulins of various sources including ovine, equine, murine, avian, llama and human have been administered orally to humans in several studies with no ill effects reported (Jones & Martino, 2016). There is, however, the need to highly purify and enzymatically digest polyclonal antibodies for products administered systemically to lessen the chances of a humoral immune response and lower the generation of ADAs that reduce treatment efficacy over time. For an oral product, these issues are of no importance since intact antibodies administered orally are unlikely to be absorbed significantly owing to their size.

There have been several attempts at delivering antibodies orally. These include antibodies that target *Candida albicans* in oral thrush, *Pseudomonas aeruginosa* bacterial infection of the mouth/throat in cystic fibrosis, diphtheria toxin affecting the throat, *Helicobacter pylori* infection in the stomach, rotavirus diarrhea and norovirus, Cryptosporidium parasite infection, *E.coli* toxin/bacterial components in the intestine, Crohn's disease, *Clostridium difficile* and bacillary dysentery affecting the large and small intestines (Jones & Martino, 2016).

For intravenous products, the generation of monovalent Fab or divalent $F(ab')_2$ fragments and removal of the Fc domain appears helpful in minimising hypersensitivity reactions and improving product safety (Newcombe & Newcombe, 2007). However, for oral administration, where little to no absorption of immunoglobulins is reported (Jasion & Burnett, 2015), it spares the need to humanise or despeciate the antibodies (Jones & Martino, 2016). In fact, intact immunoglobulin is a better choice for minimising absorption and, by bypassing the systemic circulation, it avoids eliciting a humoral immune response and the generation of ADAs, thereby enabling indefinite use.

The safety of oral antibodies is supported by two products currently on the market, EnteraGam® and Travelan®. Travelan® contains antibodies derived from bovine colostrum and is indicated for traveler's diarrhea, whereas EnteraGam®, derived from bovine serum, binds to microbial components such as toxins released by bacteria and is indicated for irritable bowel syndrome and associated diarrhea.

Orally delivered antibodies can be used to target cytokines, toxins, bacterial adhesion or virulence factors and viruses within the gastro-intestinal tract (Russell G. A. Jones & Martino, 2016). The local injection of antibodies require doses as low as one-10th to one hundredth of the required systemic dose, which reduces cost and side effects (Russell G. A. Jones & Martino, 2016). With the parental route, where purity is critical, the presence of protein impurities must be kept to a minimum. However, for oral administration it has been shown that antibodies within crude serum are less susceptible to pepsin digestion compared to purified Immunoglobulin G (IgG) (Jones & Martino, 2016). The presence of proteins such as albumin, which function as decoy proteins that are enzymatically favored substrates, reduce antibody digestion rate by more than half (Jones & Martino, 2016).

5.1.2 Peroral anti-TNFα therapy

The intravenous and subcutaneous route for anti-TNFα therapy has proven a success for IBD patients. However, its administration has proven time-consuming for healthcare professionals and has been accompanied by an extensive list of significant side effects including the reactivation of latent tuberculosis and non-Hodgkin's lymphoma owing to the neutralisation of TNFα's protective role (Scheinfeld, 2004). Despite these drawbacks, anti-TNFα expenditure is on the rise indicating their acceptance as the leading choice of therapy for IBD. Therefore, if a current intravenous product were capable of oral administration, anti-TNFα therapy would be favored.

Thalidomide and pentoxifylline have shown anti-TNFα properties when administered orally to mice with experimentally-induced oral mucositis (Lima et al., 2005). However, these two agents are absorbed and give rise to undesirable off target toxicities, particularly thalidomide, which would limit their use. An ideal therapy would be one that has the effect of intravenous anti-TNFα agents but without the side effects.

The Fab domain (the region that recognises the epitope on the antigen) in one ovine PcAb was found capable of binding up to 12 epitopes on the surface of the trimeric hTNFα structure (Abbott et al., 2013). At any one time, 8−12 Fab domains can be bound to the TNFα trimer, probably toward the lower end of this range (Abbott et al., 2013). However, for intact IgG it is likely that less IgG will be capable of binding per TNFα trimer owing to its larger size (150 kDa) compared to Fab (50 kDa). Infliximab Fab interacts with only one TNFα trimer (Liang et al., 2013).

Polyclonal antibodies are cheaper to produce than monoclonal agents. It has been reported that TNFα has a conserved structure and varies greatly between species (Worledge et al., 2000). This explains why a polyclonal antibody administered in sufficient quantity will neutralise the biological effects of murine TNFα, suggesting some shared structural homology (Worledge et al., 2000). These epitopes are not recognised by the McAb, infliximab, explaining its total ineffectiveness in this regard. Such studies support why nature itself adopts a polyclonal approach and it is becoming increasingly common to combine several different McAb in a therapeutic product as with ZMapp, which contains a cocktail of three different monoclonal antibodies for the treatment of Ebola virus disease (Bixler, Duplantier, & Bavari, 2017). Heterologous (non-human) PcAb are far less expensive to raise and purify than chimeric (mouse derived) and fully humanised McAb (Newcombe & Newcombe, 2007).

For the past 20 years, McAb therapies have dominated the market and have been the focus of research, with the possibility that polyclonal therapies have been overlooked. Considerable work has been undertaken to develop and assess the efficacy of orally active anti-TNFα therapy for IBD, as summarised in Table 2.

To date, eleven publications and one press release from eight separate groups have reported on the oral administration of antibodies or proteins for the treatment of IBD (see Table 2). The first research report, published in 1997, reported on the oral administration of non-specific IgA/IgG from human serum given to two pediatric cases of Crohn's disease who had failed to respond to conventional therapy (Tjellström et al., 1997). The outcome was positive, with lowered gut permeability observed in both children, measured using the 6-h urinary recovery of polyethylene glycols, measured prior- and post-immunoglobulin therapy.

From 2000 onwards, research focus moved to the oral administration of anti-TNFα agents. Ophidian Pharmaceuticals Ltd of Wisconsin, USA, were the first to undertake such studies (Worledge et al., 2000). "An oral anti-TNFα therapy may be a preferred approach, reducing systemic side effects and eliminating the inconvenience and expense of administering infusions." They added, "The local inhibition of TNFα activity may be a safer, more effective strategy to treat IBD". Their initial experiments examined the effects of avian-derived antibodies (IgY) toward *Clostridioides difficile* toxins A and B (Kink & Williams, 1998), but soon extended to the study of avian PcAb directed toward TNFα using 2, 4, 6-trinitrobenzene sulfate (TNBS)-induced colitis in rats. Avian antibodies appeared a highly appealing approach, especially since IgY is relatively resistant to the gastrointestinal enzymes trypsin and chymotrypsin but not pepsin (Hatta et al., 1993; Jasion & Burnett, 2015).

Hens were immunised with 20—50 μg of recombinant human TNFα together with the adjuvant Quil A to enhance antibody production, and the polyclonal antibodies (IgY) extracted from the egg yolk using a two-step polyethylene glycol procedure (Polson, von Wechmar, & Fazakerley, 1980). Antibodies from non-immunised hens acted as control. The neutralising ability of the antibodies were assessed using murine L929 cells which are sensitive to the cytotoxic effect of TNFα (Humphreys & Wilson, 1999). The results of the immunocytotoxicity assay favored the avian anti-TNFα over infliximab, with respective ND50 values of 70 ng/mL and 140 ng/mL. It was noted that the monoclonal antibody infliximab

Table 2 Summary of oral anti-TNFα publications and their outcomes (1997–2018).

Protein/antibody	Origin	Study description	References
Non-specific IgA/IgG enriched product	Human plasma	Two pediatric patients who failed to respond to conventional therapy were given human immunoglobulins orally with promising results.	(Tjellström et al., 1997)
Anti-TNFα polyclonal IgY	Avian - eggs	Rats with TNBS-induced colitis were administered avian derived antibodies to TNFα, which proved superior to sulfasalazine and dexamethasone.	(Worledge et al., 2000)
Lactococcus lactis secreting anti-TNFα nanobody	Lactococcus lactis bacteria	Bacteria secreting murine TNFα neutralizing antibodies administered orally to mice with dextran sulfate sodium induced colitis. These highly stable antibodies showed efficacy in vitro and in a DSS-induced mouse model of chronic colitis.	(Vandenbroucke et al., 2010)
Polyclonal bovine Ig toward human (AVX470) and murine TNFα (AVX470 m)	Cow colostrum	Bovine polyclonal antibodies toward human TNFα showed an in vitro profile similar to infliximab. A surrogate antibody administered to mice proved effective in treating a model of IBD with minimal systemic exposure.	(Bhol et al., 2013)
Microencapsulated nanogels delivering siRNA targeting TNFα	siRNA that targets TNFα transcription	siRNA targeting TNFα transcription. The siRNA is encapsulated and designed for release in the intestine.	(Knipe, Strong, & Peppas, 2016)
Monoclonal antibody toward TNFα (Infliximab) in a colon-specific release tablet	Monoclonal antibody	A feasibility study looking at 5 mg infliximab in an oral tablet formulation for colon-specific	(Maurer et al., 2016)

(Continued)

Table 2 Summary of oral anti-TNFα publications and their outcomes (1997–2018).—cont'd

Protein/antibody	Origin	Study description	References
		release. The product was stable for 16 months under different conditions.	
AVX-470: Anti-TNFα bovine IgG	Cow colostrum	Anti-TNFα polyclonal antibodies orally for treatment of active UC: results of a first in human trial	(Harris et al., 2016)
AVX-470 (as above)	Cow colostrum	As above	(Hartman et al., 2016)
PRX-106: A non-absorbable plant cell-expressed recombinant anti- TNFα fusion protein	Plant	Oral administration of a non-absorbable plant cell-expressed recombinant anti- TNFα fusion protein induced immunomodulatory effects and alleviated non-alcoholic steatohepatitis	(Ilan et al., 2017)
PRX-106: BY-2 plant cell-expressed recombinant anti- TNFα fusion protein	Plant	Orally administered BY-2 plant cell-expressed recombinant anti- TNFα fusion protein (PRX-106)	(Almon et al., 2017)
OPRX-106: cell-expressed recombinant human tumor necrosis factor receptor II fused to an IgG1 Fc domain (TNFRII-Fc)	Plant	Phase II clinical trial of OPRX-106 in patients with UC. OPRX-106 is a novel plant cell-expressed recombinant human tumor necrosis factor receptor II fused to an IgG1 Fc domain (TNFRII-Fc), with the plant cell functioning as a natural delivery capsule providing protection against the proteolytic enzymes of the GI tract.	('Press Releases by Refs. Protalix Biotherapeutics', 2018)
V565: anti-TNFα llama domain antibody, engineered to enhance intestinal protease resistance.	llama domain antibody	Preclinical development of a novel, orally-administered anti-tumour necrosis factor domain antibody for the treatment of IBD	(Crowe et al., 2018)

(Remicade) failed to completely neutralise human TNFα, with ND90 values approximately one hundred-fold higher than the avian PcAb.

Their work quickly progressed to animal models of experimentally-induced colitis in female Sprague-Dawley rats using TNBS rectally (Morris et al., 1989). A dose of 600 mg/kg/day was administered, which equates to an unpractical dose of 40 g for a 70 kg adult human. This study highlighted the importance and need for protecting the antibodies: "The amount of active IgY in stool extracts after oral delivery of unformulated material in rodents was about one hundred-fold less than the amount administered. IgY that has been encapsulated for release in the lower gastrointestinal tract would minimise gastrointestinal degradation".

Avian-derived polyclonal anti-TNFα antibodies were found to be superior to sulfasalazine and dexamethasone. The orally administered avian derived antibodies out-performed amino salicylates and corticosteroids, which were then considered the gold standard oral therapy. Very low concentrations of IgY were detected in the rats' systemic circulation, suggesting that the avian IgY acted topically rather than systemically. It was also observed that the polyclonal IgY neutralised TNFα of other mammalian species, whereas the monoclonal infliximab exclusively neutralised human TNFα.

The concentrations of specific IgY in egg yolk are approximately ten times less than the concentration of specific IgG in ovine antisera (Woolley & Landon, 1995), in which approximately 10% of ovine IgG is specific for TNFα (Abbott et al., 2013). However, there are two reasons for not affinity purifying anti-TNFα, namely the cost of TNFα, and the elution conditions, which are likely to dissociate parts of the non-covalently bound TNFα trimer (Abbott et al., 2013). Even crosslinking the trimer to the column could mask the epitopes on the TNFα, thereby losing potentially high affinity antibodies.

All of the work undertaken by Ophidian Pharmaceuticals Ltd. provided robust scientific knowledge, but the Ophidian story ended in failure. It seems likely that for large scale production, hens are not ideal.

Avaxia Biologics (USA) undertook similar but more advanced studies than those performed by Ophidian, with three published papers outlining their work (Bhol et al., 2013; Harris et al., 2016; Hartman et al., 2016). The first concerned a product named AVX-470, a bovine, polyclonal anti-TNFα antibody derived from cow colostrum, and reported its in-vitro activity profile (Bhol et al., 2013). Because murine and human TNFα are structurally different, cows were immunised with either recombinant human TNFα or with recombinant murine TNFα, to produce PcAb referred to as AVX-470 and AVX-470 m, respectively. The antibodies specific for murine TNFα were shown to reduce disease severity in two mouse models of IBD: the TNBS model, noted earlier, and a dextran sodium sulfate (DSS) model. At a dose of 10 mg daily, the antibodies proved useful for both treatment and prevention. Bovine antibodies could be detected in the lamina propria and muscularis mucosa of the gut wall with a dramatic reduction in TNFα, MMPs and other cytokine levels. They concluded that there was minimal systemic exposure following oral dosing, attributing detectable levels of IgG in sera to oral gavage injuries resulting in tracheal tears.

More recently, Avaxia reported the results of a first-in-human, double blind, placebo-controlled study of AVX-470 in patients with UC with a total Mayo score of 5–12 inclusive (Hartman et al., 2016). They reported on various biomarkers in five regions of the colon (ascending, transverse, descending, sigmoid and rectal). Patients were given daily divided doses of 0.2 g, 1.6 g, 3.5 g bovine immunoglobulins or placebo (starch) in delayed release enteric coated capsules designed to release their contents at pH 6 i.e. that of the small intestine/colon. The intervention proved safe and well tolerated, with evidence of clinical, endoscopic and biomarker improvements in the highest dose group (3.5 g/day), suggesting the benefit of an orally delivered locally active agent in moderate to severe UC. However, Avaxia, like Ophidian, did not take their investigations further, which is unsurprising considering the production window of antibodies in colostrum is only a few hours post calving, and further challenged by the calf competing for colostrum. Furthermore, the proportion of specific IgG in their product was less than 1% (Harris et al., 2016).

In January 2018, Protalix Biotherapeutics released positive interim data from a Phase II clinical trial of OPRX-106 in patients with UC. OPRX-106 is a novel, orally administered anti TNFα agent comprising a plant cell-expressed recombinant human TNF receptor II fused to an IgG1 Fc domain (TNFRII-Fc), with the plant cell functioning as a natural delivery capsule providing protection against the proteolytic enzymes of the GI tract. Twenty-four patients with mild to moderate UC were enrolled in an open-label, 2-arm, randomised study to receive 2 mg or 8 mg of OPRX-106, administered once daily for 8 weeks. Data from the first 14 patients to complete the 8 weeks showed clear clinical benefit: 57% of the patients achieved a clinical response (a decrease in the Mayo score of at least 3 points), with 36% achieving clinical remission (clinically symptom free, a Mayo score

≤2, with no individual sub-score exceeding 1 point after treatment) at week 8, with minimal side effects reported.

VHSquared (Cambridge) recently published their preclinical findings of using orally-administered anti-TNFα antibody for the treatment of IBD (Crowe et al., 2018). The product, V565, is derived from llama, with the antibodies (called VHH domains) being naturally resistant to intestinal protease enzymes through the lack of a light chain, and is further engineered to resist protease enzymes. Following incubation with trypsin, chymotrypsin and pancreatin, V565 retained activity, but proved sensitive to and lost activity following pepsin exposure. Enzyme-linked immunosorbent assay (ELISA) demonstrated binding, and cell-based assays using L929 and HEK-NFkB cells confirmed neutralisation of human and monkey TNFα with potencies comparable to adalimumab. V565 penetrated the lamina propria and serum of DSS-exposed mice and was undetectable in treatment-naïve mice. It is proposed that the low molecular weight (12–15 kDa) of V565 means that it will be quickly cleared from the systemic circulation through renal clearance if exposed to the systemic circulation, thus minimising systemic related side effects. Efficacy studies performed in an *ex vivo* human IBD tissue culture model demonstrated that tissue phosphoprotein levels and the production of inflammatory cytokine biomarkers were inhibited comparably by V565 and infliximab.

5.2 Circumventing the environment of the GI tract

There are formidable barriers to oral antibody administration, predominantly the highly acidic environment in the stomach and the presence of trypsin, chymotrypsin and other proteolytic enzymes in the intestine.

It is essential that antibodies reach the intestine in their intact, active form if they are to competently bind and neutralise TNFα. It has been shown that immunoglobulins are generally more resistant than dietary proteins to the proteolytic enzymes found in the GI tract, with several reports documenting the recovery of up to 25% of intact or active IgG from the ileum and feces (Jasion & Burnett, 2015). It is postulated that IgG will remain active for as long as the Fab domain remains intact and capable of binding to antigens (Jasion & Burnett, 2015). Thus, if an intact antibody administered orally undergoes some degradation during GI transit, this will not necessarily render it biologically inactive.

To minimise antibody loss, safeguards can be put in place to overcome i) the acidic environment and pepsin in the stomach, and ii) the proteolytic enzymes such as trypsin and chymotrypsin in the small intestines. Decoy proteins, encapsulation, pH modulators and masking the antibody cleavage sites with polyethylene glycol (PEG) are options to overcome attrition of biological activity of orally delivered antibodies (Jones & Martino, 2016). However, following encapsulation, the antibodies may not be equally released and distributed throughout the intestine where the disease is active. Another approach would be to provide the immunoglobulin in liquid form containing excipients to counter the protease enzymes and low pH of the stomach. This modality is more likely to allow for equal distribution of antibodies throughout the intestine.

It has been shown that pepsin in the stomach is most active at pH 3.5 or less, while at pH 6.0 pepsin is inactive (Jones & Landon, 2003). Antacids can be employed to preserve the integrity of antibodies as they transit through the stomach. Protease enzymes in the GI tract will digest the antibodies, but this can be prevented by the use of protease inhibitors, which can be divided into amino acids, modified amino acids, peptides, modified peptides, polypeptides and non-amino acids (Liu et al., 2018). The toxicity of non-amino acid enzyme inhibitors, such as diisopropyl flurophosphates, limit their use, while the low molecular weight of amino acids and their modified forms enables absorption, leading to systemic exposure and side effects (Liu et al., 2018). Of particular interest are the peptide and polypetide derived enzyme inhibitors such as chicken and duck ovomucoid (inhibitor of α-chymotrypsin and trypsin), soybean trypsin inhibitor (pancreatic endopeptidases inhibitor) and aprotinin (inhibitor of trypsin and chymotrypsin) because of their effectiveness in inhibiting GI tract enzymes and non-toxicity (Liu et al., 2018).

5.3 Advantages of oral antibody therapy

Where a rapid onset of action is needed, e.g. in the case of severe, disseminated disorders such as following snake envenomation or drug overdose, the intravenous route is favored for the administration of immunotherapeutics. Mortality in these situations is often time-dependent, requiring complete and immediate distribution of antidote to prevent further toxicity and mortality. However, there are advantages to the delivery of antibodies capable of selective targeting for the treatment of localised diseases such as macular degeneration of the eye, radiation/chemotherapy-induced mucositis and other localised inflammatory, infective or fungal infections (Jones & Martino, 2016). Systemic administration of antibodies and their consequent ubiquitous distribution is illogical in cases of localised disease (see Fig. 5). Given its site specificity, oral administration and GI-specific delivery of

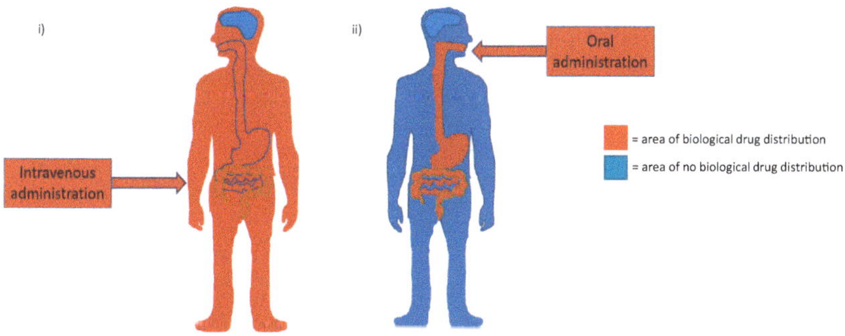

Fig. 5 A diagram to illustrate antibody distribution administered (i) intravenously, and (ii) orally.

antibodies toward hTNFα offers the potential for efficaciously superior treatment of IBD. This was well-illustrated by the successful local application of infliximab to chronic rectal fistulae in patients with CD when relatively small amounts (approximately one-10th of the recommended systemic dose) produced a rapid and significant improvement (Alessandroni et al., 2011).

Antibodies are considered non-absorbable immune modulatory compounds that will not cause immunosuppression and immunogenicity if administered orally (Jasion & Burnett, 2015). Antibodies for oral administration also require significantly less purification and safety testing than those given systemically. For instance, there is no merit in considering the use of Fab and F(ab')$_2$-based therapies as this will increase the likelihood of absorption and systemic exposure. Furthermore, their manufacture does not require the use of clean room facilities. Cost of therapy is reduced significantly for many of the aforementioned reasons including the relatively low costs associated with raising PcAb in animals, low manufacturing costs, the smaller amounts of antibodies required when using the oral route and avoiding the need for admission to hospital as day cases, and nurse/healthcare professional time to administer intravenously.

Several reports confirm that orally administered antibodies are confined to the lumen and wall of the GI tract with virtually none entering the systemic circulation (Dixon, Kuhns, Weigle, & Taylor, 1959). This has three main advantages:

a. Oral administration does not evoke a systemic humoral immune response meaning therapy can be continued indefinitely. It has been shown that neoantigen feeding in humans over a period of time induces a specific oral tolerance without any significant levels of neoantigen-specific antibody being formed in either blood or gastrointestinal secretions (Husby, Mestecky, Moldoveanu, Holland, & Elson, 1994).

b. For the same reason there is no risk of acute or delayed hypersensitivity reactions

c. Intact oral antibodies will not neutralise systemically-located hTNFα, thereby avoiding the risk of opportunistic infections such as tuberculosis and other complications such as malignancy and immunosuppression.

The manufacture of intravenous products has very stringent and costly requirements for sterile, pyrogen-free parenteral production and testing. For PcAb production, the serum source needs to be verified, often from countries of known virus free livestock, to ensure patient safety and fulfill regulatory requirements (Newcombe & Newcombe, 2007). However, an oral product can be prepared at food grade standard, at significantly lower cost.

6. Conclusion

IBD comprising UC and CD affects 2.5 to 3.0 million patients in Europe alone (Burisch et al., 2013). Its etiology involves an interplay between genetic, microbial and environmental factors that trigger an inappropriate immune response in the GI tract. Therapy aims to induce then maintain remission and prevent complications and the need for surgery.

The value of neutralising TNFα cannot be underestimated, given its early and critical role in the inflammatory cascade. Current anti-TNFα agents all comprise McAb that are administered systemically and have proven extremely beneficial in most patients with IBD. However, their use is frequently associated with adverse effects including the generation of ADAs that may limit their effectiveness over time.

There is increasing evidence that heterologous (non-human) PcAb to TNFα are more effective than their monoclonal counterparts because they bind to multiple epitopes on the cytokine with a higher avidity. Significantly, oral, as opposed to systemic administration, should avoid many of the adverse effects associated with the present use of anti-TNFα agents and offer other advantages such as being less costly to manufacture. Clearly, the antibodies need to be protected during their transit through the GI tract, which can be achieved by the use of antacids and proteolytic enzyme inhibitors.

Competing interests

No competing interests to declare.

Author contributions.

This work has been undertaken by Owen Griffiths and reviewed by his PhD supervisors.

Funding.

Owen Griffiths' work was supported by a PhD grant from Knowledge Economy Skills Scholarships (KESS 2), a major pan-Wales operation supported by European Social Funds (ESF) through the Welsh Government.

References

Abbott, W. M., Snow, M., Eckersley, S., Renshaw, J., Davies, G., Norman, R. A., et al. (2013). Characterization of the complex formed between a potent neutralizing ovine-derived polyclonal anti-TNFα Fab fragment and human TNFα. *Bioscience Reports, 33*(4). https://doi.org/10.1042/BSR20130044.

Abraham, C., & Cho, J. H. (2009). Inflammatory bowel disease. *New England Journal of Medicine, 361*(21), 2066–2078. https://doi.org/10.1056/NEJMra0804647.

Ahn, S.-H., Shah, Y. M., Inoue, J., Morimura, K., Kim, I., Yim, S., et al. (2008). Hepatocyte nuclear factor 4alpha in the intestinal epithelial cells protects against inflammatory bowel disease. *Inflammatory Bowel Diseases, 14*(7), 908–920. https://doi.org/10.1002/ibd.20413.

Alessandroni, L., Kohn, A., Cosintino, R., Marrollo, M., Papi, C., Monterubbianesi, R., et al. (2011). Local injection of infliximab in severe fistulating perianal Crohn's disease: An open uncontrolled study. *Techniques in Coloproctology, 15*(4), 407–412. https://doi.org/10.1007/s10151-011-0759-4.

Almon, E., Khoury, T., Drori, A., Gingis-Velitski, S., Alon, S., Chertkoff, R., et al. (2017). An oral administration of a recombinant anti-TNF fusion protein is biologically active in the gut promoting regulatory T cells: Results of a phase I clinical trial using a novel oral anti-TNF alpha-based therapy. *Journal of Immunological Methods, 446*, 21–29. https://doi.org/10.1016/j.jim.2017.03.023.

Angelucci, E., Cocco, A., Viscido, A., Vernia, P., & Caprilli, R. (2007). Another paradox in Crohn's disease: New onset of psoriasis in a patient receiving tumor necrosis factor-alpha antagonist. *Inflammatory Bowel Diseases, 13*(8), 1059–1061. https://doi.org/10.1002/ibd.20137.

Atzeni, F., Gianturco, L., Talotta, R., Varisco, V., Ditto, M. C., Turiel, M., et al. (2015). Investigating the potential side effects of anti-TNF therapy for rheumatoid arthritis: Cause for concern? *Immunotherapy, 7*(4), 353–361. https://doi.org/10.2217/imt.15.4.

Baumgart, D. C., & Sandborn, W. J. (2012). Crohn's disease. *The Lancet, 380*(9853), 1590–1605. https://doi.org/10.1016/S0140-6736(12)60026-9.

von Behring, E. (1901). *Nobel lecture: Serum therapy in therapeutics and medical science*. Retrieved 21 December 2018, from NobelPrize.org website https://www.nobelprize.org/prizes/medicine/1901/behring/lecture/.

Ben-Horin, S., Kopylov, U., & Chowers, Y. (2014). Optimizing anti-TNF treatments in inflammatory bowel disease. *Autoimmunity Reviews, 13*(1), 24–30. https://doi.org/10.1016/j.autrev.2013.06.002.

Bergemalm, D., Kruse, R., Sapnara, M., Halfvarson, J., & Hörnquist, E. H. (2017). Elevated fecal peptidase D at onset of colitis in Galphai2-/- mice, a mouse model of IBD. *PLoS One, 12*(3), e0174275. https://doi.org/10.1371/journal.pone.0174275.

Bhol, K. C., Tracey, D. E., Lemos, B. R., Lyng, G. D., Erlich, E. C., Keane, D. M., et al. (2013). AVX-470: A novel oral anti-TNF antibody with therapeutic potential in inflammatory bowel disease. *Inflammatory Bowel Diseases, 19*(11), 2273–2281. https://doi.org/10.1097/MIB.0b013e3182a11958.

Bixler, S. L., Duplantier, A. J., & Bavari, S. (2017). Discovering drugs for the treatment of ebola virus. *Current Treatment Options in Infectious Diseases, 9*(3), 299–317. https://doi.org/10.1007/s40506-017-0130-z.

Breese, E. J., Michie, C. A., Nicholls, S. W., Murch, S. H., Williams, C. B., Domizio, P., et al. (1994). Tumor necrosis factor alpha-producing cells in the intestinal mucosa of children with inflammatory bowel disease. *Gastroenterology, 106*(6), 1455–1466.

Burisch, J., Jess, T., Martinato, M., Lakatos, P. L., & ECCO -EpiCom. (2013). The burden of inflammatory bowel disease in Europe. *Journal of Crohn's & Colitis,* 7(4), 322–337. https://doi.org/10.1016/j.crohns.2013.01.010.

Bustos, D., Negri, G., De Paula, J. A., Di Carlo, M., Yapur, V., Facente, A., et al. (1998). Colonic proteinases: Increased activity in patients with ulcerative colitis. *Medicina, 58*(3), 262–264.

Chande, N., Townsend, C. M., Parker, C. E., & MacDonald, J. K. (2016). Azathioprine or 6-mercaptopurine for induction of remission in Crohn's disease. *Cochrane Database of Systematic Reviews, 10,* CD000545. https://doi.org/10.1002/14651858.CD000545.pub5.

Chelakkot, C., Ghim, J., & Ryu, S. H. (2018). Mechanisms regulating intestinal barrier integrity and its pathological implications. *Experimental & Molecular Medicine, 50*(8). https://doi.org/10.1038/s12276-018-0126-x.

Cherry, L. N., Yunker, N. S., Lambert, E. R., Vaughan, D., & Lowe, D. K. (2015). Vedolizumab: An α4β7 integrin antagonist for ulcerative colitis and Crohn's disease. *Therapeutic Advances in Chronic Disease, 6*(5), 224–233. https://doi.org/10.1177/2040622315586970.

Clarke, K., & Chintanaboina, J. (2018). Allergic and immunologic perspectives of inflammatory bowel disease. *Clinical Reviews in Allergy and Immunology*. https://doi.org/10.1007/s12016-018-8690-3.

Clayburgh, D. R., Shen, L., & Turner, J. R. (2004). A porous defense: The leaky epithelial barrier in intestinal disease. *Laboratory Investigation; a Journal of Technical Methods and Pathology, 84*(3), 282–291. https://doi.org/10.1038/labinvest.3700050.

Coskun, M. (2014). Intestinal epithelium in inflammatory bowel disease. *Frontiers of Medicine, 1.* https://doi.org/10.3389/fmed.2014.00024.

Coskun, M., Olsen, A. K., Holm, T. L., Kvist, P. H., Nielsen, O. H., Riis, L. B., et al. (2012). TNF-α-induced down-regulation of CDX2 suppresses MEP1A expression in colitis. *Biochimica et Biophysica Acta, 1822*(6), 843–851. https://doi.org/10.1016/j.bbadis.2012.01.012.

Crowe, J. S., Roberts, K. J., Carlton, T. M., Maggiore, L., Cubitt, M. F., Clare, S., et al. (2018). Preclinical development of a novel, orally-administered anti-tumour necrosis factor domain antibody for the treatment of inflammatory bowel disease. *Scientific Reports, 8*(1), 4941. https://doi.org/10.1038/s41598-018-23277-7.

Cumberlege, G. I. (1911). Administration of serum by the mouth. *British Medical Journal, 2*(2637), 108.

Danese, S., & Fiocchi, C. (2011). Ulcerative colitis. *New England Journal of Medicine, 365*(18), 1713–1725. https://doi.org/10.1056/NEJMra1102942.

Devkota, S., Wang, Y., Musch, M., Leone, V., Fehlner-Peach, H., Nadimpalli, A., et al. (2012). Dietary fat-induced taurocholic acid production promotes pathobiont and colitis in IL-10−/− mice. *Nature, 487*(7405), 104–108. https://doi.org/10.1038/nature11225.

Dixon, F. J., Kuhns, W., Weigle, W. O., & Taylor, P. (1959). The lack of absorption of ingested bovine antibody in humans. *The Journal of Immunology, 83,* 437–441.

van Dullemen, H. M., van Deventer, S. J., Hommes, D. W., Bijl, H. A., Jansen, J., Tytgat, G. N., et al. (1995). Treatment of Crohn's disease with anti-tumor necrosis factor chimeric monoclonal antibody (cA2). *Gastroenterology, 109*(1), 129–135.

Dwarakanath, A. D., Campbell, B. J., Tsai, H. H., Sunderland, D., Hart, C. A., & Rhodes, J. M. (1995). Faecal mucinase activity assessed in inflammatory bowel disease using 14C threonine labelled mucin substrate. *Gut, 37*(1), 58–62. https://doi.org/10.1136/gut.37.1.58.

Ebert, E. C., Wright, S. H., Lipshutz, W. H., & Hauptman, S. P. (1984). T-cell abnormalities in inflammatory bowel disease are mediated by interleukin 2. *Clinical Immunology and Immunopathology, 33*(2), 232–244.

Eri, R., & Chieppa, M. (2013). Messages from the inside. The dynamic environment that favors intestinal homeostasis. *Frontiers in Immunology, 4*, 323. https://doi.org/10.3389/fimmu.2013.00323.

Eutamene, H., Beaufrand, C., Harkat, C., & Theodorou, V. (2018). The role of mucoprotectants in the management of gastrointestinal disorders. *Expert Review of Gastroenterology & Hepatology, 12*(1), 83–90. https://doi.org/10.1080/17474124.2018.1378573.

Farrell, R. J., Alsahli, M., Jeen, Y.-T., Falchuk, K. R., Peppercorn, M. A., & Michetti, P. (2003). Intravenous hydrocortisone premedication reduces antibodies to infliximab in Crohn's disease: A randomized controlled trial. *Gastroenterology, 124*(4), 917–924. https://doi.org/10.1053/gast.2003.50145.

Feldmann, M., & Pusey, C. D. (2006). Is there a role for TNF-α in anti-neutrophil cytoplasmic antibody–associated vasculitis? Lessons from other chronic inflammatory diseases. *Journal of the American Society of Nephrology, 17*(5), 1243–1252. https://doi.org/10.1681/ASN.2005121359.

Fong, Y., Tracey, K. J., Moldawer, L. L., Hesse, D. G., Manogue, K. B., Kenney, J. S., et al. (1989). Antibodies to cachectin/tumor necrosis factor reduce interleukin 1 beta and interleukin 6 appearance during lethal bacteremia. *Journal of Experimental Medicine, 170*(5), 1627–1633.

Ford, A. C., Bernstein, C. N., Khan, K. J., Abreu, M. T., Marshall, J. K., Talley, N. J., et al. (2011). Glucocorticosteroid therapy in inflammatory bowel disease: Systematic review and meta-analysis. *American Journal of Gastroenterology, 106*(4), 590–599. quiz 600 https://doi.org/10.1038/ajg.2011.70.

Fyderek, K., Strus, M., Kowalska-Duplaga, K., Gosiewski, T., Wedrychowicz, A., Jedynak-Wasowicz, U., et al. (2009). Mucosal bacterial microflora and mucus layer thickness in adolescents with inflammatory bowel disease. *World Journal of Gastroenterology, 15*(42), 5287–5294. https://doi.org/10.3748/wjg.15.5287.

Gecse, K., Róka, R., Ferrier, L., Leveque, M., Eutamene, H., Cartier, C., et al. (2008). Increased faecal serine protease activity in diarrhoeic IBS patients: A colonic lumenal factor impairing colonic permeability and sensitivity. *Gut, 57*(5), 591–599. https://doi.org/10.1136/gut.2007.140210.

Gerardo, C. J., Quackenbush, E., Lewis, B., Rose, S. R., Greene, S., Toschlog, E. A., et al. (2017). The efficacy of crotalidae polyvalent immune Fab (ovine) antivenom versus placebo plus optional rescue therapy on recovery from copperhead snake envenomation: A randomized, double-blind, placebo-controlled, clinical trial. *Annals of Emergency Medicine, 70*(2), 233–244.e3. https://doi.org/10.1016/j.annemergmed.2017.04.034.

Ghosh, N., & Premchand, P. (2015). A UK cost of care model for inflammatory bowel disease. *Frontline Gastroenterology, 6*(3), 169–174. https://doi.org/10.1136/flgastro-2014-100514.

Halling, M. L., Kjeldsen, J., Knudsen, T., Nielsen, J., & Hansen, L. K. (2017). Patients with inflammatory bowel disease have increased risk of autoimmune and inflammatory diseases. *World Journal of Gastroenterology, 23*(33), 6137–6146. https://doi.org/10.3748/wjg.v23.i33.6137.

Hanauer, S. B., Feagan, B. G., Lichtenstein, G. R., Mayer, L. F., Schreiber, S., Colombel, J. F., ACCENT I Study Group, et al. (2002). Maintenance infliximab for Crohn's disease: The

ACCENT I randomised trial. *The Lancet, 359*(9317), 1541–1549. https://doi.org/10.1016/S0140-6736(02)08512-4.

Hanauer, S. B., Sandborn, W. J., Rutgeerts, P., Fedorak, R. N., Lukas, M., MacIntosh, D., et al. (2006). Human anti-tumor necrosis factor monoclonal antibody (adalimumab) in Crohn's disease: The CLASSIC-I trial. *Gastroenterology, 130*(2), 323–333. quiz 591 https://doi.org/10.1053/j.gastro.2005.11.030.

Harris, M. S., Hartman, D., Lemos, B. R., Erlich, E. C., Spence, S., Kennedy, S., et al. (2016). AVX-470, an orally delivered anti-tumour necrosis factor antibody for treatment of active ulcerative colitis: Results of a first-in-human trial. *Journal of Crohn's & Colitis, 10*(6), 631–640. https://doi.org/10.1093/ecco-jcc/jjw036.

Hartman, D. S., Tracey, D. E., Lemos, B. R., Erlich, E. C., Burton, R. E., Keane, D. M., et al. (2016). Effects of AVX-470, an oral, locally acting anti-tumour necrosis factor antibody, on tissue biomarkers in patients with active ulcerative colitis. *Journal of Crohn's & Colitis, 10*(6), 641–649. https://doi.org/10.1093/ecco-jcc/jjw026.

Hatta, H., Tsuda, K., Akachi, S., Kim, M., Yamamoto, T., & Ebina, T. (1993). Oral passive immunization effect of anti-human rotavirus IgY and its behaviour against proteolytic enzymes. *Bioscience Biotechnology and Biochemistry, 57*(7), 1077–1081.

Heller, F., Florian, P., Bojarski, C., Richter, J., Christ, M., Hillenbrand, B., et al. (2005). Interleukin-13 is the key effector Th2 cytokine in ulcerative colitis that affects epithelial tight junctions, apoptosis, and cell restitution. *Gastroenterology, 129*(2), 550–564. https://doi.org/10.1016/j.gastro.2005.05.002.

Herrlinger, K. R., Witthoeft, T., Raedler, A., Bokemeyer, B., Krummenerl, T., Schulzke, J.-D., et al. (2006). Randomized, double blind controlled trial of subcutaneous recombinant human interleukin-11 versus prednisolone in active Crohn's disease. *American Journal of Gastroenterology, 101*(4), 793–797. https://doi.org/10.1111/j.1572-0241.2005.00356.x.

Hilpert, H., Brüssow, H., Mietens, C., Sidoti, J., Lerner, L., & Werchau, H. (1987). Use of bovine milk concentrate containing antibody to rotavirus to treat rotavirus gastroenteritis in infants. *The Journal of Infectious Diseases, 156*(1), 158–166.

Hisamatsu, T., Kanai, T., Mikami, Y., Yoneno, K., Matsuoka, K., & Hibi, T. (2013). Immune aspects of the pathogenesis of inflammatory bowel disease. *Pharmacology & Therapeutics, 137*(3), 283–297. https://doi.org/10.1016/j.pharmthera.2012.10.008.

Horiuchi, T., Mitoma, H., Harashima, S., Tsukamoto, H., & Shimoda, T. (2010). Transmembrane TNF-alpha: Structure, function and interaction with anti-TNF agents. *Rheumatology, 49*(7), 1215–1228. https://doi.org/10.1093/rheumatology/keq031.

Hueber, W., Sands, B. E., Lewitzky, S., Vandemeulebroecke, M., Reinisch, W., Higgins, P. D. R., et al. (2012). Secukinumab, a human anti-IL-17A monoclonal antibody, for moderate to severe Crohn's disease: Unexpected results of a randomised, double-blind placebo-controlled trial. *Gut, 61*(12), 1693–1700. https://doi.org/10.1136/gutjnl-2011-301668.

Humphreys, D. T., & Wilson, M. R. (1999). Modes of L929 cell death induced by TNF-alpha and other cytotoxic agents. *Cytokine, 11*(10), 773–782. https://doi.org/10.1006/cyto.1998.0492.

Husby, S., Mestecky, J., Moldoveanu, Z., Holland, S., & Elson, C. O. (1994). Oral tolerance in humans. T cell but not B cell tolerance after antigen feeding. *The Journal of Immunology, 152*(9), 4663–4670.

Hviid, A., Svanström, H., & Frisch, M. (2011). Antibiotic use and inflammatory bowel diseases in childhood. *Gut, 60*(1), 49–54. https://doi.org/10.1136/gut.2010.219683.

Ilan, Y., Gingis-Velitski, S., Ben Ya'aco, A., Shabbat, Y., Zolotarov, L., Almon, E., et al. (2017). A plant cell-expressed recombinant anti-TNF fusion protein is biologically active in the gut and alleviates immune-mediated hepatitis and colitis. *Immunobiology, 222*(3), 544–551. https://doi.org/10.1016/j.imbio.2016.11.001.

Jasion, V. S., & Burnett, B. P. (2015). Survival and digestibility of orally-administered immunoglobulin preparations containing IgG through the gastrointestinal tract in humans. *Nutrition Journal, 14*, 22. https://doi.org/10.1186/s12937-015-0010-7.

Johansson, M. E. V., Gustafsson, J. K., Holmén-Larsson, J., Jabbar, K. S., Xia, L., Xu, H., et al. (2014). Bacteria penetrate the normally impenetrable inner colon mucus layer in both murine colitis models and patients with ulcerative colitis. *Gut, 63*(2), 281–291. https://doi.org/10.1136/gutjnl-2012-303207.

Jones, R. G. A., & Landon, J. (2003). A protocol for 'enhanced pepsin digestion': A step by step method for obtaining pure antibody fragments in high yield from serum. *Journal of Immunological Methods, 275*(1), 239–250. https://doi.org/10.1016/S0022-1759(03)00005-X.

Jones, R. G. A., & Martino, A. (2016). Targeted localized use of therapeutic antibodies: A review of non-systemic, topical and oral applications. *Critical Reviews in Biotechnology, 36*(3), 506–520. https://doi.org/10.3109/07388551.2014.992388.

Jones, J. L., Nguyen, G. C., Benchimol, E. I., Bernstein, C. N., Bitton, A., Kaplan, G. G., & Otley, A. R. (2019). The Impact of Inflammatory Bowel Disease in Canada 2018: Quality of Life. *Journal of the Canadian Association of Gastroenterology, 2*(Suppl 1), S42–S48. http://dx.doi.org/10.1093/jcag/gwy048.

Jostins, L., Ripke, S., Weersma, R. K., Duerr, R. H., McGovern, D. P., Hui, K. Y., et al. (2012). Host-microbe interactions have shaped the genetic architecture of inflammatory bowel disease. *Nature, 491*(7422), 119–124. https://doi.org/10.1038/nature11582.

Khajah, M. A. (2017). The potential role of fecal microbiota transplantation in the treatment of inflammatory bowel disease. *Scandinavian Journal of Gastroenterology, 52*(11), 1172–1184. https://doi.org/10.1080/00365521.2017.1347812.

Kink, J. A., & Williams, J. A. (1998). Antibodies to recombinant *Clostridium difficile* toxins A and B are an effective treatment and prevent relapse of C. difficile-associated disease in a hamster model of infection. *Infection and Immunity, 66*(5), 2018–2025.

Knipe, J. M., Strong, L. E., & Peppas, N. A. (2016). Enzyme- and pH-responsive microencapsulated nanogels for oral delivery of siRNA to induce TNF-α knockdown in the intestine. *Biomacromolecules, 17*(3), 788–797. https://doi.org/10.1021/acs.biomac.5b01518.

Kornbluth, A. (1998). Infliximab approved for use in Crohn's disease: A report on the FDA GI advisory committee conference. *Inflammatory Bowel Diseases, 4*(4), 328–329.

Kotlarz, D., Beier, R., Murugan, D., Diestelhorst, J., Jensen, O., Boztug, K., et al. (2012). Loss of interleukin-10 signaling and infantile inflammatory bowel disease: Implications for diagnosis and therapy. *Gastroenterology, 143*(2), 347–355. https://doi.org/10.1053/j.gastro.2012.04.045.

Kronman, M. P., Zaoutis, T. E., Haynes, K., Feng, R., & Coffin, S. E. (2012). Antibiotic exposure and IBD development among children: A population-based cohort study. *Pediatrics, 130*(4), e794–803. https://doi.org/10.1542/peds.2011-3886.

Liang, S., Dai, J., Hou, S., Su, L., Zhang, D., Guo, H., et al. (2013). Structural basis for treating tumor necrosis factor α (TNFα)-associated diseases with the therapeutic antibody infliximab. *Journal of Biological Chemistry, 288*(19), 13799–13807. https://doi.org/10.1074/jbc.M112.433961.

Lima, V., Brito, G.a. C., Cunha, F. Q., Rebouças, C. G., Falcão, B.a. A., Augusto, R. F., et al. (2005). Effects of the tumour necrosis factor-alpha inhibitors pentoxifylline and thalidomide in short-term experimental oral mucositis in hamsters. *European Journal of Oral Sciences, 113*(3), 210–217. https://doi.org/10.1111/j.1600-0722.2005.00216.x.

Lipman, N. S., Jackson, L. R., Trudel, L. J., & Weis-Garcia, F. (2005). Monoclonal versus polyclonal antibodies: distinguishing characteristics, applications, and information resources. *ILAR Journal, 46*(3), 258–268.

Liu, C., Kou, Y., Zhang, X., Cheng, H., Chen, X., & Mao, S. (2018). Strategies and industrial perspectives to improve oral absorption of biological macromolecules. *Expert Opinion on Drug Delivery, 15*(3), 223–233. https://doi.org/10.1080/17425247.2017.1395853.

Llewelyn, M. B., Hawkins, R. E., & Russell, S. J. (1992). Discovery of antibodies. *BMJ, 305*(6864), 1269–1272. https://doi.org/10.1136/bmj.305.6864.1269.

Mankertz, J., & Schulzke, J.-D. (2007). Altered permeability in inflammatory bowel disease: Pathophysiology and clinical implications. *Current Opinion in Gastroenterology, 23*(4), 379–383. https://doi.org/10.1097/MOG.0b013e32816aa392.

Marini, M., Bamias, G., Rivera-Nieves, J., Moskaluk, C. A., Hoang, S. B., Ross, W. G., et al. (2003). TNF-alpha neutralization ameliorates the severity of murine Crohn's-like ileitis by abrogation of intestinal epithelial cell apoptosis. *Proceedings of the National Academy of Sciences of the United States of America, 100*(14), 8366–8371. https://doi.org/10.1073/pnas.1432897100.

Marino, A., Giani, T., & Cimaz, R. (2018). Risks associated with use of TNF inhibitors in children with rheumatic diseases. *Expert Review of Clinical Immunology, 0*(0), 1–10. https://doi.org/10.1080/1744666X.2019.1550359.

Maurer, J. M., Hofman, S., Schellekens, R. C. A., Tonnis, W. F., Dubois, A. O. T., Woerdenbag, H. J., et al. (2016). Development and potential application of an oral ColoPulse infliximab tablet with colon specific release: A feasibility study. *International Journal of Pharmaceutics, 505*(1–2), 175–186. https://doi.org/10.1016/j.ijpharm.2016.03.027.

McCann, F. E., Perocheau, D. P., Ruspi, G., Blazek, K., Davies, M. L., Feldmann, M., et al. (2014). Selective tumor necrosis factor receptor I blockade is anti-inflammatory and reveals immunoregulatory role of tumor necrosis factor receptor II in collagen-induced arthritis. *Arthritis & Rheumatology (Hoboken, N.J.), 66*(10), 2728–2738. https://doi.org/10.1002/art.38755.

Minozzi, S., Bonovas, S., Lytras, T., Pecoraro, V., González-Lorenzo, M., Bastiampillai, A. J., et al. (2016). Risk of infections using anti-TNF agents in rheumatoid arthritis, psoriatic arthritis, and ankylosing spondylitis: A systematic review and meta-analysis. *Expert Opinion on Drug Safety, 15*(Suppl. 1), 11–34. https://doi.org/10.1080/14740338.2016.1240783.

Mitoma, H., Horiuchi, T., Hatta, N., Tsukamoto, H., Harashima, S.-I., Kikuchi, Y., et al. (2005). Infliximab induces potent anti-inflammatory responses by outside-to-inside signals through transmembrane TNF-alpha. *Gastroenterology, 128*(2), 376–392.

Mitsuyama, K., Sata, M., & Tanikawa, K. (1991). Significance of interleukin-6 in patients with inflammatory bowel disease. *Gastroenterologia Japonica, 26*(1), 20–28.

Miyoshi, J., & Chang, E. B. (2017). The gut microbiota and inflammatory bowel diseases. *Translational Research: The Journal of Laboratory and Clinical Medicine, 179*, 38–48. https://doi.org/10.1016/j.trsl.2016.06.002.

Monaco, C., Nanchahal, J., Taylor, P., & Feldmann, M. (2015). Anti-TNF therapy: Past, present and future. *International Immunology, 27*(1), 55–62. https://doi.org/10.1093/intimm/dxu102.

Morris, G. P., Beck, P. L., Herridge, M. S., Depew, W. T., Szewczuk, M. R., & Wallace, J. L. (1989). Hapten-induced model of chronic inflammation and ulceration in the rat colon. *Gastroenterology, 96*(3), 795–803.

Musch, E., Andus, T., Kruis, W., Raedler, A., Spehlmann, M., Schreiber, S., et al. (2005). Interferon-beta-1a for the treatment of steroid-refractory ulcerative colitis: A randomized, double-blind, placebo-controlled trial. *Clinical Gastroenterology and Hepatology: The Official Clinical Practice Journal of the American Gastroenterological Association, 3*(6), 581–586.

von Mutius, E. (2007). Allergies, infections and the hygiene hypothesis - the epidemiological evidence. *Immunobiology, 212*(6), 433–439. https://doi.org/10.1016/j.imbio.2007.03.002.

Nava, P., Koch, S., Laukoetter, M. G., Lee, W. Y., Kolegraff, K., Capaldo, C. T., et al. (2010). Interferon-gamma regulates intestinal epithelial homeostasis through converging beta-catenin signalling pathways. *Immunity, 32*(3), 392–402. https://doi.org/10.1016/j.immuni.2010.03.001.

Nell, S., Suerbaum, S., & Josenhans, C. (2010). The impact of the microbiota on the pathogenesis of IBD: Lessons from mouse infection models. *Nature Reviews Microbiology, 8*(8), 564–577. https://doi.org/10.1038/nrmicro2403.

Netea, M. G., Balkwill, F., Chonchol, M., Cominelli, F., Donath, M. Y., Giamarellos-Bourboulis, E. J., et al. (2017). A guiding map for inflammation. *Nature Immunology, 18*(8), 826–831. https://doi.org/10.1038/ni.3790.

Neurath, M. F. (2014). Cytokines in inflammatory bowel disease. *Nature Reviews Immunology, 14*(5), 329–342. https://doi.org/10.1038/nri3661.

Neurath, M. (2017). Current and emerging therapeutic targets for IBD. *Nature Reviews Gastroenterology & Hepatology, 14*(11), 688. https://doi.org/10.1038/nrgastro.2017.138.

Neurath, M. F. (2019). Targeting immune cell circuits and trafficking in inflammatory bowel disease. *Nature Immunology*. https://doi.org/10.1038/s41590-019-0415-0.

Neurath, M. F., Finotto, S., & Glimcher, L. H. (2002). The role of Th1/Th2 polarization in mucosal immunity. *Nature Medicine, 8*(6), 567–573. https://doi.org/10.1038/nm0602-567.

Newcombe, C., & Newcombe, A. R. (2007). Antibody production: Polyclonal-derived biotherapeutics. *Journal of Chromatography B, 848*(1), 2–7. https://doi.org/10.1016/j.jchromb.2006.07.004.

Ng, S. C., Bernstein, C. N., Vatn, M. H., Lakatos, P. L., Loftus, E. V., Tysk, C., et al. (2013). Geographical variability and environmental risk factors in inflammatory bowel disease. *Gut, 62*(4), 630–649. https://doi.org/10.1136/gutjnl-2012-303661.

O'Meara, S., Nanda, K. S., & Moss, A. C. (2014). Antibodies to infliximab and risk of infusion reactions in patients with inflammatory bowel disease: A systematic review and meta-analysis. *Inflammatory Bowel Diseases, 20*(1), 1–6. https://doi.org/10.1097/01.MIB.0000436951.80898.6d.

Parameswaran, N., & Patial, S. (2010). Tumor necrosis factor-α signaling in macrophages. *Critical Reviews in Eukaryotic Gene Expression, 20*(2), 87–103.

Paramsothy, S., Cleveland, N. K., Zmeter, N., & Rubin, D. T. (2016). The role of biosimilars in inflammatory bowel disease. *Gastroenterology and Hepatology, 12*(12), 741–751.

Paton, D. M. (1906). Serumtherapy by the mouth. *British Medical Journal, 1*(2366), 1032.

Philipose, J., Ahmed, M., Idiculla, P. S., Mulrooney, S. M., & Gumaste, V. V. (2018). Severe de novo ulcerative colitis following ixekizumab therapy. *Case Reports in Gastroenterology, 12*(3), 617–621. https://doi.org/10.1159/000493922.

Polson, A., von Wechmar, M. B., & Fazakerley, G. (1980). Antibodies to proteins from yolk of immunized hens. *Immunological Communications, 9*(5), 495–514.

Powrie, F., Leach, M. W., Mauze, S., Menon, S., Caddle, L. B., & Coffman, R. L. (1994). Inhibition of Th1 responses prevents inflammatory bowel disease in scid mice reconstituted with CD45RBhi CD4+ T cells. *Immunity, 1*(7), 553–562.

Press Releases by Protalix Biotherapeutics [Company website]. (October 25, 2018). Retrieved 25 October 2018, from http://phx.corporate-ir.net/phoenix.zhtml?c=101161&p=irol-newsArticle&ID=2324351

Qin, X. (2012). Etiology of inflammatory bowel disease: A unified hypothesis. *World Journal of Gastroenterology: WJG, 18*(15), 1708–1722. https://doi.org/10.3748/wjg.v18.i15.1708.

Qin, X. (2017). Damage of the mucus layer: The possible shared critical common cause for both inflammatory bowel disease (IBD) and irritable bowel syndrome (IBS). *Inflammatory Bowel Diseases, 23*(2), E11–E12. https://doi.org/10.1097/MIB.0000000000001010.

Ramos, G. P., & Papadakis, K. A. (2019). Mechanisms of disease: Inflammatory bowel diseases. *Mayo Clinic Proceedings, 94*(1), 155–165. https://doi.org/10.1016/j.mayocp.2018.09.013.

Reinisch, W., Hommes, D. W., Van Assche, G., Colombel, J.-F., Gendre, J.-P., Oldenburg, B., et al. (2006). A dose escalating, placebo controlled, double blind, single dose and multidose, safety and tolerability study of fontolizumab, a humanised anti-interferon gamma antibody, in patients with moderate to severe Crohn's disease. *Gut, 55*(8), 1138–1144. https://doi.org/10.1136/gut.2005.079434.

Rescigno, M. (2011). The intestinal epithelial barrier in the control of homeostasis and immunity. *Trends in Immunology, 32*(6), 256–264. https://doi.org/10.1016/j.it.2011.04.003.

Róka, R., Rosztóczy, A., Leveque, M., Izbéki, F., Nagy, F., Molnár, T., et al. (2007). A pilot study of fecal serine-protease activity: A pathophysiologic factor in diarrhea-predominant irritable bowel syndrome. *Clinical Gastroenterology and Hepatology: The Official Clinical Practice Journal of the American Gastroenterological Association, 5*(5), 550–555. https://doi.org/10.1016/j.cgh.2006.12.004.

Saenz, S. A., Taylor, B. C., & Artis, D. (2008). Welcome to the neighborhood: Epithelial cell-derived cytokines license innate and adaptive immune responses at mucosal sites. *Immunological Reviews, 226*, 172–190. https://doi.org/10.1111/j.1600-065X.2008.00713.x.

Sandborn, W. J., Feagan, B. G., Marano, C., Zhang, H., Strauss, R., Johanns, J., et al., PURSUIT-Maintenance Study Group. (2014). Subcutaneous golimumab maintains clinical response in patients with moderate-to-severe ulcerative colitis. *Gastroenterology, 146*(1), 96–109.e1. https://doi.org/10.1053/j.gastro.2013.06.010.

Sandborn, W. J., Feagan, B. G., Stoinov, S., Honiball, P. J., Rutgeerts, P., Mason, D., et al., PRECISE 1 Study Investigators. (2007). Certolizumab pegol for the treatment of Crohn's disease. *New England Journal of Medicine, 357*(3), 228–238. https://doi.org/10.1056/NEJMoa067594.

Sandborn, W. J., Hanauer, S. B., Katz, S., Safdi, M., Wolf, D. G., Baerg, R. D., et al. (2001). Etanercept for active Crohn's disease: A randomized, double-blind, placebo-controlled trial. *Gastroenterology, 121*(5), 1088–1094.

Sandborn, W. J., van Assche, G., Reinisch, W., Colombel, J.-F., D'Haens, G., Wolf, D. C., et al. (2012). Adalimumab induces and maintains clinical remission in patients with moderate-to-severe ulcerative colitis. *Gastroenterology, 142*(2), 257–265.e1-3. https://doi.org/10.1053/j.gastro.2011.10.032.

Sartor, R. B. (2008). Microbial influences in inflammatory bowel diseases. *Gastroenterology, 134*(2), 577–594. https://doi.org/10.1053/j.gastro.2007.11.059.

Scheinfeld, N. (2004). A comprehensive review and evaluation of the side effects of the tumor necrosis factor alpha blockers etanercept, infliximab and adalimumab. *Journal of Dermatological Treatment, 15*(5), 280–294. https://doi.org/10.1080/09546630410017275.

Schmitz, H., Barmeyer, C., Fromm, M., Runkel, N., Foss, H. D., Bentzel, C. J., et al. (1999). Altered tight junction structure contributes to the impaired epithelial barrier function in ulcerative colitis. *Gastroenterology, 116*(2), 301–309.

Schultsz, C., Van Den Berg, F. M., Ten Kate, F. W., Tytgat, G. N., & Dankert, J. (1999). The intestinal mucus layer from patients with inflammatory bowel disease harbors high numbers of bacteria compared with controls. *Gastroenterology, 117*(5), 1089–1097.

Silva, F. A. R., Rodrigues, B. L., Ayrizono, M. de L. S., & Leal, R. F. (2016). The immunological basis of inflammatory bowel disease. *Gastroenterology Research and Practice.* https://doi.org/10.1155/2016/2097274.

Spor, A., Koren, O., & Ley, R. (2011). Unravelling the effects of the environment and host genotype on the gut microbiome. *Nature Reviews Microbiology, 9*(4), 279–290. https://doi.org/10.1038/nrmicro2540.

Steck, N., Mueller, K., Schemann, M., & Haller, D. (2012). Bacterial proteases in IBD and IBS. *Gut, 61*(11), 1610–1618. https://doi.org/10.1136/gutjnl-2011-300775.

Strober, W., & Fuss, I. J. (2011). Pro-inflammatory cytokines in the pathogenesis of IBD. *Gastroenterology, 140*(6), 1756–1767. https://doi.org/10.1053/j.gastro.2011.02.016.

Strober, W., Fuss, I. J., & Blumberg, R. S. (2002). The immunology of mucosal models of inflammation. *Annual Review of Immunology, 20*, 495–549. https://doi.org/10.1146/annurev.immunol.20.100301.064816.

Strugala, V., Dettmar, P. W., & Pearson, J. P. (2008). Thickness and continuity of the adherent colonic mucus barrier in active and quiescent ulcerative colitis and Crohn's disease. *International Journal of Clinical Practice, 62*(5), 762–769. https://doi.org/10.1111/j.1742-1241.2007.01665.x.

Su, L., Nalle, S. C., Shen, L., Turner, E. S., Singh, G., Breskin, L. A., et al. (2013). TNFR2 activates MLCK-dependent tight junction dysregulation to cause apoptosis-mediated barrier loss and experimental colitis. *Gastroenterology, 145*(2), 407–415. https://doi.org/10.1053/j.gastro.2013.04.011.

Tannock, G. W. (2008). The search for disease-associated compositional shifts in bowel bacterial communities of humans. *Trends in Microbiology, 16*(10), 488–495. https://doi.org/10.1016/j.tim.2008.07.005.

Tilg, H., Moschen, A., & Kaser, A. (2007). Mode of function of biological anti-TNF agents in the treatment of inflammatory bowel diseases. *Expert Opinion on Biological Therapy, 7*(7), 1051–1059. https://doi.org/10.1517/14712598.7.7.1051.

Tilg, H., Ulmer, H., Kaser, A., & Weiss, G. (2002). Role of IL-10 for induction of anemia during inflammation. *The Journal of Immunology, 169*(4), 2204–2209.

Timmer, A., Patton, P. H., Chande, N., McDonald, J. W. D., & MacDonald, J. K. (2016). Azathioprine and 6-mercaptopurine for maintenance of remission in ulcerative colitis. *Cochrane Database of Systematic Reviews, 5*, CD000478. https://doi.org/10.1002/14651858.CD000478.pub4.

Tjellström, B., Stenhammar, L., Magnusson, K. E., & Sandqvist, T. (1997). Oral immunoglobulin treatment in Crohn's disease. *Acta Paediatrica, 86*(2), 221–223.

Torres, J., Mehandru, S., Colombel, J.-F., & Peyrin-Biroulet, L. (2017). Crohn's disease. *The Lancet, 389*(10080), 1741–1755. https://doi.org/10.1016/S0140-6736(16)31711-1.

Umanskiy, K., & Fichera, A. (2010). Health related quality of life in inflammatory bowel disease: The impact of surgical therapy. *World Journal of Gastroenterology, 16*(40), 5024–5034.

Ungaro, R., Bernstein, C. N., Gearry, R., Hviid, A., Kolho, K.-L., Kronman, M. P., et al. (2014). Antibiotics associated with increased risk of new-onset Crohn's disease but not ulcerative colitis: A meta-analysis. *American Journal of Gastroenterology, 109*(11), 1728–1738. https://doi.org/10.1038/ajg.2014.246.

Ungaro, R., Mehandru, S., Allen, P. B., Peyrin-Biroulet, L., & Colombel, J.-F. (2017). Ulcerative colitis. *The Lancet, 389*(10080), 1756–1770. https://doi.org/10.1016/S0140-6736(16)32126-2.

Urquhart, L. (2018). Market watch: Top drugs and companies by sales in 2017. *Nature Reviews Drug Discovery, 17*, 232. https://doi.org/10.1038/nrd.2018.42.

Van Spaendonk, H., Ceuleers, H., Witters, L., Patteet, E., Joossens, J., Augustyns, K., et al. (2017). Regulation of intestinal permeability: The role of proteases. *World Journal of Gastroenterology, 23*(12), 2106–2123. https://doi.org/10.3748/wjg.v23.i12.2106.

Vandenbroucke, K., de Haard, H., Beirnaert, E., Dreier, T., Lauwereys, M., Huyck, L., et al. (2010). Orally administered L. lactis secreting an anti-TNF nanobody demonstrate efficacy in chronic colitis. *Mucosal Immunology, 3*(1), 49–56. https://doi.org/10.1038/mi.2009.116.

Van der Sluis, M., De Koning, B. A. E., De Bruijn, A. C. J. M., Velcich, A., Meijerink, J. P. P., Van Goudoever, J. B., et al. (2006). Muc2-deficient mice spontaneously develop colitis, indicating that MUC2 is critical for colonic protection. *Gastroenterology, 131*(1), 117–129. https://doi.org/10.1053/j.gastro.2006.04.020.

Virta, L., Auvinen, A., Helenius, H., Huovinen, P., & Kolho, K.-L. (2012). Association of repeated exposure to antibiotics with the development of pediatric Crohn's diseaseâ€"A nationwide, register-based Finnish case-control study. *American Journal of Epidemiology, 175*(8), 775–784. https://doi.org/10.1093/aje/kwr400.

Wang, Y., Parker, C. E., Feagan, B. G., & MacDonald, J. K. (2016). Oral 5-aminosalicylic acid for maintenance of remission in ulcerative colitis. *Cochrane Database of Systematic Reviews, 5*, CD000544. https://doi.org/10.1002/14651858.CD000544.pub4.

Ward, M. A., Pierre, J. F., Leal, R. F., Huang, Y., Shogan, B., Dalal, S. R., et al. (2016). Insights into the pathogenesis of ulcerative colitis from a murine model of stasis-induced dysbiosis, colonic metaplasia, and genetic susceptibility. *American Journal of Physiology - Gastrointestinal and Liver Physiology, 310*(11), G973–G988. https://doi.org/10.1152/ajpgi.00017.2016.

Wehkamp, J., Götz, M., Herrlinger, K., Steurer, W., & Stange, E. F. (2016). Inflammatory bowel disease. *Deutsches Arzteblatt International, 113*(5), 72–82. https://doi.org/10.3238/arztebl.2016.0072.

Weisshof, R., & Chowers, Y. (2017). Optimization of treatment by antibodies against TNF-α in inflammatory bowel disease. *Harefuah, 156*(10), 666–669.

West, N. R., Hegazy, A. N., Owens, B. M. J., Bullers, S. J., Linggi, B., Buonocore, S., et al. (2017). Oncostatin M drives intestinal inflammation and predicts response to tumor necrosis factor-neutralizing therapy in patients with inflammatory bowel disease. *Nature Medicine, 23*(5), 579–589. https://doi.org/10.1038/nm.4307.

Wilhelm, S. M., & Love, B. L. (2017). Management of patients with inflammatory bowel disease: Current and future treatments. *Clinical Pharmacist, 9*(3). https://doi.org/10.1211/CP.2017.20202316.

Woolley, J. A., & Landon, J. (1995). Comparison of antibody production to human interleukin-6 (IL-6) by sheep and chickens. *Journal of Immunological Methods, 178*(2), 253–265.

Worledge, K. L., Godiska, R., Barrett, T. A., & Kink, J. A. (2000). Oral administration of avian tumor necrosis factor antibodies effectively treats experimental colitis in rats. *Digestive Diseases and Sciences, 45*(12), 2298–2305.

Wu, H.-M., Wei, J., Wang, K., Qi, Y., & Wang, F.-Y. (2018). Mucus protectors: Promising therapeutic strategies for inflammatory bowel disease. *Medical Hypotheses, 120*, 55–59. https://doi.org/10.1016/j.mehy.2018.08.013.

Zeissig, S., Bürgel, N., Günzel, D., Richter, J., Mankertz, J., Wahnschaffe, U., et al. (2007). Changes in expression and distribution of claudin 2, 5 and 8 lead to discontinuous tight junctions and barrier dysfunction in active Crohn's disease. *Gut, 56*(1), 61–72. https://doi.org/10.1136/gut.2006.094375.

Zelová, H., & Hošek, J. (2013). TNF-α signalling and inflammation: Interactions between old acquaintances. *Inflammation Research: Official Journal of the European Histamine Research Society, 62*(7), 641–651 [et Al.] https://doi.org/10.1007/s00011-013-0633-0.

Zheng, X., Tsuchiya, K., Okamoto, R., Iwasaki, M., Kano, Y., Sakamoto, N., et al. (2011). Suppression of hath1 gene expression directly regulated by hes1 via notch signalling is associated with goblet cell depletion in ulcerative colitis. *Inflammatory Bowel Diseases, 17*(11), 2251–2260. https://doi.org/10.1002/ibd.21611.

CHAPTER SIX

Interplay between inflammation and cancer

Rekha Khandia* and Ashok Munjal*
Department of Genetics, Barkatullah University, Bhopal, Madhya Pradesh, India
*Corresponding authors: E-mail: ak.munjal@bubhopal.ac.in; rekha.morchhale@gmail.com

Contents

Advances in Protein Chemistry and Structural Biology, Volume 119
ISSN 1876-1623
https://doi.org/10.1016/bs.apcsb.2019.09.004

Abstract

During the 19th century, for the first time, the linkage between inflammation and cancer was established. Inflammatory microenvironment is an essential component of the tumor microenvironment. Chronic inflammation due to persistent infection due to the microbes, viruses, helminths or constant exposure to non-infectious factors like smoke, silica or asbestos eventually might result in carcinogenesis. In tumor microenvironment, various inflammatory cells such as T lymphocytes (occasionally B cells), dendritic cells, macrophages, monocytes, neutrophils and natural killer (NK) cells are present. As a mediator of immune surveillance and host defense TRAIL cytokines are produced which upon binding with death receptors (DRs) initiate a cascade of apoptotic pathways. Anti-inflammatory drugs such as aspirin, celecoxib, diclofenac, diflunisal and ibuprofen etc. are being used against cancer, indicating the interplay between both the mechanisms. A deeper understanding of common pathways implicated between both the inflammation and cancer may pave the way to fight against both of these deleterious ailments.

1. Introduction

German physician, Rudolf Virchow in 1863, for the first time indicated about the association between inflammation and cancer (Balkwill & Mantovani, 2001). In fact, during the onset of chronic inflammatory conditions, humans are predisposed to several kinds of cancer including breast, liver, bowel, urinary bladder, prostate, gastric mucosa, ovary, and skin cancers. Chronic inflammation accounts for neoplastic transformation and approximately 15% of total cancers worldwide (Coussens & Werb, 2002). Various clinical and experimental studies revealed that majority of cancer related deaths is associated with chronic infection. The classical example is hepatitis by hepatitis B and hepatitis C viruses; that chronically infect the liver and if the infection is not eradicated, later it may result in hepatic carcinoma. Similarly, some inflammatory conditions caused due to the non-infectious reasons may also initiate carcinogenesis. The examples include cancer of esophagus, pancreas, and gallbladder resultant due to the inflammation of respective organ such as esophagitis, chronic pancreatitis and cholecystitis (Lu, Ouyang, & Huang, 2006).

Chronic inflammation is often characterized by tissue damage followed by damage-induced cellular proliferation, and initiation of cellular repair pathways. At the time of tissue damage, lymphocytes and macrophages are recruited at the site of inflammation. Activated macrophages release reactive oxygen species (ROS) and inflammatory cytokines heading toward the elevated nuclear factor kappa B (NF-κB) pathway and cyclooxygenase-2 (COX-2) activity. Hudson et al. (1999) revealed the presence of a unique cytokine; migration inhibitory factor (MIF) that is responsible for suppressing p53 function and creating an antiapoptosis feedback loop.

In certain tumors inflammatory cytokines like Interleukin-6 (IL-6) is highly increased and appreciable level of IL 1β is correlated with the advanced and aggressive nature of the disease. There are various mediators of inflammation including microbes, helminthes or non-living molecules like asbestos and cigarette smoke that initiates chronic inflammation.

2. Infectious inflammatory mediators

A linkage between chronic inflammation caused by infectious agents and cancer is not new; chronic infection with certain bacteria, virus, fungi, protozoans and worms have been found to enhance the risk of cancer in human being. The mechanism of cancer development may mediate through carcinogens, immune suppression, inflammation or all three (Masrour-Roudsari & Ebrahimpour, 2017). If the infection is not cured and sustained for longer period, it may bring changes in the immune cells and produce inflammatory mediators, which eventually can cause cancers. Following are the few examples of infectious inflammatory mediators:

2.1 Microbes as inflammatory mediators

The inflammation may be caused by microbes like bacterium *Helicobacter pylori*, *Bacteroides fragilis*, *Streptococcus bovis* (now *S. gallolyticus*), *Enterococcus spp.* and some members of the enterobacteriaceae family. Long term infection by *H. pylori* in gastric mucosa results in generation of significant quantities of nitric oxide that damage the host nucleotide DNA and alter the transcriptional regulation by means of DNA methyl-transferase activity. These microbes may attach to the intestinal epithelium and directly cause proliferation of epithelial cells (hyperplasia). Moreover, these microbes may damage the integrity of the epithelial barrier through secretary toxins and cause local inflammations. A strong linkage has been found between certain strains of *Escherichia coli* attachment to colon tissue and tumor infiltration. A toxin, colibactin produced by few strains of *E. coli*, *Enterobacter aerogenes*, *Citrobacter koseri* and *Klebsiella pneumoniae* can induce the DNA double-strand nicks, chromosome aberrations, and cell cycle arrest leading to cell aneuploidy/polyploidy (Faïs, Delmas, Barnich, Bonnet, & Dalmasso, 2018). The *B. fragilis* toxin can stimulate NF-kB pathway.

2.2 Viruses as inflammatory mediators

Various viral infections predispose human body to chronic inflammation and cancer. The infection with hepatitis B and C are the most common causes of chronic hepatic inflammation and hepatocellular carcinoma. Epstein—Barr virus (EBV), human T-lymphotropic virus-I (HTLV-I), Kaposi's sarcoma herpesvirus (KSHV) and Merkel cell polyomavirus (MCV) are few others that have been linked with cancer induction. During chronic viral infection, infected cells secrete cytokines such as IL-1β, tumor necrosis factor-α (TNF-α) and IL-6 that creates an inflammatory milieu. Both the viral infection and virus mediated inflammation activates NF-κB, STAT3 and the MAPK signaling pathways to promote tumor development (Read & Douglas, 2014).

During HBV and HCV infection, TNF-α, IL-6 and IL-1β is secreted by hepatocytes and infiltrating lymphocytes, which leads to the hepatocellular carcinoma. EBV, belonging to the gamma-herpes virus family, was the first identified human oncovirus. EBV infections cause various B-cell and T-cell/NK lymphoproliferative disorders such as Burkitt lymphoma, Hodgkin lymphoma, nasopharyngeal carcinoma, gastric carcinoma. Cancer cells may suppress the functioning of T lymphocytes and escape T-cell-mediated cellular cytotoxicity through an interaction between anti-PD-1 (programmed cell death-1) with its ligand PD-L1. PD1 expression is upregulated in EBV infected cells. EBV infected gastric cells express higher levels of PD-L1 via activating JAK2/STAT1/IRF-1 (Janus Kinase 2/Signal transducer and activator of transcription 1/IFN regulatory factor-1) signaling pathway (Vranic, Cyprian, Akhtar, & Al Moustafa, 2018).

HTLV-I infection causes adult T-cell leukemia. The tax gene of HTLV-I plays an important role in transcription of viral genes. Tax activates NF-κB, AP-1 and SRF mediated transcription pathways. NF-κB activation is essential to tumorigenesis and expression of antiapoptotic protein Bcl and surviving (Matsuoka, 2005). Kaposi's sarcoma herpesvirus produces homolog of human IL-6 that is supposed to increase the expression of IL-6 leading to VEGF mediated stimulation of angiogenesis (Goncalves, Ziegelbauer, Uldrick, & Yarchoan, 2017).

2.3 Fungi as inflammatory mediators

Candida albicans is a dimorphic fungal species, which is present as a part of normal fauna of human body; whereas under immunocompromised conditions, it become pathogenic. It is recognized and adhered with the endothelial cells through mannose, toll-like receptors (TLR), and dectin-1 receptors. A pro-inflammatory response against *C. albicans* involves inflammatory molecules such as TNF-α, IL-1ß and IL-18. In the work of Ramirez-Garcia et al. (2013), it was revealed that *C. albicans* adherence to the hepatic sinusoidal endothelial (HSE) cells may trigger the release of inflammatory cytokines including TNF-α and IL-18, that could lead to enhanced metastasis of B16 melanoma cells. Inhibition of IL-18 not only reduce the adhesion of B16M cells to HSE through decreased expression of VCAM-1 but the number of hepatic metastatic foci and metastatic volume was also reduced (Vidal-Vanaclocha et al., 2006). Higher risk of Hematologic malignancy, oral cavity cancer, lip cancer, pancreatic cancer, skin cancer, and thyroid cancer occurrence has been linked with Candida infection.

2.4 Protozoans as inflammatory mediators

Trichomonas vaginalis infection or serostatus has been correlated with an increased incidence of cervical cancer (Yap et al., 1995) and prostate cancer (Stark et al., 2009). The larval stage of *Taenia crassiceps* that exclusively grows inside the peritoneal cavity, down-regulates the pro-inflammatory cytokines whilst upregulates IL-4 and IL-10 and ameliorate Dextran Sodium Sulfate mediated colitis (Ledesma-Soto et al., 2015). However, the role of parasites in enhancing inflammation and cancer is controversial. *Toxoplasma gondii* is a protozoan parasite that may alter the immune response of the host and produce polarization toward Th1 responses and an increase in IFN-γ and IL-12 production promotes activation of anti-tumor response. Contrarily, *T. gondii* infection is found associated with around 1.8-folds increase in the risk of brain cancers and known to cause gliomas amongst the experimental animals (Thomas et al., 2012). Also, case reports of pituitary adenoma associated with *T. gondii* infection warns further investigation for the protumor or antitumor role (Zhang, Li, Hu, Cheng, & Huang, 2002).

2.5 Helminths as inflammatory mediators

Helminths including blood flukes (*Schistosoma haematobium, S. japonicum*, and *S. mansoni*) and liver flukes (*Clonorchis sinensis* and *Opisthorchis viverrini*) are also involved in causing cancers (Scholte, Pascoal-Xavier, & Nahum,

2018). Schistosome infection leads to immunomodulation; the eggs of *S. mansoni*, *S. japonicum*, and *S. mekong* deposited into bladder and produce IL-4, IL-5, and IL-13, which further activate the macrophages. A granulomatous host-immune response is activated to proteolytically digest the *Schistosoma* eggs but this granuloma formation induces chronic inflammation (Colley, Bustinduy, Secor, & King, 2014).

Some epigenetic factors like hypo/hypermethylation also leads to predisposal to cancer. Amongst gastric cancer patients, generally tumor suppressor genes are found hypermethylated and such epigenetic changes are present in the coding as well as non-coding areas (Díaz, Valenzuela Valderrama, Bravo, & Quest, 2018). Also chronic exposure to inflammatory cytokines leads to deregulation of the Hedgehog/GLI signaling pathway, important in maintaining the normal physiology of stomach and may lead to gastric cancer.

Hepatocellular carcinoma (HCC) is one among several most aggressive human cancers. Due to metastatic nature it is associated with high mortality. Studies have revealed that the chronic infections with viruses like hepatitis B virus and hepatitis C virus or exposure to agents like Diethylnitrosamine, 2-acetamidofluorene (2-FAA), phenobarbital, alcohol, aflatoxin B1 metabolite, biliary disease or metabolic disorders also predispose to HCC. Genetic conditions like hereditary hemochromatosis and 1-antitrypsin deficiency are also increases the risk toward HCC. Chronic inflammation leads to the continuous expression of cytokines and recruitment of immune cells to the liver. A complex cascade of interlinked reactions is then takes place that predisposes the body for development of HCC.

3. Roles of C-reactive protein (CRP) and serum amyloid A (SAA)

Some convincing evidences have been revealed by Pierce et al. (2009), who demonstrated that chronic inflammation may increase the risk of breast cancer reappearance. Considering the Systemic C-reactive protein (CRP) and serum amyloid A (SAA) as a marker of chronic inflammation, an inverse correlation was established between these markers and breast cancer survival. Both the CRP and SAA are non-specific acute phase proteins those are secreted in response to various cytokines such as IL1, IL6 and TNF-α. The CRP increases up to 1000-folds during inflammation or infection and is involved in the activation of classical complement pathway. CRP is produced in the form of homopentamer that is called native CRP (nCRP) that is capable of dissociation at site of inflammation to form monomeric unit (mCRP). Both CRP isoforms possess biological roles. nCRP has anti-inflammatory properties which upon activating classical complement pathway induce phagocytosis and promotes apoptosis. Contrarily, mCRP is inducer of chemotaxis and it recruits the white blood cells at the site of inflammation. It enhances the expression of the IL-8 and monocyte chemo-attractant protein-1 production also and induces the NO production (Sproston & Ashworth, 2018).

SAA is involved in the recruitment of inflammatory cells. In a population-based study comprising of 734 breast cancer survivors that correlated the post-treatment inflammatory markers and breast cancer survival, it was revealed that elevated CRP and SAA were linked with reduced disease-free survival. The finding also suggested that the early information regarding the reoccurrence of disease when the patients have no metastatic history (Pierce et al., 2009).

4. Inflammatory microenvironment association with cancer

Tumor microenvironment encompass fibroblasts, endothelial cells, pericytes and various cells of the immune system (Quail & Joyce, 2013). Tumor environment varies for different types of tissues as well as for different tumors of the same tissue. The presence of tumor cells is not ignored by the host immune system and it take attempts to eliminate as well as to inhibit the growth of the tumor cells. Generally, the tumors are infiltrated by the inflammatory cells and this infiltration sometimes acts as an indicator of good survival and prognosis. The type, density, and location of immune cells within the tumor may act as good indicators from the survived patients suffering from colorectal cancer; where inflammatory cells had better prognostic importance rather than histopathological findings (Galon et al., 2006). A total of 569 marker gene signatures corresponding to B cells, plasma cells, monocytes, macrophages, neutrophils, NK cells and T cells have been identified through transcriptomic data analysis and collectively known as ImSig (Nirmal et al., 2018). These markers may be used for quantitative analysis of immune cell content within the tumor or normal tissue sample. In case of Merkel cell carcinoma (MCC), which is an aggressive metastatic cancer, an association between overall survival and tumor-associated immune infiltrate has been observed. Higher CD3+ and CD8+ T-cell density in the tumor periphery indicated improved overall or disease-specific survival in patients and may act as a robust prognostic indicator (Feldmeyer et al., 2016).

After exploring the functional properties of tumor-infiltrating lymphocytes, it was observed that these cells with compromised signaling with T cell receptor, are unable to mediate tumor cytotoxicity or produce Th1-type cytokines in presence of tumor antigens (Murata, 2018).

4.1 Cells present in the tumor microenvironment

The major functions of immune cells are to maintain the tissue homeostasis, eradication of damaged cells and pathogens. Immune system is tuned in such a manner that it does not react with its own cells, but since the tumor cells acquire large number of mutations and alterations, hence they produce some tumor specific antigens which are easily recognized by the immune system as non-self that eventually lead to the clearance of the cancer cells (Chen & Mellman, 2013). However, immune cells are involved in the survival and proliferation of tumor cells also. Generally, such cells are present in the tumor microenvironment. The tumor microenvironment is comprised of dividing tumor cells, stroma, blood vessels and various inflammatory cells such as T lymphocytes (occasionally B cells), dendritic cells, macrophages, polymorphonuclear leukocytes and rare natural killer (NK) cells (Whiteside, 2007).

4.1.1 Dendritic cells

Pivotal role has been played by dendritic cells (DC)in tumor microenvironment. These cells decide whether the adaptive arm of immune system will be activated or not. DC plays instructive roles for T cells to activate and differentiate through co-stimulatory molecules and cytokines. Also it interacts with NK cells and B cells. Tumor infiltrating DC (TIDC) have been found associated with many cancers including breast, colorectal, lung, renal, head and neck, bladder, gastric and ovarian (Karthaus, Torensma, & Tel, 2012). DC infiltration have been associated with both the poor as well as good prognosis. Enhanced infiltration of activated and mature DC in tumor microenvironment (TME) of colorectal cancer is found associated with improved overall survival and good prognosis (Malietzis et al., 2015); however, an opposite outcome has been revealed by Sandel, Dadabayev, Menon, Morreau, and Melief (2005), who demonstrated a negative correlation between the number of mature TIDC and a favorable clinical outcome. This discrepancy may be due to the identification methods employed to identify DC.

Classically CD1a, S-100, CD83 and DC-SIGN are the markers used for the identification but none of such markers are expressed exclusively on DC. For instance, inflammation cause expression of S-100 proteins onto the surface of myeloid origin cells including granulocytes, macrophages and epithelial cells (Foell, Wittkowski, Vogl, & Roth, 2007); and CD1 is expressed onto the surface of macrophages and DC in case of acute viral infection (Lin, Roberts, Spence, & Brutkiewicz, 2005). On the basis of immuno-histochemical observations of S-100 antigen, it was found that less number of infiltrating S-100 DC were associated with poor survival (Reichert, Scheuer, Day, Wagner, & Whiteside, 2001). Functioning of TIDC is possibly linked with the delayed tumor progression and metastasis. High number of infiltrating DC are present in less invasive tumors and the density of these cells have an inverse correlation with tumor pathologic grade and stage, while a positive correlation with overall survival (Shurin & Lotze, 2009).

DC-LAMP + cells in TME exhibits a strong predictor of prognosis for high-grade serous ovarian carcinoma (Truxova et al., 2018) and used to determine the clinically-relevant activated anticancer immunity. Prognosis may be dependent on the shift in phenotype of TIDC phenotype instead simply degree of TIDC infiltration into the tumor. Mature and active DC recruit disease fighting effecter cells inside the tumor. Many subsets of DC are present in body with specific functions and morphology which includes Langerhans cells, monocyte-derived DC (CD14 + DCs), myeloid DC and plasmacytoid DC (Geissmann et al., 2010).

4.1.2 Tumor-associated macrophages (TAMs)

Macrophages are differentiated cells of mononuclear myeloid lineage, present in the various tissues to perform numerous important functions such as defense from pathogens, responses to a normal and pathological microenvironment, tissue homeostasis and modeling, elimination of cellular debris etc. Macrophages are induced by interferon-γ (IFN-γ)-mediated classical activation or alternatively by the helper T 2 cells(Th2) and cytokines like IL-4 and IL-13 (Gordon & Martinez, 2010). Macrophages, more specifically tumor-associated macrophages (TAMs), are abundant in most malignant tumor microenvironment. A subpopulation of metastasis-associated macrophages enables promotion of extravasation, seeding and continuous growth of tumor cells and suppression of antitumor immune response (Qian et al., 2009). These cells are also known to promote tumor angiogenesis.

The TAMs shares the properties of alternatively activated macrophages (AAMs). It has been evidenced in experimental tumor model (tumor transplanted or oncogene induced) that TAMs contribute in tumor invasion through cathepsin B and S and tumor growth is promoted through angiogenesis mediated by VEGF. The TAMs also recruit other hematopoietic cells through secretion of chemokines (Gocheva et al., 2010). AAMs mediate the growth of tumor and its metastasis via M-CSF, TNF-α, IL-10, transforming growth factor-β (TGF-β). The AAMs play role in promoting tumor is evidenced by their dependence on the IL-4 and IL-13 common receptor and receptor blockage through genetic manipulation result toward the tumor rejection in a Th1 cell dependent manner (Gordon & Martinez, 2010).

Tumor and tumor stroma generated C—C motif chemokine ligand 2 (CCL2) is helpful in recruiting the inflammatory monocytes, (those express the receptor for chemokine CCL2) and metastasis-associated macrophages and inhibition of signaling between CCL2 and CCR2 result in a blockade of recruitment of inflammatory monocytes that ultimately results in inhibition of metastasis and improves the survival rate of experimental tumor-bearing mice (Qian et al., 2011).

i) ***Origin of TAMs*****:** The origin(s) of TAMs is a topic of hot debate; initially, it was considered that TAMs are originated from circulating monocytes, but recently these have been demonstrated to originate through embryonic macrophages which are present in tissues during development. In these tissues, such progenitors persist through proliferation and are independent of adult hematopoietic system (Geissmann et al., 2010). Studies in mouse models of brain and pancreatic cancer, have demonstrated that TAMs may be originated from both the blood monocytes and embryonic macrophages. Macrophages either derived from infiltrating bone marrow-derived monocytes or tissue resident embryonic macrophages can be morphologically indistinguishable in histological slides and these may not be separated by the usage of currently available lineage-specific antibodies. It has been revealed in glioblastoma that intra-tumor over 85% of the TAMs are bone marrow-derived macrophages, while in peritumoral region embryonic macrophages (microglia) predominates (Chen et al., 2017).

ii) ***Functional plasticity of TAMs*****:** The TAMs may exhibit functional plasticity showing activation status form "classically" activated, tumoricidal (referred as M1) to "alternatively" activated tumor-promoting phenotype (referred as M2). The antitumor/pro-inflammatory or anti-inflammatory/tumor-promoting activities depend on local microenvironmental cues. The M1 polarization is associated with NF-κB,

STAT1, and IRF5 (Krausgruber et al., 2011), while M2 polarization is associated with IRF4, STAT6, MYC- Proto-Oncogene (Murray et al., 2014). There is a distinct chemokine profile of M1 and M2. The M1 macrophages express Th1 cell—attracting chemokines such as chemokine (C-X-C motif) ligand (CXCL)9 and CXCL10 while M2 macrophages express the chemokines CCL17, CCL22 and CCL24. Chemokines also may play role in polarization of macrophages. The CCL2 and CXCL4 chemokines may shift the macrophage phenotype toward an M2-like phenotype. The M1 and M2 exhibit differed iron, folate and glucose metabolism profiles.

iii) ***M1 macrophages***: M1 macrophages activate in response to the stimulation with bacterial Lipopolysaccharides (LPS), TNF-α, and/or IFN-γ. Pathogenic signals are recognized by antigen presenting cells and TNF-α is secreted, while IFN-γ is produced by NK cells and Th1 cells. Upon activation pro-inflammatory molecules including IL1, IL6, and TNF-α and effectors molecules like RNS are produced. Chemokines such as CXCL9 and CXCL0 are also produced and as a result antibacterial and tumoricidal activities are initiated.

iv) ***M2 macrophages***: Stimuli like glucocorticoids, TGF-β and IL-10 may turn into TAMs toward M2 phenotype. M2 macrophages have unique subsets. M2a macrophages express anti-inflammatory cytokines (IL-10 and TGF-β) and chemokines (CCL17 and CCL22) those possess roles in tissue remodeling. M2b macrophages produce higher amounts of IL-10 and lower amounts of pro-inflammatory cytokines such as IL-1 β, IL-6, IL-12 and TNF-α (Chistiakov, Bobryshev, & Orekhov, 2015).

v) ***Classically activated macrophages***: Classically activated M1 macrophages secrete high quantities of pro-inflammatory cytokines including IL-1β, IL-12, TNF-α and superoxide anions. Activated M1 macrophages also upregulates the iron storage protein H ferritin, while downregulating ferroportin resulting in iron retention and inflammation.

vi) ***Alternatively activated macrophages***: Macrophages are suggested to promote invasion of newly transformed cancer cells in pre-invasive areas through secretion of cathepsins, matrix metalloproteinases (MMP), cytokines, EGF, and TNF-α. These molecules help in basement membrane disruption, remodeling the extracellular matrix and migration of the cancer cells. In experimental models, it has been established that when the number of macrophages is depleted, the tumor progression is inhibited; which indicated that macrophages have imperative role in mediating the early events of tumor progression in an inducible transgenic mouse model of pre-neoplastic progression (Schwertfeger et al., 2006).

Breast cancer progress is initiated in a stepwise manner with atypical ductal hyperplasia leading to ductal carcinoma *in situ* (DCIS). Later, stages of invasive ductal carcinoma (formation of primary tumor), and metastatic ductal carcinoma comes (Wellings & Jensen, 1973). In a p53-null mouse model, PN1a and PN1b cell lines were transplanted and this transplantation made estrogen and progesterone receptor positive ductal hyperplasia (Medina et al., 2002). A significant increase of infiltrating macrophages in PN1a lesions has been observed with the dominance of TIE2+CD206 + macrophages, a subpopulation known to have pro-angiogenic and immunosuppressive functions (Carron et al., 2017; Coffelt et al., 2011). The percentage of CD45 + F480 + CD11b + macrophages are higher in PN1a lesions those were progressing toward palpable tumors, further indicated their tumor promoting roles (Carron et al., 2017).

In an experiment to determine the capacity of PN1a cell line in educating macrophages, macrophage cell line RAW 264.7 or bone marrow-derived macrophages (BMDMs) were exposed to the PN1a conditioned media or unconditioned media as control. Post exposure cellular RNA from macrophage cell line was isolated and expression profile of various genes was determined. Several tumor-promoting markers including arginase 1 (Arg1), VEGFa, TGF- β and growth arrest specific 6 (Gas6) were found to be induced. Pro-inflammatory genes *IL-12p40* and *NOS2*, that could have anticancer response were not significantly altered in PN1a educated macrophages, where Immunosuppressant IL10 was found to enhance significantly. The IL6 and TNF-α levels were increased in such educated macrophages. The experiment elucidate that few factors are secreted by tumor cells that result in polarization of macrophages in subpopulation with a tumor promoting phenotype (Carron et al., 2017).

4.1.3 Anti-cancer therapies and TAMs

4.1.3.1 Tumor protective roles

Conventional chemotherapeutic agents may inhibit effective antitumor responses owing to the elicitation of misdirected macrophage-orchestrated tissue repair response that starts the repairing of damaged tumor tissue and results in the enhancement of tumor growth as well as inhibition of antineoplastic activities (Mantovani, Biswas, Galdiero, Sica, & Locati, 2013). An enhanced recruitment of TAMs toward the tumor following the chemotherapy is often related to poor prognosis and tumor resistance to therapy and recurrence.

Various cancer cell centered therapies modulate the functions of TAMs. Post-chemotherapy tumor protecting activities of TAMs are attributed to diverse pathways. The possible pathways could be:

i) ***Increased recruitment of immunosuppressive TAMs*:** Upon cytotoxic therapies such as treatment with paclitaxil, monocyte/macrophage recruitment factors like colony stimulating factor 1 (CSF1) and IL-34 are produced which enhance the CSF1 receptor dependent macrophage infiltration. Induced or spontaneous blocking of CSF1 or its receptor has been found associated with ablated tumor angiogenesis and reduction in the primary tumor growth. Targeting TAMs by blocking of CSF-1 receptor (CSF-1R) has been shown to induce intratumoral type I interferon (type 1 IFN) signaling that enhances the efficacy of platinum based therapies. In a type 1 IFN enriched tumor microenvironment during the cisplatin therapy, antitumor immunity was found to be enhanced in a poorly immunogenic breast cancer K14cre; $Cdh1^{F/F}$; $Trp53^{F/F}$ transgenic mouse model (Salvagno et al., 2019). Depleted TAMs due to anti-CSF1 antibodies were shown to improve the efficacy of combination chemotherapy (cyclophosphamide, methotrexate, and 5-fluorouracil) in chemoresistant human breast cancer xenografts grown in immunodeficient mice (Paulus, Stanley, Schäfer, Abraham, & Aharinejad, 2006). Also depleted TAMs would enhance $CD8^+$ CTL infiltration and thereby cater an antitumor immune microenvironment (DeNardo et al., 2011).

ii) ***Pro-tumor polarization*:** Resistance to platinum containing therapies has been found associated with the increased levels of inflammatory molecules IL-6 and prostaglandin E2. Both the mediators derive differentiation of monocytes to tumor-promoting M2 macrophages. An investigation of impact of chemotherapeutic agents such as cisplatin and carboplatin on 10 different cervical and ovarian cancer cell lines as well as their effect of these cells on differentiation of monocytes revealed that the treatment enhanced the ability of tumor cells to induce IL-10 secreting M2 macrophages. Treatment with indomethacin or IL-6 receptor targeting monoclonal antibody, tamed M2-differentiation (Dijkgraaf et al., 2013).

iii) ***Blunting of antitumor activity IL17***: Gemcitabine (Gem) and 5-fluorouracil (5FU) lead to production of IL-1β by myeloid-derived suppressor cells. CD4(+) T cells secrete IL-17 under the influence of IL-1β that curtail antitumor response (Bruchard et al., 2013).

4.1.3.2 Antitumor roles

TAMs are considered to be linked with inhibited growth of tumor cells through secretion of chemo-attractants that attract T cells and thereby initiate antitumor type-1 inflammatory response as seen in colorectal cancer model (Ong et al., 2012). M1 macrophages produce Reactive oxygen species (ROS) and pro-inflammatory cytokines including IL1, IL6, and TNF-α. Also inducible nitric oxide synthase (iNOS), cluster of differentiation (CD)86, major histocompatibility complex II, and CD14 are produced (Costa da Silva et al., 2017).

4.1.4 Role of iron in reprogramming of M2 to M1 macrophage

A novel role of hemolytic RBCs, heme and iron in shaping the immune response in TME has been discovered. In iron-loaded TAMs (iTAMs), expression of iron exporter protein i.e. ferroportin is reduced and this reduction is at the level of mRNA. iTAMs are studded with high CD86, CD163, Spi-c (a macrophage-restricted transcription factor), and heme oxygenase-1 (Hmox1), whereas low CD206; and exhibit pro-inflammatory phenotype and capable of killing tumor cells. The similar results have been obtained upon applying iron nanoparticles, those have ability to reprogram M2 into M1 phenotype and kill cancer cells. Therefore, the usage of iron nanoparticle may be a therapeutic strategy to curb tumors (Costa da Silva et al., 2017).

Ferumoxytol, another iron nanoparticle composition available as an intravenous preparation for the treatment of iron deficiency (anemia) in adult patients with chronic kidney disease, is also shown to reduce lung cancer metastases in liver and lungs and exhibited higher caspase-3 activity. Hence, this drug may be used in macrophage-modulating cancer immunotherapies (Zanganeh et al., 2016). The observations are in concordance with the clinical outcomes in hemolytic diseases like sickle cell anemia and thalassemia, where heme and iron are released in the circulation and are able to polarize splenic and liver macrophages toward an M1-like phenotype, contributing to inflammation and tissues damage.

4.1.5 What selective depletion of tumor infiltrating macrophages can do?

Inhibition of myeloid cell receptors CSF1R or CCR2 present on the surface of tumor-infiltrating macrophages and inflammatory monocytes has been demonstrated to reduce the pancreatic tumor-initiating cells as shown in pancreatic cancer tissue microarray studies conducted on a cohort comprising of 60 cases of invasive pancreatic ductal adenocarcinoma patients. Inhibition of these receptor(s) enhance antitumor T cell response and leads to inhibited metastasis (Mitchem et al., 2013). Selective downregulation of CSF1 also improves the chemotherapy effects through enhancement of $CD8^+$ T cells driven antitumor response (DeNardo et al., 2011). Amongst humans, TAMs express functional TNF-related apoptosis-inducing ligand (TRAIL) receptors, which are membrane-associated death receptors.

4.1.6 TRAIL mediated cancer cell death

TRAIL is a cytokine which is produced and secreted by most of the normal tissues as a part of natural immunity to induce the apoptosis and possess a significant role in prevention of cancer cell proliferation and eradication. TRAIL ligand is trimerized to bind to death receptor 4 (DR4) and/or DR5 (Refaat, Abd-Rabou, & Reda, 2014). Binding of TRAIL with the DR4/5 leads to recruitment of Fas-associated protein with death domain (FADD) that along with procaspase 8 forms the death-inducing signaling complex (DISC). Upon activation, the procaspase 8 is converted into caspase 8.

On the basis of DISC activation, cells are named as type I and II. In the type I cells, DISC activation is robust enough to activate effector caspase-3 through caspase 8; whilst in type II cells, mitochondrial pathway is additionally required to induce apoptosis. In mitochondrial pathway, BID (BH3 interacting domain death agonist) protein is cleaved by caspase 8. The BID is member of Bcl-2 protein family that contains both pro- (Bax, Bak) and anti-apoptotic (Bcl-2, Bcl-XL) factors which forms homo and heterodimers in order to maintain a critical equilibrium between the cell death and survival. The role of BID protein is important in the sense that it integrates the intrinsic and extrinsic pathways of cell death. BID is cleaved to form truncated version of BID that is t-BID. The t-BID interacts with the protein Mtch (Mitochondrial carrier homolog 1) that is critical to the activation and oligomerization of Bax/Bak present in the outer membrane of mitochondria. Also, it leads to permeabilization of the mitochondrial membrane and release of cytochrome C from the mitochondria (Katz et al., 2012) followed by formation of apoptosome by uniting with Apaf-1 and pro-caspase-9. Afterward the effecter molecule pro-caspase 3 is activated and Apoptosis is induced (Refaat et al., 2014). The TRAIL mediated cell death has been depicted in Fig. 1.

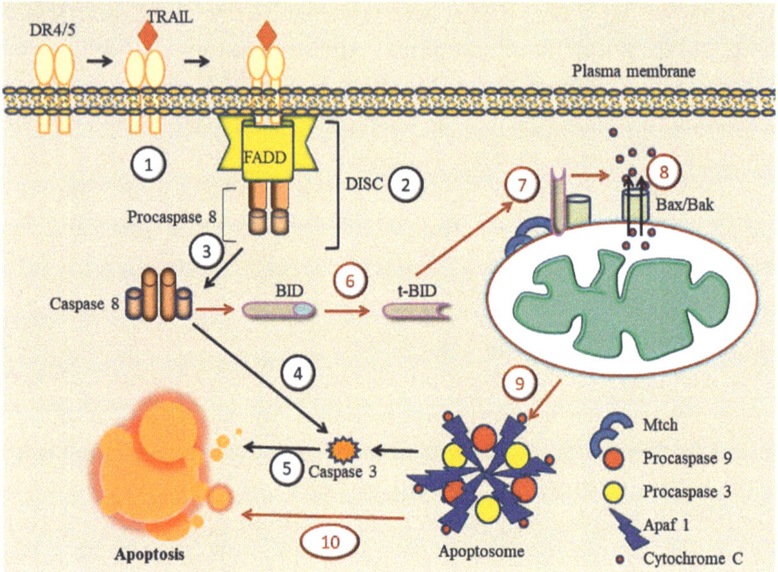

Fig. 1 Mechanism of TRAIL mediated cancer cell apoptosis. **(1)** To the death receptors (DR4/DR5), trimerized TRAIL ligand is bound **(2)** Binding of ligand with DR4/5, leads to the recruitment of Fas-associated protein with death domain (FADD) along with procaspase 8 to form death-inducing signaling complex (DISC) **(3)** Procaspase 8 is converted into active caspase 8 **(4)** In case of robust DISC activation, caspase 8 directly activates Caspase 3 **(5)** which induces apoptosis **(6)** Alternatively, mitochondrial pathway is activated. Caspase 8 cleaves BID protein to yield its truncated form, t-BID **(7)** t-BID interacts with Mtch protein and activates the oligomerization of Bax/Bak and permeabilization of mitochondrial membrane **(8)** Cytochrome C is released **(9)** Cytochrome C along with Apaf-1 and pro-caspase-9, forms apoptososme **(10)** Apoptosis is induced.

Treatment of mice with recombinant TRAIL is found to decrease the number of TAMs in tumor tissues as well as it slowed down the growth of tumor (Liguori et al., 2016). There are some natural compounds contain nutraceuticals, that upregulate or aggregate the DRs and activate caspase 8 in a TRAIL independent approach. Palmitate and Asian ginger are examples of such compounds (Prasad, Kim, Gupta, & Aggarwal, 2014).

Table 1 encompasses the list of such compounds, which have been evaluated by different groups of researchers to induce DRs dependent cancer cell killing. The information will be useful in deriving the path that will be useful in curbing the tumor-initiating cells mediated therapeutic resistance.

Table 1 Various plant derived compounds effective in killing cancer cells.

S. No	Compound	Source	Death receptor (DR) involved	Modus operandi	Cell line(s)	Model	Reference(s)
1	Curcumin	*Curcuma longa*	DR5	Formation of reactive oxygen metabolites	Caki cells	Human renal cancer cell line	Jung et al., 2005
2	Baicalein	*Scutellaria baicalensis*	DR5	Induction of apoptosis Generation of reactive oxygen species	SW480	colon cancer	Taniguchi et al., 2008
3	Withaferin	*Withania somnifera*	DR5	Increase in ROS levels c-FLIP down-regulation	Caki cells	Human renal cancer cells	Lee et al., 2009
4	Celastrol	*Celastrus hypoleucus*	DR5	Activation of caspase-8, caspase-9, and caspase-3	MDA-MB-231, MCF7, and T47D	Breast cancer cell lines	Sung, Park, Yadav, & Aggarwal, 2010
				Down-regulation of the expression of cell survival proteins including cFLIP, IAP-1, Bcl-2, Bcl-xL, survivin, and XIAP	HCT116	Colon adenocarcinoma,	
				Up-regulation of Bax expression	A293	Lung adenocarcinoma	
				Conversion of TRAIL-resistant cells to TRAIL-sensitive cells	PC3	Embryonic kidney carcinoma	

(*Continued*)

Table 1 Various plant derived compounds effective in killing cancer cells.—cont'd

S. No	Compound	Source	Death receptor (DR) involved	Modus operandi	Cell line(s)	Model	Reference(s)
5	Pterostilbene	*Pterocarpus marsupium*	DR4 and DR5	Downregulation of anti-apoptotic proteins c-FLIPS/L, Bcl-Xl, Bcl-2, survivin, and XIAP	MCF-7	Breast cancer cell lines	Chakraborty, Gupta, Ghosh, & Roy, 2010
				Up-regulation of Bax Inhibition of metastasis inducers matrix metalloproteinase 9 (MMP9) and alpha-methylacyl-CoA recemase (AMACR)	PC3	PROSTATE cancer cell lines	
		Blueberries		Apoptosis via ROS	–	Triple negative breast cancer (TNBC) cells	Hung, Liu, Ho, Lin, & Way, 2017
6	Andrographolide	*Andrographis paniculata*	DR5	Decreased anti-apoptotic Bcl-2 Up-regulation of Bak Cells arrested in sub-G1 area	SNU601, SNU638 and AGS	Gastric cancer cell lines	Lim et al., 2017
7	Berberine	*Berberis heterophylla*	DR5	Upregulation of apoptotic genes including Casp5, GADD45A, Harakiri, TNFRSF10B, TNFSF8 Downregulation of TNFRSF1B	LNCaP, DU 145	Human Prostate cancer cells	Ke et al., 2018

8	Morniga-G	*Morus nigra*	DR5 dimerization and the building of TRAIL/DR5 complexes	Activates T, B, and NK Lymphocytes and Induces Cell Death in Tn Positive Leukemia Lymphocytes	Jurkat A3	Leukemia cells	Poiroux et al., 2019
9	Methanolic extract of *Polish propolis* (contains Pinobanksin, chrysin, methoxyflavanone, p-coumaric acid, ferulic acid and caffeic acid)	*Polish propolis*	DR5	Increased apoptosis	LNCaP	Prostate cancer cells	Szliszka et al., 2013
10	Dihydroflavonol BB-1	*Blumea balsamifera*	DR5	Upregulation of DR5 through p53-independent mechanism and sensitizes TRAIL-resistant cells.	KOB and ST1	Adult T-cell leukemia/ lymphoma (ATLL) cells	Hasegawa et al., 2006
11	Apigenin	Orange, chamomile tea, onion, and wheat sprouts	DR4 and DR5	Upregulation of pro-apoptotic proteins Bad and Bax Downregulation of anti-apoptotic proteins Bcl-xl and Bcl-2 Suppression of NF-κB, AKT and ERK activation	A549 and H1299	Non-small cell lung cancer	Chen et al., 2016
		Taraxacum officinale	DR5	Production of reactive oxygen species	–	Breast cancer stem cells	Trinh, Dang, Tran, & Pham, 2016

(*Continued*)

Table 1 Various plant derived compounds effective in killing cancer cells.—cont'd

S. No	Compound	Source	Death receptor (DR) involved	Modus operandi	Cell line(s)	Model	Reference(s)
12	Piperine	*Piper Nnigrum*	DR5	Supression of survivin and p65 phosphorylation	MDA-MB-231 and MDA-MB-468	Breast cancer cells	Abdelhamed et al., 2014
13	Quercetin	Vegetables, fruits, tea, red wine, and coffee	DR5	Apoptosis via extrinsic pathway	MCF-7, BT-20	Breast cancer cells	Manouchehri, Turner, & Kalafatis, 2018
14	Silibinin	*Silybum marianum*	DR5	Apoptosis via extrinsic and intrinsic pathways	A54, NCI−H460	Non-small cell lung cancer	Dilshara et al., 2017
15	Kaempferol	*Kaempferia rotunda*	DR5	Apoptosis vis extrinsic pathway through caspase 8	A2780/CP70	Cellosaurus cell line (human ovarian cell line)	Gao, Yin, Rankin, & Chen, 2018
16	Wogonin	*Scutellaria baicalensis.*	–	Attenuate TNFα-induced NF-κB activity	CEM	T lymphoblast cell line	Fas et al., 2006
17	Pinostrobin	*Boesenbergia pandurata*		Upregulation of extrinsic pathway proteins like TRAIL R1/DR4, TRAIL R2/DR5, TNF RI/TNFRSF1A, FADD, Fas/TNFRSF6 Upregulation of intrinsic pathway proteins like Bad, Bax, HTRA2/Omi, SMAC/Diablo, cytochrome C, Pro-Caspase-3, Cleaved Caspase-3	HeLa	cervical cancer cells	Jaudan, Sharma, Malek, & Dixit, 2018

18	Sulforaphane	*Brassica oleracea*	DR4 and DR5	Up-regulation of expressions of TRAIL-R1/DR4, TRAIL-R2/DR5, Bax and Bak Inhibition of activation of NF-κB P13K/AKT and MEK/ERK pathways Inhibition of the expression of Bcl-2, Bcl-X(L), and Mcl-1	PC-3	Prostate cancer bearing mice	Shankar, Ganapathy, & Srivastava, 2008
19	Garcinol	*Garcinia indica*	DR4 and DR5	Downregulation of cell survival proteins including survivin, bcl-2, XIAP and cFLIP	HCT116/HT29	Colorectal cancer cell line	Prasad, Ravindran, Sung, Pandey, & Aggarwal, 2010
				TRAIL-resistant phenotype converted to TRAIL-sensitive	A293	Human embryonic kidney carcinoma	
					PC3	Human prostate cancer cells	
					KBM-5	Human chronic leukemic cells	
					SEG-1	Human esophageal epithelial cells	
					U266	Human multiple myeloma	
					MDA-MB-231 and MCF-7	Human breast cancer cells	

(*Continued*)

Table 1 Various plant derived compounds effective in killing cancer cells.—cont'd

S. No	Compound	Source	Death receptor (DR) involved	Modus operandi	Cell line(s)	Model	Reference(s)
20	Hispidulin	*Inula viscosa*	–	Downregulation the expression of Mcl-1, Bcl-2, and Bcl-xL Activation of caspases 8 and caspase 3	SKOV3	human ovary cancer cell line	Yang et al., 2010
21	Luteolin	*Lonicera japonica*	–	Increase in the number of intracellular autophagosomes Increase in Beclin 1 expression	SMMC-7721	Hepatocellular carcinoma	Cao et al., 2017
22	Mucin peptides	*Echinococcus granulosus*	–	Increase of activated NK cells in the spleen of immunized mice	Panc02 and TA3/Ha	Pancreatic tumor and mammary adenocarcinoma cell line	Noya et al., 2013

4.2 Tumor-associated neutrophils (TANs)

Neutrophils are known for their ability to have inflammatory roles and inducing immune system that may apparently lead to tissue damage during infection. However, in the context of tumors, the role of TANs may be immunosuppressive. Neutrophils secrete numerous chemokines and myeloperoxidase (MPO) that plays important role in recruiting monocytes/macrophages at the site of inflammation. The TANs from early tumors have inflammatory roles and these produce higher level of TNF-α, NO, and H_2O_2 as well as possess antitumor roles. Whilst in advanced tumors, these activities are hampered and pro-tumorigenic phenotype is attained. CCL17 or CCL22 are produced by TANs from established tumors and immunosuppressive regulatory T cells (Tregs)are recruited that result in blunted antitumor immunity (Mishalian et al., 2014).

In early stages of tumor, neutrophils have been found almost exclusively at the tumor periphery; whilst in advance stage, neutrophils are scattered throughout the tumor. Very much alike the M1 and M2 dichotomy, TANs also exhibit the protumorigenic (N2) and antitumor (N1) phenotypes. Depletion in N2 phenotype of neutrophil has been shown to revert the increased tumor growth, angiogenesis, and metastasis in murine models of melanoma and fibrosarcoma. Neutrophil differentiation toward the N2 phenotype is largely driven by TGF-β cytokine and its blockade results in influx of hyper-segmented and tumor cytotoxic TANs those express higher levels of pro-inflammatory cytokines. Following the TGF-β treatment if such TANs are depleted, the antitumor response is blunted (Fridlender et al., 2009). In the absence of TGF-β, antitumor N1 phenotype is generated that produces higher levels of pro-inflammatory molecules including TNF-α, MIP-1α, H_2O_2, and NO. TAN1 can also activate dendritic cells through cell—cell contact as well as secretion of TNF-α. Apart that the CD4+ T cells are activated to support antitumoral memory.

Antitumor activity is demonstrated by recruitment of CD8+ cells; and production of T-cell attracting chemokines (e.g. CCL-3, CXCL9 and CXCL10) and pro-inflammatory cytokines (e.g. IL-12, TNF-α and GM-CSF) (Fridlender & Albelda, 2012). Neutrophils are also stimulated to produce oncostatin-M by tumor cells that ultimately increases the secretion of VEGF by tumors. In TANs, there is a substantial increase in the cytokines and chemokines suggestive of immunocytes recruitment and role in maintaining the balance between immunosuppression or activation.

4.2.1 Some unique features of TANs

The cross talk between tumor and immune cells is widely recognized. TANs are a distinct population of neutrophil that exhibit different characters than the naïve neutrophil and possess following some unique features.

i) ***Structural genes***: Actin binding and polymerization genes (e.g. *Actn-1/4*, *Raf-1*, *LCP-1* and *Talin-1*), those are essential for movement of neutrophils to reach to the destination, are down regulated in TANs after infiltration into the TME and TANs lose their ability to leave the TME (Fridlender et al., 2012).

ii) ***Anti-apoptosis***: Many anti-apoptotic molecules of NF-κB have been shown to be upregulated in TANs and possibility this contributes to extraordinary longevity of TANs in comparison to other neutrophil population.

iii) ***Cytokines and chemokines***: The mRNA for chemokines CCL-2, 3, 4, 8, 12 and 17 and the CXCL-1, 2, 9 and 16 are enhanced in TANs. This is similar to the classical neutrophils those are participants of wound healing. CCL-2 and CCL-7 recruited macrophages and CCL-17 recruited Tregs are known to support tumor growth. Increased protein expression of CCL-2, CCL-17 and IL-6 also has been reported. The top-5 up-regulated chemokines were CCL-7, CCL-8 and CCL-12, which enhanced by 80 folds in TANs (Fridlender et al., 2012).

iv) ***Angiogenesis***: Neutrophils have been demonstrated to be involved in the pro-tumorigenic process of angiogenesis and neovascularization by means of secreting chemokines and MMPs. Neutrophil secretes MMP-9 that apart its role in carcinogenesis possess the role in initiating angiogenesis. In fact, it has been demonstrated that MMP-9 is mandatory to the vascularization *in* vivo. This initiation may be due to promotion of the release of VEGF or counteracting antiangiogenic factors. The mRNA level of VEGF is higher in TANs in comparison to other neutrophils. Other angiogenesis contributing factor is CXCL1/KC which participate in signaling through the CXC chemokine receptor 2 (CXCR2) present over the endothelial cells is markedly upregulated in TANs and its inhibition suppress the inflammation driven as well as spontaneous tumorigenesis (Jamieson et al., 2012).

v) **Metastasis assisting proteins**: The TANs secrete higher quantities of collagenase-IV and heparanase that assisting in tumor invasion by degrading basement membrane (Fridlender & Albelda, 2012). Neutrophil elastase (NE) is also enhanced; which enters into tumor cells, and binds IRS-1 and degrades it to activate AKT. Higher levels of NE have been found inversely associated with prognosis and found to support invasion and metastasis of several cancers. Inhibition of NE has been demonstrated to hamper hepatic metastases.

4.3 Tumor associated monocytes

Classically monocytes are considered as progenitors of macrophages and dendritic cells. Monocytes are heterogeneous population of cells. Inflammatory monocytes (CD14+ CD16−) are precursors of macrophages and dendritic cells, whilst CD14+ + CD16+ are highly phagocytic. Non-classical monocytes (CD14−CD16+) are involved in scavenging vascular debris. In contrast to the role of macrophages in cancer cell invasion and intravasation, the role of monocytes has been comparatively less studied. Fewer studies are available, which shed light on the impact of monocytes on cancer progression before it differentiates into macrophages. Studies suggested that different monocyte population behave differently in cancer metastasis. On one hand, inflammatory monocytes have been shown to facilitate the cancer cell extravasation, undifferentiated monocytes present with cancer cells reduce tumor extravasation in a non-contact dependent manner (Boussommier-Calleja et al., 2019). Inflammatory monocytes have been demonstrated to recruit to the TME through CCL2/CCR2 chemokine axis and there it become TAMs and help in promoting tumor progression, metastasis, and chemoresistance. Targeting inflammatory monocytes with a CCR2 inhibitor decreases tumor burden in a murine model (Grossman et al., 2017).

4.4 Natural killer (NK) cells

NK cells as a component of the innate immune system, is cytotoxic effecter that kills the target in a non-specific manner, contributes in defense against cancer. The evidence of antitumor activity of NK cells came from the experiment in NK depleted mice; into those fibrosarcoma tumor was induced by methylcholanthrene and as a result the growth of tumor was markedly faster in absence of NK cells. The main mechanism to kill tumor cells is Granzyme B and perforin dependent pathways though the cell killing may be perforin and granzymes independent through death-receptor pathways (involving First apoptosis signal ligand (FasL) and TRAIL. However, at the same time, in few human cases, selective NK cell deficiency did not appeared to increase the cancer incidences. Also the role of NK cells in cancer prognostic is evident as there has been found a correlation between the NK cells poor function and tumor metastasis in case of head and neck, pharyngeal and other solid tumors (Chiossone, Dumas, Vienne, & Vivier,

2018). Additionally, NK cells secrete various chemokines and cytokines including IFN-γ, TNF-α, IL-6, GM-CSF and CCL5 that may contribute into antitumor activity.

4.5 Role of inflammatory mediators in cancer

Up-regulation of several inflammatory mediator molecules result in the cancer progression; which include growth factors, cytokines, chemokines, ROS and RNS. Few of them are enlisted below:

4.5.1 Interleukin-6 (IL-6)

IL6 is one of the major cytokine, which gets dysregulated in cancer microenvironment. Its overexpression has been reported amongst most tumors along with serving for all the essential functions required for tumor growth including regulation of various signaling pathways. Also, it protects cancer cells from cancer therapy mediated damage through pro-survival signaling, anti-apoptosis and repair processes. Cell cycle is tightly regulated by tumor suppressor genes like Rb (retinoblastoma associated) and TP53 proteins. The CpG islands of promoter regions of TP53 gene are found hypermethylated in case of tumor cells. Hypermethylation of these genes results in bypassing the essential cellular check points of the cell cycle proliferation and evasion of apoptosis. IL-6 is having dual effect on the process of methylation. On one hand, it increases the expression of DNA methyltransferase (Liu et al., 2015) and its translocation to nucleus resulting in hypermethylation of CpG islands of promoter region of the p53 gene, and loss of P53 function; whilst on the other hand, it hypomethylates the retrotransposon long interspersed nuclear element-1 (LINE-1) that increases tumorigenesis (Gasche, Hoffmann, Boland, & Goel, 2011). The LINE-1 hypomethylation is associated is associated with the stage, size, severity, higher histological grade and poor prognosis of tumors. It is also related to tumor metastasis. Under normal circumstances the Rb protein is responsible for inhibition of cell entry in S phase form G1. Upon phosphorylation, Rb is unable to bind to E2F and CDK is activated facilitating the entry of cell in S phase. In case of multiple myeloma, IL-6 has been reported to increase the Rb phosphorylation. There is a delicate balance between pro-apoptotic and anti-apoptotic factors; and increased IL-6 expression may disturb this balance toward the anti-apoptotic signaling. Trans-activation of various anti-apoptotic genes including *Bcl-2, Bcl-xL, Mcl-1,* etc. has been observed in different kinds of tumors (Kumari, Dwarakanath, Das, & Bhatt, 2016). Signal transducer and activator of transcription 3 (STAT3) phosphorylation is induced by

IL-6 and phosphorylated STAT3 binds to the one of its target gene, *Survivin*, which is a member of apoptosis inhibitor protein. Thereby, it is presenting additional way to anti-apoptosis of tumor cells as demonstrated in human breast cancer cells (Gritsko et al., 2006). Functions of IL-6 have been given in brief in Fig. 2.

4.5.2 Interleukin 10 (IL-10)

The IL-10 is a major cytokine produced by immune cells such as macrophages, T lymphocytes, mast cells, granulocytes, dendritic cells, NK cells and keratinocytes. This cytokine possesses both immunosuppressive and anti-angiogenic roles. It leads to tumor proliferation and metastasis through immunosuppression by means of TNF, IL-1 and IL-12. IL-10 is also helpful in enhancing the expression of IL-6 that leads to cells proliferation through the Bcl-2 upregulation. At the same time, it also prevents the access of antigen presenting cells to tumor antigens. Contrary to tumor promoting role, it may exhibit the antitumor activities also by down-regulating the VEGF, IL-1b, TNF-α, IL-6, and MMP-9 and inhibiting the translocation of NF-KB (Sheikhpour et al., 2018).

4.5.3 Chemokines

Chemokines are the small molecules secreted mainly by immune cells but the non-immune cells like vascular endothelial cells may also produce these in order to induce angiogenesis (Lacy, 2015). At site of inflammation, inflammatory cells are recruited by the chemokines CXCL1, CXCL2, CXCL3, CXCL4, CXCL5, CXCL6, CXCL7, and CXCL8. The chemokines and their receptors have been implicated in the process of tumor development and metastasis. The CXCR2 act as receptor for various chemokines. The chemokines having glutamic acid-leucine-arginine (or ELR for short) motif binds mainly to CXCR2 and possess angiogenic properties. CXCL1 or CXCL8 have been found to overexpress in case of melanomas and tend to enhance the growth as well as metastasis (Cheng et al., 2011; Singh, Singh, Sharma, Owen, & Singh, 2010), and inhibition of their receptor, i.e., CXCR2 diminish such effects.

The CXCR2 has been found to involved in migration, invasion and angiogenesis of most common lung, prostate, breast and colorectal cancers (Jaffer & Ma, 2016). CXCL13 is a chemo-attractant for B cells, and its receptor; CXCR5, is expressed by a specific subset of T cells (Moser, 2015). CXCL13 is expressed by stromal cells, lymph nodes, spleen, myofibroblasts, CXCL13-producing $CD4^+$ follicular helper T (Th) cells, bone marrow

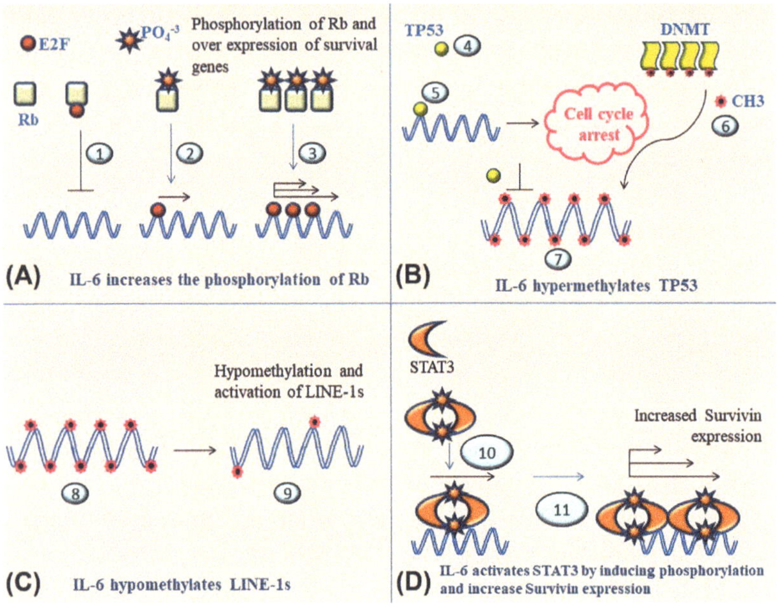

Fig. 2 Functions of Pro-inflammatory molecule, IL6, in tumor progression: (A) **IL-6 increases the phosphorylation of Rb:** (1) Unphosphorylated Retinoblastoma (Rb) protein binds to the transcription factor E2F, and therefore E2F is unable to bind to promoters of downstream genes associated with survival and proliferation and hence the transcription of these genes are halted (2) Phosphorylated Rb is unable to bind to E2F and transcription of genes associated with survival and proliferation occurs (3) IL-6 increases the phosphorylation of Rb and in turn cell cycle progression and survival genes are overexpressed leading to tumor growth. (B) **IL-6 hypermethylates TP53**: (4) TP53 is tumor suppressor (5) which is induced by DNA damage and oncogene activation; and leads to cell cycle arrest (6) A class of DNA methyltransferases (DNMT) is responsible for methylation of the CpG islands of TP53 gene and its inactivation. Several tumors are found associated with inactivated TP53 gene (7) IL-6 increases the DNMT and resulting in inactivation of TP53, and makes the gene inaccessible to transcription factor. (C) **IL-6 hypomethylates LINE-1s**: (8) Retrotransposons long interspersed nuclear element-1s (LINE-1s or L1s), which play an important role in the gene regulation; which is further being controlled by means of methylation (9) Hypomethylation of LINE-1s has been linked with various tumors. Under the influence of IL-6, LINE-1s are hypomethylated and this leads to tumorigenesis. (D) **IL-6 activates STAT3 by inducing phosphorylation and increase survivin expression**: STAT3 transcriptionally up-regulates several genes associated with cell survival, cell cycle progression, and homeostasis (10) STAT3 is activated thorough phosphorylation via several receptor and non-receptor cellular kinases and STAT3 activation induces the anti-apoptotic protein Survivin (11) IL-6 induce the phosphorylation of STAT3, which enhances expression of anti-apoptotic protein Survivin, that inhibits tumor cell apoptosis.

endothelial cells, osteoblasts and tumor cells (Tan et al., 2018). CXCL13-CXCR5 axis is reported to play a critical role in tumor growth, invasion, and ultimately metastasis of cancer; and high levels of CXCR5 and CXCL13 are found linked with poor prognosis (Qi et al., 2014). CXCL5 is able to induce endothelial cell proliferation, tube formation and migration by activating the AKT/NF-κB/FOXD1/VEGF-A pathway (Chen et al., 2019) and promotes tumor angiogenesis. However, its prognostic value is controversial since in the same type of tumor, contradictory results have been observed. Its overexpression has positive association with tumor stage, lymph node metastasis, and worse survival (Hu, Fan, Lv, Chen, & Shao, 2018).

CXCL10 and its receptor CXCR3, both expressed by cancer cells is exceptional in the sense that this chemokine suppresses the growth of cancer unlike other chemokines such as CCL2, CXCL12, CCL3/4/5, CXCL8; those are also produced by cancer cells, but promotes tumor (Karin & Razon, 2018). Higher level of CXCL10 reduces the tumor vasculature as well as tumor burden and enhances the T cell response in case of high-grade serous ovarian tumor microenvironment (Au et al., 2017). Also CXCL9 and CXCL10 could serve as independent predictors of an improved overall survival in high-grade serous ovarian cancer and $CXCL9^{high\ expression}$/ $CXCL10^{high\ expression}$ tumors exhibit a significantly better overall patient survival than tumors overexpressing only one of the two chemokines (Bronger et al., 2016).

4.5.4 Nuclear Factor-κB (NF-κB)

The NF-κB family is composed of five transcription factors, which include NF-κB1/p105, NF-κB2/p100, RelA/p65, RelB and c-Rel; these form homo or heterodimers in order to bind to the promoter region of the target gene. It plays an important role in the expression of several genes involved in both inflammation and tumorigenesis; hence, the molecule is key to both the inflammation as well as cancer. All the members of NF-κB family contains a Rel homology domain (RHD), comprising nuclear localization signal (NLS). Their homo or heterodimer bind to the sequence specific DNA and interact with the ankyrin repeat motifs present in the members of inhibitors of NF-κB family (IκB family).

The IκB family composes 7 members (IκB, IκBα, IκBβ, IκBγ, IκBε, IκBζ, IκBNS and Bcl-3). The IκBζ, IκBNS, and Bcl-3 are present in the nucleus; where these interact with the NF-κB family members in order to regulate the transcription. Remaining members of IκB family are present in cytoplasm; where these interact with NLS and thereby preventing the entry of NF-κB family members inside the nucleus. The NF-κB transcription factors are kept transcriptionally inactive by the members of IκB family (Inoue, Gohda, Akiyama, & Semba, 2007).

Pro-inflammatory chemokines including CCL20, CXCL13, and CXCL8, that are the ligands of CXCR2 in case of ovarian cancer, are induced by TNF-activated NF-κB signaling. Other inflammatory genes, like *IL1*, *IL6*, *IL8*, and *CCL2* are also found abundantly expressed in glioma-cell lines. NF-κB is activated to increase the expression of pro-inflammatory genes that leads to the acceleration of tumor development. The mechanism is governed through a positive feedback loop. IL1 is able to phosphorylate the MKK4 which is an essential step in the processing of NF-κB p100 into the active form p52.

Berbamine, a bisbenzylisoquinoline alkaloid, identified from the traditional Chinese medicinal plant, *Berberis amurensis*, has anti-inflammatory potential through inhibition of NF-κB and MAPK (Jia et al., 2017). Its anti-cancer potential also has been identified against lung cancer (Hou et al., 2014) and myeloma (Liang, Xu, Zhang, & Zhao, 2009).

4.5.5 Interleukin-8 (IL-8)

IL-8/CXCL8, is 99 amino acids long, and its expression is regulated by NF-κB. IL-8 binds to CXCR1 and CXCR2 receptors. Upon exposure to IL-1 or TNF-α, leukocytes and endothelial cells produce IL-8. Fibroblasts and malignant tumor cells also secrete IL-8 in response to hypoxic conditions or chemotherapy (Xie, 2001). Its expression is found significantly higher in various tumor types including brain, breast, cervical, colon, gastric, lung, melanoma, mesothelioma, ovarian, prostate, renal, and thyroid AML, CLL, Hodgkin's lymphoma; and its positive correlation with tumor size and stage has been established (Chen et al., 2003).

The cancer patients with higher IL-8 concentration, often exhibit poor survival rate (Alfaro et al., 2017). Serum IL-8 levels very linearly; it correlates with the tumor burden and metastatic changes in the melanoma and NSCLC patients (Sanmamed et al., 2017). IL-8 has shown to induce angiogenesis and simultaneously recruits the neutrophils at the tumor site. IL-8 can be targeted by miR (microRNA)-203 and miR-23a; and miR-203 is able to inhibit the IL-8 (Wei et al., 2013) and impedes tumor invasion and metastasis.

The epithelial-mesenchymal transition (EMT) is an important step of tumor progression and metastasis, where epithelial cells are trans-differentiate into aggressive mesenchymal cells. Tumor cells experiencing EMT secrete more IL8 and TAMs; and neutrophils are recruited to tumor site (Long et al., 2016).

4.5.6 *Interleukin-17 (IL-17)*

IL-17 is produced by Th17 cells, and six members of IL-17 family (IL-17A to IL-17F). Its over-abundance in tumor microenvironment clearly indicates its role in the early tumor formation. In a study conducted on 82 patients suffering with gastric cancer, IL-17 has been found to upregulate and it has a positive correlation with the tumor tissue depth, lymph-vascular invasion and lymph node involvement. Number of vascular endothelial cells and angiogenesis was also increased indicating an obvious relationship between tumor and IL-17 (Iida et al., 2011).

It encourages CCL-2 expression mediated entry of IL-17 secreting monocytes to enhance local inflammatory response (Mizutani et al., 2009). IL-17 driven activation of STAT3 and NF-κB pathway further leads to an expression of antiapoptotic genes including *Bcl-2*, *A1*, and *Mcl 1* and are known to function in a co-operate manner for development and progression of colon, gastric and liver cancers (Grivennikov & Karin, 2010).

4.5.7 *Interleukin-23 (IL-23)*

TLR receptor signaling in tissues induces the secretion of IL-23 from the immune cells (dendritic cells and macrophages). It acts as a player in autoimmune diseases as well as in tumorigenesis. It is known to promote tumor growth and tumor associated inflammatory response including infiltration of M2 macrophages, granulocytes and neutrophils along with immunosuppressive cytokines and vascular endothelial growth factor (Nie, Yu, Sang, & Gao, 2017). Also IL-23 mediated immune-response aggravates inflammation in gut and promotes the colon cancer. It expression has been found upregulated in both inflammatory bowel diseases and colon cancer (Neurath, 2019). A balance between cytokines IL-12 and IL-23 is responsible for shaping antitumor or pro-tumor immunity respectively. Anti-IL-23 treatment, therefore, could be an antitumor therapeutic and it could be used along with other immunotherapies (Yan, Smyth, & Teng, 2017).

4.6 Reactive oxygen and nitrogen species

Under the chronic inflammatory conditions, ROS/RNS are produced by the inflammatory and the epithelial cells. The oxidative DNA damage gives rise to 8-oxo-7,8-dihydro-2′-deoxyguanosine (8-oxodG); which is considered to be mutagenic, as during replication, it leads to misincorporation of adenine opposite to 8-oxodG, resulting in G:C to T:A transversions. The ROS/RNS mediated organ damage under inflammatory conditions leads to the development of cancer (Ohnishi et al., 2013). In fact, urinary 8-oxodG conveniently can be adapted as an inflammation-related cancer biomarker. Peroxynitrite (ONOO−), a RNS; and forms 8-nitroguanine in DNA that is chemically highly unstable and released from the DNA strand and leaves apurinic site (Ohnishi et al., 2013).

Inflammation mediated ROS/RNS damage also modifies the proteins and carbonylate them. Carbonylation is irreversible and irreparable protein damage due to oxidative stress. Damaged transferrin protein may liberate iron ions which may mediate Fenton reaction and generates ROS to contribute in carcinogenesis (Murata, 2018).

4.7 Inflammation and angiogenesis

Angiogenesis is a key process into which new blood vessels are formed from the pre-existing blood vessels. Rapidly growing tumor cells have a high demand of nutrition and O_2, which is fulfilled by increasing the number of new blood vessels. Hence, enhanced angiogenesis may indirectly support the tumor growth. Hypoxia acts as a common stimulant leading to inflammation as well as angiogenesis. Hypoxia inducible factor (HIF) induction is O_2 independent and initiated by STAT3 and NF-κB. HIF activates various genes including *IL-6*, *MMP9*, *cyclooxygenase 2* and pro-survival genes like *Bcl-2*. In all solid tumors, hypoxia and expression of HIF-1α as well as HIF-2α are the common factors. In tumor associated inflammation, mutual relationship between HIF and NF-κB is evident (D'Ignazio, Batie, & Rocha, 2017). miRNAs are single stranded short oligonucleotides of 22bp, those are capable in regulating gene expression at the level of transcription. miRNA interacts with mRNA due to complementarity and degrade it. Many of the miRNAs have been found associated with inflammation and angiogenesis. Of many example, one is miR-126, which is constitutively produced mainly in the endothelial cells and is responsible for maintaining vascular integrity. The up-regulation of miR-126 has been found in case of spinal cord injury rat model, where it increased angiogenesis by degrading the mRNAs of SPRED1 and PIK3R2; the inhibitors of angiogenesis. At the same time, miR-126 inhibits the inflammation by reducing VCAM1 expression, an adhesion molecule that mediate the adherence of leukocytes to the endothelial cells (Hu, Zeng, Huang, Wang, & Lu, 2015). M1 and M2 macrophages have opposite impact on process of angiogenesis. M1 are shown to inhibit the cell proliferation and angiogenesis, whilst M2 promotes it. TAMs are able to increase the angiogenesis via release of angiogenic stimulators including VEGF, TNF-α, basic FGF (bFGF), IL-8, or insulin-like growth factor 1 (IGF-1) (Szade, Grochot-Przeczek, Florczyk, Jozkowicz, & Dulak, 2015).

5. Utility of anti-inflammatory drugs against cancer

Numerous epidemiological studies have revealed the significant decrease in the malignancy and cancer incidence after long term usage of nonsteroidal anti-inflammatory drugs (NSAID) such as aspirin, celecoxib, diclofenac, diflunisal, ibuprofen (Motrin, Advil), indomethacin (Indocin), naproxen (Aleve, Anaprox, Naprelan, Naprosyn), oxaprozin (Daypro), piroxicam (Feldene), salsalate (Disalsate), sulindac and tolmetin. These are diverse in nature but commonly block the enzyme cyclooxygenase (COX) or prostaglandin endoperoxide H synthase (PGHS). Prostaglandins (PGs) are synthesized by COX thorough action on arachidonic acid.

On the basis of inhibitory action on COX, NSAID may be divided into two isoforms i.e., COX-1 and COX-2. Both isoforms produce prostaglandins, COX 1 is expressed ubiquitously in all cells and produce PGs mediating role in platelet function, gastrointestinal cytoprotection and other physiological functions; whereas the COX2 is produced in several cell types in response to various cytokines, growth factors or pro-inflammatory molecules and mediate both chronic and acute inflammation. Another classification of NSAID is based on its intrinsic ability to selectively inhibit COX1 or COX2.

The therapeutic implication like anti-inflammatory, antipyretic, and analgesic effects of NSAID is due to COX2 inhibition, whilst the side effects exhibited by NSAID are due to COX1 inhibition. COX2 overexpression is found linked with enhanced angiogenesis and carcinogenesis through inhibition of T cell, B cell and specifically NK cells proliferation. Improved cell motility and invasiveness in breast cancer has been observed with COX2 overexpression (Singh, Berry, Shoher, Ramakrishnan, & Lucci, 2005). In case of pancreatic adenocarcinomas, COX2 over-expressed and two NSAIDs (sulindac sulfide and NS398) inhibited cell proliferation in a dose dependent manner (Molina, Sitja-Arnau, Lemoine, Frazier, & Sinicrope, 1999).

A list of various patents (filed/granted) for the compounds possessing both anti-cancer and anti-inflammatory activities has been depicted in Table 2.

Table 2 A list of various patents for compounds having both anticancer and anti-inflammatory activities.

S. No.	Title of patent	Patent number	Modus operandi/ function	Inventers	Date of publication	Status	Reference
1	8-Anilinoimidazopyridines and their use as anti-cancer and/or anti-inflammatory agents	AU2008343062B2	Inhibit MEK kinase activity.	Robert Heald, Stephen Price, Pascal Pierre Alexandre Savy	2013-03-07	Granted	Heald, Price, Pierre, & Savy, 2013
2	Extracts of shark cartilage having anti-collagenolytic, anti-inflammatory, anti-angiogenic and anti-tumoral activities; process of making, methods of using and compositions thereof	US6025334A	The extract from shark cartilage is useful as anti-angiogenic, anti-tumor, anti-inflammatory and anti-collagenolytic compound	Eric Dupont, Paul Brazeau, Christina Juneau, Daniel H. Maes, Kenneth Marenus	2000-02-15	Granted	Dupont, Brazeau, Juneau, Maes, & Marenus, 2000
3	Compositions for treatment of cancer and inflammation with curcumin and at least one NSAID	WO2005077394A1	Cyclooxygenase-2(COX-2)" synthesizes prostaglandins and is involved in inflammation and carcinogenesis. The patent application comprise of use of curcumin and at least one non-steroidal Anti-inflammatory Drugs	Nadir Arber, Shahar Lev-Ari, Dov Lichtenberg	2005-02-10	Application	Arber, Lev-Ari, & Lichtenberg, 2005
4	Substituted imidazoles having anti-cancer and cytokine inhibitory activity	CA2234066C	The formula can inhibit cytokines including IL-1, IL-5, IL-A and TNF during rheumatoid arthritis, rheumatoid spondylitis, osteoarthritis, gouty arthritis and cancer	Harold G. Selnick, David A. Claremon, Nigel J. Liverton	2005-12-13	Grant	Selnick, Claremon, & Liverton, 2005

5	5-substituted quinazolinone derivatives as anti-cancer agents	EP2428513B1	The compound is able to manage or prevent undesired angiogenesis, macular degeneration an asbestos-related disorder and atherosclerosis and also manages lymphomas	Muller GW, Man H	2017-05-31	Granted	Muller & Man, 2017
6	Stapled peptide inhibitors of nemo as potential anti-inflammatory and anti-cancer drugs	EP3184541A1	A peptide inhibitor of NF-κB essential modulator (NEMO)inhibits the NF-κB signaling pathway	Fabrice Agou, Alix Boucharlaty, ves-Marie Coic, Françoise Baleux	2015-12-23	Application	Agou, Boucharlaty, Coic, & Baleux, 2015
7	Phosphonates as anti-cancer agents	US5369097A	The use of phosphonates in the treatment of inflammatory diseases including arthritis, inflammatory bowel diseases, colitis, and pulmonary inflammation	Salari H, Bittman R	1994-11-29	Granted	Salari & Bittman, 1994
8	Novel anti-cd38 antibodies for the treatment of cancer	CA2663209C	Humanized antibodies capable of killing CD38+ (a transmembrane glycoprotein, upregulated in several hemopoitic origin cancers) cells by apoptosis, antibody-dependent cell-mediated cytotoxicity (ADCC), and/or complement-dependent cytotoxicity (CDC).	Peter U. Park, Laura M. Bartle, Anna Skaletskaya, Viktor S. Golmakher, Daniel Tavares, Jutta Deckert, Vincent Mikol, Veronique Blanc	2018-02-13	Granted	Park et al., 2018

(Continued)

Table 2 A list of various patents for compounds having both anticancer and anti-inflammatory activities.—cont'd

S. No.	Title of patent	Patent number	Modus operandi/ function	Inventers	Date of publication	Status	Reference
9	Thieno pyrimidinone for the treatment of inflammatory diseases and cancer	JP5313909B2	The compound is selective inhibitor of PI3K [delta], and used to treat abnormal hematopoietic cells proliferation, and other conditions characterized by inflammation	Stephen Elle White, Edward A. Keshiki, Eugene Torset, Fukiing Luang, Francine Fellowes	2013-10-09	granted	White et al., 2013
10	Methods for the treatment and prevention of cancer using anti-CD40 antibodies	US6843989B1	Anti CD40 antibody that enhances binding of CD40 ligand to CD40	Clay (B) Siegall, Alan (F) Wahl, Joseph (A) Francisco, Henry Perry Fell, Jr.	2005-01-18	Granted	Siegall et al., 2005
11	Compositions and methods for the treatment of inflammatory diseases using topoisomerase inhibitors	US8883856B2	The composition is anti-inflammatory and anti angiogenic	John Jackson, Helen M. Burt, Stephen K. Dordunoo	2014-11-11	Granted	Jackson, Burt, & Dordunoo, 2014

6. Outlook

Inflammation and cancer are interlinked phenomena. Various steps and mediators of the inflammation and cancer are common. This chronic inflammatory microenvironment is associated with the release of various pro-inflammatory and oncogenic mediators such as nitric oxide (NO), cytokines (IL-1β, IL-2, IL-6, and TNF-α), growth factors, and chemokines. Interleukins such as IL-6, IL-8, IL-10, IL-17, IL-23 and chemokines like CXCL1, CXCL2, CXCL3, CXCL4, CXCL5, CXCL6, CXCL7, and CXCL8 along with ROS/RNS result in an elevated NF-κB pathway and cyclooxygenase-2 (COX-2) activity facilitating inflammation-mediated tumorigenesis. The tight association between cancer and inflammation is depicted by the fact that monoclonal antibodies directed against TNF-α, VEGF, and IL-6 reduces the tumor burden and inflammation, whilst IL-2 regress tumor growth. Tumor microenvironment encompasses various immune cells including dendritic cells, macrophage, monocytes and neutrophils. TAMs and TANs have dual role in facilitating the cancer. In both the TAMs and TANs a dichotomy is present. TAM-1 and TAN-1 have antitumor phenotype, whilst TAM-2 and TAN-2 have pro-tumor effects and depletion in TAM-2 and TAN-2 may be linked with enhanced tumor growth, invasion and metastasis. Inflammation mediated generation of ROS and RNS modifies DNA and protein and exert mutagenic effect leading to carcinogenesis. SAA recruits inflammatory cells and its increased level is associated with reduced disease free survival time. Hypoxia is also common in both the inflammation and cancer and various miRNA like miR-126 are common in both inflammation and angiogenesis, a key participant in solid tumor progression. DR4/5 receptors are generally involved in cancer cell death via binding to TRAIL ligands and various therapies are based on activating the DRs to kill tumor cells. Inflammation and cancer are coupled in such a way that various anti-inflammatory drugs are being used against cancer like aspirin, celecoxib, diclofenac, diflunisal, ibuprofen (Motrin, Advil), indomethacin (Indocin), naproxen (Aleve, Anaprox, Naprelan, Naprosyn), oxaprozin (Daypro), piroxicam (Feldene), salsalate (Disalsate), sulindac and tolmetin. Conclusively, it may be stated that inflammation and cancer are tightly interlined process and by curbing chronic inflammation, up to some extent cancer may be controlled.

Acknowledgments

Authors are thankful to the Prof. R.J. Rao, Hon'ble Vice-Chancellor, Barkatullah University for extending the all kind of support.

References

Abdelhamed, S., Yokoyama, S., Refaat, A., Ogura, K., Yagita, H., Awale, S., et al. (2014). Piperine enhances the efficacy of TRAIL-based therapy for triple-negative breast cancer cells. *Anticancer Research, 34*(4), 1899.

Agou, F., Boucharlaty, A., Coic, V. M., & Baleux, F. (2015). *Stapled peptide inhibitors of nemo as potential anti-inflammatory and anti-cancer drugs.* Patent EP3184541A1, 13 December, 2015.

Alfaro, C., Sanmamed, M. F., Rodríguez-Ruiz, M. E., Teijeira, Á., Oñate, C., González, Á., et al. (2017). Interleukin-8 in cancer pathogenesis, treatment and follow-up. *Cancer Treatment Reviews, 60,* 24–31. http://dx.doi.org/10.1016/j.ctrv.2017.08.004.

Arber, N., Lev-Ari, S., & Lichtenberg, D. (2005). *Compositions for treatment of cancer and inflammation with curcumin and at least one NSAID.* Patent WO2005077394A1, 10 February, 2005.

Au, K., Peterson, N., Truesdell, P., Reid-Schachter, G., Khalaj, K., Ren, R., et al. (2017). CXCL10 alters the tumour immune microenvironment and disease progression in a syngeneic murine model of high-grade serous ovarian cancer. *Gynecologic Oncology, 145*(3), 436–445. http://dx.doi.org/10.1016/j.ygyno.2017.03.007.

Balkwill, F., & Mantovani, A. (2001). Inflammation and cancer: Back to Virchow? *Lancet, 357*(9255), 539–545. http://dx.doi.org/10.1016/S0140-6736(00)04046-0.

Boussommier-Calleja, A., Atiyas, Y., Haase, K., Headley, M., Lewis, C., & Kamm, R. D. (2019). The effects of monocytes on tumor cell extravasation in a 3D vascularized microfluidic model. *Biomaterials, 198,* 180–193. http://dx.doi.org/10.1016/j.biomaterials.2018.03.005.

Bronger, H., Singer, J., Windmüller, C., Reuning, U., Zech, D., & Delbridge, C. (2016). CXCL9 and CXCL10 predict survival and are regulated by cyclooxygenase inhibition in advanced serous ovarian cancer. *British Journal of Cancer, 115*(5), 553–563. http://dx.doi.org/10.1038/bjc.2016.172.

Bruchard, M., Mignot, G., Derangère, V., Chalmin, F., Chevriaux, A., Végran, F., et al. (2013). Chemotherapy-triggered cathepsin B release in myeloid-derived suppressor cells activates the Nlrp3 inflammasome and promotes tumor growth. *Nature Medicine, 19*(1), 57–64. http://dx.doi.org/10.1038/nm.2999.

Cao, Z., Zhang, H., Cai, X., Fang, W., Chai, D., Wen, Y., et al. (2017). Luteolin promotes cell apoptosis by inducing autophagy in hepatocellular carcinoma. *Cellular Physiology and Biochemistry, 43*(5), 1803–1812. http://dx.doi.org/10.1159/000484066.

Carron, E. C., Homra, S., Rosenberg, J., Coffelt, S. B., Kittrell, F., Zhang, Y., et al. (2017). Macrophages promote the progression of premalignant mammary lesions to invasive cancer. *Oncotarget, 8*(31), 50731–50746. http://dx.doi.org/10.18632/oncotarget.14913.

Chakraborty, A., Gupta, N., Ghosh, K., & Roy, P. (2010). In vitro evaluation of the cytotoxic, anti-proliferative and anti-oxidant properties of pterostilbene isolated from Pterocarpus marsupium. *Toxicology in Vitro, 24*(4), 1215–1228. http://dx.doi.org/10.1016/j.tiv.2010.02.007.

Chen, Z., Feng, X., Herting, C. J., Garcia, V. A., Nie, K., Pong, W. W., et al. (2017). Cellular and molecular identity of tumor-associated macrophages in glioblastoma. *Cancer Research,* 77(9), 2266–2278.

Cheng, W. L., Wang, C. S., Huang, Y. H., Tsai, M. M., Liang, Y., & Lin, K. H. (2011). Overexpression of CXCL1 and its receptor CXCR2 promote tumor invasion in gastric cancer. *Annals of Oncology, 22*(10), 2267–2276. http://dx.doi.org/10.1093/annonc/mdq739.

Chen, D. S., & Mellman, I. (2013). Oncology meets immunology: The cancer-immunity cycle. *Immunity, 39*(1), 1–10. http://dx.doi.org/10.1016/j.immuni.2013.07.012.

Chen, M., Wang, X., Zha, D., Cai, F., Zhang, W., He, Y., et al. (2016). Apigenin potentiates TRAIL therapy of non-small cell lung cancer via upregulating DR4/DR5 expression in a p53-dependent manner. *Scientific Reports, 6*, 35468. http://dx.doi.org/10.1038/srep35468.

Chen, C., Xu, Z. Q., Zong, Y. P., Ou, B. C., Shen, X. H., Feng, H., et al. (2019). CXCL5 induces tumor angiogenesis via enhancing the expression of FOXD1 mediated by the AKT/NF-κB pathway in colorectal cancer. *Cell Death & Disease, 10*(3), 178. http://dx.doi.org/10.1038/s41419-019-1431-6.

Chen, J. J., Yao, P. L., Yuan, A., Hong, T. M., Shun, C. T., Kuo, M. L., et al. (2003). Up-regulation of tumor interleukin-8 expression by infiltrating macrophages: Its correlation with tumor angiogenesis and patient survival in non-small cell lung cancer. *Clinical Cancer Research, 9*, 729–737.

Chiossone, L., Dumas, P. Y., Vienne, M., & Vivier, E. (2018). Natural killer cells and other innate lymphoid cells in cancer. *Nature Reviews Immunology, 18*(11), 671–688. http://dx.doi.org/10.1038/s41577-018-0061-z.

Chistiakov, D. A., Bobryshev, Y. V., & Orekhov, A. N. (2015). Changes in transcriptome of macrophages in atherosclerosis. *Journal of Cellular and Molecular Medicine, 19*(6), 1163–1173. http://dx.doi.org/10.1111/jcmm.12591.

Coffelt, S. B., Chen, Y. Y., Muthana, M., Welford, A. F., Tal, A. O., Scholz, A., et al. (2011). Angiopoietin 2 stimulates TIE2-expressing monocytes to suppress T cell activation and to promote regulatory T cell expansion. *The Journal of Immunology, 186*(7), 4183–4190. http://dx.doi.org/10.4049/jimmunol.1002802.

Colley, D. G., Bustinduy, A. L., Secor, W. E., & King, C. H. (2014). Human schistosomiasis. *Lancet, 383*(9936), 2253–2264. http://dx.doi.org/10.1016/S0140-6736(13)61949-2.

Costa da Silva, M., Breckwoldt, M. O., Vinchi, F., Correia, M. P., Stojanovic, A., Thielmann, C. M., et al. (2017). Iron induces anti-tumor activity in tumor-associated macrophages. *Frontiers in Immunology, 8*, 1479. http://dx.doi.org/10.3389/fimmu.2017.01479.

Coussens, L. M., & Werb, Z. (2002). Inflammation and cancer. *Nature, 420*(6917), 860–867. http://dx.doi.org/10.1038/nature01322.

D'Ignazio, L., Batie, M., & Rocha, S. (2017). Hypoxia and inflammation in cancer, focus on HIF and NF-κB. *Biomedicines, 5*(2). http://dx.doi.org/10.3390/biomedicines5020021. pii: E21.

DeNardo, D. G., Brennan, D. J., Rexhepaj, E., Ruffell, B., Shiao, S. L., Madden, S. F., et al. (2011). Leukocyte complexity predicts breast cancer survival and functionally regulates response to chemotherapy. *Cancer Discovery, 1*(1), 54–67. http://dx.doi.org/10.1158/2159-8274.cd-10-0028.

Díaz, P., Valenzuela Valderrama, M., Bravo, J., & Quest, A. F. G. (2018). *Helicobacter pylori* and gastric cancer: Adaptive cellular mechanisms involved in disease progression. *Frontiers in Microbiology, 9*, 5. http://dx.doi.org/10.3389/fmicb.2018.00005.

Dijkgraaf, E. M., Heusinkveld, M., Tummers, B., Vogelpoel, L. T., Goedemans, R., Jha, V., et al. (2013). Chemotherapy alters monocyte differentiation to favor generation of cancer-supporting M2 macrophages in the tumor microenvironment. *Cancer Research, 73*(8), 2480–2492. http://dx.doi.org/10.1158/0008-5472.CAN-12-3542.

Dilshara, M. G., Jayasooriya, R. G. P. T., Molagoda, I. M. N., Jeong, J. W., Lee, S., Park, S. R., et al. (2017). Silibinin sensitizes TRAIL-mediated apoptosis by upregulating DR5 through ROS-induced endoplasmic reticulum stress-Ca2+-CaMKII-Sp1 pathway. *Oncotarget, 9*(12), 10324–10342. http://dx.doi.org/10.18632/oncotarget.23129.

Dupont, E., Brazeau, P., Juneau, C., Maes, D. H., & Marenus, K. (2000). *Extracts of shark cartilage having anti-collagenolytic, anti-inflammatory, anti-angiogenic and anti-tumoral activities; process of making, methods of using and compositions thereof.* Patent US6025334A, 15 February, 2000.

Faïs, T., Delmas, J., Barnich, N., Bonnet, R., & Dalmasso, G. (2018). Colibactin: More than a new bacterial toxin. *Toxins (Basel), 10*(4), E151. http://dx.doi.org/10.3390/toxins10040151.

Fas, S. C., Baumann, S., Zhu, J. Y., Giaisi, M., Treiber, M. K., Mahlknecht, U., et al. (2006). Wogonin sensitizes resistant malignant cells to TNF alpha- and TRAIL-induced apoptosis. *Blood, 108*(12), 3700–3706. http://dx.doi.org/10.1182/blood-2006-03-011973.

Feldmeyer, L., Hudgens, C. W., Ray-Lyons, G., Nagarajan, P., Aung, P. P., Curry, J. L., et al. (2016). Density, distribution, and composition of immune infiltrates correlate with survival in Merkel cell carcinoma. *Clinical Cancer Research, 22*(22), 5553–5563. http://dx.doi.org/10.1158/1078-0432.CCR-16-0392.

Foell, D., Wittkowski, H., Vogl, T., & Roth, J. (2007). S100 proteins expressed in phagocytes: A novel group of damage-associated molecular pattern molecules. *Journal of Leukocyte Biology, 81*, 28–37. http://dx.doi.org/10.1189/jlb.0306170.

Fridlender, Z. G., & Albelda, S. M. (2012). Tumor-associated neutrophils: Friend or foe? *Carcinogenesis, 33*(5), 949–955. http://dx.doi.org/10.1093/carcin/bgs123.

Fridlender, Z. G., Sun, J., Kim, S., Kapoor, V., Cheng, G., Ling, L., et al. (2009). Polarization of tumor-associated neutrophil phenotype by TGF-beta: "N1" versus "N2" TAN. *Cancer Cell, 16*(3), 183–194. http://dx.doi.org/10.1016/j.ccr.2009.06.017.

Fridlender, Z. G., Sun, J., Mishalian, I., Singhal, S., Cheng, G., Kapoor, V., et al. (2012). Transcriptomic analysis comparing tumor-associated neutrophils with granulocytic myeloid-derived suppressor cells and normal neutrophils. *PLoS One, 7*(2), e31524. http://dx.doi.org/10.1371/journal.pone.0031524.

Galon, J., Costes, A., Sanchez-Cabo, F., Kirilovsky, A., Mlecnik, B., Lagorce-Pagès, C., et al. (2006). Type, density, and location of immune cells within human colorectal tumors predict clinical outcome. *Science, 313*(5795), 1960–1964. http://dx.doi.org/10.1126/science.1129139.

Gao, Y., Yin, J., Rankin, G. O., & Chen, Y. C. (2018). Kaempferol induces G2/M cell cycle arrest via checkpoint kinase 2 and promotes apoptosis via death receptors in human ovarian carcinoma A2780/CP70 cells. *Molecules, 23*(5), E1095. http://dx.doi.org/10.3390/molecules23051095.

Gasche, J. A., Hoffmann, J., Boland, C. R., & Goel, A. (2011). Interleukin-6 promotes tumorigenesis by altering DNA methylation in oral cancer cells. *International Journal of Cancer, 129*(5), 1053–1063. http://dx.doi.org/10.1158/1078-0432.CCR-04-1752.

Geissmann, F., Manz, M. G., Jung, S., Sieweke, M. H., Merad, M., & Ley, K. (2010). Development of monocytes, macrophages, and dendritic cells. *Science, 327*, 656–661. http://dx.doi.org/10.1126/science.1178331.

Gocheva, V., Wang, H. W., Gadea, B. B., Shree, T., Hunter, K. E., Garfall, A. L., et al. (2010). IL-4 induces cathepsin protease activity in tumor-associated macrophages to promote cancer growth and invasion. *Genes & Development, 24*(3), 241–255. http://dx.doi.org/10.1101/gad.1874010.

Goncalves, P. H., Ziegelbauer, J., Uldrick, T. S., & Yarchoan, R. (2017). Kaposi sarcoma herpesvirus-associated cancers and related diseases. *Current Opinion in HIV and AIDS, 12*(1), 47–56. http://dx.doi.org/10.1097/COH.0000000000000330.

Gordon, S., & Martinez, F. O. (2010). Alternative activation of macrophages: Mechanism and functions. *Immunity, 32*(5), 593–604. http://dx.doi.org/10.1016/j.immuni.2010.05.007.

Gritsko, T., Williams, A., Turkson, J., Kaneko, S., Bowman, T., Huang, M., et al. (2006). Persistent activation of stat3 signaling induces survivin gene expression and confers resistance to apoptosis in human breast cancer cells. *Clinical Cancer Research, 12*(1), 11–19. http://dx.doi.org/10.1158/1078-0432.CCR-04-1752.

Grivennikov, S., & Karin, M. (2010). Dangerous liaisons: STAT3 and NF-kappaB collaboration and crosstalk in cancer. *Cytokine & Growth Factor Reviews, 21*(1), 11–19. http://dx.doi.org/10.1016/j.cytogfr.2009.11.005.

Grossman, J. G., Timothy, M., Nywening, T. M., Belt, B., Ahlers, M., Hawkins, W. G., et al. (2017). Targeting inflammatory monocytes in human metastatic colorectal cancer. *Journal of Clinical Oncology, 35*(4), 605. http://dx.doi.org/10.1200/JCO.2017.35.4_suppl.605.

Hasegawa, H., Yamad, Y., Komiyama, K., Hayashi, M., Ishibashi, M., Yoshida, T., et al. (2006). Dihydroflavonol BB-1, an extract of natural plant *Blumea balsamifera*, abrogates TRAIL resistance in leukemia cells. *Blood, 107*(2), 679–688. http://dx.doi.org/10.1182/blood-2005-05-1982.

Heald, R., Price, S., Pierre, P., & Savy, A. (2013). *8-Anilinoimidazopyridines and their use as anti-cancer and/or anti-inflammatory agents*. Patent AU2008343062B2, 07 March, 2013.

Hou, Z. B., Lu, K. J., Wu, X. L., Chen, C., Huang, X. E., & Yin, H. T. (2014). *In vitro* and *in vivo* antitumor evaluation of berbamine for lung cancer treatment. *Asian Pacific Journal of Cancer Preview, 15*, 1767–1769. http://dx.doi.org/10.7314/apjcp.2014.15.4.1767.

Hudson, J. D., Shoaibi, M. A., Maestro, R., Carnero, A., Hannon, G. J., & Beach, D. H. (1999). A proinflammatory cytokine inhibits p53 tumor suppressor activity. *The Journal of Experimental Medicine, 190*, 1375–1382. http://dx.doi.org/10.1084/jem.190.10.1375.

Hu, B., Fan, H., Lv, X., Chen, S., & Shao, Z. (2018). Prognostic significance of CXCL5 expression in cancer patients: A meta-analysis. *Cancer Cell International, 18*, 68. http://dx.doi.org/10.1186/s12935-018-0562-7.

Hung, C. M., Liu, L. C., Ho, C. T., Lin, Y. C., & Way, T. D. (2017). Pterostilbene enhances TRAIL-induced apoptosis through the induction of death receptors and downregulation of cell survival proteins in TRAIL-resistance triple negative breast cancer cells. *Journal of Agricultural and Food Chemistry, 65*(51), 11179–11191. http://dx.doi.org/10.1021/acs.jafc.7b02358.

Hu, J., Zeng, L., Huang, J., Wang, G., & Lu, H. (2015). miR-126 promotes angiogenesis and attenuates inflammation after contusion spinal cord injury in rats. *Brain Research, 1608*, 191–202. http://dx.doi.org/10.1016/j.brainres.2015.02.036.

Iida, T., Iwahashi, M., Katsuda, M., Ishida, K., Nakamori, M., Nakamura, M., et al. (2011). Tumor-infiltrating CD4+ Th17 cells produce IL-17 in tumor microenvironment and promote tumor progression in human gastric cancer. *Oncology Reports, 25*(5), 1271–1277. http://dx.doi.org/10.3892/or.2011.1201.

Inoue, J., Gohda, J., Akiyama, T., & Semba, K. (2007). NF-kappaB activation in development and progression of cancer. *Cancer Science, 98*(3), 268–274. http://dx.doi.org/10.1111/j.1349-7006.2007.00389.x.

Jackson, J., Burt, H. M., & Dordunoo, S. K. (2014). *Compositions and methods for the treatment of inflammatory diseases using topoisomerase inhibitors*. Patent US8883856B2, 11 November, 2014.

Jaffer, T., & Ma, D. (2016). The emerging role of chemokine receptor CXCR2 in cancer Progression. *Translational Cancer Research, 5*(Suppl. 4), 616–628.

Jamieson, T., Clarke, M., Steele, C. W., Samuel, M. S., Neumann, J., Jung, A., et al. (2012). Inhibition of CXCR2 profoundly suppresses inflammation-driven and spontaneous tumorigenesis. *The Journal of Clinical Investigation, 122*(9), 3127–3144. http://dx.doi.org/10.1172/JCI61067.

Jaudan, A., Sharma, S., Malek, S. N. A., & Dixit, A. (2018). Induction of apoptosis by pinostrobin in human cervical cancer cells: Possible mechanism of action. *PLoS One, 13*(2), e0191523. http://dx.doi.org/10.1371/journal.pone.0191523.

Jia, X. J., Li, X., Wang, F., Liu, H. Q., Zhang, D. J., & Chen, Y. (2017). Berbamine exerts anti-inflammatory effects via inhibition of NF-κB and MAPK signaling pathways.

Cellular Physiology and Biochemistry, 41(6), 2307–2318. http://dx.doi.org/10.1159/000475650.

Jung, E. M., Lim, J. H., Lee, T. J., Park, J. W., Choi, K. S., & Kwon, T. K. (2005). Curcumin sensitizes tumor necrosis factor-related apoptosis-inducing ligand (TRAIL)-induced apoptosis through reactive oxygen species-mediated upregulation of death receptor 5 (DR5). *Carcinogenesis, 26*(11), 1905–1913. http://dx.doi.org/10.1093/carcin/bgi167.

Karin, N., & Razon, H. (2018). Chemokines beyond chemo-attraction: CXCL10 and its significant role in cancer and autoimmunity. *Cytokine, 109*, 24–28. http://dx.doi.org/10.1016/j.cyto.2018.02.012.

Karthaus, N., Torensma, R., & Tel, J. (2012). Deciphering the message broadcast by tumor-infiltrating dendritic cells. *American Journal of Pathology, 181*, 733–742. http://dx.doi.org/10.1016/j.ajpath.2012.05.012.

Katz, C., Zaltsman-Amir, Y., Mostizky, Y., Kollet, N., Gross, A., & Friedler, A. (2012). Molecular basis of the interaction between proapoptotic truncated BID (tBID) protein and mitochondrial carrier homologue 2 (MTCH2) protein: Key players in mitochondrial death pathway. *The Journal of Biological Chemistry, 287*(18), 15016–15023. http://dx.doi.org/10.1074/jbc.M111.328377.

Ke, R., Vishnoi, K., Viswakarma, N., Santha, S., Das, S., Rana, A., et al. (2018). Involvement of AMP-activated protein kinase and Death Receptor 5 in TRAIL-Berberine-induced apoptosis of cancer cells. *Scientific Reports, 8*, 5521. http://dx.doi.org/10.1038/s41598-018-23780-x.

Krausgruber, T., Blazek, K., Smallie, T., Alzabin, S., Lockstone, H., Sahgal, N., et al. (2011). IRF5 promotes inflammatory macrophage polarization and TH1-TH17 responses. *Nature Immunology, 12*(3), 231–238. http://dx.doi.org/10.1038/ni.1990.

Kumari, N., Dwarakanath, B. S., Das, A., & Bhatt, A. N. (2016). Role of interleukin-6 in cancer progression and therapeutic resistance. *Tumor Biology, 37*(9), 11553–11572. http://dx.doi.org/10.1007/s13277-016-5098-7.

Lacy, P. (2015). Secretion of cytokines and chemokines by innate immune cells. *Frontiers in Immunology, 6*, 190. http://dx.doi.org/10.3389/fimmu.2015.00190.

Ledesma-Soto, Y., Callejas, B. E., Terrazas, C. A., Reyes, J. L., Espinoza-Jiménez, A., González, M. I., et al. (2015). Extra-intestinal helminth infection limits pathology and proinflammatory cytokine expression during DSS-induced ulcerative colitis: A role for alternatively activated macrophages and prostaglandins. *BioMed Research International, 2015*, 563425. http://dx.doi.org/10.1155/2015/563425.

Lee, T. J., Um, H. J., Min do, S., Park, J. W., Choi, K. S., & Kwon, T. K. (2009). Withaferin A sensitizes TRAIL-induced apoptosis through reactive oxygen species-mediated up-regulation of death receptor 5 and down-regulation of c-FLIP. *Free Radical Biology and Medicine, 46*(12), 1639–1649. http://dx.doi.org/10.1016/j.freeradbiomed.2009.03.022.

Liang, Y., Xu, R. Z., Zhang, L., & Zhao, X. Y. (2009). Berbamine, a novel nuclear factor kappaB inhibitor, inhibits growth and induces apoptosis in human myeloma cells. *Acta Pharmacologica Sinica, 30*, 1659–1665. http://dx.doi.org/10.1038/aps.2009.167.

Liguori, M., Buracchi, C., Pasqualini, F., Bergomas, F., Pesce, S., Sironi, M., et al. (2016). Functional TRAIL receptors in monocytes and tumor-associated macrophages: A possible targeting pathway in the tumor microenvironment. *Oncotarget*, 7(27), 41662–41676. http://dx.doi.org/10.18632/oncotarget.9340.

Lim, S. C., Jeon, H. J., Kee, K. H., Lee, M. J., Hong, R., & Han, S. I. (2017). Andrographolide induces apoptotic and non-apoptotic death and enhances tumor necrosis factor-related apoptosis-inducing ligand-mediated apoptosis in gastric cancer cells. *Oncology Letters, 13*(5), 3837–3844. http://dx.doi.org/10.3892/ol.2017.5923.

Lin, Y., Roberts, T. J., Spence, P. M., & Brutkiewicz, R. R. (2005). Reduction in CD1d expression on dendritic cells and macrophages by an acute virus infection. *Journal of Leukocyte Biology*, 77(2), 151–158. http://dx.doi.org/10.1189/jlb.0704399.

Liu, C. C., Lin, J. H., Hsu, T. W., Su, K., Li, A. F., Hsu, H. S., et al. (2015). IL-6 enriched lung cancer stem-like cell population by inhibition of cell cycle regulators via DNMT1 upregulation. *International Journal of Cancer, 136*(3), 547–559. http://dx.doi.org/10.1002/ijc.29033.

Long, X., Ye, Y., Zhang, L., Liu, P., Yu, W., Wei, F., et al. (2016). IL-8, a novel messenger to cross link inflammation and tumor EMT via autocrine and paracrine pathways (Review). *International Journal of Oncology, 48*(1), 5–12. http://dx.doi.org/10.3892/ijo.2015.3234.

Lu, H., Ouyang, W., & Huang, C. (2006). Inflammation, a key event in cancer development. *Molecular Cancer Research, 4*(4), 221–233.

Malietzis, G., Lee, G. H., Jenkins, J. T., Bernardo, D., Moorghen, M., Knight, S. C., et al. (2015). Prognostic value of the tumour-infiltrating dendritic cells in colorectal cancer: A systematic review. *Cell Communication and Adhesion, 22*(1), 9–14. http://dx.doi.org/10.3109/15419061.2015.1036859.

Manouchehri, J. M., Turner, K. A., & Kalafatis, M. (2018). TRAIL-induced apoptosis in TRAIL-resistant breast carcinoma through quercetin cotreatment. *Breast Cancer (Auckl), 12*. http://dx.doi.org/10.1177/1178223417749855, 1178223417749855.

Mantovani, A.1, Biswas, S. K., Galdiero, M. R., Sica, A., & Locati, M. (2013). Macrophage plasticity and polarization in tissue repair and remodelling. *The Journal of Pathology, 229*, 176–185. http://dx.doi.org/10.1002/path.4133.

Masrour-Roudsari, J., & Ebrahimpour, S. (2017). Causal role of infectious agents in cancer: An overview. *Caspian Journal of Internal Medicine, 8*(3), 153–158. http://dx.doi.org/10.22088/cjim.8.3.153.

Matsuoka, M. (2005). Human T-cell leukemia virus type I (HTLV-I) infection and the onset of adult T-cell leukemia (ATL). *Retrovirology, 2*, 27. http://dx.doi.org/10.1186/1742-4690-2-27.

Medina, D., Kittrell, F. S., Shepard, A., Stephens, L. C., Jiang, C., Lu, J., et al. (2002). Biological and genetic properties of the p53 null preneoplastic mammary epithelium. *Federation of American Societies for Experimental Biology Journal, 16*(8), 881–883. http://dx.doi.org/10.1096/fj.01-0885fje.

Mishalian, I., Bayuh, R., Eruslanov, E., Michaeli, J., Levy, L., Zolotarov, L., et al. (2014). Neutrophils recruit regulatory T-cells into tumors via secretion of CCL17–a new mechanism of impaired antitumor immunity. *International Journal of Cancer, 135*(5), 1178–1186.

Mitchem, J. B., Brennan, D. J., Knolhoff, B. L., Belt, B. A., Zhu, Y., Sanford, D. E., et al. (2013). Targeting tumor-infiltrating macrophages decreases tumor-initiating cells, relieves immunosuppression, and improves chemotherapeutic responses. *Cancer Research, 73*(3), 1128–1141. http://dx.doi.org/10.1158/0008-5472.CAN-12-2731.

Mizutani, K., Sud, S., McGregor, N. A., Martinovski, G., Rice, B. T., Craig, M. J., et al. (2009). The chemokine CCL2 increases prostate tumor growth and bone metastasis through macrophage and osteoclast recruitment. *Neoplasia, 11*(11), 1235–1242. http://dx.doi.org/10.1593/neo.09988.

Molina, M. A., Sitja-Arnau, M., Lemoine, M. G., Frazier, M. L., & Sinicrope, F. A. (1999). Increased cyclooxygenase-2 expression in human pancreatic carcinomas and cell lines: Growth inhibition by nonsteroidal anti-inflammatory drugs. *Cancer Research, 59*(17), 4356–4362.

Moser, B. (2015). CXCR5, the defining marker for follicular B helper T (TFH) cells. *Frontiers in Immunology, 6*, 296. http://dx.doi.org/10.3389/fimmu.2015.00296.

Muller, G. W., & Man, H. (2017). *5-substituted quinazolinone derivatives as anti-cancer agents*. Patent EP2428513B1, 31 May, 2017.

Murata, M. (2018). Inflammation and cancer. *Environmental Health and Preventive Medicine, 23*, 50. http://dx.doi.org/10.1186/s12199-018-0740-1.

Murray, P. J., Allen, J. E., Biswas, S. K., Fisher, E. A., Gilroy, D. W., Goerdt, S., et al. (2014). Macrophage activation and polarization: Nomenclature and experimental guidelines. *Immunity, 41*(1), 14–20. http://dx.doi.org/10.1016/j.immuni.2014.06.008.

Neurath, M. F. (2019). IL-23 in inflammatory bowel diseases and colon cancer. *Cytokine and Growth Factor Review, 45*, 1–8. http://dx.doi.org/10.1016/j.cytogfr.2018.12.002.

Nie, W., Yu, T., Sang, Y., & Gao, X. (2017). Tumor-promoting effect of IL-23 in mammary cancer mediated by infiltration of M2 macrophages and neutrophils in tumor microenvironment. *Biochemical and Biophysical Research Communications, 482*(4), 1400–1406. http://dx.doi.org/10.1016/j.bbrc.2016.12.048.

Nirmal, A. J., Regan, T., Shih, B. B., Hume, D. A., Sims, A. H., & Freeman, T. C. (2018). Immune cell gene signatures for profiling the microenvironment of solid tumors. *Cancer Immunology Research, 6*(11), 1388–1400. http://dx.doi.org/10.1158/2326-6066.CIR-18-0342.

Noya, V., Bay, S., Festari, M. F., García, E. P., Rodriguez, E., Chiale, C., et al. (2013). Mucin-like peptides from *Echinococcus granulosus* induce antitumor activity. *International Journal of Oncology, 43*(3), 775–784. http://dx.doi.org/10.3892/ijo.2013.2000.

Ohnishi, S., Ma, N., Thanan, R., Pinlaor, S., Hammam, O., Murata, M., et al. (2013). DNA damage in inflammation-related carcinogenesis and cancer stem cells. *Oxidative Medicine and Cellular Longevity, 2013*, 387014. http://dx.doi.org/10.1155/2013/387014.

Ong, S. M., Tan, Y. C., Beretta, O., Jiang, D., Yeap, W. H., Tai, J. J., et al. (2012). Macrophages in human colorectal cancer are pro-inflammatory and prime T cells towards an anti-tumour type-1 inflammatory response. *European Journal of Immunology, 42*(1), 89–100. http://dx.doi.org/10.1002/eji.201141825.

Park, P. U., Bartle, L. M., Skaletskaya, A., Golmakher, V. S., Tavares, D., Deckert, J., et al. (2018). *Novel anti-cd38 antibodies for the treatment of cancer.* Patent CA2663209C, 13 February, 2018.

Paulus, P., Stanley, E. R., Schäfer, R., Abraham, D., & Aharinejad, S. (2006). Colony-stimulating factor-1 antibody reverses chemoresistance in human MCF-7 breast cancer xenografts. *Cancer Research, 66*, 4349–4356. http://dx.doi.org/10.1158/0008-5472.CAN-05-3523.

Pierce, B. L., Ballard-Barbash, R., Bernstein, L., Baumgartner, R. N., Neuhouser, M. L., Wener, M. H., et al. (2009). Elevated biomarkers of inflammation are associated with reduced survival among breast cancer patients. *Journal of Clinical Oncology, 27*(21), 3437–3444. http://dx.doi.org/10.1200/JCO.2008.18.9068.

Poiroux, G., Barre, A., Simplicien, M., Pelofy, S., Segui, B., Van Damme, E. J. M., et al. (2019). Morniga-g, a T/Tn-specific lectin, induces leukemic cell death via caspase and DR5 receptor-dependent pathways. *International Journal of Molecular Sciences, 20*(1), E230. http://dx.doi.org/10.3390/ijms20010230.

Prasad, S., Kim, J. H., Gupta, S. C., & Aggarwal, B. B. (2014). Targeting death receptors for TRAIL by agents designed by Mother Nature. *Trends in Pharmacological Sciences, 35*(10), 520–536. http://dx.doi.org/10.1016/j.tips.2014.07.004.

Prasad, S., Ravindran, J., Sung, B., Pandey, M. K., & Aggarwal, B. B. (2010). Garcinol potentiates TRAIL-induced apoptosis through modulation of death receptors and antiapoptotic proteins. *Molecular Cancer Therapy, 9*(4), 856–868. http://dx.doi.org/10.1158/1535-7163.MCT-09-1113.

Qian, B., Deng, Y., Im, J. H., Muschel, R. J., Zou, Y., Li, J., et al. (2009). A distinct macrophage population mediates metastatic breast cancer cell extravasation, establishment and growth. *PLoS One, 4*(8). http://dx.doi.org/10.1371/journal.pone.0006562. e6562.

Qian, B. Z., Li, J., Zhang, H., Kitamura, T., Zhang, J., Campion, L. R., et al. (2011). CCL2 recruits inflammatory monocytes to facilitate breast-tumour metastasis. *Nature, 475*(7355), 222–225. http://dx.doi.org/10.1038/nature10138.

Qi, X. W., Xia, S. H., Yin, Y., Jin, L. F., Pu, Y., Hua, D., et al. (2014). Expression features of CXCR5 and its ligand, CXCL13 associated with poor prognosis of advanced colorectal cancer. *European Review for Medical and Pharmacological Sciences, 18*(13), 1916–1924.

Quail, D. F., & Joyce, J. A. (2013). Microenvironmental regulation of tumor progression and metastasis. *Nature Medicine, 19*(11), 1423–1437. http://dx.doi.org/10.1038/nm.3394.

Ramirez Garcia, A., Arteta, B., Abad Diaz-de-Cerio, A., Pellon, A., Antoran, A., Marquez, J., et al. (2013). *Candida albicans* increases tumor cell adhesion to endothelial cells *in vitro*: Intraspecific differences and importance of the mannose receptor. *PLoS One, 8*(1), e53584. http://dx.doi.org/10.1371/journal.pone.0053584.

Read, S. A., & Douglas, M. W. (2014). Virus induced inflammation and cancer development. *Cancer Letters, 345*(2), 174–181. http://dx.doi.org/10.1016/j.canlet.2013.07.030.

Refaat, A., Abd-Rabou, A., & Reda, A. (2014). TRAIL combinations: The new 'trail' for cancer therapy (Review). *Oncology Letters,* 7(5), 1327–1332. http://dx.doi.org/10.3892/ol.2014.1922.

Reichert, T. E., Scheuer, C., Day, R., Wagner, W., & Whiteside, T. L. (2001). The number of intratumoral dendritic cells and zeta-chain expression in T cells as prognostic and survival biomarkers in patients with oral carcinoma. *Cancer, 91*(11), 2136–2147. http://dx.doi.org/10.1002/1097-0142(20010601)91:11<2136::AID-CNCR1242>3.0.CO;2-Q.

Salari, H., & Bittman, R. (1994). *Phosphonates as anti-cancer agents.* Patent US5369097A, 29 November, 1994.

Salvagno, C., Ciampricotti, M., Tuit, S., Hau, C. S., van Weverwijk, A., Coffelt, S. B., et al. (2019). Therapeutic targeting of macrophages enhances chemotherapy efficacy by unleashing type I interferon response. *Nature Cell Biology, 21*(4), 511–521. http://dx.doi.org/10.1038/s41556-019-0298-1.

Sandel, M. H., Dadabayev, A. R., Menon, A. G., Morreau, H., & Melief, C. J. M. (2005). Prognostic value of tumor-infiltrating dendritic cells in colorectal cancer: Role of maturation status and intratumoral localization. *Clinical Cancer Research, 11,* 2576–2582. http://dx.doi.org/10.1158/1078-0432.CCR-04-1448.

Sanmamed, M. F., Perez-Gracia, J. L., Schalper, K. A., Fusco, J. P., Gonzalez, A., Rodriguez Ruiz, M. E., et al. (2017). Changes in serum interleukin-8 (IL-8) levels reflect and predict response to anti-PD-1 treatment in melanoma and non-small cell lung cancer patients. *Annals of Oncology, 208,* 1988–1995. http://dx.doi.org/10.1093/annonc/mdx190.

Scholte, L. L. S., Pascoal-Xavier, M. A., & Nahum, L. A. (2018). Helminths and cancers from the evolutionary perspective. *Frontiers of Medicine, 5,* 90. http://dx.doi.org/10.3389/fmed.2018.00090.

Schwertfeger, K. L., Xian, W., Kaplan, A. M., Burnett, S. H., Cohen, D. A., & Rosen, J. M. (2006). A critical role for the inflammatory response in a mouse model of preneoplastic progression. *Cancer Research, 66*(11), 5676–5685. http://dx.doi.org/10.1158/0008-5472.CAN-05-3781.

Selnick, H. G., Claremon, D. A., & Liverton, N. J. (2005). *Substituted imidazoles having anti-cancer and cytokine inhibitory activity.* Patent CA2234066C, 13 December, 2005.

Shankar, S., Ganapathy, S., & Srivastava, R. K. (2008). Sulforaphane enhances the therapeutic potential of TRAIL in prostate cancer orthotopic model through regulation of apoptosis, metastasis, and angiogenesis. *Clinical Cancer Research, 14*(21), 6855–6866. http://dx.doi.org/10.1158/1078-0432.CCR-08-0903.

Sheikhpour, E., Noorbakhsh, P., Foroughi, E., Farahnak, S., Nasiri, R., & Neamatzadeh, H. (2018). A survey on the role of interleukin-10 in breast cancer: A narrative. *Reports of Biochemistry and Molecular Biology,* 7(1), 30–37.

Shurin, M. R., & Lotze, M. T. (2009). *Dendritic cells in cancer: Emergence of the discipline* (pp. 11–30). Springer.

Siegall, C. B., Wahl, A. F., Francisco, J. A., & Fell, H. P., Jr. (2005). *Methods for the treatment and prevention of cancer using anti-CD40 antibodies*. Patent US6843989B1, 18 January, 2005.

Singh, B., Berry, J. A., Shoher, A., Ramakrishnan, V., & Lucci, A. (2005). COX-2 overexpression increases motility and invasion of breast cancer cells. *International Journal of Oncology, 26*(5), 1393–1399.

Singh, S., Singh, A. P., Sharma, B., Owen, L. B., & Singh, R. K. (2010). CXCL8 and its cognate receptors in melanoma progression and metastasis. *Future Oncology, 6*(1), 111. http://dx.doi.org/10.2217/fon.09.128.

Sproston, N. R., & Ashworth, J. J. (2018). Role of C-reactive protein at sites of inflammation and infection. *Frontiers in Immunology, 9*, 754. http://dx.doi.org/10.3389/fimmu.2018.00754.

Stark, J. R., Judson, G., Alderete, J. F., Mundodi, V., Kucknoor, A. S., Giovannucci, E. L., et al. (2009). Prospective study of *Trichomonas vaginalis* infection and prostate cancer incidence and mortality: Physicians' health study. *Journal of the National Cancer Institute, 101*(20), 1406–1411. http://dx.doi.org/10.1093/jnci/djp306.

Sung, B., Park, B., Yadav, V. R., & Aggarwal, B. B. (2010). Celastrol, a triterpene, enhances TRAIL-induced apoptosis through the down-regulation of cell survival proteins and up-regulation of death receptors. *The Journal of Biological Chemistry, 285*(15), 11498–11507. http://dx.doi.org/10.1074/jbc.M109.090209.

Szade, A., Grochot-Przeczek, A., Florczyk, U., Jozkowicz, A., & Dulak, J. (2015). Cellular and molecular mechanisms of inflammation-induced angiogenesis. *IUBMB Life, 67*(3), 145–159. http://dx.doi.org/10.1002/iub.1358.

Szliszka, E., Sokół-Łętowska, A., Kucharska, A. Z., Jaworska, D., et al. (2013). Ethanolic extract of polish propolis: Chemical composition and TRAIL-R2 death receptor targeting apoptotic activity against prostate cancer cells. *Evidence-based Complementary and Alternative Medicine, 2013*, 757628. http://dx.doi.org/10.1155/2013/757628.

Taniguchi, H., Yoshida, T., Horinaka, M., Yasuda, T., Goda, A. E., Konishi, M., et al. (2008). Baicalein overcomes tumor necrosis factor-related apoptosis-inducing ligand resistance via two different cell-specific pathways in cancer cells but not in normal cells. *Cancer Research, 68*(21), 8918–8927. http://dx.doi.org/10.1158/0008-5472.CAN-08-1120.

Tan, P., Shi, M., Lai, L., Tang, Z., Xie, N., Xu, H., et al. (2018). Regulative role of the CXCL13-CXCR5 axis in the tumor microenvironment. *Precision Clinical Medicine, 1*(1), 49–56.

Thomas, F., Lafferty, K. D., Brodeur, J., Elguero, E., Gauthier-Clerc, M., & Missé, D. (2012). Incidence of adult brain cancers is higher in countries where the protozoan parasite Toxoplasma gondii is common. *Biology Letters, 8*(1), 101–103. http://dx.doi.org/10.1098/rsbl.2011.0588.

Trinh, N., Dang, N., Tran, D., & Pham, P. (2016). *Taraxacum officinale* dandelion extract efficiently inhibited the breast cancer stem cell proliferation. *Biomedical Research and Therapy, 3*(07), 733–741.

Truxova, I., Kasikova, L., Hensler, M., Skapa, P., Laco, J., Pecen, L., et al. (2018). Mature dendritic cells correlate with favorable immune infiltrate and improved prognosis in ovarian carcinoma patients. *Journal for Immunotherapy of Cancer, 6*(1), 139. http://dx.doi.org/10.1186/s40425-018-0446-3.

Vidal-Vanaclocha, F., Mendoza, L., Telleria, N., Salado, C., Valcárcel, M., Gallot, N., et al. (2006). Clinical and experimental approaches to the pathophysiology of interleukin-18 in cancer progression. *Cancer Metastasis Reviews, 25*, 417–434. http://dx.doi.org/10.1007/s10555-006-9013-3.

Vranic, S., Cyprian, F. S., Akhtar, S., & Al Moustafa, A. E. (2018). The role of epstein-barr virus in cervical cancer: A brief update. *Frontiers in Oncology, 8*, 113. http://dx.doi.org/10.3389/fonc.2018.00113.

Wei, T., Xu, N., Meisgen, F., Ståhle, M., Sonkoly, E., & Pivarcsi, A. (2013). Interleukin-8 is regulated by miR-203 at the posttranscriptional level in primary human keratinocytes. *European Journal of Dermatology*. http://dx.doi.org/10.1684/ejd.2013.1997.

Wellings, S. R., & Jensen, H. M. (1973). On the origin and progression of ductal carcinoma in the human breast. *Journal of the National Cancer Institute, 50*(5), 1111–1118. http://dx.doi.org/10.1093/jnci/50.5.1111.

White, S. E., Keshiki, E. A., Torset, E., Luang, F., & Fellowes, F. (2013). *Thieno pyrimidinone for the treatment of inflammatory diseases and cancer*. Patent JP5313909B2, 09 October, 2013.

Whiteside, T. L. (2007). The local tumor microenvironment. In *General principles of tumor immunotherapy: Basic and clinical applications of tumor immunology* (pp. 145–167). Springer. http://dx.doi.org/10.1007/978-1-4020-6087-8.

Xie, K. (2001). Interleukin-8 and human cancer biology. *Cytokine & Growth Factor Reviews, 12*, 375–391.

Yang, J. M., Hung, C. M., Fu, C. N., Lee, J. C., Huang, C. H., Yang, M. H., et al. (2010). Hispidulin sensitizes human ovarian cancer cells to TRAIL-induced apoptosis by AMPK activation leading to Mcl-1 block in translation. *Journal of Agriculture and Food Chemistry, 58*(18), 10020–10026. http://dx.doi.org/10.1021/jf102304g.

Yan, J., Smyth, M. J., & Teng, M. W. L. (2017). Interleukin (IL)-12 and IL-23 and their conflicting roles in cancer. *Cold Spring Harbor Perspectives in Biology, 10*(7), a028530.

Yap, E. H., Ho, T. H., Chan, Y. C., Thong, T. W., Ng, G. C., Ho, L. C., et al. (1995). Serum antibodies to *Trichomonas vaginalis* in invasive cervical cancer patients. *Genitourinary Medicine, 6*, 402–404.

Zanganeh, S., Hutter, G., Spitler, R., Lenkov, O., Mahmoudi, M., Shaw, A., et al. (2016). Iron oxide nanoparticles inhibit tumour growth by inducing pro-inflammatory macrophage polarization in tumour tissues. *Nature Nanotechnology, 11*(11), 986–994. http://dx.doi.org/10.1038/nnano.2016.168.

Zhang, X., Li, Q., Hu, P., Cheng, H., & Huang, G. (2002). Two case reports of pituitary adenoma associated with Toxoplasma gondii infection. *Journal of Clinical Pathology, 55*(12), 965–966.

CHAPTER SEVEN

Microglial NLRP3 inflammasome activation in multiple sclerosis

Melis Olcum[a], Bora Tastan[a,b], Cagla Kiser[a,b], Sermin Genc[a,b,c] and Kursad Genc[c,*]

[a]Izmir Biomedicine and Genome Center, Dokuz Eylul University Health Campus Balcova, Izmir, Turkey
[b]Izmir International Biomedicine and Genome Institute (iBG-Izmir), Dokuz Eylul University Health Campus, Balcova, Izmir, Turkey
[c]Department of Neuroscience, Institute of Health and Science, Dokuz Eylul University Health Campus, Balcova, Izmir, Turkey
*Corresponding author: E-mails: kkursadgenc@hotmail.com, kemal.genc@deu.edu.tr

Contents

Advances in Protein Chemistry and Structural Biology, Volume 119
ISSN 1876-1623
https://doi.org/10.1016/bs.apcsb.2019.08.007

Abstract

Multiple sclerosis (MS) is a chronic, autoimmune and neuroinflammatory disease of the central nervous system (CNS) mediated by autoreactive T cells directed against myelin antigens. Although the crucial role of adaptive immunity is well established in MS, the contribution of innate immunity has only recently been appreciated. Microglia are the main innate immune cells of the CNS. Similar to other myeloid cells, microglia recognize both exogenous and host-derived endogenous danger signals through pattern recognition receptors (PRRs) localized on their cell surface such as Toll Like receptor 4, or in the cytosol such as NLRP3. The second one is the sensor protein of the multi-molecular NLRP3 inflammasome complex in activated microglia that promotes the maturation and secretion of proinflammatory cytokines, interleukin-1β and interleukin-18. Overactivation of microglia and aberrant activation of the NLRP3 inflammasome have been implicated in the pathogenesis of MS. Indeed, experimental data, together with post-mortem and clinical studies have revealed an increased expression of NLRP3 inflammasome complex elements in microglia and other immune cells. In this review, we focus on microglial NLRP3 inflammasome activation in MS. First, we overview the basic knowledge about MS, microglia and the NLRP3 inflammasome. Then, we summarize studies about microglial NLRP3 inflammasome activation in MS and its animal models. We also highlight experimental therapeutic approaches that target different steps of NLRP inflammasome activation. Finally, we discuss future research avenues and new methods in this rapidly evolving area.

List of Abbreviations

AD	Alzheimer's Disease
AIM	Absent in Melanoma
ALS	Amyotrophic Lateral Sclerosis
ASC	Apoptosis-associated Speck-like Protein
ATP	Adenosine Triphosphate
BBB	Blood Brain Barrier

BDNF	Brain Derived Neurotrophic Factor
CARD	Caspase Recruitment Domain
CNS	Central Nervous System
CSF	Cerebrospinal Fluid
DAMP	Damage-related Molecular Patterns
DC	Dendritic Cell
DMD	Disease Modifying Drug
DMF	Dimethyl Fumarate
EAE	Experimental Autoimmune Encephalomyelitis
EBV	Epstein Barr Virus
GM-CSF	Granulocyte-macrophage Colony Stimulating Factor
GSDMD	Gasdermin D
HLA	Human Leukocyte Antigen
IFN	Interferon
IGF	Insulin-like Growth Factor
IL	Interleukin
JNK	c-Jun N-terminal Kinase
LPS	Lipopolysaccharide
LRR	Leucine Rich Repeats
MBP	Myelin Basic Protein
MHC	Major Histocompatibility Complex
MMP	Matrix Metalloproteinase
MOG	Myelin Oligodendrocyte Glycoprotein
MRI	Magnetic Resonance Imaging
MS	Multiple Sclerosis
NF-KB	Nuclear Factor kappa-light-chain-enhancer of Activated B Cells
NIREG	Neuro-immune-regulator
NK	Natural Killer
NLRP3	Nucleotide-binding Domain and Leucine-rich Repeat Containing Protein 3
NOD	Nucleotide-binding Domain and Oligomerization Domain
OPC	Oligodendrocyte Precursor Cell
PAMP	Pathogen-associated Molecular Patterns
PBMC	Peripheral Blood Mononuclear Cell
PD	Parkinson's Disease
PLP	Proteolipid Protein
PNS	Peripheral Nervous System
PPMS	Primary Progressive Multiple Sclerosis
PRR	Pattern Recognition Receptors
PYD	Pyrin Domain
ROS	Reactive Oxygen Species
RRMS	Relapsing-remitting Multiple Sclerosis
SNP	Single Nucleotide Polymorphism
SPMS	Secondary Progressive Multiple Sclerosis
TBI	Traumatic Brain Injury
Th	T helper
TLR	Toll Like Receptor
Treg	T regulator

1. Multiple sclerosis

Multiple sclerosis (MS) is a chronic autoimmune disease of the central nervous system (CNS) characterized by demyelination and diffuse neurodegeneration that is observed both in the brain and spinal cord (Filippi et al., 2018). Autoreactive $CD4^+$ T cells have a central role in disease pathogenesis and they respond to myelin specific antigens, such as myelin basic protein (MBP), myelin oligodendrocyte glycoprotein (MOG) and proteolipid protein (PLP). Approximately 2.5 million people worldwide are affected by this disorder (Browne et al., 2014). MS is more common in young women and has a huge impact on quality of life and economic burden on society. Inflammatory attacks on myelinated axons may occur anywhere within the CNS, including the optic nerves, brainstem, periventricular white matter and cervical spinal cord.

Although the etiology of MS remains unclear, several genetic, environmental, and epigenetic factors are involved in disease pathogenesis (Olsson, Barcellos, & Alfredsson, 2017). Smoking, vitamin D deficiency, obesity, and infectious agents such as Epstein-Barr virus (EBV) are known environmental risk factors in the development of MS. Human leukocyte antigen (HLA) DRB1 *1501 has been associated with MS in many populations since the 1970s (Thompson, Baranzini, Geurts, Hemmer, & Ciccarelli, 2018). Recent genome-wide association studies in MS have identified several single nucleotide polymorphisms (SNPs) in both adaptive and innate immunity system genes (Parnell & Booth, 2017). Further functional studies are required to understand how these SNPs contribute to disease pathogenesis.

The clinical course of MS is classically categorized into four subtypes: Clinically isolated syndrome, relapsing-remitting multiple sclerosis (RRMS), secondary progressive multiple sclerosis (SPMS) and primary progressive multiple sclerosis (PPMS) (Filippi et al., 2018). About 85% of MS patients are initially diagnosed with RRMS that is characterized by recurrent attacks following total or partial recovery. Approximately 90% of untreated patients with RRMS evolve into SPMS within 20–25 years. 15% of patients can present PPMS which is characterized by the progressive worsening of symptoms from the onset of disease with no relapses (Klineova & Lublin, 2018).

The diagnosis of MS is based on clinical findings supported by laboratory evidences by neuroimaging and cerebrospinal fluid (CSF) analysis. Magnetic resonance imaging (MRI) evidence of demyelination is present of T2 hyperintense white matter lesions in the CNS. Spatial and temporal dissemination of MRI lesions is accepted as an indicator of disease progression. Gadolinium enhancement in T1-weighted MRI images is considered the hallmark of active plaques that represent the presence of inflammatory cells that penetrate the impaired blood-brain barrier (BBB) (Filippi et al., 2019). Presence of oligoclonal bands in CSF and brain imaging findings are included in the newly revised McDonald diagnostic criteria (2017) (Thompson, Banwell, et al., 2018).

A pathological hallmark of MS is focal demyelinating plaques which are located in both the white and gray matter of the brain, spinal cord, and optic nerves (Lassmann, 2018). Active demyelinating plaques are accompanied by densely populated phagocytic microglia and macrophages. Although the number of microglial cells in the center of plaques is reduced in chronic inactive lesions, a limited number of microglia are still present in periplaques area (Filippi et al., 2018). Additionally, chronic active plaques are sharply demarcated lesions and contain demyelination, partial axonal preservation, and reactive gliosis. Apart from these focal lesions, diffuse changes including perivascular inflammation, diffuse microglial activation, axonal injury, and astrogliosis in normal appearing white and gray matter are observed in patients with progressive MS (Lassmann, 2018). Cortical atrophy is a pathological hallmark of the progressive phase of disease that leads to cognitive dysfunction.

The underlying pathogenesis of the MS attack is demyelination caused by peripheral and central immune activation. Oligodendrocytes are the main glial cells that produce myelin in the CNS and exert metabolic support to neurons (Patel & Balabanov, 2012; Philips & Rothstein, 2017). Demyelination and tissue injury are partly mediated by the toxic products secreted by innate immune cells (Correale, Marrodan, & Ysrraelit, 2019; Patel & Balabanov, 2012) (Fig. 1). Besides, metabolic defects such as mitochondrial deficit, energy failure, reactive oxygen species (ROSs), excess of glutamate, ionic imbalance, and abnormality in iron metabolism contribute to oligodendrocyte apoptosis, subsequent neuronal damage and impaired remyelination (Adiele & Adiele, 2019; Correale et al., 2019). Reduced mitochondrial density in MS lesions and mitochondrial dysfunction are attributed as the main causes of neurodegeneration (Campbell & Mahad, 2018). Accumulation of excessive ROS is another cause of oligodendrocyte injury in MS (Ohl, Tenbrock, & Kipp, 2016). Impairment in the iron metabolism has a significant role in the pathogenesis of MS. Iron is mainly stored in microglia and it is essential trophic factor for myelin synthesis and

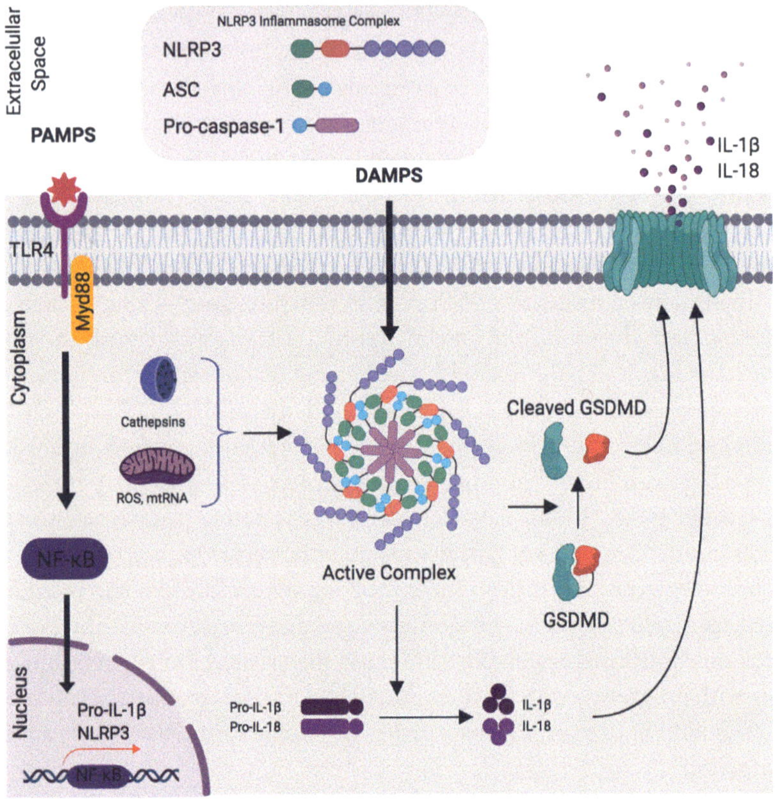

Fig. 1 Basic Mechanism of NLRP3 Inflammasome Activation.* DAMPs and/or PAMPs upregulates expression of NLRP3, pro-IL-1β and pro-IL-18 driven by nuclear translocation of NF-kB. Various stimuli such as ATP, K efflux, ROS and mtDNA activates formation of NLRP3 inflammasome complex. NLRP3 oligomerization in turn recruits ASC and pro-caspase-1 and causes caspase-1 autoactivation. Active caspase-1 cleaves pro-IL-1β and pro-IL-18 and induces pyroptosis through cleavege of Gasdermin D which promotes secretion of and IL-1β and IL-18. Simplified for clarity. See the text for details. *Created with BioRender.

oligodendrogenesis (Filippi et al., 2019). The reduced repair capacity of oligodendrocytes and irreversible axonal damage due to the lack of trophic factor support are other important factors that contribute to the pathogenesis of disease progression (Adiele & Adiele, 2019; Correale et al., 2019) (Fig. 1).

At the present time, there is no cure for MS. Interferon beta (IFN-β) was the first effective drug to be FDA approved for the treatment of RRMS in 1993 (Tintore, Vidal-Jordana, & Sastre-Garriga, 2019). Then, several disease-modifying drugs (DMDs) were introduced for MS treatment, including glatiramer acetate, teriflunomide, fingolimod, dimethyl fumarate, natalizumab, alemtuzumab, rituximab, andocrelizumab and cladribine. All of these mentioned drugs target the immunologic etiology of the disease. They diminish the frequency and severity of acute attacks and improve patient's quality of life by reducing their disabilities. Due to their serious adverse effects, long-term usage of DMDs have been limited (Filippi et al., 2018). In addition, these drugs do not prevent the chronic progressive disability. Clinical trials that attenuate the progression of disease by inducing neurodegeneration with different stem cells are still ongoing (Genc, Bozan, Genc, & Genc, 2019). Therefore, there is still a need to find effective and safe treatments for MS.

2. Animal models

Even though MS has been known since the 18th century, access to biologic samples to study MS pathophysiology has been restricted to post-mortem tissues of MS patients (Praet, Guglielmetti, Berneman, Van Der Linden, & Ponsaerts, 2014). Animal models allow researchers to use different aspects to elucidate the possible mechanisms that underlie MS pathology including demyelination, inflammation and neurodegeneration. These models include experimental autoimmune encephalomyelitis (EAE), toxin-induced demyelination and virus-induced models (Praet et al., 2014). These models mimic certain aspects of the disease instead of its entire model due to the complex nature of MS (Kipp, Nyamoya, Hochstrasser, & Amor, 2017).

In EAE model, animals are immunized with myelin derived peptides including MOG, MBP and PLP (Tuusa, Raasakka, Ruskamo, & Kursula, 2017). These peptides are administrated with a bacterial adjuvant such as complete Freund's adjuvant or incomplete Freund's Adjuvant (Billiau & Matthys, 2001). For EAE induction, C57BL/6 and SJL/J mice strains and Lewis rats are frequently used to mimic the clinical and immunopathological aspects of human MS (Constantinescu, Farooqi, O'brien, & Gran, 2011). The EAE model is one of the most studied animal model as it has allowed researcher to develop treatments for MS when compared to other MS-mimicking models (Lassmann & Bradl, 2017). Ascending hind limb-tail paralysis and progressive loss of body weight are observed two weeks after immunization (Klaren, Motl, Woods, & Miller, 2014).

In the toxin-induced demyelinating models, administration of toxins such as cuprizone, lysophosphatidyl, lysolecithin and ethidium bromide initiate demyelination and mimic MS in rodents (Lassmann & Bradl, 2017; Praet et al., 2014). In virus-induced MS models, usage of viral agents such as single-stranded RNA picornaviruses, Theiler's murine encephalomyelitis virus initiate demyelination and clinically mimic MS in animals (Gerhauser, Hansmann, Ciurkiewicz, Loscher, & Beineke, 2019).

3. Immunopathogenesis

3.1 Adaptive immunity

Both innate and adaptive immune systems are involved in the immunopathogenesis of MS. Exacerbation of disease is a result of the interaction between the peripheral immune cells including T cells, B cells, dendritic cells (DCs) and the immune cells of brain, especially microglia. There are two main hypotheses for initiation of disease: the outside-in and the inside-out (Gharagozloo et al., 2017) (Fig. 2). The outside-in hypothesis is the classical and most widely accepted one where peripheral immune cells are first activated out-side of the brain, then cross to the CNS via the damaged BBB and ultimately lead to immune mediated tissue injury (Thompson, Baranzini et al., 2018). T cells activation occurs in the presence of molecular mimicry between foreign peptides and self-peptides presented by DCs (Tai, Wang, Korner, Zhang, & Wei, 2018). In the inside-out hypothesis, disease starts within the CNS, results in oligodendroglial and axonal injury without the involvement of peripheral inflammatory cells and continues with an autoimmune peripheral reaction (Gharagozloo et al., 2017). Oligodendroglial and axonal injury can be caused by developmental abnormalities, mitochondrial dysfunction, ROS, infectious agents (viruses or bacteria) and environmental toxins (Filippi et al., 2019). Post-translationally modified myelin proteins formed after oligodendrocyte injury can enter peripheral circulation via the glymphatic system, and then activate the peripheral immune cells.

The role of adaptive immune responses in MS pathogenesis has been studied extensively. Basically, aberrantly activated myelin proteins-specific $CD4^+$ T helper (Th) cells and $CD8^+$ T cells to pass into the brain parenchyma and cause perivascular lesions (Gharagozloo et al., 2017). When $CD4^+$ Th cells are activated by antigen-presenting cells (APCs), they differentiate into various subtypes, such as Th1, Th2, Th17 and alter the immune response by secreting different cytokines (Baecher-Allan, Kaskow, & Weiner, 2018) (Fig. 2). While Th1 cells contribute to the clearance of

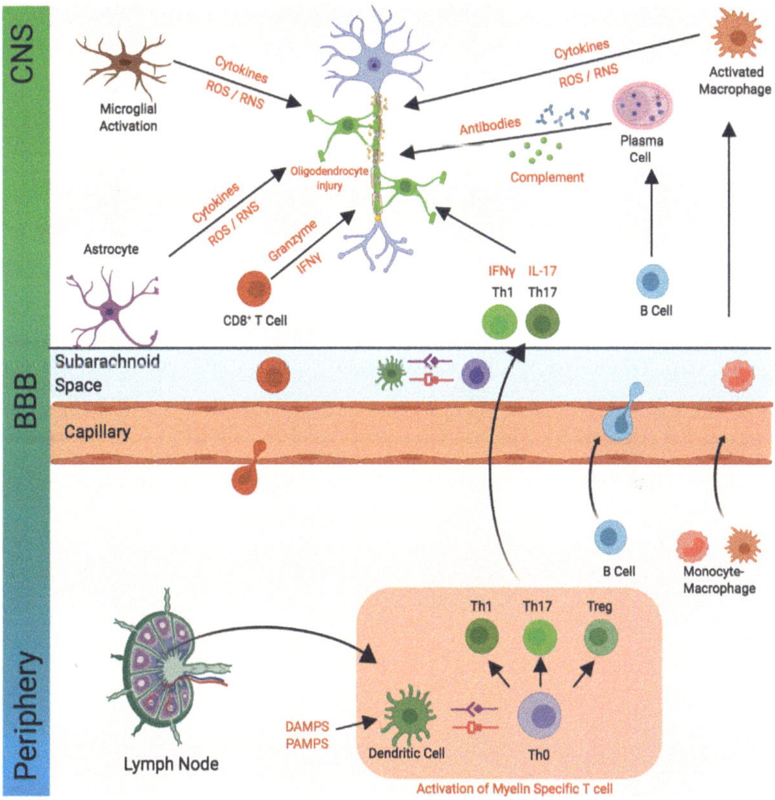

Fig. 2 Immunopathogenesis of Multiple Sclerosis.* Innate and adaptive immune responses lead demyelination and oligodendrocyte injury. *Created with BioRender. (*DAMPs*, Damage-associated molecular patterns; *PAMPs*, Pathogen-associated molecular pattern molecules; *Th*, T-helper cell; *IFN*, interferon; *IL*, interleukin; *TNF*, tumor necrosis factor; *NO*, nitric oxide). Simplified for clarity. See the text for details.

extracellular pathogens by releasing the proinflammatory cytokine, interferonγ (IFNγ), Th2 cells have an opposing effect on the response of Th1 cells. Naive CD4$^+$ T cells differentiate into interleukin-17 (IL-17) producing Th17 cells in the presence of interleukin-23 (IL-23). Both Th1 and Th17 cells are critically involved in the pathogenesis of MS, especially in the initial stages of lesion formation. CD8$^+$ cytotoxic T cells are the most common type of lymphocytes in MS lesions. IFN γ, perforin and granzyme secretion from these cells are responsible for the axonal and oligodendrocyte death.

CD4$^+$ regulatory T (Treg) cells repress cell proliferation by secreting interleukin-10 (IL-10) (Baecher-Allan et al., 2018). Several defects in suppressive effect of Treg cells have been linked to MS pathogenesis (Astier, Meiffren, Freeman, & Hafler, 2006; Danikowski, Jayaraman, & Prabhakar, 2017). Lack of inhibitory function of $FoxP3^+$ specific subtypes of Tregs has been associated with clinical exacerbation of MS.

$\gamma\delta$ (gamma—delta) T cells constitute about 2% of the total blood lymphocytes (Baecher-Allan et al., 2018). They do not require antigen presentation via major histocompatibility complex (MHC) molecules for activation and secrete several cytokines, including IFN-γ, interleukin-4 (IL-4), and IL-17 after activation by non-peptide bacterial products. $\gamma\delta$ T cells secrete IL-17 that enhance the generation of Th17 cells (Malik, Want, & Awasthi, 2016). The number of these cells has particularly been increased in around both active and chronic demyelinating lesions (Monteiro et al., 2018).

Recent anti-CD20 antibody treatment has revealed the importance of B cells in the immunopathogenesis of MS (Li, Patterson, & Bar-Or, 2018). Increased granulocyte-macrophage colony-stimulating factor (GM-CSF) and decreased IL-10 production have been detected in B cells of MS patients (Li, Rezk, et al., 2015). $CD80^+$ B cells were increased in PBMCs of MS patients, while IFN-β therapy was able to reduce this number (Genc, Dona, & Reder, 1997). B cells and plasma cells found in the brain parenchyma, meninges, and CSF of MS patients can produce anti-myelin antibodies that can be detected by the presence of oligoclonal bands (Michel et al., 2015).

Alteration in mature B cell count and activity exhibit a correlation between disease activity and treatment response (Arneth, 2019; Michel et al., 2015). Antibody-independent functions of B cells are to attract and activate T cells and myeloid cells for recruitment into the CNS and thus enhance cellular immune responses. Functional immunoglobins secreted from B cells and plasma cells contribute to myelin destruction through activating the classical complement system (Hemmer, Kerschensteiner, & Korn, 2015; Liu et al., 2017). Recent studies have confirmed that complement system is activated in MS (Plantone, Inglese, Salvetti, & Koudriavtseva, 2018).

3.2 Innate immunity

Innate immunity is a rapid responding system that is the first step of host defense mechanism (Heneka, Kummer, & Latz, 2014). Innate immunity response is not specific to the antigen. Innate immunity includes physical and chemical barriers and biological components. Biological components of innate immunity include several cell types and soluble inflammatory mediators. Innate immune cells are neutrophils, monocytes, macrophages, dendritic cells, natural killer (NK) cells, innate lymphoid cells, mast cells and NK T cells in the PNS; and microglia, CNS-resident non-parenchymal macrophages (meningeal, perivascular and choroid plexus), and astrocytes in the CNS (Brown & Weinberg, 2018; Cui & Wan, 2019; Gross, Schulte-Mecklenbeck et al., 2016; Pierson, Wagner, & Goverman, 2018; Van Kaer, Postoak, Wang, Yang, & Wu, 2019). All of these cells have been implicated in MS immunopathogenesis (Mammana et al., 2018; Ponath, Park, & Pitt, 2018; Sie & Korn, 2017). Innate immune responses begin with recognition of potential external threats such as pathogen-associated molecular patterns (PAMPs) or internal threats such as damage-related molecular patterns (DAMPs) by pattern recognition receptors (PRRs) on myeloid cells.

Soluble mediators including cytokines, chemokines, proteins (cell adhesion molecules and complement proteins), microRNA (miRNA), enzymes (matrix metalloproteinases- MMPs, myeloperoxidase, inducible nitric oxide synthase, NADPH oxidases, and cyclo-oxygenase 2), and nucleosides such as adenosine triphosphate (ATP) enable cell-to-cell communication in innate immunity (Hannocks et al., 2019; Kothur, Wienholt, Brilot, & Dale, 2016; Wang et al., 2018). Cytokines, chemokines, nucleosides and cell adhesion molecules exert their function via their cognate receptors (Wang et al., 2018). ROS and reactive nitrogen species induce oxidative and nitrative stress, respectively (Ohl et al., 2016). Finally, pro-resolving mediators such as resolvins and maresines have been shown to promote resolution of inflammation (Schett & Neurath, 2018; Serhan & Levy, 2018). All of these soluble factors have been implicated in MS immunopathogenesis (Baecher-Allan et al., 2018; Filippi et al., 2018; Wang et al., 2018).

4. Microglia

Microglia are tissue-resident macrophages that comprise approximately 10% of the cells in the CNS (Wolf, Boddeke, & Kettenmann, 2017). They arise from yolk-sac primitive erythromyeloid progenitor cells which migrate into the brain at early prenatal embryogenic developmental stages (Guttenplan & Liddelow, 2019). Migration and colonization of microglia into the brain begin before the BBB formation between embryonic day 8 and 10 (E8-E10) in mice (Reu et al., 2017) and embryonic day 4,5 to 5 weeks in human (Sominsky, De Luca, & Spencer, 2018).

Microglia have distinct morphology in the adult brain. Prenatal and early postnatal microglia are mostly in the non-ramified state, indicating that microglia in the developing brain is continuously active (Wolf et al., 2017). At the end of the second week postnatally, microglia switch to a mature phenotype indicated by the expression of transmembrane protein 119 (Tmem119) and gain a ramified morphology (Lenz & Nelson, 2018).

4.1 Homeostatic microglia

Microglia play a crucial role in the development of the CNS. During the prenatal period, microglia contribute to synaptic elimination, neuronal cell death and also promote neural precursor cell proliferation and survival. Microglia regulate wiring of the forebrain circuits and modulate axonal outgrowth in prenatal mice (Tay, Savage, Hui, Bisht, & Tremblay, 2017). During development, microglia have an essential role in vasculogenesis and vascular sprouting by secreting soluble factors such as vascular endothelial growth factor (Kierdorf & Prinz, 2017).

During postnatal development, microglia eliminate the neurons that are not involved in functional circuits (Colonna & Butovsky, 2017; Ikegami, Haruwaka, & Wake, 2019). Microglia also shape neuronal synapses via synaptic pruning, which is the elimination of dendritic spines that are not receiving signals from synaptic contacts (Colonna & Butovsky, 2017). In early postnatal stage, microglia enhance cortical apoptosis which is essential for synaptic plasticity and behavioral adaptation (Bar & Barak, 2019; Nonaka & Nakanishi, 2019; Sominsky et al., 2018).

Together with their immune roles, microglia are essential modulators of processes including synaptogenesis, survival of synapses, neuronal maturation and activity of neurons in adults (Wolf et al., 2017). Microglia contribute to the maintenance of homeostasis of brain by continuously scanning the microenvironment with their ramified processes. Adult microglia express numerous surface molecules on their cell membrane to immediately respond to changes in their microenvironment by the release of several cytokines, chemokines, hormones, purines, neurotransmitters and neurotrophic factors. Microglial brain-derived neurotrophic factor (BDNF) is also a significant contributor to the regulation of learning-induced synapse formation in the healthy brain (Parkhurst et al., 2013). To maintain homeostasis, microglia express surface markers that include fractalkine receptor CX3C chemokine receptor 1 (CX3CR1), colony stimulating factor 1 receptor (CSF-1R), the integrin CD11b, surface glycoproteins F4/80 and CD68, ionized calcium-binding adapter molecule 1 (IBA1), and pan-hematopoietic CD45 (Li & Barres, 2018; Tay et al., 2017).

4.2 Cell to cell interaction of microglia with other CNS cells

4.2.1 Interaction with neuron

Cell surface receptors and their ligands enable a bidirectional interaction between microglia with neurons. For instance, neurons express a ligand CX3L1 (also known as fractalkine) that is specific to the microglial receptor, CX3CR1 (Kabba et al., 2018). Neuro-immune-regulators (NIREGs) are proteins that regulate both the severity and duration of microglial responses (Bedoui, Neal, & Gasque, 2018). Constitutive expression of CD200, CD47 and chemokine (C-X-C motif) ligand 1 (CXCL1) on the neuronal surface are important in enhancing tissue resilience. Microglia remain in a steady state through interactions via their co-receptors CD200R, CD172a and CX3CR1 (Wolf et al., 2017). Neurons express numerous complement NIREGs, including CD55, CD46, CD59, and factor H. NIREGs are also involved in the regulation of cell stress, inflammatory responses and insurance of 'don't eat me' signal in order to prevent phagocytosis by microglia (Bedoui et al., 2018). Microglia can also modulate neuronal activity at the synaptic level (Marinelli, Basilico, Marrone, & Ragozzino, 2019).

4.2.2 Interaction with oligodendrocyte

There is a well-established balance between microglia and oligodendrocytes, which are responsible for myelin production. Microglia secrete growth factors that stimulate oligodendrocyte precursor cell (OPC) differentiation and myelination by promoting the expression of myelination-related proteins (Bar & Barak, 2019). Microglia can cross-talk with oligodendrocytes through CXCR1, CD200R, CSF-1R, cytokines, chemokines and neurotrophic factors during developmental stages. Additionally, oligodendrocytes can also activate microglia by releasing chemokines and cytokines (Kabba et al., 2018).

4.2.3 Interactions with astrocyte

Astrocytes account for almost 50% of all glial cell in the CNS (Kabba et al., 2018). They have key roles in the regulation of homeostasis, synaptic plasticity and neuroprotection (Li, Li, Zheng, & Qin, 2019). Astrocytes are critical players in the pathogenesis of EAE and MS (Brambilla, 2019; Ponath et al., 2018). Microglia-astrocyte cross-talk contributes to synaptic pruning during development (Thion, Ginhoux, & Garel, 2018). Astrocytes play a central role in the synaptic maturation and ramification of microglia. They can also stimulate microglial proliferation by secreting soluble factors (Reemst, Noctor, Lucassen, & Hol, 2016). Activated microglia can stimulate reactive A1 astrocytes by secreting interleukin-1β (IL-1β), tumor necrosis factor-α (TNF-α), and complement component 1q both *in vitro* and *in vivo*. Activated A1 astrocytes then secrete unidentified neurotoxin(s) that can lead to neuronal and oligodendrocyte death (Hinkle, Dawson, & Dawson, 2019; Liddelow et al., 2017).

4.3 Immune functions of microglia

Microglia express variety of receptors related to the myeloid lineage, such as PPRs that recognize PAMPs and DAMPs (Wolf et al., 2017). In addition, to maintain brain homeostasis phagocytic microglia are known to express antigen presentation genes (Dubbelaar, Kracht, Eggen, & Boddeke, 2018). Resting microglia transform into an activated state and migrate to the lesion site once a signal is detected from an infection, trauma, neurodegenerative disease, loss of brain homeostasis, or programmed cell death (Eyo & Wu, 2019).

4.3.1 Phagocytosis

Phagocytic microglia are essential for normal development, injury and brain regeneration. In addition to removing complete or part of cells, microglia also have an important role in the clearance of misfolded proteins and myelin debris (Kettenmann, Hanisch, Noda, & Verkhratsky, 2011). Microglia respond to demyelination injury and facilitate the remyelination process by phagocytosis of myelin debris, remodeling the extracellular matrix and secreting trophic factors that is required for OPCs (Lloyd, Davies, & Miron, 2017). Microglial cells phagocyte pathogens, apoptotic cells and cellular debris through secreting cytokines and producing ROS (Tay et al., 2017).

4.3.2 Antigen presentation

Phagocytic and endocytic microglia have receptors such as TLRs that can effectively mediate antigen capture (Fiebich, Akter, & Akundi, 2014). Activated microglia also possess a lysosomal machinery in order to process antigens and express MHC Class II along with costimulatory molecules required for myelin peptide presentation to antigen specific $CD4^+$ T cells in the CNS (Schetters, Gomez-Nicola, Garcia-Vallejo, & Van Kooyk, 2017).

4.3.3 Microglial polarization

Microglia can polarize into distinct phenotypes depending on the nature of stimuli. Various conditions including age and CNS disorders, microenvironmental factors can influence microglial polarization. In the classical activation, M1 microglia comprise the first defense of innate immunity that accounts for the first few hours to days after stimulation. Microglia polarize into the M1 phenotype by lipopolysaccharide (LPS), interferon-γ and bacterial debris (Kabba et al., 2018), then secrete proinflammatory cytokines IL-1β, IL-6, and TNF-α that contribute to innate responses.

Microglia can also polarize into the M2 phenotype by IL-4 and interleukin-13 (IL-13) (alternative activation). M2 microglia play role in tissue repair once activation signals are received from damaged and dysfunctional neurons. To provide resolution of inflammation microglia then secrete several anti-inflammatory cytokines and neurotrophic factors that include IL-4, IL-10, insulin-like growth factor-1 (IGF-1), transforming growth factor-β and BDNF. However, microglial activation status is now considered to be a highly dynamic process that is tightly regulated. After single-cell transcriptomics and mass cytometry studies in both mice and human, the dichotomic view remains oversimplified.

5. Microglia in EAE and MS

Microglia play a fundamental role in all MS lesions (Zrzavy et al., 2017). After inflammation or CNS injury, microglia become activated (Wang et al., 2019). Activated microglia or disease associated microglia found in lesions and white matter in MS patients have an increased expression of pro-inflammatory genes (Wang et al., 2019). The relationship between microglial activation and its contribution to disease progression was demonstrated by a decrease in P2Y purinoceptor 12^+ homeostatic microglia and an increase in TMEM119^+ microglia (Zrzavy et al., 2017). The role of activated microglia in the EAE model have also been studied. Centonze et al. demonstrated that activated microglia triggered excitation of post-synaptic currents by triggering TNF-α release and caused subsequent glutamate excitoxicity (Centonze et al., 2009, 2010).

Microglia and T cells are found in MS lesions (Luo et al., 2017). Activated microglia cause myelin sheath and oligodendrocyte damage via secreting ROS, reactive nitrogen species and glutamate (Luo et al., 2017; Voet, Prinz, & Van Loo, 2019). Pro-inflammatory cytokines secreted from microglia exert a neurotoxic effect in MS (Surace & Block, 2012; Voet et al., 2019). Microglia also secrete chemokines for the recruitment of infiltrating cells (monocyte, macrophage and lymphocyte).

Microglia have also beneficial effects including phagocytosis, BDNF secretion and remyelination in MS (Yamasaki et al., 2014). Microglial triggering receptor expressed on myeloid cells 2, CR3 and signal regulatory protein-α receptors take place in the phagocytosis of myelin debris (Voet et al., 2019). Microglia contribute to remyelination by secreting IGF-1 and fibroblast growth factor (FGF-2) and induce proliferation of OPCs (Luo et al., 2017).

6. NLRP3 inflammasome

Inflammasomes are intracellular multiprotein complexes that mediate innate immune responses against PAMPs and DAMPs. The components and activation mechanisms of inflammasomes has been demonstrated by Tschopp and his group in 2002 (Martinon, Burns, & Tschopp, 2002). Activation of inflammasomes ultimately result in proteolytic cleavage and secretion of proinflammatory cytokines, pro-IL-1β and IL-18 that are crucial for the clearance of pathogens or injured cells (Hanamsagar, Torres, & Kielian, 2011). However, overactivation or dysregulation of inflammasomes are known to contribute to the pathogenesis of several disorders, including infections, autoimmune, and neurodegenerative diseases.

6.1 Sensors

Inflammasome sensor proteins are grouped based on their structural features. The nucleotide-binding, leucine-rich repeat containing proteins (NLR) represent a family of cytosolic sensors that are key components of the inflammasome complex (Delbridge & O'riordan, 2007). Each family member contains a C-terminal leucine-rich repeat region (LRR) required for ligand detection, a central nucleotide-binding and oligomerization domain (NOD or NACHT), and an N-terminal effector domain which differs in each NLR subfamily proteins, such as caspase recruitment domain (CARD), and pyrin domain (PYD) (Areschoug & Gordon, 2008). Various inflammasome sensors can recognize diverse molecules, including nucleic acids, bacterial proteins, toxins, metabolites and protein aggregates (Mangan et al., 2018).

6.2 NLRP3 triggers

The NLRP3 inflammasome is the most extensively studied inflammasome complex and prototype of NLRP proteins. Activation of the NLRP3 inflammasome triggered by LPS and ATP has been characterized by Mariathasan and his group in 2006. The NLRP3 inflammasome can be activated by a wide range of triggers including pathogen-derived ligands, such as cell wall components, nucleic acids, and toxins; environmental crystalline particles like silica, asbestos, and alum; and endogenous danger signals like ATP, uric acid crystals and aggregated proteins (Braga et al., 2017; Leemans, Cassel, & Sutterwala, 2011; Yeon, Yang, Lee, & Lee, 2017).

6.3 Components of NLRP3 complex and their domains

The NLRP3 inflammasome is formed by a sensor protein (NLRP3), an adaptor molecule (apoptosis-associated speck-like protein-ASC); and an effector enzyme (caspase-1) (Broz & Dixit, 2016) (Fig. 3). NLRP3 has three domains: a pyrin domain, a nucleotide binding NACHT domain and a LRR domain. The NACHT domain binds ATP and exerts ATPase activity. The pyrin domain is involved in homotypic interactions with the ASC adaptor protein. ASC contains two distinct domains: the N-terminal pyrin and the C-terminal CARD domains. ASC has a unique adaptor function that brings together PYD- and CARD-containing proteins to assemble an inflammasome. When ASC specks are generated one speck per cell, it is accepted as an evidence of inflammasome activation. Nucleation of ASC allows formation of CARD—CARD interactions with pro-caspase-1 (Kumar, Kawai, & Akira, 2011). Subsequently, caspase-1 undergoes auto cleavage and promotes the maturation and secretion of proinflammatory mediators IL1b and IL-18 (Mangan et al., 2018; Schroder & Tschopp, 2010) (Fig. 3).

6.4 Mechanisms of NLRP3 inflammasome activation

6.4.1 Priming

Canonical activation of the NLRP3 inflammasome occurs in two steps: priming and activation. In many resting cells, the basal expression of NLRP3 and IL-1β protein levels are not sufficient to activate the NLRP3 inflammasome. The priming signal leads to nuclear factor kappa B (NF-kB) translocation into nucleus and is subsequently accompanied with an increase in the messenger ribonucleic acid (mRNA) levels of both NLRP3 and pro-IL-1β (Sun, 2011; Sutterwala, Haasken, & Cassel, 2014; Green et al., 2018). The priming step can be triggered various stimuli such as LPS,

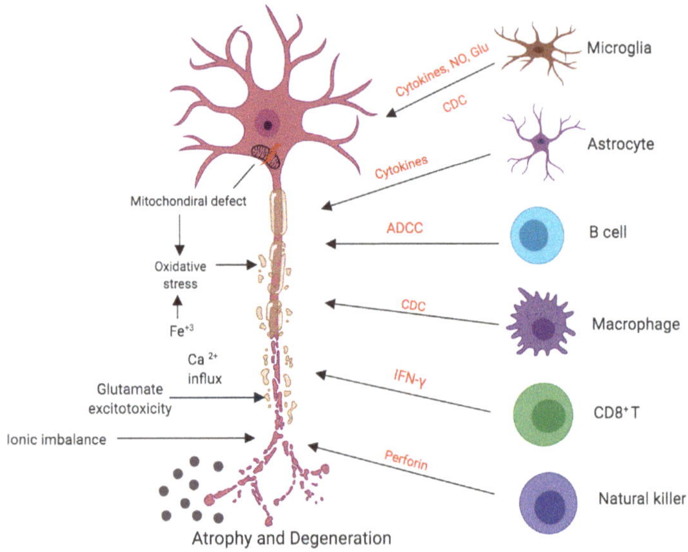

Fig. 3 Mechanisms of cell injury in MS.* Immune dependent and independent mechanisms induce demyelination and neuronal degeneration. * Created with BioRender. (*NO*, nitric oxide, *CDC*, complement dependent cytotoxicity, *ADCC*, antibody dependent cellular cytotoxicity). See the text for further detail.

cytokines, high mobility group box 1 and advanced glycation end products through toll Like Receptor 4 (TLR4); TNF-α and IL-1β via their cognate receptors (Mukherjee et al., 2009). In addition to the transcriptional priming step, recent studies suggest that non-transcriptional priming mechanisms can also effectively activate NLRP3 within minutes through post-translational modifications, such as phosphorylation of NLRP3 by c-Jun N-terminal kinase (JNK) or mitogen-activated protein kinase (Sun, 2011).

6.4.2 Activation

Diverse endogenous and exogenous signals trigger the assembly of the inflammasome components. However, the exact mechanism whether the same inflammasome sensor is activated by various danger signals remains unknown. One plausible explanation is that NLRP3 can sense these stimuli indirectly via intracellular upstream cellular stress signals, including ion flux, ROS, lysosomal disruption and Golgi disassembly (Groslambert & Py, 2018).

The most common ion flux that activates the NLRP3 inflammasome is potassium (K^+) efflux. Various stimuli like ATP, crystalline and nigericin decrease the intracellular concentration of K^+ in cells. But, K^+ efflux is not specific for NLRP3 inflammasome activation (Munoz-Planillo et al., 2013). Increase in cytosolic calcium (Ca^{++}) leads to NLRP3 inflammasome activation through increasing mitochondrial ROS production (Csordas & Hajnoczky, 2009; Lemasters, Theruvath, Zhong, & Nieminen, 2009). Sodium (Na^+) influx and chloride (Cl^-) efflux are also involved in NLRP3 inflammasome activation (Yang, Wang, Kouadir, Song, & Shi, 2019).

ROS and especially mitochondrial ROS (mtROS) are well known endogenous triggers for NLRP3 inflammasome activation. Several NLRP3 inflammasome agonists increase ROS production, and ROS inhibition suppress NLRP3 inflammasome activity. Although these findings support the role of ROS in the activation of the NLRP3 inflammasome, the exact mechanism of how NLRP3 inflammasome sense ROS is still not known. It is possible to think that NEK7, a NLRP3 interacting protein, can either sense ROS production or K^+ efflux instead of NLRP3 itself (Gross, Mishra et al., 2016). Intracellular ROS can also indirectly activate the NLRP3 inflammasome by enhancing the interaction between thioredoxin-interacting protein and NLRP3 (Tschopp & Schroder, 2010).

Mitochondrial dysfunction also contributes to inflammasome activation. Anti-apoptotic mitochondrial proteins B-cell lymphoma 2 and B-cell lymphoma-extra-large inhibit the NLRP1 inflammasome (Faustin et al., 2009). Chemicals that induce mitochondrial membrane pore formation can activate the NLRP3 inflammasome through the release of mitochondrial deoxyribonucleic acid or by altering mitophagy (Allam et al., 2014). Mitochondrial localization of NLRP3 and its specific interactions with mitochondrial proteins like mitofusin2 and cardiolipin have been implicated to be an activation mechanism for inflammasomes (Iyer et al., 2013).

Lysosomal destabilization acts on both the priming and activation steps for inflammasomes. The inefficient clearance of large foreign particles such as silica may cause lysosomal ruptures and the release of the lysosomal enzyme Cathepsin B can then activate the NLRP3 inflammasome (Hornung et al., 2008). Lysosomes are involved in the regulation of intracellular calcium homeostasis. Lysosomal calcium signaling acts at the priming step by stabilizing pro-IL-1β mRNA (Weber & Schilling, 2014). Lysosomal membrane rupture activates the NLRP3 inflammasome due to the K^+ efflux after pore opening (Munoz-Planillo et al., 2013).

Recent studies have shown the role of the Golgi apparatus in inflammasome activation. NLRP3 first triggers the disassembly of the trans-golgi network into vesicles, and then induces NLRP3 aggregation (Chen & Chen, 2018). NLRP3 is translocated from the endoplasmic reticulum to Golgi by cholesterol biosynthesis regulator proteins (sterol regulatory element-binding protein2 and sterol regulatory element-binding protein cleavage-activating protein), which has been proposed to be a requirement for inflammasome activation (Guo et al., 2018).

6.5 Other activation mechanisms of NLRP3 inflammasome

Caspase-4/5 in humans, and caspase-11 in mice are responsible for noncanonical inflammasome activation (Yi, 2018). Cytosolic LPS is the main inducer of the noncanonical pathway. Caspase-11 senses cytosolic LPS through binding to the lipid A portion of LPS and leads to pyroptosis without the involvement of caspase-1. Active caspases cleave gasdermin-D (GSDMD) and cause the release of the N-terminal fragment that drives pyroptosis. Consequent, K^+ efflux is responsible for the release of inflammatory cytokines. The N-terminal fragment of GSDMD can also activate the NLRP3 inflammasome via an undefined mechanism.

Alternative activation of the NLRP3 inflammasome is mediated by the TLR4 signaling pathway (Yang et al., 2019). Alternative activation exerts specific features including requirement of ASC and caspase-1, independency on K efflux and lack of ASC speck formation and pyroptosis. Signaling cascade continues TLR4- TIR-domain-containing adapter-inducing interferon-β - receptor-interacting serine/threonine-protein kinase 1-Fas-associated protein with death domain-caspase-8 to induce NLRP3 inflammasome activation and subsequently leads to IL-1β and IL-18 secretion (Gurung et al., 2014). The role of caspase-8 activation in the NLRP3 inflammasome by alternative pathway has not yet been completely elucidated. Caspase-8 activation may act as a priming signal that directly cleaves pro-IL-1β and contributes to the secretion of cytokines. In the absence of inhibitor of apoptosis protein (IAP), caspase-8 mediated cell death signal may act as an inflammasome signal (Gurung & Kanneganti, 2015).

6.6 Regulation

Inflammasome function is tightly regulated by several mechanisms (Rathinam, Vanaja, & Fitzgerald, 2012), as uncontrolled activation may lead to a variety of autoimmune diseases and metabolic disorders. Regulation of NLRP3 may occur at the transcriptional, post-transcriptional and post-translational levels (Song & Li, 2018).

6.6.1 Negative regulators of NLRP3 inflammasome

Negative regulators limit inflammasome activity and can interfere at different steps of inflammasome formation (Tozser & Benko, 2016). For example, the heat shock protein tripartite motif-containing protein 30, acts as a negative regulator through the inhibition of ROS production. Nitric oxide, carbon monoxide, small heterodimer partner protein, inhibitor of nuclear factor Kappa-B kinase subunit α, and G protein signaling modulator-3 have all been reported to act as negative regulators of the NLRP3 inflammasome. Autophagy also negatively regulates the NLRP3 inflammasome by several mechanisms, including the clearance of intracellular inflammasome inducer sources, suppression of IL-1β release, and degradation of inflammasome complex proteins (Rodgers, Bowman, Liang, & Jung, 2014).

6.6.2 Post-transcriptional regulation

Regulatory molecules like microRNAs (miRNAs) and RNA binding proteins can limit the amount and stability of mRNAs that encode essential proteins for the priming and/or activation steps, thus ultimately regulate NLRP3 inflammasome activity (Tezcan et al., 2019). miRNAs are 20–23 nt long noncoding RNAs that control gene expression via binding to the 3′UTR of coding mRNAs. Several miRNAs have been identified as post-transcriptional regulatory mechanisms for NLRP3 activity. miRa-146a is a negative regulator of the NLRP3 inflammasome at priming step and acts by targeting the NF-κB signaling molecules TNF receptor associated factor 6, and interleukin-1 receptor-associated kinase 1 (Singer et al., 2018). miR-223 can bind the 3′ UTR region of NLRP3 mRNA, and reduce NLRP3 expression. Due to their higher expression in myeloid cells, miR-223 plays a crucial role in innate immune responses (Zhao et al., 2018).

6.6.3 Post-translational regulation

Common post-translational modifications of proteins, such as phosphorylation, methylation, acetylation, glycosylation, ubiquitination, sumoylation and s-nitrosylation are involved in the regulation process. Ubiquitination type modifications are crucial for the regulation of the NLRP3 inflammasome. A20 is a NF-kB responsive deubiquitinase that can either activate or suppress inflammasome activation based on cellular signals (Das, Chen, Hendriks, & Kool, 2018; Rothschild, Mcdaniel, Ringel-Scaia, & Allen, 2018; Yue, Stone, & Lin, 2018). While the deubiquitinating enzyme BRCA1/BRCA2-containing complex subunit 3 induces NLRP3 activation, E3 ubiquitin ligase F-box L2 ubiquitinates the lysine-689 residue on

NLRP3 to promote its proteosomal degradation (Py, Kim, Vakifahmetoglu-Norberg, & Yuan, 2013). Phosphorylation of NLRP3 is another regulatory mechanism for the inflammasome activation. The protein tyrosine phosphatase non-receptor type 22 activates NLRP3 by dephosphorylating the tyrosine-861 residue (Spalinger et al., 2016). Phosphorylation of NLRP3 at the serine-295 residue prevents inflammasome assembly formation by inhibiting the ATPase activity (Mortimer, Moreau, Macdonald, & Chadee, 2016). Phosphorylation of NLRP3 can also act as a positive regulator of inflammasome activation. A recent study demonstrated that the serine-194 residue phosphorylated by JNK-1 can drive NLRP3 assembly formation (Song et al., 2017).

6.7 Consequences of NLRP3 inflammasome activation

6.7.1 Secretion of cytokines

IL-1β is a crucial player for proper inflammasome functioning in the CNS (Dinarello, 2018). By damaging endothelial cells, IL-1β disrupts the structural integrity of the BBB. When astrocytes secrete the chemokine, CCR2, peripheral immune cells start infiltrating into the CNS through the impaired BBB (Mccandless et al., 2009). Microglia and astrocytes are also activated by IL-1 β, and in turn can stimulate T cells and generate pro-inflammatory cytokines such as IL-6 and TNF-α (Ferrari et al., 2004). IL-1β mediates neuronal injury via glutamate excitotoxicity that is detected in the pathogenesis of MS (Gosselin & Rivest, 2007; Kostic, Zivkovic, & Stojanovic, 2013; Lin & Edelson, 2017; Rossi et al., 2012).

IL-18 is another cytokine processed by the NLRP3 inflammasome activation in MS (Sedimbi, Hagglof, & Karlsson, 2013). Recent studies have revealed the involvement of IL-18 in disease pathology in both *in vivo* animal models and in clinical studies (Dinarello, 2018). IL-18 has similar effects to IL-1β on T and B cells (Nakanishi, 2018). It also upregulates the expressions of caspase-1, MMPs, and pro-inflammatory cytokines by activating several signaling pathways in microglia (Bossu et al., 2009).

6.7.2 Pyroptosis

Caspase-1 activation by the inflammasome leads to programmed cell death mediated by GSDMD, namely pyroptosis. When GSDMD is cleaved by caspase-1, the C terminal fragment is removed, and its inhibition at the N terminal of gasdermin (GSDMD-NT) is abolished. Then, GSDMD-NT translocates and binds to phosphatidylinositol phosphates and phosphatidylserine in the inner leaflet of the membrane and oligomerizes to form

~15 nm pores (Rathkey et al., 2018). These pores let water into the cell, increase intracellular pressure causing membrane rupture, and finally induce the release of pro-inflammatory cytokines. Non-canonical inflammasome activation by caspases 4, 5 and 11 also activate the cleavage of GSDMD to induce pyroptosis (Liu, Zhang et al., 2016). Pyroptotic cell death attracts leukocytes to the site of inflammation, induces subsequent inflammatory responses, and leads to severe tissue damage (Bortolotti, Faure, & Kipnis, 2018).

6.8 NLRP3 inflammasome informs adaptive immunity

The IL-1 family cytokine signaling is important in adaptive immunity (Garlanda, Dinarello, & Mantovani, 2013). IL-1β provides survival signals for naive T cells and is crucial for the differentiation of T helper cell subtype Th17. This connection is involved in sterile autoimmune activity in MS (Wang, Ma, Wu, & Zhu, 2013).

Similar to IL-1β, IL-18 also plays role in the induction of adaptive immunity (Raupach, Peuschel, Monack, & Zychlinsky, 2006). IL-18 is described as IFN-γ inducing factor for T cells under pathogenic insults, and mediates differentiation of Th1 cell subtype and NK cells (Chaix et al., 2008; Harrison et al., 2015).

7. NLRP3 in CNS disorders

Microglia has been the focus of many NLRP3 inflammasome studies as they express a variety of inflammation sensing proteins. Microglial NLRP3 inflammasome activation has been extensively studied in acute and chronic CNS disorders, including Alzheimer's disease (AD), Parkinson's disease (PD), amyotrophic lateral sclerosis (ALS), frontotemporal dementia, stroke, traumatic brain and spinal cord injuries. *In vitro* studies revealed that aggregated ß-amyloid (Aβ) and hyperphosphorylated tau proteins induced the activation of the NLRP3 inflammasome in microglia (Stancu et al., 2019). A recent postmortem study has reported the increased expression of ASC, caspase-1, IL-1β in the cerebral cortex of AD patients (Li, Ismael et al., 2019).

Similar to Aβ, aggregated αSyn, a pathological protein accumulated in PD, can act as DAMPs to activate microglial NLRP3 inflammasome, thereby inducing mitochondrial impairment, ROS production and Cathepsin B activity (Bai Yang et al., 2018; Mouton-Liger et al., 2018;

Panicker et al., 2019; Sarkar et al., 2017). *In vivo* studies using either genetic (mutation in α-synuclein, parkin, PTEN-induced kinase 1) or toxin-based (1-methyl-4-phenyl-1,2,3,6-tetrahydropyridine, 6-hydroxydopamine) models have demonstrated the contribution of microglial NLRP3 inflammasome to PD pathogenesis (Lee et al., 2019; Mao et al., 2017; Mouton-Liger et al., 2018; Zhou et al., 2016). Microglial NLRP3 inflammasome activation has been observed in patients with ALS and frontotemporal dementia in which pathological proteins (mutant superoxide dismutase and TAR DNA-binding protein 43) have been accumulated (Johann et al., 2015; Leal-Lasarte, Franco, Labrador-Garrido, Pozo, & Roodveldt, 2017).

NLRP3 inflammasome activation is predominantly observed in microglia in animal models of traumatic brain (TBI) and spinal cord injury (Lin et al., 2017; Mortezaee, Khanlarkhani, Beyer, & Zendedel, 2018; Xu et al., 2018). NLRP3 inhibition in these models were able to rescue neurons from microglia mediated cell death (Mortezaee et al., 2018; Xu et al., 2018). In addition, the concentration of NLRP3 was elevated in the CSF of children with severe TBI, supporting the idea that the NLRP3 inflammasome is activated upon trauma (Wallisch et al., 2017). Post-ischemic inflammatory responses exert deleterious effects on stroke sequelae. Microglial NLRP3 inflammasome activation was also detected at the early stages in ischemic stroke animal models (Fann et al., 2013; Gong, Pan, Shen, Li, & Peng, 2018).

In addition to microglia, recent studies point out that NLRP3 inflammasome activation is also observed in other CNS cells, such as astrocytes, neurons, cerebral endothelial cells and pericytes in experimental models of CNS disorders. Immune cells (T cells and myeloid cells) express components of the NLRP3 inflammasome complex in disease conditions, such as MS. Further studies are required to gain insight and a comprehensive understanding of the role of NLRP3 inflammasome activation in the CNS and peripheral immune cells.

8. Microglial NLRP3 in EAE

The critical role of NLRP3 inflammasome activity in MS pathology has been demonstrated in several animal models. The NLRP3 inflammasome complex components NLRP3, ASC and pro-caspase-1 has been activated in EAE (Place & Kanneganti, 2017) (Table 1). NLRP3 inflammasome amplifies the neuroinflammation and contributes the progression of EAE (Inoue & Shinohara, 2013; Jafarzadeh & Nemati, 2018).

One of the hallmarks of NLRP3 inflammasome activation is the production and secretion of pro-inflammatory cytokines, IL-1β and IL-18 (Malik & Kanneganti, 2017). IL-1β has a fundamental role in MS (Lin & Edelson, 2017; Mendiola & Cardona, 2018). Many earlier studies have demonstrated an upregulation of these pro-inflammatory cytokines at both the mRNA and protein level (Lukens, Barr, Chaplin, Chi, & Kanneganti, 2012; Mckenzie et al., 2018; Zhang et al., 2018; Znalesniak et al., 2016). In a study by Lukens et al., IL-1β protein expression was significantly increased in EAE and this increase was shown to be specifically mediated by caspase-1 activity (Lukens et al., 2012). EAE induced mice demonstrated a significant increase in IL-1β and other inflammasome components protein levels in the cerebellum and spinal cord (Znalesniak et al., 2016). Similarly, another study showed that EAE induction significantly increased IL-1β mRNA levels in the hindbrain and spinal cord, whereas IL-1β protein expression was only upregulated in the spinal cord (Mckenzie et al., 2018). EAE induction in IL-1β $^{-/-}$ mice demonstrated that this deficiency led to a decrease in CD4^{+} T cells together with a subsequent reduction of GM-CSF secreted by these cells (Lukens et al., 2012). Another study in EAE induced mice revealed that IL-1β deficient microglia secreted less inflammatory cytokines and chemokines including IL-6, IL-13, CXCL-1 and chemokine (C-X-C motif) ligand 2 and failed to enhance EAE progression (Zhang et al., 2018).

Activation of the NLRP3 inflammasome is required for GM-CSF production, which contributes to the development of EAE. It has been demonstrated that IL-1β produced by the NLRP3 inflammasome complex is required for the regulation of GM-CSF production along with the MYD88 adaptor protein. The experiments with IL-1R knock out mice revealed that IL-1R is required for the production GM-CSF and this deficiency reduced the clinical score in EAE induced mice. In addition, the number of MHC-II positive microglia was reduced in EAE induced IL-1R $^{-/-}$ mice (Lukens et al., 2012). IL-18 also plays a critical role in the pathogenesis of MS exacerbations (Karni, Koldzic, Bharanidharan, Khoury, & Weiner, 2002). In the EAE model, IL-18 protein expression was significantly increased and its deficiency led to a significant decrease in the clinical score of disease (Gris et al., 2010).

The alterations in the level of NLRP3 inflammasome complex proteins in EAE have been reported in several studies. The expression of NLRP3 was markedly increased both at the mRNA (Gris et al., 2010; Znalesniak et al., 2016; Mckenzie et al., 2018) and protein level (Bai, Wang et al., 2018b; Ke et al., 2017). Caspase-1 mRNA and protein levels together with the NLRP3

Table 1 NLRP3 in EAE models.

Organism	EAE model	Inflammasome components identified	Site of detection	Method of detection	Clinical outcome	Outcome	References
Mouse (C57BL/6, *Nlrp3*$^{-/-}$, *Casp-1*$^{-/-}$, *Il-18*$^{-/-}$)	MOG_{35-55}	NLRP3, IL-1β, IL-18, GFAP	spinal cord	clinical score, RT-PCR, ELISA	Decreased clinical score in *Nlrp3*$^{-/-}$ and *Il-18*$^{-/-}$ mice	Increased NLRP3 mRNA expression in EAE induced mice Reduced demyelination and astrogliosis in *Nlrp3*$^{-/-}$ mice Reduced IL-18 cytokine expression, MOG-specific Th1 and Th17 T cell response and reduced inflammatory infiltrate in the CNS in *Nlrp3*$^{-/-}$ mice Reduced IFN-γ and IL-17 in *Il-18*$^{-/-}$ mice	(Gris et al., 2010)
Mouse (C57BL/6, *Nlrp3*$^{-/-}$, *Casp1*$^{-/-}$, *Il-1β*$^{-/-}$, *Il-18*$^{-/-}$)	MOG_{35-55}	N/A	spinal cord	clinical score	Decreased clinical score in *Nlrp3*$^{-/-}$ mice	Reduced demyelination in *Nlrp3*$^{-/-}$ mice	(Jha et al., 2010)

Mouse (C57BL/6, *Nlrp3*$^{-/-}$, *Casp1*$^{-/-}$, *Il-1β*$^{-/-}$, *Il-18*$^{-/-}$)	8-10 week-old male mice, 0.2% cuprizone, 6 weeks	NLRP3, IL-1β, IBA1, GFAP	corpus callosum	RT-PCR, ELISA	N/A	Increased NLRP3 expression and IL-1β Decreased microgliosis and astrogliosis in *Nlrp3*$^{-/-}$ mice Delayed demyelination and decreased mature oligodendrocyte death in *Nlrp3*$^{-/-}$ mice Delayed demyelination and decreased astrogliosis, microgliosis and mature oligodendrocyte death in *Casp1*$^{-/-}$ mice	(Jha et al., 2010)
Mouse (C57BL/6, *Nlrp3*$^{-/-}$, *Casp1*$^{-/-}$, *Asc*$^{-/-}$)	$MOG_{35\text{-}55}$	N/A	spinal cord	clinical score	Decreased clinical score in *Asc*$^{-/-}$ and *Casp1*$^{-/-}$ mice	Decreased MOG-specific T cells	(Shaw et al., 2010)

(*Continued*)

Table 1 NLRP3 in EAE models.—cont'd

Organism	EAE model	Inflammasome components identified	Site of detection	Method of detection	Clinical outcome	Outcome	References
Mouse (C57BL/6, *Casp1*$^{-/-}$, *Il-1β*$^{-/-}$, *Il-1R*$^{-/-}$)	7-12 week-sex-matched mice, MOG_{35-55}	IL-1β	spinal cord	clinical score, Flow cytometry, ELISA	Decreased EAE clinical score in *Il-1R*$^{-/-}$	Reduced number of MHC-II positive microglia in EAE induced *Il-1R*$^{-/-}$ mice Decreased IL-1β expression in EAE induced *Casp1*$^{-/-}$	(Lukens et al., 2012)
Mouse C57BL/6	8-12 week-old male mice, MOG_{35-55}	NLRP3, IL-1β	spinal cord cerebellum	RT-PCR	N/A	Increased expression of NLRP3 and IL-1β mRNA	(Znalesniak et al., 2016)
Mouse (C57BL/6, *Nlrp3*$^{-/-}$, *Nlrc4*$^{-/-}$, *Asc*$^{-/-}$, *Casp1*$^{-/-}$, *Casp11*$^{-/-}$, *Il-1β*$^{-/-}$, *Il-18*$^{-/-}$)	8-10 week-old male mice, 0.2% cuprizone, 3–4 weeks	IL-1β, Caspase-1, IBA1, GFAP	BMDM	ELISA,WB, IF	N/A	Increased NLRC4 protein expression in IBA1 and GFAP positive cells in cuprizone induced mice Decreased microgliosis, astrogliosis and demyelination in *Nlrp3*$^{-/-}$ *Nlrc4*$^{-/-}$ DKO mice	(Freeman et al., 2017)

Mouse (C57BL/6)	10-12 week-old female mice, MOG_{35-55}	NLRP3, IL-1β, Caspase-1, NLRP1, Caspase-11, GSDMD, IBA1	hind brain spinal cord	IF, IHC, RT-PCR	N/A	Increased IL-1β, Caspase-1, NLRP3 and GSDMD mRNA expression in EAE induced mice Increased microgliosis and pyroptosis in EAE induced mice	(Mckenzie et al., 2018)
Mouse (C57BL/6, $CX3Cr1Cre^{EREYFP}$, $CX3Cr1^{GFP}$, $Nlrp3^{-/-}$, $Casp8^{fl/fl}$, $IRAKM^{fl/fl}$, $Casp8^{-/-}$, $Ripk3^{-/-}$, $Il\text{-}1\beta^{-/-}$	MOG_{35-55}, Adoptive immunization	IL-1β,ASC, Caspase-8, NLRP3, Caspase-1, IBA1	brain spinal cord	clinical score, ELISA, RT-PCR, Flow cytometry	Decreased clinical score in $Asc^{\Delta microglia}$, $Ripk3^{-/-}$, $Casp8^{\Delta microglia}$ mice	Decreased IL-1β mRNA expression in EAE induced $Asc^{\Delta microglia}$ mice Caspase-8 activity in NLRP3/ASC dependent manner in EAE induced mice Increased Caspase-8 activity in microglia in brain of EAE induced mice Microglia-intrinsic ASC increased Th1-and Th17 induced EAE in mice.	(Zhang et al., 2018)

Casp, Caspase; *NLRC*, NLR family CARD domain-containing protein 4; *Ripk*, Receptor interacting protein kinase; *IRAKM*, interleukin 1 receptor-associated kinase M.

expression was also reported to be increased in EAE induced mice (Bai, Wang et al., 2018; Ke et al., 2017; Mckenzie et al., 2018; Shao et al., 2014).

Knock out animal studies have confirmed the crucial role of NLRP3 inflammasome activation in the pathogenesis of EAE. Deficiency of these inflammasome complex proteins reduced disease progression and improved clinical scores (Gris et al., 2010; Jha et al., 2010; Mckenzie et al., 2018; Zhang et al., 2018; Znalesniak et al., 2016). EAE induction in *Nlrp3*$^{-/-}$ mice caused demyelination and astrogliosis that was accompanied with a reduced clinical score. Jha et al. demonstrated the critical role of NLRP3 inflammasome activation by using the cuprizone model to mimic MS. Deficiency in NLRP3 induced demyelination and caused mature oligodendrocyte death. *Nlrp3*$^{-/-}$ mice also displayed reduced microgliosis and astrogliosis following cuprizone induction. Furthermore, mice lacking caspase-1 were presented with delayed demyelination and reduced gliosis (Jha et al., 2010).

The role of ASC, another component of the NLRP3 inflammasome complex, was reported in EAE induced ASC KO mice with delayed disease progression, reduced MOG-specific T cells in the lymph node and improved clinical score (Shaw et al., 2010). The requirement of microglia specific ASC at the effector stage of EAE has been reported (Zhang et al., 2018). ASC deficiency in microglia led to a reduction in infiltration of immune cells, including CD4^{+} T cells, B cells, neutrophils, and macrophages and attenuation of EAE. Furthermore, IL-1β is produced via IL-1 Receptor-Associated Kinase M (IRAKM)/ASC-NLRP3—caspase-8 axis and contributes to pathogenesis of EAE IRAKM-caspase-8 inflammasome activation is also necessary in microglia in EAE induced mice.

Another inflammasome complex, NLR family CARD domain-containing protein 4 (NLRC4) together with NLRP3 elicit disease progression in cuprizone-induced demyelination model. The expression of NLRC4 was increased in the corpus callosum of cuprizone-induced mice, especially in astrocytes and microglia. The use of *Nlrc4*$^{-/-}$, *Nlrp3*$^{-/-}$, and *Nlrp3*$^{-/-}$ *Nlrc4*$^{-/-}$ mice revealed that deficiency in NLRC4 and NLRP3 reduced microglia accumulation and astrocyte positive cells in the corpus callosum of cuprizone induced mice. Furthermore, reduced demyelination in these mice was reported (Freeman et al., 2017).

The noncanonical activation of the NLRP3 inflammasome and pyroptosis play role in the pathogenesis of EAE. The mRNA expression of NLRP3, IL-1β, caspase-1, GSDMD, caspase-11, NLRC4, and absent in melanoma 2 (AIM2) was increased in the hindbrain of EAE induced mice. Additionally, GSDMD expression was elevated in spinal cord lesions and was colocalized with Iba-1 positive cells. GSDMD and caspase-1 positive microglia and oligodendrocytes suggest that these cells undergo pyroptosis (Mckenzie et al., 2018).

NLRP3 inflammasome activation also informs adaptive immunity (Deng, Yu, & Wang, 2019; Evavold & Kagan, 2018). NLRP3 deficiency diminished the Th1 and Th17 T cell response and reduced infiltration of inflammatory cells, including macrophages, $CD4^+$, and $CD8^+$ T cells in the spinal cord and brain (Gris et al., 2010; Inoue, Williams, Gunn, & Shinohara, 2012). NLRP3 inflammasome signaling may enhance the chemotactic ability of immune cells by increasing their chemotaxis-related protein expressions such as $\alpha4\beta1$ integrin, chemokine (C-C motif) ligand 7, chemokine (C-C motif) ligand 8, and chemokine (C-X-C motif) ligand 16 (Inoue, Shinohara et al., 2012).

9. Experimental therapeutic implications

Although there is currently no cure for MS, several treatment options that provide symptom management are available. The drugs developed for this purpose target different molecular mechanisms that underlie MS. Inflammasome activation is one of the mechanisms that contribute greatly to MS progression. Several drugs that are currently in use have been shown to be effective against inflammasome activation in MS.

One of these drugs is IFN-β which has been widely used (Scheu et al., 2019) and is the first effective drug to be FDA approved for the treatment of MS (Tintore et al., 2019). The effect and mechanism of IFN-β on NLRP3 inflammasome activation has been shown in the EAE model (Inoue, Williams et al., 2012, 2016) (Table 2). The studies revealed that the efficacy of IFN-β treatment in EAE was remarkably dependent on the activation of the NLRP3 inflammasome. IFN-β treatment was effective as long as EAE progression relied on NLRP3 inflammasome activation (Inoue, William et al., 2012). Interestingly, the occurrence of NLRP3 inflammasome-independent EAE subtype called Type-B EAE showed resistance to IFN-β treatment. The high immunization in Type-B EAE caused strong stimulation of an innate immune response by subsequently bypassing the NLRP3 inflammasome in the EAE model (Inoue et al., 2016).

Another drug shown to be effective in suppressing NLRP3 inflammasome activation in MS is prednisolone (Yu et al., 2018) (Table 2).

Table 2 Experimental NLRP3 inflammasome inhibitors in EAE Models.

Name of therapeutic agent	Class of therapeutic agent	Organism	EAE model	Inflammasome components affected by treatment	Site of detection	Method of detection	Outcome	References
Ac-YVAD-cmk	Caspase-1 inhibitor	Mouse (C57BL/6)	MOG_{35-55}	IL-18		Flow cytometry, EAE clinical score	Reduced EAE clinical Score in caspase-1 inhibitor treated EAE induced mice Increased IL-18 expression in $CD4^+$ T cells from EAE induced mice	(Lalor et al., 2011)
IFNβ	Cytokine	Mouse (C57BL/6, *Asc*$^{-/-}$, *Nlrp3*$^{-/-}$, *Ifnar1*$^{-/-}$, 2D2 TCR Tg)	Active: MOG_{35-55} Passive: Transfer of $CD4^+$ T cells	IL-1β, Caspase-1	serum spleen	ELISA,WB	Decreased IL-1β and Caspase-1 protein expression in *Asc*$^{-/-}$ and *Nlrp3*$^{-/-}$ EAE-induced mice Decreased IL-1β and Caspase-1 protein expression in IFNβ treated EAE induced mice Increased IL-1β and Caspase-1 protein expression in EAE induced *Ifnar1*$^{-/-}$ mice	(Inoue et al., 2012b)

HU-308	Agonist for CB2 (a peripheral cannabinoid receptor)	Mouse (C57BL/6, CB2R-KO)	8-9 week-old female mice, MOG_{35-55}	NLRP3, IL-1β, Caspase-1	brain spinal cord	WB, RT-PCR	Decreased NLRP3 mRNA; IL-1β, Caspase-1 protein expression in HU-308 treated EAE-induced mice	(Shao et al., 2014)
DRα1-mMOG-35-55	Modified MOG	Mouse (C57BL/6, DR*1501-Tg and DR*1502-Tg mice)	8-12 week-old female mice, MOG_{35-55}	NLRP3, IL-1β	spinal cord	RT-PCR, Flow cyto-metry	Decreased NLRP3 and IL-1β in DRα1-mMOG-35-55 treated EAE-induced DR*1501-Tg mice Increased number of M2 polarized microglia	(Benedek et al., 2015)
MCC950	NLRP3 inflammasome inhibitor	Mouse (C57BL/6)	MOG_{35-55}			EAE clinical score	Attenuation of EAE in MCC950 treated EAE induced mice	(Coll et al., 2015)
IFNβ	Cytokine	Mouse (C57BL/6, *Asc*$^{-/-}$, *Nlrp3*$^{-/-}$, *Cxcr2*$^{fl/fl}$)	6-8 week-old female mice, MOG_{35-55}, Passive induction	IL-1β	spinal cord	ELISA	Increased EAE clinical Score in *Nlrp3*$^{-/-}$ and *Asc*$^{-/-}$ mice Decreased IFNβ efficiency in severe EAE induced mice	(Inoue et al., 2016)

(*Continued*)

Table 2 Experimental NLRP3 inflammasome inhibitors in EAE Models.—cont'd

Name of therapeutic agent	Class of therapeutic agent	Organism	EAE model	Inflammasome components affected by treatment	Site of detection	Method of detection	Outcome	References
Progesterone	Hormone	Mouse (C57BL/6)	6-8 week-old female, mice, 0.2% cuprizone, 5 weeks	NLRP3, IL-18, IBA1, GFAP	corpus callosum	RT-PCR, WB, IF	Decreased NLRP3 and IL-18 mRNA and protein expression in progesterone treated cuprizone induced mice Decreased IBA1 and GFAP positive cells in progesterone treated cuprizone induced mice	(Aryanpour et al., 2017)
JC-171	NLRP3 Inflammasome Inhibitor	Mouse (C57BL/6)	MOG_{35-55}	IL-1β	spinal cord	ELISA	Decreased IL-1β in spinal cord of JC-171 treated EAE induced mice	(Guo et al., 2017)
PNU282987	α7 nAChR Agonist	Mouse (C57BL/6, B6.129P2-$Cnr2^{tm1Dgen}$/J)	8-9 week-old female mice, MOG_{35-55}	NLRP3, Caspase-1, IL-1β, IL-18	spinal cord	WB	Decreased expression of NLRP3, IL-1β, IL-18, Caspase-1, protein expression in spinal cord of PNU282987 treated EAE induced mice	(Ke et al., 2017)

Name of therapeutic agent	Class of therapeutic agent	Organism	EAE model	Inflammasome components affected by treatment	Site of detection	Method of detection	Outcome	References
2ccPA	Natural Phospholipid Mediator	Mouse (C57BL/6)	10 week-old male mice, 0.2% cuprizone, 5-6-10 weeks	NLRP3, IL-1β, P2X7R, IBA1, GFAP	corpus callosum	RT-PCR, IF	Decreased NLRP3, IL-1β, P2X7R, IBA1 and GFAP mRNA expression in 2ccPA treated cuprizone induced mice Decreased IBA1 positive cells in 2cc PA treated cuprizone induced mice	(Yamamoto et al., 2017)
Tetramethylpyrazine	Alkaloid	Mouse (C57BL/6)	12-week-old female mice, MOG_{35-55}	NLRP3, Caspase-1, IL-18, IBA1, GFAP	spinal cord	WB, ELISA, IF	Decreased NLRP3, Caspase-1 and IL-18 protein level in tetramethyl-pyrazine treated EAE-induced mice Decreased microgliosis and astrogliosis in tetramethyl-pyrazine treated EAE-induced mice	(Bai et al., 2018b)

(Continued)

Table 2 Experimental NLRP3 inflammasome inhibitors in EAE Models.—cont'd

Name of therapeutic agent	Class of therapeutic agent	Organism	EAE model	Inflammasome components affected by treatment	Site of detection	Method of detection	Outcome	References
VX-765	Caspase-1 inhibitor	Mouse (C57BL/6)	10-12 week-old female mice, MOG_{35-55}	NLRP3, IL-1β, Caspase-1, NLRP1, Caspase-11, GSDMD, IBA1	hind brain spinal cord	IF, IHC, RT-PCR	Decreased IL-1β, Caspase-1, GSDMD and subsequently microgliosis and pyroptosis in VX-765 treated EAE induced mice Decreased IL-1β, NLRP3, NLRP1, Caspase-1, Caspase-11, mRNA expression	(Mckenzie et al., 2018)
PMX205	Antagonist of C5a receptor	Mouse (Biozzi AB/H)	7-8 week-old, syngeneic Biozzi AB/H spinal cord homogenate (SCH)	NLRP3, IL-1β, ASC, IBA1, AIM2, NLRP1, NLRC4	spinal cord	IHC, RT-PCR, IF	Decreased IL-1β and IBA1 protein expression; NLRP3, IL-1β, ASC, IBA1, AIM2, NLRP1, NLRC4 mRNA expression in PMX205 treated EAE induced mice	(Michailidou et al., 2018)

							Decreased microglial inflammasome activation in C6 antisense treated EAE induced mice	
Prednisone	Corticosteroid	Mouse (C57BL/6)	8 week-old male, mice, 0.3%, cuprizone, 3 weeks	NLRP3, IL-1β, Caspase-1, IBA1, GFAP	corpus callosum	WB, IF	Decreased NLRP3, Caspase-1 and IL-1β protein expression in prednisone treated cuprizone induced mice Decreased IBA1 and GFAP positive cells in prednisone treated cuprizone induced mice	(Yu et al., 2018)
Oligodendrocyte secreted conditioned medium		Mouse (C57BL/6)	10-week-old female mice, MOG_{35-55}	NLRP3, IL-1β, IBA1, GFAP	spinal cord	WB, RT-PCR	Decreased expression of NLRP3, IL-1β, IBA1, GFAP protein levels and IL-1β and GFAP mRNA expression in spinal cord of 100xCM treated mice	(Jahanbazi Jahan-Abad et al., 2019)

(*Continued*)

Table 2 Experimental NLRP3 inflammasome inhibitors in EAE Models.—cont'd

Name of therapeutic agent	Class of therapeutic agent	Organism	EAE model	Inflammasome components affected by treatment	Site of detection	Method of detection	Outcome	References
Rapamycin & MCC950	mTORC1 complex inhibitor & NLRP3 inflammasome inhibitor	Mouse (C57BL/6)	8-10 week-old female, MOG_{35-55}	IL-1β	brain	WB	Decreased IL-1β protein expression in MCC950 treated EAE induced mice	(Xu et al., 2019)

Ac-YVAD-cmk, selective and irreversible caspase-1 inhibitor, *HU-308*, CB2 receptor agonist, *MCC950*, NLRP3 inhibitor, *JC-171*, Inhibitor of IL-1β release, *2ccPA*, 2-carba cyclic phosphatidic acid, *VX765*, Caspase-1 inhibitor, *PMX-205*, Suppressor of ROS-induced activation of the NLRP3 inflammasome.

Prednisolone or prednisone, a prodrug which is metabolized into prednisolone in the liver, is an immunosuppressive drug used in several autoimmune diseases, including asthma and rheumatic disorders (Becker, 2013). A recent study demonstrated the underlying mechanism of the effects of prednisone in MS by using the cuprizone-induced demyelination model (Yu et al., 2018). Prednisone treatment decreased disease scores, improved cognitive function, and reversed demyelination and gliosis. Furthermore, prednisone attenuated NLRP3 inflammasome activation and the subsequent inflammatory cytokine secretion, supporting the idea that NLRP3 inflammasome suppression could be a key mediator for prednisone activity.

Dimethyl fumarate (DMF), another DMD used in MS has been shown to ameliorate NLRP3 inflammasome activation. DMF is an immunomodulatory drug approved by US Food and Drug Administration (FDA) for the treatment of the relapsing forms of multiple sclerosis (RRMS) (Liu, Zhou et al., 2016). The exact mechanism of action of DMF has not been elucidated, but studies showed that DMF modulates nuclear factor erythroid 2-related factor 2-dependent and independent signaling pathways (Yadav, Soin, Ito, & Dhib-Jalbut, 2019) *in vitro* inflammasome model in THP-1 monocytes (Miglio, Veglia, & Fantozzi, 2015) and *in vivo* colitis model (Liu, Zhou et al., 2016). Both studies demonstrated that DMF ameliorated NLRP3 inflammasome activation and decreased the expression of inflammasome markers. However, the effect of DMF on NLRP3 activation in microglial cells has yet to be investigated.

The effects of natural compounds in the amelioration of NLRP3 inflammasome activation have been extensively studied. A myriad of natural compounds have been shown to have anti-inflammatory effect and suppress NLRP3 inflammasome activity in the CNS, including resveratrol (Fu et al., 2013), sulforaphane (Greaney, Maier, Leppla, & Moayeri, 2016), quercetin (Wang, Pan, Zhang, Wang, & Kong, 2012), and curcumin (Li, Wang et al., 2015). These natural compounds possess anti-inflammatory and anti-oxidative effects that ameliorate NLRP3 inflammasome activation. For instance, tetramethylpyrazine found in the herbal medicine chuanxiong has been demonstrated to decrease the expression of inflammasome markers, NLRP3, caspase-1 and IL-18. Additionally, treatment improved the clinical score and reduced microgliosis and astrogliosis in the EAE-induced mice (Bai, Wang et al., 2018). Another natural compound 2-carba-cyclic phosphatidic acid, a phospholipid mediator, improved the clinical score, prevented axonal injury and reduced Iba + microglia in the corpus callosum in the cuprizone model, supporting the potential use of natural compounds

(Yamamoto et al., 2017). Although these tested compounds have different action mechanisms in the suppression of the NLRP3 inflammasome pathway, combinatorial therapies of these natural compounds could have a synergistic effect for MS treatment.

Inhibition of NLRP3 inflammasome complex proteins by small compounds could be a rationale therapeutic approach for autoimmune disorders. The use of caspase-1 inhibitors for MS treatment has been well studied (Lalor et al., 2011; Mckenzie et al., 2018). Caspase-1, the effector protein of the NLRP3 inflammasome complex, is responsible for the maturation of IL-1β and IL-18 that is known to contribute to disease progression. The use of Ac-YVAD-cmk, an inhibitor of caspase-1, led to the suppression of IL-17 and IFN-γ production by $CD4^+$ T cells and subsequently mitigated EAE (Lalor et al., 2011). Another caspase-1 inhibitor, VX-765 has also been shown to be a potent candidate molecule for the treatment of MS. In the study, inhibition of caspase-1 by VX-765 in a EAE induced mice model was sufficient to reduce neuroinflammation, inhibit axonal injury and improve neurobehavioral outcomes. Furthermore, EAE induced mice treated with VX-765 had reduced expressions of IL-1β, GSDMD, caspase-1 proteins and several inflammasome/inflammation related genes in their spinal cords. Finally, VX-765 also reduced NLRP3 inflammasome activation in nigericin induced human fetal primary microglial cells (Mckenzie et al., 2018).

NLRP3 inhibitors have demonstrated to be potential therapeutic targets in MS. A number of studies focused on the use of NLRP3 inhibitors such as MCC950 (Coll et al., 2015; Xu et al., 2019), JC-171 (Guo et al., 2017) for the treatment of MS. Studies revealed that a small molecule inhibitor, MCC950, decreased IL-17 and IFN-γ producing $CD3^+$ T cells and attenuated the severity of disease (Coll et al., 2015). MCC950 treated EAE induced mice had reduced nerve damage, astrogliosis and IL-1β protein expression. Another inhibitor, JC-171, had a similar effect on the EAE progression. Histopathological evaluation of the spinal cord revealed that JC-171 reduced myelin damage and slowed disease progression by decreasing IL-1β protein expression and the number of $IL17A^+$ $CD4^+$ Th17 cells in EAE induced mice (Guo et al., 2017).

A recent study with a novel therapeutic approach revealed the use of 3D-culture system in which neurotrophic factors in oligodendrocyte-derived conditioned media to be effective in reducing demyelination, and the infiltration of immune cells in EAE mice (Jahanbazi Jahan-Abad et al., 2019). Furthermore, conditioned media increased myelin marker expression, suppressed microglial and astrocytic activation, and reduced inflammasome markers NLRP3 and Il-1β by ultimately reducing the severity of EAE. Another novel approach using modified MOG reversed EAE disease progression by reducing immune cell infiltration including monocytes, activated microglia ($CD11b^{+}CD45hi$) and $CD3^{+}$ T cells, expression of pro-inflammatory genes (NLRP3, IL-1β and CD74), altering the polarization state of macrophages and activating critical genes involved in neuronal survival and regeneration (Huwe1, MBP and histone deacetylase 5) (Benedek et al., 2015).

Several candidate molecules have been shown to be potent for the treatment of MS. For example, HU-308, cannabinoid receptor 2 (CB2R) agonist (Shao et al., 2014), progesterone, a hormone (Aryanpour et al., 2017), PNU282987, α7 nicotinic acetylcholine receptors agonist (Ke et al., 2017) and PMX205, C5a receptor antagonist (Michailidou et al., 2018) have all attenuated NLRP3 inflammasome activation and decreased the clinical score in EAE and cuprizone animal models.

HU-308, an agonist for CB2R, leads to autophagy and ameliorates NLRP3 inflammasome activity in the EAE model. By activating the autophagy pathway, HU-308 was able to reduce demyelination and inflammatory cell infiltration and the expression of inflammasome markers both in the brain and spinal cord (Shao et al., 2014). Progesterone, a natural anti-inflammatory hormone, decreases NLRP3 and IL-18 mRNA and protein expressions, protects oligodendrocytes against demyelination and improves behavioral score in EAE induced mice. Progesterone also alteres the polarization state of microglial cells from M1 into M2 phenotype (Aryanpour et al., 2017). A study with PNU282987, a selective α7nAChR agonist, revealed that PNU282987 modulates β-arrestin-1 expression in the spinal cord and decreases the expression of inflammasome markers NLRP3, caspase-1, IL-1β and IL-18 in a β-arrestin-1-mediated manner (Ke et al., 2017).

PMX205, a specific inhibitor of the C5a receptor 1, suppressed NLRP3 inflammasome activation in different cells (Laudisi et al., 2013; Triantafilou, Hughes, Triantafilou, & Morgan, 2013). As a result, inhibition of the complement system by PMX205 decreased genes that are key for inflammasome-related microglial activation: NLRP3, IL-1β, ASC, AIM2, NLR Family Pyrin Domain Containing 1 -NLRP1, NLRC4. PMX205 was also able to reduce IL-1β and Iba1 protein expressions that correlated with reduced demyelination, the extent of axonal injury and improve clinical scores. (Michailidou et al., 2018).

Taken together, there is still a need for potent treatment strategies for MS. The NLRP3 inflammasome pathway could be an ideal candidate for the development of new therapeutic strategies. The regulation of the NLRP3 inflammasome pathway can contribute greatly to the management and treatment of MS. A study using miR-223 mimic and miR-223 deficient mice in EAE could serve as good example for the modulation of the NLRP3 signaling pathway for potential treatment strategies (Cantoni et al., 2017).

10. NLRP3 in MS

Epidemiological studies suggest that the genetic susceptibility as one of the main causes of MS pathology aside from viral infections of EBV or environmental reasons. Gene association studies aim to explain the genetic susceptibility parameters critical in MS development. (Baranzini & Oksenberg, 2017). SNPs in the NLRP3 gene encoding region is of additional importance as inflammasome activity has been previously associated with autoimmune diseases (Table 3). There are about 60 SNPs in the NLRP3 gene which have been linked to several diseases such as cryopyrin-associated periodic syndromes, Muckle Well's syndrome, and AD (Aksentijevich et al., 2002; Compeyrot-Lacassagne, Tran, Guillaume-Czitrom, Marie, & Kone-Paut, 2009; Hoffman, Mueller, Broide, Wanderer, & Kolodner, 2001; Schuh et al., 2015; Zhang et al., 2011). A study in the Iranian population with MS revealed lower frequency of CG rs10754558, and higher frequency of CC rs3806265 in NLRP3 (Imani et al., 2018). In a Brazilian cohort, peripheral blood mononuclear cell (PBMC) analysis for 8 SNPs and inflammasome elements were evaluated. The NLRP3 gene rs35829419 C > A SNP was found to be related to MS severity (Soares, Oliveira, & Pontillo, 2019). This study supports experimental models regarding a constitutive activation of inflammasome in disease pathology that in turn triggers the release of pro-inflammatory cytokines, IL-1β and IL1-18. Elevated IL-18 is reported to be relevant to the clinical progression of MS. In a previous study, same polymorphism exhibited a non-significant trend for the association between IFN- β responders (Malhotra et al., 2015). However, in a larger cohort, the same group reported that the results could not be replicated (Malhotra et al., 2018). The most recent study relates several increased rare variants of NLRP3 and CASP1 genes to MS patients (Vidmar et al., 2019). These mutations reportedly play a key role in the inflammasome signaling pathway and inactivate the inflammasome via autophagy/mitophagy and type-1 interferon response.

Table 3 NLRP3 in multiple sclerosis.

Subjects/(population)	Inflammasome components identified	Method	Main findings	References
Genotype: 403 responders and 386 non-responders (European) Expression: 97 MS patients (28 IFN-β responders, 69 non responder), 14 healthy controls	NLRP3	Genotyping qPCR	A non-significant trend for association between rs35829419 and IFN- β response Baseline mRNA expression levels of NLRP3 increased in PBMC samples of non-responders NLRP3 mRNA expression increased in responders after IFN- β treatment	(Malhotra et al., 2015)
421 IFN-β responders, 198 non responders (European)	14 NLRP3 polymorphisms	TaqMan genotyping	No significant associations between the response to IFN-β and NLRP3 polymorphisms	(Malhotra et al., 2018)
Genotyping: 209 MS, 36 NMO, 233 healthy controls (Brazil)	8 SNPs in NLRP1, NLRP3, NLRC4,	Genotyping qPCR	C > A at rs35829419 in NLRP3 gene related to MS severity	(Soares et al., 2019)

(*Continued*)

Table 3 NLRP3 in multiple sclerosis.—cont'd

Subjects/(population)	Inflammasome components identified	Method	Main findings	References
Expression: after LPS + ATP treatment: 9 MS and 10 healthy controls			The expression of inflammasome genes up-regulated in LPS-treated MS monocytes	
Genotyping: 187 RRMS, 122 healthy controls (Iranian)	NLRP3 (rs10754558, rs3806265, rs4612666 and rs35829419)	TaqMan genotyping qPCR	C > T at rs3806265 NLRP3 are associated with MS risk	(Imani et al., 2018)
			Lower CG genotype at rs10754558 in NLRP3 gene in MS patients	
Expression: 37 MS (18 relapse, 19 remission), 22 healthy controls			NLRP3 expression decreased with IFN- β treatment	
4 MS patients and 9 healthy control brain tissue samples	NLRP3, ASC, Caspase-1	immunohistochemistry	NLRP3, ASC and Caspase-1 and IL-1β expressed in active lesions of MS, reduced in chronic inactive lesions	(Kawana et al., 2013)

15 MS patients and 12 other disease controls, brain tissue samples	Caspase-1, NLRP1, NLRP3, AIM2	qPCR immunohistochemistry	Upregulation of Caspase-1, NLRP1, NLRP3, AIM2 at the transcript level in white matter of MS patients, IL-1β immunoreactivity detected in brain monocytic cells.	(Mckenzie et al., 2014)
7 MS patients, 4 other disease control brain tissue samples and CSF	NLRP3, Caspase-1	qPCR Bioplex ELISA	NLRP3 and IL-1β gene expression levels increased in MS plaques. IL-18 cytokine secretion is also increased in CSF	(Voet et al., 2018)
32 MS patients and 120 age-matched controls serum	Caspase-1, ASC	Protein expression Simple plex assay	Caspase-1, ASC, and IL-18 are elevated in the serum of MS patients	(Keane et al., 2018)
47 MS patients and 46 healthy controls PBMC	Caspase-1	Competitive RT-PCR Western blot	Caspase-1 and IL-18 expression increased in PBMC of MS	(Huang et al., 2004)
MS and control patients after IFN- β treatment PBMC culture	Caspase-1	WB	IFN-β Inhibits Caspase-1 expression in activated monocytes from healthy person (*in vitro*) Lower IL-1β were seen in serum of IL-1 β treated MS patients.	(Guarda et al., 2011)

(*Continued*)

Table 3 NLRP3 in multiple sclerosis.—cont'd

Subjects/(population)	Inflammasome components identified	Method	Main findings	References
32 MS patients and 37 healthy controls	NLRP3 and Caspase-1	qPCR	NLRP3 and Caspase-1 mRNA levels were significantly higher in RRMS	(Peelen et al., 2015)
PBMC in ex vivo assays: 18 MS patients and 21 age-matched healthy controls			Culture supernatant derived from LPS/ATP stimulated PBMC promotes IL-17 and suppresses IL-10 in $CD4^+$ T cells	
30 MS patients (22 women and 8 men) PBMC	NLRP3, ASC, Caspase-1	NLRP3 and ASC: qPCR	mRNA expressions of NLRP3 decreased with IFN-β 1a	(Noroozi et al., 2017)
		Caspase-1: WB	Plasma levels of IL-1β decreased with IFN-β 1a	

NMO, Neuromyelitis optica.

In earlier studies, IL-1β secretion from MHC II^{+} microglia in brain lesions draw attention to the role of inflammasome activation in MS in the CNS (Burm et al., 2016). Inflammasome components have also been evaluated and perivascular macrophages and astrocytes were found to be predominantly located in active MS lesions (Kawana et al., 2013). In addition to former immunohistochemical analysis, significant up-regulation of inflammasome-associated genes (caspase-1, NLRP1, NLRP3, AIM2) and IL-1β in the white matter of MS patients were reported by quantitative PCR (qPCR) (Mckenzie, Reinke, Branton, Lu, & Power, 2014; Voet et al., 2018). Additionally, NLRP3 inflammasome activation end product IL-18 secretion was increased in the CSF of MS patients (Voet et al., 2018).

Peripheral activation of the NLRP3 inflammasomes was detected in serum samples collected from 120 normal donors and 32 MS patients. The protein levels of caspase-1, ASC, and IL-18 in the serum of MS patients were higher when compared to the control group (Keane, Dietrich, & De Rivero Vaccari, 2018). This study suggests ASC and caspase-1 to be biomarkers for MS with high sensitivities at 90% and 80%, respectively.

PBMC derived from MS patients have also been frequently used in studies. IFN- treatment suppress the level of IL1b in serum (Guarda et al., 2011). Elevated caspase-1 mRNA levels were reported in PBMCs derived from MS patients when compared to controls (Huang, Huang, & Hillert, 2004; Peelen et al., 2015). IFN-β modulates the expression of inflammasomes at the mRNA level, thereby decreasing IL-1β secretion and improving the clinical presentation of MS (Noroozi, Meimand, Arababadi, Nakhaee, & Asadikaram, 2017). Women are more sensitive to IFN-β treatment, and a decrease in NLRP3 expression has been reported after 6 months of therapy in females patients but not in males. IFN-β pre-activation enables activated memory T cells to reduce IL-1β release from monocytes. Preactivated human memory T cells can also downregulate the P2X purinoceptor 7 mRNA expression and extracellular calcium following ATP stimulation (Beynon, Quintana, & Weiner, 2012).

There is a clear consensus in the literature that NLRP3 plays a central role in response to IFN-β. Even after IFN-β treatment, responders maintain a decreased level of NLRP3 and IL-1β. Clinical studies have common limitations such as: treatment naïve patients are hard to find, groups are mostly heterogeneous and low in patient number, and studies fail to include ethnicities or sex differences.

11. Future perspective

Since the contribution of microglia to the pathophysiology of MS is well established, they have been the subject of MS research for decades. Up to this point, researchers have been focused on the origin and roles of microglia in disorders of the CNS. The advancement in life science technologies have enabled researchers to identify specific microglial phenotypes, which revealed remarkable differences among healthy or disease associated microglia. However, there are likely sub-microglial phenotypes present in the CNS, and the identification of these sub groups certainly will provide a better understanding of MS (Ajami et al., 2018; Yeh & Ikezu, 2019). Single cell technologies such as mass cytometry will further assist in the identification of new disease associated sub-microglial and oligodendroglial phenotypes in MS (Clark, Lee, Smallwood, Kelsey, & Reik, 2016; Mrdjen et al., 2018; Van Bruggen, Agirre, & Castelo-Branco, 2017). Furthermore, omics studies including genomics, transcriptomics, and epigenomics will play an important role in the characterization of sub-microglial populations in healthy and disease-associated states (Cuevas-Diaz Duran, Wei, & Wu, 2017; Shema, Bernstein, & Buenrostro, 2019). Single-cell high-throughput analysis of the CSF and PBMC samples from MS patients will increase our understanding about MS pathogenesis (Cuevas-Diaz Duran et al., 2017).

The interactions between microglia and other cells in the CNS, including astrocytes, oligodendrocytes, neurons, CNS-resident macrophages and T cells direct the course of disease in MS and its animal models. The characterization of these cell-to-cell interactions using organoids, co-cultures, 3D culture systems, embryonic stem cell or induced pluripotent stem cell technologies will boost our scientific knowledge in MS pathophysiology (Cuascut & Hutton, 2019; Di Ruscio, Patti, Welner, Tenen, & Amabile, 2015; Ormel et al., 2018; Pocock & Piers, 2018; Song, Yan, Marzano, & Li, 2019; Watson, Kavanagh, Allenby, & Vassey, 2017). Future studies using microglial cell type-specific deletion of NLRP3 inflammasome genes and *in vivo* molecular imaging techniques are needed in new knockout and transgenic animal models (Guttenplan & Liddelow, 2019; Voet et al., 2019).

Animal models will continue to contribute to MS research for the development of new treatments and better understanding of the underlying disease mechanism. However, existing animal models could not completely fulfill the complexity and heterogeneity of MS, so novel animal models will be required to recapitulate all aspects of this disorder (Lassmann & Bradl, 2017).

The improvements in basic life science should be translated to the clinical research. New imaging techniques like MRI, optical coherence tomography and positron emission tomography may be of great help in demonstrating the microglial states more effectively in patients (Filippi et al., 2019). Establishment of post-mortem brain tissue banks from healthy and MS patients will immensely contribute to MS research and be an invaluable source for human studies.

In conclusion, these newly developed methods and approaches will certainly elucidate our understanding of the complete role of microglia in MS and give rise to the development of novel, more specific and effective strategies for MS treatment.

Acknowledgments

The authors thank Assistant Prof. Dr. Cigdem TOSUN for her valuable critical reading of the manuscript.

References

Adiele, R. C., & Adiele, C. A. (2019). Metabolic defects in multiple sclerosis. *Mitochondrion, 44*, 7–14.

Ajami, B., Samusik, N., Wieghofer, P., Ho, P. P., Crotti, A., Bjornson, Z., et al. (2018). Single-cell mass cytometry reveals distinct populations of brain myeloid cells in mouse neuroinflammation and neurodegeneration models. *Nature Neuroscience, 21*, 541–551.

Aksentijevich, I., Nowak, M., Mallah, M., Chae, J. J., Watford, W. T., Hofmann, S. R., et al. (2002). De novo CIAS1 mutations, cytokine activation, and evidence for genetic heterogeneity in patients with neonatal-onset multisystem inflammatory disease (NOMID): A new member of the expanding family of pyrin-associated autoinflammatory diseases. *Arthritis & Rheumatism, 46*, 3340–3348.

Allam, R., Lawlor, K. E., Yu, E. C., Mildenhall, A. L., Moujalled, D. M., Lewis, R. S., et al. (2014). Mitochondrial apoptosis is dispensable for NLRP3 inflammasome activation but non-apoptotic caspase-8 is required for inflammasome priming. *EMBO Reports, 15*, 982–990.

Areschoug, T., & Gordon, S. (2008). Pattern recognition receptors and their role in innate immunity: Focus on microbial protein ligands. *Contributions to Microbiology, 15*, 45–60.

Arneth, B. M. (2019). Impact of B cells to the pathophysiology of multiple sclerosis. *Journal of Neuroinflammation, 16*, 128.

Aryanpour, R., Pasbakhsh, P., Zibara, K., Namjoo, Z., Beigi Boroujeni, F., Shahbeigi, S., et al. (2017). Progesterone therapy induces an M1 to M2 switch in microglia phenotype and suppresses NLRP3 inflammasome in a cuprizone-induced demyelination mouse model. *International Immunopharmacology, 51*, 131–139.

Astier, A. L., Meiffren, G., Freeman, S., & Hafler, D. A. (2006). Alterations in CD46-mediated Tr1 regulatory T cells in patients with multiple sclerosis. *Journal of Clinical Investigation, 116*, 3252–3257.

Baecher-Allan, C., Kaskow, B. J., & Weiner, H. L. (2018). Multiple sclerosis: Mechanisms and immunotherapy. *Neuron, 97*, 742–768.

Bai, H., Yang, B., Yu, W., Xiao, Y., Yu, D., & Zhang, Q. (2018a). Cathepsin B links oxidative stress to the activation of NLRP3 inflammasome. *Experimental Cell Research, 362*, 180–187.

Bai, X. Y., Wang, X. F., Zhang, L. S., Du, P. C., Cao, Z., & Hou, Y. (2018b). Tetramethylpyrazine ameliorates experimental autoimmune encephalomyelitis by modulating the inflammatory response. *Biochemical and Biophysical Research Communications, 503*, 1968–1972.

Bar, E., & Barak, B. (2019). Microglia roles in synaptic plasticity and myelination in homeostatic conditions and neurodevelopmental disorders. *Glia*. http://dx.doi.org/10.1002/glia.23637. PMID: 31058364. [Epub ahead of print] Review.

Baranzini, S. E., & Oksenberg, J. R. (2017). The genetics of multiple sclerosis: From 0 to 200 in 50 years. *Trends in genetics, 33*, 960–970.

Becker, D. E. (2013). Basic and clinical pharmacology of glucocorticosteroids. *Anesthesia Progress, 60*, 25–31. quiz 32.

Bedoui, Y., Neal, J. W., & Gasque, P. (2018). The neuro-immune-regulators (NIREGs) promote tissue resilience; a vital component of the host's defense strategy against neuroinflammation. *Journal of Neuroimmune Pharmacology, 13*, 309–329.

Benedek, G., Meza-Romero, R., Jordan, K., Keenlyside, L., Offner, H., & Vandenbark, A. A. (2015). HLA-DRalpha1-mMOG-35-55 treatment of experimental autoimmune encephalomyelitis reduces CNS inflammation, enhances M2 macrophage frequency, and promotes neuroprotection. *Journal of Neuroinflammation, 12*, 123.

Beynon, V., Quintana, F. J., & Weiner, H. L. (2012). Activated human CD4+CD45RO+ memory T-cells indirectly inhibit NLRP3 inflammasome activation through downregulation of P2X7R signalling. *PLoS One, 7*, e39576.

Billiau, A., & Matthys, P. (2001). Modes of action of Freund's adjuvants in experimental models of autoimmune diseases. *Journal of Leukocyte Biology, 70*, 849–860.

Bortolotti, P., Faure, E., & Kipnis, E. (2018). Inflammasomes in tissue damages and immune disorders after trauma. *Frontiers in Immunology, 9*, 1900.

Bossu, P., Salani, F., Cacciari, C., Picchetto, L., Cao, M., Bizzoni, F., et al. (2009). Disease outcome, alexithymia and depression are differently associated with serum IL-18 levels in acute stroke. *Current Neurovascular Research, 6*, 163–170.

Braga, T. T., Forni, M. F., Correa-Costa, M., Ramos, R. N., Barbuto, J. A., Branco, P., et al. (2017). Soluble uric acid activates the NLRP3 inflammasome. *Scientific Reports, 7*, 39884.

Brambilla, R. (2019). The contribution of astrocytes to the neuroinflammatory response in multiple sclerosis and experimental autoimmune encephalomyelitis. *Acta Neuropathologica, 137*, 757–783.

Brown, M. A., & Weinberg, R. B. (2018). Mast cells and innate lymphoid cells: Underappreciated players in CNS autoimmune demyelinating disease. *Frontiers in Immunology, 9*, 514.

Browne, P., Chandraratna, D., Angood, C., Tremlett, H., Baker, C., Taylor, B. V., et al. (2014). Atlas of multiple sclerosis 2013: A growing global problem with widespread inequity. *Neurology, 83*, 1022–1024.

Broz, P., & Dixit, V. M. (2016). Inflammasomes: Mechanism of assembly, regulation and signalling. *Nature Reviews Immunology, 16*, 407–420.

Burm, S. M., Peferoen, L. A., Zuiderwijk-Sick, E. A., Haanstra, K. G., T Hart, B. A., Van Der Valk, P., et al. (2016). Expression of IL-1beta in rhesus EAE and MS lesions is mainly induced in the CNS itself. *Journal of Neuroinflammation, 13*, 138.

Campbell, G., & Mahad, D. J. (2018). Mitochondrial dysfunction and axon degeneration in progressive multiple sclerosis. *FEBS Letters, 592*, 1113–1121.

Cantoni, C., Cignarella, F., Ghezzi, L., Mikesell, B., Bollman, B., Berrien-Elliott, M. M., et al. (2017). Mir-223 regulates the number and function of myeloid-derived suppressor cells in multiple sclerosis and experimental autoimmune encephalomyelitis. *Acta Neuropathologica, 133*, 61–77.

Centonze, D., Muzio, L., Rossi, S., Cavasinni, F., De Chiara, V., Bergami, A., et al. (2009). Inflammation triggers synaptic alteration and degeneration in experimental autoimmune encephalomyelitis. *Journal of Neuroscience, 29*, 3442–3452.

Centonze, D., Muzio, L., Rossi, S., Furlan, R., Bernardi, G., & Martino, G. (2010). The link between inflammation, synaptic transmission and neurodegeneration in multiple sclerosis. *Cell Death & Differentiation, 17*, 1083–1091.

Chaix, J., Tessmer, M. S., Hoebe, K., Fuseri, N., Ryffel, B., Dalod, M., et al. (2008). Cutting edge: Priming of NK cells by IL-18. *The Journal of Immunology, 181*, 1627–1631.

Chen, J., & Chen, Z. J. (2018). PtdIns4P on dispersed trans-Golgi network mediates NLRP3 inflammasome activation. *Nature, 564*, 71–76.

Clark, S. J., Lee, H. J., Smallwood, S. A., Kelsey, G., & Reik, W. (2016). Single-cell epigenomics: Powerful new methods for understanding gene regulation and cell identity. *Genome Biology, 17*, 72.

Coll, R. C., Robertson, A. A., Chae, J. J., Higgins, S. C., Munoz-Planillo, R., Inserra, M. C., et al. (2015). A small-molecule inhibitor of the NLRP3 inflammasome for the treatment of inflammatory diseases. *Nature Medicine, 21*, 248–255.

Colonna, M., & Butovsky, O. (2017). Microglia function in the central nervous system during Health and neurodegeneration. *Annual Review of Immunology, 35*, 441–468.

Compeyrot-Lacassagne, S., Tran, T. A., Guillaume-Czitrom, S., Marie, I., & Kone-Paut, I. (2009). Brain multiple sclerosis-like lesions in a patient with Muckle-Wells syndrome. *Rheumatology, 48*, 1618–1619.

Constantinescu, C. S., Farooqi, N., O'brien, K., & Gran, B. (2011). Experimental autoimmune encephalomyelitis (EAE) as a model for multiple sclerosis (MS). *British Journal of Pharmacology, 164*, 1079–1106.

Correale, J., Marrodan, M., & Ysrraelit, M. C. (2019). Mechanisms of neurodegeneration and axonal dysfunction in progressive multiple sclerosis. *Biomedicines, 7*.

Csordas, G., & Hajnoczky, G. (2009). SR/ER-mitochondrial local communication: Calcium and ROS. *Biochimica et Biophysica Acta, 1787*, 1352–1362.

Cuascut, F. X., & Hutton, G. J. (2019). Stem cell-based therapies for multiple sclerosis: Current perspectives. *Biomedicines, 7*.

Cuevas-Diaz Duran, R., Wei, H., & Wu, J. Q. (2017). Single-cell RNA-sequencing of the brain. *Clinical and Translational Medicine, 6*, 20.

Cui, Y., & Wan, Q. (2019). NKT cells in neurological diseases. *Frontiers in Cellular Neuroscience, 13*, 245.

Danikowski, K. M., Jayaraman, S., & Prabhakar, B. S. (2017). Regulatory T cells in multiple sclerosis and myasthenia gravis. *Journal of Neuroinflammation, 14*, 117.

Das, T., Chen, Z., Hendriks, R. W., & Kool, M. (2018). A20/Tumor necrosis factor alpha-induced protein 3 in immune cells controls development of autoinflammation and autoimmunity: Lessons from mouse models. *Frontiers in Immunology, 9*, 104.

Delbridge, L. M., & O'riordan, M. X. (2007). Innate recognition of intracellular bacteria. *Current Opinion in Immunology, 19*, 10–16.

Deng, J., Yu, X. Q., & Wang, P. H. (2019). Inflammasome activation and Th17 responses. *Molecular Immunology, 107*, 142–164.

Di Ruscio, A., Patti, F., Welner, R. S., Tenen, D. G., & Amabile, G. (2015). Multiple sclerosis: Getting personal with induced pluripotent stem cells. *Cell Death & Disease, 6*, e1806.

Dinarello, C. A. (2018). Overview of the IL-1 family in innate inflammation and acquired immunity. *Immunological Reviews, 281*, 8–27.

Dubbelaar, M. L., Kracht, L., Eggen, B. J. L., & Boddeke, E. (2018). The kaleidoscope of microglial phenotypes. *Frontiers in Immunology, 9*, 1753.

Evavold, C. L., & Kagan, J. C. (2018). How inflammasomes inform adaptive immunity. *Journal of Molecular Biology, 430*, 217–237.
Eyo, U. B., & Wu, L. J. (2019). Microglia: Lifelong patrolling immune cells of the brain. *Progress in Neurobiology, 179*, 101614.
Fann, D. Y., Lee, S. Y., Manzanero, S., Tang, S. C., Gelderblom, M., Chunduri, P., et al. (2013). Intravenous immunoglobulin suppresses NLRP1 and NLRP3 inflammasome-mediated neuronal death in ischemic stroke. *Cell Death & Disease, 4*, e790.
Faustin, B., Chen, Y., Zhai, D., Le Negrate, G., Lartigue, L., Satterthwait, A., et al. (2009). Mechanism of Bcl-2 and Bcl-X(L) inhibition of NLRP1 inflammasome: Loop domain-dependent suppression of ATP binding and oligomerization. *Proceedings of the National Academy of Sciences of the U S A, 106*, 3935–3940.
Ferrari, C. C., Depino, A. M., Prada, F., Muraro, N., Campbell, S., Podhajcer, O., et al. (2004). Reversible demyelination, blood-brain barrier breakdown, and pronounced neutrophil recruitment induced by chronic IL-1 expression in the brain. *American Journal Of Pathology, 165*, 1827–1837.
Fiebich, B. L., Akter, S., & Akundi, R. S. (2014). The two-hit hypothesis for neuroinflammation: Role of exogenous ATP in modulating inflammation in the brain. *Frontiers in Cellular Neuroscience, 8*, 260.
Filippi, M., Bar-Or, A., Piehl, F., Preziosa, P., Solari, A., Vukusic, S., et al. (2018). Multiple sclerosis. *Nat Rev Dis Primers, 4*, 43.
Filippi, M., Bruck, W., Chard, D., Fazekas, F., Geurts, J. J. G., Enzinger, C., et al.Attendees of the Correlation Between, P., and Workshop, M.R.I.F.I.M. (2019). Association between pathological and MRI findings in multiple sclerosis. *The Lancet Neurology, 18*, 198–210.
Freeman, L., Guo, H., David, C. N., Brickey, W. J., Jha, S., & Ting, J. P. (2017). NLR members NLRC4 and NLRP3 mediate sterile inflammasome activation in microglia and astrocytes. *Journal of Experimental Medicine, 214*, 1351–1370.
Fu, Y., Wang, Y., Du, L., Xu, C., Cao, J., Fan, T., et al. (2013). Resveratrol inhibits ionising irradiation-induced inflammation in MSCs by activating SIRT1 and limiting NLRP-3 inflammasome activation. *International Journal of Molecular Sciences, 14*, 14105–14118.
Garlanda, C., Dinarello, C. A., & Mantovani, A. (2013). The interleukin-1 family: Back to the future. *Immunity, 39*, 1003–1018.
Genc, B., Bozan, H. R., Genc, S., & Genc, K. (2019). Stem cell therapy for multiple sclerosis. *Advances in Experimental Medicine & Biology, 1084*, 145–174. http://dx.doi.org/10.1007/5584_2018_247. PMID: 30039439.
Genc, K., Dona, D. L., & Reder, A. T. (1997). Increased CD80(+) B cells in active multiple sclerosis and reversal by interferon beta-1b therapy. *Journal of Clinical Investigation, 99*, 2664–2671.
Gerhauser, I., Hansmann, F., Ciurkiewicz, M., Loscher, W., & Beineke, A. (2019). Facets of Theiler's murine encephalomyelitis virus-induced diseases: An update. *International Journal of Molecular Sciences, 20*.
Gharagozloo, M., Gris, K. V., Mahvelati, T., Amrani, A., Lukens, J. R., & Gris, D. (2017). NLR-dependent regulation of inflammation in multiple sclerosis. *Frontiers in Immunology, 8*, 2012.
Gong, Z., Pan, J., Shen, Q., Li, M., & Peng, Y. (2018). Mitochondrial dysfunction induces NLRP3 inflammasome activation during cerebral ischemia/reperfusion injury. *Journal of Neuroinflammation, 15*, 242.
Gosselin, D., & Rivest, S. (2007). Role of IL-1 and TNF in the brain: Twenty years of progress on a Dr. Jekyll/Mr. Hyde duality of the innate immune system. *Brain, Behavior, and Immunity, 21*, 281–289.

Greaney, A. J., Maier, N. K., Leppla, S. H., & Moayeri, M. (2016). Sulforaphane inhibits multiple inflammasomes through an Nrf2-independent mechanism. *Journal of Leukocyte Biology, 99*, 189–199.

Green, J. P., Yu, S., Martin-Sanchez, F., Pelegrin, P., Lopez-Castejon, G., Lawrence, C. B., et al. (2018). Chloride regulates dynamic NLRP3-dependent ASC oligomerization and inflammasome priming. *Proceedings of the National Academy of Sciences of the U S A, 115*, E9371–E9380.

Gris, D., Ye, Z., Iocca, H. A., Wen, H., Craven, R. R., Gris, P., et al. (2010). NLRP3 plays a critical role in the development of experimental autoimmune encephalomyelitis by mediating Th1 and Th17 responses. *The Journal of Immunology, 185*, 974–981.

Groslambert, M., & Py, B. F. (2018). Spotlight on the NLRP3 inflammasome pathway. *Journal of Inflammation Research, 11*, 359–374.

Gross, C. C., Schulte-Mecklenbeck, A., Wiendl, H., Marcenaro, E., Kerlero De Rosbo, N., Uccelli, A., et al. (2016a). Regulatory functions of natural killer cells in multiple sclerosis. *Frontiers in Immunology, 7*, 606.

Gross, C. J., Mishra, R., Schneider, K. S., Medard, G., Wettmarshausen, J., Dittlein, D. C., et al. (2016b). K(+) efflux-independent NLRP3 inflammasome activation by small molecules targeting Mitochondria. *Immunity, 45*, 761–773.

Guarda, G., Braun, M., Staehli, F., Tardivel, A., Mattmann, C., Forster, I., et al. (2011). Type I interferon inhibits interleukin-1 production and inflammasome activation. *Immunity, 34*, 213–223.

Guo, C., Chi, Z., Jiang, D., Xu, T., Yu, W., Wang, Z., et al. (2018). Cholesterol homeostatic regulator SCAP-SREBP2 integrates NLRP3 inflammasome activation and cholesterol Biosynthetic signaling in macrophages. *Immunity, 49*, 842–856 e847.

Guo, C., Fulp, J. W., Jiang, Y., Li, X., Chojnacki, J. E., Wu, J., et al. (2017). Development and characterization of a hydroxyl-sulfonamide analogue, 5-chloro-N-[2-(4-hydroxysulfamoyl-phenyl)-ethyl]-2-methoxy-benzamide, as a novel NLRP3 inflammasome inhibitor for potential treatment of multiple sclerosis. *ACS Chemical Neuroscience, 8*, 2194–2201.

Gurung, P., Anand, P. K., Malireddi, R. K., Vande Walle, L., Van Opdenbosch, N., Dillon, C. P., et al. (2014). FADD and caspase-8 mediate priming and activation of the canonical and noncanonical Nlrp3 inflammasomes. *The Journal of Immunology, 192*, 1835–1846.

Gurung, P., & Kanneganti, T. D. (2015). Novel roles for caspase-8 in IL-1beta and inflammasome regulation. *American Journal Of Pathology, 185*, 17–25.

Guttenplan, K. A., & Liddelow, S. A. (2019). Astrocytes and microglia: Models and tools. *Journal of Experimental Medicine, 216*, 71–83.

Hanamsagar, R., Torres, V., & Kielian, T. (2011). Inflammasome activation and IL-1beta/IL-18 processing are influenced by distinct pathways in microglia. *Journal of Neurochemistry, 119*, 736–748.

Hannocks, M. J., Zhang, X., Gerwien, H., Chashchina, A., Burmeister, M., Korpos, E., et al. (2019). The gelatinases, MMP-2 and MMP-9, as fine tuners of neuroinflammatory processes. *Matrix Biology, 75–76*, 102–113.

Harrison, O. J., Srinivasan, N., Pott, J., Schiering, C., Krausgruber, T., Ilott, N. E., et al. (2015). Epithelial-derived IL-18 regulates Th17 cell differentiation and Foxp3(+) Treg cell function in the intestine. *Mucosal Immunology, 8*, 1226–1236.

Hemmer, B., Kerschensteiner, M., & Korn, T. (2015). Role of the innate and adaptive immune responses in the course of multiple sclerosis. *The Lancet Neurology, 14*, 406–419.

Heneka, M. T., Kummer, M. P., & Latz, E. (2014). Innate immune activation in neurodegenerative disease. *Nature Reviews Immunology, 14*, 463–477.

Hinkle, J. T., Dawson, V. L., & Dawson, T. M. (2019). The A1 astrocyte paradigm: New avenues for pharmacological intervention in neurodegeneration. *Movement Disorders, 34*, 959–969.

Hoffman, H. M., Mueller, J. L., Broide, D. H., Wanderer, A. A., & Kolodner, R. D. (2001). Mutation of a new gene encoding a putative pyrin-like protein causes familial cold autoinflammatory syndrome and Muckle-Wells syndrome. *Nature Genetics, 29*, 301–305.

Hornung, V., Bauernfeind, F., Halle, A., Samstad, E. O., Kono, H., Rock, K. L., et al. (2008). Silica crystals and aluminum salts activate the NALP3 inflammasome through phagosomal destabilization. *Nature Immunology, 9*, 847–856.

Huang, W. X., Huang, P., & Hillert, J. (2004). Increased expression of caspase-1 and interleukin-18 in peripheral blood mononuclear cells in patients with multiple sclerosis. *Multiple Sclerosis, 10*, 482–487.

Ikegami, A., Haruwaka, K., & Wake, H. (2019). Microglia: Lifelong modulator of neural circuits. *Neuropathology, 39*, 173–180.

Imani, D., Azimi, A., Salehi, Z., Rezaei, N., Emamnejad, R., Sadr, M., et al. (2018). Association of nod-like receptor protein-3 single nucleotide gene polymorphisms and expression with the susceptibility to relapsing-remitting multiple sclerosis. *International Journal of Immunogenetics, 45*, 329–336.

Inoue, M., Chen, P. H., Siecinski, S., Li, Q. J., Liu, C., Steinman, L., et al. (2016). An interferon-beta-resistant and NLRP3 inflammasome-independent subtype of EAE with neuronal damage. *Nature Neuroscience, 19*, 1599–1609.

Inoue, M., & Shinohara, M. L. (2013). NLRP3 inflammasome and MS/EAE. *Autoimmune Diseases, 2013*, 859145.

Inoue, M., Williams, K. L., Gunn, M. D., & Shinohara, M. L. (2012a). NLRP3 inflammasome induces chemotactic immune cell migration to the CNS in experimental autoimmune encephalomyelitis. *Proceedings of the National Academy of Sciences of the U S A, 109*, 10480–10485.

Inoue, M., Williams, K. L., Oliver, T., Vandenabeele, P., Rajan, J. V., Miao, E. A., et al. (2012b). Interferon-beta therapy against EAE is effective only when development of the disease depends on the NLRP3 inflammasome. *Science Signaling, 5*, ra38.

Iyer, S. S., He, Q., Janczy, J. R., Elliott, E. I., Zhong, Z., Olivier, A. K., et al. (2013). Mitochondrial cardiolipin is required for Nlrp3 inflammasome activation. *Immunity, 39*, 311–323.

Jafarzadeh, A., & Nemati, M. (2018). Therapeutic potentials of ginger for treatment of multiple sclerosis: A review with emphasis on its immunomodulatory, anti-inflammatory and anti-oxidative properties. *Journal of Neuroimmunology, 324*, 54–75.

Jahanbazi Jahan-Abad, A., Karima, S., Sahab Negah, S., Noorbakhsh, F., Borhani-Haghighi, M., & Gorji, A. (2019). Therapeutic potential of conditioned medium derived from oligodendrocytes cultured in a self-assembling peptide nanoscaffold in experimental autoimmune encephalomyelitis. *Brain Research, 1711*, 226–235.

Jha, S., Srivastava, S. Y., Brickey, W. J., Iocca, H., Toews, A., Morrison, J. P., et al. (2010). The inflammasome sensor, NLRP3, regulates CNS inflammation and demyelination via caspase-1 and interleukin-18. *Journal of Neuroscience, 30*, 15811–15820.

Johann, S., Heitzer, M., Kanagaratnam, M., Goswami, A., Rizo, T., Weis, J., et al. (2015). NLRP3 inflammasome is expressed by astrocytes in the SOD1 mouse model of ALS and in human sporadic ALS patients. *Glia, 63*, 2260–2273.

Kabba, J. A., Xu, Y., Christian, H., Ruan, W., Chenai, K., Xiang, Y., et al. (2018). Microglia: Housekeeper of the central nervous system. *Cellular and Molecular Neurobiology, 38*, 53–71.

Karni, A., Koldzic, D. N., Bharanidharan, P., Khoury, S. J., & Weiner, H. L. (2002). IL-18 is linked to raised IFN-gamma in multiple sclerosis and is induced by activated CD4(+) T cells via CD40-CD40 ligand interactions. *Journal of Neuroimmunology, 125*, 134–140.

Kawana, N., Yamamoto, Y., Ishida, T., Saito, Y., Konno, H., Arima, K., et al. (2013). Reactive astrocytes and perivascular macrophages express NLRP3 inflammasome in active demyelinating lesions of multiple sclerosis and necrotic lesions of neuromyelitis optica and cerebral infarction. *Clinical and Experimental Neuroimmunology, 4*, 296–304.

Ke, P., Shao, B. Z., Xu, Z. Q., Chen, X. W., Wei, W., & Liu, C. (2017). Activating alpha7 nicotinic acetylcholine receptor inhibits NLRP3 inflammasome through regulation of beta-arrestin-1. *CNS Neuroscience and Therapeutics, 23*, 875–884.

Keane, R. W., Dietrich, W. D., & De Rivero Vaccari, J. P. (2018). Inflammasome proteins as biomarkers of multiple sclerosis. *Frontiers in Neurology, 9*, 135.

Kettenmann, H., Hanisch, U. K., Noda, M., & Verkhratsky, A. (2011). Physiology of microglia. *Physiological Reviews, 91*, 461–553.

Kierdorf, K., & Prinz, M. (2017). Microglia in steady state. *Journal of Clinical Investigation, 127*, 3201–3209.

Kipp, M., Nyamoya, S., Hochstrasser, T., & Amor, S. (2017). Multiple sclerosis animal models: A clinical and histopathological perspective. *Brain Pathology, 27*, 123–137.

Klaren, R. E., Motl, R. W., Woods, J. A., & Miller, S. D. (2014). Effects of exercise in experimental autoimmune encephalomyelitis (an animal model of multiple sclerosis). *Journal of Neuroimmunology, 274*, 14–19.

Klineova, S., & Lublin, F. D. (2018). Clinical course of multiple sclerosis. *Cold Spring Harb Perspect Med, 8*.

Kostic, M., Zivkovic, N., & Stojanovic, I. (2013). Multiple sclerosis and glutamate excitotoxicity. *Reviews in the Neurosciences, 24*, 71–88.

Kothur, K., Wienholt, L., Brilot, F., & Dale, R. C. (2016). CSF cytokines/chemokines as biomarkers in neuroinflammatory CNS disorders: A systematic review. *Cytokine, 77*, 227–237.

Kumar, H., Kawai, T., & Akira, S. (2011). Pathogen recognition by the innate immune system. *International Reviews of Immunology, 30*, 16–34.

Lalor, S. J., Dungan, L. S., Sutton, C. E., Basdeo, S. A., Fletcher, J. M., & Mills, K. H. (2011). Caspase-1-processed cytokines IL-1beta and IL-18 promote IL-17 production by gammadelta and CD4 T cells that mediate autoimmunity. *The Journal of Immunology, 186*, 5738–5748.

Lassmann, H. (2018). Multiple sclerosis pathology. *Cold Spring Harb Perspect Med, 8*.

Lassmann, H., & Bradl, M. (2017). Multiple sclerosis: Experimental models and reality. *Acta Neuropathologica, 133*, 223–244.

Laudisi, F., Spreafico, R., Evrard, M., Hughes, T. R., Mandriani, B., Kandasamy, M., et al. (2013). Cutting edge: The NLRP3 inflammasome links complement-mediated inflammation and IL-1beta release. *The Journal of Immunology, 191*, 1006–1010.

Leal-Lasarte, M. M., Franco, J. M., Labrador-Garrido, A., Pozo, D., & Roodveldt, C. (2017). Extracellular TDP-43 aggregates target MAPK/MAK/MRK overlapping kinase (MOK) and trigger caspase-3/IL-18 signaling in microglia. *The FASEB Journal, 31*, 2797–2816.

Lee, E., Hwang, I., Park, S., Hong, S., Hwang, B., Cho, Y., et al. (2019). MPTP-driven NLRP3 inflammasome activation in microglia plays a central role in dopaminergic neurodegeneration. *Cell Death & Differentiation, 26*, 213–228.

Leemans, J. C., Cassel, S. L., & Sutterwala, F. S. (2011). Sensing damage by the NLRP3 inflammasome. *Immunological Reviews, 243*, 152–162.

Lemasters, J. J., Theruvath, T. P., Zhong, Z., & Nieminen, A. L. (2009). Mitochondrial calcium and the permeability transition in cell death. *Biochimica et Biophysica Acta, 1787*, 1395–1401.

Lenz, K. M., & Nelson, L. H. (2018). Microglia and beyond: Innate immune cells as regulators of brain development and behavioral function. *Frontiers in Immunology, 9*, 698.

Li, Q., & Barres, B. A. (2018). Microglia and macrophages in brain homeostasis and disease. *Nature Reviews Immunology, 18*, 225–242.

Li, L., Ismael, S., Nasoohi, S., Sakata, K., Liao, F. F., Mcdonald, M. P., et al. (2019b). Thioredoxin-interacting protein (TXNIP) associated NLRP3 inflammasome activation in human alzheimer's disease brain. *Journal of Alzheimer's Disease, 68*, 255–265.

Li, Y., Li, J., Li, S., Li, Y., Wang, X., Liu, B., et al. (2015b). Curcumin attenuates glutamate neurotoxicity in the hippocampus by suppression of ER stress-associated TXNIP/NLRP3 inflammasome activation in a manner dependent on AMPK. *Toxicology and Applied Pharmacology, 286*, 53–63.

Li, K., Li, J., Zheng, J., & Qin, S. (2019a). Reactive astrocytes in neurodegenerative diseases. *Aging Dis, 10*, 664–675.

Li, R., Patterson, K. R., & Bar-Or, A. (2018). Reassessing B cell contributions in multiple sclerosis. *Nature Immunology, 19*, 696–707.

Li, R., Rezk, A., Miyazaki, Y., Hilgenberg, E., Touil, H., Shen, P., et al. (2015a). Proinflammatory GM-CSF-producing B cells in multiple sclerosis and B cell depletion therapy. *Science Translational Medicine, 7*, 310ra166.

Liddelow, S. A., Guttenplan, K. A., Clarke, L. E., Bennett, F. C., Bohlen, C. J., Schirmer, L., et al. (2017). Neurotoxic reactive astrocytes are induced by activated microglia. *Nature, 541*, 481–487.

Lin, C. C., & Edelson, B. T. (2017). New insights into the role of IL-1beta in experimental autoimmune encephalomyelitis and multiple sclerosis. *The Journal of Immunology, 198*, 4553–4560.

Lin, Z. H., Wang, S. Y., Chen, L. L., Zhuang, J. Y., Ke, Q. F., Xiao, D. R., et al. (2017). Methylene Blue Mitigates acute neuroinflammation after spinal cord injury through inhibiting NLRP3 inflammasome activation in microglia. *Frontiers in Cellular Neuroscience, 11*, 391.

Liu, X., Zhang, Z., Ruan, J., Pan, Y., Magupalli, V. G., Wu, H., et al. (2016a). Inflammasome-activated gasdermin D causes pyroptosis by forming membrane pores. *Nature, 535*, 153–158.

Liu, X., Zhou, W., Zhang, X., Lu, P., Du, Q., Tao, L., et al. (2016b). Dimethyl fumarate ameliorates dextran sulfate sodium-induced murine experimental colitis by activating Nrf2 and suppressing NLRP3 inflammasome activation. *Biochemical Pharmacology, 112*, 37–49.

Liu, Y., Given, K. S., Harlow, D. E., Matschulat, A. M., Macklin, W. B., Bennett, J. L., et al. (2017). Myelin-specific multiple sclerosis antibodies cause complement-dependent oligodendrocyte loss and demyelination. *Acta Neuropathol Commun, 5*, 25.

Lloyd, A. F., Davies, C. L., & Miron, V. E. (2017). Microglia: Origins, homeostasis, and roles in myelin repair. *Current Opinion in Neurobiology, 47*, 113–120.

Lukens, J. R., Barr, M. J., Chaplin, D. D., Chi, H., & Kanneganti, T. D. (2012). Inflammasome-derived IL-1beta regulates the production of GM-CSF by CD4(+) T cells and gammadelta T cells. *The Journal of Immunology, 188*, 3107–3115.

Luo, C., Jian, C., Liao, Y., Huang, Q., Wu, Y., Liu, X., et al. (2017). The role of microglia in multiple sclerosis. *Neuropsychiatric Disease and Treatment, 13*, 1661–1667.

Malhotra, S., Rio, J., Urcelay, E., Nurtdinov, R., Bustamante, M. F., Fernandez, O., et al. (2015). NLRP3 inflammasome is associated with the response to IFN-beta in patients with multiple sclerosis. *Brain, 138*, 644–652.

Malhotra, S., Sorosina, M., Rio, J., Peroni, S., Midaglia, L., Villar, L. M., et al. (2018). NLRP3 polymorphisms and response to interferon-beta in multiple sclerosis patients. *Multiple Sclerosis, 24*, 1507–1510.

Malik, A., & Kanneganti, T. D. (2017). Inflammasome activation and assembly at a glance. *Journal of Cell Science, 130*, 3955–3963.

Malik, S., Want, M. Y., & Awasthi, A. (2016). The emerging roles of gamma-delta T cells in tissue inflammation in experimental autoimmune encephalomyelitis. *Frontiers in Immunology, 7*, 14.

Mammana, S., Fagone, P., Cavalli, E., Basile, M. S., Petralia, M. C., Nicoletti, F., et al. (2018). The role of macrophages in neuroinflammatory and neurodegenerative pathways of alzheimer's disease, amyotrophic lateral sclerosis, and multiple sclerosis: Pathogenetic cellular effectors and potential therapeutic targets. *International Journal of Molecular Sciences, 19.*

Mangan, M. S. J., Olhava, E. J., Roush, W. R., Seidel, H. M., Glick, G. D., & Latz, E. (2018). Targeting the NLRP3 inflammasome in inflammatory diseases. *Nature Reviews Drug Discovery, 17*, 588–606.

Mao, Z., Liu, C., Ji, S., Yang, Q., Ye, H., Han, H., et al. (2017). The NLRP3 inflammasome is involved in the pathogenesis of Parkinson's disease in rats. *Neurochemical Research, 42*, 1104–1115.

Marinelli, S., Basilico, B., Marrone, M. C., & Ragozzino, D. (2019). Microglia-neuron cross-talk: Signaling mechanism and control of synaptic transmission. *Seminars in Cell & Developmental Biology, 94*. pii: S1084-9521(18)30170-8. https://doi.org/10.1016/j.semcdb.2019.05.017. PMID: 31112798, [Epubahead of print] Review

Martinon, F., Burns, K., & Tschopp, J. (2002). The inflammasome: A molecular platform triggering activation of inflammatory caspases and processing of proIL-beta. *Molecular Cell, 10*, 417–426.

Mccandless, E. E., Budde, M., Lees, J. R., Dorsey, D., Lyng, E., & Klein, R. S. (2009). IL-1R signaling within the central nervous system regulates CXCL12 expression at the blood-brain barrier and disease severity during experimental autoimmune encephalomyelitis. *The Journal of Immunology, 183*, 613–620.

Mckenzie, B., Reinke, S., Branton, W., Lu, J.-Q., & Power, C. (2014). Activation of multiple inflammasomes within the central nervous system during experimental autoimmune encephalomyelitis and multiple sclerosis. *Journal of Neuroimmunology, 275*, 163.

Mckenzie, B. A., Mamik, M. K., Saito, L. B., Boghozian, R., Monaco, M. C., Major, E. O., et al. (2018). Caspase-1 inhibition prevents glial inflammasome activation and pyroptosis in models of multiple sclerosis. *Proceedings of the National Academy of Sciences of the U S A, 115*, E6065–E6074.

Mendiola, A. S., & Cardona, A. E. (2018). The IL-1beta phenomena in neuroinflammatory diseases. *Journal of Neural Transmission, 125*, 781–795.

Michailidou, I., Jongejan, A., Vreijling, J. P., Georgakopoulou, T., De Wissel, M. B., Wolterman, R. A., et al. (2018). Systemic inhibition of the membrane attack complex impedes neuroinflammation in chronic relapsing experimental autoimmune encephalomyelitis. *Acta Neuropathol Commun, 6*, 36.

Michel, L., Touil, H., Pikor, N. B., Gommerman, J. L., Prat, A., & Bar-Or, A. (2015). B cells in the multiple sclerosis central nervous system: Trafficking and contribution to CNS-compartmentalized inflammation. *Frontiers in Immunology, 6*, 636.

Miglio, G., Veglia, E., & Fantozzi, R. (2015). Fumaric acid esters prevent the NLRP3 inflammasome-mediated and ATP-triggered pyroptosis of differentiated THP-1 cells. *International Immunopharmacology, 28*, 215–219.

Monteiro, A., Cruto, C., Rosado, P., Martinho, A., Rosado, L., Fonseca, M., et al. (2018). Characterization of circulating gamma-delta T cells in relapsing vs remission multiple sclerosis. *Journal of Neuroimmunology, 318*, 65–71.

Mortezaee, K., Khanlarkhani, N., Beyer, C., & Zendedel, A. (2018). Inflammasome: Its role in traumatic brain and spinal cord injury. *Journal of Cellular Physiology, 233*, 5160–5169.

Mortimer, L., Moreau, F., Macdonald, J. A., & Chadee, K. (2016). NLRP3 inflammasome inhibition is disrupted in a group of auto-inflammatory disease CAPS mutations. *Nature Immunology, 17*, 1176–1186.

Mouton-Liger, F., Rosazza, T., Sepulveda-Diaz, J., Ieang, A., Hassoun, S. M., Claire, E., et al. (2018). Parkin deficiency modulates NLRP3 inflammasome activation by attenuating an A20-dependent negative feedback loop. *Glia, 66*, 1736–1751.

Mrdjen, D., Pavlovic, A., Hartmann, F. J., Schreiner, B., Utz, S. G., Leung, B. P., et al. (2018). High-dimensional single-cell Mapping of central nervous system immune cells reveals distinct myeloid subsets in Health, aging, and disease. *Immunity, 48*, 380–395 e386.

Mukherjee, S., Chen, L. Y., Papadimos, T. J., Huang, S., Zuraw, B. L., & Pan, Z. K. (2009). Lipopolysaccharide-driven Th2 cytokine production in macrophages is regulated by both MyD88 and TRAM. *Journal of Biological Chemistry, 284*, 29391–29398.

Munoz-Planillo, R., Kuffa, P., Martinez-Colon, G., Smith, B. L., Rajendiran, T. M., & Nunez, G. (2013). K(+) efflux is the common trigger of NLRP3 inflammasome activation by bacterial toxins and particulate matter. *Immunity, 38*, 1142–1153.

Nakanishi, K. (2018). Unique action of interleukin-18 on T cells and other immune cells. *Frontiers in Immunology, 9*, 763.

Nonaka, S., & Nakanishi, H. (2019). Microglial clearance of focal apoptotic synapses. *Neuroscience Letters, 707*, 134317.

Noroozi, S., Meimand, H.a. E., Arababadi, M. K., Nakhaee, N., & Asadikaram, G. (2017). The effects of IFN-beta 1a on the expression of inflammasomes and apoptosis-associated speck-like proteins in multiple sclerosis patients. *Molecular Neurobiology, 54*, 3031–3037.

Ohl, K., Tenbrock, K., & Kipp, M. (2016). Oxidative stress in multiple sclerosis: Central and peripheral mode of action. *Experimental Neurology, 277*, 58–67.

Olsson, T., Barcellos, L. F., & Alfredsson, L. (2017). Interactions between genetic, lifestyle and environmental risk factors for multiple sclerosis. *Nature Reviews Neurology, 13*, 25–36.

Ormel, P. R., Vieira De Sa, R., Van Bodegraven, E. J., Karst, H., Harschnitz, O., Sneeboer, M.a. M., et al. (2018). Microglia innately develop within cerebral organoids. *Nature Communications, 9*, 4167.

Panicker, N., Sarkar, S., Harischandra, D. S., Neal, M., Kam, T. I., Jin, H., et al. (2019). Fyn kinase regulates misfolded alpha-synuclein uptake and NLRP3 inflammasome activation in microglia. *Journal of Experimental Medicine, 216*, 1411–1430.

Parkhurst, C. N., Yang, G., Ninan, I., Savas, J. N., Yates, J. R., 3rd, Lafaille, J. J., et al. (2013). Microglia promote learning-dependent synapse formation through brain-derived neurotrophic factor. *Cell, 155*, 1596–1609.

Parnell, G. P., & Booth, D. R. (2017). The multiple sclerosis (MS) genetic risk factors indicate both acquired and innate immune cell subsets contribute to MS pathogenesis and identify novel therapeutic opportunities. *Frontiers in Immunology, 8*, 425.

Patel, J., & Balabanov, R. (2012). Molecular mechanisms of oligodendrocyte injury in multiple sclerosis and experimental autoimmune encephalomyelitis. *International Journal of Molecular Sciences, 13*, 10647–10659.

Peelen, E., Damoiseaux, J., Muris, A. H., Knippenberg, S., Smolders, J., Hupperts, R., et al. (2015). Increased inflammasome related gene expression profile in PBMC may facilitate T helper 17 cell induction in multiple sclerosis. *Molecular Immunology, 63*, 521–529.

Philips, T., & Rothstein, J. D. (2017). Oligodendroglia: Metabolic supporters of neurons. *Journal of Clinical Investigation, 127*, 3271–3280.

Pierson, E. R., Wagner, C. A., & Goverman, J. M. (2018). The contribution of neutrophils to CNS autoimmunity. *Clinical Immunology, 189*, 23–28.

Place, D. E., & Kanneganti, T. D. (2017). Recent advances in inflammasome biology. *Current Opinion in Immunology, 50*, 32–38.

Plantone, D., Inglese, M., Salvetti, M., & Koudriavtseva, T. (2018). A perspective of coagulation dysfunction in multiple sclerosis and in experimental allergic encephalomyelitis. *Frontiers in Neurology, 9*, 1175.

Pocock, J. M., & Piers, T. M. (2018). Modelling microglial function with induced pluripotent stem cells: An update. *Nature Reviews Neuroscience, 19*, 445–452.

Ponath, G., Park, C., & Pitt, D. (2018). The role of astrocytes in multiple sclerosis. *Frontiers in Immunology, 9*, 217.

Praet, J., Guglielmetti, C., Berneman, Z., Van Der Linden, A., & Ponsaerts, P. (2014). Cellular and molecular neuropathology of the cuprizone mouse model: Clinical relevance for multiple sclerosis. *Neuroscience & Biobehavioral Reviews, 47*, 485–505.

Py, B. F., Kim, M. S., Vakifahmetoglu-Norberg, H., & Yuan, J. (2013). Deubiquitination of NLRP3 by BRCC3 critically regulates inflammasome activity. *Molecular Cell, 49*, 331–338.

Rathinam, V. A., Vanaja, S. K., & Fitzgerald, K. A. (2012). Regulation of inflammasome signaling. *Nature Immunology, 13*, 333–342.

Rathkey, J. K., Zhao, J., Liu, Z., Chen, Y., Yang, J., Kondolf, H. C., et al. (2018). Chemical disruption of the pyroptotic pore-forming protein gasdermin D inhibits inflammatory cell death and sepsis. *Sci Immunol, 3*.

Raupach, B., Peuschel, S. K., Monack, D. M., & Zychlinsky, A. (2006). Caspase-1-mediated activation of interleukin-1beta (IL-1beta) and IL-18 contributes to innate immune defenses against *Salmonella enterica* serovar Typhimurium infection. *Infection and Immunity, 74*, 4922–4926.

Reemst, K., Noctor, S. C., Lucassen, P. J., & Hol, E. M. (2016). The indispensable roles of microglia and astrocytes during brain development. *Frontiers in Human Neuroscience, 10*, 566.

Reu, P., Khosravi, A., Bernard, S., Mold, J. E., Salehpour, M., Alkass, K., et al. (2017). The lifespan and turnover of microglia in the human brain. *Cell Reports, 20*, 779–784.

Rodgers, M. A., Bowman, J. W., Liang, Q., & Jung, J. U. (2014). Regulation where autophagy intersects the inflammasome. *Antioxidants and Redox Signaling, 20*, 495–506.

Rossi, S., Furlan, R., De Chiara, V., Motta, C., Studer, V., Mori, F., et al. (2012). Interleukin-1beta causes synaptic hyperexcitability in multiple sclerosis. *Annals of Neurology, 71*, 76–83.

Rothschild, D. E., Mcdaniel, D. K., Ringel-Scaia, V. M., & Allen, I. C. (2018). Modulating inflammation through the negative regulation of NF-kappaB signaling. *Journal of Leukocyte Biology*. http://dx.doi.org/10.1002/JLB.3MIR0817-346RRR. PMID:29389019. [Epub ahead of print] Review.

Sarkar, S., Malovic, E., Harishchandra, D. S., Ghaisas, S., Panicker, N., Charli, A., et al. (2017). Mitochondrial impairment in microglia amplifies NLRP3 inflammasome proinflammatory signaling in cell culture and animal models of Parkinson's disease. *NPJ Parkinsons Dis, 3*, 30.

Schetters, S. T. T., Gomez-Nicola, D., Garcia-Vallejo, J. J., & Van Kooyk, Y. (2017). Neuroinflammation: Microglia and T Cells get ready to tango. *Frontiers in Immunology, 8*, 1905.

Schett, G., & Neurath, M. F. (2018). Resolution of chronic inflammatory disease: Universal and tissue-specific concepts. *Nature Communications, 9*, 3261.

Scheu, S., Ali, S., Mann-Nuttel, R., Richter, L., Arolt, V., Dannlowski, U., et al. (2019). Interferon beta-mediated protective functions of microglia in central nervous system Autoimmunity. *International Journal of Molecular Sciences, 20*.

Schroder, K., & Tschopp, J. (2010). The inflammasomes. *Cell, 140*, 821–832.

Schuh, E., Lohse, P., Ertl-Wagner, B., Witt, M., Krumbholz, M., Frankenberger, M., et al. (2015). Expanding spectrum of neurologic manifestations in patients with NLRP3 low-penetrance mutations. *Neurol Neuroimmunol Neuroinflamm, 2*, e109.

Sedimbi, S. K., Hagglof, T., & Karlsson, M. C. (2013). IL-18 in inflammatory and autoimmune disease. *Cellular and Molecular Life Sciences, 70*, 4795–4808.

Serhan, C. N., & Levy, B. D. (2018). Resolvins in inflammation: Emergence of the proresolving superfamily of mediators. *Journal of Clinical Investigation, 128*, 2657–2669.

Shao, B. Z., Wei, W., Ke, P., Xu, Z. Q., Zhou, J. X., & Liu, C. (2014). Activating cannabinoid receptor 2 alleviates pathogenesis of experimental autoimmune encephalomyelitis via activation of autophagy and inhibiting NLRP3 inflammasome. *CNS Neuroscience and Therapeutics, 20*, 1021–1028.

Shaw, P. J., Lukens, J. R., Burns, S., Chi, H., Mcgargill, M. A., & Kanneganti, T. D. (2010). Cutting edge: Critical role for PYCARD/ASC in the development of experimental autoimmune encephalomyelitis. *The Journal of Immunology, 184*, 4610–4614.

Shema, E., Bernstein, B. E., & Buenrostro, J. D. (2019). Single-cell and single-molecule epigenomics to uncover genome regulation at unprecedented resolution. *Nature Genetics, 51*, 19–25.

Sie, C., & Korn, T. (2017). Dendritic cells in central nervous system autoimmunity. *Seminars in Immunopathology, 39*, 99–111.

Singer, J. W., Fleischman, A., Al-Fayoumi, S., Mascarenhas, J. O., Yu, Q., & Agarwal, A. (2018). Inhibition of interleukin-1 receptor-associated kinase 1 (IRAK1) as a therapeutic strategy. *Oncotarget, 9*, 33416–33439.

Soares, J. L., Oliveira, E. M., & Pontillo, A. (2019). Variants in NLRP3 and NLRC4 inflammasome associate with susceptibility and severity of multiple sclerosis. *Mult Scler Relat Disord, 29*, 26–34.

Sominsky, L., De Luca, S., & Spencer, S. J. (2018). Microglia: Key players in neurodevelopment and neuronal plasticity. *The International Journal of Biochemistry & Cell Biology, 94*, 56–60.

Song, L., Yan, Y., Marzano, M., & Li, Y. (2019). Studying heterotypic Cell(-)Cell interactions in the human brain using pluripotent stem cell models for neurodegeneration. *Cells, 8*.

Song, N., & Li, T. (2018). Regulation of NLRP3 inflammasome by phosphorylation. *Frontiers in Immunology, 9*, 2305.

Song, N., Liu, Z. S., Xue, W., Bai, Z. F., Wang, Q. Y., Dai, J., et al. (2017). NLRP3 phosphorylation is an essential priming event for inflammasome activation. *Molecular Cell, 68*, 185–197 e186.

Spalinger, M. R., Kasper, S., Gottier, C., Lang, S., Atrott, K., Vavricka, S. R., et al. (2016). NLRP3 tyrosine phosphorylation is controlled by protein tyrosine phosphatase PTPN22. *Journal of Clinical Investigation, 126*, 1783–1800.

Stancu, I. C., Cremers, N., Vanrusselt, H., Couturier, J., Vanoosthuyse, A., Kessels, S., et al. (2019). Aggregated Tau activates NLRP3-ASC inflammasome exacerbating exogenously seeded and non-exogenously seeded Tau pathology in vivo. *Acta Neuropathologica, 137*, 599–617.

Sun, S. C. (2011). Non-canonical NF-kappaB signaling pathway. *Cell Research, 21*, 71–85.

Surace, M. J., & Block, M. L. (2012). Targeting microglia-mediated neurotoxicity: The potential of NOX2 inhibitors. *Cellular and Molecular Life Sciences, 69*, 2409–2427.

Sutterwala, F. S., Haasken, S., & Cassel, S. L. (2014). Mechanism of NLRP3 inflammasome activation. *Annals of the New York Academy of Sciences, 1319*, 82–95.

Tai, Y., Wang, Q., Korner, H., Zhang, L., & Wei, W. (2018). Molecular mechanisms of T cells activation by dendritic cells in autoimmune diseases. *Frontiers in Pharmacology, 9*, 642.

Tay, T. L., Savage, J. C., Hui, C. W., Bisht, K., & Tremblay, M.-È. (2017). Microglia across the lifespan: From origin to function in brain development, plasticity and cognition. *The Journal of Physiology, 595*, 1929–1945.

Tezcan, G., Martynova, E. V., Gilazieva, Z. E., Mcintyre, A., Rizvanov, A. A., & Khaiboullina, S. F. (2019). MicroRNA post-transcriptional regulation of the NLRP3 inflammasome in immunopathologies. *Frontiers in Pharmacology, 10*, 451.

Thion, M. S., Ginhoux, F., & Garel, S. (2018). Microglia and early brain development: An intimate journey. *Science, 362*, 185–189.

Thompson, A. J., Banwell, B. L., Barkhof, F., Carroll, W. M., Coetzee, T., Comi, G., et al. (2018a). Diagnosis of multiple sclerosis: 2017 revisions of the McDonald criteria. *The Lancet Neurology, 17*, 162–173.

Thompson, A. J., Baranzini, S. E., Geurts, J., Hemmer, B., & Ciccarelli, O. (2018b). Multiple sclerosis. *Lancet, 391*, 1622–1636.

Tintore, M., Vidal Jordana, A., & Sastre-Garriga, J. (2019). Treatment of multiple sclerosis - success from bench to bedside. *Nature Reviews Neurology, 15*, 53–58.

Tozser, J., & Benko, S. (2016). Natural compounds as regulators of NLRP3 inflammasome-mediated IL-1beta production. *Mediators of Inflammation, 2016*, 5460302.

Triantafilou, K., Hughes, T. R., Triantafilou, M., & Morgan, B. P. (2013). The complement membrane attack complex triggers intracellular Ca2+ fluxes leading to NLRP3 inflammasome activation. *Journal of Cell Science, 126*, 2903–2913.

Tschopp, J., & Schroder, K. (2010). NLRP3 inflammasome activation: The convergence of multiple signalling pathways on ROS production? *Nature Reviews Immunology, 10*, 210–215.

Tuusa, J., Raasakka, A., Ruskamo, S., & Kursula, P. (2017). Myelin-derived and putative molecular mimic peptides share structural properties in aqueous and membrane-like environments. *Multiple Sclerosis and Demyelinating Disorders, 2*.

Van Bruggen, D., Agirre, E., & Castelo-Branco, G. (2017). Single-cell transcriptomic analysis of oligodendrocyte lineage cells. *Current Opinion in Neurobiology, 47*, 168–175.

Van Kaer, L., Postoak, J. L., Wang, C., Yang, G., & Wu, L. (2019). Innate, innate-like and adaptive lymphocytes in the pathogenesis of MS and EAE. *Cellular and Molecular Immunology, 16*, 531–539.

Vidmar, L., Maver, A., Drulovic, J., Sepcic, J., Novakovic, I., Ristic, S., et al. (2019). Multiple Sclerosis patients carry an increased burden of exceedingly rare genetic variants in the inflammasome regulatory genes. *Scientific Reports, 9*, 9171.

Voet, S., Mc Guire, C., Hagemeyer, N., Martens, A., Schroeder, A., Wieghofer, P., et al. (2018). A20 critically controls microglia activation and inhibits inflammasome-dependent neuroinflammation. *Nature Communications, 9*, 2036.

Voet, S., Prinz, M., & Van Loo, G. (2019). Microglia in central nervous system inflammation and multiple sclerosis pathology. *Trends in Molecular Medicine, 25*, 112–123.

Wallisch, J. S., Simon, D. W., Bayir, H., Bell, M. J., Kochanek, P. M., & Clark, R. S. B. (2017). Cerebrospinal fluid NLRP3 is increased after severe traumatic brain injury in infants and children. *Neurocritical Care, 27*, 44–50.

Wang, C., Pan, Y., Zhang, Q. Y., Wang, F. M., & Kong, L. D. (2012). Quercetin and allopurinol ameliorate kidney injury in STZ-treated rats with regulation of renal NLRP3 inflammasome activation and lipid accumulation. *PLoS One, 7*, e38285.

Wang, K., Song, F., Fernandez-Escobar, A., Luo, G., Wang, J. H., & Sun, Y. (2018). The properties of cytokines in multiple sclerosis: Pros and cons. *The American Journal of the Medical Sciences, 356*, 552–560.

Wang, J., Wang, J., Wang, J., Yang, B., Weng, Q., & He, Q. (2019). Targeting microglia and macrophages: A potential treatment strategy for multiple sclerosis. *Frontiers in Pharmacology, 10*, 286.

Wang, X., Ma, C., Wu, J., & Zhu, J. (2013). Roles of T helper 17 cells and interleukin-17 in neuroautoimmune diseases with emphasis on multiple sclerosis and Guillain-Barre syndrome as well as their animal models. *Journal of Neuroscience Research, 91*, 871–881.

Watson, P. M. D., Kavanagh, E., Allenby, G., & Vassey, M. (2017). Bioengineered 3D glial cell culture systems and applications for neurodegeneration and neuroinflammation. *SLAS Discov, 22*, 583–601.

Weber, K., & Schilling, J. D. (2014). Lysosomes integrate metabolic-inflammatory cross-talk in primary macrophage inflammasome activation. *Journal of Biological Chemistry, 289*, 9158–9171.

Wolf, S. A., Boddeke, H. W., & Kettenmann, H. (2017). Microglia in physiology and disease. *Annual Review of Physiology, 79*, 619–643.
Xu, L., Zhang, C., Jiang, N., He, D., Bai, Y., & Xin, Y. (2019). Rapamycin combined with MCC950 to treat multiple sclerosis in experimental autoimmune encephalomyelitis. *Journal of Cellular Biochemistry, 120*, 5160–5168.
Xu, X., Yin, D., Ren, H., Gao, W., Li, F., Sun, D., et al. (2018). Selective NLRP3 inflammasome inhibitor reduces neuroinflammation and improves long-term neurological outcomes in a murine model of traumatic brain injury. *Neurobiology of Disease, 117*, 15–27.
Yadav, S. K., Soin, D., Ito, K., & Dhib-Jalbut, S. (2019). Insight into the mechanism of action of dimethyl fumarate in multiple sclerosis. *Journal of Molecular Medicine (Berlin), 97*, 463–472.
Yamamoto, S., Yamashina, K., Ishikawa, M., Gotoh, M., Yagishita, S., Iwasa, K., et al. (2017). Protective and therapeutic role of 2-carba-cyclic phosphatidic acid in demyelinating disease. *Journal of Neuroinflammation, 14*, 142.
Yamasaki, R., Lu, H., Butovsky, O., Ohno, N., Rietsch, A. M., Cialic, R., et al. (2014). Differential roles of microglia and monocytes in the inflamed central nervous system. *Journal of Experimental Medicine, 211*, 1533–1549.
Yang, Y., Wang, H., Kouadir, M., Song, H., & Shi, F. (2019). Recent advances in the mechanisms of NLRP3 inflammasome activation and its inhibitors. *Cell Death & Disease, 10*, 128.
Yeh, H., & Ikezu, T. (2019). Transcriptional and epigenetic regulation of microglia in Health and disease. *Trends in Molecular Medicine, 25*, 96–111.
Yeon, S. H., Yang, G., Lee, H. E., & Lee, J. Y. (2017). Oxidized phosphatidylcholine induces the activation of NLRP3 inflammasome in macrophages. *Journal of Leukocyte Biology, 101*, 205–215.
Yi, Y. S. (2018). Regulatory roles of the caspase-11 non-canonical inflammasome in inflammatory diseases. *Immune Netw, 18*, e41.
Yu, H., Wu, M., Lu, G., Cao, T., Chen, N., Zhang, Y., et al. (2018). Prednisone alleviates demyelination through regulation of the NLRP3 inflammasome in a C57BL/6 mouse model of cuprizone-induced demyelination. *Brain Research, 1678*, 75–84.
Yue, Y., Stone, S., & Lin, W. (2018). Role of nuclear factor kappaB in multiple sclerosis and experimental autoimmune encephalomyelitis. *Neural Regen Res, 13*, 1507–1515.
Zhang, A. Q., Zeng, L., Gu, W., Zhang, L. Y., Zhou, J., Jiang, D. P., et al. (2011). Clinical relevance of single nucleotide polymorphisms within the entire NLRP3 gene in patients with major blunt trauma. *Critical Care, 15*, R280.
Zhang, C. J., Jiang, M., Zhou, H., Liu, W., Wang, C., Kang, Z., et al. (2018). TLR-stimulated IRAKM activates caspase-8 inflammasome in microglia and promotes neuroinflammation. *Journal of Clinical Investigation, 128*, 5399–5412.
Zhao, G., Jiang, K., Yang, Y., Zhang, T., Wu, H., Shaukat, A., et al. (2018). The potential therapeutic role of mir-223 in Bovine endometritis by targeting the NLRP3 inflammasome. *Frontiers in Immunology, 9*, 1916.
Zhou, Y., Lu, M., Du, R. H., Qiao, C., Jiang, C. Y., Zhang, K. Z., et al. (2016). MicroRNA-7 targets Nod-like receptor protein 3 inflammasome to modulate neuroinflammation in the pathogenesis of Parkinson's disease. *Molecular Neurodegeneration, 11*, 28.
Znalesniak, E. B., Fu, T., Guttek, K., Handel, U., Reinhold, D., & Hoffmann, W. (2016). Increased cerebral Tff1 expression in two murine models of neuroinflammation. *Cellular Physiology and Biochemistry, 39*, 2287–2296.
Zrzavy, T., Hametner, S., Wimmer, I., Butovsky, O., Weiner, H. L., & Lassmann, H. (2017). Loss of 'homeostatic' microglia and patterns of their activation in active multiple sclerosis. *Brain, 140*, 1900–1913.

CHAPTER EIGHT

Sleep deprivation, oxidative stress and inflammation

Fatin Atrooz and Samina Salim*
Department of Pharmacological and Pharmaceutical Sciences, College of Pharmacy, University of Houston, Houston, TX, United States
*Corresponding author: E-mail: ssalim@uh.edu

Contents

Abstract

Adequate sleep is essential for normal brain function, especially during early life developmental stages as postnatal brain maturation occurs during the critical period of childhood and adolescence. Therefore, sleep disturbance and/or deficit during this period can have detrimental consequences. Many epidemiological and clinical studies have linked early life sleep disturbance with occurrence of later life behavioral and cognitive impairments. Role of oxidative stress and inflammation has been implicated in sleep deprivation-related impairments. This review article presents a detailed description of the current state of the literature on the subject.

Advances in Protein Chemistry and Structural Biology, Volume 119
ISSN 1876-1623
https://doi.org/10.1016/bs.apcsb.2019.03.001

1. Introduction

It is well known that sleep, especially during early life, is essential for proper brain development and function (Orzel-Gryglewska, 2010). Consequently, sleep deprivation (SD) in children and adolescents has been associated with affective and behavioral difficulties (Astill, Van der Heijden, Van Ijzendoorn, & Van Someren, 2012; Dewald, Meijer, Oort, Kerkhof, & Bogels, 2010). Relevant to this, in a longitudinal study, SD in children, 2.5–6 years old, were found to be associated with hyperactivity and behavioral abnormalities (Touchette et al., 2009). Later onset of anxiety and depression has also been associated with early life sleep problems (Gregory et al., 2005). In fact, some longitudinal studies suggest that early life sleep problems are highly predictive of future affective and behavioral problems (Gessa, Pani, Fadda, & Fratta, 1995). The role of sleep in several neurodevelopmental processes including synaptogenesis, synaptic pruning, neuronal myelination, and neurogenesis has been proposed. Consequently, sleep loss has been implicated in disruption of synaptic integrity and neural circuits maturation (Frank, Issa, & Stryker, 2001; Lopez et al., 2008). Oxidative stress, inflammation, and glial dysfunction are suggested as an underlying mechanisms (Atrooz, Liu, Kochi, & Salim, 2019; Cirelli, 2006). Before a detailed description of relevant studies, basic literature related to sleep physiology must be discussed.

2. Sleep physiology

Sleep is a physiological state characterized by lack of response to environmental stimuli. In vertebrates, sleep is defined as a specific pattern of synchronized electrical activity of the cortical area of the brain. Sleep is typically evaluated by polysomnography (PSG), which involves simultaneous recording of brain's cortical activity using electroencephalogram (EEG), eye movement using electrooculogram (EOG), and skeletal muscles' activity using electromyogram (EMG). In humans and other mammals, sleep consists of two main phases: rapid eye movement (REM) sleep and non-REM (NREM) sleep. NREM sleep is characterized by high amplitude low frequency EEG waves known as slow wave sleep, decreased muscle tone, and slow eye movement. While REM sleep is characterized by low amplitude high frequency waves known as active sleep, muscle atonia, and rapid eye movement. In humans, NREM sleep is further divided into three stages; N1, N2, and N3, each stage has a defined EEG waves. During sleep, these phases alternate in a highly regulated pattern forming sleep cycles (Stenberg & Porkka-Heiskanen, 1990). Sleep/wakefulness state is regulated by the interaction of two processes; the circadian system (process C) and the sleep homeostasis (process S) (Borbely, 1982a; 1982b). Process C is controlled by the suprachiasmatic nucleus (SCN) within the hypothalamus. The SCN serves as the neural pacemaker of circadian timing cycle. It is mainly synchronized to environmental light/dark cycle and projects signals that control proper timing of physiological functions including sleep/wakefulness cycle. The daily circadian rhythm is 24 h under normal light/dark cycles, with sleep onset and wakefulness onset occurring at same time every day. Sleep homeostasis or process S is regulated by the sleep pressure generated after a period of wakefulness, hence, the level of process S increases with extended wakefulness and decreases after sleep onset. There are two hypothesis for sleep pressure generation; one is accumulation of sleep promoting substances such as adenosine and nitric oxide, second is the need for restoration of energy resources (Abrahamson & Moore, 2006). The interaction of the sleep homeostasis and the circadian rhythm regulates the timing, the depth and the duration of sleep. In fact, the alignment between the two processes is essential for body metabolism and brain function. Furthermore, disruption in sleep/circadian rhythm is associated with many metabolic, psychiatric, and neurodegenerative diseases (Wulff, Gatti, Wettstein, & Foster, 2010).

The wakefulness state is coordinated by several defined nuclei in the pons and midbrain areas known as ascending reticular activating system (ARAS). These wakefulness promoting cells are; noradrenergic (NE) cells in locus coeruleus, serotonergic (5-HT) cells in raphe nuclei, cholinergic (Ach) cells in pedunculopontine tegmentum and latero-dorsal tegmentum, glutamatergic cells (Glu) in midbrain, and dopaminergic (DA) cells in substantia nigra and ventral tegmental area. Projections of these waking promoting cells activate thalamo-cortical, hypo-thalamo-cortical and basalo-cortical systems. In addition to ARAS, there are five other groups of cells that promote wakefulness these groups include; histaminergic cells of posterior hypothalamic area, the hypocretin/orexin cells in lateral hypothalamus, cholinergic cells in basal forebrain, neuropeptide Y(NPY) containing cells in suprachiasmic nucleus, and glutamatergic neurons in ventro medial prefrontal cortex (vmPFC). Activation of these systems maintain wakefulness by activation of cortex, however, lesion of one specific wakefulness promoting group may not induce changes in amount of wakefulness, suggesting that all these groups of brain regions together contribute in promotion and maintenance of wakefulness but none of them is absolutely necessary for generation of wakefulness. Understanding sleep initiation and maintenance has been a challenge for decades. Initiation of sleep is suggested to be a result of successive passive and active physiological processes which leads to blockage of cortical sensory gates (Datta, 2010). The passive process that contributes to sleep initiation results from accumulation of neuronal activity-dependent metabolites. During wakefulness, metabolic products such as adenosine, nitric oxide, cytokines, and prostaglandins accumulate leading to slow down of wakefulness-prompting neuronal activity, which ultimately slows down the production of metabolites. Reducing the activity of wake promoting neurons represents the active process of sleep initiation. Metabolite-dependent neuronal activity is known as metabolite homeostasis (Datta, 2010). Lately, electrophysiological studies have suggested that the thalamic reticular nucleus is the pacemaker of sleep spindles generation (Steriade, McCormick, & Sejnowski, 1993). The thalamic reticular nucleus consists exclusively of GABAergic neurons, it also serves as the sensory and internal signal at the gateway to the cerebral cortex. The thalamic reticular nucleus contains two different types of neurons; the thalamo-cortical relay neurons which relay incoming sensory signals to the cerebral cortex, and thalamo-reticular neurons which prevents the formal one from sending the sensory signals to the cerebral cortex. During wakefulness, the activity of the thalamo-cortical relay neurons is proportional to the activity of wake promoting noradrenergic, serotonergic, and cholinergic cells, while the thalamic-reticular cells remain inactive. During the passive step of sleep initiation, reduction in wake-promoting cells leads to reduction in activity of thalamo-cortical relay and enhancement of the thalamic-reticular cell. Excitation of thalamic-reticular relay further inhibits thalamo-cortical relay by activation of the inhibitory postsynaptic GABA-B receptors. Therefore, the gate for cerebral cortex sensory signals is closed and the cerebral cortex is deprived of external information, which is reflected by high voltage and slow brain waves in NREM sleep, an indication of cortical inactivity (Datta, 2010; Kalia, 2006; Stenberg & Porkka-Heiskanen, 1990).

Sleep occurs in all organisms with neuronal/glial network, suggesting that sleep is a property of every neuronal network. While many theories have been presented to explain the function of sleep such as; energy restoration, waste elimination, thermoregulation, and neuronal connectivity and plasticity augmentation, sleep is still a challenging enigma for scientists

(Krueger, Frank, Wisor, & Roy, 2016; Krueger & Obal, 2003). Overall, sleep is essential for optimum health, and particularly for optimal mental health as discussed below.

3. Sleep and mental health

One of the leading theories of sleep function is the synaptic homeostasis. The synaptic homeostasis hypothesis proposes that; extensive strengthening of synapses during wakefulness increases the need for energy resources and hence saturates learning processes (Ringli & Huber, 2011; Tononi & Cirelli, 2014). During sleep, spontaneous neuronal activity normalizes the synaptic strength and restores the cellular homeostasis. The synchronized neuronal activity during sleep forms high amplitude slow oscillation reflected by increased SWA in EEG. Slow wave oscillation results from repeated sequences of depolarization and hyperpolarization which leads to reduction in synaptic strength. Ultimately, this leads to reduction in synaptic strength which reduces the amplitude and the synchronization of the slow oscillation reflected by the decrease of the SWA with time after sleep. Hence, by recalibrating synaptic strength to the baseline level, sleep promotes synaptic homeostasis (Ringli & Huber, 2011; Tononi & Cirelli, 2014). Accordingly, sleep plays an essential role in energy restoration and neuronal plasticity and connectivity. And, neuronal plasticity underlies sleep-dependent memory consolidation. In fact, many studies have linked alterations of sleep dependent-plasticity and memory functions to neurobehavioral and psychiatric disorders especially when sleep deprivation occurred during developmental stages of early life.

Another proposed function of sleep is the regulation of affective brain function. Neuroimaging studies have showed that the activity of the emotion related brain regions including the amygdala, striatum, hippocampus, and the prefrontal cortex increases during REM sleep. Enhanced activity of emotional regulation regions is associated with reduction in level of adrenergic locus coeruleus tone during REM sleep (Dang-Vu et al., 2010; Kametani & Kawamura, 1990; Ouyang, Hellman, Abel, & Thomas, 2004). This is important because affective experiences are associated with burst of adrenergic tone during the time of traumatic and/or stressful experiences. Elevation of adrenergic tone and autonomic reactions tag these affective experiences with emotion forming salient emotional memory (Goldstein & Walker, 2014). During REM sleep, this emotional memory is recalled with reduced adrenergic tone leading to decoupling of emotions from the information of the experience. Removal of the affective emotions that originally tagged the emotional experiences is a preventive mechanism from developing anxiety disorders that result from persistence of affective charges within memory networks. Hence, the emotional regulation function of sleep is considered as a mechanism to forget the emotional tone of affective experiences, while retaining the memory of those experiences (Goldstein & Walker, 2014). Additionally, serval studies have suggested that reduction of the locus coeruleus activity during REM sleep recalibrates next day noradrenergic response to emotional stimuli. This allows a balance between emotional sensitivity and specificity to salient stimuli governed by top-down prefrontal cortex control of the amygdala (Goldstein & Walker, 2014; Hermans et al., 2011; Mallick & Singh, 2011; van Marle, Hermans, Qin, & Fernandez, 2009). Emotional regulation function of sleep might explain the complex relationship between sleep, sleep deprivation and psychiatric disorders.

4. Consequences of sleep deprivation

While sleep has an essential role in maintenance of body and brain functions, consequently, sleep deprivation (SD) has been associated with many physiological and psychological disorders. For example, in healthy individuals, SD has been linked to metabolic disorders including diabetes 2 and obesity (Knutson, Spiegel, Penev, & Van Cauter, 2007), and increased the risk of cardiovascular diseases (Cappuccio, Cooper, D'Elia, Strazzullo, & Miller, 2011; Dettoni et al., 2012). The association between SD and mental health has been suggested in many clinical and epidemiological studies. The detrimental effects of SD on memory encoding and learning have been extensively reported in human and animal studies (Drummond et al., 2000; Guan, Peng, & Fang, 2004; Harrison & Horne, 2000). Moreover, in both human and animal models of fear conditioning, SD negatively affects fear extinction following exposure to traumatic event contributing to development of post-traumatic stress disorder (PTSD) (Pace-Schott, Germain, & Milad, 2015). Additionally, affective disorders including anxiety and depression are highly correlated with sleep loss (Babson, Trainor, Feldner, & Blumenthal, 2010; Kahn-Greene, Killgore, Kamimori, Balkin, & Killgore, 2007). We will discuss studies implicating sleep loss with several mental impairments including depression, anxiety disorders and cognitive impairment.

4.1 Sleep deprivation and depression

Several epidemiological studies have indicated the remarkable link between sleep and psychiatric disorders. For instance, 75% of depressed subjects have insomnia symptoms, and 20% of patients with insomnia experienced depressive symptoms (Nutt, Wilson, & Paterson, 2008; Tsuno, Besset, & Ritchie, 2005). Furthermore, sleep EEG in depressed patients showed alterations in sleep architecture including; a decrease in REM latency (the time from sleep start and first period of REM), an increase in total REM sleep time and density, and reduction in slow wave sleep (SWA), additionally, high risk studies including relatives of depressed patients indicated that REM sleep alterations may precede the onset of depression and hence, might be useful in identifying subjects at high risk for depression (Palagini, Baglioni, Ciapparelli, Gemignani, & Riemann, 2013). In fact, one hypothesis has suggested the involvement of REM sleep dysregulation in the etiology and pathophysiology of depression (Palagini et al., 2013). Indeed, prospective studies have suggested that sleep deprivation in adolescents increases the risk for major depression which in turn increases the risk of sleep reduction (Roberts & Duong, 2014). Data from animal studies suggest that chronic sleep restriction may gradually induce changes in neuroendocrine stress systems, serotonergic neurotransmission, neurogenesis and neuronal plasticity (Meerlo, Havekes, & Steiger, 2015). Alteration of synaptic plasticity and strength by chronic SD might lead to alteration in connectivity within the different brain regions involved in the regulation of emotion and mood contributing to the pathophysiology of depression (Meerlo et al., 2015; Meerlo, Sgoifo, & Suchecki, 2008).

4.2 Sleep deprivation and anxiety disorders

In healthy adults, acute sleep deprivation is reported to increase self-reported symptoms of affective psychopathology (Babson et al., 2010; Kahn-Greene et al., 2007). Some studies have suggested that anxiety disorders and sleep problems are prevalent and comorbid. In a German survey, examination of the relationships between anxiety disorders and sleep quality revealed that most anxiety disorders are moderately associated with poor sleep quality. Moreover, individuals with anxiety disorders and poor sleep have compromised mental health and increased disability relative to those with anxiety disorders alone (Ramsawh, Stein, Belik, Jacobi, & Sareen, 2009). Other studies have suggested that sleep disturbance might contribute to anxiety disorders and it might exacerbate the severity of the symptoms in anxiety and related disorders. Sleep disturbance may also diminish treatment efficacy in these disorders suggesting that addressing sleep problems in the treatment of anxiety disorders may enhance treatment efficacy (Cox & Olatunji, 2016).

Animal models of SD are very important for investigating the link between sleep deprivation and anxiety, however, the effect of SD on anxiety produced inconsistent results in rodents. Some studies have reported that SD induces anxiety-like behavior, while others have reported reduced anxiety-like behavior following SD which makes it hard to reproduce sleep deprivation-induced anxiety in humans (Pires, Bezerra, Tufik, & Andersen, 2016). The lack of consistency in animal models, might be attributed to the variation of SD methods and protocols used (Alkadhi, 2013), or the lack of the sensitivity of methodologies used for the evaluation of the anxiety-like behavior (Pires et al., 2016). With respect to the methodology, some studies have suggested the analysis of self-grooming for evaluation of anxiety-like behavior following SD (Pires et al., 2012; Pires, Tufik, & Andersen, 2013).

4.3 Sleep deprivation and cognitive impairments

Impairment of memory processing by sleep loss has been addressed in human and animal models of SD (Havekes, Vecsey, & Abel, 2012). In humans, functional magnetic resonance imaging (fMRI) studies involved sleep-deprived and well-rested brains clearly demonstrated the importance of sleep for optimal cognitive function and learning (Chee & Chuah, 2008). Chronic sleep-restriction experiments which mimic sleep loss experienced by many individuals in modern societies and by individuals with sleep disorders demonstrate that over time, cognitive deficits accumulate to severe levels. Functional neuroimaging has revealed that sleep deprivation associated cognitive deficits, involve scattered changes in the brain regions including frontal and parietal control areas, secondary sensory processing areas, and thalamic areas. However, the degree of cognitive vulnerability to sleep loss varies among individuals which may be attributed to the basis of genes involved in sleep homeostasis and circadian rhythms (Goel, Rao, Durmer, & Dinges, 2009). Animal models of SD provided useful insights for the molecular processes that might play a role in interaction between sleep and memory. SD studies indicate that hippocampus-dependent memory formation and working memory are mainly sensitive for SD, and that there is a specific period of time following training during which SD impacts memory consolidation. The most sensitive period for SD was found to be 5−6 h following training, however, the sensitive period varied depending on the nature of the training (Havekes et al., 2012). Electrophysiological studies were conducted both in vivo and in vitro to determine the effect of SD on hippocampal synaptic plasticity. SD was reported to inhibit synaptic potentiation in the hippocampus but facilitating certain forms of synaptic depression (Hagewoud et al., 2010; Kopp, Longordo, Nicholson, & Luthi, 2006). And brief period of SD (5−6 h) impairs the maintenance of long-term potentiation (LTP). LTP is a form of synaptic plasticity critical for memory consolidation which depends on cyclic AMP (cAMP) and protein kinase a (PKA) pathway. The cAMP- PKA pathway, by phosphorylation of GluA1 subunit of α-amono-3-hydroxy-methyl-4-isoxazole propionic acid receptors (AMPARs), controls AMPAR function and hence, synaptic plasticity. Long periods of total SD impaired spatial working memory and reduced phosphorylation of GluA1 in mice hippocampus (Hagewoud et al., 2010). Additionally, cAMP-PKA pathway and the MAP kinase (MAPK) pathway represented by the extracellular signal-regulated kinase (ERK), together, those pathways regulate changes in synaptic efficacy which is essential for memory formation. Seventy five hours of REM sleep deprivation using platform over water method, decreased synaptic plasticity and transmission which were associated with reduced ERK phosphorylation and GluA1 expression in mice hippocampus (Ravassard et al., 2009). The role of protein synthesis in sleep-dependent cortical plasticity during memory consolidation has been suggested by several studies (Sweatt & Hawkins, 2016). Translational initiation is a critical step in protein synthesis which involves the translation initiation factors 4E and 4G in eukaryotes (eIF4E and eIF4G). In the brain, eIF4E is sequestered by 4E binding protein 2 (4EBP2) which prevents its interaction with eIF4G. The rapamycin complex 1 (mTORC1) is essential for release of eIF4E by phosphorylation of 4EBP2 allowing eIF4E-eIF4G binding and subsequent protein synthesis initiation (Sweatt & Hawkins, 2016). A series of experiments have demonstrated that protein synthesis regulated by mTORC1-dependent dephosphorylation of 4EBP2 is a critical signaling mechanism that underlies memory deficits induced by sleep loss (Graves, Heller, Pack, & Abel, 2003; Hernandez & Abel, 2008; Tudor et al., 2016). In summary, SD impacts memory and cognition potentially through alteration of synaptic plasticity and protein synthesis in critical brain regions including hippocampus and prefrontal cortex. The molecular mechanisms by which SD alters protein synthesis and synaptic plasticity is not fully addressed, oxidative stress and inflammation might have a role in such mechanisms, more details are discussed in this review.

5. Sleep deprivation in children and adolescents

According to a national survey conducted in 2014 by the National Sleep Foundation, approximately 55% of children and adolescents don't obtain adequate sleep per night. Further, inadequate sleep is more common at older ages; for example, 31% of children 6–11 years old sleep less than the recommended 11 h per night, while 56% of adolescents 15–17 years old sleep less than the recommended sleep hours per night (Buxton et al., 2015) (National Sleep Foundation, 2014 sleep in America poll). Comparisons between cross sectional studies conducted between 2003 and 2012 by the National Survey of Children's Health on children 6–17 years old (Hawkins & Takeuchi, 2016) found a consistent increase of inadequate sleep among all studied age groups, and the shorter sleep duration increased with age. Sleep deprivation in youth has been associated with adverse physical, mental and behavioral outcomes, therefore, increasing the amount of sleep in youth has become a public health priority in the United States. In fact, members of the American Academy of Sleep medicine have released a consensus statement of recommended amount of sleep for youth to promote optimal physical and mental health (Paruthi et al., 2016). Several studies investigated the causes of a decrease in sleep duration among youth. Bedtime delay and short sleep duration in school-aged children and adolescents, have been consistently related to the extensive exposure of electronic media including television viewing, use of computers, electronic gaming, mobile telephones, and music (Cain & Gradisar, 2010). Early school start times and academic workload are also lead to insufficient sleep in school aged children and adolescents (Wheaton, Chapman, & Croft, 2016). Furthermore, sleep disturbances are common among youth with psychiatric disorders such as anxiety, depression, autism, or schizophrenia (Alfano, Pina, Zerr, & Villalta, 2010; Gregory & Sadeh, 2016; Hodge, Carollo, Lewin, Hoffman, & Sweeney, 2014; Yilmaz, Sedky, & Bennett, 2013) and in children who exposed to violent events (Spilsbury, Babineau, Frame, Juhas, & Rork, 2014). The detrimental effects of insufficient sleep in youth on mental and behavioral outcomes have been reported in many epidemiological and clinical studies, some are discussed in the next section.

5.1 Consequences of sleep deprivation in children and adolescents

In otherwise healthy children, insufficient sleep has been linked to poor school performance (Astill et al., 2012; Dewald et al., 2010), behavioral problems such as attention deficit, and emotional symptoms such as anxiety and depression (Gregory & Sadeh, 2012; Maski & Kothare, 2013). In a longitudinal study, sleep deprivation in children 2.5–6 years old was associated with hyperactivity and poor behavior at school (Touchette et al., 2008, 2009). Later onset of anxiety and depression are also associated with early life (childhood and adolescent) sleep disturbances (Gessa et al., 1995; Gregory et al., 2005). The longitudinal studies suggest that early life sleep deprivation are highly predictive of future affective and behavioral problems (Maski & Kothare, 2013). How sleep at early life modulate neurobehavioral functioning and cognition is not fully understood. Some investigators have suggested that sleep spindles and slow wave activity, which show significant changes through childhood and adolescents might have a role in neurobehavioral and executive functional development. However, further research are needed to investigate the association between sleep and neurobehavioral development (Kurth, Olini, Huber, & LeBourgeois, 2015; Lopez, Hoffmann, & Armitage, 2010; Maski & Kothare, 2013).

6. Neurobiological processes and early life sleep deprivation

6.1 Sleep and postnatal brain development

Brain development starts prenatally and continues postnatally in all mammals. Postnatal brain development is characterized by cortical gray matter expansion/regression and white matter development. Gray matter maturation is indicated by a massive increase of synapse (synaptogenesis), that peaks at childhood (2–3 years old) followed by rapid elimination and refinement of excess synapses (synaptic pruning) which continues until adolescent stage. However, the increase in synaptic density and synaptic pruning is regionally specific, for instance, synaptic density peaks in visual cortex at 6–8 months of age, while in prefrontal cortex at age of 2–4 years. White matter development is indicated by neuronal myelination which occur during early life stages (childhood and adolescence) and continues until early adult stage. These processes are important for optimization of neuronal connectivity and maturation of neurobehavioral functions (Huttenlocher, 1979; Semple, Blomgren, Gimlin, Ferriero, & Noble-Haeusslein, 2013).

Interestingly, sleep architecture shows remarkable changes during development that parallel the time course of postnatal brain maturation, suggesting a relationship between postnatal brain development and sleep (Kurth et al., 2015; Semple et al., 2013). REM sleep is highly concentrated in newborns consisting around 50% of their total sleep. During the first two years of life, REM sleep diminishes to 20%–25% of total sleep time that maintained throughout development (Louis, Cannard, Bastuji, & Challamel, 1997). REM sleep found to promote cortical plasticity necessary for consolidation of waking experiences in developing brain (Dumoulin Bridi et al., 2015). Furthermore, localization, distribution and coherence of sleep EEG from early childhood to late adolescence reflect the brain maturational processes. Cortical maturation follows a posterior to anterior trajectory, similarly, SWA shifts from posterior to anterior brain regions with maturation (Kurth, Ringli, et al., 2010). In addition, the coherence of EEG activity, which measures the functional connectivity strengthen by neuronal myelination, increases with maturation in a region-specific manner (Kurth, Achermann, Rusterholz, & Lebourgeois, 2013; Tarokh, Carskadon, & Achermann, 2010). Myelination is important for brain connectivity and functional network maturation. Oligodendrocytes wrap the axons with myelin sheaths forming multiple insulating layers that increase the action potential conduction by 1000-folds. Neuronal myelination is reflected by the increase of the volume of the white matter in the brain. In humans, neuronal myelination started prenatally and continues through the early adult life. In rodents, neuronal myelination continues until at least postnatal day (PND) 30–40. Interestingly, oligodendrocytes proliferation and myelin synthesis occur preferentially during sleep (Toth & Neumann, 2013), which suggests that neuronal activity during sleep, by inducing neuronal myelination, enhances functional connectivity during brain development (Kurth et al., 2013, 2015). Hence, sleep is essential for neuronal network connectivity and brain maturation during the sensitive window of childhood.

Another important process during postnatal brain development is synaptogenesis. Synaptogenesis is the process of formation of new synapses between neurons. During brain development, there is a period of synapse overproduction followed by synapse pruning and elimination. These processes reflect the refinement of neuronal circuits during childhood and adolescence inducing synaptic plasticity and cortical maturation essential for efficient processing of adult cognition. In humans, density of synapses increases rapidly after birth to reach 50% over the adult level by age of 2–3 years (Huttenlocher, 1979; Huttenlocher, 1984; Huttenlocher & Dabholkar, 1997; Huttenlocher, de Courten, Garey, & Van der Loos,

1982). In rodents, synaptic density peaks during the second week after birth and reaches the adult level by week 3–4 of age (Crain, Cotman, Taylor, & Lynch, 1973; Semple et al., 2013). However, the timing of appearance of synapse peak and elimination is region specific. The increase in synaptic density is correlated with the increase of N-Methyl-D-Aspartic Acid Receptors (NMDARs) density in the cortex which peaks at age of 1–22 years in humans and at PND28 in rats (McDonald, Johnston, & Young, 1990; Zhang, 2006; Zhong, Carrozza, Williams, Pritchett, & Molinoff, 1995). Interestingly, Studying the synaptic density using two-photon microscopy in adolescent mice showed that sleep is associated with a net of cortical spine loss while net gain of spine was increased during wakefulness, (Maret, Faraguna, Nelson, Cirelli, & Tononi, 2011). Furthermore, in a longitudinal study of sleep EEG across childhood and adolescence, (Campbell & Feinberg, 2009; Feinberg & Campbell, 2010), a very steep decline of NREM delta and theta waves was reported during adolescent stage (11–16.5 years). The study suggested that EEG changes might reflect synaptic pruning indicated by reduction in cortical thickness as measured by MRI in adolescents (Shaw et al., 2008). In a cross sectional study including children and adolescents, the topography of SWA was highest over the posterior brain region in children then shifted to the frontal cortex in adolescents, which matches the course of gray matter maturation (Kurth, Jenni, et al., 2010; Smith, Wilkins, Mogavero, & Veenema, 2015). The fact that SWA amplitude increases during childhood to reach maximum during puberty, then decreases during adolescence, suggests that SWA might be the driving mechanism underlying brain maturation processes (Ringli & Huber, 2011). Indeed, measuring the cortical volume and the synaptic density across development in humans and rats found a clear correlation between the trajectories of SWA coherence and cortical maturation (Kurth et al., 2015). This proposed role of SWA in brain maturation is further strengthened by the emergence of synaptic homeostasis hypothesis mentioned above. Hence, SWA can be an indicator of synaptic density and strength during development (Ringli & Huber, 2011). Cortical maturation is also correlated with progressive changes in behavioral and cognitive functions from childhood to adulthood, this behavioral and cognitive development is thought to rely on synaptic pruning and neuronal myelination (Luna & Sweeney, 2004), supporting the link between SWA, cortical maturation and behavioral development. Therefore, this window of development is highly sensitive to sleep deprivation. Yet the exact relationship between brain maturation, SWA and behavior needs further investigation, as several neurobehavioral disorders are associated with sleep problems, suggesting a bidirectional relationship between sleep and neurobehavioral disorders.

7. Sleep deprivation and allostatic load

Allostatic load is a measure of cumulative physiological dysregulation across biological systems. Allostasis is the process of maintaining homeostasis, it is an active process that involves metabolic mediators such as those of the autonomic nervous system, the neuroendocrine system and the immune system (McEwen & Wingfield, 2003). Chronic stress or deficits of homeostasis regulating systems enhance allostatic load/overload promoting brain and body dysfunction (McEwen & Stellar, 1993; McEwen & Wingfield, 2003). Consequences of SD and circadian disruption involves elevation of allostatic load mediators such as, pro-inflammatory cytokines, cortisol, oxidative stress, glycogen, and insulin (Hirotsu, Tufik, & Andersen, 2015; McEwen, 2006). Accordingly, SD is reported to induce hypertension, reduce parasympathetic tone, increase risk for obesity, and increase risk of cardiovascular diseases and diabetes (Hirotsu et al., 2015). The consequences of sleep deprivation suggested that SD is a stressor that contribute to allostatic load leading to physiological and behavioral dysfunction and precipitation of physiological and psychological diseases (McEwen, 2006; McEwen & Karatsoreos, 2015).

8. Sleep deprivation, oxidative stress and inflammation

Oxidative stress occurs when the production of reactive oxygen species (ROS) or reactive nitrogen species (RNS) overwhelms the antioxidant capacity of the cells (Betteridge, 2000). ROS and RNS comprise of free radical species and non-radical species/oxidants (Pham-Huy, He, & Pham-Huy, 2008). Free radicals are molecules or atoms with unpaired electrons in their outer shell such as superoxide ($O_2^{\cdot}$), hydroxyl ($OH^{\cdot}$), peroxyl ($ROO^{\cdot}$), nitric oxide ($NO^{\cdot}$) and nitrogen dioxide ($NO_2^{\cdot}$). Free radicals are highly unstable and readily participate in further reactions forming non-radical species that are also called oxidants. Examples of non-radical species are peroxynitrite ($ONOO-$), hydrogen peroxide (H_2O_2), ozone (O_3), hypochlorous acid (HOCl), nitrous acid (HNO_2), etc. These non-radicals in turn can easily produce free radicals by losing one or more electrons (Halliwell, 2007).

Normally, ROS and RNS are produced in the body as a consequence of redox reactions that accompany different metabolic processes such as oxidative phosphorylation, prostaglandin synthesis or various enzymatic reactions that involve cytochrome P450 enzyme complex (Pacher, Beckman, & Liaudet, 2007). Activation of pathways associated with inflammation, stress, and aging also result in production of ROS and RNS. At physiologically low to moderate levels, ROS and RNS play significant roles in performing different cellular functions and are critical for optimum cellular health. For instance, ROS/RNS participate in various signaling process and cascades in cardiac, epithelial, vascular and neuronal cells. Nitric oxide is an example of oxidant which serves as an intercellular signaling molecule that regulates dilation of arteries, clotting of blood, gastric motility and transmission between neurons (Pacher et al., 2007). Also, ROS plays an important role in LTP which is a form of synaptic plasticity considered essential for learning and memory (Serrano & Klann, 2004). ROS causes activation of mitogen activated protein kinases (MAPKs), protein kinases that regulate cellular signal transduction (Son et al., 2011). Moreover, ROS are also a critical part of cellular immune response as they lead to activation of proinflammatory cytokines such as IL-1β and TNF-α (Arsenijevic et al., 2000; Wang, Malo, & Hekimi, 2010). Oxidants such as H_2O_2 oxidize proteins thereby altering their structure and function which then leads to transcription of specific genes or activates certain signaling cascades that regulate normal cellular proliferation, maturation or controlled degradation (Reczek & Chandel, 2015; Schieber & Chandel, 2014).

Generally, antioxidant defense systems in the body ensure that ROS and RNS production in the body is just enough to achieve physiologically beneficial effects. The antioxidant defense mechanisms include enzymatic and non-enzymatic systems. Enzymatic antioxidant defenses include superoxide dismutase (SOD), glutathione peroxidase (GPx), and catalase (CAT). Non-enzymatic antioxidants include ascorbic acid (Vitamin C), α-tocopherol (Vitamin E), glutathione (GSH), carotenoids, flavonoids, and others. SOD exists in two forms: cytosolic Cu/Zn-SOD, and mitochondrial Mn-SOD. SOD catalyzes the dismutation of the highly reactive superoxide anion $O_2^{\cdot}$ to the less reactive species; H_2O_2 and O_2. Hydrogen peroxide can be destroyed by CAT or GPX reactions. CAT reacts very efficiently with H_2O_2 to form water and molecular oxygen. Glutathione peroxidase (GPx) catalyzes the reduction of hydro peroxides using GSH (Kleinova et al., 2007). Glutathione system is one of the most essential anti-oxidative defense mechanisms. Glutathione (GSH) is a tripeptide that contains

L-cysteine, L-glutamic acid and glycine. Glutathione exists in reduced (GSH) and oxidized (GSSG) states. Reduced glutathione (GSH) is a major antioxidant molecule in cells. It provides reducing equivalents for the GPx which results in formation of a disulfide bond between two GSH molecules generating oxidized glutathione (GSSG). The enzyme glutathione reductase (GSR) recycles GSSG to GSH (Masella, Di Benedetto, Vari, Filesi, & Giovannini, 2005).

In normal conditions, there is a balance between pro-oxidant production and the intracellular levels of antioxidants. This balance is essential for the survival of organisms and their health (Valko et al., 2007). However, various factors lead to excessive production of these reactive species setting off the balance maintained by the antioxidants, thus resulting in oxidative stress. Once the levels of ROS and RNS increase beyond an optimum level, the resultant oxidative stress leads to cellular damage by oxidizing lipids, proteins and DNA. Oxidative stress-associated cellular damage and alteration of cellular components initiates a cascade of underlying mechanisms that eventually lead to different diseases. Increase in oxidative stress induces an inflammatory response via release of proinflammatory cytokines such as TNF-α and IL-6. Other mediators of inflammation such as nuclear factor-kappa B (NF-κB), vascular cell adhesion molecule-1 (VCAM-1) are also activated by ROS and RNS. This inflammatory response is an underlying causal mechanism for various diseases such as diabetes, chronic renal failure, hypertension, chronic obstructive pulmonary diseases (COPD) and rheumatoid arthritis as well as neurodegenerative disorders like Parkinson's disease and multiple sclerosis (Aruoma, Grootveld, & Bahorun, 2006; Butterfield, Castegna, Drake, Scapagnini, & Calabrese, 2002; Hoshino & Mishima, 2008; MacNee, 2001; Prabhakar, 2013).

The central nervous system (CNS) is especially vulnerable to the effects of oxidative stress owing to relatively low level of antioxidants in the brain and high level of transition metals such as Fe^{2+} that form reactive unstable complexes and generate more free radicals (Rahal et al., 2014). Also, levels of polyunsaturated fatty acids (PUFAs) and lipids are very high in the CNS. These lipids and PUFAs are well-known targets of oxidative stress and undergo free-radical induced lipid peroxidation and oxidation (Cherubini, Ruggiero, Polidori, & Mecocci, 2005). Moreover, various redox reactions that result in production of ROS and RNS occur in the brain in order to meet the high oxygen and energy requirement of the brain (Butterfield et al., 2002). Therefore, it seems likely that excessive levels of ROS and RNS in the brain might alter the structure and function of different brain regions resulting in neurological and psychological conditions. However, neuronal response to oxidative stress is not uniform, which makes some regions of the brain more vulnerable to oxidative stress than others. For example, it has been reported that the cortex and the hippocampus are the most sensitive brain regions to oxidative stress (Wang & Michaelis, 2010).

Both clinical and preclinical studies have indicated that behavioral and memory deficits are associated with oxidative stress elevation. For example, in an animal model of stress, elevation in markers of oxidative stress in hippocampus of socially defeated rats was associated with induction of anxiety, depression-like behavior and memory impairment (Patki, Solanki, Atrooz, Allam, & Salim, 2013). Moreover, early life SD increased plasma 8-isoprostane levels and induced expression of antioxidant enzymes in the prefrontal cortex of rats. Elevation of oxidative stress markers was associated with anxiety-like behavior at early life which developed into depression-like behavior at adult life (Atrooz et al., 2019). In humans, depressed patients showed an increase in oxidative stress markers in serum indicated by a decrease in antioxidant enzymes and an increase in the lipid peroxidation marker, malondialdehyde (MDA), as compared to age-matched control group (Stefanescu & Ciobica, 2012). Anxiety disorders in humans were also associated with elevation of lipid peroxidation products and alteration of antioxidant enzymes (Ng, Berk, Dean, & Bush, 2008). Additionally, children and adolescents with anxiety disorders showed plasma elevation of oxidative stress markers (Guney et al., 2014).

One of the proposed functions of sleep is promoting anti-oxidative mechanisms. This perhaps is an adaptive response to sleep loss/deprivation as SD or sleep loss might induce oxidative stress. For instance, it has been suggested that sleep promotes removal of free radicals accumulated during wakefulness (Reimund, 1994). Peroxide infusion into preoptic/anterior hypothalamus region of brain induced sleep in rats by promoting the release of neuromodulators, nitric oxide and adenosine (Ikeda et al., 2005). Furthermore, intraventricular infusion of the oxidized glutathione (GSSG) enhanced the SWA sleep and REM sleep (Honda, Komoda, & Inoue, 1994). Indeed, some studies have suggested that oxidative stress is the underlying pathophysiological mechanism for development of cardiovascular and neurobehavioral complications mediated by obstructive sleep apnea (Gozal & Kheirandish-Gozal, 2008). Animal models also have provided important insights into the relationship between oxidative stress and sleep deprivation (Villafuerte et al., 2015). Chronic SD in rats decreased SOD activity in the hippocampus and brainstem (Ramanathan, Gulyani, Nienhuis, & Siegel, 2002), and decreased total glutathione (GSH) levels and catalase activity in liver, but increased glutathione peroxidase (GPx) activity in the heart (Everson, Laatsch, & Hogg, 2005). Short periods of SD (96 h) decreased the GSH levels in rats' hippocampus (D'Almeida et al., 1998). Twenty four hours sleep deprivation in rats reduced lipid peroxidation in hippocampus (Melgarejo-Gutierrez et al., 2013) and increased the level of glyoxalase (GLO-1) and glutathione reductase (GSR-1) in prefrontal cortex, hippocampus, and amygdala (Vollert et al., 2011). While acute SD (6 h) in rats by gentle handling increased the level of the reduced glutathione (GSH) levels in the cortex, brain stem, and forebrain and enhanced the activity of GPx in hippocampus and cerebellum (Ramanathan, Hu, Frautschy, & Siegel, 2010). Prolonged SD, for 5−11 days, significantly decreased SOD activity in hippocampus and brain stem of adult rats (Ramanathan et al., 2002). Adult rats exposed to 24 h SD showed behavioral and cognitive deficits associated with plasma elevation of 8-ioprostane (Solanki, Atrooz, Asghar, & Salim, 2016). However, other animal models of SD did not find any changes in oxidative stress markers or antioxidant capacity in peripheral blood or brain regions following SD (D'Almeida et al., 1997; Gopalakrishnan, Ji, & Cirelli, 2004). The inconsistency of results might due to the variation in the methods used for sleep deprivation, the duration of SD, or the rodent strains used for SD. Collectively, these data suggest that while short periods of SD enhance anti-oxidant response in brain and other organs, long SD periods reduce the anti-oxidant response suggesting that extended wakefulness induces chronic oxidative stress that lead to failure of antioxidant mechanisms to sustain the accumulation of pro-oxidants.

Moreover, SD has been implicated in inflammation and immune dysfunction. In healthy individuals, acute or chronic SD is associated with increased serum levels of IL-1, TNF-α, IL-6, IL-17, and NFκB, in addition to alteration of numbers and activity of macrophages and natural killer cells (Irwin et al., 2008, 2015; van Leeuwen et al., 2009; Wright Jr et al., 2015). In preclinical studies, SD induced elevation of inflammatory markers such as; IL-1, IL-6, and TNF-α, in peripheral blood and different brain regions, also has been reported (Atrooz et al., 2019; Chennaoui et al., 2015). While the immune system has the potential to induce brain plasticity and neuronal networks functioning, elevation of neuroinflammatory mediators can cause impairment of synaptic plasticity (Hong, Mills, Loredo, Adler, & Dimsdale, 2005; Tancredi et al., 2000). In rat's hippocampus slices, treatment with IL-6 decreased the synaptic plasticity indicated by reduction of LTP potentially through inhibition of MAP/ERK activation. The effect of IL-6 on the synaptic plasticity was associated with the activation of the signal transducer and activator of transcription-3 (STAT3), Phosphorylation of STAT3 is mediated via gp 130-associated JAK tyrosine kinases, accordingly, inhibition of synaptic plasticity by IL-6 was counteracted by simultaneous treatment with the tyrosine kinases inhibitor lavendustin A, while inactivation of MAP/ERK might be mediated by stimulation of tyrosine and/or dual-specificity phosphatases (Tancredi et al., 2000).

In vitro studies showed that as a response to oxidative stress, the activity of P38 and JNK MAPKs increased which in turn mediated the production of pro-inflammatory cytokines including IL-6. Additionally, activation of the MAPKs pathway was also essential for regulating the expression of the antioxidant enzymes including HO and Mn-SOD (Nahirnyj, Livne-Bar, Guo, & Sivak, 2013). Prolonged activation of MAPKs is detrimental to cells due to their role in mediating biosynthesis of proinflammatory cytokines, hence, activation of MAPKs, induces the expression of MAPK phosphatases such as (MKP1) which in turn dephosphorylates MAPKs and therefore restraints the MAPKs-mediated inflammatory response (Collins, Downer, Toulouse, & Nolan, 2015). This mechanism of negative feedback regulation is critical for cell survival. Hence, MKP1 is considered as a key factor in regulating the stress response, and its expression is highly regulated transcriptionally, post-transcriptionally, and post-translationally by numerous factors (Kuwano & Gorospe, 2008). It is well known that MKP1 regulates the magnitude and duration of MAPKs signaling, and as the strength of MAPKs signaling determines the duration of biological responses and many physiological outcomes, therefore, the spatial and temporal titration of MKP1 has a fundamental regulatory role. MKP1, by dephosphorylation of $ERK_{1/2}$ and MEK, alters the neurotrophic downstream signaling pathway which is essential for neuronal growth, plasticity and cell survival (Duman, 2004; Valjent, Caboche, & Vanhoutte, 2001). Interestingly, in rat models of early life SD, SD caused enhanced expression of MKP1 and also caused long lasting reduction in synaptic density and plasticity in rats prefrontal cortex that was evident at adult stage (Atrooz et al., 2019).

In summary, while sleep has a role in regulation of synaptic plasticity and protein synthesis, sleep deprivation might alter protein synthesis, and synaptic plasticity through oxido-inflammatory mechanisms. During early developmental stage, synaptic growth and synaptic plasticity are essential for neural circuit formation and maturation, therefore SD during these critical periods might permanently alter neural circuit maturation in brain regions that regulate emotion and cognition leading to development of psychiatric disorders later in life.

Disclosure of interest

The authors report no conflict of interest. Funding for this research was provided by an NIH grant awarded to Samina Salim (2R15MH093918-02).

References

Abrahamson, E. E., & Moore, R. Y. (2006). Lesions of suprachiasmatic nucleus efferents selectively affect rest-activity rhythm. *Molecular and Cellular Endocrinology, 252*(1–2), 46–56. http://dx.doi.org/10.1016/j.mce.2006.03.036.

Alfano, C. A., Pina, A. A., Zerr, A. A., & Villalta, I. K. (2010). Pre-sleep arousal and sleep problems of anxiety-disordered youth. *Child Psychiatry and Human Development, 41*(2), 156–167. http://dx.doi.org/10.1007/s10578-009-0158-5.

Alkadhi, K. (2013). Neurobiological consequences of sleep deprivation. *Current Neuropharmacology, 11*, 19.

Arsenijevic, D., Garcia, I., Vesin, C., Vesin, D., Arsenijevic, Y., Seydoux, J., & Richard, D. (2000). Differential roles of tumor necrosis factor-alpha and interferon-gamma in mouse hypermetabolic and anorectic responses induced by LPS. *European Cytokine Network, 11*(4), 662–668.

Aruoma, O. I., Grootveld, M., & Bahorun, T. (2006). Free radicals in biology and medicine: From inflammation to biotechnology. *BioFactors, 27*(1–4), 1–3.

Astill, R. G., Van der Heijden, K. B., Van Ijzendoorn, M. H., & Van Someren, E. J. (2012). Sleep, cognition, and behavioral problems in school-age children: A century of research meta-analyzed. *Psychological Bulletin, 138*(6), 1109–1138. http://dx.doi.org/10.1037/a0028204.

Atrooz, F., Liu, H., Kochi, C., & Salim, S. J. N. (2019). *Early life sleep deprivation: Role of oxido-inflammatory processes.*

Babson, K. A., Trainor, C. D., Feldner, M. T., & Blumenthal, H. (2010). A test of the effects of acute sleep deprivation on general and specific self-reported anxiety and depressive symptoms: An experimental extension. *Journal of Behavior Therapy and Experimental Psychiatry, 41*(3), 297–303. http://dx.doi.org/10.1016/j.jbtep.2010.02.008.

Betteridge, D. J. (2000). What is oxidative stress? *Metabolism, 49*(2 Suppl. 1), 3–8.

Borbely, A. A. (1982a). Sleep regulation. Introduction. *Human Neurobiology, 1*(3), 161–162.

Borbely, A. A. (1982b). A two process model of sleep regulation. *Human Neurobiology, 1*(3), 195–204.

Butterfield, D. A., Castegna, A., Drake, J., Scapagnini, G., & Calabrese, V. (2002). Vitamin E and neurodegenerative disorders associated with oxidative stress. *Nutritional Neuroscience, 5*(4), 229–239. http://dx.doi.org/10.1080/10284150290028954.

Buxton, O. M., Chang, A. M., Spilsbury, J. C., Bos, T., Emsellem, H., & Knutson, K. L. (2015). Sleep in the modern family: protective family routines for child and adolescent sleep. *Sleep Health, 1*(1), 15–27. PubMed PMID: 26779564; PubMed Central PMCID: PMC4712736.

Cain, N., & Gradisar, M. (2010). Electronic media use and sleep in school-aged children and adolescents: A review. *Sleep Medicine, 11*(8), 735–742. http://dx.doi.org/10.1016/j.sleep.2010.02.006.

Campbell, I. G., & Feinberg, I. (2009). Longitudinal trajectories of non-rapid eye movement delta and theta EEG as indicators of adolescent brain maturation. *Proceedings of the National Academy of Sciences of the United States of America, 106*(13), 5177–5180. http://dx.doi.org/10.1073/pnas.0812947106.

Cappuccio, F. P., Cooper, D., D'Elia, L., Strazzullo, P., & Miller, M. A. (2011). Sleep duration predicts cardiovascular outcomes: A systematic review and meta-analysis of prospective studies. *European Heart Journal, 32*(12), 1484–1492. http://dx.doi.org/10.1093/eurheartj/ehr007.

Chee, M. W., & Chuah, L. Y. (2008). Functional neuroimaging insights into how sleep and sleep deprivation affect memory and cognition. *Current Opinion in Neurology, 21*(4), 417–423. http://dx.doi.org/10.1097/WCO.0b013e3283052cf7.

Chennaoui, M., Gomez-Merino, D., Drogou, C., Geoffroy, H., Dispersyn, G., Langrume, C., & Sauvet, F. (2015). Effects of exercise on brain and peripheral inflammatory biomarkers induced by total sleep deprivation in rats. *Journal of Inflammation, 12*, 56. http://dx.doi.org/10.1186/s12950-015-0102-3.

Cherubini, A., Ruggiero, C., Polidori, M. C., & Mecocci, P. (2005). Potential markers of oxidative stress in stroke. *Free Radical Biology and Medicine, 39*(7), 841–852. http://dx.doi.org/10.1016/j.freeradbiomed.2005.06.025.

Cirelli, C. (2006). Cellular consequences of sleep deprivation in the brain. *10*(5), 307–321.

Collins, L. M., Downer, E. J., Toulouse, A., & Nolan, Y. M. (2015). Mitogen-activated protein kinase phosphatase (MKP)-1 in nervous system development and disease. *Molecular Neurobiology, 51*(3), 1158–1167. http://dx.doi.org/10.1007/s12035-014-8786-6.

Cox, R. C., & Olatunji, B. O. (2016). A systematic review of sleep disturbance in anxiety and related disorders. *Journal of Anxiety Disorders, 37*, 104–129. http://dx.doi.org/10.1016/j.janxdis.2015.12.001.

Crain, B., Cotman, C., Taylor, D., & Lynch, G. (1973). A quantitative electron microscopic study of synaptogenesis in the dentate gyrus of the rat. *Brain Research, 63*, 195–204.

D'Almeida, V., Hipólide, D. C., Azzalis, L. g. A., Lobo, L. c. L., Junqueira, V. n. B., & Tufik, S. J. N. l. (1997). Absence of oxidative stress following paradoxical sleep deprivation in rats. *235*(1–2), 25–28.

D'Almeida, V., Lobo, L. L., Hipolide, D. C., de Oliveira, A. C., Nobrega, J. N., & Tufik, S. (1998). Sleep deprivation induces brain region-specific decreases in glutathione levels. *NeuroReport, 9*(12), 2853–2856.

Dang-Vu, T. T., Schabus, M., Desseilles, M., Sterpenich, V., Bonjean, M., & Maquet, P. (2010). Functional neuroimaging insights into the physiology of human sleep. *Sleep, 33*(12), 1589–1603.

Datta, S. (2010). Cellular and chemical neuroscience of mammalian sleep. *Sleep Medicine, 11*(5), 431–440. http://dx.doi.org/10.1016/j.sleep.2010.02.002.

Dettoni, J. L., Consolim-Colombo, F. M., Drager, L. F., Rubira, M. C., Souza, S. B., Irigoyen, M. C., & Lorenzi-Filho, G. (2012). Cardiovascular effects of partial sleep deprivation in healthy volunteers. *Journal of Applied Physiology, 113*(2), 232–236. http://dx.doi.org/10.1152/japplphysiol.01604.2011.

Dewald, J. F., Meijer, A. M., Oort, F. J., Kerkhof, G. A., & Bogels, S. M. (2010). The influence of sleep quality, sleep duration and sleepiness on school performance in children and adolescents: A meta-analytic review. *Sleep Medicine Reviews, 14*(3), 179–189. http://dx.doi.org/10.1016/j.smrv.2009.10.004.

Drummond, S. P., Brown, G. G., Gillin, J. C., Stricker, J. L., Wong, E. C., & Buxton, R. B. (2000). Altered brain response to verbal learning following sleep deprivation. *Nature, 403*(6770), 655–657. http://dx.doi.org/10.1038/35001068.

Duman, R. S. (2004). Role of neurotrophic factors in the etiology and treatment of mood disorders. *NeuroMolecular Medicine, 5*(1), 11–25. http://dx.doi.org/10.1385/NMM:5:1:011.

Dumoulin Bridi, M. C., Aton, S. J., Seibt, J., Renouard, L., Coleman, T., & Frank, M. G. (2015). Rapid eye movement sleep promotes cortical plasticity in the developing brain. *Science Advances, 1*(6), e1500105. http://dx.doi.org/10.1126/sciadv.1500105.

Everson, C. A., Laatsch, C. D., & Hogg, N. (2005). Antioxidant defense responses to sleep loss and sleep recovery. *American Journal of Physiology - Regulatory, Integrative and Comparative Physiology, 288*(2), R374–R383. http://dx.doi.org/10.1152/ajpregu.00565.2004.

Feinberg, I., & Campbell, I. G. (2010). Sleep EEG changes during adolescence: An index of a fundamental brain reorganization. *Brain and Cognition, 72*(1), 56–65. http://dx.doi.org/10.1016/j.bandc.2009.09.008.

Frank, M. G., Issa, N. P., & Stryker, M. P. (2001). Sleep enhances plasticity in the developing visual cortex. *Neuron, 30*(1), 275–287.

Gessa, G. L., Pani, L., Fadda, P., & Fratta, W. (1995). Sleep deprivation in the rat: An animal model of mania. *European Neuropsychopharmacology, 5*(Suppl. l), 89–93.

Goel, N., Rao, H., Durmer, J. S., & Dinges, D. F. (2009). Neurocognitive consequences of sleep deprivation. *Seminars in Neurology, 29*(4), 320–339. http://dx.doi.org/10.1055/s-0029-1237117.

Goldstein, A. N., & Walker, M. P. (2014). The role of sleep in emotional brain function. *Annual Review of Clinical Psychology, 10,* 679–708. http://dx.doi.org/10.1146/annurev-clinpsy-032813-153716.

Gopalakrishnan, A., Ji, L. L., & Cirelli, C. (2004). Sleep deprivation and cellular responses to oxidative stress. *Sleep, 27*(1), 27–35.

Gozal, D., & Kheirandish-Gozal, L. (2008). Cardiovascular morbidity in obstructive sleep apnea: Oxidative stress, inflammation, and much more. *American Journal of Respiratory and Critical Care Medicine, 177*(4), 369–375. http://dx.doi.org/10.1164/rccm.200608-1190PP.

Graves, L. A., Heller, E. A., Pack, A. I., & Abel, T. (2003). Sleep deprivation selectively impairs memory consolidation for contextual fear conditioning. *Learning & Memory, 10*(3), 168–176. http://dx.doi.org/10.1101/lm.48803.

Gregory, A. M., Caspi, A., Eley, T. C., Moffitt, T. E., Oconnor, T. G., & Poulton, R. (2005). Prospective longitudinal associations between persistent sleep problems in childhood and anxiety and depression disorders in adulthood. *Journal of Abnormal Child Psychology, 33*(2), 157–163.

Gregory, A. M., & Sadeh, A. (2012). Sleep, emotional and behavioral difficulties in children and adolescents. *Sleep Medicine Reviews, 16*(2), 129–136. http://dx.doi.org/10.1016/j.smrv.2011.03.007.

Gregory, A. M., & Sadeh, A. (2016). Annual Research Review: Sleep problems in childhood psychiatric disorders–a review of the latest science. *Journal of Child Psychology and Psychiatry, 57*(3), 296–317. http://dx.doi.org/10.1111/jcpp.12469.

Guan, Z., Peng, X., & Fang, J. (2004). Sleep deprivation impairs spatial memory and decreases extracellular signal-regulated kinase phosphorylation in the hippocampus. *Brain Research, 1018*(1), 38–47. http://dx.doi.org/10.1016/j.brainres.2004.05.032.

Guney, E., Fatih Ceylan, M., Tektas, A., Alisik, M., Ergin, M., Goker, Z., & Erel, O. (2014). Oxidative stress in children and adolescents with anxiety disorders. *Journal of Affective Disorders, 156,* 62–66. http://dx.doi.org/10.1016/j.jad.2013.11.016.

Hagewoud, R., Havekes, R., Novati, A., Keijser, J. N., Van der Zee, E. A., & Meerlo, P. (2010). Sleep deprivation impairs spatial working memory and reduces hippocampal AMPA receptor phosphorylation. *Journal of Sleep Research, 19*(2), 280–288. http://dx.doi.org/10.1111/j.1365-2869.2009.00799.x.

Halliwell, B. (2007). Biochemistry of oxidative stress. *Biochemical Society Transactions, 35*(Pt 5), 1147–1150. http://dx.doi.org/10.1042/BST0351147.

Harrison, Y., & Horne, J. A. (2000). Sleep loss and temporal memory. *Quarterly Journal of Experimental Psychology A, 53*(1), 271–279. http://dx.doi.org/10.1080/713755870.

Havekes, R., Vecsey, C. G., & Abel, T. (2012). The impact of sleep deprivation on neuronal and glial signaling pathways important for memory and synaptic plasticity. *Cellular Signalling, 24*(6), 1251–1260.

Hawkins, S. S., & Takeuchi, D. T. (2016). Social determinants of inadequate sleep in US children and adolescents. *Public Health, 138*, 119–126. http://dx.doi.org/10.1016/j.puhe.2016.03.036.

Hermans, E. J., van Marle, H. J., Ossewaarde, L., Henckens, M. J., Qin, S., van Kesteren, M. T., & Fernandez, G. (2011). Stress-related noradrenergic activity prompts large scale neural network reconfiguration. *Science, 334*(6059), 1151–1153. http://dx.doi.org/10.1126/science.1209603.

Hernandez, P. J., & Abel, T. (2008). The role of protein synthesis in memory consolidation: Progress amid decades of debate. *Neurobiology of Learning and Memory, 89*(3), 293–311. http://dx.doi.org/10.1016/j.nlm.2007.09.010.

Hirotsu, C., Tufik, S., & Andersen, M. L. (2015). Interactions between sleep, stress, and metabolism: From physiological to pathological conditions. *Sleep Science, 8*(3), 143–152. http://dx.doi.org/10.1016/j.slsci.2015.09.002.

Hodge, D., Carollo, T. M., Lewin, M., Hoffman, C. D., & Sweeney, D. P. (2014). Sleep patterns in children with and without autism spectrum disorders: Developmental comparisons. *Research in Developmental Disabilities, 35*(7), 1631–1638. http://dx.doi.org/10.1016/j.ridd.2014.03.037.

Honda, K., Komoda, Y., & Inoue, S. (1994). Oxidized glutathione regulates physiological sleep in unrestrained rats. *Brain Research, 636*(2), 253–258.

Hong, S., Mills, P. J., Loredo, J. S., Adler, K. A., & Dimsdale, J. E. (2005). The association between interleukin-6, sleep, and demographic characteristics. *Brain, Behavior, and Immunity, 19*(2), 165–172. http://dx.doi.org/10.1016/j.bbi.2004.07.008.

Hoshino, Y., & Mishima, M. (2008). Redox-based therapeutics for lung diseases. *Antioxidants and Redox Signaling, 10*(4), 701–704. http://dx.doi.org/10.1089/ars.2007.1961.

Huttenlocher, P. R. (1979). Synaptic density in human frontal cortex - developmental changes and effects of aging. *Brain Research, 163*(2), 195–205.

Huttenlocher, P. R. (1984). Synapse elimination and plasticity in developing human cerebral cortex. *American Journal of Mental Deficiency, 88*(5), 488–496.

Huttenlocher, P. R., & Dabholkar, A. S. (1997). Regional differences in synaptogenesis in human cerebral cortex. *The Journal of Comparative Neurology, 387*(2), 167–178.

Huttenlocher, P. R., de Courten, C., Garey, L. J., & Van der Loos, H. (1982). Synaptogenesis in human visual cortex–evidence for synapse elimination during normal development. *Neuroscience Letters, 33*(3), 247–252.

Ikeda, M., Ikeda-Sagara, M., Okada, T., Clement, P., Urade, Y., Nagai, T., & Inoue, S. (2005). Brain oxidation is an initial process in sleep induction. *Neuroscience, 130*(4), 1029–1040. http://dx.doi.org/10.1016/j.neuroscience.2004.09.057.

Irwin, M. R., Wang, M., Ribeiro, D., Cho, H. J., Olmstead, R., Breen, E. C., & Cole, S. (2008). Sleep loss activates cellular inflammatory signaling. *Biological Psychiatry, 64*(6), 538–540.

Irwin, M. R., Witarama, T., Caudill, M., Olmstead, R., & Breen, E. C. (2015). Sleep loss activates cellular inflammation and signal transducer and activator of transcription (STAT) family proteins in humans. *Brain, Behaviour, and Immunity, 47*, 86–92.

Kahn-Greene, E. T., Killgore, D. B., Kamimori, G. H., Balkin, T. J., & Killgore, W. D. (2007). The effects of sleep deprivation on symptoms of psychopathology in healthy adults. *Sleep Medicine, 8*(3), 215–221. http://dx.doi.org/10.1016/j.sleep.2006.08.007.

Kalia, M. (2006). Neurobiology of sleep. *Metabolism, 55*(10 Suppl. 2), S2–S6. http://dx.doi.org/10.1016/j.metabol.2006.07.005.

Kametani, H., & Kawamura, H. (1990). Alterations in acetylcholine release in the rat hippocampus during sleep-wakefulness detected by intracerebral dialysis. *Life Sciences, 47*(5), 421–426.

Kleinova, M., Hewitt, M., Brezova, V., Madden, J. C., Cronin, M. T., & Valko, M. (2007). Antioxidant properties of carotenoids: QSAR prediction of their redox potentials. *General Physiology and Biophysics, 26*(2), 97–103.

Knutson, K. L., Spiegel, K., Penev, P., & Van Cauter, E. (2007). The metabolic consequences of sleep deprivation. *Sleep Medicine Reviews, 11*(3), 163–178. http://dx.doi.org/10.1016/j.smrv.2007.01.002.

Kopp, C., Longordo, F., Nicholson, J. R., & Luthi, A. (2006). Insufficient sleep reversibly alters bidirectional synaptic plasticity and NMDA receptor function. *Journal of Neuroscience, 26*(48), 12456–12465. http://dx.doi.org/10.1523/JNEUROSCI.2702-06.2006.

Krueger, J. M., Frank, M. G., Wisor, J. P., & Roy, S. (2016). Sleep function: Toward elucidating an enigma. *Sleep Medicine Reviews, 28*, 46–54. http://dx.doi.org/10.1016/j.smrv.2015.08.005.

Krueger, J. M., & Obal, F., Jr. (2003). Sleep function. *Frontiers in Bioscience, 8*, d511–519.

Kurth, S., Achermann, P., Rusterholz, T., & Lebourgeois, M. K. (2013). Development of brain EEG connectivity across early childhood: Does sleep play a role? *Brain Sciences, 3*(4), 1445–1460. http://dx.doi.org/10.3390/brainsci3041445.

Kurth, S., Jenni, O. G., Riedner, B. A., Tononi, G., Carskadon, M. A., & Huber, R. (2010). Characteristics of sleep slow waves in children and adolescents. *Sleep, 33*(4), 475–480.

Kurth, S., Olini, N., Huber, R., & LeBourgeois, M. (2015). Sleep and early cortical development. *Current Sleep Medicine Reports, 1*(1), 64–73. http://dx.doi.org/10.1007/s40675-014-0002-8.

Kurth, S., Ringli, M., Geiger, A., LeBourgeois, M., Jenni, O. G., & Huber, R. (2010). Mapping of cortical activity in the first two decades of life: A high-density sleep electroencephalogram study. *Journal of Neuroscience, 30*(40), 13211–13219. http://dx.doi.org/10.1523/JNEUROSCI.2532-10.2010.

Kuwano, Y., & Gorospe, M. (2008). Protecting the stress response, guarding the MKP-1 mRNA. *Cell Cycle*, 7(17), 2640–2642. http://dx.doi.org/10.4161/cc.7.17.6534.

van Leeuwen, W. M., Lehto, M., Karisola, P., Lindholm, H., Luukkonen, R., Sallinen, M., & Alenius, H. (2009). Sleep restriction increases the risk of developing cardiovascular diseases by augmenting proinflammatory responses through IL-17 and CRP. *PLoS One, 4*(2), e4589.

Lopez, J., Hoffmann, R., & Armitage, R. (2010). Reduced sleep spindle activity in early-onset and elevated risk for depression. *Journal of the American Academy of Child & Adolescent Psychiatry, 49*(9), 934–943. http://dx.doi.org/10.1016/j.jaac.2010.05.014.

Lopez, J., Roffwarg, H. P., Dreher, A., Bissette, G., Karolewicz, B., & Shaffery, J. P. (2008). Rapid eye movement sleep deprivation decreases long-term potentiation stability and affects some glutamatergic signaling proteins during hippocampal development. *Neuroscience, 153*(1), 44–53. http://dx.doi.org/10.1016/j.neuroscience.2008.01.072.

Louis, J., Cannard, C., Bastuji, H., & Challamel, M. J. (1997). Sleep ontogenesis revisited: A longitudinal 24-hour home polygraphic study on 15 normal infants during the first two years of life. *Sleep, 20*(5), 323–333.

Luna, B., & Sweeney, J. A. (2004). The emergence of collaborative brain function: FMRI studies of the development of response inhibition. *Annals of the New York Academy of Sciences, 1021*, 296–309. http://dx.doi.org/10.1196/annals.1308.035.

MacNee, W. (2001). Oxidative stress and lung inflammation in airways disease. *European Journal of Pharmacology, 429*(1–3), 195–207.

Mallick, B. N., & Singh, A. (2011). REM sleep loss increases brain excitability: Role of noradrenaline and its mechanism of action. *Sleep Medicine Reviews, 15*(3), 165–178. http://dx.doi.org/10.1016/j.smrv.2010.11.001.

Maret, S., Faraguna, U., Nelson, A. B., Cirelli, C., & Tononi, G. (2011). Sleep and waking modulate spine turnover in the adolescent mouse cortex. *Nature Neuroscience, 14*(11), 1418–1420. http://dx.doi.org/10.1038/nn.2934.

van Marle, H. J., Hermans, E. J., Qin, S., & Fernandez, G. (2009). From specificity to sensitivity: How acute stress affects amygdala processing of biologically salient stimuli. *Biological Psychiatry, 66*(7), 649–655. http://dx.doi.org/10.1016/j.biopsych.2009.05.014.

Masella, R., Di Benedetto, R., Vari, R., Filesi, C., & Giovannini, C. (2005). Novel mechanisms of natural antioxidant compounds in biological systems: Involvement of glutathione and glutathione-related enzymes. *The Journal of Nutritional Biochemistry, 16*(10), 577–586. http://dx.doi.org/10.1016/j.jnutbio.2005.05.013.

Maski, K. P., & Kothare, S. V. (2013). Sleep deprivation and neurobehavioral functioning in children. *International Journal of Psychophysiology, 89*(2), 259–264. http://dx.doi.org/10.1016/j.ijpsycho.2013.06.019.

McDonald, J. W., Johnston, M. V., & Young, A. B. (1990). Differential ontogenic development of three receptors comprising the NMDA receptor/channel complex in the rat hippocampus. *Experimental Neurology, 110*(3), 237–247.

McEwen, B. S. (2006). Sleep deprivation as a neurobiologic and physiologic stressor: Allostasis and allostatic load. *Metabolism, 55*(10 Suppl. 2), S20–S23. http://dx.doi.org/10.1016/j.metabol.2006.07.008.

McEwen, B. S., & Karatsoreos, I. N. (2015). Sleep deprivation and circadian disruption: Stress, allostasis, and allostatic load. *Sleep Medicine Clinics, 10*(1), 1–10. http://dx.doi.org/10.1016/j.jsmc.2014.11.007.

McEwen, B. S., & Stellar, E. (1993). Stress and the individual. Mechanisms leading to disease. *Archives of Internal Medicine, 153*(18), 2093–2101.

McEwen, B. S., & Wingfield, J. C. (2003). The concept of allostasis in biology and biomedicine. *Hormones and Behavior, 43*(1), 2–15.

Meerlo, P., Havekes, R., & Steiger, A. (2015). Chronically restricted or disrupted sleep as a causal factor in the development of depression. *Current Topics in Behavioral Neurosciences, 25*, 459–481. http://dx.doi.org/10.1007/7854_2015_367.

Meerlo, P., Sgoifo, A., & Suchecki, D. (2008). Restricted and disrupted sleep: Effects on autonomic function, neuroendocrine stress systems and stress responsivity. *Sleep Medicine Reviews, 12*(3), 197–210. http://dx.doi.org/10.1016/j.smrv.2007.07.007.

Melgarejo-Gutierrez, M., Acosta-Pena, E., Venebra-Munoz, A., Escobar, C., Santiago-Garcia, J., & Garcia-Garcia, F. (2013). Sleep deprivation reduces neuroglobin immunoreactivity in the rat brain. *NeuroReport, 24*(3), 120–125. http://dx.doi.org/10.1097/WNR.0b013e32835d4b74.

Nahirnyj, A., Livne-Bar, I., Guo, X., & Sivak, J. M. (2013). ROS detoxification and proinflammatory cytokines are linked by p38 MAPK signaling in a model of mature astrocyte activation. *PLoS One, 8*(12), e83049. http://dx.doi.org/10.1371/journal.pone.0083049.

Ng, F., Berk, M., Dean, O., & Bush, A. I. (2008). Oxidative stress in psychiatric disorders: Evidence base and therapeutic implications. *The International Journal of Neuropsychopharmacology, 11*(6), 851–876. http://dx.doi.org/10.1017/S1461145707008401.

Nutt, D., Wilson, S., & Paterson, L. (2008). Sleep disorders as core symptoms of depression. *Dialogues in Clinical Neuroscience, 10*(3), 329–336.

Orzel-Gryglewska, J. (2010). Consequences of sleep deprivation. *International Journal of Occupational Medicine & Environmental Health, 23*(1), 95–114. http://dx.doi.org/10.2478/v10001-010-0004-9.

Ouyang, M., Hellman, K., Abel, T., & Thomas, S. A. (2004). Adrenergic signaling plays a critical role in the maintenance of waking and in the regulation of REM sleep. *Journal of Neurophysiology, 92*(4), 2071–2082. http://dx.doi.org/10.1152/jn.00226.2004.

Pace-Schott, E. F., Germain, A., & Milad, M. R. (2015). Effects of sleep on memory for conditioned fear and fear extinction. *Psychological Bulletin, 141*(4), 835–857. http://dx.doi.org/10.1037/bul0000014.

Pacher, P., Beckman, J. S., & Liaudet, L. (2007). Nitric oxide and peroxynitrite in health and disease. *Physiological Reviews, 87*(1), 315–424. http://dx.doi.org/10.1152/physrev.00029.2006.

Palagini, L., Baglioni, C., Ciapparelli, A., Gemignani, A., & Riemann, D. (2013). REM sleep dysregulation in depression: State of the art. *Sleep Medicine Reviews, 17*(5), 377–390. http://dx.doi.org/10.1016/j.smrv.2012.11.001.

Paruthi, S., Brooks, L. J., D'Ambrosio, C., Hall, W. A., Kotagal, S., Lloyd, R. M., & Wise, M. S. (2016). Recommended amount of sleep for pediatric populations: A consensus statement of the American Academy of sleep medicine. *Journal of Clinical Sleep Medicine, 12*(6), 785–786. http://dx.doi.org/10.5664/jcsm.5866.

Patki, G., Solanki, N., Atrooz, F., Allam, F., & Salim, S. (2013). Depression, anxiety-like behavior and memory impairment are associated with increased oxidative stress and inflammation in a rat model of social stress. *Brain Research, 1539*, 73–86. http://dx.doi.org/10.1016/j.brainres.2013.09.033.

Pham-Huy, L. A., He, H., & Pham-Huy, C. (2008). Free radicals, antioxidants in disease and health. *International Journal of Biomedical Sciences, 4*(2), 89–96.

Pires, G. N., Alvarenga, T. A., Maia, L. O., Mazaro-Costa, R., Tufik, S., & Andersen, M. L. (2012). Inhibition of self-grooming induced by sleep restriction in dam rats. *Indian Journal of Medical Research, 136*(6), 1025–1030.

Pires, G. N., Bezerra, A. G., Tufik, S., & Andersen, M. L. (2016). Effects of experimental sleep deprivation on anxiety-like behavior in animal research: Systematic review and meta-analysis. *Neuroscience & Biobehavioral Reviews, 68*, 575–589. http://dx.doi.org/10.1016/j.neubiorev.2016.06.028.

Pires, G. N., Tufik, S., & Andersen, M. L. (2013). Grooming analysis algorithm: Use in the relationship between sleep deprivation and anxiety-like behavior. *Progress In Neuro-Psychopharmacology & Biological Psychiatry, 41*, 6–10. http://dx.doi.org/10.1016/j.pnpbp.2012.11.006.

Prabhakar, O. (2013). Cerebroprotective effect of resveratrol through antioxidant and anti-inflammatory effects in diabetic rats. *Naunyn-Schmiedeberg's Archives of Pharmacology, 386*(8), 705–710. http://dx.doi.org/10.1007/s00210-013-0871-2.

Rahal, A., Kumar, A., Singh, V., Yadav, B., Tiwari, R., Chakraborty, S., et al. (2014). Oxidative stress, prooxidants, and antioxidants: The interplay. *BioMed Research International, 2014*, 761264. http://dx.doi.org/10.1155/2014/761264.

Ramanathan, L., Gulyani, S., Nienhuis, R., & Siegel, J. M. (2002). Sleep deprivation decreases superoxide dismutase activity in rat hippocampus and brainstem. *NeuroReport, 13*(11), 1387–1390.

Ramanathan, L., Hu, S., Frautschy, S. A., & Siegel, J. M. (2010). Short-term total sleep deprivation in the rat increases antioxidant responses in multiple brain regions without impairing spontaneous alternation behavior. *Behavioural Brain Research, 207*(2), 305–309. http://dx.doi.org/10.1016/j.bbr.2009.10.014.

Ramsawh, H. J., Stein, M. B., Belik, S. L., Jacobi, F., & Sareen, J. (2009). Relationship of anxiety disorders, sleep quality, and functional impairment in a community sample. *Journal of Psychiatric Research, 43*(10), 926–933. http://dx.doi.org/10.1016/j.jpsychires.2009.01.009.

Ravassard, P., Pachoud, B., Comte, J. C., Mejia-Perez, C., Scote-Blachon, C., Gay, N., et al. (2009). Paradoxical (REM) sleep deprivation causes a large and rapidly reversible decrease in long-term potentiation, synaptic transmission, glutamate receptor protein levels, and ERK/MAPK activation in the dorsal hippocampus. *Sleep, 32*(2), 227–240.

Reczek, C. R., & Chandel, N. S. (2015). ROS-dependent signal transduction. *Current Opinion in Cell Biology, 33*, 8–13. http://dx.doi.org/10.1016/j.ceb.2014.09.010.

Reimund, E. (1994). The free radical flux theory of sleep. *Medical Hypotheses, 43*(4), 231–233.

Ringli, M., & Huber, R. (2011). Developmental aspects of sleep slow waves: Linking sleep, brain maturation and behavior. *Progress in Brain Research, 193*, 63–82. http://dx.doi.org/10.1016/B978-0-444-53839-0.00005-3.

Roberts, R. E., & Duong, H. T. (2014). The prospective association between sleep deprivation and depression among adolescents. *Sleep, 37*(2), 239–244. http://dx.doi.org/10.5665/sleep.3388.

Schieber, M., & Chandel, N. S. (2014). ROS function in redox signaling and oxidative stress. *Current Biology, 24*(10), R453–R462. http://dx.doi.org/10.1016/j.cub.2014.03.034.

Semple, B. D., Blomgren, K., Gimlin, K., Ferriero, D. M., & Noble-Haeusslein, L. J. (2013). Brain development in rodents and humans: Identifying benchmarks of maturation and vulnerability to injury across species. *Progress in Neurobiology, 106–107*, 1–16. http://dx.doi.org/10.1016/j.pneurobio.2013.04.001.

Serrano, F., & Klann, E. (2004). Reactive oxygen species and synaptic plasticity in the aging hippocampus. *Ageing Research Reviews, 3*(4), 431–443. http://dx.doi.org/10.1016/j.arr.2004.05.002.

Shaw, P., Kabani, N. J., Lerch, J. P., Eckstrand, K., Lenroot, R., Gogtay, N., et al. (2008). Neurodevelopmental trajectories of the human cerebral cortex. *Journal of Neuroscience, 28*(14), 3586–3594. http://dx.doi.org/10.1523/JNEUROSCI.5309-07.2008.

Smith, C. J., Wilkins, K. B., Mogavero, J. N., & Veenema, A. H. (2015). Social novelty investigation in the juvenile rat: Modulation by the mu-opioid system. *Journal of Neuroendocrinology, 27*(10), 752–764. http://dx.doi.org/10.1111/jne.12301.

Solanki, N., Atrooz, F., Asghar, S., & Salim, S. J. N. l. (2016). Tempol protects sleep-deprivation induced behavioral deficits in aggressive male Long–Evans rats. *612*, 245–250.

Son, Y., Cheong, Y. K., Kim, N. H., Chung, H. T., Kang, D. G., & Pae, H. O. (2011). Mitogen-activated protein kinases and reactive oxygen species: How can ROS activate MAPK pathways? *Journal of Signal Transduction, 2011*, 792639. http://dx.doi.org/10.1155/2011/792639.

Spilsbury, J. C., Babineau, D. C., Frame, J., Juhas, K., & Rork, K. (2014). Association between children's exposure to a violent event and objectively and subjectively measured sleep characteristics: A pilot longitudinal study. *Journal of Sleep Research, 23*(5), 585–594. http://dx.doi.org/10.1111/jsr.12162.

Stefanescu, C., & Ciobica, A. (2012). The relevance of oxidative stress status in first episode and recurrent depression. *Journal of Affective Disorders, 143*(1–3), 34–38. http://dx.doi.org/10.1016/j.jad.2012.05.022.

Stenberg, D., & Porkka-Heiskanen, T. (1990). Regulation of sleep. *Duodecim, 106*(22), 1608–1615.

Steriade, M., McCormick, D. A., & Sejnowski, T. J. (1993). Thalamocortical oscillations in the sleeping and aroused brain. *Science, 262*(5134), 679–685.

Sweatt, J. D., & Hawkins, K. E. (2016). The molecular neurobiology of the sleep-deprived, fuzzy brain. *Science Signaling, 9*(425), fs7. http://dx.doi.org/10.1126/scisignal.aaf6196.

Tancredi, V., D'Antuono, M., Cafè, C., Giovedì, S., Buè, M. C., D'Arcangelo, G., & Benfenati, F. J. (2000). The inhibitory effects of interleukin-6 on synaptic plasticity in the rat hippocampus are associated with an inhibition of mitogen-activated protein kinase ERK. *Journal of Neurochemistry, 75*(2), 634–643.

Tarokh, L., Carskadon, M. A., & Achermann, P. (2010). Developmental changes in brain connectivity assessed using the sleep EEG. *Neuroscience, 171*(2), 622–634. http://dx.doi.org/10.1016/j.neuroscience.2010.08.071.

Tononi, G., & Cirelli, C. (2014). Sleep and the price of plasticity: From synaptic and cellular homeostasis to memory consolidation and integration. *Neuron, 81*(1), 12–34. http://dx.doi.org/10.1016/j.neuron.2013.12.025.

Toth, I., & Neumann, I. D. (2013). Animal models of social avoidance and social fear. *Cell and Tissue Research, 354*(1), 107–118. http://dx.doi.org/10.1007/s00441-013-1636-4.

Touchette, E., Cote, S. M., Petit, D., Liu, X., Boivin, M., Falissard, B., & Montplaisir, J. Y. (2009). Short nighttime sleep-duration and hyperactivity trajectories in early childhood. *Pediatrics, 124*(5), e985–993. http://dx.doi.org/10.1542/peds.2008-2005.

Touchette, E., Petit, D., Tremblay, R. E., Boivin, M., Falissard, B., Genolini, C., et al. (2008). Associations between sleep duration patterns and overweight/obesity at age 6. *Sleep, 31*(11), 1507–1514.

Tsuno, N., Besset, A., & Ritchie, K. (2005). Sleep and depression. *Journal of Clinical Psychiatry, 66*(10), 1254–1269.

Tudor, J. C., Davis, E. J., Peixoto, L., Wimmer, M. E., van Tilborg, E., Park, A. J., & Abel, T. (2016). Sleep deprivation impairs memory by attenuating mTORC1-dependent protein synthesis. *Science Signaling, 9*(425), ra41. http://dx.doi.org/10.1126/scisignal.aad4949.

Valjent, E., Caboche, J., & Vanhoutte, P. (2001). Mitogen-activated protein kinase/extracellular signal-regulated kinase induced gene regulation in brain: A molecular substrate for learning and memory? *Molecular Neurobiology, 23*(2–3), 83–99. http://dx.doi.org/10.1385/MN:23:2-3:083.

Valko, M., Leibfritz, D., Moncol, J., Cronin, M. T., Mazur, M., & Telser, J. (2007). Free radicals and antioxidants in normal physiological functions and human disease. *The International Journal of Biochemistry & Cell Biology, 39*(1), 44–84. http://dx.doi.org/10.1016/j.biocel.2006.07.001.

Villafuerte, G., Miguel-Puga, A., Rodriguez, E. M., Machado, S., Manjarrez, E., & Arias-Carrion, O. (2015). Sleep deprivation and oxidative stress in animal models: A systematic review. *Oxidative Medicine and Cellular Longevity, 2015*, 234952. http://dx.doi.org/10.1155/2015/234952.

Vollert, C., Zagaar, M., Hovatta, I., Taneja, M., Vu, A., Dao, A., et al. (2011). Exercise prevents sleep deprivation-associated anxiety-like behavior in rats: Potential role of oxidative stress mechanisms. *Behavioural Brain Research, 224*(2), 233–240. http://dx.doi.org/10.1016/j.bbr.2011.05.010.

Wang, D., Malo, D., & Hekimi, S. (2010). Elevated mitochondrial reactive oxygen species generation affects the immune response via hypoxia-inducible factor-1 alpha in long-lived Mclk1+/- mouse mutants. *The Journal of Immunology, 184*(2), 582–590. http://dx.doi.org/10.4049/jimmunol.0902352.

Wang, X., & Michaelis, E. K. (2010). Selective neuronal vulnerability to oxidative stress in the brain. *Frontiers in Aging Neuroscience, 2*, 12. http://dx.doi.org/10.3389/fnagi.2010.00012.

Wheaton, A. G., Chapman, D. P., & Croft, J. B. (2016). School start times, sleep, behavioral, health, and academic outcomes: A review of the literature. *Journal of School Health, 86*(5), 363–381. http://dx.doi.org/10.1111/josh.12388.

Wright, K. P., Jr., Drake, A. L., Frey, D. J., Fleshner, M., Desouza, C. A., Gronfier, C., et al. (2015). Influence of sleep deprivation and circadian misalignment on cortisol, inflammatory markers, and cytokine balance. *47*, 24–34.

Wulff, K., Gatti, S., Wettstein, J. G., & Foster, R. G. (2010). Sleep and circadian rhythm disruption in psychiatric and neurodegenerative disease. *Nature Reviews Neuroscience, 11*(8), 589–599. http://dx.doi.org/10.1038/nrn2868.

Yilmaz, E., Sedky, K., & Bennett, D. S. (2013). The relationship between depressive symptoms and obstructive sleep apnea in pediatric populations: A meta-analysis. *Journal of Clinical Sleep Medicine, 9*(11), 1213–1220. http://dx.doi.org/10.5664/jcsm.3178.

Zhang, Z. W. (2006). Canadian association of neurosciences review: Postnatal development of the mammalian neocortex: Role of activity revisited. *The Canadian Journal of Neurological Sciences, 33*(2), 158–169.

Zhong, J., Carrozza, D. P., Williams, K., Pritchett, D. B., & Molinoff, P. B. (1995). Expression of mRNAs encoding subunits of the NMDA receptor in developing rat brain. *Journal of Neurochemistry, 64*(2), 531–539.

FSC
www.fsc.org
MIX
Papier | Fördert
gute Waldnutzung
FSC® C083411

Kolibri 360 GmbH
Ferdinand-Jühlke-Straße 7
99095 Erfurt, Deutschland
produktsicherheit@kolibri360.de